Current Developments in Monetary and Financial Law

Volume

Current Developments in Monetary and Financial Law

5

International Monetary Fund

Cataloging-in-Publication Data

Current developments in monetary and financial law. — Washington, D.C. :
International Monetary Fund. 1999-
        p. : cm.

    Includes bibliographical references.
    ISBN 978-1-55775-796-8 (volume 1)
    ISBN 978-1-58906-176-7 (volume 2)
    ISBN 978-1-58906-334-1 (volume 3)
    ISBN 978-1-58906-507-9 (volume 4)
    ISBN 978-1-58906-773-8 (volume 5)

    1. Banking law—Congresses. 2. Monetary policy—Law and
legislation—Congresses. 3. Financial policy—Law and legislation—
Congresses. 4. Financial crises—Congresses. 5. Banks and banking—State
supervision—Congresses. 6. Banks and banking, International—Congresses.
7. Bank and banking, Central—Congresses. 8. Economic and Monetary
Union—Congresses. 9. Payment systems—Congresses. I. International
Monetary Fund. Legal Dept. II. IMF Institute.
K1066.C97

Please send orders to:
International Monetary Fund, Publication Services
700 19th Street, N.W., Washington, D.C. 20431, U.S.A.
Telephone: (202) 623-7430; Fax: (202) 623-7201

E-mail: publications@imf.org
Internet: www.imfbookstore.org

Contents

PREFACE

The Legal Department and the Institute of the IMF held the tenth biennial seminar for legal advisers of central banks of member countries on October 23-27, 2006. The theme of the seminar was *Law and Financial Stability*. The Hon. Randall Kroszner, Governor, Board of Governors of the Federal Reserve System of the United States, delivered the keynote address, while Mr. Rodrigo de Rato, IMF Managing Director, and Mr. John Lipsky, IMF First Deputy Managing Director, also addressed the seminar. Presentations were made by officials of the IMF and other international organizations, officials of central banks, representatives of the private sector, lawyers, and scholars. The papers published in this volume are based on those presentations. The views expressed are those of the authors and should not necessarily be attributed to the IMF or to any institution with which they are affiliated.

The seminar covered many topics and was intended to enhance understanding of financial stability generally and of the legal instruments available to central banks, supervisors, international institutions and others to promote it. Particular attention was devoted to the legal framework for central banking, banking regulation, payments and securities settlement systems, and anti-money laundering and terrorist financing. Also discussed were capital markets issues, including the rationale for regulating hedge funds and derivatives.

The sponsorship of an international seminar, with participants from many central banks and speakers from different parts of the world, is a complex matter. Many people contributed to the preparation of the seminar and the publication of this volume. I wish to express our particular gratitude to Messrs. Barend Jansen and Roy Baban of the Legal Department for the role they played in organizing and preparing the seminar. Thanks also go to Ms. Linda Byron, Mr. Henry Wright and Ms. Nan Wang of the Legal Department who provided administrative and organizational assistance. Mr. Peter Whitten, a private consultant, Ms. Patricia Loo of the External Relations Department and Ms. Duangratai Jayanan of the Legal Department provided editorial expertise with respect to the composition of this volume. Mr. John Austin and Mr. Ayodeji

Badaki, both of the Legal Department, also played important roles in facilitating the publication of this volume.

SEAN HAGAN

The General Counsel
Director of the Legal Department

I. LEGAL DEVELOPMENTS IN THE IMF

1

The International Monetary Fund's Legal Instruments to Promote Financial Stability

ROSS LECKOW

This chapter examines the legal instruments available to the International Monetary Fund to promote financial stability in and among its member countries. The instruments are derived from the Fund's functions under its Articles of Agreement and the manner in which the Fund performs these functions.

The chapter first provides a definition of financial stability. It then turns to the Fund's legal framework, starting with some basic principles and then examining the purposes of the Fund and their relationship to financial stability. The chapter then discusses three important functions of the Fund as they relate to financial stability: surveillance, technical assistance, and financial assistance.

Defining Financial Stability

There is no generally accepted definition of financial stability. Rather, it is an evolving concept and can mean different things in different contexts. A narrow definition would refer only to the stability of a country's banking system, but financial stability cannot be ensured by focusing on a country's banks alone. A country's financial system also includes its payments system and, more broadly, its securities exchanges, pension funds, insurers, and other entities that provide a framework for carrying out economic transactions and channeling savings into investment. A broader definition of financial stability can therefore refer to a concern for stability at all these levels, including the efficient operation of a country's financial markets.

Further, a definition of financial stability can have both a domestic and an international element. It can refer not only to the stability of the domestic financial system but also the stability of the global financial system and avoidance of situations in which a financial or economic crisis in one country has ripple effects that lead to crises in others.

This chapter adopts the broad definition of financial stability. For our purposes, a stable financial system is one in which major shocks that could disrupt the smooth functioning of the financial system are prevented, one which can withstand such shocks when they occur, and one in which such shocks do not spill over into neighboring countries or into other regions of the world.

The Fund's Legal Framework: Basic Principles

To understand the Fund's legal framework and the manner in which it approaches the issue of financial stability, it is important to keep a few principles in mind.

First, the Fund's legal framework is largely an aspect of public international law. Thus the focus of the chapter is not on how member countries promote their domestic financial stability but on the legal framework governing the operations of the International Monetary Fund and the manner in which the Fund interacts with its member countries to promote financial stability.

Second, it is important to keep in mind that the Fund is an international organization established by a multilateral treaty, the Articles of Agreement. The two most important sources of law for the Fund are the Articles of Agreement and decisions of the Executive Board. The Articles specify the purposes of the Fund and certain functions that the Fund is to perform in furtherance of these purposes. The Articles also establish certain obligations that member countries are required to observe, some of which are relevant to the question of financial stability. To make an analogy to a domestic legal system, the Articles of Agreement represents the Fund's constitution.

The second important source of law for our purposes consists of decisions of the Fund's Executive Board. In addition to governing the Fund's day-to-day operations, the Board adopts decisions of general applicability that specify how the Fund will interact with its members on different issues and how specific provisions of the Fund's Articles will be implemented. These decisions of general applicability are roughly analogous to legislation in a domestic legal system.

The Fund's Legal Framework: Purposes

If one looks at the Fund's purposes under Article I of the Fund's Articles of Agreement, one will not see a reference to financial stability. Yet financial stability has become central to the achievement of many of the purposes set out in Article I.

To understand their relationship to financial stability, it is useful to highlight two of these purposes:

- First, "to promote exchange stability, to maintain orderly exchange arrangements among members, and to avoid competitive exchange depreciation" (Article I (iii));

- Second, "to assist in the establishment of a multilateral system of payments in respect of current transactions and in the elimination of foreign exchange restrictions which hamper the growth of world trade" (Article I (iv)).

Thus if one were to boil the purposes of the Fund down to their essence, it might consist of the following: to build an international monetary system in which current payments and transfers between countries move freely, and the system of exchange rates between the currencies of different members are stable and supported by prudent economic and financial policies implemented by each of the Fund's members. By building a stable international monetary system, the Fund will create the basis upon which global trade and investment will continue to grow and contribute to growth throughout the global economic system.

Viewed from this perspective, the importance of financial stability to the Fund is obvious. It would be impossible for the Fund to ensure the stability of the international monetary system without first ensuring the stability of members' financial systems. A sound financial system in each of its member countries is essential to support macroeconomic stability. Problems in a country's financial system can reduce the effectiveness of monetary policy, create large fiscal costs related to the rescue of troubled financial institutions, trigger capital flight, and deepen economic recession.

Moreover, it would be impossible for the Fund to ensure the stability of the international monetary system without also ensuring that the linkages between the financial markets of different countries are given adequate attention. The globalization of financial markets now means that many issues related to financial stability need to be dealt with at the global level: financial weaknesses in one country can rapidly spill over and contaminate others.

The Fund has learned this lesson from bitter experience. There have been far too many examples of crises in a member country's financial system that have sent shock waves through the member's economy and have triggered a major balance of payments crisis in that country and, in some cases, in others. Clearly, the promotion of financial stability has become closely linked to the purposes of the Fund.

The Fund's Legal Framework: Functions

Insofar as the Articles relate to the promotion of financial stability, the principal functions of the Fund are surveillance, technical assistance, and financial assistance.

Surveillance under Article IV

Surveillance under Article IV is perhaps the Fund's most important function. It is conducted in both the bilateral and multilateral contexts. This section focuses on surveillance at the bilateral level.

Article IV is concerned primarily with the promotion of a stable system of exchange rates among the currencies of all the Fund's members. Member countries are required under Article IV to observe certain obligations respecting their domestic economic and financial policies and their exchange rate policies that are designed to promote orderly exchange arrangements and a stable system of exchange rates. Article IV assumes that if members implement the right macroeconomic policies, stability in the global system of exchange rates will be assured.

With this objective in mind, the Fund is required under Article IV to exercise surveillance over members' compliance with these obligations. While the provisions of Article IV contemplate that the Fund would engage in a compliance exercise with each of its members, in practice it has evolved into a broader exercise. Beyond such questions of compliance, the surveillance process has evolved into a policy dialogue in which the Fund seeks to persuade the authorities of member countries to follow domestic and external policies that will contribute to external stability. On a regular basis (normally annually), the Fund discusses economic developments and policy with the authorities of each of its members and communicates its views to the member on its policies and on those areas that may be a cause for concern.

Three important features of this process should be noted. First, the purpose of surveillance is essentially crisis prevention, to persuade the authorities of a member to change their policies before they may lead to a macroeconomic crisis.

Second, the surveillance process is mandatory and universal in its application. It applies to all of the Fund's members, each one of which is required to participate in the process, to consult with the Fund, and to provide the Fund with the information it needs for this purpose.

Third, given the broad range of policies that could theoretically be relevant to the questions of macroeconomic stability that are at the heart of an Article IV discussion, there is generally some discretion on the part of the Fund as to the particular issues and policies it will raise with a member. Some types of policies are very closely related to the obligations of members under Article IV and will inevitably be discussed in an Article IV consultation. Other policies may only be important in the circumstances of a particular member and may only be discussed with respect to that member.

How does this relate to financial stability? One area of policy that has been a growing subject of attention in the Article IV process concerns the financial systems of members and their linkages with other members' financial systems. While there was a time when these issues received comparatively little attention in an Article IV consultation, this is no longer the case. The financial sector is now an important area that is frequently discussed with members under Article IV.

As part of its medium-term strategy, the Fund is in the process of implementing several important changes to strengthen its analysis of financial sector issues in the context of bilateral surveillance. It is expected that Article IV reports will incorporate analyses of financial sector and balance sheet vulnerabilities, drawing their implications for macroeconomic aggregates and capital flows, and the scope for domestic and external spillovers. To strengthen the quality of the Fund's financial sector work in the Article IV process, a new department, the Monetary and Capital Markets Department, has been created to focus on these issues and work closely with the Fund's area departments in their surveillance work.

Technical Assistance

As a mechanism for the promotion of financial stability, surveillance has the advantage of its universal application and global reach. Its principal drawback, however, is the level of detail with which it examines the financial sector. Surveillance is concerned with broad macroeconomic policy and developments in a member country. It is not possible for the Fund to examine the member's financial sector in great detail in this process. This is where the Fund's second mechanism for the promotion of financial stability, technical assistance (TA), comes into play.

Under Article IV, Section 2(b), the Fund may perform financial and technical services for members. These technical services generally take the form of expert advice that the Fund provides to its members to help them strengthen their institutional capacity in areas of importance to the Fund. TA is voluntary, both for the member and for the Fund. The Fund is not required to provide it, and will only do so if a member requests it.

In the area of financial stability, the Fund has an active TA program that is focused primarily on the institutional capacity of member countries in the financial sector. Fund staff works closely with the authorities of member countries, in particular to help them to strengthen the organizational structure and operations of their central banks and financial supervisory agencies and to transfer know-how, on, for example, the conduct of monetary policy and other central bank operations, and the supervision of financial institutions and payments systems.

The Fund's Legal Department provides legal technical assistance to member countries on issues related to the financial sector. The Department has a very active program of assistance in legislative drafting in the financial sector and in training lawyers and judges in member countries in principles of financial law and in international best practices in these areas.

Financial Sector Assessment Program

A particularly important component of the Fund's TA activities in the financial sector concerns the Financial Sector Assessment Program (FSAP). The FSAP is conducted jointly by the Fund and the World Bank. It was launched in 1999, partly in response to the Asian crisis and to the call by the international community for intensified cooperative efforts to monitor the financial systems of member countries. Its purpose is to provide member countries with a comprehensive evaluation of their financial systems, to alert national authorities to likely vulnerabilities in their financial sectors, and to assist them in the design of measures that would reduce these vulnerabilities.

An FSAP focuses on the linkages between the operations of the financial sector and macroeconomic performance. In particular, it examines developments in the financial sector, risks and vulnerabilities using a range of financial soundness indicators and macrofinancial stress tests, and also examines different aspects of the institutional framework for the financial sector.

Since the program's inception, approximately 120 countries, or two-thirds of the Fund's membership, have requested and received an FSAP. A particularly important feature of the FSAP exercise is its relationship to surveillance. Because an FSAP will examine the financial sector in more detail than is contemplated in an Article IV consultation, the information and findings in an FSAP for a member are often used to inform the Fund's surveillance work with respect to that member.

International Codes and Standards

An important related initiative concerns the work of the Fund and World Bank to encourage compliance with international standards and codes in the financial sector. As part of a broader initiative, the Fund and Bank have adopted several standards and codes that specify good practices that countries should observe in designing and implementing their institutional frameworks governing different aspects of the financial sector.

While some of these standards were developed by the Fund, many others were developed by other international bodies with expertise in particular areas, including:

- Basel Committee's *Core Principles on Banking Supervision*;

- International Organization of Securities Commission's *Objectives for Securities Regulation*;

- International Association of Insurance Supervisors' *Insurance Supervisory Principles*;

- Committee on Payments and Settlements Systems' *Recommendations for Securities Settlement Systems*;

- Financial Action Task Force's *Recommendations* in the area of Anti-money Laundering and Combating the Financing of Terrorism.

Other standards address such issues as the conduct of monetary and financial policy, corporate governance, accounting, and auditing.

The Fund and Bank assess a member's compliance with these standards and issue a report known as a Report on the Observance of Standards and Codes (ROSC). The purpose of the ROSC exercise is to identify in a member's institutional framework areas that need to be strengthened. Many such areas may be addressed through subsequent technical assistance from the Fund.

As part of the standards initiative, the Fund has developed standards for reporting economic data to the markets—the Special Data Dissemination Standard (SDDS) and the General Data Dissemination System (GDDS). These focus on the practices that member countries employ in reporting economic statistics to the market. They recognize that the stability of a country's financial markets is likely to be strengthened by making accurate and timely economic data available to investors and market participants. If investors are fully informed of developments, they are less likely to overreact when market conditions deteriorate.

Transparency

The Fund's concern for transparency in economic reporting extends beyond the standards and codes initiative and beyond its TA activities. Beyond TA, a particularly important development in this regard is the Fund's Transparency Policy.

The policy is a relatively recent initiative under which the Fund seeks to publish its own reports on members' economies and economic policies. It is a departure from the Fund's traditional approach to the publication of such information, which was one of confidentiality. Historically, the Fund did not publish its reports on member economies or its views on their policies. The philosophy behind this approach was that it would be easier for the Fund to provide frank policy advice to a member and a member to accept that advice if the discussions were to take place behind closed doors.

This philosophy began to change in the midst of the emerging market crises of the mid- and late 1990s. The Fund began to recognize that the absence of timely and accurate economic information may actually undermine the stability of a country's economy. It therefore began to encourage members to consent to the publication of particular Fund staff reports on their economies and to the summaries of Executive Board discussions of these reports.

Still, there are rather strict limits within the Fund's legal framework that define the circumstances under which the Fund can publish any of these documents without a member's consent. Many such documents contain confidential information that members have provided to the Fund, and their consent is, of course, necessary before such information can be made public. Moreover, the Articles establish very stringent conditions under which the Fund can publish its views on a member's policies without that member's consent.

Notwithstanding these limitations, an enormous amount of material produced by the Fund on members' economies is now being published. The reason is that members have recognized the benefits of transparency and have generally consented to publication. This development has dramatically improved the quality of information available to the markets.

Fund Financial Assistance

The two tools discussed above—surveillance and technical assistance—are effective instruments that the Fund can use to prevent financial crises from occurring in its member countries. But what can it do if a crisis does occur? Imagine a country that has suffered a major financial meltdown that has mushroomed into a full-blown balance of payments crisis. In these circumstances the Fund will seek to stabilize the member's external position but, as part of this process, will also help restore its financial system to health. Some of the instruments already mentioned, such as technical assistance, may prove useful. But the principal mechanism that will be used is the Fund's financial assistance.

Under the Articles, the Fund may provide financial assistance to members to help them address a balance of payments problem. But the Fund will only extend financial assistance if the member is prepared to implement a program of economic reform that is designed to resolve that problem. The financial assistance will be phased over the life of the member's program, and the conditionality attached to each disbursement will effectively require the member to implement particular features of its program, either by meeting specified economic targets or by implementing key structural measures, if it is to continue receiving disbursements.

In a country where problems in the financial sector were an important reason for the member's balance of payments crisis, the member's program will often focus on restoring the financial system to health. The implementation of measures designed to help strengthen the member's financial system may become explicit conditions attached to particular disbursements to the member. For example, such conditions may include the enactment of legislation designed to strengthen the legal and institutional framework for dealing with insolvent banks. Other important measures may focus on strengthening the corporate insolvency framework to facilitate the resolution of claims that domestic and foreign creditors may hold against insolvent corporate borrowers.

Financial stability in a member country is also restored by the resolution of claims held against the member country at the international level. These include claims held by foreign creditors on debt of the member government that is either overdue or that the member is unlikely to be able to service when it falls due. For a Fund-supported program to be viable, it is often necessary for various classes of creditors to agree to reschedule these claims in a manner that is consistent with the member's ability to pay.

The Fund and the creditor community have historically cooperated in seeking the orderly resolution of these claims. In recent years, this cooperative relationship has begun to experience difficulties, in particular as a result of changes in the ways in which governments in emerging-market countries have borrowed. While historically they have raised money in the form of syndicated loans from a limited group of large international banks, more recently they have relied upon public bond issues purchased by a myriad of different investors. Reliance upon public bond issues has dramatically complicated the restructuring of such debt if the government is unable to pay. Stated simply, it is difficult to get a large and diverse group of bondholders to agree to a restructuring.

To address these problems of collective action, the official sector, including the Fund, has been promoting the development of a legal framework that would enable a qualified majority of creditors to make key restructuring decisions that would bind all creditors. In regard to the legal basis of such a mechanism, two alternative approaches have been proposed. One would be based on the contractual terms of the sovereign bonds. The other would be based on an international treaty, to be implemented through an amendment of the Fund's Articles of Agreement. The contractual approach, through the inclusion of collective action clauses in bond instruments, is clearly the preferred approach at this time. Because these issues are of central importance to Fund operations, the Legal Department will continue to closely monitor developments in this area.

Conclusion

The promotion of financial stability has become an important objective of the Fund. The Fund pursues this objective through all of its principal activities, including surveillance, technical assistance, and financial assistance. But an important feature of much of the Fund's approach is its emphasis on advice, persuasion, and ultimately cooperation. This approach stems from a recognition that the promotion of financial stability is a responsibility that is shared by the Fund, its members, financial institutions, and everyone within the international financial community.

II. CENTRAL BANK LAW

CHAPTER 2 | The Price Stability Mandate of the European System of Central Banks: A Legal Perspective

NIALL J. LENIHAN

> The ESCB is entrusted with one overriding objective: to maintain price stability. This goal is its single most important objective, the reason for which the System is created, briefly: its raison d'être. It is with a view to this that the central banks of the European Community are to be endowed with a large measure of independence: it is with the ultimate objective of maintaining price stability that the ESCB will be put on a separate footing from the political organs of the Community.

—René Smits[1]

The European System of Central Banks (ESCB), comprising the European Central Bank (ECB) and the national central banks (NCBs) of the member states of the European Union (EU), was established under the provisions of the Treaty Establishing the European Community (the Treaty or the EC Treaty), to which the 27 EU member states are party.[2] Under the Treaty the primary objective of the ESCB is to maintain price stability and, without prejudice to this primary objective, the ESCB shall support the general economic policies of member states in the Community.[3]

This chapter examines the ESCB's objectives from a legal perspective. In doing so, it outlines the relevant provisions of the Treaty setting out the ESCB's mandate. In doing so, it will:

1. Explain the overriding importance that the Treaty has assigned to the ESCB's objective to maintain price stability, and summarize the main economic and historical influences on the evolution of this objective.

2. Explore the ESCB's price stability objective in more precise terms, and outline the extent to which this objective is susceptible to judicial oversight by the European Court of Justice.

17

3. Describe the key link identified by the Court of Justice in the *OLAF* case[4] between the principle of central bank independence and the objective of price stability.

4. Discuss the ESCB's secondary objective to support the general economic policies in the Community, against the background of a coordinated, but not a single, economic and fiscal policy in the euro area.

5. Explain how the ESCB's mandate helped to clarify the constitutional position of the ECB within the Community legal order in the *OLAF* case, where the Court of Justice showed a strong appreciation that the objective to maintain price stability is one of the cornerstones of economic and monetary union, and, therefore, of the European Community as a whole.

6. Explore whether the ESCB price stability mandate is applicable to all 27 national central banks in the ESCB, and not only the ECB and the central banks of member states which have adopted the euro.

7. Assess the manner in which the recently signed Treaty of Lisbon, currently scheduled to enter into force on 1 January, 2009, addresses the mandate of the ESCB.

Treaty-Based Mandate of the ESCB

The objectives of the ESCB are set out in Article 105(1) of the Treaty, which provides as follows:

> The primary objective of the ESCB shall be to maintain price stability. Without prejudice to the primary objective of price stability, the ESCB shall support the general economic policies in the Community with a view to contributing to the achievement of the objectives of the Community as laid down in Article 2 of the Treaty. The ESCB shall act in accordance with the principle of an open market economy with free competition, ensuring an efficient allocation of resources, and in compliance with the principles set out in Article 4.

The objectives of the Community laid down in Article 2 are as follows:

> The Community shall have as its task, by establishing a common market and an economic and monetary union and by implementing common policies or activities referred to in Articles 3 and 4, to promote throughout the Community a harmonious, balanced and sustainable development of economic activities, a high level of employment and of social protection, equality between men and women, sustainable and non-inflationary growth, a high degree of competitiveness and convergence of economic performance, a high level of protection and improvement of the quality of the environment, the raising of the standard of living and quality of life, and economic and social cohesion and solidarity among member states.

For the purposes set out in Article 2, Article 3(1) of the Treaty identifies the full range of the Community's activities, including the prohibition of customs duties and quantitative restrictions on the import and export of goods between member states; a common commercial policy; an internal market characterized by the abolition, as between member states, of obstacles to the free movement of goods, persons, services and capital; the approximation of the laws of member states to the extent required for the functioning of the common market; a system ensuring that competition in the internal market is not distorted; measures concerning the entry and movement of persons; common policies in the spheres of agriculture, fisheries and transport; coordination between employment policies; policies in the social sphere (the European Social Fund), the environment and development cooperation; the strengthening of economic and social cohesion and the competitiveness of industry; the promotion of research and technological development; the development of trans-European networks; contributions to health and consumer protection, education, training and culture; and measures in the spheres of energy, civil protection and tourism.

As noted above, the ESCB is required under Article 105(1) of the Treaty to act in compliance with the principles of Article 4, which identifies the activities of the member states and the Community concerning economic and monetary union. In particular, Article 4(3) provides as follows:

> These activities of the member states and the Community shall entail compliance with the following guiding principles: stable prices, sound public finances and monetary conditions and a sustainable balance of payments.

Overriding Importance of Price Stability

The Treaty establishes a clear hierarchy of objectives for the ESCB and assigns overriding importance to maintaining price stability.[5] The maintenance of price stability can be properly characterized as the *Grundnorm*, or *raison d'être*, of the ESCB.[6] Because the primary objective of price stability is written into the EC Treaty, it can only be amended by means of an intergovernmental conference followed by ratification of the amendments by all the member states in accordance with their respective constitutional requirements.[7]

The ESCB's primary objective to maintain price stability has often been contrasted with the multiple goals of the U.S. Federal Reserve System, whose Board of Governors and Federal Open Market Committee are required to "maintain long run growth of the monetary and credit aggregates commensurate with the economy's long run potential to increase production, so as to promote effectively the goals of maximum employment, stable prices and moderate long-term interest rates."[8] The basic thinking behind setting price stability as the primary objective of the ESCB's monetary policy is, first, that it is the task of other economic actors than central banks, notably those responsible for fiscal and structural policies, to enhance the growth potential of the economy, and, second, that assigning to monetary policy an objective for real income or employment would be problematic since, apart from the positive impact of price stability, monetary policy has no scope for exerting any lasting influence on real income or employment.[9] By focusing the monetary policy of the ESCB on this primary objective, the Treaty makes it clear that ensuring price stability is the most important contribution that monetary policy can make to achieve a favorable economic environment and a high level of employment.[10]

Historically, the formulation of the ESCB's primary objective to maintain price stability evolved out of the blueprint for economic and monetary union put forward in the 1989 Delors Report, which was based in large part on a contribution by the Deutsche Bundesbank.[11] Commentators have noted that this objective, together with the independence of the new ESCB, was a precondition to the willingness of the German authorities to sacrifice their national currency, the Deutsche Mark, which had become the strongest of European currencies because of its long record of low inflation.[12] Commentators have also drawn attention to the particularly strong antipathy to inflation among the German public, dating back to the disastrous experience Germany had with hyperinflation during the 1920s.[13]

In broader international terms, commentators have noted that the "oil shock" of 1973—the quadrupling of oil prices that contributed to plunging much of the industrialized world into an era of soaring inflation and low and volatile growth, known in economic jargon as stagflation—is the historical development that marked a turning point in the understanding of the need for price stability. The oil shock destroyed the post-war pattern in which governments tried to buy a little more growth with a little more inflation (following the Phillips curve), and instead entrenched price stability as their primary concern. This development has had important legal implications nationally and internationally, particularly in the 1990s, as a substantial number of domestic laws, as well as international treaties such as the EC Treaty, have made this objective the primary goal of central banks and monetary agencies.[14]

Precise Interpretation of ESCB's Price Stability Mandate

The Treaty does not precisely define what is meant by "price stability." The term is generally understood to denote internal price stability, meaning the volume of goods and services that can be obtained for one euro, as opposed to the stability or strength of the currency in terms of third currencies such as the U.S. dollar, Japanese yen, or British sterling.[15] This interpretation is supported by the fact that under the Treaty the decision as to which member states fulfill the necessary conditions for the adoption of the euro is made on the basis of a number of economic convergence criteria, including the achievement of a high degree of price stability.[16] This standard of price stability means, in particular, that a member state has a price performance that is sustainable and an average rate of inflation, observed over a period of one year before the examination, that does not exceed by more than 1.5 percent that of, at most, the three best performing member states in terms of price stability.[17] This demonstrates that the term "price stability," as referred to in the Treaty, refers exclusively to internal price performance.[18]

In the absence of any clarification in the Treaty regarding the specific level of price stability to be maintained by the ESCB, the ECB is in a position to determine for itself what level of price stability it considers acceptable.[19] The ECB has defined this price stability in quantitative terms as a year-on-year increase in the Harmonised Index of Consumer Prices (HICP) for the euro area of below, but close to, 2 percent over the medium term, which makes clear that not only inflation above 2 percent, but also deflation, would be inconsistent with price stability.[20]

As a matter of strict legal theory, the European Court of Justice (the Court), as the final arbiter regarding the interpretation of the Treaty, may be called upon to determine whether particular measures adopted by the ECB are consistent with the ESCB's primary objective to maintain price stability.[21] In this respect, some commentators have argued that particular inflation ranges expressed in precise quantitative terms (e.g., 0 to 3 percent, or less than 2 percent) would be compatible with price stability, and even that the ECB is legally bound to respect such precise limits.[22] It is likely, however, that the Court would be reluctant to curtail the discretion of the ECB on what is essentially a matter of monetary policy. In *Roquette Frères*[23] the Court stated that where "the evaluation of a complex economic situation is involved," the Commission "enjoys a wide measure of discretion," and that "[i]n reviewing the legality of the exercise of such discretion, the Court must confine itself to examining whether it contains a manifest error or constitutes a misuse of power or whether the authority did not clearly exceed the bounds of its discretion." The Court may be expected to accord the ECB a similarly large degree of discretion with respect to the precise formulation of monetary policy, provided that the ECB's elaboration of what is meant by price stability is based on economically reasonable grounds.[24]

ESCB's Price Stability Mandate and Central Bank Independence

In the *OLAF* case[25] the Court was confronted with the question of whether conferring powers on the European Anti-Fraud Office (OLAF)—a bureau within the European Commission charged with combating fraud, corruption, and other illegal activities affecting the Community's financial interests—to conduct internal investigations within the ECB would infringe the ECB's independence under the Treaty. The ECB's independence is established under Article 108 of the Treaty, which provides that when exercising the powers and carrying out the tasks and duties conferred upon them by the Treaty, neither the ECB, nor a national central bank, nor any member of their decision-making bodies shall seek or take instructions from Community institutions (including the Commission) or bodies, from any government of a member state, or from any other body.

Although the Court ruled against the ECB on the facts of *OLAF*, it did note that "it is appropriate to state at the outset that the draftsmen of the EC Treaty clearly intended to ensure that the ECB should be in a position to carry out independently the tasks conferred upon it by the Treaty."[26] In considering the scope of the ECB's independence, both the Court and the advocate general, in his advisory opinion to the Court,[27] made a number of observations highlighting the important link between the objective of price stability and the principle of central bank independence.

Advocate General Francis Jacobs expressed the following opinion regarding this matter:

> It is … clear that the independence thus established is not an end in itself; it serves a specific purpose. By shielding the decision-making process of the ECB from short-term political pressures the principle of independence aims to enable the ECB effectively to pursue the aim of price stability and, without prejudice to that aim, support the economic policies in the Community as required by Article 105(1) EC.[28]

Advocate General Jacobs also noted that "[c]entral bank independence is thought to serve economic policy goals, notably to reduce inflation and, perhaps, promote economic growth."[29] In this respect, he referred the Court to specific economic literature for what he referred to as "an overview of the, not entirely conclusive, empirical evidence."[30] The economic literature cited by the advocate general notes that "[t]he foremost argument put forward in favor of an independent monetary authority is that of price stability" because "governments are tempted to create money for their own ends and in order to produce economic benefits in the short term, which eventually leads to an increase in the rate of inflation."[31] On the crucial question of the rate (as distinct from the variability) of inflation, the literature cited by the advocate general concludes that "[t]heoretical considerations on the relationship between central bank independence and the rate of inflation are backed by empirical evidence. On the basis of comparisons of the degree of independence of central banks and the inflation record of the respective country a negative correlation between the degree of independence and the inflation record has been generally acknowledged."[32]

The Court echoed the advocate general's view in more succinct, but trenchant, terms:

> Article 108 EC seeks, in essence, to shield the ECB from *all* political pressure in order to enable it effectively to pursue the objectives attributed to its tasks, through the independent exercise of the specific powers conferred on it for that purpose by the EC Treaty and the ESCB Statute.[33]

ESCB's Secondary Objective to Support General Economic Policies in the European Community

The Treaty provides that without prejudice to the primary objective of price stability, the ESCB shall support the general economic policies in the Community with a view to contributing to the achievement of the objectives of the Community.[34] A number of points can be noted regarding this provision.

First, it is clear that the ESCB has only one overriding objective—price stability—and that the ESCB's secondary objective to support general economic policies does not imply any goal sharing.[35] This is not to suggest that this secondary objective is meaningless. One commentator has argued that where the ECB has the choice between two measures of monetary policy, both of which comply with the primary objective of price stability, but only one of which has the additional quality of assisting general economic policies, then the ECB must give priority to that measure.[36] It is emphasized, however, that the decision in this respect lies solely with the ECB.[37]

Second, the secondary objective of the ESCB is to support the general economic *policies* (plural) *in* (rather than *of*) the Community. This wording reflects the fact that, under the Treaty arrangements for economic and monetary union, the primary responsibility for economic policy rests with the member states rather than the Community, subject to the obligation of member states to coordinate their economic policies within the EU Council and to avoid excessive government deficits, as further detailed in the EU Stability and Growth Pact.[38] The ESCB's primary objective to maintain price stability has to be understood against this background of a coordinated, but not a single, economic and fiscal policy.

Third, the ESCB's secondary objective is to support *general,* rather than *specific,* economic policies in the Community, implying that the ESCB should have regard to general trends in economic policies.[39] One practical way in which the ECB can support the general economic policies pursued in the Community is by expressing its views regarding economic developments and, like any central bank, offering suggestions for improvement.[40] The mandate to support the general economic policies in the Community does not require the ECB to coordinate its independently formulated monetary policy *ex ante* with the economic policies in the Community. The existence of this secondary objective is, however, part of the rationale behind the ongoing dialogue between the ECB and economic policy makers at Community level.[41] This dialogue is underpinned by a number of institutional provisions in the Treaty. For example, the President of the EU Council of Finance Ministers (ECOFIN) and a member of the Commission may participate, without having the right to vote, in meetings of the Governing Council of the ECB.[42] The President of the ECB shall be invited to participate in ECOFIN meetings when the Council is discussing matters relating to the objectives and tasks of the ESCB.[43] The member states, the Commission, and the ECB each appoint not more than two members of the Economic and Financial Committee (EFC), which has the tasks, *inter alia*, of keeping under review the economic and financial situation of the member states and of the Community, reporting thereon regularly to the ECOFIN and to the Commission, and contributing to the ECOFIN's work on the co-ordination and multilateral surveillance of the economic policies of member states and the avoidance of excessive government deficits in connection with the Stability and Growth Pact.[44]

Constitutional Implications of ESCB's Mandate

Prior to the *OLAF* case the precise constitutional relationship be-tween the ECB and the European Community was the subject of aca-demic controversy. Based, *inter alia*, on the ECB's independence and separate legal personality under the Treaty,[45] some commentators argued that the ECB is "an independent specialised organisation of Community law, independent from (albeit associated with) the Euro-pean Communities," while others regarded the ECB, quite simply, as "the Central Bank of the European Community."[46]

In the *OLAF* case the Court considered the ESCB's mandate to be particularly relevant to understanding the constitutional position of the ECB within the Community legal order. Advocate General Jacobs made the following observations on this point:

> [I]t may be recalled that Article 105(1) EC provides that '[w]ithout prejudice to the objective of price stability, the ESCB shall support the general economic policies in the Community with a view to contributing to the achievement of the objectives of the Community as laid down in Article 2'. That provision corresponds to Article 4 EC ... which provides that '[f]or the purposes set out in Article 2, the activities of the member states and of the Community shall include ... the adoption of an economic policy' and that '[c]oncurrently with the foregoing ... these activities shall include the ... definition and conduct of a single monetary policy and exchange-rate policy the primary objective of both of which shall be to maintain price stability and, without prejudice to this objective, to support the general economic policies in the Community in accordance with the principle of an open market economy with free competition'.... It follows ... that the ECB forms an integral part of the Community framework.... The ECB is subject to the general principles of law which form part of the Community and promotes the goals of the

Community set out in Article 2 EC through the implementation of the tasks and duties laid upon it. It may therefore be described as the Central Bank of the *European Community*; it would be inaccurate to characterise it, as have some writers, as an organisation which is 'independent of the European Community', a 'Community within the Community', [or] a 'new Community.'[47]

Again, the Court echoed the opinion of the advocate general:

[U]nder Article 4(2) and Article 105(1) EC, the primary objective of the ESCB, at the heart of which is the ECB, is to maintain price stability and, without prejudice to this objective, to lend support to the general economic policies in the European Community, with a view to contributing to the achievement of the objectives of the Community as laid down in Article 2 EC, which include an economic and monetary union and also the promotion of sustainable and non-inflationary growth. It follows that the ECB, pursuant to the EC Treaty, falls squarely within the Community framework.[48]

In addition to clarifying the constitutional position of the ECB within the Community legal order, the *OLAF* case indicates a strong appreciation on the part of the Court that the ESCB's primary objective to maintain price stability is one of the cornerstones of economic and monetary union and, therefore, of the Community itself.[49] A number of Treaty provisions in addition to those cited by the Court and the advocate general point towards the central role accorded to the objective of maintaining price stability within the Community legal order.[50] First, the preamble to the Treaty on European Union, under which the provisions on economic and monetary union were introduced into Community law, notes the resolve of the member states to establish "a single and stable currency."[51] Second, the activities of the Community and the member states concerning economic and monetary union entail compliance with stable prices as a guiding principle.[52] Third, as noted above, the decision as to which member states fulfill the necessary conditions for the adoption of the euro is made on the basis of an examination of, *inter alia*, the achievement of a high degree of price stability.[53] Fourth, as part of the legal integration of national central banks into the ESCB, most national central banks' statutes were required to be adapted in order to reflect the primary objective of the ESCB to maintain price stability.[54] Fifth, in order to prevent central bank financing of the public sector from fuelling inflation, the Treaty imposes on ESCB central banks a prohibition on monetary financing.[55] Sixth, while the EU Council may, in the absence of an exchange-rate system for the euro in relation to non-Community currencies (such as the old Bretton Woods system of near-fixed exchange rates), formulate general orientations for exchange-rate policy in relation to these currencies, these general orientations shall be without prejudice to the primary objective of the ESCB to maintain price stability.[56]

It is interesting to note the advocate general's suggestion that the close identification of the ESCB's mandate with the European Community itself is also reflected in the obligation of the ESCB to act in accordance with the principle of an open market economy with free competition, favoring an efficient allocation of resources. In this respect, the adherence of the ESCB to the principles of an open market economy must be seen against the ECB's place within the framework of a Community, one of whose main tasks is to establish an internal market based on the free movement of persons, goods, services, and capital.[57]

Application of ESCB Mandate to Central Banks Outside the Euro Area

At the time of writing, only 15 of the current 27 EU member states have adopted the euro. The remaining member states are treated, in the jargon of the Treaty, as "member states with a derogation," which means that the key Treaty provisions relating to monetary union do not apply to those member states.[58] While all 27 national central banks are members of the ESCB, the central banks of member states with a derogation retain their powers in the field of monetary policy according to national law.[59]

The Treaty is unclear as to when the central banks of member states with a derogation must comply with the primary objective of price stability (i.e., either straightaway, or only from the time the euro is adopted as the currency of the member state in question).[60] There is a technical inconsistency within the wording of the Treaty regarding whether the price stability objective is applicable to the central banks of member states with a derogation. Within the main body of the Treaty, it is stipulated that a derogation shall entail that various specified Treaty articles, including Article 105(1) (the provision that sets out the ESCB's primary objective to maintain price stability), do not apply to the member states concerned.[61] However, the Treaty further stipulates that the exclusion of such a member state and its national central bank from rights and obligations within the ESCB is laid down in Chapter IX of the Protocol on the Statute of the European System of Central Banks and of the ESCB Statute, annexed as a protocol to the Treaty.[62] Chapter IX of the ESCB Statute in turn stipulates that a derogation shall entail that various specified articles of the ESCB Statute shall not confer any rights or impose any obligations on the member state concerned, but surprisingly does not list Article 105(1) among the excluded provisions.[63] This suggests that the primary objective of maintaining price stability applies to all ESCB central banks, not only to the ECB and the central banks of member states that have adopted the euro (commonly referred to collectively as the Eurosystem).

In regard to this conflict within the text of the Treaty, a number of points would appear to support the interpretation that the primary objective of the ESCB to maintain price stability applies to all ESCB central banks.[64]

First, from a textual perspective the primary objective of the ESCB to maintain price stability is an objective that applies to the central bank members of the ESCB, rather than their respective member states as such. Insofar as the main body of the Treaty sets out the legal implications of a derogation for member states only, and then refers to the ESCB Statute for an understanding regarding the exclusion of both member states *and* their national central banks from rights and obligations within the ESCB, the ESCB Statute would appear to be more directly relevant to understanding the specific implications of a derogation for the central bank of a member state with a derogation.[65]

Second, it is an established principle of interpretation endorsed by the European Court of Justice that every provision of Community law must be placed in its context and interpreted in the light of the provisions of Community law as a whole, regard being paid to the objectives thereof and to its state of evolution at the date on which the provision in question is to be applied.[66] In this respect, the objective to maintain price stability is accorded a central role in the Community legal order. As noted above, the objectives of the Community include the promotion of noninflationary growth,[67] and the activities of the member states and the Community concerning economic and monetary union entail compliance with stable prices as a guiding principle.[68] The application of the primary objective of the ESCB to maintain price stability to the central banks of member states with a derogation would therefore appear more consistent with the overall scheme and purpose of the EC Treaty.[69]

Third, this conclusion is also based on the underlying rationale of central bank independence, which is only justified if the overall objective of price stability has primacy[70] consistent with the close link between the ESCB's objective of price stability and the principle of central bank independence identified by the Court of Justice in the *OLAF* case.

Price Stability and the Treaty of Lisbon

In what was intended to mark an important step in the history of European integration, the heads of state or government of the EU member states signed the Treaty establishing a Constitution for Europe (the European Constitution) in October 2004. Ratification of the European Constitution was rejected, however, in referenda in France and the Netherlands in mid-2005. Following this, the more modest Treaty of Lisbon amending the Treaty on European Union and the Treaty Establishing the European Community (the Treaty of Lisbon) was signed in late 2007.

It is of particular interest in the current context that similar to the text of the European Constitution on which it is based, the Treaty of Lisbon confirms that the primary objective of the ESCB shall be to maintain price stability and, without prejudice to that objective, to support the general economic policies in the European Union in contributing to the achievement of the Union's objectives.[71] During the discussions of the draft Constitution in the Convention on the Future of Europe (the Convention), some Convention members proposed that supporting sustainable growth and high levels of employment should be added, on an equal footing, to the primary objective of price stability. The vast majority of Convention members rejected this suggestion on the ground that the ESCB's current mandate to pursue price stability as a primary objective is based on a broad consensus of policy makers and economists that maintaining price stability is the best contribution monetary policy can make toward the achievement of other economic goals, including growth and employment.[72]

Members of the Convention also touched upon the question of the extent to which price stability should be an objective not only for the ESCB but also for the member states and the Union as a whole. There was general agreement that the Constitution should confirm that the activities of the member states and the Union in connection with the single currency entail compliance with stable prices as a guiding principle.[73] A debate ensued, however, on whether price stability should continue to be listed among the overarching objectives of the Union. In its contribution to this debate, the ECB stressed three points. First, noninflationary growth is mentioned as one of the Community's objectives in the existing EC Treaty. Second, price stability is not only the ESCB's primary objective, but it also forms part of the heart of monetary union for all European citizens; in this sense stable prices clearly benefit society. Third, the introduction of a simplified procedure to amend the part of the Constitution that includes the ESCB's primary objective of price stability rendered it necessary to include a reference to price stability among the Union's objectives in order to strengthen the Union's commitment to price stability.[74] The ECB's arguments were accepted, and the key objectives of the Union enshrined in both the Lisbon Treaty and the Constitution were reformulated to include the following reference to price stability:

> The Union ... shall work for the sustainable development of Europe based on balanced economic growth and price stability, a highly competitive social market economy, aiming at full employment and social progress, and a high level of protection and improvement of the quality of the environment. It shall promote scientific and technological advance.[75]

Summary and Conclusions

This chapter has explored the price stability mandate of the ESCB from a legal perspective. The EC Treaty establishes a clear hierarchy of objectives for the ESCB, within which it assigns overriding importance to maintaining price stability. Without prejudice to the ESCB's primary objective to maintain price stability, the ESCB has the secondary objective to support the general economic policies in the European Community (soon to be replaced under the Treaty of Lisbon by the European Union[76]).

The ESCB's mandate is often contrasted with that of the U.S. Federal Reserve System, which is required to promote the multiple goals of maximum employment, stable prices, and moderate long-term interest rates, without establishing any hierarchy among these goals. By focusing the monetary policy of the ESCB on the primary objective of price stability, the EC Treaty makes it clear that ensuring price stability is the most important contribution that monetary policy can make to achieving a favorable economic environment and a high level of employment.

Because the ESCB's primary objective of price stability is written into the Treaty, it can only be amended by means of an inter-governmental conference followed by ratification of the amendments by all member states in accordance with their respective constitutional requirements. This makes the objective of price stability more robust than if it were a statutory objective enshrined in secondary legislation, as is the case for central banks in most countries, which are typically chartered under parliamentary legislation rather than international treaties.

The Treaty does not give a precise definition of what is meant by price stability. The term is generally understood as denoting internal price stability, meaning the volume of goods and services which can be obtained for one euro, as opposed to the stability or strength of the currency in terms of other currencies such as the U.S. dollar. In the absence of any clarification in the Treaty regarding the specific level of price stability to be maintained by the ESCB, the ECB is in a position to determine for itself what level of price stability it considers acceptable. The ECB has defined this price stability in quantitative terms as a year-on-year increase in the Harmonised Index of Consumer Prices (HICP) for the euro area of below, but close to, 2 percent over the medium term. This makes clear that not only inflation above 2 percent, but also deflation, would be inconsistent with price stability. As a matter of strict legal theory, the European Court of Justice, as the final arbiter regarding the interpretation of the Treaty, may be called upon to determine whether particular measures adopted by the ECB are consistent with the ESCB's primary objective to maintain price stability. In practice, the Court may be expected to accord the ECB a large degree of discretion with respect to the precise formulation of monetary policy, provided that the ECB's elaboration of what is meant by price stability is based on economically reasonable grounds.

In the *OLAF* case the Court highlighted the important link between the ESCB's objective of price stability and the principle of central bank independence. In particular, the Court emphasized that the independence granted to the ECB under the Treaty seeks in essence to shield the ECB from all political pressure in order to enable the ECB effectively to pursue the aim of price stability and, without prejudice to that aim, to support the economic policies in the Community.

Regarding the ESCB's secondary objective to support general economic policies in the Community/Union, it is emphasized that the ESCB's secondary objective is to support general, rather than specific, economic policies in the Community/Union. This implies that the ESCB should have regard for general trends in economic policies. This secondary objective partly explains the ongoing dialogue between the ECB and economic policy makers at the Community/Union level, which is underpinned by a number of institutional provisions in the Treaty. In this respect, it is recalled that the ESCB must pursue its objectives in an environment of a coordinated, but not a single, economic and fiscal policy, since the main responsibility for economic and fiscal policy remains at the national rather than the Community/Union level.

In the *OLAF* case the European Court of Justice considered the ESCB's mandate to be of particular relevance to understanding the constitutional position of the ECB as falling squarely within the Community (soon Union) legal order. In addition, the Court indicated a strong appreciation that the ESCB's primary objective to maintain price stability is one of the cornerstones of economic and monetary union and, therefore, of the Community/Union itself. In this regard, this chapter argues that the primary objective of maintaining price stability applies to the central banks of all EU member states, not only to the ECB and the central banks of member states which have adopted the euro.

The Treaty of Lisbon, which is scheduled to enter into force on January 1, 2009, confirms that the primary objective of the ESCB is to maintain price stability and, without prejudice to that objective, to support the general economic policies in the European Union. The Convention on the Future of Europe, which prepared the constitutional text on which the Lisbon Treaty was based, rejected the arguments of some members that supporting sustainable growth and high levels of employment should be added, on an equal footing, to the primary objective of price stability. Indeed, the overarching objectives of the Union enshrined in the final text of the Lisbon Treaty make explicit reference to the Union working for the sustainable development of Europe based, *inter alia*, on balanced economic growth and price stability.

Notes

Note: The author wishes to thank Inigo Arruga, Principal Legal Counsel, ECB, Kristine Drevina, Legal Counsel, and Andres Tupits, Senior Legal Counsel, ECB, for their helpful comments on this paper. Any views expressed in this paper are those of the author, and may not be attributed to the ECB.

[1] René Smits, *The European Central Bank: Institutional Aspects* (Kluwer Law International, 1997), at 184.

[2] The central banking system of the euro is comprised only of the ECB and the national central banks of the (at the time of writing) 15 EU member states that have adopted the euro, commonly referred to as the Eurosystem.

[3] Treaty Establishing the European Community [hereinafter the EC Treaty], Article 105(1), first and second sentences.

[4] Case C-11/00, *Commission of the European Communities v. European Central Bank*, [2003] E.C.R. I-7147.

[5] *See* European Central Bank, *The Monetary Policy of the ECB* (2004), at 9–10.

[6] *See* Smits, *supra* note 1, at 184; Chiara Zilioli and Martin Selmayr, *The Law of the European Central Bank* (Hart Publishing, 2001), 35–36.

[7] Article 48, Treaty on European Union; *see also* Matthias J. Herdegen, "Price Stability and Budgetary Restraints in the Economic and Monetary Union: The Law as Guardian of Economic Wisdom," *Common Market Law Report* 9 (1998), at 21.

[8] U.S. Federal Reserve Act, § 2A, 12 U.S.C. § 225a. For a comparative commentary regarding the respective goals of the ESCB and the U.S. Federal Reserve System, see Carel C.A. van den Berg, *The Making of the Statute of the European System of Central Banks* (Dutch University Press, 2004), at 51–60.

[9] *See* European Central Bank, *supra* note 5, at 43-44; Hanspeter Scheller, *The European Central Bank: History, Role and Functions* (European Central Bank, 2004), 45–47.

[10] *See* European Central Bank, *supra* note 5, at 10; Jean-Victor Louis, *L'Union économique et monétaire*, in Commentaire Megret, *Le Droit de la CEE* (Editions de l'Université de Bruxelles, 1995), at 58; Scheller, *supra*

note 9, at 45–47; Jean-Claude Trichet, *Why Price Stability?* (European Central Bank, 2001), at 220.

[11] Committee for the Study of Economic and Monetary Union, *Report on Economic and Monetary Union in the European Community* (Office for Official Publications of the European Communities, 1989), para. 32; Karl Otto Pöhl, "The further development of the European Monetary System," published in the collection of papers submitted to the Committee for the Study of Economic and Monetary Union, *Report on Economic and Monetary Union in the European Communities* (Office for Official Publications of the European Communities, 1989), para. IIB.1; *see also* van den Berg, *supra* note 8, at 60–71.

[12] *See* Louis, *supra* note 10, at 58; Philippe-Emmanuel Partsch, "La Politique Monétaire," in *Union européenne/ Communauté européenne, Commentaire article par article des traités UE et CE*, (Helbing & Lichtenhahn, 2000), at 1000; van den Berg, *supra* note 8, at 51–52.

[13] See Rosa M. Lastra, *Legal Foundations of International Monetary Stability* (Oxford University Press, 2006), at 56; van den Berg, *supra* note 8, at 52–53; Christian Waigel, *Die Unabhängigkeit der Europäischen Zentralbank* (Nomos Verlagsgesellschaft, 1999), at 21.

[14] *See* Lastra, *supra* note 13, at 37–38.

[15] *See* Charlotte Gaitanides, *Das Recht der Europäischen Zentralbank* (Mohr Siebeck, 2005), 18–20; Smits, *supra* note 1, at 184; Rainer Stadler, *Der rechtliche Handlungsspielraum des Europäischen Systems der Zentralbanken* (Nomos Verlagsgesellschaft, 1996), at 100.

[16] EC Treaty, Articles 121(1) and 122(2).

[17] Protocol (No. 6) annexed to the EC Treaty on the convergence criteria referred to in Article 121 (ex Article 109j) of the Treaty, Article 1.

[18] See Martin Selmayr, "Wie unabhänig ist die Europäische Zentralbank?" 49 *Wertpapier Mitteilungen* (1999), 2429, at 2431–32.

[19] *See* Partsch, *supra* note 12, at 1001; Smits, *supra* note 1, at 186.

[20] *See* European Central Bank, *supra* note 5, at 50–55.

[21] EC Treaty, Articles 230 (1)–(2), 232 (1), (4), 234; *see also* D.R.R. Dunnett, "Legal and Institutional Issues Affecting Economic and Monetary Union," in *Legal Issues of the Maastricht Treaty* (Wiley Chancery Law, 1994),

at 137; Prof. Dr. Bernhard Kempen, *EUV/EGV Vertrag über die Europäische Union und Vertrag zur Gründung der Europäischen Gemeinschaft (Art. 105 EGV)*, (Verlag C.H. Beck, 2003), at 1309; Smits, *supra* note 1, at 186.

[22] *See* Selmayr, *supra* note 18, at 2432; Smits, *supra* note 1, at 185-86; Stadler, *supra* note 15, at 103-4.

[23] Case 29/77, *S.A. Roquette Frères v. French State* [1977] E.C.R. 1835, paras. 19-20; see also Case 74-74, *Comptoir national technique agricole (CNTA) SA v. Commission of the European Communities* [1975] E.C.R. 533, paras. 16, 21-23.

[24] *See* Gaitanides, *supra* note 15, at 39-40.

[25] Case C-11/00, *Commission of the European Communities v. European Central Bank*, [2003] E.C.R. I -7147.

[26] *Id.*, para. 130.

[27] Under the Treaty it is the duty of the advocate-general, acting with complete impartiality and independence, to make, in open court, reasoned submissions on cases brought before the Court of Justice, in order to assist the Court in the performance of its task. *See* EC Treaty, Article 222, second para.

[28] Case C-11/00, *Commission of the European Communities v. European Central Bank*, [2003] E.C.R. I-7147, Advocate General Jacobs on 3 October 2002, paras. 150 and 155.

[29] *Id.*, para. 150, note 115.

[30] *Id.* (citing Fabian Amtenbrink, *The Democratic Accountability of Central Banks* (Hart Publishing, 1999), 11–17 and 23–26).

[31] *See* Amtenbrink, *supra* note 30, at 12–14.

[32] *Id.*, 15 (citing, e.g., A. Alesina and L.H. Summers, "Central Bank Independence and Macroeconomic Performance: Some Comparative Evidence," 25 *Journal of Money Credit & Banking* No. 2 (1993), at 151–62, at 159; A. Cukierman, S.B. Webb, and B. Neyapti, "Measuring the Independence of Central Banks and Its Effects on Policy Outcomes," 6 *The World Economic Review* No. 3 (1992), 353-98, at 383).

[33] Case C-11/00, *Commission of the European Communities v. European Central Bank*, [2003] E.C.R. I-7147, para. 134 (emphasis added). For an

analysis of this aspect of the Court's decision, see Frank Elderson and Hans Weenink, "The European Court of Justice redefined? A landmark judgement of the European Court of Justice," *Euredia* 2003 - 2, 273, at 291-94, 300.

[34] EC Treaty, Article 105(1), second sentence.

[35] *See* Prof. Dr. Ulrich Häde, *Kommentar des Vertrages über die Europäische Union und des Vertrages zur Gründung der Europäischen Gemeinschaft – EUV/EGV (Art. 105)*, Luchterhand, at 1347; Kempen, *supra* note 21, at 1310; Louis, *supra* note 10, at 59; Selmayr, *supra* note 18, at 2431; van den Berg, *supra* note 8, at 55.

[36] *See* Louis, *supra* note 10, at 59.

[37] *Id.*

[38] EC Treaty, Articles 98, 99 and 104; Protocol annexed to the Treaty on the excessive deficit procedure; Resolution of the European Council on the Stability and Growth Pact, Amsterdam, 17 June 1997; Council Regulation (EC) No 1466/97 of 7 July 1997 on the strengthening of the surveillance of budgetary positions and the surveillance and coordination of economic policies, as amended; Council Regulation (EC) No 1467/97 of 7 July 1997 on speeding up and clarifying the implementation of the excessive deficit procedure, as amended; *see also* Häde, supra note 35, at 1347; Kempen, *supra* note 21, at 1310; Louis, *supra* note 10, at 59; Smits, *supra* note 1, at 181-82, 187-88; van den Berg, *supra* note 8, at 55; Dr. Andreas Zahraknik, *Kommentar zu EU- und EG- Vertrag: Art. 105-124 EGV,* (Manzsche Verlags- und Universitätsbuchhandlung, 2004), at 5.

[39] *See* Smits, *supra* note 1, at 188.

[40] *Id.*, at 189.

[41] *See* Scheller, *supra* note 9, at 47.

[42] EC Treaty, Article 113(1). The President of the ECOFIN may also submit a motion for deliberation to the Governing Council of the ECB.

[43] EC Treaty, Article 113(2).

[44] EC Treaty, Article 114(2), (4).

[45] EC Treaty, Articles 107(2), 108.

[46] *Compare* Zilioli and Selmayr, *supra* note 6, at 1-35, especially at 29–32, with Ramon Torrent, "Whom is the European Central Bank the central bank of?: Reaction to Zilioli and Selmayr," *Common Market Law Report* 1229 (1999), at 1129-34.

[47] Opinion of Advocate General Jacobs, *supra* note 28, at paras. 57-60.

[48] Case C-11/00, *Commission of the European Communities v. European Central Bank*, [2003] E.C.R. I-7147, at paras. 91-92. For an interesting analysis of this aspect of the *OLAF* case, see Elderson and Weenink, *supra* note 33, at 281–87.

[49] *See generally* Herdegen, *supra* note 7, at 10-11, 14-17, 20-22.
[50] *See* Gaitanides, *supra* note 15, at 16; Stefan Tilch, *Europäische Zentralbank und Europäisches System der Zentralbanken* (Peter Lang), at 154.

[51] Treaty on European Union, Recital 6.

[52] EC Treaty, Article 4(3).

[53] EC Treaty, Articles 121(1) and 122(2); Protocol (No. 6) annexed to the EC Treaty on the convergence criteria referred to in Article 121 (ex Article 109j) of the Treaty, Article 1.

[54] EC Treaty, Article 109; see European Monetary Institute, *Convergence Report* (March 1998), 296, 307, 310, 313, 315-16, 318, 322, 330, 333, 337, 340, 344, 348.

[55] EC Treaty, Article 101(1), which provides that overdraft facilities or any other type of credit facility with the ECB or with the national central banks in favor of Community institutions or bodies, central governments, regional, local or other public authorities, other bodies governed by public law, or public undertakings of member states shall be prohibited, as shall the purchase directly from them by the ECB or national central banks of debt instruments. When drafting the Treaty prohibition on monetary financing, the Committee of Governors of the Central Banks of the member states of the (then) European Economic Community noted that the prohibition "is generally regarded as necessary to ensure the System's ability to achieve its primary objective" of price stability. See Committee of Governors, *Explanatory Note on Certain Articles Contained in the Proposed Statute of the ESCB and of the ECB* (2 September 1991), at 3.

[56] EC Treaty, Article 111(2). Moreover, the EU Council may only conclude formal agreements on such an exchange-rate system for the euro in relation to non-Community currencies, and adopt, adjust, or abandon the central rates of

the euro within the exchange-rate system, after consulting the ECB in an endeavor to reach a consensus consistent with price stability. EC Treaty, Article 111(1).

[57] *See* Smits, *supra* note 1, at 190-92.

[58] EC Treaty, Article 122.
   Denmark has an exemption, the effect of which is that all provisions of the Treaty and the ESCB Statute referring to a derogation are applicable to Denmark. As for the abrogation of Denmark's exemption, the procedure for deciding whether Denmark fulfils the necessary conditions for the adoption of the euro shall only be initiated at the request of Denmark. See the Protocol annexed to the EC Treaty on certain provisions relating to Denmark.
   Unless the United Kingdom notifies the EU Council that it intends to move to the third stage of economic and monetary union, it shall be under no obligation to do so. The full legal consequences of the special status of the United Kingdom are spelled out in the Protocol annexed to the EC Treaty on certain provisions relating to the United Kingdom of Great Britain and Northern Ireland (the UK Protocol).

[59] Article 43(2) of the ESCB Statute. In the case of the United Kingdom, the United Kingdom (as distinct from the Bank of England) shall retain its powers in the field of monetary policy according to national law. UK Protocol, paragraph 4.

[60] *See* European Central Bank, *Convergence Report* (December 2006), at 24, available on the ECB's website at www.ect.int/pub/pdf/conrep/cr200612en.pdf.

[61] EC Treaty, Article 122(3), first sentence. Similarly, the UK Protocol stipulates that Article 105(1) of the Treaty shall not apply to the United Kingdom. UK Protocol, paragraph 5, first sentence.

[62] EC Treaty, Article 122(3), second sentence.

[63] ESCB Statute, Article 43.1 (which fails to refer to Article 2 of the ESCB Statute). Similarly, when identifying the articles of the ESCB Statute that shall not apply to the United Kingdom, the UK Protocol fails to refer to Article 2 of the ESCB Statute. UK Protocol, paragraph 8.

[64] The case of the Bank of England is less straightforward in view of the particular provisions of the UK Protocol. *See* notes 65, 68 and 70, *infra*.

[65] This particular argument would appear less persuasive in the case of the Bank of England given that the UK Protocol stipulates that Article 105(1) of

the Treaty shall not apply to the United Kingdom, and that in this provision "references to national central banks shall not include the Bank of England." UK Protocol, paragraph 5.

[66] *See, e.g.*, Case 283/81, *CILFIT v. Italian Ministry of Health* [1982] E.C.R. 3415, 3430.

[67] EC Treaty, Article 2.

[68] EC Treaty, Article 4(3). The activities of the member states and the Community concerning monetary union set out in Article 4(2) of the Treaty, to which Article 4(3) refers in part, shall not apply to the United Kingdom. UK Protocol, paragraph 5. However, the activities of the member states and the Community concerning economic policy coordination set out in Article 4(1) of the Treaty, to which Article 4(3) also refers in part, apply to the United Kingdom, and these particular activities of the United Kingdom would therefore appear to entail compliance with "stable prices" as a guiding principle.

[69] *See* European Central Bank, *supra* note 60, at 24.

[70] *See* European Central Bank, *supra* note 60, at 24. This particular point is not persuasive in the case of the United Kingdom insofar as the UK Protocol stipulates that Article 108 of the Treaty, which enshrines the independence of ESCB central banks, shall not apply to the United Kingdom, and that in this provision references to national central banks shall not include the Bank of England. UK Protocol, paragraph 5.

[71] Article 2, Treaty of Lisbon (amending Article 105(5), EC Treaty, whose title is to be renamed the "Treaty on the Functioning of the European Union"); *see also* Articles I-30(2), second sentence, and III-85(1), Treaty establishing a Constitution for Europe.

[72] *See* European Central Bank, "The European Constitution and the ECB," *ECB Monthly Bulletin* (August 2004), at 58-59; Jean-Victor Louis, "Monetary Policy and Central Banking in the Constitution," published in European Central Bank, *Legal Aspects of the European System of Central Banks: Liber Amicorum Paolo Zamboni Garavelli* (2005), 27, at 36; Dominique Servais and Rudolphe Ruggeri, "The EU Constitution: Its Impact on Economic and Monetary Union and Economic Convergence," published in European Central Bank, *Legal Aspects of the European System of Central Banks: Liber Amicorum Paolo Zamboni Garavelli* (2005), 43, at 45-46.

[73] Article III-177(3), Treaty establishing a Constitution for Europe.

[74] *See* Letter from Jean-Claude Trichet, President, European Central Bank, to Brian Cowen, President, Council of the European Union, 16 April 2004, "Negotiations on the draft Treaty establishing a Constitution for Europe," 1, published on the ECB's website at www.ecb.int/pub; *see also* European Central Bank, *supra* note 72, at 59; Servais and Ruggeri, *supra* note 72, at 45.

[75] Article 1, Treaty of Lisbon (introducing new Article 3(3), first para., Treaty on European Union); *see also* Article I-3(3), first para., Treaty establishing a Constitution for Europe. Some commentators have questioned whether this wording refers to price stability as a goal, or rather as a means to achieve the sustainable development of Europe alongside balanced economic growth, a competitive social market economy, and so on. See Servais and Ruggeri, *supra* note 72, at 45.

[76] Article 1, Treaty of Lisbon (introducing new Article 1, third para., third sentence, Treaty on European Union).

3 | Should a Central Bank Also Be a Banking Supervisor?

FRANCISCO JOSÉ DE SIQUEIRA

This chapter examines the tension between ensuring a stable monetary system and supervising commercial banks, with specific focus on the Latin American experience. It addresses the key question of whether the banking supervisory function should be located within a central bank, whose first obligation is price stability, and presents the arguments both for and against separation of the functions.

The Latin American Experience

As late as the second half of the nineteenth century, banks in Latin America were not under state regulation. The financial systems existed basically for commercial transactions, and currency was issued by many banks. Because central banks did not exist at the time, the functions that would otherwise be exercised by central banks were decentralized.

Eventually, currency instability and its consequent impact on the means of payment made it clear that it was necessary to regulate both issuing and credit. Although several countries centralized their issuing in the late nineteenth and early twentieth centuries, until World War I the only central bank in the region was the Central Bank of Uruguay, created in 1896. It was only after World War I that the region improved regulation and control of its monetary systems by institutionalizing central banks.

The Brussels International Financial Conference, convened by the League of Nations in 1920, played a decisive role in the creation of central banks in Latin America. At the conference, countries that did not yet have their own central banks were advised to constitute one. The central bank would be both the basis upon which the monetary systems of the post-war world would rise and the mechanism that would facilitate a country's financial relationships. A central bank's autonomy from the direct influence of its national government was considered a key force in opposing budgetary deficits and, consequently, in preventing inflationary surges.

From 1923 on, central banks were founded in several Latin American countries: Colombia (1923), Chile (1925), Guatemala (1925), Mexico (1925), Ecuador (1927), Bolivia (1929), Peru (1931), El Salvador (1934), Argentina (1935), Costa Rica (1936), Venezuela (1939), Nicaragua (1941), Paraguay (1944), Dominican Republic (1947), Cuba (1949), Honduras (1951), Brazil (1964), and Haiti (1979). In contrast to the Central Bank of Uruguay, which had been inspired by the English model, most of those institutions were influenced either by the Federal Reserve System (Fed) of the United States or by the past experience of the region.

The process of determining which functions should be assigned to the nascent central banks was more the result of political decisions than a response to economic necessity. In the natural course of events, banking supervision was added to the list of central bank responsibilities due to each country's legislative policy and governmental structure.

Latin American central banks have evolved to adapt themselves to macroeconomic environments that are in constant change. This experience has, in turn, played a key role in determining how the financial systems have developed. Central banks in the region have become vital actors in supporting economic development as well as decisive instruments in rebuilding the financial stability once missing during episodes of monetary expansionism. Yet in the 1970s they still had to face external disturbances resulting from severe instabilities in world economy. And in the 1980s, having become established institutions, national central banks possessed the capabilities to withstand the external debt crisis that damaged countries like Mexico and Brazil.

Monetary Policy and Banking Supervision

In general, there are two complementary views in regard to governmental structures for monetary policy and banking supervision. The first would diminish a central bank's role as a banking supervisor in order to strengthen the central bank's autonomy. The second view, which is increasingly being followed, defends the combination of banking, securities, and insurance supervision in a single entity, distinct from the central bank, as the way to improve consolidated supervision of financial groups.

The latter trend argues that banking supervision should not be among a central bank's responsibilities, so that the principal objective of the institution—price stability—is emphasized. Thus, assembled in a different entity, the supervision of banking, securities, and insurance would make the activity of supervising groups that act in every segment more efficient.

Reasons for the Separation of the Functions

Central bank autonomy is a powerful argument for removing the monetary authority's responsibility for banking supervision. The need to protect a central bank's monetary functions has justified the political choice of locating banking supervision in another entity.

Central bank and *monetary policy* are relatively recent concepts. Until the midst of the 19th century, currency was a piece of commonly accepted merchandise (gold or silver). The concept of monetary policy only became relevant with the appearance of banknotes and bank money, when currency became a sort of security (banknote) or a bank account balance (bank money) instead of a sort of good.

The adoption of fiduciary currencies (legal tender and inconvertible) did not happen entirely peacefully or without traumas. Public opinion, governments, and politicians from the developed world did notice the episodes of hyperinflation that occurred in Germany and other Eastern Europe countries in the 1930s. These events led to a last attempt to keep international monetary rules under the Bretton Woods system, according to which the North American currency was convertible into gold, whereas the remaining currencies were convertible into American dollars.

The post-war period was a time of economic progress and transformation, in part because of the strong influence of the economist John Maynard Keynes. At that time, two distinct schools of economic thought appeared in the debate over the role of currency in the economy. Keynesians understood that variations in the money supply affected the real economy, and accordingly they supported the discretionary conduct of monetary policy. On the other hand, monetarists argued that currency caused little impact on real economy, at least in the long run. Consequently, monetarists insisted on the management of monetary policy according to strict rules.

It was also a time when the debate on central bank autonomy fueled the controversy over regulation versus discretion of monetary policy. With the gold standard abolished in the early 1970s, what would be chosen to replace it: a new system or the discretion of an autonomous central bank? The truth is that economists do not have a clear and unequivocal answer to this question. There are theoretical arguments that favor the establishment of a rule for monetary policy (inflation targeting, currency boards, etc.), but there is no consensus on the design of such a definitive rule. There is also empirical evidence favorable to central bank autonomy, but there is no consensus on the precise institutional format of this autonomy.

The trend that seems to prevail today is to maintain a discretionary monetary policy in which the money supply is set according to economic necessities. Moreover, it is important to mention that most democratic societies do not seem to be willing to confer this discretionary power to the government, but prefer delegating it to an autonomous central bank. This view reflects what has become a consensus among economists: monetary stability is a precondition for long-term growth and inflation is a socially regressive tax.

When discussing the subject of central bank autonomy, two aspects must be highlighted. First, the desired autonomy of the central bank is basically restricted to monetary policy. Second, once it is not possible for a central bank to have absolute control over the economy, the right degree of autonomy is a matter of political decision.

There is also concern about how a governmental institution can have a mandate—in this case for monetary policy—that may, when exercised, conflict with other areas of the government. A central bank that is autonomous from the government is better able to make decisions aimed at preserving stability of prices.

Because central bank autonomy is justified by its important role in determining monetary policy, the imposition of other aims and functions, such as banking supervision, is seen as harmful to the central bank's autonomy because it weakens and compromises the main objective of price stability. The more singularly the objective of a central bank to maintain monetary stability is defined, the greater its autonomy. If the central bank is also a banking supervisor, it can be vulnerable to political pressure to act in a way that is beneficial to banks but not to monetary stability.

Despite the importance of the opinions according to which banking supervision should not be one of the functions of an autonomous central bank, there is no consensus that monetary policy would actually be better if the central bank were not a supervising entity. The last two chairmen of the U.S. Federal Reserve were eloquent defenders of the maintenance of its power in the area of banking supervision. The arguments of this defense are normally related to macroeconomic concerns about price stability and sound payments systems, as well as to the rediscount window, since the information obtained in the course of supervisory actions can also be used for purposes of monetary regulation. For example, in 1994 the Fed chairman Alan Greenspan, in a statement before the Committee of Banking, Housing and Urban Affairs of the U.S. Senate, asserted that joint responsibility produces better results for supervision and monetary policy than would be obtained by a supervisor that had no macroeconomic responsibilities or an executor of macroeconomic policy with no involvement in overseeing banking transactions.

The argument is that if the central bank has better information on commercial banks' health, it will avoid providing rediscount to insolvent banks, in order to protect monetary policy. Furthermore, the access to confidential information derived from the activity of supervision may help monetary policy, not only because of the important role that banks play in the economy but also because problems in banks usually precede other economic problems. There is clear evidence that a central bank's privileged access to confidential information can be substantially useful.

Reasons Against the Separation of the Functions

Once the two objectives (price and banking system stability) are seen as complementary, there are strong reasons, mainly based on the fact that the central bank is the lender of last resort for commercial banks, *not* to separate the functions.

Commercial banks are not only part of payments systems but, together with other financial institutions, they also intermediate currency and credit of economic agents, performing operations in which interest rates are formed. Thus there is a strong correlation between macroeconomic stability and the health of financial systems. A country's macroeconomic difficulties affect the solvency and liquidity of the banking system. Banks and financial institutions in insolvency jeopardize both the sound functioning of the economy and the government's economic policy.

In general, banking insolvency is caused by bad management, assumption of excessive risks, fraud, and unexpected changes in the economy that negatively affect the returns of loans and investments. There is a saying that the financial system is always a highly sensitive thermometer of a country's economy, for changes in the economic environment have a direct influence in the solvency of banks and financial institutions due to their operations with clients and the quality of their loans.

Similarly, economic policy is affected by a fragile and debilitated financial system, principally because of budgetary and monetary impacts caused by bankruptcy of banks and financial institutions. In effect, insolvent financial institutions do not respond to stimulations from the market or the government's economic policy, especially from monetary policy. A fragile banking system is an obstacle to a contracting monetary policy as well, impeding the rise of interest rates.

Supervision of Cross-Border Institutions

With exponential increases in international financial and economic transactions, the preoccupation with stability and solvency of financial systems has also become an international issue. Because economic and financial markets have become interdependent across national boundaries, there is a risk that local problems will become contagious.

The creation of an international supervising entity is not viable. But at the end of 1974 the Bank for International Settlements (BIS) created the Committee on Banking Supervision, commonly called the Basel Committee. Its purpose is to promote the adoption of certain mechanisms and to exchange information among national supervisory bodies, with the goal of controlling the international financial system by influencing national banking systems. The Basel Committee also promulgates qualitative standards for banking supervision and recommends the autonomy of supervising institutions, though without taking a position about the location of the supervising body (whether within the central bank or outside of it).

Nonetheless, the great concern of several countries in regard to supervision is in fact related to banking insolvency. There is little disagreement about the traditional supervisory instruments of the banking safety net: licensing, regulation, and supervision of financial institutions. The conflicts occur in regard to the remaining instruments of the safety net, e.g., the rediscount window, the mechanisms of intervention and liquidation of banks, and deposit insurance. In this case, the classical discussion regarding deposit insurance—the problem of moral hazard—might be invoked.

Deposit Insurance and Moral Hazard

The protection of depositors by means of deposit insurance is frequently condemned under the argument of moral risk, mainly when the protection is limitless. However, in the absence of deposit insurance the negative effect of moral hazard can be worse if large depositors and banks themselves are certain that government will always intervene in these situations, saving everyone. A proper deposit insurance mechanism, besides preventing the government from reimbursing depositors, eliminates much of the discretion in dealing with these cases, thus reducing the moral hazard caused by the repetitive governmental practice of stepping in to save all.

In sum, the prudential policy is to foster cooperation between the supervising and the monetary authorities, precisely because the central bank has the duty to be the banks' lender of last resort, one of the classic instruments of the banking sector's safety net. In this regard, there is legitimate concern (well explored in the specific literature on deposit insurance) about the danger of moral risk, which recommends avoiding loan authorizations by the central banks to insolvent banks.

Advantages and Disadvantages of Supervision

A frequent argument for separating banking supervision and monetary policy is that there can be a conflict of interest between the two activities. The basis of this argument is the importance of protecting the autonomy of the central bank in its role of preserving the stability of prices. The pressure to rescue a bank through the rediscount window may sometimes be excessive, compromising the monetary policy. Under pressure from bankers or politicians, the central bank may be tempted to give priority to the protection of banks, to the detriment of public policy.

The more important conflict is related to the setting of interest rates. A central bank that also performs the role of supervisor might resist raising interest rates to curb inflation because the measure could harm the financial health of the very banks it supervises. Usually, the greater the dissimilarities between the level of a commercial bank's short-term or fixed-rate borrowing and its long-term or pre-fixed-interest-rate lending, the greater the potential harm to the institution as a result of a rise in interest rates.

On the other hand, the same argument of potential conflict can be used to support the maintenance of supervision within the central bank. The reasoning from this point of view is that a central bank without responsibilities of supervision would tend to neglect the impacts of monetary policy on the banking system and, consequently, on the economy as a whole. In response, the defenders of central bank autonomy argue that most difficulties the banking system faces are not caused by monetary policy but, among other factors, by assets of bad quality, capital insufficiency, and fraud.

Two main reasons are posed by supporters of maintaining banking supervision within the monetary authority. The first is associated to the strategic role of payments systems, through which systemic risk is transmitted in the economy. This was the argument of Alan Greenspan in 1994, when he defended the role of the Fed in banking supervision before the U.S. Congress. The second is related to the solution of systemic crises, for the central bank is the lender of last resort to the banking system. The practical issue consists of identifying the moment when the rediscount window must be used to aid banks, considering that supervision utilizes other mechanisms to prevent undesired behaviors deriving from moral hazard.

Rediscount is not an absolute right of a commercial bank. The monetary authority must be aware of the danger of lending to a bank that is in an illiquidity situation but is not insolvent. This rule is valid for the liquidation of small and medium banks but not for bigger banks, because their bankruptcy can eventually produce systemic risk. Nevertheless, how can the central bank know that a bank is insolvent, if it is not the supervising agency? How can a situation that is not likely to represent systemic risk be identified?

These questions constitute the basis of the argument by those who defend the importance of a central bank having supervisory powers. They maintain that the central bank assumes vital importance in moments of crisis because it can quickly obtain information if it is also the banking supervisor. It would be impossible to transmit the needed information and analysis in a timely way if it had to come from another entity. Moreover, supervisory powers enable more efficient action by a central bank than coordinated action between two distinct entities.

On the other hand, the defenders of separation argue that better information is acquired when different institutions hold those two functions. Supporters of central bank autonomy also argue that in crisis situations the central bank, invested in the role of banking supervisor, would be more vulnerable to political pressure. In order to protect the reputation of the central bank, the defenders of central bank autonomy further argue that the monetary authority should not be involved with intervention and liquidation of banks.

An important argument for the separation of monetary and supervising authorities into two distinct institutions is market regulation, particularly in regard to deposit insurance and the danger of moral hazard. If rediscount regulation were more difficult, making it harder to access central bank credit, it is probable that banks (and the banking supervisor itself), even in moments of crisis, would act more correctly and efficiently because they would be liable for their occasional economic shortcomings.

Nonetheless, diminishing the role of the central bank in banking supervision does not necessarily mean that the moral risk problem is eliminated. Even without deposit insurance, the supervising authorities and banks can still believe that they will always be helped by the central bank and still neglect supervision or market regulation. Such moral hazard can be as great as the size of the bank in difficulty ("too big to fail"), which may compel central bank intervention as a way to prevent systemic risk. This problem can be minimized by a deposit insurance mechanism not managed by the central bank, but it does not entirely solve the problem.

In the past decade, economic theory has paid considerable attention to the issue of market regulation. There is evidence that fewer bank bankruptcies occur in countries in which the central bank is invested with banking supervision powers. There is also evidence that in these countries less public resources are used in the assistance of insolvent banks because bank insolvencies are dealt with mainly by means of resources of both the central bank and banking institutions. One possible explanation is that a central bank with supervisory powers can more quickly recognize and respond to banking problems, therefore not allowing them to assume great proportions.

The international trend, however, seems to be towards removing banking supervision from central banks and committing it to a specialized institution, as demonstrated in the attached comparative tables[1] on the institutional organization of central banks and agencies of supervision of the banking system.

The Basel Core Principles of Consolidated Supervision

One of the main contributions of the Basel Committee on Banking Supervision is its recommendation of consolidated supervision over financial conglomerates. As a response to the concern about the soundness of bank financial groups, the Committee asserted the principle of consolidated supervision over international financial groups. The issue is so important that it was included in the Basel Core Principles for Effective Banking Supervision. Core Principle 20 states:

> An essential element of banking supervision is the ability of the supervisors to supervise the banking group on a consolidated basis.

This recommendation comprises nonbanking activities, since these activities can expose banking activity to risks.

Evidently, this concern is not directed exclusively at banking financial activities. It also reaches other sectors of financial systems, such as securities and insurance markets. Because of that, in 1996 the Joint Forum on Financial Conglomerates was established under the aegis of the Basel Committee on Banking Supervision, the International Organisation of Securities Commissions (IOSCO), and the International Association of Insurance Supervisors (IAIS).

The Joint Forum has already produced several papers with recommendations. The most important are "Capital Adequacy Principles," "Principles for Supervisory Information Sharing," and "Coordinator," which is a guide for the coordination of joint supervisions over financial conglomerates by different supervisory bodies.[2] It is important to emphasize that, except for defending a certain degree of autonomy for the supervisory bodies, the international entities concerned with the supervision of banking, securities, and insurance sectors have avoided making recommendations about the political and institutional organization of member countries and have only dealt with technical and operational aspects of banking supervision.

Conclusion

It is important that each country seek the model of banking supervision that best fits its specific circumstances, whether within the central bank or outside of it. There has been a strong international trend towards a simpler bank model, transferring the role of banking supervision to a specialized supervisory body. Removing the supervisory role from the monetary authority, on its turn, seems to constitute a political choice in favor of autonomy, so that the central bank does not become a fourth branch of the state. Additionally, banking supervision is usually a burden that imposes costs, risks, and responsibilities. It therefore demands different specialization and qualification from those expected of a classical central bank.

The main concern, however, is the costs of bank liquidation, principally of big banks that may bring risks to the system, forcing expenses with the recuperation. Such costs may be high and, if not supported, they may affect the monetary policy. This concern can be partly addressed with the maintenance of an adequate deposit insurance system, although the ultimate responsibility for liquidity would lie with the government and with the central bank, even when the latter is not the supervisory entity, because it will always have the role of lender of last resort to the banking system.

While the trend today is to grant autonomy to central banks, according to the classical model, it is important that central banks which are not yet autonomous perform both the tasks of implementing monetary policy and those of banking supervision. Otherwise, there is a risk of weakening the conduct of monetary policy and the ability to face systemic crisis. As a matter of fact, the joint operation, performed by only one body, through the consolidated supervision of financial conglomerates, is an option to be considered by countries that have not gone through the process of separating monetary policy and banking supervision.

ANNEX

Country	Monetary Policy	Supervision				Comments
		Banking	**Payments System**	**Insurance**	**Securities**	
Germany	Deutsche Bundesbank	Federal Banking Supervisory Office			Federal Securities Supervisory Office/ Federal Supervisory Office for Securities Trading	CB independent since its creation, in 1957. At present it is part of the European CB.
Argentina	Banco Central de la República Argentina	Superintendencia de Entidades Financieras y Cambiarias	Banco Central de la República Argentina	Superintendencia de Seguros de la Nación (Ministerio de Economía)	Comisión Nacional de Valores	CB independent (currency board). The Superintendencia is directly subordinate to the CB President (Article 43 of Law 24144 of 23.9.1992).

Annex: Institutional Organisation of Central Banks and Supervisory Bodies

Australia	Reserve Bank of Australia	Australian Prudential Regulation Authority (APRA)	Reserve Bank of Australia	Australian Prudential Regulation Authority (APRA)	APRA and Australian Securities and Investments Commission (ASIC)	CB independent since 1959. 1998 – separation of the banking supervision from the RBA and merger with the Insurance and Superannuation Commission.
Bolivia	Banco Central de Bolivia	Superintendencia de Bancos y Entidades Financieras	BCB's regulatory power	separate	mixed	CB independent since 1995. 1987 – creation of Superintendencia de Bancos y Entidades Financieras.
Canada	Bank of Canada	Office of the Superintendent of Financial Institutions	Bank of Canada	Office of the Superintendent of Financial Institutions	Office of the Superintendent of Financial Institutions	CB independent. 1925 – creation of Office of the Inspector General of Bank (OIGB). 1987 – merger of OIGB with Department of Insurance.
Chile	Banco Central de Chile	Superintendencia de Bancos e Instituciones Financeiras	Banco Central de Chile	Superintendencia de Valores y Seguros	Superintendencia de Valores y Seguros	CB independent since 1989. 1925 – creation of Superintendencia.

Colombia	Banco de la República de Colombia	Superintendencia Bancaria de Colombia (MF)	Banco de la República de Colombia	Superintendencia Bancaria de Colombia	Superintendencia Bancaria de Colombia	BRC independent since 1991, but Ministro de Hacienda presides the Monetary Board (Junta Monetaria – 7 members, 6 from the BRC).
Costa Rica	Banco Central de Costa Rica	Superintendencia General de Entidades Financieras		Separate	Superintendencia General de Valores	CB is not independent. The Superintendencia General de Entidades Financieras is a subsidiary of CB.
El Salvador	Banco Central de Reserva de El Salvador	Superintendencia del Sistema Financiero		Superintendencia del Sistema Financiero	Superintendencia de Valores	CB is no independent.
Ecuador	Banco Central del Ecuador	Superintendencia de Bancos	Banco Central del Ecuador	Superintendencia de Bancos	Superintendencia de Compañías del Ecuador	CB is not independent. 1927 – creation of Superintendencia de Bancos after CB split-up.
Spain	Banco de España	Banco de España	Banco de España	Dirección General de Seguros	Comisión Nacional del Mercado de Valores	CB independent (European CB). 1994 – Banco de España independence.

France	Banque de France	Banking and Financial Regulatory Committee (BC)/ Credit Institutions and Investment Firms Committee/ Banking Commission (BC)	Banque de France		Banking and Financial Regulatory Committee (BC)/ Capital Markets Council/ Stock Exchange Commission	CB independent (European Central Bank). 1996 – Banque de France independence.
Honduras	Banca Central de Honduras	Banking supervisor		Banking supervisor	Banking supervisor	Conforme Aguirre (1997).
Hong Kong	Hong Kong Monetary Authority	Hong Kong Monetary Authority	Hong Kong Monetary Authority		Hong Kong Securities and Futures Commission	CB independent (currency board). 1993 – merger of supervision with the Central Bank.
England	Bank of England	Financial Services Authority	Bank of England	Financial Services Authority	Financial Services Authority	CB independent since 1997. 1997 – separation of banking supervision from Bank of England and merger of supervisions.
Ireland	Central Bank of Ireland	Central Bank of Ireland	Central Bank of Ireland			CB independent (European Central Bank).

Country	Central Bank					Independence
Israel	Bank of Israel	Bank of Israel	Bank of Israel			CB independent.
Italy	Banca d'Italia	Banca d'Italia	Banca d'Italia			CB independent (European Central Bank).
Japan	Bank of Japan	Financial Supervisory Agency	Bank of Japan	Financial Supervisory Agency	Financial Supervisory Agency	CB is not independent.
Luxembourg	Luxembourg Monetary Institute	Luxembourg Monetary Institute	Luxembourg Monetary Institute			CB independent (European Central Bank).
Mexico	Banco de México	Comisión Nacional Bancaria y de Valores	Banco de México/ Comisión Nacional Bancaria y de Valores	Comisión Nacional de Seguros y Finanzas	Comisión Nacional Bancaria y de Valores	CB independent since 1993 (constitutional reform). 1995 – creation of CNBV, by merger of banking supervision with securities supervision.
Nicaragua	Banco Central de Nicaragua	Banking Supervisor		Banking supervisor	Banking supervisor	Conforme Aguirre (1997).
New Zealand	Reserve Bank of New Zealand	Reserve Bank of New Zealand	Reserve Bank of New Zealand		Reserve Bank of New Zealand	CB independent since 1989.
Panama	Banco Central	Banking Supervisor		Separate	separate	Conforme Aguirre (1997).
Paraguay	Banco Central	Banco Central		separate	separate	Conforme Aguirre (1997).

Peru	Banco Central de Reserva del Perú	Superintendencia de Banca y Seguros	Banco Central de Reserva del Perú		Comisión Nacional Supervisora de Empresas y Valores (CONASEV)	CB is not independent. 1931 – creation of Superintendencia. 1979 – administrative and personnel Superintendencia independence.
Portugal	Banco de Portugal	Banco de Portugal	Banco de Portugal			CB independent (European Central Bank).
Switzerland	Swiss National Bank	Federal Banking Commission	Swiss National Bank			CB independent.
Uruguay	Banco Central	Banco Central	Banco Central			Conforme Aguirre (1997).
Venezuela	Banco Central de Venezuela	Superintendencia de Banca y Outras Instituciones Financieras		separate	separate	1993 – creation of Superintendencia

Notes

[1] See annex to this chapter.

[2] The papers released by the Joint Forum are available at the BIS website at www.bis.org.

III. FINANCIAL STABILITY: OVERVIEW

4 | Understanding Financial Stability: Towards a Practical Framework

GARRY J. SCHINASI

Safeguarding financial stability is now widely recognized as an important part of maintaining macroeconomic and monetary stability and a key to the achievement of sustainable growth. Central banks in many advanced countries, as well as the International Monetary Fund, devote considerable resources to monitoring and assessing financial stability and to publishing financial stability reports. A casual reading of these publications would suggest that financial stability practitioners share some common understandings. To cite a few, it is more or less taken for granted that:

• finance is fundamentally different from other economic functions such as exchange, production, and resource allocation;

• finance contributes to other economic functions and facilitates economic development, growth, efficiency, and ultimately social prosperity;

• financial stability is an important social objective—a public good—even if it is not widely seen as being on a par with monetary stability;[1]

• monetary and financial stability are closely related, if not inextricably intertwined, even though there is no consensus on why this is so.

There is also a growing academic literature on financial stability, much of it covering specific topics in considerable depth, and some of it providing rigorous anchors for debating substantive and policy issues. For example, there are extensive literatures on the special role and fragility of banks in finance, the costs and benefits of deposit insurance, and the causes, consequences, and remedies for bank failures. There are also new and growing literatures on market sources of financial fragility and systemic risk more generally (for example, see Allen, 2006).[2]

Despite considerable practical and intellectual progress in recent years, the discipline of financial stability analysis is still in a formative stage, compared to macroeconomic and monetary analysis. The various literatures taken together do not yet provide cohesive and practical approaches or tool kits for assessing financial stability, for analyzing systemic issues and controversies, and for designing policies to optimize the net social benefits of finance. In short, the discipline lacks a widely accepted and useful framework.

Nevertheless, the practice of assessing and safeguarding financial stability is ongoing. This chapter specifically addresses three questions.

• Why have concerns about financial stability increased in recent decades?

• What are the important conceptual challenges faced by policy makers in safeguarding financial stability?

• What are the essential ingredients of a practical framework for safeguarding financial stability in real time, and the challenges in implementing such a framework?

Why Have Financial Stability Issues Recently Become Important?

Since the early 1990s, safeguarding financial stability has become an increasingly dominant objective in economic policymaking, as illustrated by the financial stability reports published by more than 50 central banks and several international financial institutions (including the IMF), as well as by the more prominent place given to financial stability in the organizational structures and mandates of many of these institutions.[3]

Recent Trends in Financial Systems

During the past several decades, significant structural changes in financial systems have been associated with the expansion, liberalization, and subsequent globalization of financial systems, all of which have increased the possibility of larger adverse consequences of financial instability on economic performance. The four major trends:

- Expansion of financial systems relative to the real economy

- Changes in the composition of financial systems

- Increased integration of financial systems

- Greater complexity of financial systems

Expansion of Financial Systems

Financial systems have expanded at a significantly higher pace than the real economy. In advanced economies, total financial assets now represent a multiple of annual economic production. Table 1 illustrates this expansion from 1970 to 2000 for a heterogeneous group of advanced economies with relatively mature financial systems. For example, while currency remained relatively steady as a percentage of GDP over the 30-year period, total assets in financial institutions grew from 110 percent of GDP in 1980 to 377 percent in 2000 in the United Kingdom, from 182 percent in 1980 to 353 percent in 2000 in Germany, and from 111 percent in 1980 to 257 percent in 2000 in the United States.

The growth of assets in the equity and bond markets is just as phenomenal. While differences between countries reflect their more market or bank-oriented financial systems, most aggregates have increased. The broad measures of an economy's total financial assets invariably involve some double counting due to claims between financial institutions, but even these mutual holdings are relevant for financial stability because they represent the links, interactions, and complexities in the financial system.

Changes in the Composition of Financial Systems

The process of financial expansion has been accompanied by changes in the composition of the financial system, with a declining share of monetary assets (aggregates), an increasing share of nonmonetary assets, and, by implication, greater leverage of the monetary base. The amount of currency relative to GDP has been broadly stable or decreased in all countries except Japan. In the United States, even the sizes of both M1 and M2 have fallen as financial innovation has progressed. For outlier Japan, the increasing importance of narrow money in the 1990s may be attributable to greater incentives to hold money due to the Japanese financial sector's fragile state and enduring deflationary pressure.

Table 1. Development of Key Financial Aggregates (In percent of GDP)

	1970	1980	1990	2000
United States				
1 Currency	6	5	5	6
2 M1	21	15	14	11
3 M2	60	57	56	50
4 M3	65	72	72	73
5 Total bank assets	54	54	53	58
6 Total financial institutions assets	...	111	171	257
7 Equity	34	25	35	132
8 Bonds	47	53	108	157
6+7+8	...	189	314	546
United Kingdom				
1 Currency	8	5	3	4
2 M4	52	50	86	93
3 Total bank assets	51	47	108	156
4 Total financial institution assets	...	110	242	377
5 Equity	41	23	57	167
6 Bonds	52	31	33	74
4+5+6	...	164	332	618
France				
1 Currency	10	5	4	3
2 M1	29	24	25	23

3 M2	44	51	44	44
4 M3	62	69	74	65
5 Total bank assets	...	...	...	...
6 Total financial institutions assets	...	...	...	...
7 Equity	6	4	14	84
8 Bonds	14	19	42	55
6+7+8	...	...	...	...
Canada				
1 Currency	4	3	3	3
2 M1	11	9	7	11
3 M2	38	47	56	48
4 M3	46	63	64	65
5 Total bank assets	...	...	...	...
6 Total financial institutions assets	...	...	...	...
7 Equity	9	18	26	87
8 Bonds	33	52	68	76
6+7+8	...	...	...	...
Germany				
1 Currency	5	6	7	6
2 M1	15	17	22	28
3 M2	25	29	39	...
4 M3	42	48	59	68
5 Total bank assets	121	160	216	303
6 Total financial institutions assets	...	182	259	353
7 Equity	11	7	17	48
8 Bonds	26	37	67	112
6+7+8	...	226	343	513
Japan				
1 Currency	8	9	10	13
2 M1	29	29	27	48
3 M2	74	86	114	127
4 M3	127	136	180	219
5 Total bank assets	66	77	134	127
6 Total financial institutions assets	122	157	269	260
7 Equity	41	25	76	70
8 Bonds	23	60	78	124
6+7+8	186	242	423	454
Italy				
1 Currency	10	7	6	7
2 M1	44	42	35	18

3 M2	76	79	67	...
4 M3	76	89	88	...
5 Total bank assets	...	...	...	...
6 Total financial institutions assets	...	...	...	...
7 Equity	7	3	10	57
8 Bonds	...	39	65	108
6+7+8	...	...	...	...
Netherlands				
1 Currency	8	6	7	5
2 M1	23	21	25	35
3 M2	...	...	...	...
4 M3	53	60	77	92
5 Total bank assets	71	129	184	254
6 Total financial institutions assets	116	191	285	431
7 Equity	41	16	38	185
8 Bonds	11	25	73	85
6+7+8	168	232	396	701

Note: Currency is coins and bank notes in circulation; M1, M2, M3, and M4 are national definitions. Total assets of financial institutions consist of total bank assets and (depending on data availability) assets of insurers, pension funds, and mutual funds. Equity is total stock market capitalization; bonds are total debt securities outstanding (government and corporate).

Sources: Thomson Financial, International Monetary Fund, Bank for International Settlements, Merrill Lynch, Salomon Smith Barney, and various national sources.

The simple average expansion of the financial systems shown in Table 1 is illustrated in Figure 1, in which total assets of financial institutions are reflected by the triangle's surface. Figure 1 shows rather dramatically that between 1970 and 2000 the size of these assets almost tripled relative to GDP. Note also how the average of the financial systems has become more highly leveraged, in the sense that the broader monetary and financial assets represent a much greater share of the triangle in 2000 than in 1970 relative to central bank money (or currency).

Figure 1. Composition of Key Financial Aggregates in 1970 and 2000

(In percent of GDP, average of the United States, Germany, the United Kingdom, Japan, France, Italy, Canada, and the Netherlands)

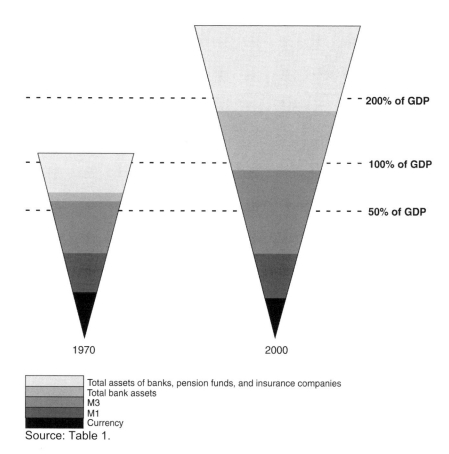

200% of GDP

100% of GDP

50% of GDP

1970   2000

Total assets of banks, pension funds, and insurance companies
Total bank assets
M3
M1
Currency
Source: Table 1.

Figure 2 shows the change in composition of the financial system over the past decades by expressing key financial aggregates as a percentage of their value in 1970 (all deflated by GDP). Clearly, the relative importance of monetary aggregates has decreased, while non-monetary components have increased rapidly.

Figure 2. Development of Key Financial Aggregates, 1970–2000

(Average for the United States, Japan, Germany, the United Kingdom, France, Italy, Canada, and the Netherlands, 1970=100)

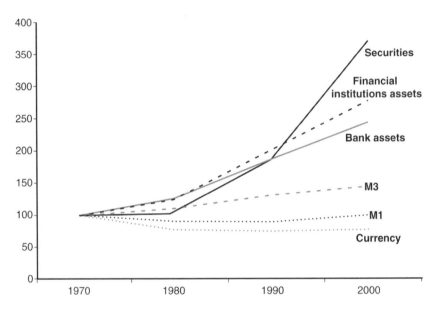

Source: Table 1.

Increased Integration of Financial Systems

As a result of increasing cross-industry and cross-border integration, financial systems are more integrated, both nationally and internationally. Financial institutions now encompass a broader range of activities than that of a traditional bank, which takes deposits and extends loans. This is reflected in the rise in financial conglomerates, which provide a vast array of banking, underwriting, brokering, asset-management, and insurance products and/or services.[4] In the 1990s, the number of mergers and acquisitions within the financial sector soared (Figure 3).

Figure 3. Financial Sector Mergers and Acquisitions, 1990-1999

(Number of M&As in G10 countries)

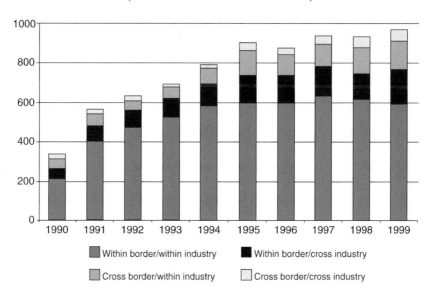

Within border/within industry   Within border/cross industry

Cross border/within industry   Cross border/cross industry

Source: Group of Ten, *Consolidation of the Financial Sector* (Basel, 2001).

Some of these transactions involved different industries or countries, especially in Europe, where roughly half of the deals in this period were either cross-border, cross-industry, or both (Table 2). In addition, cooperation between financial institutions intensified through joint ventures and strategic alliances.[5] The greater international orientation of financial systems is also reflected in the increasing size of cross-border transactions in bonds and equity relative to GDP (see Table 3). On this score, the amount of outstanding international debt securities surged over the past decades (Table 4).

Table 2. Financial Sector Mergers and Acquisitions, 1991–1999 Distribution (percentages)

	North America	Europe	Japan/Australia
Within Border/within industry	80	53	64
Within Border/cross industry	12	19	16
Cross Border/within industry	6	21	14
Cross Border/cross industry	2	8	5
Total	100	100	100

Source: Group of Ten, *supra* Figure 3.

Table 3. Cross-Border Transactions in Bonds and Equities
(In percent of GDP)

	1975–79	1980–84	1985–89	1990–94	1995–99	2000–03	2001	2002	2003
United States									
Bonds	4.0	9.4	63.6	93.9	139.0	188.0	161.4	208.4	262.1
Equities	1.9	3.6	9.9	14.7	45.0	90.8	87.4	85.0	82.1
Japan									
Bonds	2.2	9.8	115.3	72.9	63.7	70.2	73.7	73.8	77.8
Equities	1.1	4.4	14.9	9.6	17.2	36.5	36.7	33.1	35.3
Germany									
Bonds	5.3	9.7	37.8	86.5	208.7	350.5	378.7	351.1	394.0
Equities	1.9	3.4	11.7	14.9	48.6	132.6	133.6	115.6	112.2
France									
Bonds	...	6.8	21.9	108.6	233.5	293.9	288.1	299.3	362.0
Equities	...	2.4	12.1	16.9	56.1	150.7	140.2	138.1	154.0
Canada									
Bonds	1.2	3.9	29.3	104.5	216.6	149.5	135.6	157.0	175.8
Equities	3.3	6.5	14.8	19.2	52.3	122.8	101.9	151.5	132.1
Italy[1]	0.9	1.4	9.4	114.7	518.8	1,126.5	821.9	1,197.0	1,705.2

Sources: Bank for International Settlements and national balance of payments data.
Note: Gross purchases and sales of securities between residents and nonresidents.
[1] No breakdown in bonds and equities is available.

Table 4. Outstanding International Debt Securities by Nationality of Issuer (percent of GDP)

	1970	1980	1990	2000	2003	2004
United States	0.1	0.7	3.1	17.8	27.9	28.6
Japan	0.0	1.5	10.5	6.0	6.3	6.4
Germany	0.1	0.4	4.5	47.9	80.5	86.4
France	0.1	2.1	7.8	24.0	42.2	45.9
Italy	0.1	0.5	4.6	19.4	35.8	40.6
United Kingdom	0.2	2.3	14.9	40.8	63.0	68.0
Canada	0.2	13.4	18.6	27.9	31.0	29.9
Netherlands	0.6	2.4	13.0	79.4	112.6	118.6
Sweden	0.3	7.5	20.1	44.5	52.4	52.4
Switzerland	0.5	1.7	4.5	41.2	49.0	72.9
Belgium	0.4	2.1	15.0	57.3	82.5	85.9

Sources: Bank for International Settlements, IMF, *World Economic Outlook* database.

[1] Figure in 1970 column is from 1971.
[2] Figure in 1970 column is from 1972.

Greater Complexity of Financial Systems

Financial systems have become more complex in terms of the intricacy of financial instruments, the diversity of activities, and the concomitant mobility of risks. Deregulation and liberalization created scope for financial innovation and enhanced the mobility of risks. In general, this greater complexity, especially the increase in risk transfers, has made it more difficult for market participants, supervisors, and policymakers alike to track the development of risks within the system and over time.

To further illustrate the globalization of finance, and the greater mobility of risks across global markets, Table 5 and Table 6 present the worldwide development and use of derivative instruments since the mid-1980s, for exchange-traded derivatives, and since the 1990s, for over-the-counter derivatives. Regarding exchange-traded derivatives, in nominal terms the total notional amounts outstanding have increased more than 60 times since the mid-1980s, while the number of derivative contracts traded has increased more than sevenfold. Regarding over-the-counter derivatives, the notional value of contracts increased from US$80 trillion at end-December 1998 to nearly US$285 trillion at end-December 2005—tripling of the notional value of contracts in 8 years. The gross market value (or replacement cost) of these contracts, which is a proxy for the credit-risk or counterparty exposures associated with the notional values, increased from around US$3 trillion at end-December 1998 to around US$9 trillion at end-December 2005, also a tripling. Note that the majority of derivative transactions were interest-rate contracts.

Table 5. Exchange-Traded Derivative Financial Instruments: Notional Principal Amounts Outstanding and Annual Turnover

	1986	1990	1995	2000	2005	2006 Q3
National principle amounts outstanding	(In billions of U.S. dollars)					
Interest rate futures	370.0	1454.8	5876.2	7907.8	20708.7	24699.0
Interest rate options	144.0	595.4	2741.8	4734.2	31588.2	43369.3
Currency futures	10.2	17.0	33.8	74.4	107.6	139.9
Currency options	39.2	56.5	120.4	21.4	66.1	68.0
Stock market index futures	13.5	69.1	172.2	377.5	802.9	985.6
Stock market index options	37.8	93.6	337.7	1148.4	4542.6	6316.5
Total	614.8	2286.4	9282.0	14263.8	57816.2	75578.4
North America	514.6	1264.4	4852.3	8168.0	36394.2	45898.7
Europe	13.1	461.4	2241.2	4197.9	17982.4	24631.4
Asia-Pacific	87.0	560.5	1990.1	1611.8	3014.0	4534.8
Other	0.1	0.1	198.4	286.2	425.5	513.5
Annual turnover	(In millions of contracts traded)					
Interest rate futures	91.0	219.1	561.0	781.2	2110.4	669.3
Interest rate options	22.2	52.0	225.5	107.7	430.8	146.7
Currency futures	19.9	29.7	99.6	43.5	143.0	55.5
Currency options	13.0	18.9	23.3	7.0	19.4	6.4
Stock market index futures	28.4	39.4	114.8	225.2	918.7	291.6
Stock market index options	140.4	119.1	187.3	481.5	3139.8	773.4
Total	314.9	478.2	1211.5	1646.0	6762.0	1942.9
North America	288.7	312.3	455.0	461.3	1926.8	648.9
Europe	10.3	83.0	354.8	718.6	1592.8	466.5
Asia-Pacific	14.3	79.1	126.4	331.3	2932.4	722.2
Other	1.6	3.8	275.5	134.9	310.0	105.4

Source: Bank for International Settlements

Table 6. Global Over-the-Counter Derivatives Markets: Notional Amounts and Gross Market Values of Outstanding Contracts by Counterparty, Remaining Maturity, and Currency [1]
(In billions of U.S. dollars)

	National Amounts			Gross Market Values		
	End-Dec 1998	End-Dec 2000	End-Jun 2006	End-Dec 1998	End-Dec 2000	End-Jun 2006
Total	80,309	95,199	369,906	3,232	3,183	10,074
Foreign exchange	18,011	15,666	38,111	786	849	1,134
By counterparty						
With other reporting dealers	7,284	5,729	15,281	336	271	367
With other financial institutions	7,440	6,597	15,120	297	357	471
With nonfinancial customers	3,288	3,340	7,710	153	222	296
By remaining maturity						
Up to one year[2]	15,791	12,888	29,578	...	...	...
One to five years[2]	1,624	1,902	5,841	...	...	...
Over five year[2]	592	876	2,692	...	...	...
By major currency						
U.S. dollar[3]	15,810	14,073	31,771	698	771	967
Euro[3]	...	5,981	15,348	...	361	472
Japanese yen[3]	5,319	4,254	9,510	370	274	242
Pound sterling[3]	2,612	2,391	5,219	62	82	148
Other[3]	12,283	4,633	14,374	442	210	439
Interest rate[4]	50,015	64,668	262,296	1,675	1,426	5,549
By counterparty						
With other reporting dealers	24,442	31,494	114,474	748	638	2,219
With other financial institutions	19,790	27,048	115,089	683	610	2,613
With nonfinancial customers	5,783	6,126	32,734	244	179	718
By remaining maturity						
Up to one year[2]	18,185	24,107	90,582	...	...	...
One to five years[2]	21,405	25,923	101,795	...	...	...
Over five year[2]	10,420	14,638	69,918	...	...	...
By major currency						
U.S. dollar	13,763	19,421	88.094	370	486	2,149
Euro	...	21,311	103,607	...	477	2,358
Japanese yen	9,763	13,107	32,214	212	232	472
Pound sterling	3,911	4,852	19,079	130	113	296
Other	22,578	5,977	19,302	963	118	276
Equity-linked	1,488	1,891	6,783	236	289	671
Commodity[5]	408	662	6,394	43	133	718
Other	10,387	12,313	35,969	492	485	1,707

Source: Bank for International Settlements.

[1] All figures are adjusted for double-counting. Notional amounts outstanding have been adjusted by halving positions vis-à-vis other reporting dealers. Gross market values have been calculated as the sum of the total gross positive market value of contracts and the absolute value of the gross negative market value of contracts with non-reporting counterparties.
[2] Residual maturity.
[3] Counting both currency sides of each foreign exchange transaction means that the currency breakdown sums to twice the aggregate.
[4] Single-currency contracts only.
[5] Adjustments for double-counting are estimated.

Risks and Vulnerabilities

The four trends discussed above reflect important advances in finance that have contributed substantially to economic efficiency, both nationally and internationally. They also have implications for the nature of financial risks and vulnerabilities and the potential impact of these risks and vulnerabilities on real economies, as well as implications for the role of policymakers in promoting financial stability. Consider financial system and market developments in the 1990s and early 2000s, a period during which global inflation pressures subsided and in many countries were eliminated. During this period, reflecting in part the above-mentioned trends, national financial systems around the world either experienced, or were exposed to, repeated episodes of unpleasant financial-market dynamics, including asset-price volatility and misalignments; volatile if not unsustainable financial and capital flows; extreme market turbulence, at times leading to concerns about potential systemic consequences; and a succession of costly country crises in 1994–95, 1997, 1998, 1999, and the early 2000s (Table 7). The experiences of, and fallout from, these financial stresses and strains occurred within both advanced countries with highly sophisticated financial markets and developing countries with financial systems of varying degrees of immaturity and dysfunction. As these developments were occurring, economic and financial policymakers became increasingly concerned that global financial stability was becoming more difficult to safeguard.

Table 7. Market Turbulence and Crises in the 1990s and Early 2000s

1992	ERM Exchange rate crises involving Italy and the United Kingdom.
1994	Bond market turbulence in G-10 Countries.
1994-95	Mexican (tesobono) Crisis.
	Failure of Barings.
1996	Bond market turbulence in United States.
1997	U.S. equity market correction.
1997-98	Asian crises (Thailand, Idonesia, South Korea).
1998	Russian default.
	Long-Term Capital Management crisis and market turbulence.
1999	Argentina and Turkey crises.
2000	Global bursting of equity price bubble.
2001	Corporate governance problems—Enron, Marchoni, Global Crossing, etc.
	September 11 Terrorist Attack.
2001-2	Argentina crisis and default.
	Parmalat.

Source: G. Schinasi, *Safeguarding Financial Stability: Theory and Practice* (Washington, D.C.: International Monetary Fund, 2006).

These episodes were a rude awakening for some policy makers about the stability implications of these otherwise beneficial structural changes. It is not too dramatic to say that they were a wake-up call to many about the darker side of modern finance. Several lessons can be taken from these episodes, and three such episodes are representative of what can be learned: bond market turbulence in 1994; the Asian crises in 1997–98; and the Russian and Long-Term Capital Management (LTCM) hedge fund crises in the autumn of 1998.

The bond market turbulence of 1994 is an example of how a long-anticipated monetary policy change, which was delayed in part for financial system concerns, led to turbulence—not just in U.S. financial markets and in the deepest most liquid market for U.S. treasury securities but also in European and Asian markets. When the U.S. Federal Reserve System increased policy interest rates by 25 basis points on February 6, 1994, the long end of the U.S. treasury yield curve increased by more than 175 basis points, and Europe followed suit as well. This created significant turbulence in global financial markets for several weeks, and even posed, in the view of some, the risk of systemic financial consequences. The lesson is that monetary policy changes in one country can threaten financial stability in another, and in the extreme can cause a risk of systemic global financial consequences.

The Asian crises are an example of how exchange rate policies can lead to massive economic and financial disruptions in economies that had been seen as growth machines for close to a decade. At the time, these were seen as one crisis, but in actuality they were quite separate. What connected them was that once Thailand went into crisis, international investors understood that finance and financial stability is an economic fundamental factor that must be considered in international investment portfolio decisions. They hypothesized that if Thailand had a weak financial system and could grow fast, maybe other Asian economies had the same problem. When they paid attention to this, they decided that both Indonesia and South Korea had some of the same underlying weaknesses.

The combination of the Russian default and the collapse of the hedge fund LTCM demonstrated how a default by a country like Russia on a relatively small amount of debt ultimately became part of a scenario—one of credit-spread tightening and then liquidity runs—that not only led to the collapse of a relatively large hedge fund (although a small financial institution) but also threatened the systemic stability of some of the deepest, most liquid, and most efficient securities markets in the world, notably in the U.S. securities markets.

The bottom line is that there have been periods of structural changes that have created a new and ever-changing financial landscape that is not fully understood. The 1990s and early 2000s demonstrated clearly some of the characteristics of this new financial landscape and suggests that a more systematic approach to safeguarding financial stability is required.

The turbulence experienced during the 1990s and early 2000s raised, and continues to challenge us with, questions about the structure and nature of the existing regulatory and supervisory regimes around the world for addressing some of the problems that surfaced. Table 8 classifies the main public-policy issues and concerns raised by the turbulence during these decades. There are three broad areas where policy issues arise to varying degrees from cross-border banks, foreign exchange, and other global markets, and hedge funds: protecting investors and markets, dealing with safety-net issues and moral hazard, and assessing and mitigating cross-border and systemic risk. All three issues are important for banks generally, for cross-border banks in particular, and for global markets. Investor protection and safety-net issues are seen widely as not being relevant for hedge funds, while many, though not all, believe that hedge funds can pose systemic risk. The potential systemic risk associated with the collapse of the hedge fund LTCM is a case in point.

Table 8. Public Policy Issues and Concerns

Issues and Concerns	Cross-Border Institutions	International Markets	Hedge Funds
Protection/ Integrity?	Investor Protection	Market Integrity	No; Possibly for Retail Investors (of funds of funds)
Moral Hazard from Safety Net?	Yes; and Home/Host Burden Sharing Issues	Possibly from G-3 Central Bank Liquidity	No
Cross-Border and Systemic Risks?	Maybe: Depends on Size, Complexity, etc.	Yes, via OTC markets and infrastructure Linkages	Yes?, via opacity, complexity, and w/ Institutions and markets

Source: G. Schinasi, "Causes and Conditions for Cross-Border Threats to Financial Stability," remarks at the Federal Reserve Bank of Chicago conference, "Cross-Border Banking and National Regulation," October 5-6, 2006 (in George G. Kaufman et al., eds., *Cross-Border Banking and National Regulation* (London: World Scientific Publishing Company, 2007)).

In view of the classification in Table 8, how are these risks and public-policy concerns addressed through financial policies? That is, to what extent are the tools of financial policies used to address these concerns? Table 9 is one (perhaps exaggerated) way of answering this question.

As indicated in the column labeled "Cross-Border Institutions" in Table 9, large cross-border banking groups, including the large internationally active banks, are probably the most closely regulated and supervised organizations on the planet, and for good reasons:

• These institutions pose financial risks for depositors, investors, markets, and even unrelated financial stakeholders because of their size, scope, complexity, and risk taking.

• Some of them are intermediaries, investors, brokers, dealers, insurers, reinsurers, infrastructure owners and participants, all rolled up into a single complex institution.

• The institutions are systemically important: all of them within their national systems, many of them regionally, and about twenty of them globally.

• Protection, safety-net, and systemic risks issues are key pubic policy challenges.

• Oversight occurs at the national level, through both market discipline and official involvement, and at the international level through committees and groups.

Table 9. Oversight Regimes

Oversight	Cross-Border Institutions	International Markets	Hedge Funds
Regulation	National with cooperation	Not really; over-the-counter transactions	No
Supervision	National and Home/Host Issues	n.a.	No
Surveillance	Indirect, as participant	Direct; National and International	Indirect, as participant
Market Discipline	Partially	Primarily	Exclusively

Source: Schinasi, supra Table 8.

At the other extreme of regulation and supervision are hedge funds, as can be seen in the right-hand column of Table 9.

• They are neither regulated nor supervised. Many of the financial instruments hedge funds use are not subject to securities regulation, and the markets in which they operate are, by and large, the least regulated and supervised. This is part of their investment strategy, and it defines the scope of their profit making.

• Hedge funds are forbidden in some national jurisdictions. In jurisdictions where they are partially regulated, this is tantamount to being forbidden—given the global nature and fungibility of the hedge-fund business model.

• Their market activities are subject to market surveillance just like other institutions, but this does not make transparent who is doing what, how they are doing it, and with whom they are doing it.

• Investor protection is not an issue for most individual hedge funds, for they restrict their investor base to wealthy individuals and institutions willing to invest with relatively high minimum amounts.

• Investor protection is becoming an issue with the advent of funds-of-hedge-funds that allow minimum investments of relatively small amounts less than US$100,000 or even less than US$50,000.

• Probably beginning with the Asian crisis and then LTCM, and intensifying with the their tremendous growth over the past several years, hedge funds are increasingly being seen as potentially giving rise to concerns about systemic risk, a topic that is discussed later in the chapter.

Global markets fall in between being regulated and not being regulated or supervised. Examples of global markets are the FX markets and their associated derivatives markets (both exchange-traded and over-the-counter) and the G-3 fixed-income markets, as well as others associated with international financial centers (pound, Swiss franc, etc) as well as their associated derivatives markets. Dollar, euro, and yen government bonds are traded in a continuous global market, and the associated derivatives activities are also global.

Global markets are only indirectly regulated. They are subject to surveillance through private international networks and business-cooperation agreements, through information sharing by central banks and supervisory and regulatory authorities, and through official channels, committees, and working groups. Parts of these markets are linked to national clearance, settlement, and payments infrastructures, so they are also subject to surveillance through these channels. The risks they potentially pose are less of a concern to the extent that the major players in them—the large internationally active banks—are effectively supervised and market-disciplined by financial stakeholders.

Regarding infrastructure, the financial activities represented in the columns of Tables 8 and 9 all pass through the third transmission channel, or at least their balance sheet transactions involving securities trading. Large internationally active banks typically are major participants in domestic and international clearance, settlement, and payments infrastructures, both public and private, as well as the major trading exchanges. Many of them co-own parts of the national and international infrastructures and have a natural interest in their performance and viability. Incentives are to some extent aligned to achieve both private and collective net benefits.[6] Increasingly, however, internationally active banks are becoming more heavily involved in over-the-counter transactions, which do not pass through these infrastructures. This poses systemic risk challenges.

In summary, financial structural changes have brought tremendous benefits for the world economy. But there is also a darker side of modern finance, as revealed in the experiences during the 1990s and early 2000s. The costs of these experiences have not been evenly distributed among emerging markets, developing countries, transition countries and mature markets. The United States was not spared, even though it has the deepest, most liquid markets in the world. Nor was Europe spared, and Japan certainly wasn't spared. By and large, oversight regimes still have a national focus, so there are challenges for which the nationally oriented regimes are not keeping pace, such as financial innovation. Private finance can be likened to a greyhound running fast around a track, whereas regulation is more like a bloodhound slowly sniffing out the clues, not quite able to keep pace with the greyhound.

The Conceptual Challenges

The situation described above calls for a more systematic method for assessing the sources of financial risks and vulnerabilities. A more disciplined process is required, key concepts need to be defined as precisely as is practical, measures of the degree of financial stability or instability need to be developed, and there need to be internally consistent ways of adding this all up. The challenges of assessing risks and vulnerabilities in financial systems, as well as the likelihood of threats to financial stability can be likened to asking geophysicists to come up with reliable models for predicting earthquakes, with the obvious additional complexity that finance involves human trust, decisions, and fallibility (see Shubik (1999 and 2001).[7] The assessment of risks and the identification of financial vulnerabilities require an analytical framework, for which there currently is no consensus.

The Financial Stability Challenge: A Balancing Act

There are many ways to characterize the challenges faced in achieving and maintaining financial stability. Moreover, the nature of the challenge will depend to some extent on the structure and maturity of the economic system being studied. For mature financial systems, the financial stability challenge can be characterized as *maintaining the smooth functioning of the financial system and its ability to facilitate and support the efficient functioning and performance of the economy.*

To achieve financial stability, it is necessary to have in place mechanisms designed to *prevent financial problems from becoming systemic and/or threatening the stability of the financial and economic system, while maintaining (or not undermining) the economy's ability to sustain growth and perform its other important functions.*

For two reasons, the challenge is not necessarily to prevent all financial problems from arising:

• First, it is not practical to expect that a dynamic and effective financial system would avoid instances of market volatility and turbulence, or that all financial institutions would be capable of perfectly managing the uncertainties and risks involved in providing financial services and enhancing financial stakeholder value.

• Second, it would be undesirable to create and impose mechanisms that are overly protective of market stability or overly constraining of the risk taking of financial institutions. Constraints could be so intrusive and inhibiting that they could reduce the extent of risk taking to the point where economic efficiency is inhibited. Moreover, the mechanisms of protection or insurance could, if poorly designed and implemented, create the moral hazard of even greater risk taking.

An important aspect of the challenge of financial stability is *maintaining the economy's ability to sustain growth and perform its other important functions*. But the challenge of financial stability analysis and policymaking is that maintenance of financial stability must be balanced against other and perhaps higher-priority objectives, such as economic efficiency. Finance is not an end in itself but plays a supporting role in improving the ability of the economic system to perform its functions.

The challenge of financial stability, therefore, is a balancing act. The likelihood of systemic problems could be limited in practice by designing a set of rules and regulations that restrict financial activities in such a way that the incidence or likelihood of destabilizing asset price volatility, asset market turbulence, or individual bank failures could be eliminated. But it is also likely that this type of 'stability' would be achieved at the expense of economic and financial efficiency.

This reasoning leads to the impression, if not conclusion, that there is an *ex ante* trade-off between achieving, on the one hand, economic and financial efficiency and on the other economic and financial stability. That is, if one is concerned solely with stability, then it may be possible to achieve and maintain it by trading off some efficiency.

The possibility of an *ex ante* trade-off can be illustrated by narrowing the definitions of stability and efficiency. Consider a market for a good whose price is sensitive to incoming information, a characteristic of many asset markets. In principle one could limit the variability of the asset price by imposing restrictions in the market that would inhibit the ability of traders to price-in every small piece of information. But from a trader's and investor's perspective, such restrictions would inhibit the efficiency of the market's ability to price and allocate resources in the presence of uncertainty.

On the other hand, it is possible to try to maintain efficiency, and even enhance it, while still allowing the financial system room to innovate, evolve, and better support the economic system. If the cost of doing so is greater asset price volatility or capital flow volatility, it is up to society to choose a point along this continuum of trade-offs.

Some have characterized the difference between the American financial system and the European financial system as choices of different points along this trade-off continuum. The American system is more market-oriented in that the financing of both household and corporate activities is accomplished more through markets than in Europe, where there is much greater reliance on bank funding and less reliance on tradable securities (although this is changing in Europe). While one might argue that the American system of finance has led to greater economic productivity and efficiency, this greater efficiency is accompanied by greater asset market volatility and turbulence, and a greater propensity to financial stress.

From a broader perspective, the challenge of achieving and maintaining financial stability goes well beyond the stability of asset prices, or prices generally. This is not to say that authorities, and central banks in particular, should not be concerned with asset price volatility, and price volatility more generally, because they determine the value of money. Instead, the challenge of financial stability is broader than, and in fact encompasses, the need to limit the impact of price instability on the functioning of the overall financial system. In fact, if the financial system is stable, it will be able to tolerate higher levels of asset price volatility as well as other financial problems, including weaknesses in financial institutions.

At the highest level of generality, one can see that the challenge of financial stability is to create a framework for managing the risk of a system-wide problem, or what is known as systemic financial risk. But what is systemic risk, and how should we think of it? That is the subject of the next section.

The Required Conceptual Elements of a Framework

A framework for financial stability can best be understood as a set of definitions, concepts, and organizing principles that impose discipline on the analysis of a financial system. Such a framework is not merely and academic exercise but a practical tool for early identification of risks and vulnerabilities that might threaten the maintenance of stability.

An effective framework would have to meet three important standards:

• There must be rigorous definitions and understandings of key concepts, such as what is meant by the terms financial system, financial stability and instability, and systemic, just to name a few.

• To be most useful for monitoring and policy, the framework's concepts and definitions ultimately must be either directly measurable or correlated with measures. In other words, the concepts and definitions must have useful and policy-relevant empirical counterparts; they must match the real world.

• The set of definitions, concepts, and organizing principles along with their empirical counterparts must serve the purpose of ensuring internal consistency in the identification of sources of risks and vulnerabilities and in the design and implementation of policies aimed at resolving difficulties should they emerge.

Defining Key Concepts

It is important to define the relevant concepts, especially what is meant by the terms *financial system, financial stability and instability*, and *systemic risk*.

Financial System

Broadly, the financial system can be seen as being comprised of three separate but closely related components. First, there are *financial intermediaries* that pool funds and risks and then allocate them to their competing uses. Today financial institutions are providing a growing range of services, not just the traditional banking services of taking deposits and making loans. Insurance companies, pension funds, hedge funds, and financial-nonfinancial hybrids (such as General Electric) supply a range of financial services. Second, there are *financial markets* that directly match savers and investors—for example, through the issuance and sale of bonds or equities directly to investors. Third, there is the *financial infrastructure*, comprised of both privately and publicly owned and operated institutions—such as clearance, payment, and settlements systems for financial transactions—as well as monetary, legal, accounting, regulatory, supervisory, and surveillance infrastructures.[8]

Notably, both private and public persons participate in financial markets and in vital components of the financial infrastructure. Governments borrow in markets, hedge risks, operate through markets to conduct monetary policy and maintain monetary stability, and own and operate payments and settlement systems. Accordingly, the term *financial system* encompasses the monetary system with its official understandings, agreements, conventions, and institutions, as well as the processes, institutions, and conventions of private financial activities.[9] Any analysis of how the financial system works and how well it is performing its key functions requires an understanding of these components.

From this definition, one could reasonably expect that considerations of financial stability and monetary stability are related in some meaningful ways. These relationships will become more transparent in what follows.

Financial Stability and Instability

There is as yet no widespread agreement on a useful working definition of financial stability. Some authors define financial *instability* instead of stability,[10] while others prefer to define the problem in terms of managing systemic risk rather than as maintaining or safeguarding financial stability.[11] Consistent with some aspects of these alternative definitions, Schinasi (2004b and 2006a) proposes and analyzes a definition of financial stability that has three important characteristics.

• First, the financial system is efficiently and smoothly facilitating the inter-temporal allocation of resources from savers to investors and the allocation of economic resources generally.

• Second, forward-looking financial risks are being assessed and priced reasonably accurately, and they are also being relatively well managed.

• Third, the financial system is in such condition that it can comfortably, if not smoothly, absorb financial and real economic surprises and shocks.

If any one or a combination of these characteristics is not maintained, it is likely that the financial system is moving in the direction of becoming less stable and at some point might exhibit instability. For example, inefficiencies in the allocation of capital or shortcomings in the pricing of risk can, by laying the foundations for imbalances and vulnerabilities, compromise future financial system stability.

All three of these aspects of the definition can and do entail both endogenous and exogenous elements. For example, surprises that can impinge on financial stability can emanate both from within and from outside the financial system. Moreover, the inter-temporal and forward-looking aspects of this particular way of defining financial stability serve to emphasize that threats to financial stability arise not only from shocks or surprises but also from the possibility of disorderly adjustments of imbalances that have built endogenously over a period of time—because, for example, expectations of future returns were misperceived and therefore mispriced.[12]

There are several important implications of defining financial stability in this way.

First, judgments about the performance of the financial system entail an evaluation of how well the financial system is facilitating economic resource allocation, the savings and investment process, and ultimately economic growth. There are two-way linkages; the real economy can be positively or negatively affected by the financial system, and the performance of the financial system can be affected by the performance of the real economy. A framework useful for assessing financial stability must pay attention to these linkages.

Disturbances in financial markets or at individual financial institutions need not be considered threats to financial stability if they are not expected to damage economic activity at large. In fact, the incidental closing of a minor financial institution, a rise in asset-price volatility, and sharp and even turbulent corrections in financial markets may be the result of competitive forces, the efficient incorporation of new information, and the economic system's self-correcting and self-disciplining mechanisms. By implication, in the absence of contagion and the high likelihood of systemic effects, such developments may be viewed as welcome—if not healthy—from a financial stability perspective. Just as in Schumpeterian business cycles, where the adoption of new technologies and recessions have both constructive and destructive implications, a certain amount of instability can be tolerated from time to time because it may encourage long-term financial system efficiency. [13]

Second, financial stability is a broad concept, encompassing the different aspects of the financial system—infrastructure, institutions, and markets. Because of the interlinkages between these components, expectations of disturbances in any one component can affect overall stability, requiring a systemic perspective. Consistent with the definition of the financial system, at any given time, stability or instability could be the result of either private institutions and actions, or official institutions and actions, or both simultaneously and/or iteratively.

Third, financial stability not only implies that the financial system adequately fulfills its role in allocating resources, transforming and managing risks, mobilizing savings, and facilitating wealth accumulation and growth, but also that within this system the system of payments throughout the economy functions smoothly (across official and private, retail and wholesale, and formal and informal payment mechanisms). This requires that money—both central bank money and its close substitute, derivative monies (such as demand deposits and other bank accounts)—adequately fulfills its role as a means of payment and unit of account and, when appropriate, as a short-term store of value. In other words, financial stability and what is usually regarded as a vital part of monetary stability overlap to a large extent. [14]

Fourth, financial stability requires the absence of financial crises and the ability of the financial system to limit and deal with the emergence of imbalances before they constitute a threat to stability. In a well-functioning and stable financial system, this occurs in part through self-corrective, market-disciplining mechanisms that create resilience and that endogenously prevent problems from festering and growing into system-wide risks. In this respect, there may be a policy choice between allowing market mechanisms to work to resolve potential difficulties and intervening quickly and effectively—through liquidity injections via markets, for example—to restore risk taking and/or to restore stability. Thus financial stability entails both preventive and remedial dimensions.

Finally, but not least important, financial stability can be thought of as occurring along a continuum, reflecting different possible combinations of conditions of the financial system's constituent parts. An analogy is the health of an organism, which also occurs along a continuum. A healthy organism can usually reach for a greater level of health and well-being, and the range of what is normal is broad and multi-dimensional. In addition, not all states of illness are significant, systemic, or life-threatening, and some illnesses, even temporarily serious ones, allow the organism to continue to function reasonably productively and return to a state of health without permanent damage. One implication of viewing financial stability in this way is that maintaining financial stability does not necessarily require that each part of the financial system operates persistently at peak performance; it is consistent with the financial system operating on a "spare tire" from time to time.[15]

The concept of a financial-stability continuum is relevant because finance fundamentally involves uncertainty, is dynamic (meaning both inter-temporal and innovative), and is composed of many interlinked and evolutionary elements (infrastructure, institutions, markets). Accordingly, financial stability is expectations-based, dynamic, and dependent on many parts of the system working reasonably well. What might represent stability at one time might be more stable or less stable at some other time, depending on other aspects of the economic system, such as technological, political, and social developments. Moreover, financial stability can be seen as being consistent with various combinations of the conditions of its constituent parts, such as the soundness of financial institutions, financial markets conditions, and effectiveness of the various components of the financial infrastructure.

Systemic Risk

According to the G-10 Report on financial consolidation and risk:

> Systemic financial risk is the risk that an event will trigger a loss of economic value or confidence in, and attendant increases in uncertainly about, a substantial portion of the financial system that is serious enough to quite probably have significant adverse effects on the real economy. Systemic risk events can be sudden and unexpected, or the likelihood of their occurrence can build up through time in the absence of appropriate policy responses. The adverse real economic effects from systemic problems are generally seen as arising from disruptions to the payment system, to credit flows, and from the destruction of asset values."[16]

The G-10 study notes that this definition encompasses much of what is in the literature but it is stricter in two respects. One is that the negative externalities of a systemic event must have the potential to adversely affect the real economy; that is, to be a systemic event, a financial event must have the potential to affect the real economy. The second is that the potential impact on the real economy occurs with relatively high probability. The emphasis on real effects reflects the view that it is the output of real goods and services and the accompanying employment implications that are the primary concern of economic policymakers. "In this definition, a financial disruption that does not have a high probability of causing a significant disruption of real economic activity is not a systemic risk event." [17]

Taken together, a good understanding of what is meant by financial stability and what is meant by financial instability can serve to define boundaries around the scope of the analysis. The safeguarding of financial stability should not be understood as a zero tolerance of bank failures or of an avoidance of market volatility, but that it should avoid financial disruptions that lead to real economic costs. [18]

Toward a Practical Framework for Assessing Financial Stability

With working definitions of the financial system, financial stability, and systemic risk in hand, it becomes possible to discuss the key role that financial stability assessments play in safeguarding financial stability. The core objectives of a framework for safeguarding financial stability are the *prevention* and *resolution* of systemic financial problems. That is, safeguarding financial stability fundamentally requires a framework to prevent problems from occurring and to resolve problems if prevention fails.

A key to prevention is the early identification of risks to stability and of potential sources of vulnerability in the financial system before they lead to unsustainable and potentially damaging imbalances and consequences. For example, weaknesses and vulnerabilities could exist in any of the components of the financial system—institutions, markets, infrastructure—and could entail all three simultaneously. Along with identifying potential sources of risks and vulnerabilities, it is also desirable to attempt to calibrate their intensity and potential for (or probability of) leading to financial-system problems and possible systemic effects. Financial stability assessments are a key part of prevention.

The key to resolution is to have mechanisms in place and policy tools available to remedy situations in which the financial system seems to be in the early stages of moving towards instability. Such tools would include, for example, moral suasion and intensified supervision and/or market surveillance. Should remedial measures fail, or undetected endogenous factors or unanticipated exogenous factors lead to instability, tools should be available for resolving problems and instabilities quickly and with minimum spillovers and contagion, either to the financial system or the economy. Such tools would include emergency liquidity assistance.

Figure 4 represents a schematic that might be considered as a reasonable model for such a framework for prevention and resolution. Both prevention and resolution of financial difficulties are part of the framework (although resolution is well beyond the scope of this chapter and is not discussed). [19]

In order to prevent problems from occurring or becoming significant enough to pose a risk to financial stability, it would be desirable to have a continuous process of information gathering, technical analysis, monitoring, and assessment. Because of the linkages between the real economy and the financial system, and also the various components of the financial system, this continuous process would be most useful if it encompassed economic and financial dimensions as well as institutional knowledge about institutions, markets, and the financial infrastructure. In effect, the process needs to be comprehensive and analytical (see the top bar in Figure 4). Note that ongoing and more fundamental research into the changing structure of the financial system and its changing linkages to the real economy, as well as the further development of measurement techniques for detecting growing imbalances and calibrating risks and vulnerabilities, are vital for keeping this important monitoring phase up to date.

The process entails information gathering about, and monitoring of, the macroeconomy (and at times microeconomic aspects as well) and the various aspects of the financial system through supervisory, regulatory, and surveillance mechanisms. Each of the financial-system monitoring components could entail both macro- and micro-prudential characteristics. For example, in gathering information about and monitoring individual institutions, the supervisory process could be aided by knowledge about where the economy is along the business and credit cycles and how markets have been performing overall. This is important because the macroeconomy and markets provide the background against which the operational performance of individual institutions should be assessed. Likewise, an assessment of the condition of financial markets could be different depending on whether the major institutions operating in the markets were well-capitalized and profitable, or not. This is another way of observing that there are tradeoffs, even in the assessment process, in safeguarding financial stability.

The reason for gathering information, analyzing it, and continuously monitoring the various components of, and influences on, the financial system is to enable systematic and periodic assessments of whether the financial system is performing its main functions well enough to be judged to be within a corridor of financial stability along the continuum discussed earlier. Such an assessment could lead to three conclusions, each of them having quite different implications for action (see the middle bar in Figure 4 labeled assessment and the arrows). The financial system can be judged to be in a zone or corridor of financial stability, as approaching a boundary of stability/instability, or outside a zone or corridor of stability. Within the third category, the financial system could be further judged to be in a position in which self-corrective processes and mechanisms are judged to be likely to move the system back toward the corridor of stability or alternatively to need prompt remedial and even emergency measures to reverse the instability.[20]

Figure 4. Framework for Maintaining Financial System Stability

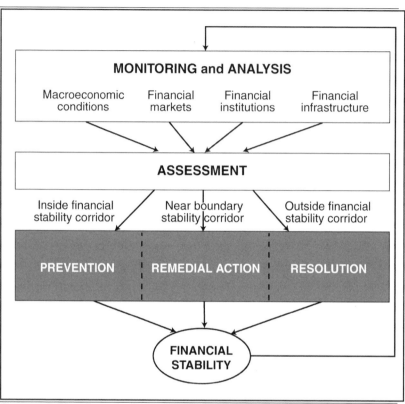

Source: Schinasi, *supra* Table 7; A. Houben, J. Kakes, and G. Schinasi, "Framework for Safeguarding Financial Stability," IMF Working Paper 04/101 (Washington, DC: July 2004).

One could also develop a delineation of financial conditions and potential difficulties according to their intensity, scope, and potential threat to systemic stability. For example, potential financial difficulties can be thought of as falling into one of the following fairly broad categories:

• difficulties in a single institution or market not likely to have system-wide consequences for either the banking or financial system;

- difficulties that involve several relatively important institutions involved in market activities with some nontrivial probability of spillovers and contagion to other institutions and markets; and

- problems likely to spread to a significant number and types of financial institutions and across usually unrelated markets for managing liquidity needs, such as forward, interbank, and equity markets.

Problems occurring within each of these categories would require different diagnostic tools and policy responses, ranging from doing nothing to intensifying supervision or surveillance of a specific institution or market, to liquidity injections into the markets to dissipate strains, or to interventions into particular institutions.

Challenges in Implementing a Framework

While the categories of possible assessments may be easy to discuss in principle, they are difficult to identify in actual practice. How, for example, should the boundary of stability be defined and measured? When does a small, isolated problem threaten to become a systemic one? There would also seem to be a bias toward being prudent and overreaching in identifying both potential sources of risks and vulnerability, and in overestimating their likelihood and importance. Thus it would be useful to establish ground rules or guidelines for applying discipline to the continuous process of information gathering, analysis, and monitoring—and, most importantly, for identifying sources of risks and vulnerabilities. A check list of questions for identifying risks and vulnerabilities and for assessing where they lie along the stability spectrum could include the following:[21]

- Is the process systematic?

- Are the risks identified plausible?

- Are the identified risks systemically relevant?

- Can linkages and channels of transmission (or contagion) be identified?

- Have risks and linkages been cross-checked?

- Has the identification of risks and the assessment been consistent over time?

In practice, the process of assessing financial stability entails a *systematic* identification and analysis of the sources of risk and vulnerability that could impinge on stability in the circumstances in which the assessment is being made. For example, consider the comprehensive list of sources of risks in Table 10. An operationally significant distinction is made between endogenous sources of risk that are present within the financial system and exogenous sources of risk that might emanate from outside the realm of finance.

In keeping with the broad definition of the financial system outlined above, endogenous sources of risk can arise in financial institutions, financial markets, or the infrastructures, or in any combination of the three. For instance, credit, market, or liquidity risks may be present in financial institutions which, if they materialize, could hamper the process of reallocating financial resources between savers and investors. Financial markets can be a source of endogenous risk not only because they offer alternative sources of finance to nonfinancial sectors but also because they entail systemic linkages between financial institutions, and more directly between savers and investors. Financial infrastructures are also an important endogenous source of risk, in part because they entail linkages between market participants as well, but also because they provide the institutional framework in which financial institutions and markets operate.

Outside the financial system, the macroeconomic environment can be an exogenous source of risk for financial stability because it directly influences the ability of economic and financial actors (households, companies, and even the government) to honor their financial obligations. Financial stability assessments should entail a systematic and periodic process of monitoring of each of these sources of risks, both individually and collectively, by taking account of cross-sector and also cross-border linkages. This process should satisfy at least the list of questions above.

There are also formidable measurement and modeling challenges in the ability to assess the strength and robustness of the various risks, to calibrate their plausibility and importance, or to appraise quantitatively the potential costs should the risks materialize. In actual practice, many shortcuts and qualitative judgments must be made in order to produce an overall assessment.

For most macroeconomic or monetary policy objectives (for example, unemployment, external or budgetary equilibrium, price inflation) there are widely accepted measurable indicators that define, and measure deviations from, the objective, even if still subject to methodological and analytical debate, even controversy. In the fields of both macroeconomics and monetary economics, it took each of the disciplines some 20–30 years of practice, trial, and error, measurement and modeling development, and fundamental research to achieve these indicators. As noted earlier, financial stability analysis is still in its early stage of development. Thus there is as yet no widely accepted set of measurable indicators of financial stability that can be monitored and assessed over time. In part, this reflects the multifaceted nature of financial stability, as it relates to both the stability and resilience of financial institutions, and to the smooth functioning of financial markets and settlement systems over time.[22] Moreover, these diverse factors need to be weighed in terms of their potential ultimate influence on real economic activity. But it also reflects the relatively young age of the discipline of assessing financial stability. Because measurement is not highly developed yet, it is reasonable to see the current practice of making financial stability assessments more as an art form than as a rigorous scientific discipline.

Table 10. Sources of Risk to Financial Stability

Endogenous	Exogenous
Institutions-based:	*Macroeconomic disturbances:*
• Financial risks	Economic-environment risk
○ Credit	Policy imbalances
○ Market	*Event risk*
○ Liquidity	Natural disaster
○ Interest rate	Political events
○ Currency	Large business failures
• Operational risk	
• Information technology weaknesses	
• Legal/integrity risk	
• Reputation risk	
• Business strategy risk	
• Concentration risk	
• Capital adequacy risk	
Market-based:	
• Counterparty risk	
• Asset price misalignment	
• Run on markets	
○ Credit	
○ Liquidity	
• Contagion	
Infrastructure-based :	
• Clearance, payment and settlement system risk	
• Infrastructure fragilities	
○ Legal	
○ Regulatory	
○ Accounting	
○ Supervisory	
• Collapse of confidence leading to runs	
• Domino effects	

Source: Schinasi and Houben, Kakes, and Schinasi, supra Figure 4.

Challenges in measuring financial system stability reach well beyond the challenges of measuring the degree of stability in each individual sub-component of the financial system. Financial stability requires that the constituent components of the system—financial institutions, markets, and infrastructures—are jointly stable. Weaknesses and vulnerabilities in one component may or may not compromise the stability of the system as a whole, depending on size and linkages, including the degree and effectiveness of risk-sharing between different components. Moreover, as different parts of the system perform different tasks, there are challenges to aggregating information across the system. For example, in diversified financial systems, where both financial institutions and markets are important providers of finance, there is no commonly accepted way of aggregating information on the degree of stability in both the banking system and financial markets to form an overall assessment of system stability. If the banking system is functioning well but, at the same time, there are signs of strains in financial markets, the overall assessment of financial system stability is likely to be *ex ante* ambiguous, particularly if the respective shares of the two components as providers of finance are similar. The more complex and sophisticated a financial system, the more complex is the task of measuring overall stability in a precise way.

Financial stability assessments carry a higher degree of uncertainty than ordinarily associated with forecasts based on macroeconometric models. This is because there are four formidable practical challenges to measuring, modeling, and assessing the consequences of rare events:

• If past crises were prevented or tackled by policy actions, assessments of the likely costs of a selected scenario, based on simulations drawn from historical data-sets, will likely prove to be biased unless sufficient account is taken of policy reactions. It is doubtful that past policy responses to episodes of financial stress could be summarized by a mechanical reaction function, particularly if the authorities were mindful of avoiding the moral hazards that typically follow from predictable behavior. Moreover, even in cases that did not lead to policy responses, the frequency of crises in historical data-sets may be too low to facilitate precision in estimating the likely "policy neutral" consequences of a stylized scenario.

• Confidence intervals around the expected output losses associated with the materialization of a specified scenario may be neither well-defined statistically nor defined at all. For instance, simulations based on historical episodes tend to be founded on statistical relationships that reflect the central tendency of probability distributions, rather than the tails. Moreover, for hypothetical scenarios that have not occurred in the past, it may not be possible to compute a confidence interval around the simulation because the events themselves may be subject to Knightian uncertainty—or unquantifiable risk.[23]

• Most macroeconometric models used for stress-testing tend to be built on the basis of log-linear relationships. For simulations, this means that a doubling of the size of a shock will result in a proportionate change in the effect. In reality, however, it can never be excluded that in situations of financial stress, unpredictable nonlinearities may surface—due, for instance, to threshold effects.

• As witnessed during the near collapse of Long Term Capital Management in 1998, unexpected linkages may surface during crises, such as correlations between financial markets that ordinarily tend to be uncorrelated. Given such uncertainties, the real economic costs associated with a particular scenario could well prove to be larger than those predicted by an empirical model. Such considerations would suggest that the output of any stress-testing exercise should only be viewed as indicative of how, or if, the financial system would endure adverse disturbances. In order to avoid complacency, this calls for a high degree of caution and judgment in forming financial assessments.

In order to advance the practice of financial stability assessment from what is essentially an art towards a science, progress is necessary on at least three fronts: data, models, and understanding of linkages. A priority for data gathering must be microeconomic balance-sheet data covering financial institutions, households, and firms. While a picture of the aggregate risks borne within each of these sectors can be useful for financial stability analysis, far more important is an understanding of the way in which the risks are distributed across sectors and especially whether or not concentrations or pockets of vulnerabilities can be pinpointed. In mature economies, the availability and comprehensiveness of such data is rather mixed, particularly for the household sector.

There are two areas where more and better analytical research on financial stability modeling appears necessary: (1) models for identifying risks and vulnerabilities and (2) models for assessing the consequences of adverse disturbances.[24] Concerning the identification of risks, the literature suggests that it is doubtful that models will ever be capable of predicting crises, particularly with precise timing. Nevertheless, this should not stand in the way of developing models for assessing vulnerabilities. Even simple single-indicator approaches can be useful for gauging risks to financial stability,[25] and current work holds promise for the development of more comprehensive frameworks for pinpointing the sets of variables[26] and the conditions that raise the likelihood of financial stress.[27] As for the prediction of crises, it cannot be excluded that drawing on the intellectual advances made in other disciplines in the modeling of complex and discontinuous processes—such as the prediction of earthquakes—may offer insights for financial stability assessment.

Conclusion

This chapter has explored the various challenges in safeguarding financial stability, which have become more important over the past three decades. There are formidable conceptual challenges in defining financial stability and in analyzing it. From the perspective of assessing the performance of financial systems, and their likelihood of encountering difficulties, those who work in the financial-stability "discipline"—if it can as yet be labeled as such—do not yet know how to integrate knowledge and information about financial institutions and financial markets. Nor do they know how to conceptualize usefully and model empirically the important systemic linkages between financial processes and the real economic processes that finance is designed to facilitate. In short, the discipline lacks a widely accepted framework.

The challenges that lie ahead for financial stability analysis concern both measurement and theory. The challenges are formidable, in part because financial stability assessments must not only take stock of disturbances as they emerge but also identify and examine the vulnerabilities that could lead to such disturbances occurring in the future. A forward-looking approach is required in order to identify the potential build-up of financial imbalances and to account for the transmission lags in policy instruments. The real difficulty is that financial crises are inherently difficult, if not impossible, to predict, in part because of contagion effects and likely nonlinearities in both the build-up of imbalances and their transmission to the real economy. In addition, financial stability risks often reflect the far-reaching consequences of unlikely events. This implies that the focus of the attention is not the mean, median or mode of possible outcomes but the entire distribution of outcomes, in particular the "left tail."

While many conceptual and methodological challenges lie ahead, it is important to acknowledge that significant progress has been made in recent years. Even though there is no obvious framework for summarizing developments in financial stability in a single quantitative measure, a growing number of central banks around the world are making financial stability assessments and publishing financial stability reports, many of them based on a broad and forward-looking conception of financial stability.

The three major challenges to financial stability—the globalization of finance, the increasing use of sophisticated instruments, and the entrance of new large participants in global markets—lead, separately and collectively, to the strong conclusion that further and continuous reforms are desirable and should be aimed at striking a better balance between relying on market discipline and relying on official or private-collective action. In some countries—most of them advanced countries with mature markets—a rebalancing toward greater reliance on market discipline is desirable. In other countries—many with poorly developed markets—strong efforts need to be made to improve the financial infrastructure through private-collective and government expenditures and commitments, and to target the role of government to enhance the effectiveness and efficiency of market mechanisms for finance.

Reforms in seven areas would go a long way in improving the prospects for safeguarding financial stability where it presently exists, and in promoting it where it is yet to be achieved:

• Improve internal governance at the board-of-directors level, management and risk controls, and the alignment of incentives of board, management, and staff by realigning private incentives within all financial institutions.

• Reduce moral hazard and other adverse incentives by reevaluating and reforming existing regulatory incentives and their consistency with private market incentives.

• Improve market discipline and strengthen private-collective and official surveillance and supervision by enhancing financial transparency through disclosure by a wide range of financial and nonfinancial entities.

• Reduce informational asymmetries and the tendency toward adverse selection by improving financial market transparency.

• Reduce, and if possible eliminate, legal uncertainties where laws are still ambiguous (such as with close-out procedures for credit derivatives and other complex structured financial instruments) by introducing new legislation developed in a coordinated fashion by private financial industry, official, and legislative representatives.

• Improve the ability to monitor, assess, and safeguard financial stability, and to restore it when this fails by aggressively developing and implementing comprehensive and appropriately targeted frameworks, analytical tools, and the necessary data and information.

• Reduce opportunities for international regulatory arbitrage, and eliminate international gaps of information and analyses by enhancing international cooperation and coordination in financial-system regulation, surveillance, and supervision.

The complexity of the challenges and the rapidity and creativity with which new financial instruments are developed and disseminated require a systemic approach to safeguarding financial stability. The financial system, working within the context of the broader economic, social, and political systems, affects the performance of the economy and well-being of society. In turn, those systems must operate hand in hand to safeguard the stability of the financial system, and the constellation of tools they provide must be used to ensure economic stability.

Ultimately, the goal is to maintain financial stability so that the financial system is capable of performing its three key functions: the intertemporal allocation of resources from savers to investors and the allocation of economic resources generally; the assessment, pricing, and allocation of forward-looking financial risks; and the absorption of financial and real economic shocks and surprises.

Notes

[1] *See* James Tobin, "Money as a Social Institution and Public Good," in J. Eatwell, M. Milgate, and P. Newman, eds., *The New Palgrave Dictionary of Money and Finance* (London: Macmillan, 1992).

[2] *See* F. Allen, "Modeling Financial Stability," *National Institute Economic Review*, Vol. 192 (April 2005).

[3] See O. Oosterloo, J. de Haan, and R. Jong-A-Pin, "Financial Stability Reviews: A first Empirical Analysis," paper presented at the Federal Reserve Bank of Chicago Conference, "International Financial Instability: Cross-Border Banking and National Regulation," October 5, 2006.

[4] *See* various issues of the IMF's *International Capital Markets* and Group of Ten, *Consolidation of the Financial Sector* (Basel, 2001).

[5] Van der Zwet discusses this blurring of distinctions between financial sectors and across countries, including by looking at variables such as the share of financial institutions' cross-border and cross-sector revenues. *See* A.van der Zwet, "The Blurring of Dinstinctions between Financial Sectors: Fact or Fiction," Occasional Studies No. 2 (Amsterdam: De Nederlandsche Bank, 2003).

[6] The phrase "to some extent" needs to be emphasized. Consider, for example, that the G-10 central banks decide to get out of the business of providing clearance, settlement, and payment services on foreign-exchange transactions—as might have been considered years ago when they challenged private institutions to eliminate Herstatt risk, the risk of losses of principal on foreign-exchange transactions owing to time-zone differences. If this decision were taken, the major international banks would have the incentive to organize fully the clearance, settlement, and payment on FX transactions. But if this were to happen, this private organization could become too big to fail or even to liquidate in a timely manner without global systemic consequences.

[7] Martin Shubik, *Theory of Money and Financial Institutions* (Cambridge, MA: MIT Press, 1999).

[8] On the role of the legal system see, for example, R. Levine, "Law, Finance and Economic Growth," *Journal of Financial Intermediation*, Vol. 8 (1999), at 8–35; M. Leahy, S. Schich, G. Wehinger, F. Pelgrin, and T. Thorgeirsson, "Contributions of Financial Systems to Growth in OECD Countries," *OECD*

Working Paper No. 280 (Paris, 2001); T. Beck, A. Demirgüç-Kunt, and R. Levine, "Bank Concentration and Crises," *NBER Working Paper* No. 9921 (Cambridge, MA: NBER, 2003).

[9] This particular formulation is an adaptation of "international financial system" in Edwin Truman, *Inflation Targeting in the World Economy* (Washington, D. C.: Institute for International Economics, 2003).

[10] *See, e.g.,* the definitions in the following: J. Chant, "Financial Stability as a Policy Goal," in J. Chant, A. Lai, M. Illing, and F. Daniel, eds., *Essays on Financial Stability*, Bank of Canada Technical Report No. 95 (Ottawa, 2003); A. Crockett, "The Theory and Practice of Financial Stability," *De Economist*, Vol. 144, No. 4 (1996); Deutsche Bundesbank, "Report on the stability of the German financial system," *Monthly Report* (Frankfurt, December 2003); W.F. Duisenberg, "The Contribution of the Euro to Financial Stability," in *Globalization of Financial Markets and Financial Stability—Challenges for Europe* (Baden-Baden, 2001); R. Ferguson, "Should Financial Stability Be An Explicit Central Bank Objective?" (Washington, D.C.: Federal Reserve Board of Governors, 2002); M. Foot, "What is 'Financial Stability' and How Do We Get It?" The Roy Bridge Memorial Lecture (London: Financial Services Authority, 2003); A. Large, "Financial Stability: Maintaining Confidence in a Complex World," *Financial Stability Review* (2003), at 170–74 (London: Bank of England); F.S. Mishkin, "Global Financial Instability: Framework, Events, Issues," *Journal of Economic Perspectives*, Vol. 13, No. 4 (1999); Norwegian Central Bank, 2003, *Financial Stability Review*, Vol. 1 (2003); T. Padoa-Schioppa, "Central Banks and Financial Stability: Exploring a Land in Between," in V. Gaspar, P. Hartmann, O. Sleijpen, eds., *The Transformation of the European Financial System* (Frankfurt: European Central Bank, 2003); A.J. Schwartz, "Real and Pseudo-Financial Crises," in F. Capie and G.E. Woods, eds., *Financial Crises and the World Banking System* (New York: St Martin's, 1986); and A.H.E.M. Wellink, "Current Issues in Central Banking," speech at the Central Bank of Aruba, Oranjestad, Aruba, 2002. All of these definitions are surveyed in G. Schinasi, "Defining Financial Stability," IMF Working Paper 04/187 (Washington D.C.: International Monetary Fund, 2004) and G. Schinasi, *Safeguarding Financial Stability: Theory and Practice* (Washington, D.C.: International Monetary Fund, 2006). A typology of instability is developed in E.P. Davis, "A Typology of Financial Instability," *Financial Stability Report*, No. 2 (Wenen: Oesterreichische Nationalbank, 2002).

[11] From a policy perspective, a positive approach focusing on financial stability is more useful than a negative one focusing on financial instability.

See Garry Schinasi, *Safeguarding Financial Stability: Theory and Practice* (Washington, D.C.: International Monetary Fund, 2006.

[12] That financial stability should not be thought of simply as a static concept of shock absorption capacity has been emphasized by others. *See*, for example, H.M. Minsky, *Inflation, Recession and Economic Policy* (Wheatsheaf, Sussex: MIT Press, 1982) and C.P. Kindleberger, *Manias, Panics and Crashes* (Cambridge: Cambridge University Press, 1996).

[13] *See* J. Schumpeter, *The Theory of Economic Development* (Cambridge, MA: Harvard University Press, 1934.

[14] On the role of central banks in financial stability, see T. Padoa-Schioppa, "Central Banks and Financial Stability: Exploring a Land in Between," in V. Gaspar, P. Hartmann, O. Sleijpen, eds., *The Transformation of the European Financial System* (Frankfurt: European Central Bank, 2003) and G. Schinasi, "Responsibility of Central Banks for Stability in Financial Markets," IMF Working Paper 03/121 (2003).

[15] *See* A. Greenspan, "Do Efficient Markets Mitigate Financial Crises?" Speech delivered before the 1999 Financial Markets Conference of the Federal Reserve Bank of Atlanta.

[16] Group of Ten, *Consolidation of the Financial Sector* (Basel: Group of Ten, 2001).

[17] *Id.*

[18] For papers that focus on aspects of systemic risk, see D. Hoelscher, and Marc Quintyn, "A Framework for Managing Systemic Banking Crises," *IMF Occasional Paper* (forthcoming) and M. Summer, "Banking Regulation and Systemic Risk," *Open Economies Review*, Vol. 14 (2003), at 43–70.

[19] For a brief discussion of the resolution phase, see Schinasi, *Safeguarding Financial Stability, supra* note 11, at 114–118. Also see the conference papers discussed at the Federal Reserve Bank of Chicago conference, "International Financial Instability: Cross-Border Banking and National Regulation," which deal in part with the challenges in resolving cross-border banking problems in a world in which regulation and supervision are nationally oriented. See D.D. Evanoff, G.G. Kaufman, and J.R. LaBrosse, eds., *International Financial Instability: Global Banking and National Regulation*, (World Scientific Publishing Company, 2007).

[20] As Kindleberger puts it, "markets work well, on the whole, and can normally be relied upon to decide the allocation of resources and, within limits, the distribution of income, but that occasionally markets will be overwhelmed and need help." *See* Kindleberger, *Manias, Panics and Crashes, supra* note 12.

[21] These ideas are developed in detail in J. Fell and G. Schinasi, "Assessing Financial Stability: Exploring the Boundaries of Analysis," *National Institute Economic Review*, Vol. 192 (April 2005).

[22] Sets of indicators have been developed, and are widely used, for assessing the soundness of banking institutions. See, for example, the IMF Soundness Indicators, both core and encouraged sets, in International Monetary Fund/World Bank, *Analytical Tools of the Financial Sector Assessment Program* (Washington D.C., 2003); and International Monetary Fund/World Bank, *Compilation Guide on Financial Soundness Indicators* (Washington D.C., 2004).

[23] *See* F.H. Knight, *Risk, Uncertainty, and Profit* (Cambridge, MA: The Riverside Press, 1921).

[24] For an overview of early warning systems used by some G-10 authorities, see R. Sahajwala and P. van den Berg, "Supervisory risk assessment and early warning systems," Basel Committee on Banking Supervision Working Paper No. 4 (2000). On the use of financial market indicators, see M. Persson and M. Blåvarg, "The Use of Market Indicators in Financial Stability Analysis," *Economic Review* (Sveriges Riksbank, 2003), at 5–28.

[25] See J. Campbell and R. Shiller, "Valuation Ratios and the Long-Run Stock Market Outlook: An Update," NBER Working Paper No. 8221 (Cambridge, Massachusetts: NBER, 2001).

[26] International Monetary Fund, *Compilation Guide on Financial Soundness Indicators* (Washington D.C., 2004).

[27] O.C. Aspachs, C. Goodhart, M. Segoviano, D. Tsomocos, and L. Zicchino, "Searching for a Metric for Financial Stability," paper presented at the U.S. FDIC's 6th Annual Bank Research Conference, September 13-15, 2006.

5 | Institutional Responses to Recent Episodes of Financial Instability

CHARLES ENOCH

It has been estimated that more than half the membership of the IMF has experienced at least one episode of financial instability over the past thirty years. In the last fifteen years alone, countries hit by financial instability include Mexico, Argentina, Uruguay, Russia, the countries of Scandinavia, the countries of southeastern Europe and the Baltics, as well as Japan, Thailand, Indonesia, and Korea. While these countries have all recovered, to a greater or lesser extent, there remains in many of them an institutional legacy that is likely to persist long beyond the crisis itself.

By the beginning of the 1990s there was a worldwide trend towards reform of central banks in order to make their operation of monetary policy more effective. Studies by Cuckierman and others[1] had demonstrated that countries where the central bank was independent had a better track record of controlling inflation. Chile and New Zealand led the trend in revising their respective laws in order to give independence to their central banks, with promising subsequent results. The move towards the European Union, with the associated work in advance of the Maastricht Treaty and the focus on the characteristics and performance of the Bundesbank, gave a wider audience to the arguments in favor of central bank independence.

Just as perceived monetary policy failures led to institutional changes to improve the workings of monetary policy, so the failures to maintain financial stability—particularly from 1990 onwards—have led to institutional changes in that area as well. These changes have been essentially of three kinds:

- In many countries, to establish an agency outside the central bank tasked with supervising the financial system;

- To enhance independence and accountability of these new supervisory institutions;

- To clarify what a customer of a bank could expect to recover in the event of bank failure, whether a blanket guarantee on all liabilities during the actual period of instability, or a clearly specified limited amount that is insured once the system recovered from instability.

In general, there has also been a pattern of increasing openness to the international economy after a period of financial instability.

This chapter looks briefly at these emerging trends, then presents a brief overview of country experience of financial instability since 1990. Finally, it looks more closely at three particular cases—Bulgaria, Indonesia, and Turkey—before offering some concluding observations.

Separation of Monetary and Supervisory Responsibilities

Banking supervision has traditionally been a responsibility of the central bank in most countries, at least outside Latin America, where there is long experience of specialist "superintendence" institutions. Under that arrangement, a central bank was the agency with overall oversight for the monetary and financial systems, which involved operating monetary policy and the payments system and hence keeping watch over the major players in the banking system. In some countries, such as the United Kingdom, the central bank also acted as a promoter of the financial sector, frequently lobbying on behalf of financial institutions on, for instance, tax issues with the government. Over time, instances of supervisory difficulties led to codification of the central banks' responsibilities in this area. In the United Kingdom, for example, the 1979 Banking Law was a response to the failure of some smaller banks earlier that decade, and put the Bank of England's supervisory powers over the banks on to a more formal statutory basis.

Unquestionably, there are important synergies between the monetary policy and the supervisory responsibilities of a central bank. The information required to operate monetary policy overlaps considerably with that needed to perform effective banking supervision. And some operations, such as the execution of a central bank's function as lender of last resort, have a direct impact both on the monetary stance and the ability of the commercial bank to function.

Nevertheless, there is now widespread recognition of possible conflicts. A central bank's overriding objective is to contain inflation, which generally means raising interest rates when inflationary pressures seem to be rising. However, raising interest rates may have an adverse impact on the banks since higher rates may mean that borrowers cannot repay their loans, causing a rise in nonperforming loans. Fear of causing difficulties for the banks may cause a central bank responsible also for the commercial banks to hesitate over implementing a rise in interest rates when inflationary pressures call for it. Hence excess deference to the short-term needs of the banking sector may conflict with a central bank's monetary policy objectives—which in turn may not even help the banks beyond the short term, since lower inflation benefits the economy as a whole, and hence also the banks. Fear of this conflict of interest led to widespread support for separating responsibility for monetary and supervisory policy. In many cases this has involved establishing a separate supervisory agency outside the central bank, and transferring to it the central bank's responsibility for banking supervision.

It is worth noting three important factors that supported such institutional change. First, there has been a breakdown of barriers in the financial sector between banks and nonbank financial institutions (NBFIs). Indeed, since banks in many countries were the major owners of the nonbank financial institutions such as insurance and leasing companies, and active in a range of securities business, this meant that the important synergies for the authorities were not so much between the monetary and the financial aspects of the banking sector as between the banking and the nonbank parts of the financial sector. NBFIs have traditionally been supervised outside the central bank, often by the ministry of finance or ministry of commerce, so combining NBFI supervision with supervision of banks did not carry a presumption that supervision would be in the central bank. Thus in many cases the countries where the financial sector was broadest, in the sense that banking was not the overwhelming financial sector activity, were also where the establishment of a separate overall supervisor seemed to make most sense.

Second, with independence being granted to central banks to operate monetary policy, it was not immediately clear that similar independence should be given to the operation of banking supervision. Analytic studies had not shown with similar persuasiveness that independence was related to better supervision. Also, governments might feel that public money was more directly at stake where banking supervision was concerned, so they had a right to direct oversight of supervision even if they were prepared to concede independence in the operation of monetary policy. Perhaps this dichotomous relationship was felt most strongly in the case of the countries preparing for European Monetary Union. Under Maastricht, all central banks of countries participating in the common currency must be independent of national authorities. Countries were prepared to concede this independence in order to achieve lower inflation, but it was not clear what would be achieved by conceding a similar independence on the supervisory side. Thus the transfer of monetary responsibility to the European Central Bank was accompanied by a serious reconsideration of the role of supervision within a central bank, even if not all national authorities subsequently took it out of the central bank. The Netherlands Bank, for instance, retained supervisory responsibility for the banks and indeed managed to broaden its supervisory responsibilities into part of the nonbank financial sector.

The third factor was that in a number of cases central banks were deemed to have done an inadequate job in supervising the banks. As noted above, many countries experienced periods of serious financial instability in roughly the past fifteen years. Such episodes required in many cases the expenditure of substantial amounts of public money, and led to public investigations and recrimination. Generally, the central bank was blamed. A natural response would be to remove responsibility for supervision from the central bank—the Bank of Japan was a clear example. Similar factors underlay the establishment of the separate banking regulation agency outside the central bank in China.

It is briefly worth noting also that this change is not universally considered a panacea for supervision of the financial sector. A number of countries have had serious coordination problems between the new agency and the central banks that can undermine the safety of the banking system. Also, central banks—even those that no longer have supervisory responsibilities—have not walked away from their financial oversight obligations. Financial stability is often seen as a twin to the monetary stability objective of central banks. Amongst the most important innovations of central banks in recent years has been the introduction and refinement of the Financial Stability Report.[2]

Independence and Accountability

As noted above, the early movement towards central bank independence derived from arguments on the monetary side rather than out of concern for financial stability. Indeed, some institutional reforms at the time focused on separating the banking from the monetary agency so that the government could keep control over banking even while it was ceding independence over monetary policy to the central bank. Thus for a period it seemed that banking supervision might become subject to more, not less, official control.

Three broad factors, however, ensured that this did not occur. First, the trend towards greater autonomy or independence for public bodies is broad, and not just restricted to the operation of monetary policy. Accountability is today seem as an integral element of the working of any public institution. Independence has a number of dimensions, including on the legal side. These encompass the terms of appointment and dismissal of management; the governance of the institution; and its openness and transparency. Accountability may relate to responsibilities to report to parliament, to exchange information with the executive, to have clear legal criteria for actions, and to maintaining contacts with the public, for instance through regular publications and public appearances, careful explanation of decisions, and participation in public discussions. Particularly where institutional failing undermined the credibility of the institution, enhanced accountability could be an important tool for credibility to be restored.

Second, linkage of supervision with official control again very clearly leads to potential conflicts of interest. Taking firm action against a bank may cause difficulties for the government. Perhaps friends of the government own the bank, or allow the bank to be used for the government's purposes, or perhaps the government itself owns the bank. In other cases, perhaps, the government is concerned not to upset the customers of the bank, who may be harmed if the supervisor takes firm action against the bank. Thus if it has the power, a government may seek to discourage supervisors from taking necessary actions against the bank—meaning that the ultimate cost from the banks' problems may be much greater if necessary supervisory interventions have been delayed.

Third, once again, was the experience of financial instability, where official interventions had either led to the instability, or had delayed redress and thereby exacerbated the costs, and where the institutions themselves had lost credibility. The U.S. savings and loan and other banking failures at the time had shown the cost of delay and had led to the introduction of mandatory rules for the supervisors so as to minimize the possibility of political interference In other cases as well, official control over the supervisors was seen to have seriously undermined the supervisors' ability to carry out their function effectively. And if one could not fully trust official oversight of a regulatory institution, the institution would also have to be directly accountable to the public: enhancing accountability provisions was an integral element of institutional restructuring.

These moves towards independence and accountability have been formally codified. As a result of financial instability in the early 1990s, specifically the 1994 Mexican crisis, the Basel Core Principles for Effective Banking Supervision (BCP) were devised. The first Core Principle addresses the need for operational independence of the supervisor, making it clear that such independence is a critical element for supervision to become effective. As countries seek to meet the requirements of the BCP, in some cases following the analysis of the IMF/World Bank Financial Sector Assessment Program, which itself was introduced as an institutional response by the IMF and World Bank to financial instability, they have introduced reforms to ensure such independence.

Nevertheless, while there has been progress in establishing independence of regulatory agencies in recent years, this is far from complete. A recent study of 32 countries that have recently restructured their regulatory agencies found that only in 70 percent of them has the agency been given operational independence.[3]

Blanket Guarantees and Deposit Insurance: The Problem of Moral Hazard

An initial institutional change in response to recent major financial instability has been the introduction of a blanket guarantee on deposits and credits, in order to maintain confidence in the system. In Thailand and Indonesia, for instance, promulgations of blanket guarantees were early and important steps in handling the unfolding banking crises. Where effective, such action has served to prevent financial sector meltdown, and provided time to the authorities to remedy the situation. But blanket guarantees in many countries have proven expensive, leaving the public sector with a stock of debt of a significant proportion of GDP and with a large repayment obligation.

While the cost may well be justified in the time of instability—the cost of a meltdown could be devastating—it is undesirable to keep a blanket guarantee once the instability has abated, for it raises the danger of moral hazard. The moral hazard effect is that under a blanket guarantee many of the most important signals for ensuring an efficient allocation of savings and investment, and of a sound system, no longer operate. Hence many countries that experienced financial instability have by now replaced the earlier blanket guarantee with a limited deposit insurance scheme, and others are on a path to doing so.

Japan, for instance, delayed the replacement of its blanket guarantee with a limited insurance fund, fearing that confidence in its banking system had not been sufficiently restored, but has now completed the transition. Russia was one of a number of countries seeking to use the deposit insurance fund to create a level playing field for the different types of banks, by implicitly including the Sberbank—the state owned savings bank, and the dominant bank for household deposits—within the limited deposit insurance fund. This was done despite the fact that such banks—with their implicit blanket guarantee even when no formal guarantee was in effect—had served as havens in flights to safety during the periods of financial instability. In 2002 the International Association of Deposit Insurers was created to devise and disseminate best practices in deposit insurance, and this continues to provide useful guidance and research, including on how insurance premia might be matched to the relative riskiness of individual banks.

Financial Instability Since the 1990s

Monetary and financial instability cannot always be disentangled. Monetary instability can frequently be the cause or the catalyst for financial instability. Thus the inability of Sweden in 1992 to keep the krona within its European Exchange Rate Mechanism led to the floating and swift depreciation of the exchange rate, and a resultant banking crisis, as banks had left their foreign currency exposures unhedged following many years of exchange rate stability. As the economy went into recession, much of the criticism was directed at the central bank. A key part of the response was to separate out supervision from the central bank into a new dedicated supervisory agency, the Swedish Financial Supervisory Authority.

In 1997 in the United Kingdom, shortly after he had given independence to the Bank of England, the Chancellor of the Exchequer extracted banking supervision from the Bank and placed it with supervision of other financial institutions within the new Financial Supervision Agency (FSA). In part, this was probably done so the government could restrict its loss of control over the Bank of England's monetary policy responsibilities; but in part it also reflected a series of banking failures that, while not leading to systemic problems, had left some unease about the Bank's record in the supervisory area. Put together, there was an argument that with the Bank of England being given full responsibility for the operation of monetary policy, its credibility in that regard was so important that one would not wish to risk it being jeopardized by problems that might emerge in other parts of its mandate.

During the 1990s there were widespread banking problems across much of central and eastern Europe. The establishment of commercial banks after the fall of communism had not always been matched by a strong supervisory capacity, sound accounting principles, a fit and proper licensing regime, reform of state enterprises, or a legal system to ensure payment of debt obligations. Addressing the resultant instability required a whole range of institutional reforms, including strengthening the central bank, in some cases (Lithuania, for instance), establishing a separate asset resolution agency, and passing banking, bankruptcy, and bank bankruptcy legislation. In many cases reforms were put in place so that a significant part of the banking system would be bought by foreigners. In Estonia, for instance, virtually the entire banking system is now foreign-owned.

Russia fell into serious financial instability in 1998, following macroeconomic and governance problems similar to those that affected other transition economies. Banking supervision remained within the central bank, although the supervisory function was substantially enhanced. A new asset-resolution agency was established to handle the assets of the failed banks. This agency was subsequently refocused to manage the newly introduced deposit insurance system; the Central Bank of Russia used the initiation of this system effectively to re-license the banking system, to apply fit-and-proper criteria to bank owners and managers, and try to enhance the governance of the system. A separate nonbank regulator was established, and it is not clear whether this will be the basis for an eventual consolidated regulator.

In 1994 Mexico had also experienced a major banking crisis, described by IMF Managing Director Michel Camdessus as the first crisis of the twenty-first century. Institutional responses included enhancing the independence and accountability practices of the central bank and the regulators. More broadly, Mexico sought to open itself further to the international economic and financial community. Foreign banks now dominate the Mexican banking system, and Mexico is now a full member of the OECD, the organization of developed nations. Indeed, Angel Gurria, Mexico's chief debt negotiator of the earlier 1980s crisis, served as OECD's secretary-general from 1996 to 2006.

Finally, a number of Asian countries experienced serious financial instability beginning in late 1997. In all cases the exchange rate fell substantially, and a significant part of the countries' banking sectors was found to be insolvent, with high levels of nonperforming loans across the system. Even those countries not in full crisis (such as Malaysia) undertook significant institutional reform in response. China, Japan, and Korea established regulatory agencies outside the central bank. Malaysia and the countries hit by crisis established asset management and bank resolution agencies, either separate or in a single institution. Also, in many countries in the region, laws were passed to give independence to the central bank.

Financial Instability: Three Case Studies

The range of countries falling into banking crisis was wide, including post-communist transition economies, emerging Asian economies, and economies that had demonstrated large macroeconomic imbalances over many years. It is instructive to look at examples of each of these types.

Bulgaria

In 1996 Bulgaria fell into a full monetary and banking crisis. Monetary, fiscal, and structural policies had been weak, with unreconstructed state-owned enterprises experiencing continuing losses and the government accumulating unsustainable levels of debt. From late 1995, the exchange rate had been depreciating substantially. Although the authorities closed two banks in April 1996 in the face of revealed solvency problems, payments delays, and intensifying bank runs, this action was seen as "too little too late," and it only prompted further runs across much of the banking system. Although the government announced a blanket guarantee, levels of government indebtedness made the cost of such a guarantee clearly unsupportable and the announcement therefore not credible; indeed, the government seemed to recognize the problem since the payout from the guarantee was to be delayed and, in the case of payments for foreign currency deposits, was to be made in several stages over time.

Several more banks, both public and private, were closed over the summer of 1996, but the government seemed unable to take more fundamental action to address the situation. With credibility in the government and in official institutions evaporating, there were growing calls for the introduction of a currency board arrangement. Such a structure had just been introduced in Bosnia and Estonia, and earlier into Argentina, where it had seemed to stabilize the economy after a long period of economic turmoil. For several months it proved impossible to get consensus on how to take such a proposal forward. During this period the exchange rate collapsed, the country went into hyperinflation, and several more banks failed. The government ultimately resigned, and elections brought the opposition to power.

The months of economic collapse in late 1996 and early 1997, while devastating to many individuals, broadened the options available in the subsequent institutional reconstruction, since the liabilities of the banking system had been very largely eroded by inflation, and the credibility of existing institutions eliminated. The currency board arrangement (CBA) created by the new central bank law passed by parliament was therefore able to cover a large share of the remaining liabilities with the country's foreign exchange reserves without imposing restrictions on withdrawals, and indeed could guarantee the free exchange of domestic currency for the deutsche mark, the currency chosen as the peg. Bulgaria therefore used the establishment of the CBA as an opportunity for international integration, with entry into the EU as a long-term end-point (finally achieved at the start of 2007). Another example showing the desire to integrate with the international community following the perceived failure of existing institutions was seen in the results of a newspaper survey, asking the public who should be represented on the board of the CBA. The most popular response, over 40 percent of the total, was that it should be composed of a mixture of Bulgarians and foreigners. More surprisingly, was the next most popular response: over 30 percent wanted the board comprised *only* of foreigners.

The result of these institutional changes was a substantially reformed central bank that operated essentially as a currency board, although with some minor but important modifications from the "pure" model. In response to public concerns that the central bank had fed the banking crisis and the subsequent hyperinflation by providing excessive liquidity support, the newly established banking department of the Bulgarian National Bank (BNB) was tightly constrained in the amount of liquidity support it could provide and the conditions under which it could supply it. A bank receiving such support would have to be demonstrably solvent, and of systemic importance. Meanwhile, supervision fell to a separate supervision department, with the head of supervision personally responsible for the quality and the results of the supervision. Supervision thus remained inside the BNB, but as a distinct, autonomous department, with departmental mandates ensuring that supervision staff would not be subject to outside pressures or to conflicts of interest. Related legal reforms included laws on banking and bank bankruptcy, so that the authorities would be able to better handle banking sector problems in the future.

In short, the financial instability in Bulgaria led to reconstitution of the central bank as a currency board. The new law gave it independence from the government and required higher reporting and accountability provisions. Credibility also hinged critically on its commitment to freely exchange local currency for the peg foreign currency at the specified exchange rate. Strong barriers between the departments of the central bank served to eliminate traditional conflicts of interest; restrictions on the provision of funding for the banks severely limited the possibility of a liquidity explosion; and the vesting of responsibility for supervision of the banks within the banking supervision department, together with the exiting of weak banks from the system and the subsequent sale of remaining state banks, largely to foreign banks, served to enhance incentives and capacity for high-quality banking supervision.

These arrangements have so far served Bulgaria well. The country's economy has grown rapidly since the crisis and the government has substantially reduced the outstanding debt that it incurred before and during that time. An ultimate exit from the CBA is envisaged in the context of Bulgaria's entry into European Economic and Monetary Union.

Indonesia

In late 1997, as Thailand fell into financial crisis, the Indonesian currency depreciated rapidly, and runs developed at a significant number of banks. Indonesia turned to the IMF for assistance, and as part of its IMF-supported program at the start of November 1997 closed 16 banks (3 percent of the banking system) that had been found to be insolvent. This initially seemed to stabilize the system, but problems soon intensified: only a limited deposit insurance was in effect, and those who lost money included some very powerful groups with strong incentives to destabilize the situation, including for instance by harassing the management of the central bank.

It was also unclear to what extent the government was committed to the program it had signed with the IMF, when it reversed a number of its actions. For instance, a relative of the president was allowed in essence to reacquire a bank of his that had been closed. Equally important, it was not clear that the bank strategy had been comprehensive, so there was a widespread fear of further closings, and by December 1997 relentless runs resumed across the banking sector, and the exchange rate continued to depreciate rapidly. A revised IMF program in mid-January 1998 had no perceptible effect on the exchange rate, or on the pressure on the banks.

In late January 1998 the authorities reversed course, introduced a blanket guarantee, and established the Indonesian Bank Restructuring Agency (IBRA). This had a substantial immediate effect, with a bounce-back in the exchange rate, but continuing uncertainties about government policies—and the apparent non-functioning of IBRA—meant that the benefits were soon dissipated, and the banking runs resumed. Bank Indonesia (BI) provided substantial liquidity support for the banks up to the beginning of April 1998. At that point there was a major intervention by IBRA, with bank closings and takeovers. The blanket guarantee finally gained credibility, as all deposits from failed banks were available to depositors the next business day, and the runs tailed off over the next few weeks. Although selective runs against some banks regarded as Chinese-owned resumed in the following months, apparently politically inspired, and in June 1998 there were limited runs in response to government announcements of further bank closings, there were no further instances of system-wide runs. IBRA handled the resolution of the banks and of the taken-over assets (although governance problems meant that the overall costs escalated rapidly from earlier estimates), and was closed in 2004 with its job completed. With confidence restored and the economy growing robustly, the authorities have begun the progressive replacement of the blanket guarantee with limited deposit insurance. A dedicated agency is in the process of being established to take on this role.

A generally held view from early in the crisis was that the crisis reflected the failure of BI, firstly because it had failed to adequately supervise the banks that were insolvent, and also because it had fed the crisis through providing liquidity to the banks. It was also thought that this failure was due to pervasive political interference. Commercial banks had been directed to lend to politically connected individuals, and BI had been directed not to require banks to classify nonperforming loans to such individuals. Liquidity support was hard to manage in the crisis, with retrenchment by foreign interests and capital flight by Indonesians, and BI did seek written assurances from owners that they would repay the liquidity support if their banks were found to be in breach of regulations. These assurances did later yield some reflows, but governance problems severely constrained the amounts.

Meanwhile, President Suharto announced that his response to the crisis was that he would introduce a currency board arrangement along the lines of those in Argentina and Bulgaria. This was supported by some U.S. academics, who argued that it would cut BI's liquidity support to the banks, and hence stop the outflows. However, Suharto's proposal was conditional on the peg being at a rate 30 percent over the rate then prevailing in the market. He claimed that it would demonstrate the strength of the rupiah and its economy. Clearly, however, a peg at such a rate would not have been sustainable, and indeed it would have been seen as an invitation to capital flight. Eventually, opinion coalesced against the proposal, and Suharto withdrew it.

Once Suharto was replaced in May 1998, reform of BI could begin. The key need was universally recognized to be independence. Strong provisions to ensure independence from the government were put into the new banking law. Stability of the currency is defined as BI's objective. Appointments of the governor and the board are made through parliament rather than government, and regular external auditing and reporting to parliament is required. A study found that the new banking law puts Indonesia at the very top of the list of the

32 countries studied in terms of independence, after being below the average level before the new law was in place.[4]

Banking supervision is left in the central bank for the moment, but the law specified that preparations should begin for the establishment of a unified supervisor. With the crisis now behind, however, and BI expending energy in enhancing its supervisory capacity, preparations for the unified supervisor are being pushed further into the future.

Turkey

Turkey suffered major instability in its financial sector in 2001, after more limited crises in 1994 and 2000. The 2001 instability was attributed in part to continuing deficiencies in macroeconomic performance, as well as governance problems in the banking sector. The banks' financial figures had seemed satisfactory, and their exposures hedged. However, when the exchange rate depreciated, it became clear that the situation of a number of banks was much weaker. For several, the apparent hedging had been with fictitious or related partners, or with partners who walked away when their obligations were due. Moreover, some banks' customers were unable to service foreign currency debts that they had incurred. At the same time, huge politically related, or "duty," losses emerged at the state banks. The authorities introduced a number of measures to handle the failing banks; overall, the number of banks fell from 81 in 2001 to 35 in 2006. Meanwhile, substantial amounts of public money were provided to recapitalize the state banks for their duty losses, and the system of duty losses was eliminated.

An early institutional response was to establish a dedicated agency for supervising the banks, the Bank Regulation and Supervision Agency (BRSA). The agency was created to bring together two sets of supervisors, the sworn bank auditors, who conducted onsite examinations, and the offsite supervisors, and to integrate the two formerly disparate teams. Staff were initially provided from a number of agencies, including the central bank and the treasury, as well as from outside the official side, as capacity was built up. The BRSA was given a large degree of operational independence, although it was still subject to the Ministry of Finance for its budget, and its staff not fully protected from legal proceedings.

In addition, the Savings and Deposit Insurance Fund (SDIF) was taken out of the central bank and established as an independent agency. This agency was tasked with administering the blanket guarantee that had been introduced in response to the instability, resolving failing banks passed to it by the BRSA, and to selling the assets that it acquired through its handling of the failing banks. Good progress has been made in selling the assets, and a bridge bank is being used to handle the remaining banks under SDIF control. Meanwhile the blanket guarantee has been replaced by a limited deposit insurance scheme, the administration of which will increasingly be the main focus of the SDIF's work as the resolution of the 2001 crisis is concluded.

There are other important elements worth mentioning in the Turkish context. The central bank law granted operational independence to the central bank, and a further banking law in 2005 enhanced the power of the BRSA to carry out its supervisory functions. This latter law became operational once the BRSA published and implemented the consequent sub-regulations, twelve months after the passage of the law. The BRSA has also taken over responsibility for nonbanks, e.g., leasing and factoring companies, as a start towards consolidated supervision. In the future it may also take over from the treasury responsibility for insurance companies, and ultimately from the capital markets board responsibility for securities firms. Thus Turkey seems to be adopting a gradualist approach to creating a single supervisor.

Finally, it is worth noting that, like other countries that have been through periods of financial instability—such as Mexico and Bulgaria—Turkey is seeking to integrate itself more into the international economic and financial community. The authorities have adopted a welcoming attitude to foreign banks wishing to purchase banks in Turkey, and the share of foreign banks in the Turkish banking system is now rising rapidly. And underlying Turkey's economic program across the entire range of issues is the objective of harmonization with EU standards so as to be able to achieve eventual entry into the EU.

Conclusions

There have been four major institutional trends following recent periods of financial instability, although none of them has applied in every country that has been through financial instability.

First, in many countries the supervisory function has been taken out of the central bank. This has in some cases, but not all, been related to the establishment of a consolidated supervisor, covering financial institutions other than the banks.

Second, the regulatory function, whether inside or outside the central bank, is now subject to higher levels of independence and accountability than before. Moreover, the individuals conducting the supervision in many cases have legal protection for actions taken in furtherance of their responsibilities.[5]

Third, in many cases there is now greater transparency as to participants' rights and responsibilities as regards a commercial bank. In particular, there is a formal system of limited deposit insurance. Individuals thus are given more information, and are expected to take more responsibility in making their banking decisions.

Finally, in many countries there has been a subsequent opening to the international economic and financial community, perhaps to help restore credibility in institutions that are perceived to have failed. Countries have opened up their banking systems to foreign banks and sought integration into regional economic communities. In doing so, they have sought to demonstrate adherence to international financial standards.

To some extent these trends might well have occurred without the periods of financial instability. On the other hand, such instability demonstrated the weaknesses in the prior systems and stimulated the various authorities to make the needed changes. And even without there being further periods of instability, one may expect these trends to continue.

Notes

[1] *See, e.g.*, Alex Cuckierman, *A Central Bank Strategy, Credibility, and Autonom*, (Cambridge, MA: MIT Press, 1992)

[2] *See* Chapter 7 *infra* in this volume: Martin Čihák, "Central Banks and Financial Stability: A Survey of Financial Stability Reports."

[3] *See* Marc Quintyn, Silvia Ramrez, and Michael W. Taylor, "The Fear of Freedom," IMF Working Paper, WP/07/25.

[4] *Id.*

[5] *See*, for example, Chapter 11 *infra* in this volume: Ross Delston and Andrew Campbell, "To Protect or Not to Protect, That is the Question: Statutory Protections for Financial Supervisors—How to Promote Financial Stability by Enacting the Right Laws."

6 The Fund's Role in Sovereign Liquidity Crises

KERN ALEXANDER

Traditionally, the main threat to financial stability has been the classic bank-run problem, in which a credit institution with a balance sheet principally composed of liquid liabilities and illiquid assets was forced to sell its assets at a deep discount because of a sudden call on its deposit liabilities. Because most of the bank's liabilities were denominated in the local currency, the central bank could intervene to provide liquidity to the ailing institution. Bagehot's law would apply, permitting the central bank to lend in an emergency only to banks that were illiquid but not insolvent, at a penal rate of interest, while taking the bank's securities as good collateral.[1] Systemic risk in the domestic economy could thus be controlled.

Unlike earlier bank-run problems, most financial crises today arise because of some element of foreign-exchange risk. The growing risk to financial stability because of a counterparty default precipitated by a bank or nonbank finance firm with large foreign currency exposures is substantial. The potential contagion through the interbank payment system and across jurisdictions and currencies is considerable. If a large bank or G10 country experiences a default, the bank or sovereign debtor will normally have the ability to borrow in its own currency to cover its exposures.[2] The probability of default is thus lower because a bank can usually access the central bank's discount window; in the case of a sovereign debtor, it can issue more bonds but at a higher interest rate, or simply print more money.[3]

In contrast, because most of the international debt obligations of sovereign debtors and large financial institutions in developing and emerging market countries are denominated in G10 reserve currencies, their ongoing access to these funds is limited by demand and supply in the foreign exchange market and the willingness of foreign investors or lenders (including G10 central banks) to extend credit. Essentially, their default obligations are in currencies for which there is no central bank support. The debtors in non-G10 countries have a currency-mismatch problem, which restricts their ability to raise capital in a crisis.

How can international financial institutions provide liquidity for these obligations? Admittedly, the International Monetary Fund (IMF) has limited resources and cannot provide adequate assistance in a major banking or financial crisis.[4] Although there has been much debate regarding the future role of the IMF, the size of today's globalized capital markets make it unlikely that the Fund's limited resources could stem a sovereign debt or other financial crisis by acting on its own.

This chapter explores alternative roles for the Fund to act through existing institutional arrangements with G10 countries to provide supplementary resources to sovereign debtors in a liquidity crisis. The role of the Fund is addressed in terms of how it can coordinate the operation of a lender-of-last-resort mechanism for countries experiencing the equivalent of a bank-run scenario when foreign investors lose confidence and refuse to renew short-term investments or loans. The central question is, what mechanism or procedures could be used to allow sovereign debtors that are illiquid but solvent to access adequate foreign exchange to stabilize a crisis situation?

The chapter suggests that international economic law has an important role to play in promoting financial stability by applying public international law principles—such as the doctrine of *pacta sunt servanda*, which provides that states must adhere to obligations they have assumed through international agreements—that can enhance legal certainty in international economic and financial relations. The chapter further argues that legal certainty is a necessary component in the exercise of an effective lender-of-last-resort authority and that globalized financial markets require clearer institutional linkages and legal rules regarding how the function of an international lender of last resort (ILOLR) would operate. In this regard, the institutional linkages between the IMF and the G10 industrial countries should be made more transparent and legally binding under the existing General Arrangements to Borrow so that the Fund has the authority to access adequate currencies to stabilize a financial crisis in a non-G10 country or region.

The problem of moral hazard should be addressed by a clear rule-based framework with binding legal obligations regarding the allocation of responsibilities for lending by the G10 countries and the Fund's role in ensuring repayment and in facilitating lending in a financial crisis. Indeed, the role of international law in designing an effective ILOLR should be informed by the need to manage the sub-optimal incentives of investors and states acting without adequate information and coordination so that a rule-based procedure can be devised to allow states in exceptional circumstances to access foreign exchange to preempt or recover from a financial crisis caused by a sudden loss of investor confidence.

Devising an international legal framework to govern the operation of emergency lending by central banks and the Fund to sovereign debtors can be linked to the policy objective of controlling systemic risk in globalized financial markets and preventing the spread of contagion from one country or region to others, as occurred in the Asian financial crisis in 1997–98. International economic law has a crucial function to play in building a more robust international lender-of-last-resort mechanism that can effectively control the negative externality of cross-border sovereign debt risk. Generally, this would involve developing *ex ante* prudential regulatory structures and *ex post* measures for financial crisis resolution.

The chapter focuses mainly on the *ex post* crisis resolution measures that the Fund should take when a non-G10 sovereign debtor is experiencing payment difficulties or related financial distress. In the Asian financial crisis, the Fund's emergency lending proved inadequate to stem the crisis. Since then, Fund resources have been underutilized, in part because many sovereign debtors are unwilling to submit to stringent conditionality requirements, which have often exacerbated a borrowing country's economic and financial difficulties.[5]

The chapter suggests that the Fund should have enhanced authority to make calls for reserve currency loans from G10 countries through an amended General Arrangements to Borrow (GAB).The

GAB was adopted in 1962 primarily as a guarantee that each G10 state would have the ability to borrow reserve currencies (mainly U.S. dollars and UK sterling) from other G10 states in order to smooth the transition to currency convertibility while adhering to the Fund's fixed exchange rate parities. The GAB authorized the IMF to act as intermediary between the G10 states by facilitating consultations, assessing how much should be borrowed, and in guaranteeing repayment. The GAB contained a provision, however, that allowed G10 countries to refuse to lend even if the Fund and a majority of G10 countries had approved the loan.

When it was created, the GAB framework was an appropriate response to the exigencies of the international monetary system that required states to maintain fixed exchange rate parities and to adopt currency convertibility. The GAB applied only to G10 states because they held most of the foreign currency reserves, and it was necessary for them to cooperate in lending to advanced economies that were gradually liberalizing and needed access to reserve currencies during the transition. Financial crises did not occur often, and when they did they were generally contained in domestic jurisdictions by capital controls. Today, financial crises are mainly microeconomic in origin and arise because of bank-run-type panics and sudden losses of investor confidence, and are exacerbated by asymmetries of information that lead to problems of moral hazard. Existing Fund lending programs and the GAB framework are not adequate for effective crisis management in today's globalized financial markets.

The chapter proposes two reforms. First, the GAB should be amended so that G10 countries have an obligation to lend once the IMF Managing Director has made a call for reserve currency loans with majority consent of the Executive Board and majority approval of GAB participants. The GAB and its sister lending arrangement, the New Arrangements to Borrow, should be consolidated, and the credit arrangements of its present participants should be increased substantially beyond the present 34 billion SDRs. Second, for countries to be eligible for GAB emergency lending, they must comply with disclosure standards under the Fund's existing programs, such as the Special Data Dissemination Standard, and purchase credit-risk insurance on all their sovereign debt instruments.

The chapter proceeds as follows. The first section reviews the background to the Fund's involvement in financial crises and how the changing nature of financial crises in globalized financial markets requires an international lender-of-last-resort mechanism. The second section examines the evolution of Fund lending programs and the role of the General Arrangements to Borrow. The third section analyzes recent proposals for crisis management and the major issues confronting an international lender of last resort. The fourth section examines some *ex ante* and *ex post* regulatory approaches. The *ex ante* approach involves the Fund exercising its conditionality powers to require sovereign debtors to purchase credit protection on the debt instruments they issue and to comply with existing Fund disclosure standards and related financial sector regulatory practices. The *ex post* approach would involve the Fund and G10 states amending the General Arrangements to Borrow and New Arrangements to Borrow programs to allow the Fund to make binding calls on the G10 states to lend currencies up to their prescribed credit limit to the Fund so that it can lend them to sovereign debtors or their central banks in a crisis. Before making calls on the G10 states, the Fund would be expected to exhaust its own emergency loan programs and to ensure that the sovereign debtors receiving assistance have complied with Fund disclosure standards and conditionality programs.

The Fund's Evolving Role

Under the Bretton Woods system, developed countries had relative autonomy in pursuing their domestic macroeconomic policy objectives, which included unemployment, interest rate policy, and inflation control. The concerns of central bankers and financial regulators were shaped mainly by macroeconomic imbalances that arose in part from current account deficits and capital flows between countries. The Fund's chief function was to oversee the parity values of its members's currencies and to provide temporary liquidity support to members experiencing macroeconomic imbalances. Most countries sought reserve currencies, such as the U.S. dollar or sterling, to finance current-account or capital-account deficits. When most G10 countries began to liberalize their current accounts in the early 1960s, there was an increase in the demand for reserve currencies that could be used to finance any resulting imbalances. The breakdown of the Bretton Woods system in 1971 resulted in the floating of the main reserve currencies, and cost of foreign exchange risk was shifted from the state to the market.[6] As a result, most developed countries and some developing countries have adopted capital-account convertibility to allow firms and investors to freely access foreign exchange assets in order to cover their exposure to foreign exchange risk and to speculate in currency values.

Consequently, there has been a dramatic and substantial increase in private-sector cross-border capital flows, which has led to a deepening of financial markets but has also resulted in greater financial fragility for many countries, especially developing countries and emerging market economies. Since the early 1980s there has been a growing number of banking and currency crises in both developed and developing countries, and the resulting social costs have been greatly magnified by contagion across markets and by the lack of an effective lender of last resort for many of these countries. Indeed, the floating exchange rates and liberalized capital markets of the post-Bretton Woods system means that the Fund can no longer directly influence foreign exchange policy and control liquidity creation.

Due to this paradigm shift, the Fund found a new role of managing financial crises, mainly in developing and emerging market economies. In the 1980s the Fund orchestrated the programs for lending into arrears that helped stabilize the Latin American sovereign debt crisis. In the early 1990s it provided assistance for some developed and developing countries that were suffering currency crises, and played the lender of last resort along with the U.S. government in bailing out the Mexican banking system in 1994–95. In return for its financial assistance, the IMF exercised its conditionality powers to ensure that Fund resources were protected by devising economic restructuring programs and policies for members that draw on Fund resources.

The Asian financial crisis, however, demonstrated the difficulties confronting the Fund in providing adequate liquidity to ailing sovereign debtors and central banks in a crisis situation. The slow economic recovery of these countries also called into question the effectiveness of the recovery program the IMF had prescribed for these countries. The growth of global capital markets and cross-border financial liberalization since the Asian crisis has continued unabated, and the role of the IMF has been called into question because the Fund's limited resources would probably be inadequate to stem a sovereign debt crisis for a major country and would certainly be inadequate to stabilize a cross-border banking crisis involving a major financial center.[7] Nevertheless, in recent years there have been some monetary and banking crises in peripheral economies in which the Fund played a stabilizing role and served as "de facto international lender of last resort."[8]

The role of the Fund therefore has been the topic of debate regarding whether it should have an expanded role as (1) a global lender of last resort or (2) a more limited role in its lending activities, so that it would not be considered the only or the main lender in a financial crisis.[9] The latter view suggests that the private sector should play a greater role in providing funding to resolve financial crises, whether in the form of bond issuance or other forms of debt offered to the capital markets or through private bank loans, with the IMF merely playing a facilitative role in reducing agency problems between the private lenders and the state borrowers.[10] This notion is reinforced by the fact that the value of cross-border trading in securities in today's globalized capital markets far exceeds the limited resources controlled by the Fund. Accordingly, a solution to sovereign debtor liquidity crises must necessarily involve the private sector along with certain public-sector actors, such as central banks, who have the resources to provide bridge financing to a debtor state in a crisis.

Despite its more limited role in lending, some academics and policymakers envision a broader role for the Fund that could involve enhanced surveillance powers over the macroeconomic policies of countries and financial systems, including monitoring compliance with the IMF codes of conduct, as well as elaborating and overseeing implementation of some standards of regulatory conduct. In addition to enhanced surveillance, the IMF would offer more intensive technical assistance to developing countries and emerging market economies and would be expected to engage in "ruthless truth-telling" to member countries that abandon economic fundamentals or fail to achieve financial stability objectives.[11] Finally, in the case of a crisis, the Fund should play the role of a neutral third-party advisor in assisting financial negotiations and facilitating a sovereign debtor's access to emergency finance.[12]

Fund Lending Arrangements

Although quota subscriptions are the prime source of IMF funding, several supplementary borrowing and lending programs are available to the Fund to provide short-term emergency lending to members experiencing temporary economic or payment difficulties. Traditionally, the most important of these programs have been the General Arrangements to Borrow (GAB), the Stand-by Arrangements, and, more recently, the New Arrangements to Borrow (NAB) and the Supplemental Reserve Facility (SRF).[13] These bilateral arrangements are essentially agreements between the Fund and a member country that wishes to draw on its resources. The arrangements are not legally binding, but they create expectations and conditions regarding the use of the Fund's resources. This section describes these arrangements and examines their role in providing emergency lending assistance to IMF members. These bilateral arrangements provide the institutional framework on which to build a more effective function for the Fund as international lender of last resort.

Stand-by Arrangements

The stand-by arrangement provides the Fund with the opportunity to examine a state's economic activities and policies before entering into an arrangement that would allow the state to draw against Fund resources.[14] Article XXX (b) of the Amended Articles defines a stand-by arrangement as "a decision of the Fund by which a member is assured that it will be able to make purchases from the General Resources Account in accordance with the terms of the decision during a specified period and up to a specified amount."[15] Stand-by arrangements enter into force once the Executive Board approves the stand-by in consideration of a letter of intent to the Managing Director signed by the minister of finance or the governor of the central bank of the applicant state.

The letter of intent lays out the undertakings the Fund requires in return for granting the line of credit. The legal status of stand-by arrangements has been debated. While former IMF general counsel Sir Joseph Gold argued that a stand-by is an "arrangement" and not an agreement creating legal obligations, others consider the letter of intent, together with the stand-by arrangements, to "constitute a legally binding agreement."[16]

The Executive Board of the Fund itself has issued a comprehensive decision on "the Use of the Fund's General Resources and Stand-by Arrangements of 1979" that expressly denies any contractual function and binding language of the stand-by arrangements.[17] For instance, a state that fails without justification to fulfill a commitment under a stand-by arrangement is not regarded as having breached the Articles of Agreement, and is not subject to sanctions. Nonetheless, nonfulfilment of a commitment may lead the Fund to refuse to renew the stand-by or to limit the state's future ability to draw against the stand-by. It has been therefore argued that "it is not unfair to regard a stand-by arrangement as constituting an obligation of a state on whose behalf a Letter of Intent is signed and to which a stand-by has been granted."[18] This narrower contractual view of the stand-by, however, does not adequately take into account the broader legal authority of the Fund under Article V of the Articles to impose conditions on its members regarding their use of Fund resources.[19]

Precautionary Stand-by Arrangements

Precautionary stand-by arrangements are facilities that certain states may draw against to prevent a capital account crisis. Under such an arrangement the country indicates its intention not to draw upon the Fund's resources unless its economic circumstances deteriorate. The use of these stand-bys was first discussed by the Executive Board in June 2003 to determine whether there was a possibility that precautionary arrangements might, to some extent, replace the IMF Contingent Credit Line (CCL). The CCL was created in 1999 to provide eligible states with "a precautionary line of defense" for members with economic and financial policies that do not put the Fund's resources at risk but which may nevertheless be vulnerable to financial-market crises. The CCL had not been used when it expired in November 2003. The newly proposed precautionary stand-by arrangements replaced the CCL and serve the purpose of promoting crisis prevention.

Since the expiration of the Contingent Credit Line in 2003, views of the Executive Directors have been divided regarding whether or not there remain any gaps in Fund emergency lending instruments. The effect of this could potentially be that in a capital-account crisis arising from exogenous factors, such as the loss of confidence by foreign investors, a country that maintains strong domestic policies under Fund surveillance may still not be able to avoid a crisis unless a new emergency funding policy were in place to provide *ex ante* assurances of appropriate financial support.[20]

Extended Arrangements

Another area of IMF reform was the plan to increase affordable funding for developing countries for longer terms. The first official initiative in this area occurred when the Fund adopted so-called "extended arrangements" in 1974 by establishing the Extended Fund Facility (EEF), whereby member states could conclude stand-by arrangements for longer-term assistance both with respect to time (longer periods of borrowing) and quota limits (larger amounts) than under the original stand-by arrangements. In addition to these extended arrangements, the IMF introduced six other types of special conditions for stand-by arrangements, all regrouped under the term of *special facility*.[21] These extended stand-by arrangements could be utilized by the Fund to make longer-term loans to a country that has suffered a financial shock and as a result has experienced severe economic contraction with a substantial impact on its long-term economic development. In this situation, the ability to make long-term loans for economic recovery following a crisis should be considered a complementary policy tool to emergency lender-of-last-resort lending.

General Arrangements to Borrow

By the early 1960s, post-war economic recovery in Western economies was leading to a number of structural changes in the international monetary and financial system. The first steps towards currency convertibility for the current account were taken by the six countries that established the European Economic Community in 1957 when they adopted the European Monetary Agreement of 1955.[22] As the Bretton Woods regime of fixed exchange rates took full effect for the main Western European countries in 1959 following the termination of the European Payments Union, the IMF began to push for currency convertibility for these countries to promote global trade and to relieve some of the pressure on the IMF exchange parities.[23] Convertibility, however, had the potential to lead to volatile capital movements that could undermine financial stability and could potentially lead to a deficit of reserve currencies (dollars or sterling) for some countries trying to finance trade deficits.[24] In response, the Fund issued a decision in 1961 that it had the authority to make its resources available to assist members having balance-of-payments problems that are caused or exacerbated by capital flows.[25] During this period, IMF membership was growing faster than the increases in its membership quotas, and because the subscriptions of member states of 75 percent of their quota did not add to the pool of freely usable Fund resources, the Executive Board began debating the merits of creating a funding source that would allow it to borrow the reserve currencies at market interest rates and lend these funds to other G10 members to cover their current account imbalances when these imbalances were perceived to threaten the Fund's exchange rate parities.[26]

To address these concerns, the General Arrangements to Borrow (GAB) was created in 1962 by a decision of the Fund's Executive Board.[27] The GAB was an international agreement that was interpreted at the time to be a set of bilateral credit arrangements between the Fund and each government or central bank of the main industrial countries.[28] The Fund's competence to act in the GAB derives from Article VII (1) of the Articles of Agreement, which contains broad language permitting the Fund to borrow currencies from any source whether within or outside IMF member states.[29] The GAB was not part of the Articles, but it had the purpose of supporting the Fund's treaty objective of promoting international monetary stability by giving the Fund access to the currencies of the G10 countries in order to lend them to other G10 members or approved IMF members that were experiencing economic imbalances or temporary payment difficulties on a large scale that exceeded the Fund's resources.[30]

The GAB created a framework whereby the Fund was authorized to make calls for currency from the G10 countries (GAB participants), but only after it had consulted with GAB participants and had obtained majority approval of the Executive Board and special-majority approval of GAB participants. Once these conditions had been met, the Fund could borrow the currency and lend it to the GAB participant country that had sought the loan to cover an imbalance in its current or capital accounts. Specifically, the Fund's role was to act as an intermediary between the GAB participants to replenish their holdings of reserve currencies by borrowing from participants in surplus and lending to participants in deficit.[31]

The Managing Director's call to borrow currencies can only take effect if approved by the Executive Board.[32] When the IMF borrows under the GAB from GAB participants, it has a legal obligation to repay the loan to the lending state(s) within five years and to allocate its repayments proportionally to reflect the proportional commitments of each participant.[33] If the IMF does not perform its obligation to repay the loan (e.g., late payment of the loan is considered non-fulfillment), it will be considered in arrears. GAB loans are enforceable contracts, with a legally binding effect between the IMF and the lender.[34]

One of the weaknesses of the GAB in its role as an effective lender of last resort was that each GAB participant country that was called upon to loan its currency to the Fund was not legally bound to do so, even though the Executive Board and a special majority of GAB participants had approved the loan and the Fund was obliged to repay the loan over a period of up to five years.[35] This created a level of uncertainty regarding whether the Fund could borrow adequate reserve currencies in a financial crisis.[36] The absence of a specific legal obligation to lend was a political compromise for the benefit of the United States or any other GAB participant that wanted the flexibility, during "the world dollar shortage", of retaining its dollar assets for national economic policy objectives.[37]

Nevertheless, the GAB created legal relationships between the Fund and the G10 countries by which the latter agreed they would cooperate to strengthen the Fund and the international monetary system.[38] In practice, the effectiveness of the GAB depended on the

IMF Managing Director consulting and negotiating with the Executive Board and the GAB participants in advance over the terms and conditions by which the participants would lend their currencies to the IMF.[39] These negotiations addressed a number of issues, including whether the currencies and amounts to be called from a participant under its credit arrangements reflected its economic ability to lend its currency and how much of that currency the Fund held along with the allocation of responsibilities across different participants for lending the currencies.[40] The negotiations also addressed the type of transaction through which the Fund would make the funds available—for instance, either an exchange transaction, an exchange transaction under stand-by arrangement, or an extended arrangement.[41] Indeed, Gold notes that it was intended but not required that calls would be made under several credit arrangements to provide financing for a participant's borrowing from the Fund or for a stand-by arrangement with the Fund.[42]

A participant was expected to make its currency available upon a call by the IMF Managing Director.[43] The call would be in proportion to the participant's commitment of funds. Between 1962 and 1983 the total value of credit commitments by GAB participants was SDR 6,344 million, and the country with the largest single credit commitment was the United States with SDR 1.883 billion, which was 29 percent of the total commitments.[44] By 1983, several amendments were made to the GAB to bring it up to date with the Second Amendment of the Articles of Agreement, which became effective in 1978, and this resulted in GAB participants agreeing to enlarge their credit arrangements to enhance the capacity of the Fund to draw on reserve currencies for emergency lending in a financial crisis.[45] The total value of credit commitments was substantially increased to SDR 1.7 billion, and the United States remained the largest individual contributor with an individual amount of SDR 4.25 billion, which was 25 percent of the total commitments.[46] This means that today if the Fund issued a call for currencies, and if a special majority of GAB participants including the United States approved along with the IMF Executive Board, the United States would be obliged therefore to contribute 25 percent of the total value of the approved call.

Besides increasing the credit arrangements of GAB participants to reflect their size and role in the global economy and capacity to provide loans to the Fund, the revised GAB contained other amendments, the most important of which was that the IMF could now borrow under the GAB for the benefit of nonparticipants. Conditions applied, however, including that members benefiting from such loans must have been approved for adjustment programs with the IMF.[47] The Managing Director may only initiate calls for the benefit of a nonparticipant if certain criteria are met: (1) that the Fund has inadequate resources to meet expected or actual requests for financial assistance and (2) the occurrence is an exceptional situation associated with a member's balance of payments problems of a size that could threaten the stability of the international monetary system.[48] These criteria are more stringent for nonparticipants than for participants, as there is a requirement that the Managing Director make a determination that an exceptional situation "threatens" international monetary stability, which is not required for GAB participants.[49] Moreover, the Managing Director has a responsibility to pay due regard that loans for the benefit of nonparticipants do not prejudice GAB participants' access to these resources. The rate of interest charged on GAB loans was increased to a minimum of 4 percent per annum, which provided additional revenue for the Fund to offset any losses associated with fluctuations in exchange rates during the period for repaying the loan.[50]

Since its inception, the GAB has been invoked by the Fund and approved by GAB participants on ten occasions. The most recent occurred in 1998, when the GAB approved a Fund request of SDR 6.3 billion in connection with an extended financing arrangement for the Russian government to support its currency and government bond market, both of which had collapsed in the 1998 Russian financial crisis.[51] After disbursing only SDR 1.4 billion, the Fund terminated the arrangement in response to the Russian government's default on its government bonds and its failure to fulfill other conditionality commitments.[52] The GAB has resulted in an institutional framework that allows the Fund to play the role of a lender of last resort by borrowing surplus reserve currencies, the value of which far exceed its own resources, so that it can lend them to GAB participants suffering economic imbalances or a financial crisis.[53] The Fund's role as an intermediary in providing short-term emergency loan assistance to GAB members creates coordination benefits between countries and reduces transaction costs in allocating surplus currencies from GAB participants in surplus to other participants in deficit and in need of immediate assistance.

The GAB system has worked well for the benefit of the G10 countries and other approved GAB participants[54] that were expected to provide reserve currency liquidity at market rates to the IMF, which would then lend the currency to another GAB participant experiencing a deficit in that currency. The GAB allowed the Fund to play a limited role as lender of last resort by borrowing directly from GAB participants and then lending to GAB borrowers in order to cover temporary imbalances that were putting pressure on the Fund's fixed exchange rate parities.

The GAB system, however, has been criticized as being for the benefit of the prosperous industrial countries Developing countries were disadvantaged by not being able to access reserve currency assets on such generous terms. This LOLR function for the G10 seemed to work well for GAB participants but not for the majority of IMF member countries, which were not participants in the GAB and not generally able to access reserve currencies through the GAB. Moreover, GAB participants even proved reluctant to make their funds available to other GAB members because the special-majority requirement to approve calls for funds by the IMF Managing Director was often a difficult threshold to reach.

In addition, the requirements for non-GAB countries to qualify for GAB loans proved difficult to meet. Although paragraph 21 (a) allowed the Fund to make calls for foreign exchange for non-GAB members in one of four circumstances which most members could meet based on their usual drawings from Fund accounts, the approval of a proposal for calls depended on acceptance by a special majority of GAB participants and approval by the IMF Executive Board. Even if the special majority and Board approval were obtained, an individual GAB participant could still unilaterally decide, based on its balance of payments and reserve position, that "calls should not be made on it, or that calls should be made for a smaller amount than that proposed."[55] These obstacles explain in part why no country outside the GAB membership was approved for a GAB loan until

1998, when Russia obtained a loan because of the consensus among GAB countries that the Russian financial crisis was a serious threat to international financial stability and to the financial institutions in their countries. In addition, the absence of legal obligation for an individual GAB participant to make a loan according to an approved call raises serious issues regarding the stability of expectations and legal certainty of the function of an emergency lender of last resort.

New Arrangements to Borrow and the Supplemental Reserve Facility

The New Arrangements to Borrow (NAB) emerged as a result of the Mexican financial crisis of 1994–95 and the conviction by IMF members that more resources should be made available to the Fund to stabilize financial crises for developing and emerging market economies.[56] The NAB contains a set of bilateral credit arrangements between the Fund and 26 IMF members and institutions that enable the Fund to borrow their currencies in order to forestall or prevent an impairment of the international monetary system or to deal with a threat to financial stability. The larger membership of the NAB also includes a number of developing countries, such as Korea, Malaysia, and Thailand, but its membership is primarily composed of wealthy developed countries.[57]

The NAB contains total credit arrangements of SDR 17 billion, equal to the GAB arrangements and resulting in a combined total of SDR 34 billion for both programs. NAB is not intended to replace the GAB, but rather to enhance the amount of resources available to the Fund from which it can borrow to forestall a financial crisis. The NAB was designed to allow the Fund to have access to substantially more resources than were available under the GAB so that it could address systemic problems in the global financial system. Like the GAB, NAB participants are eligible to draw on Fund resources through GAB and NAB financing, and non-NAB states that are Fund members are eligible for NAB financing subject to the same terms and repayment conditions as NAB participants, whereas non-GAB states are subject to less favorable repayment terms than GAB participants.[58] Under NAB financing, therefore, there is no discrimination between NAB and non-NAB members in the financing conditions for an approved NAB credit, whereas under the GAB,

GAB participants receive more favorable treatment than non-GAB members.

Any IMF member wishing to draw on resources in the NAB must apply and conclude a stand-by arrangement with the Fund and to present a letter of intent with the Fund before it can draw on resources. As with other stand-by facilities, such as the Poverty Reduction Strategy Program (PRSP) or Supplemental Reserve Facility (SRF), a failure to meet the objectives of the program does not lead to sanctions or punishment, but only to a suspension of the right to draw or the denial of a renewal under the stand-by arrangements.[59] Fund conditionality, therefore, plays an important role in the member having continued access to NAB financing.

As mentioned above, the GAB has only been invoked on ten occasions, and in each instance financial support was provided to a G10 or G8 country that was either in deficit or needed assistance to purchase part of its reserve holdings. In contrast, the NAB has been activated only once, when it was used to provide a stand-by arrangement for Brazil in December 1998, when the country experienced a temporary loss of confidence by foreign investors that led to a collapse in its currency. Acting through the NAB, the Fund made a call for SDR 9.1 billion, of which SDR 2.9 billion was used to support the Brazilian currency and its government bond market.

The actual drawing from the Fund by the borrowing member under the NAB (or GAB) is considered a legal act. For example, it is considered a purchase, which is given in exchange for the obligation to repurchase special drawing rights or "freely usable currencies."[60] Moreover, as with the GAB, the Fund, when borrowing from NAB participants, assumes a legal obligation to repay the NAB lenders within five years.[61] The NAB does not replace the GAB, but the NAB is the facility of first and principal recourse for non-GAB members, with the exception that if a country is a member of both the NAB and the GAB, it may request funding under either facility.

Another short-term financing facility approved by the Fund in the late 1990s was the Supplemental Reserve Facility (SRF), which was established in 1997 during the Asian financial crisis. The SRF facility provided the Fund with another lending mechanism to make short-term loans at market rates to members suffering from a financial crisis. Member borrowers would have to comply with a Fund restructuring program in order to maintain eligibility to draw on the facility.

The NAB and SRF provided needed additional facilities for IMF members to access reserve currencies in a crisis. However, the available credit under these programs is inadequate, even when supplemented by existing Fund programs, to stem a major financial crisis. Although these lending programs may provide adequate resources for countries experiencing temporary economic and financial imbalances, the amount that the Fund could borrow under the GAB, NAB, and SRF would likely be inadequate to stabilize a contagion-like crisis similar to the crisis that affected the East Asian countries in 1997–98. This undermines the Fund's ability to play a credible role as lender of last resort .

Based on the inadequacies of the GAB, NAB, and other emergency lending facilities in serving an LOLR role, high-level debates have occurred involving former senior officials of the Fund regarding what role the Fund should play in providing emergency lending in a financial crisis with systemic proportions. Should the Fund have an enhanced role with an added institutional dimension, or are the existing borrowing arrangements adequate? One view holds that the emergence of a globalized financial system requires an international lender of last resort, and the IMF is in the best position to play this role because of its experience in dealing with a number of financial crises.[62] Former IMF Managing Director Michel Camdessus has argued that the Fund has been performing and adapting to this role for the last fifty years and that it would be important for promoting financial stability to reaffirm its role in this area so it can more effectively fulfill this vital function. Furthermore, the Fund's experience and expertise provide it with enough judgment to avoid any influence of moral hazard either from governments or market participants. Similarly, Paul Krugman and Stanley Fischer assert that the Fund has become a de facto international LOLR because of its many interventions on behalf of countries in financial distress. They argue that because there is a general acceptance of a domestic lender of last resort, by analogy there needs to be an international LOLR to stem a bank-run-like scenario when foreign investors lose confidence in a country and began to liquidate their exposures.[63]

On the other hand, Horst Köhler recognizes that the Fund is not an LOLR in the traditional sense and that its inability to act quickly with substantial resources precludes it from preventing most crises or stabilizing a country undergoing one. Moreover, the political constraints on providing financial support in the GAB or NAB and the lack of legal certainty once a special majority has approved financial support undermines the Fund's credibility to be able to act decisively and obtain adequate resources through the GAB and NAB to stem a major crisis. The absence of legal certainty regarding the Fund's powers to obtain the necessary supplementary resources from the pre-existing credit arrangements of GAB participants means that its effectiveness in exercising the LOLR function is undermined. Although it is important on moral hazard grounds for the market not to know at what point the Fund might intervene to provide liquidity support, it is also equally important that investors believe that the Fund has the capacity and willingness to stabilize a crisis if necessary. Otherwise, it will be more difficult to incentivize foreign investors to play their part by not exiting the market so quickly when there is an apparent loss of confidence in the market.[64]

Crisis Management and the Lender of Last Resort

The financial crises of the 1990s triggered vigorous discussions among economic policymakers and academics about how to reform the IMF and World Bank so that they could more effectively address financial disruptions in international markets, and how to avoid financial crises. Following the Asian crisis, the debate focused on achieving greater financial stability through a two-pronged approach, namely, crisis prevention and crisis management. A vast literature has arisen on crisis prevention,[65] which addresses how to improve the predictability of a financial crisis and how to minimize the social costs once it occurs. By contrast, crisis management focuses on measures that should be adopted *ex post,* once a crisis has occurred or is imminent, and how to manage the contagion across countries and the potential spill-overs on the rest of economic activity.[66]

The following section examines existing approaches to crisis management, highlights the main problems, and suggests a reformed international LOLR framework that would address the need to provide more legal certainty in the *ex post* crisis lending mechanism for GAB and NAB participants to lend reserve currencies to non-G10 countries who are experiencing a financial crisis. The GAB and NAB credit arrangements would be consolidated and substantially increased to SDR 100,000 million. The Fund would play the role of intermediary by certifying when a financial crisis is occurring and assessing the amount and composition of reserve currencies needed to stem the crisis. In doing so, the Fund's Managing Director, after consultation with the Executive Board, would consult with GAB participants and consider any objections to the use or composition of GAB currencies and then a make a call for loans. Once the special majority requirement is reached, the Managing Director would have the legal authority to obtain the respective currencies in their prescribed allocations and disburse them through Fund drawing operations for the borrowing sovereign debtor. Legal certainty would be enhanced because once the special majority requirement was reached, all GAB and NAB participants for whom the proposal for calls applied would be obliged to lend according to the call. Moreover, procedural transparency would be enhanced because the authority of the Managing Director would be recognized to make a determination when a financial crisis or sovereign debt crisis was occurring, and then to consult and obtain approval from the Executive Board and from GAB members to make a call for currencies. Transparency would be further enhanced because the composition of currencies required for any bailout would depend on the relative proportion of currencies in which the defaulted sovereign debt was denominated. Thus, central banks would be on notice regarding their potential exposure in a bailout. The most practicable approaches to crisis management will now be reviewed.

Managing a Financial Crisis

The management of a financial crisis is usually an essential function of a central bank. Remedial action in managing a crisis must target the source of the crisis, and there must be adequate resources at hand and sufficient legal discretion for the central bank to take the necessary measures. If these conditions are in place, the impact and potential contagion of the crisis to other sectors of the economy or financial system as a whole may be minimized or even prevented.

If crisis prevention cannot avoid the occurrence of a crisis, crisis management becomes all the more important for the soundness of the financial system. Barry Eichengreen notes, however, that the achievements of crisis management have been particularly small in comparison with prevention efforts.[67] The lack of progress in the field not only lies in its intrinsic challenges, such as moral hazard, distinguishing between insolvency and illiquidity, and determining adequate levels of assistance; it is also due to the prevailing rigidity of the institutionalized approach and the need for reform of institutions and their mandates.

Inevitably, most of the debate over reform has focused on the institutions and tools that so far have been responsible for crisis management. Financial crises have traditionally been addressed and managed with financial assistance by the Fund, other IFIs, and the G10 countries. The subsequent sections describe the actors and tools outside the GAB framework involved, and discuss an array of alternatives, comparing their benefits and shortcomings with existing crisis-management techniques.

Financial Assistance

Lack of sufficient, adequate, and speedy emergency financing is often considered to be one of the main threats to financial stability. This poses a considerable strain on crisis management, particularly when countries with sound macroeconomic fundamentals are victims of capital volatility.[68] A general consensus has emerged that improved access to financial assistance in a crisis is necessary to provide liquidity for countries experiencing a shock to their financial systems.[69] This has led to the design of various proposals and recommendations concentrating on other components of crisis management beyond mere financial assistance, such as institutional reform, participation and cooperation, and new instruments and tools.

Furthermore, the lack of clarity and consensus on how to proceed partly explains why only limited progress has been made. For instance, IMF emergency lending to a country in crisis may be accompanied by a temporary suspension of international debt service payments. Although IMF emergency measures in recent years have provided a needed respite for countries in arrears and suffering from liquidity problems, the real detriment of the IMF programs has been the stringent conditionality arrangements imposed on sovereign debtors as a result of the country accepting emergency financing support. These Fund programs have led to substantial economic and financial sector restructuring in the debtor country's economy that has proved to be socially costly and in most cases has failed to achieve economic recovery and financial stability.

Official assistance has come in the form of persuading and sometimes requiring private lenders and investors to incur some of the costs of the bailout and a restructuring of debt servicing, often at a high cost for the country in question. This is known as bailing in the private sector. Until the financial crises of the 1990's, however, institutions like the IMF and other institutional and international creditors often did not consider the fundamental reason why a country should receive temporary assistance in a crisis. Rather, the main objective of the official international lending community was whether further lending to the country in crisis would enable it to resume making payments on its debt and eventually whether it could cure its arrears. Very little emphasis was placed on the systemic impact of the country's inability to continue making payments on its debts.

During the financial crises of the late 1990s, there was a growing awareness that the decision to provide emergency lending should depend on factors other than the ability of a country to resume servicing its debts to private and official creditors. Instead, the focus was placed on the systemic effects of providing a country or financial sector with financial support, and when to offer assistance by distinguishing between illiquidity and insolvency as a source of financial crises. In essence, this new approach raised questions about the efficiency considerations of financial assistance. Eichengreen has observed that "[t]he bottom line is that the IMF must make a judgement of whether limited assistance will help a country to surmount its financial difficulties and resume business as usual, in which case it should lend, or whether lending is unlikely to have its effect, in which case the fund should stand aside...."[70]

Crisis management, as envisaged today by the IFIs, was conceptualized and tailored during the financial crises of the 1990s. In particular, many proposals materialized as part of a broader approach to the design of an international financial architecture. In particular, the G-7 Köln summit laid the groundwork by recognizing the Fund's efforts in the Asian crisis and proposing a series of recommendations. For debt restructuring and reduction of Fund programs, a series of operational guidelines were laid down, such as medium-term financial sustainability, the need for broad comparability and fairness of treatment where both private and institutional creditors were involved, clarity in official financing terms, and public disclosure of policy approaches adopted by the IMF. Further, the G-7 urged the Fund to continue reforming its specific lending facilities according to a set of principles, such as offering institutional support for prevention of crises, sound macroeconomic policy design, and the observance of standards, among others.[71]

Sovereign Debt Restructuring

Sovereign debt restructuring is often an alternative for countries with an unsustainable debt burden. This may be the only way out of an insolvency crisis, when the borrowing country is unable to meet its long-term repayment obligations. Under such circumstances, creditors will call in their loans and subsequent efforts such as standstills and creditor committees will be enacted to try and deal with the debt overhang of the insolvent country.[72]

Private creditors, however, may resist engaging in orderly debt renegotiations, especially if individual creditors believe they will obtain improved conditions if they "hold out" after a debt restructuring process. As such, cooperation to achieve a balanced distribution of responsibility and losses is often undermined by the pursuit of individual interests, which may harm the indebted country, cooperative creditors, and international financial markets.[73] To address this problem, leading banks and financial institutions, acting through the Institute of International Finance (IIF), have developed a set of principles for debt restructuring.[74]

The IIF principles are organized under four pillars that offer an approach to debt restructuring that will ensure stability of capital flows and minimize the likelihood of unmanageable market disruptions. The four IIF pillars are: (1) transparency and timely flow of information; (2) close debtor–creditor dialogue and cooperation in order to avoid restructuring; (3) good-faith actions in debt restructuring situations, and (4) fair treatment of all parties. They are accompanied by a set of principles and a set of recommendations that are based on a market-oriented approach, which would be nonbinding and flexible for sovereigns and creditors to adopt in the event of a debt crisis.

The IMF has commented positively on the IIF principles, but it has also stressed that it holds a different view from the IIF in relation to measures that the IIF recommends for a sovereign having difficulties in making its debt payments. The IMF notes that the IIF principles recommend "that the creditor community should consider appropriate requests for voluntary and temporary maintenance of trade lines and inter-bank lines to support a borrowing country's efforts to avoid a broad debt restructuring,"[75] but considers this recommendation as problematic if linked to continued debt servicing. The IMF argues that creditors could decide in favor of the country's request for an emergency loan if interest and inter-bank payments and other debts are serviced, but that such a condition may place the sovereign debtor in a riskier position, since the creditors' option of withdrawing trade and inter-bank lines could pose the threat of a greater default.

Other relevant considerations in sovereign debt management are linked with the conditions of IMF financing. Such financing could alleviate a sovereign debt liquidity crisis if the interest rate on IMF loans was sufficiently subsidized so as to cover the debt overhang of the borrowing country. The cost of subsidizing the illiquid country would then have to be borne by either the creditors or the borrowers.[76] An alternative to financing would be for the firms in the indebted country to negotiate and sign write-downs, depending on the share of the debt that is private versus public and also the willingness of the indebted country to take over the private debt. Such a write-down would avoid a default and the suspension of credit from private banks, thereby ensuring the uninterrupted flow of capital. However, neither of these alternatives will be effective if IMF lending is limited in both the amount and speed of the bailout. If private creditors expect IMF subsidized funds to be available, they would have an incentive to withdraw funds available in the form of equity investment and channel these to IMF lending, since these resources will be bailed out if there is a crisis. Further, such positioning will in turn raise the return on investment, given that the expected value of the subsidy will be greater, and thus pose a moral hazard.[77]

In light of the debate over these issues, the Fund staff developed and proposed the Sovereign Debt Restructure Mechanism (SDRM).[78] The SDRM was proposed as a tool for equitable sovereign debt restructuring, having the dual objectives of avoiding the risk of default while restoring sustainability and growth in the affected economies.[79] It consisted of a standstill mechanism that allowed for a sovereign to depart temporarily from its contractual obligations to make debt payments in a way that would adhere to the following four approaches:

- The debt restructuring process is initiated and maintained on the basis of consent by a qualified majority of creditors in each creditor class whose claims are being restructured, and it is binding on all creditors of the class.

- It eliminated the incentive for individual creditors to start litigation by deducting whatever they may have recovered in the litigation from the residual claim submitted in the restructuring agreement.

- It offered protection of creditor interests by including safeguards.

- It allowed for the exclusion of new financing for restructuring unless there is qualified majority consent by each creditor class.

The Fund Executive Board, however, rejected the SDRM proposal. This action was partly due to U.S. opposition, as well as to the fears of many developing countries that it could affect their ability to raise capital in financial markets, and in particular that it could affect the cost of sovereign debt issuance.[80] Further, it was also argued that SDRM would create moral hazard,[81] since the availability of an IMF-imposed creditor standstill could reduce the incentives for sovereign debtors to fulfill their contractual obligations.[82]

At this time, the IMF continues to offer large-scale lending packages in crisis situations based on the acceptance by the borrowing country of strict conditionality.[83] These packages are constructed with instruments intended to offer bridge financing, such as the GAB, the NAB, the SRF, or the Lending-into-Arrears policy. None of these instruments, however, necessarily distinguishes between illiquidity and insolvency or addresses the specific questions regarding the unintended incentives and social costs they may impose on the debtor country or on creditor-debtor relations. Indeed, former Managing Director Rodrigo de Rato has recognized that a wide range of views exists regarding what the extent and scope of the Fund's financial assistance programs should be. As a result, there is a need for a review of the existing instruments for crisis resolution, in terms of their efficiency, the limits of the Fund's resources, and the moral hazard they may create in international capital markets.[84]

Lender of Last Resort

The concept of the lender of last resort (LOLR) originated in the theoretical contributions of Thornton and Bagehot.[85] The LOLR function has become the essential role for central banks. The growing importance of an LOLR function may also be considered a symptom of the increase in banking and currency crises in recent years, as these types of crises originate from a sudden loss of confidence by private investors and lenders in a country's banking sector and in the ability of the state or sovereign agency to manage its finances.

In addition, central banks are confronted with yet another major challenge that involves the collapse of a certain financial institution or group of financial institutions as a result of a sudden loss of confidence by depositors or lenders when these institutions are "too big to fail." The resulting speculative attacks can threaten to infect the whole financial system, as well as other sectors of the economy. In this sense, insofar as financial crises prevail and international financial markets remain exposed to systemic risk and contagion, the need for an LOLR is justified, since it goes beyond traditional financial assistance activities targeting a particular country.

Functional Challenges of the International LOLR

Although an international LOLR function is attractive in theory, its feasibility has been questioned on the grounds that there is no political consensus regarding what type of powers such an institution would exercise or who would provide it with adequate resources. Since the early 1990s, the IMF has played an increasing role as a de facto lender of last resort, especially in the Mexican and Asian crises. The Fund's performance in resolving these crises, however, was strongly criticized.[86] There are several explanations for this criticism.

First, it relates to the difficulty of identifying whether a financial crisis stems from a liquidity or solvency problem.[87] The absence of a clear demarcation between the two types of crisis resulted in the IMF following a policy that had the effect of providing indiscriminate assistance to any member state in crisis. This created a moral hazard among private lenders, who perceived the private costs they had incurred in making investments in these countries as having been shifted to, and subsequently shared with, official-sector agencies.

Ideally, the LOLR function should be exercised on behalf of countries that are encountering liquidity problems, rather than for countries with solvency problems. In offering the same type of assistance, the IMF does not discriminate between countries in crisis because of irresponsible financial management and overexposure to risk provoked by speculators and private-sector participants, and those which have fundamental shortcomings underlying their macroeconomic and financial management. The former generally are illiquid because of speculative moves, which dry out reserves and other assets in speedy capital exits. The latter reflect weak government performance in macroeconomic management, which can eventually result in an inability to pay or even service debts acquired with foreign creditors.[88]

Indiscriminate lending disrupts market order because private lenders that under normal circumstances would not lend to a particular country have the incentive to take the risk, since they know they will be eventually paid with Fund resources. Evidently, private creditors taking this approach increase their risk exposure beyond prudent levels, thereby transferring part of their costs to the country acquiring the debt.

A second reason for the inadequacy of the IMF as a LOLR can be seen in the peculiarities of Fund lending policies. According to Stephanie Griffith-Jones and Jenny Kimmis, serious problems arise from the timing, scale, and conditionalities of lending.[89] Excessive focus on satisfying lending conditionalities has disregarded the importance of timely assistance and has resulted in burdensome and lengthy consultation processes with the countries in crisis, in turn resulting in an increased need for more funds once the actual assistance comes through. In addition, the way in which Fund lending has been based on periodic arrears poses considerable strain on financial recovery expectations. The inability to assess whether the next arrear will come through or be suspended tends to trigger speculative reaction in financial markets. This behavior became evident in the Russian and Argentinean crises, contributing to an even deeper downfall of those economies.

Although the IMF tried to solve the problem of timely assistance through the creation of contingent credit lines in 1999 as well as with the Emergency Finance Mechanism and the Supplementary Reserve Facility, its efforts have been inadequate. It has been observed that the actual amount needed for liquidity assistance by most countries in distress exceeds the Fund's capacities and that more funds are necessary.[90] Furthermore, current IMF lending has a negative effect on market discipline. As Eichengreen states, "Repeated rescues create moral hazard ... weakening market discipline. IMF support allows governments to cling to unsustainable policies even longer than they would otherwise do, which allows financial vulnerabilities to build up, leading to more severe fallout when the collapse finally comes."[91]

A third consideration as to why the Fund is an inadequate LORL relates to surveillance. Rosa Lastra notes that, together with an LORL role, enhanced surveillance and transparency is required, in order to monitor supervisory and regulatory policies. In this sense, the IMF would need to strengthen its mandate on surveillance, contained in Article IV of the Articles of Agreement. In addition, the organization would need to develop a ratings system based on a set of parameters to monitor the financial systems of its member countries.[92] The Fund, however, began to address the surveillance concern in 2002 by establishing the Capital Markets Department, which has a remit for reviewing the financial sector policies of members and the impact of member financial policies on global and regional financial stability.

A fourth critique relates to the role of an LOLR as an undisputed function of central banks. At the national level, this may be a lesser problem, as most nations have a central bank or an institution vested with central bank functions. At the international level, however, this creates a considerable array of problems concerning which institution should exercise this function and how much sovereignty countries may be willing to cede to such an international organization.[93] The main challenge therefore lies in the political will to devise an effective international institution for a lender of last resort.

A fifth, and perhaps the main, reason for contesting the IMF as an LOLR lies in how its differs from the approach of national central banks in acting as a lender of last resort. At the national level, emergency liquidity would usually be provided in three types of crises: (1) payment system crisis, (2) general liquidity crisis, and (3) classic liquidity crisis.[94]

A payment system crisis can occur when there is a breakdown in the payment system between central banks and the main money center banks. As most payments are settled through the banking system, it is difficult to separate the supervision of the payment system from the supervision of individual banks. In this regard, the IMF could facilitate emergency loans through GAB to large money center banks or central banks in countries that were experiencing a payment system crisis. Presently, however, as discussed above, the Fund does not possess the resources or the legal and political authority to require G10 central banks to provide reserve currency loans through the GAB to provide an effective intervention in a payment crisis.

A general liquidity crisis can arise from a collapse of the financial markets in the form of a stock market collapse or a loss of confidence by banks and investors in each other. The central bank can inject liquidity to the market through open market operations, which involves the central bank entering repurchase agreements for the debt securities of major financial institutions in order to increase the supply of money into the banking system. This can in theory lead to a reduction of interest rates on the loans made by banks to each other in the short-term loan market. During the 2007 world credit crisis, the ECB used open market operations to enter repurchase agreements with major Eurozone banks in order to make more liquidity available to the Eurozone financial system. Presently, the IMF lacks the legal authority and the institutional capacity to conduct open market operations in this manner to inject liquidity into its member states

The classic response to a market liquidity crisis involves an individual financial institution providing sound collateral to the central bank in return for an emergency loan at a penal interest rate. The central bank's objective is not to cure a problem originating in the broader financial markets (e.g., the payment system), but rather to address the short-term financial difficulties of an individual bank whose illiquidity could potentially spread to other banks and to the broader market. In the EU, national central banks and supervisory authorities and finance ministries are responsible for deciding whether to provide emergency lending based on good collateral.[95] In this capacity, the central bank is providing a service in its capacity as a "banker's bank."[96] These institutional attributes and capacities are what the Fund presently lacks.

Private-Sector Involvement

Critiques of the current state of crisis management also voice concerns about private-sector involvement. The IMF's financial assistance, as well as that of other IFIs, does not apply to the private sector.[97] As such, a private-sector crisis, such as a banking crisis, will only receive assistance once the country's authorities decide to assume part of the private-sector's obligations and apply for financial assistance in order to cancel the private-sector debt. Further, the Fund has abstained from involving the private sector by directly lending to it to resolve a crisis, though proposals for extending financial assistance to the private sector already exist.[98]

Proposals to assist the private sector directly were made at the Köln Summit in 1999, where government and central bank representatives envisaged a framework for involving the private sector in crisis resolution. The focus was on cooperative solutions to manage crises with communication and dialogue. This approach was intended for creditors and debtors in the financial sector, as well as for countries and other market participants in the broader financial system. Several principles were suggested to address risk and responsibility sharing, adequate risk assessment, debt financing and payment, and equal treatment of private creditors and claims, seeking effective dialogue, cooperation, and market-based solutions.[99]

In 2000, at the G7 summit in Fukuoka, Japan, heads of state further clarified the particularities of private-sector involvement in crisis prevention and resolution. The proposals called for operational guidelines to enhance IMF lending program and a facilitative role in mediating negotiations between private creditors and sovereign debtors. Specifically, the proposals distinguished between the functions of the IMF and the Paris Club by stating that "in cases where a contribution from official bilateral creditors (primarily the Paris Club) is needed, the IMF financing plan would need to provide for a broad comparability desired and achieved between the contributions of official bilateral and private creditors. The Paris Club, if involved, should of course continue to assess the comparability desired and achieved between its agreement and those to be reached with other creditors."[100] Since then, the IMF has recognized the efforts of the Paris Club to foster support for consultation and coordination procedures between official and private bilateral creditors.[101] However, the way that the Fund can respond to a financial crisis distinguishes it from that of private creditors in terms of speed, form, process, and comparability of restructuring.[102] Further, joint consultations between the Paris Club and the IMF in seeking to improve the process of restructuring have led to the proposition of alternative solutions in cases where both official and private claims are significant.[103]

The involvement of the private sector in supporting a country in a financial crisis should be encouraged on efficiency grounds because private-sector foreign investors often do not calculate the full social costs of their risky investments and therefore have an incentive to invest too much speculative short-term capital in countries with inadequate regulatory institutions and fragile financial systems. To address this problem, academics and policymakers have advocated various mechanisms of private-sector involvement in crisis prevention and resolution that takes the form of "bailing in" the private sector or "burden sharing."[104]

The best approaches for involving the private sector should be determined on a case-by-case basis and take into account such factors as the severity of the crisis, the type of debt instruments issued and their term structure, the extent of foreign exchange exposure, and whether the state appears to be suffering a liquidity or solvency crisis. Indeed, Goodhart has noted that because financial crises have gone beyond the scope and abilities of central banks, their management cannot solely depend on these institutions. He also notes, however, that private-sector participation in the form of assistance is by far more challenging than before, given the incentive structure against financial assistance in the private sector. He argues that "multinational banks will claim that the home country forces, whether shareholders, regulators, or their own domestic law, prevent them from risking their own capital in any co-ordinated rescue exercise in another country. If the multinationals will not play, then competition will prevent the domestically headquartered banks from doing so either."[105]

Previous efforts to involve the private sector in crisis prevention and resolution have been inadequate, and the absence of an effective framework that involves creditors in negotiations on debt relief schemes and crisis management undermines financial stability. Not only is the allocation of responsibilities and risk burdens absent, the needed dialogue for fostering accountability and benefiting from private-sector expertise in crisis management so far remains a lost opportunity. Perhaps the Fund could play a more active role in coordinating the involvement of private-sector actors, in order to assume more of the responsibility of managing the risks of financial crises.

Alternatives to Current and Future Financial Assistance

Various alternatives to Fund lending programs have been suggested, including (1) presumptive lending limits on IMF lending; (2) standstills to protect a country and lend into arrears (e.g., bridge financing); (3) approved debt roll-overs with a penalty for liquidity shortages; (4) enforcement of collective-action clauses.

Presumptive Lending Limits

Presumptive lending limits are viewed as more efficient alternatives to Fund lending programs because they address the moral hazard problem that became apparent in the Mexican and Asian crises in the 1990s, where Fund rescue packages were much greater than the actual quotas maintained by these countries with the Fund. Generally, Fund bailout programs would total, at the maximum, 100 percent of a country's quota, but in the Mexican and Asian crises, rescues packages amounted to between 500 and 700 percent for Mexico and approximately 1,900 percent of the actual quotas of Asian members. Eichengreen has suggested that the Fund should apply lending limits that aim to maintain the 100 percent rule in the first year of the bailout while committing a maximum of 300 percent for a whole lending program. The goal would be to restore the belief among foreign investors that the Fund would not continuously offer financing for a debtor country after it exhausts its Fund quota and will not provide indefinite support in the event of a prolonged or recurring crisis.[106]

This approach, however, may be more difficult to implement than envisaged. Though financial assistance is determined on the basis of quotas, so too are voting powers on the Fund's Executive Board. Current quotas may not reflect actual or potential country needs of a bailout. Such differentiation could pose difficulties under systemic risk and contagion, or may actually favor some countries more than others, thus inadequately targeting the impact of a given financial crisis. In addition, reviewing current quotas would pose an immediate conflict of interest among IMF members seeking to maintain the voting status quo.[107]

Finally, although setting limits on financial assistance may be the optimal solution, ultimately the question of credibility remains an issue. There is no point in establishing such limits if the IMF waives the rule, no matter how well justified additional financing in a particular case may be.

Temporary Payment Standstills

Temporary payment standstills (standstills), either sanctioned or endorsed by the IMF, are considered an alternative to current financial bail-outs in the event of a liquidity crisis. If a country were suffering from capital flight, a Fund-imposed standstill on debt payments could give the country enough time to seek an orderly solution, which could allow creditors adequate time to coordinate their actions and to allow the state debtor to make the necessary commitments to undertake economic reforms.[108] This would reduce the risk of precipitating a solvency crisis because of creditor runs, and provide for the opportunity of corrective and timely action. In addition, the IMF could provide bridge financing during the time of the standstill in order to stabilize the economic situation.

An alternative could also be to shift the sanctioning power of standstills to an independent institution, other than the Fund, allowing for a clear separation of the financial assistance role of the Fund from the actual decision to impose a standstill on debt repayments. Another variant on this approach might involve the sovereign borrower declaring the standstill, subject to approval by an independent international panel. Negotiations for debt rescheduling between the sovereign borrower and the creditors would be limited in time and subject to terms imposed by the panel if no agreement were reached within a given period. Under this approach, the IMF could simply endorse the standstill, which was imposed by another institution, in order to send a message of stability and credibility to the markets, and follow its endorsement with bridge loans that could stabilize the debtor country during the standstill.

Debt Roll-overs with a Penalty for Liquidity Shortages

A debt roll-over envisages the incorporation of clauses in debt contracts that allow for a one-time-only opportunity to defer the interest payments while rolling over the principal debt. The debtor wishing to roll over debt would pay a penalty fee and would have a deadline to pay the deferred service (e.g., ninety days).[109] This alternative presumes that the problems of liquidity could be solved by providing an extension of the period for servicing the debt. As with a standstill, the period during which the country is waived from its debt payments allows for corrective action and a return to stability in the market (i.e., speculative creditor reactions). If the sovereign's payment difficulty, however, were of a solvency nature, such a mechanism would only offer a truce for initiating negotiations for major debt restructuring and a bail out.

Collective Action Clauses

Following the Fund's rejection of the SDRM, the collective-action clause (CAC) in sovereign bond contracts has emerged as an effective device to allow sovereign debtors and their bondholders to renegotiate the terms of their payments and possibly to restructure their debt in the event of payment difficulties. Traditionally, most sovereign bond contracts have been governed by New York law and usually contained clauses that required a bond issuer to obtain unanimous consent from all bondholders of a particular class of bonds before a change in payment terms could be agreed upon. Bond contracts under New York law made it difficult for sovereign debtors to restructure repayment terms because a single creditor (or small group) could object to the proposed renegotiated terms and block any restructuring. For instance, a small group of bondholders could hold out and attempt to enforce repayment under the original terms of the contract, while at the same time a majority of bondholders were negotiating with the sovereign debtor for a restructuring that might lead to a reduction in the principal or interest rate. By contrast, bond contracts under English law usually contain CACs that allow the issuers of the bonds to restructure the payment terms of the principal and interest if they can persuade the bondholders who hold a super-majority of the value of the class of bonds to vote for the restructuring.[110]

CACs offer a flexible mechanism for debtors and bondholders to renegotiate payment terms and provide an incentive for all bondholders to participate in restructuring negotiations and not to ride free on the willingness of other bondholders to renegotiate their claims.[111] CACs also ensure a more orderly and coordinated action by bondholders if the servicing or payment of debts is disrupted. As mentioned above, it incentivizes bondholders to act in unison, eliminating the incentive of a few bondholders to institute litigation at the expense of the majority of bondholders. The advantage of CACs lies in their transparency, since creditors are bound to proceed in a particular manner in the event of a suspension of debt payments, as specified by the clause. By vesting the power to file suit in the hands of a trustee, and eventually also the decision to initiate buy-ups and distribute the proceeds of such buy-ups among the creditors, these clauses offer additional predictability and lower the levels of uncertainty for creditors, since the trustee will be expected to act for the benefit of all creditors bound by the clause.

However, the incentives for some bondholders to abstain from participating in collective restructuring remain high, as dissident bondholders may try to enforce their claims in sympathetic jurisdictions. Further, the proliferation of bond holders in sovereign debt markets points to a greater number and diffusion of creditors, and, given the shift away from syndicated commercial bank lending to direct issuance of debt instruments, has resulted in a sophisticated secondary market of tradeable sovereign debt instruments. Finally, changes in legal systems have weighed in favor of more litigation, where limitations on "sovereign immunity" allow creditors to bring civil actions to recovers damages or to enforce specific performance in foreign courts. This partly explains why CACs, though potentially effective, may be increasingly difficult to implement because of the ability of individual bondholders to bring their claims against debtor states in court.[112]

Nevertheless, CACs are being used in a growing majority of bond contracts under both English and New York law, and represent a flexible market-based approach to addressing the problems faced by countries experiencing liquidity crises and other types of payment difficulties. Notwithstanding the difficulties, international bodies have proposed modified CAC structures.[113] Also, other jurisdictions outside New York and England are adopting modified CACs in their international sovereign bond contracts.[114]

Although the above proposals have addressed many of the challenges of building a durable institutional and legal framework to govern the LOLR function, each proposal contains inherent flaws that range from enhancing the powers of the Fund beyond what would be acceptable in today's international political climate to the misalignment of incentives between creditors and debtors in the proposal for an SDRM. The CAC approach creates incentives for bondholders and the sovereign to renegotiate payment terms in light of changes in the economic environment and provides an effective *ex ante* set of rules for bondholders to coordinate their actions for the benefit of a super majority of claimants. Nevertheless, greater coordination in the provision of, and access to, liquidity on a cross-border basis is needed to support a crisis-management situation, especially where a sovereign's debt exposure is denominated in one or more of the reserve currencies of G10 countries for which it does not have central bank support. This becomes particularly important in a financial crisis when a sovereign debtor or a large financial institution in its jurisdiction loses the ability to make current payments on its liabilities and therefore is in need of emergency funding for a short period of time until investor and/or depositor confidence is restored. The premise for such emergency lending is that the debtor state or bank is simply illiquid and not insolvent. The following section argues for a revised GAB framework that would support the Fund in providing a more effective international lender of last resort.

The Need for Multilateral Coordination of Central Bank Intervention

Recent non-G10 sovereign debt and banking crises (Mexico 1994–95, Russia 1998, and Argentina 2001) demonstrate that the Fund does not have adequate resources to act on its own in stemming a financial crisis or, in particular, to play the role of lender of last resort. Fund negotiations with G10 countries such as the United States to obtain reserve currency financing for non-G10 sovereigns in a crisis is *ad hoc* and often results in delayed disbursement of badly needed liquidity, which has led in many cases to a deepening of the crisis. Moreover, there is a concern regarding the adequacy of the Fund's resources to deal with a full-blown financial crisis that occurs on a regional or global basis. Only with the support of one or more of the G10 central banks could the Fund preempt or stabilize a crisis in a large developing country (e.g., Mexico) or in a country with a large financial sector. Although the Fund's authority is clear regarding how it would intervene to stem a crisis in a member state, its role is not so clear regarding how it would raise capital in a major financial crisis where its own resources were inadequate and it would be required to obtain resources from the central banks of the G10 countries.

It is essential to ask what type of institutional framework could be devised to address a financial crisis caused by a sudden loss of investor confidence in a country or region's economy and a resulting need to provide liquidity assistance to sovereign debtors whose cost for accessing international capital markets has become prohibitively high. Specifically, how might the Fund coordinate an emergency financial rescue of an ailing sovereign debtor? It does not have the resources to act on its own; rather, it would have to coordinate with a group of central banks from reserve-currency countries and agree on procedures and obligations to ensure that adequate liquidity can be made available to a sovereign borrower or state-owned or controlled bank that cannot meet its obligations. How might a group of central banks share responsibility for providing liquidity support to a sovereign debtor whose access to foreign lending in reserve currencies has been drastically curtailed because of an external shock to its economy or imbalance in its own economy or financial system?

As described earlier, since 1962 the GAB has allowed the G10 countries to voluntarily lend to one another and to other IMF members by lending reserve currencies to the Fund, which in turn would make these funds available through exchange transactions or stand-by arrangements to a GAB participant that was experiencing imbalances in its current or capital accounts. In 1998 the New Arrangements to Borrow was adopted that allows NAB participants, of which there are 26 (including GAB participants), to lend their currencies to the Fund if a special majority approves the Managing Director's proposal for calls to lend and the Executive Board approves. As with the GAB, however, a NAB participant does not have a legal obligation to lend its currency to the Fund in proportion to its pre-existing credit arrangements for the benefit of a country in a financial crisis. This creates legal uncertainty precisely at a time when there needs to be stability of expectations on the part of foreign investors that an ailing state is able to access emergency loans to stabilize a liquidity crisis or to prevent a further deterioration of its finances.

On the few occasions when GAB participants have loaned their currencies in response to the Fund's call for loans, the Fund was borrowing the currencies to support another GAB participant that was experiencing persistent current account or fiscal deficits.[115] Generally, non-GAB participants (non-G10 countries) have not been able to borrow assets through the GAB and have had instead to borrow from other, more limited, Fund lending programs. In the NAB, however, any IMF member is able to borrow from NAB countries (which includes GAB countries), but must be supported by the Managing Director and approved by the Executive Board. Moreover, even if the Managing Director proposes a call for loans from NAB countries, individual NAB members are not legally bound to lend. Despite the large number of banking and currency crises that have occurred since 1998, only one call for loans under NAB was approved—to Brazil in 1999. As with the GAB, the NAB has been underutilized as an international lender of last resort.

The GAB and NAB processes have suffered from a lack of legal stability due to the absence of a legal obligation of GAB and NAB participating countries to lend their currencies once the Fund has approved a call for loans. This chapter argues that the Fund can play an enhanced role in serving as the intermediary through which developed-country central banks can lend to developing countries to prevent or stabilize a financial crisis. In doing so, the Fund can act as payment agent for disbursing funds on behalf of the G10 countries and by exercising enhanced surveillance over non-G10 countries that borrow reserve currencies in a crisis. This can only be accomplished by establishing a transparent institutional framework through which the Fund would act with G10 central bank support along with enhanced legal certainty regarding the Fund's authority to coordinate central bank intervention in a sovereign debt or other financial crisis.

An important aspect of the Fund's inability to intervene decisively in a crisis are the political and legal uncertainties regarding the willingness and obligation of GAB participants to provide adequate resources to the Fund so that it can preempt an impending crisis. A major weakness in the GAB and NAB in confronting modern financial crises is that the consultations and decision making by GAB participants and with the Fund and its Executive Board can be time-consuming and, if there is a proposal for calls, involve extensive negotiations between the Managing Director and each GAB participant in order to decide the allocation of GAB lending to individual members. Once an announcement is made that a commitment to lend is in place, an individual participant that did not vote with the special majority does not have to participate in the call. Moreover, a participant that commits itself to participate in the call can later decide to withdraw upon giving notice to the Managing Director and other GAB participants that its involvement will have an adverse impact on its currency reserves or create other significant economic imbalances. There are no specific tests to determine precisely what a participant has to prove in order to refuse, or withdraw from, participation in the call. Under both the GAB and NAB, the participants appear to exercise almost complete discretion whether to participate in a call for loans with the exception that they have an obligation to engage in consultations and to notify other participants and the Fund of any change in the circumstances that affect their decision either to be involved or not.

The GAB framework should be amended to enhance the legal certainty of the lending obligation of a GAB participant once the Fund makes a determination that a financial crisis or impairment of the international monetary system is occurring, and when that determination has been supported by a majority of the Executive Board. Once the Managing Director has consulted with the GAB participants and the Executive Board, and obtained a majority approval from the Executive Board and a special majority of the GAB, the Fund could compel GAB members to lend in proportion to the relative amounts of their credit arrangements.

Each time lending is requested, a G10 central bank would be designated to take the lead in coordinating the provision of reserve currencies from other G10 countries to meet the specific needs of the crisis. The Fund would consult with GAB participants to determine which participant should take the lead in lending to the Fund and in possibly encouraging others to lend to the Fund. An important criterion for determining which participant should take the lead in lending for a bailout would be the portion of that participant's currency that was denominated in the debt instruments issued by the ailing sovereign debtor and/or any related state-owned corporations. For example, if a state defaults on debt instruments of different classes that have a value in denominated currencies of US$60 million, CH30 million, and £10 million, the Fund should ask the U.S. participant to coordinate the lending effort because more than half of the value of the debt instruments are denominated in U.S. dollars. Moreover, there would be a presumption that each participating central bank would lend a portion of the emergency loan that amounted to the relative share its currency composed of the defaulted debt instruments. The relative portion of each participating central bank's exposure would be valued in Special Drawing Rights (SDRs).[116] Only in exceptional circumstances—where, for example, a designated participant could show that by lending according to the formula it would have an adverse effect on its capital or current account—would it be excused from its proportional responsibility. This would promote more transparency in the Eurocurrency markets and create incentives for participants that issue their currencies to oversee and supervise the trading book of financial intermediaries that use their currencies in cross-border debt investment.[117]

In addition, an enhanced GAB framework would require some *ex ante* regulatory safeguards that members should undertake to be eligible for GAB financing. All countries seeking GAB support would be required to have their economies and financial sectors subject to enhanced surveillance and oversight by the Fund so that more market information is available to foreign investors about these countries' financial markets. Moreover, there would be a requirement that states seeking GAB assistance purchase credit-risk protection in advance, which could take the form of sovereign credit default swaps or other synthetic credit derivative instruments.[118] The Fund could act as an agent in selling the credit-risk protection on behalf of a private-sector financial intermediary or by directly providing the credit protection itself. Moreover, it could approve and monitor the provision of credit-risk insurance by third-party intermediaries to sovereign debtors. In return for complying with these *ex ante* safeguards, a member state would be eligible to access GAB members' currencies by conducting exchange transactions or stand-by arrangements with the Fund.

Finally, the GAB and the NAB should be consolidated so that their credit arrangements can be pooled and enhanced to at least SDR 100,000 million. The new GAB framework would apply the same rules regarding lending and consultations and repayment requirements to all of its participants and to all IMF members who obtain resources through the new GAB lending arrangements. All participants and nonparticipants in the funding framework would be subject to the same requirements regarding conditionality and economic restructuring, which the Fund may impose in its discretion.

Devising an effective international institutional arrangement to cope with or forestall an impairment to the international monetary and financial system requires that the cross-border dimension and externality of financial risk be controlled. As discussed above, sovereign debt crises raise serious concerns for international economic policymakers because of the threat that the financial failure of a sovereign or a large state-managed banking system could create significant spill-over effects on other economies and financial systems. Addressing these threats to financial stability in a way that promotes the treaty objectives of the Articles of Agreement, while still adhering to the more narrow objectives of maintaining currency stability for GAB participants, requires that the Fund play the role of intermediary and monitor in the provision of emergency liquidity assistance to a member country. This would involve devising *ex ante* disclosure standards and financial practices for states to enhance their credibility with foreign investors. The Fund would also take on a more robust role in monitoring the global financial system and members' economic and financial policies, but it would recognize that the sources of market failure can vary from country to country and that a one-size-fits-all approach to economic and financial policy should be replaced with a more flexible surveillance function that dispenses with strict conditionality and allows states to experiment with different economic policies and regulatory approaches.

Moreover, it is necessary to enhance legal certainty in a consolidated GAB and NAB framework—GAB II—to ensure that if a financial crisis occurs and a sovereign is suffering from a liquidity problem, the Fund can access adequate G10 or GAB/NAB participants' currencies by making calls for loans which, if approved by a special majority, would oblige all GAB II participants to make loans according to a pro rata portion of the relative sizes of their credit arrangements.

Devising an institutional and international legal framework to address these issues would not involve a substantial reform and modification of the present international financial regulatory and legal regime. For instance, Article VII (1) of the Articles of Agreement provides the IMF with authority to negotiate agreements with its members to borrow capital to support Fund objectives. It was pursuant to this authority that the original General Arrangements to Borrow was agreed to in 1962, so the Fund could borrow the currencies that were being used increasingly for cross-border capital transactions in order to lend them to other G10 countries to cover their economic imbalances. The GAB, however, was not available to non-G10 countries, mainly because when it was adopted strict capital controls were still in force in most countries and there was little need for these countries, which had not liberalized their capital and current accounts, to borrow reserve currencies. In today's liberalized and globalized capital markets, however, all developed countries and many developing countries and emerging market economies have adopted some form of capital account liberalization, which means they are exposed to potential imbalances in the capital account that can shift quickly because of a change in investor sentiments. These countries therefore are in need of an emergency financing mechanism that would allow them to borrow currencies for which they have liabilities in the capital account and to finance substantial imbalances in the current account.

Conclusion

The IMF is confronted with demands to change its policy of "replacing private capital flows" to one of "dealing with market failures in private markets." The main challenge before the IMF is the definition of its role in managing a financial crisis. Specifically, the question has arisen whether it should lend to sovereign debtors or large systemically important banks to help resolve an insolvency or liquidity crisis. If so, should the Fund lend into arrears in order to provide temporary liquidity to stabilize a crisis, especially in today's globalized capital markets, when it has inadequate funds at its disposal?[119] In the area of crisis management, the main challenges for the IMF are, on the one hand, coordinating policy with the G-7, the Financial Stability Forum, the G10 central bankers, and financial regulators in order to share responsibility for bail-outs and guarantees from the IMF to central banks; and, on the other hand, playing the role of broker in assisting sovereign debtors by liaising with private creditors and central bankers to find alternative sources of liquidity in order to stabilize a financial crisis.[120] The first task involves being a full actor; its second task is that of a facilitator. Under either approach, the Fund will have to accept a more limited role in directly intervening in financial crises and in using its lending activities as a policy instrument to bring about economic and financial reform.

The IMF's existing lending programs were adopted in the late 1990s, along with other emergency programs for liquidity assistance. But most of these programs have been underutilized by non-G10 sovereign debtors in need of emergency lending because of strict conditionality requirements that have often resulted in poorly designed economic policies and financial sector reform. The chapter therefore proposed the following steps to establish a more proactive role for the Fund in promoting financial stability by enhancing its facilitative role as a lender of last resort.

- First, the *ex ante* role would involve the Fund requiring that sovereign debtors comply with the disclosure requirements of Fund programs such as the General Data Dissemination standard. Also, to be eligible for emergency lending under the GAB framework, the Fund would facilitate and require the purchase by its members of credit-risk protection on their bonds or other debt instruments and loans.

- Second, the Fund's role in crisis resolution would be to coordinate access to reserve currency assets by consolidating the GAB and NAB into one credit arrangement and increase the aggregate credit amount available to borrow to SDR 100,000 million. Once the requirements for making a call for loans are fulfilled, each participating country (or regional organization) would have an obligation to lend a proportion of the call that reflected the proportion that its currency constituted in the defaulted sovereign debt instruments. The country or participating central bank with the largest percentage would take the lead in coordinating the other lending participants. The Fund would play a facilitative role in providing technical advice regarding how the loans should be disbursed to the sovereign debtor.

Although these proposals do not significantly enhance the Fund's role in overseeing and maintaining financial stability, its key role as an intermediary in the provision of credit-risk insurance and in accessing emergency reserves from G10 countries keeps it at the heart of the international monetary system.

These proposals set forth a realistic role for the Fund to play in contributing to financial stability and assisting countries to borrow reserve currencies during a financial crisis. Moreover, these proposals would only require an amendment of the GAB and not the Fund Articles of Agreement. Under this approach, the Fund would facilitate the provision of emergency financing, and there would be a principled framework for allocating financial responsibility among G10 countries and institutions so as to coordinate the disbursement of reserve currencies to an ailing sovereign debtor through the Fund.

Finally, these suggested reforms are based on economic and legal theories that support the role of international economic law in regulating the negative externalities (or social costs) of international economic activity. In this regard, creating a more effective international lender of last resort to control the social costs of sovereign debt failure necessitates a Bagehot-like institution to play an effective role in providing reserve currency loans to sovereigns during liquidity crises. The GAB framework potentially allows the leading developed countries, acting together, to play the role of international lender of last resort by acting through the Fund to minimize the social costs of sovereign debt failure.

Notes

[1] Walter Bagehot, *Lombard Street: A Description of the Money Market* (1873; repr., Homewood, Illinois: Richard D. Irwin, Inc., 1962). Bagehot described the maxim this way: "[I]n a crisis, the lender of last resort should lend freely, at a penalty rate, on the basis of collateral that is marketable in the ordinary course of business when there is no panic." *See* discussion in Forrest Capie and Geoffrey E. Wood, *The Lender of Last Resort* (Abingdon, Oxon: Routledge, 2007), at 423–24. The Bank was an incorporated joint stock company that had competed for business against other London banks in the eighteenth and nineteenth centuries. In 1830 the Bank for the first time allowed bill brokers (the forerunners of the discount houses) to open "discount accounts" with the Bank. This allowed specialist dealers in bills of exchange to take bills of a certain standard to the Bank to be exchanged for Bank of England notes, thereby providing them with last-resort facilities. Richard Roberts, "The Bank and the City" in Richard Roberts and David Kynaston, eds., *The Bank of England: Money, Power and Influence 1694–1994* (Oxford : Clarendon Press, 1995), at 156–57.

[2] Through the General Arrangements to Borrow of 1962, G10 countries have always had the ability to borrow G10 reserve currencies in times of crisis. *See* discussion below.

[3] This can create moral hazard on the part of depositors and investors who perceive that the central bank or government will cover the liabilities of the bank or sovereign debtor.

[4] John Taylor, "The IMF's Virtuous Loan Circle," editorial, *Wall Street Journal* (March 23, 2006), at 23. Taylor is a professor of economics at Stanford University and former U.S. Undersecretary of the Treasury for International Affairs. He was one of the leading opponents of the IMF's proposed sovereign debt restructuring mechanism.

[5] *See* Joseph Stiglitz, *Globalization and its Discontents* (London: Allen Lane, 2002), at 43–52.

[6] John Eatwell and Lance Taylor, *Global Finance at Risk: The Case for International Regulation* (Cambridge: Polity Press, 2000), at 54–95.

[7] The Fund's role in liquidity assistance has been reduced even more in the face of the dramatic growth in private-sector-led global capital flows. *See*

Andrew Crockett, David Vines, and Christopher Gilbert *The IMF and its Critics* (Cambridge: Cambridge University Press, 2004) at 46–54.

[8] *See* discussion of de facto international lender of last resort in Rosa M. Lastra, "The IMF in Historical Perspective," 3 *Journal of International Economic Law* (September 2000), at 521.

[9] Malcolm Knight, Laurence Schembri, and Andrew Powell, "Reforming the Global Financial Architecture: Just Tinkering around the Edges?" in Vines and Gilbert, eds., *supra* note 7, at 14–149.

[10] *Id.* at 146–47.

[11] Mervyn King, "Reform of the International Monetary Fund," Speech at the Indian Council for Research on International Economic Relations in New Delhi, India, at 9 (quoting John Maynard Keynes's phrase at the Bretton Woods conference in 1944).

[12] Knight et al*., supra* note 9, at 145.

[13] Other short-term borrowing arrangements include the Compensatory Financing Facility and the Exogenous Shocks Facility. Longer-term borrowing facilities include the Extended Fund Facility and Poverty Reduction and Growth Facility. *See* IMF Financial Activities—Update September 30, 2004. Some joint Fund-World Bank programs include the Comprehensive Development Framework, Country Assistance programs, and Highly Indebted Poor Countries Debt Relief Strategies. *See* http://www.worldbank.org/hipc/.

[14] Sir Joseph Gold, *The Legal and Institutional Aspects of the International Monetary System: Selected Essays*, vol. 1 (Washington D.C.: International Monetary Fund, 1979), at 462–66. Stand-by arrangements are the main instrument by which Fund resources are made available to its members. Stand-by arrangements were not contained in the original Articles of Agreement but came about through decisions of the Executive Board (Dec. No. 155-(52/57) (1 October 1952) (formalizing the practice of stand-by arrangements that are recognized today in Article V, Section 3 of the Amended Articles).

[15] Articles of Agreement, Article XXX (b).

[16] *See* Andreas Lowenfeld, *International Economic Law* (Oxford: Oxford University Press, 2002), at 516.

[17] The Board's Decision states that "[s]tand-by arrangements are not international agreements and therefore language having a contractual connotation will be avoided in stand-by arrangements and letters of intent," Executive Board Decision No. 6056-(79/38) March 2, 1979. This reaffirmed an earlier decision by the Board in 1968 that "[i]n view of the character of stand-by arrangements, language having a contractual flavor will be avoided in the stand-by documents." *See* Gold, supra note 14, pp. 464–65, citing para. 7, Decision No. 2603-(68/132), September 20, 1968, *Selected Decisions*, Fourth Issue (1970), at 31.

[18] *See* Lowenfeld, *supra* note 16, at 519.

[19] Article V, Section 3 (a) of the Articles of Agreement requires the Fund to "adopt policies on the use of its general resources ... that will establish adequate safeguards." It states:

> The Fund shall adopt policies on the use of its general resources, including policies on stand-by or similar arrangements, and may adopt special policies for special balance of payments problems, that will assist members to solve their balance of payments problems in a manner consistent with the provisions of this Agreement and that will establish adequate safeguards for the temporary use of the general resources of the Fund.

[20] *See* "IMF Discusses Status Report on Crisis Prevention and Precautionary Arrangements," Public Information Notice (PIN) No. 04/117, October 6, 2004, also available at www.imf.org/external/np/sec/pn/2004/pn04117.htm:

> Fundamental differences of view exist about the need for and desirability of a policy for using exceptional amounts of financing under precautionary arrangements ... [d]irectors holding this view[desirability to use exceptional amounts of funding] feel that regular precautionary arrangements—while useful in cases where pressures are likely to emerge in the current account—are not an effective tool of crisis prevention for members that pursue sound policies but still remain exposed to exogenous shocks and contagion. They regret the lack of progress in designing a policy on exceptional access under precautionary

arrangements, and urge that this issue remain a high priority on the Fund's agenda

See also "Crisis Prevention and Precautionary Arrangements—Status Report," Prepared by the Policy Development and Review Department in consultation with other Departments (September 3, 2004), also available at www.imf.org/external/np/pdr/cp/eng/2004/090304.htm (last visited 7 October 2004, on which the Executive Board's discussions are based).

[21] These long-term special facilities include the Comprehensive Development Framework (CDF), which seeks to direct the development agenda for a country so that it can meet the United Nations's Millennium Development Goals (MDGs). Other facilities are the Country-Assistance Programs (CAS), and the Highly Indebted Poor Countries Debt Relief Strategies (HIPC). *See* http://www.worldbank.org/hipc/. A country becomes eligible for HIPC debt relief only when it establishes a poverty-reduction strategy program, in which a country may become eligible for either concessional IMF lending for low-income members under the Poverty Reduction and Growth Facility (PRGF) financed by the PRGF Trust, or for debt relief under the Enhanced Heavily Indebted Poor Country (HIPC) Initiative *See* IMF, "Financial Activities— Update September 30, 2004," available at: www.imf.org./external/np/tre/ activity/2004 (last visited 23 July 2006). The PRGF, formerly known as the Enhanced Structural Adjustment Facility (ESAF), provides loans at concessional interest rate to eligible, low-income countries. In contrast, the HIPC Initiative is a debt relief program, whereby the IMF makes cumulative grant commitments to the members eligible under the HIPC Initiative for financial assistance with the requirement that these grants be used to "help meet debt service payments" to the IMF.

[22] This led to a final decision to adopt convertibility by the EEC countries and the United Kingdom in late 1958. *See* P.L. Cottrell, "The Bank in its International Setting" in Richard Roberts and David Kynaston, eds., *The Bank of England: Money, Power and Influence 1694-1994* (Oxford : Clarendon Press, 1995), at 130–132.

[23] *Id.*

[24] *Id.* In the early 1960s the U.S. dollar and sterling financed approximately 27 percent of world trade.

[25] Decision No. 1238-(61/43), July 28, 1961, *Selected Decisions, Fourth Issue* (1970), p. 19.

[26] Joseph Gold, *Legal and Institutional Aspects of the International Monetary Financial System supra* note 14, at 448–455 (discussing origins of the GAB and the role of US economic imbalances).

[27] Para. 4, Entry into Force:

> This decision shall become effective when it has been adhered to by at least seven of the members or institutions included in the Annex with credit arrangements amounting in all to not less than the equivalent of five and one-half billion United States dollars of the weight and fineness in effect on July 1, 1944.

[28] These industrial countries formed the G10 later in 1962. They included the central bank governors or ministers of finance from Belgium, Canada, the German Bundesbank, France, Italy, Japan, Netherlands, the Swedish Riksbank, United Kingdom, and the United States, and later the Swiss National Bank. The G10 plus the Swiss National Bank comprise the participants today in the General Arrangements to Borrow, along with Saudi Arabia, which became an associated member in 1985.

[29] Article VII, Section 1, Measures to replenish the Fund's holdings of currencies:

> The Fund may, if it deems such action appropriate to replenish its holdings of any member's currency in the General Resources Account needed in connection with its transactions, take either or both of the following steps:
> (1)propose to the member that, on terms and conditions agreed between the Fund and the member, the latter lend its currency to the Fund or that, with the concurrence of the member, the Fund borrow such currency from some other source either within or outside the territories of the member, but no member shall be under any obligation to make such loans to the Fund or to concur in the borrowing of its currency by the Fund from any other source;

[30] The General Arrangements to Borrow, Preamble:

> In order to enable the International Monetary Fund to fulfill more effectively its role in the international monetary system, the main industrial countries have agreed that they will, in a spirit of broad and willing cooperation, strengthen the Fund by general arrangements under which they will stand ready to make loans to the Fund up to specified amounts under Article VII, section 1 of the Articles of Agreement when supplementary resources are needed to forestall or cope with an impairment of the international monetary system.

See IMF, *Selected Decisions, Thirtieth Issue* (Washington D.C.: International Monetary Fund, 2005).

[31] In contrast, the World Bank replenishes its resources by borrowing money from the private sector, a method that has been suggested for the IMF. To borrow from the private sector, the Fund would not need to amend the Articles of Agreement because it has such authority under Article VII, Section 1 (i).

[32] *See* Letter from Mr. Wilfrid Baumgartner, Minster of Finance, France, to Mr. Douglas Dillon, Secretary of Treasury, United States, December 15, 1961. Paragraph C of the letter states, *inter alia*, "[a] favorable decision [to lend] shall require the following majorities of the participants", … (1) a two-thirds majority of the number of participants voting; and (2) a three-fifths majority of the weighted votes of the participants voting, weighted on the basis of the commitments to the Supplementary Resources."

[33] Para. 11 (d) of GAB states that repayment "shall be made in proportion to the Fund's indebtedness to the participants that made transfers in respect of which repayment is being made."

[34] *See* Sir Joseph Gold, *supra* note 26, at 464–66.

[35] Para. 11, GAB, Repayment by the Fund:

> (a) the Fund, five years after a transfer by a participant, shall repay the participant an amount equivalent to the transfer.

[36] There was a real concern among G10 countries that the United States would create a dollar shortage by drawing on its own IMF quota to finance its growing imbalances in the current and capital account. Moreover, the

reserve currency status of the dollar and sterling, combined with growing economic imbalances for both countries, caused concern that there would be inadequate reserve currencies available for countries that would need to borrow reserve currencies to finance imbalances in their current and capital accounts. *See* statement of President Kennedy, February 6, 1961, that the U.S. quota in the Fund of US$4,125 billion could be drawn by the United States and that the U.S. quota had to be considered as part of the country's international reserves. *See* Joseph Gold, *The Legal and Institutional Aspects of the International Monetary System: Selected Essays* vol. 2 (Washington, DC : IMF, 1984), p. 479.

[37] The fear of "the world dollar shortage" was discussed in P.L. Cottrell,"The Bank in its International Setting," in Richard Roberts and David Kynaston, eds., *The Bank of England, supra* note 1, at 130–32. *See also* Gold, *supra* note 26, at 479–80.

[38] Gold, *supra* note 26, at 457.

[39] Para. 7, Calls:

> (a) The Managing Director shall make a proposal for calls for an exchange transaction or for future calls for exchange transactions under a stand-by or extended arrangement only after consultation with Executive Directors and participants.

[40] Para. 7 (b) states that "[t]he currencies and amounts to be called under one or more of the credit arrangements shall be based on the present and prospective balance of payments and reserve position of participating members or members whose institutions are participants and on the Fund's holdings of currencies."

[41] Paragraph 7 (a) provides for "a proposal for calls for an exchange transaction or for future calls for exchange transactions under a stand-by or extended arrangement."

[42] *See* Gold, *supra* note 26, at 458 (citing GAB para. 7 (b)).

[43] Para. 7, Calls:

> (a) The Managing Director shall make a proposal for calls for an exchange transaction or for future calls for exchange transactions

under a stand-by or extended arrangement only after consultation with Executive Directors and participants.

[44] The credit commitments in SDR million of the GAB members between 1962 and 1983 were Belgium 143; Canada 165; Germany Bundesbank 1,476; France 395; Italy 235; Japan 1,161; Netherlands 244; Swedish Riksbank 79; and United Kingdom 565.

[45] Enhancing the GAB's credit arrangements was seen as necessary, especially in the aftermath of the Latin American sovereign debt crisis, where the Fund was unable to stabilize the crisis without U.S. financial support.

[46] In 1983 the credit commitments of GAB members were increased in absolute terms and reduced in relative terms because Saudi Arabia was approved in 1985 to have an associated arrangement with the GAB. See Decision of the Executive Board No. 7403-(83/73) of 20 May 1983. The enlarged credit commitments of the GAB in SDR million from 1983 to 2008 are Belgium 595 (.035 percent); Canada 893 (.053); German Bundesbank 2,380 (.14); France 1,700 (.10); Italy 1,105 (.065); Japan 2,125 (.125); Netherlands 850 (.05); Swedish Riksbank 383 (.02); Swiss National Bank 1,020 (.06); United Kingdom 1.700 (.10); and Saudi Arabia 1500 (.09).

[47] *See* discussion in Gold, *supra* note 36, at 500. The transactions that the Fund can finance for non-GAB participants are those that are in the higher tranches of the credit tranche policy, and under stand-by arrangements going beyond the first credit tranche, or in the first tranche if the transaction is requested as part of an extended arrangement or stand-by arrangement.

[48] *Id.* at 500–501.

[49] *See* Decision of the Executive Board No. 7337-(83/37) of 24 February 1983, para. 21 (b), as amended, states that the Managing Director may institute a procedure if "he considers that the Fund faces an inadequacy of resources to meet actual and expected requests for financing that reflect the existence of an exceptional situation associated with balance of payments problems of members of a character or aggregate size that could threaten the stability of the monetary system."

[50] Also, gold was eliminated as a means of payment and was replaced by Special Drawing Right (SDRs), while a GAB participant's credit arrangements continued to be expressed in its own currency.

[51] Other recent Fund interventions through the GAB were in 1977 when the Fund borrowed reserve currencies from GAB participants and loaned them to the United Kingdom and Italy, respectively, under stand-by arrangements to provide temporary financing to these countries, which were suffering substantial current and capital account imbalances; and in 1978, when the Fund obtained surplus U.S. dollars to lend to the United States in order to finance its reserve tranche purchase.

[52] The Fund cancelled the lending arrangement for Russia in 1999 after the Fund repaid the outstanding amount owed to GAB creditors following the Fund's receipt of increased quota payments by IMF members as required under the Eleventh General Review of Quotas. *See* International Monetary Fund, "IMF Borrowing Arrangements: GAB and NAB," Factsheet, 2006.

[53] The GAB has been renewed nine times, beginning in December 1962, for approximately five-year intervals, and was most recently renewed for a period beginning December 2003 for five years.

[54] GAB participants include the G10 countries plus Saudi Arabia as an associate member.

[55] Baumgartner letter, *supra* note 32, para. C. Gold also interpreted the GAB paragraph 7 (b) and paragraph C of the Baumgartner letter to mean that the GAB "[does] not bind the participants to lend, and do not require the Fund to borrow." Gold, *supra* note 26, at 457.

[56] The NAB was adopted by decision of the Executive Board in 1997 and entered into force in 1998, when it was immediately used to finance an extended arrangement for Brazil. *See* Decision of the Executive Board No. 11428-(97/60) of 27 January 1997. *See also* International Monetary Fund, "IMF's New Arrangements to Borrow Enter into Force," Press Release No. 98/57 (November 19, 1998).

[57] All GAB participants are also participants in NAB plus the following countries/institutions: Australia, Austria, Banco Central de Chile, Denmark, Finland, Hong Kong Monetary Authority, Korea, Kuwait, Luxembourg, Malaysia, Norway, Singapore, Spain, and Thailand.

[58] NAB, para. 6., Initiation of Procedure:

(b) The Managing Director may initiate the procedure set out in paragraph 7A for exchange transactions requested by members that are not participants if [the conditions are fulfilled].

[59] This means a failure to follow through with the program or plan laid out in the arrangement does not therefore amount to a failure to perform a legal obligation, and, consequently, there are no legal sanctions or enforcement mechanisms for not fulfilling conditions in the stand-by.

[60] *Id.* Freely usable currencies are the currencies generally acceptable for settlement of international accounts, such as G10 reserve currencies and other floating currencies traded in the foreign exchange markets.

[61] Para. 11, Repayment by the Fund, which states in relevant part:

(a) [t]he Fund, five years after a transfer by a participant, shall repay the participant an amount equivalent to the transfer calculated in accordance with paragraph 12. If the drawer for whose purchase participants make transfers is committed to repurchase at a fixed date earlier than five years after its purchase, the Fund shall repay the participants at that date.

[62] Michel Camdessus, "International Financial Institutions: Dealing with New Global Challenges" (Washington D.C.: Per Jacobssen Institute, 2005/06)(a Per Jacobssen Lecture on file with the author.)

[63] *See* V. V. Chari and P.J. Kehoe, "Asking the Right Questions About the IMF" (Minneapolis: Federal Reserve Bank of Minneapolis, 1999), at 2 (citing Krugman and Fischer), available at www.minneapolisfed.org/pubs/ar/1998/ar1998.cfm, accessed 17 July 2007

[64] Michel Camdessus, Jacques de Larosiere, and Horst Köhler, "How should the IMF be Reshaped: Three Points of View on the IMF in the Twenty First Century," 41 *Finance and Development* (September 2004), at 27–29.

[65] *See* Eatwell and Taylor, *supra* note 6, at 25–26.

[66] John Eatwell, "International Financial Contagion: What Should We Be Looking For?" in Mardi Dungey and Demosthenes Tambakis*, eds., Identifying International Financial Contagion: Progress and Challenges* (Oxford : Oxford University Press, 2005), 3–34.

[67] Barry Eichengreen, *Financial Crises and What to do About Them* (New York: Oxford University Press, 2002), chapter 3.

[68] Ariel Buira, "The Governance of the IMF in a Global Economy" in A. Buira, ed., *Challenges to the World Bank and IMF: Developing Countries Perspectives* (London: Anthem Press, 2003), at 13–36.

[69] Barry Eichengreen, *Toward a New International Financial Architecture: A Practical Post-Asia Agenda* (Washington DC: Institute for International Economics,1999), at 65–69.

[70] Eichengreen, *supra* note 67, at 61.

[71] Group of Seven, "Strengthening the International Financial Architecture: Report from the G7 Finance Ministers to the Heads of State and Government," Fukuoka, Japan, July 8, 2000.

[72] *See* David Vines and Christopher Gilbert, "The IMF and International Financial Architecture," in D. Vines and C. Gilbert, eds., *The IMF and its Critics supra* note 7, at 24–25.

[73] *See* IMF, "Progress Report to the International Monetary and Financial Committee on Crisis Resolution," April 12, 2005. Debt restructuring is perhaps one of the topics of crisis management that has been intensively discussed by diverse institutions, private-sector participants, and academics, given the numerous and repeated country experiences of unsustainable debt payment and servicing in recent years.

[74] Institute of International Finance, "Principles for Stable Capital Flows and Fair Debt Restructuring in Emerging Markets," March 11, 2005.

[75] For a summary of previous efforts and relevant literature of the different efforts see IMF, "Progress Report," *supra* note 73, at 12.

[76] Vines and Gilbert, *supra* note 72, at 24–25.

[77] *Id.* at 25–26.

[78] *See* IMF, "Proposed Features of a Sovereign Debt Restructuring Mechanism," prepared by the Legal and Policy Department and Review

Departments, February 12, 2003 (providing a detailed study of the SDRM proposal).

[79] The SDRM, also known as the "Krueger Proposal," was developed by Anne Krueger, the First Deputy Managing Director of the IMF. *See* Anne Krueger, "International Financial Architecture for 2002: A New Approach to Sovereign Debt Restructuring," address delivered on November 26, 2001.

[80] *See* Barry Herman, "Mechanisms for Dialogue and Debt-Crisis Workout that Can Strengthen Sovereign Lending to Developing Countries," in A. Buira, ed., *Challenges to the World Bank and IMF*, *supra* note 68, at 203–226.

[81] The moral hazard created because of a perception of a bailout can lead to an under-pricing of the financial risk to which the investors and depositors may be exposed and potentially increase systemic risk.

[82] International Law Association, "International Monetary Law Committee Report," *Report of the Seventy-First Conference*, Berlin, 2004, at 122–124.

[83]A. Haldane and M. Kruger, "The Resolution of International Financial Crises: An Alternative Framework," in Vines and Gilbert (eds.), *The IMF and its Critics*, *supra* note 7, at 207–224.

[84] IMF, "Report of the Managing Director to International Monetary and Financial Committee on the IMF's Policy Agenda," September 22, 2005, at 10.

[85] Henry Thornton discussed the role of a lender of last resort in "An Enquiry into the Nature and Effects of the Paper Credit of Great Britain," published in 1802. Bagehot later developed the concept in his renowned work *Lombard Street: A Description of the Money Markets*, in 1873. *See* Capie and Wood, *supra* note 1. The term later became commonly used in the late nineteenth century, after an observation made in 1879 by Sir Francis Baring, who described the Bank of England as a *dernier resort* for banks in need of liquidity during crises.

[86] *See* Rosa M. Lastra, "The International Monetary Fund in Historical Perspective," 3 *Journal of International Economic Law* (2000), at 507–537.

[87] *See* Eatwell and Taylor, *supra* note 6, at 43, 46–47.

[88] *See* Eichengreen, *supra* note 67, chapter 3 (discussing crisis management).

[89] *See* Stephanie Griffith-Jones and Jenny Kimmis, "Stabilizing Capital Flows," in Jonathan Michie and Grieve Smith, eds., *Global Instability:The Political Economy of World Economic Governance* (New York : Routledge, 1999), pp. 87–96.

[90] *See* Rosa M. Lastra, "Member of Last Resort: An International Perspective," 48 *International and Comparative Law Quarterly* (April 1999), at 340–361.

[91] Eichengreen, *Financial Crises*, *supra* note 67, at 52.

[92] *See* Rosa M. Lastra, "The International Monetary Fund in Historical Perspective," *supra* note 86, at 514–517.

[93] *Id.* Indeed, prudential regulation and financial-crisis management pose different types of challenges in today's financial markets, and therefore the optimal institutional model at the national level could involve the central bank coordinating with the Finance Ministry and potentially with an autonomous domestic supervisor.

[94] See Rosa M. Lastra *The Legal Foundation of International Monetary Stability* (Oxford: Oxford University Press, 2006) pp. 304-306.

[95] The definition of what types of collateral to take is not harmonised at the EU level, nor is it defined in the ESCB statute.

[96] Lastra, *supra* note 92, at 340–361, fn. 2.

[97] *See* Eatwell and Taylor, *supra* note 6, at chapter 3.

[98] *See* Eichengreen, *supra* note 67, at 52–53.

[99] Group of Seven, "Report of G7 Finance Ministers to the Köln Economic Summit," Cologne, June 18–20, 1999, paragraph 45.

[100] Group of Seven, "Report from the G7 Finance Ministers to the Heads of State and Government," Fukuoka, Japan, July 8, 2000, paragraph 21 (b).

[101] In parallel to the official creditor's Paris Club, there is a forum for private creditors, known as the London Club. Its origins were inspired in the Paris Club, and it serves as a venue for private commercial banks.

[102] IMF, "Reviewing the Process for Sovereign Debt Restructuring within the Existing Legal Framework," August 1, 2003, prepared by Policy Development and Review, International Capital Markets, and Legal Departments.

[103] IMF, "Involving the Private Sector in the Resolution of Financial Crises— The Treatment of the Claims of Private Sector and Paris Club Creditors— Preliminary Considerations," June 27, 2001.

[104] Rosa M. Lastra, "The International Monetary Fund in Historical Perspective," *supra* note 92, at 507–537.

[105] Goodhart, "The Organisational Structure of Banking Supervision," *FSI Occasional Papers* 1, November, 2002, at 26.

[106] *Id.* at 76–80.

[107] *Id.* at 78.

[108] *Id.* at 80–83.

[109] *Id.* at 83–85.

[110] The most important provision of the CAC specifies the proportion of shareholders that qualify as a majority and is entitled to initiate a debt restructuring process that will bind all parties of the clause.

[111] These clauses establish decision-making rules and specify how bondholders are to be represented in the event of a renegotiation of debt payments.

[112] International Law Association, "International Monetary Law Committee Report," *Report of the Seventy-First Conference*, Berlin, 2004, at 122–156.

[113] *See* Group of Ten, "Report of the G-10 Working Group on Contractual Clauses," September 26, 2002, for the G10 proposal. The IIF together with the Emerging Markets Traders Association, the International Primary Market

Association, The Bond Market Association, the Securities Industry Association, the International Securities Market Association, and the Emerging Markets Creditors Association developed the "Model for Collective Action Clauses for Sovereign Bonds" and issued it as a discussion draft on January 31, 2003. For a detailed report of advances in the field, see IMF, "Progress Report to the International Monetary and Financial Committee on Crisis Resolution," April 12, 2005.

[114] International Law Association, *supra* note 115.

[115] For instance, GAB loans were made to the United Kingdom on four occasions: 1964 (SDR 405 million), 1965 (SDR 525 million), 1967 (SDR 476 million), 1969 (SDR 200 million), and 1977 (1.4935 billion). One loan has been made to Italy, in 1977 for SDR 82.5 million. *See* Gold, *supra* note 36, Table 2, at 510.

[116] The benchmark value for determining the value of reserve currency lending would be Special Drawing Rights (SDRs). In this example, based on the published IMF currency conversion rates into SDRs for October 2007, US$60 million (US$1=.6415 SDRs) would be SDRs 38.49 million, Swiss franc 30 million would be SDRs 16.49 million, and UK£10 million (£1= 1.307 SDRs) would be SDRs 13.07 million. Therefore, the US portion of the emergency loan would be 56.6 percent, the Swiss portion would be 24.2 percent, and the UK portion would be 19.2 percent.

[117] This chapter adopts the traditional definition of eurocurrency that it is a reserve currency, or a hard currency, that is a traded in a jurisdiction in which it is not the currency of issue.

[118] Credit derivatives are financial instruments that allow debtors to insure against losses on their debt. Their use is growing rapidly for sovereign debtors.

[119] *See* Vines and Gilbert, *supra* note 42, at 33.

[120] *See* Knight et al., *supra* note 10, at 144–148.

7 | Central Banks and Financial Stability: A Survey of Financial Stability Reports

MARTIN ČIHÁK

In the last three decades, financial stability has emerged as an important public policy objective. The main reasons for the increased interest in financial stability include the increased frequency and high costs of financial crises, the explosive growth in the volume of financial transactions within nations and worldwide, and the increased complexity of new financial instruments.[1]

One of the most visible signs of this increased focus on financial stability has been the rapid growth in the past decade in the number central banks publishing a financial stability report (FSR). As of the end of 2005, almost fifty central banks were publishing FSRs, and many others were considering publication.

This chapter builds extensively on the author's work, which was the first comprehensive survey of the available FSRs (hereinafter Čihak 2006 or the survey).[2] It surveyed 160 FSRs published in 47 countries over a period of more than 10 years (altogether, more than 10,000 pages of text, graphs, and tables).[3] Relying on this research, the chapter focuses on the definition of financial stability, the aim of FSRs, and the central bank's role in financial stability.

The chapter first discusses what an FSR is and how it differs from other central bank reports, then presents a survey of which central banks publish FSRs. The ensuing section describes several important features of FSRs, in particular the definition of financial stability in FSRs, objectives of an FSR, its role in central bank accountability, and the overall assessments in FSRs. Finally, the chapter illustrates, based on the survey of Čihák 2006, areas of needed improvement in the existing FSRs.

What Is an FSR?

Defining an FSR is far from straightforward. Central banks and other institutions have been producing a number of outputs covering the financial sector, but varying widely in a number of respects. Virtually every central bank publishes an annual report or another report with some coverage of the financial sector. An FSR, however, is a more specific product.

For the purpose of this chapter, an FSR is defined as a regular, self-contained central bank publication that focuses on risks and exposures in the financial system. The key elements of this definition are as follows:

- *Focus on risks and exposures.* General-interest publications, such as annual reports with a section describing the performance of the banking sector, do not qualify as FSRs if they only discuss performance without covering risks and exposures. Also, central banks in some countries publish separate reports on financial system structure or related development issues (e.g., the European Central Bank (ECB) publishes a regular report on banking structures in the European Union). These reports have an important function, but are not considered an FSR for the purposes of this study.

- *Systemic coverage.* Some rating agencies publish reports on the soundness of specific institutions or even groups of institutions, focusing on individual institutions. By contrast, FSRs cover financial systems. Even though some calculations in FSRs are based on an individual institution's data, most results are presented in aggregate form and the focus of the report is on systemic issues rather than on soundness of individual institutions.[4] The systemic focus of the FSR reflects its role in the framework of financial sector regulation and supervision. In particular, an FSR is part of a central bank's macroprudential surveillance function (see Table 1).

- *Publisher.* Most FSRs are published by central banks. In several countries, a report on risks in the financial system is also published by a separate regulatory agency (these are not included in the survey of FSRs). At a global level, stability reports are also published by international organizations, in particular the IMF (the Global Financial Stability Report), which is a broader survey of financial stability than the country-specific reports. There have also been several reports on financial stability published by private-sector participants. Those reports, while interesting, tend to be one-off endeavors rather than regular documents.[5] This chapter (and the Čihák survey) focuses on regular reports published by central banks.

- ***Self-contained nature.*** FSRs are generally stand-alone documents, even though in some cases they are a part of another publication (e.g., an annual report or a bulletin). To qualify as an FSR, a text has to be relatively self-contained and have analytical depth. For example, a short section or several paragraphs describing banking sector developments in an annual report would generally not qualify as an FSR. A table of macroprudential indicators with a short commentary would not qualify. By contrast, Deutsche Bundesbank's roughly 80-page "Report on the stability of the German financial system" in 2004 clearly qualified as an FSR, even though it was only a chapter in the central bank's monthly report.[6]

- ***Regularity of publication.*** FSRs are regular (typically annual or semi-annual) publications. A one-off report on the financial sector is not considered an FSR.

FSRs also have secondary features that vary from country to country. For example, they use different titles, such as *Financial Stability Review* (Bank of England or Bank Indonesia), *Financial System Review* (Bank of Canada), *Monetary and Financial Stability Report* (Hong Kong Monetary Authority), or *Macroprudential Analysis* (Croatian National Bank). Structure, length, and format also vary substantially.

Table 1. General Structure of Financial Sector Regulation and Supervision

Type of Market Failure	Systemic Instability	Asymmetric Information	Market Misconduct	Anticompe titive Behavior
Regulatory/ supervisory area	Macro-prudential surveillance (financial stability)	Micro-prudential supervision (individual institutions)	Business supervision (consumer protection)	Competition
Banks	Central bank, monetary authority	One	One	Separate agency responsible for competition in general
Insurance companies		Or	Or	
Capital market firms		More	More	
Other financial firms		agencies	Agencies	

Source: The author, adapted from Martin Čihák and Richard Podpiera, "Is One Watchdog Better Than Three? International Experience with Integrated Financial Sector Supervision," IMF Working Paper No. 06/57 (Washington, D.C.: International Monetary Fund, 2006).

Who Publishes FSRs?

The first FSRs were published in the mid-1990s in the United Kingdom and several Nordic countries. Since then, the number of central banks publishing FSRs has increased rapidly, from two in 1995 to almost fifty at the end of 2005 (Figure 1).[7] In addition, several central banks produce FSRs internally and are considering their publication in the future.[8]

Figure 1. The Number of Countries Publishing FSRs, 1995–2005

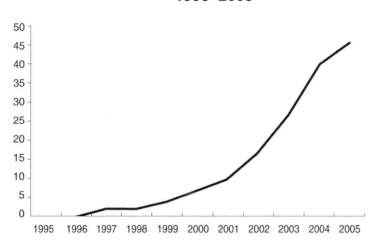

Source: Author's calculations, based on information available from individual central banks.

The characteristics of central banks that publish FSRs can be summarized as follows (see also Table 3):

- **Income level.** The FSRs are published by central banks in high- and medium-income countries (Figure 2). Low-income country central banks do not generally publish FSRs, even though many cover financial sector issues to some extent in their annual reports or other publications. Also, some countries publish general reports on financial sector performance, while others publish separate reports on financial sector structure and development.

- **Geography of FSRs.** Europe accounts for a majority of the published FSRs. In the euro area, FSRs are published both by the ECB and by the individual central banks. Of the 30 OECD countries, 25 publish FSRs.

- **Institutional basis for financial stability analysis.** Despite the growing interest in financial stability in central banks, it is rare to find a direct reference to financial stability as a central bank's objective in its basic founding legislation. If financial stability is included, it is more likely to be found among "tasks" than among "objectives." Financial stability is often bundled together with other standard tasks, such as the support for smooth functioning of the payment system, regulation and supervision of the banking system, or lender-of-last resort functions.[9] Financial stability and the central bank's role in it is more commonly specified in other documents, such as mission statements or memoranda of understanding (if there is an integrated financial supervisory agency outside the central bank). Central banks typically explain their interest in the stability and general health of the financial system by their role of lender of last resort and their monetary policy objectives.[10] The correlation between the publication of an FSR and the explicit inclusion of financial stability among objectives in central bank legislation is therefore positive, but rather weak (see Table 3).

- *Organizational structure.* The emphasis on financial stability is often reflected also in the organizational structure of the central bank. Central banks publishing FSRs are more likely to have a separate organizational unit covering financial stability, but the relationship is not one-to-one (some FSR-publishing central banks have the financial stability function located in bank supervision, research, or another organizational unit; and there are central banks that have a separate organizational unit, but do not publish an FSR).

- *Financial Sector Assessment Program.* In 1999 the IMF and the World Bank launched the Financial Sector Assessment Program (FSAP), which provides countries with independent assessments of their financial sector and its regulatory framework. Participation in the program is voluntary. Interestingly, most FSRs published in the early years of the program (up to 2004) were by central banks that have participated or volunteered to participate (Table 3). This indicates that the reasons for publishing FSRs were similar to those prompting countries to volunteer early for the FSAP.

Figure 2. Countries Publishing FSRs, by Income Level

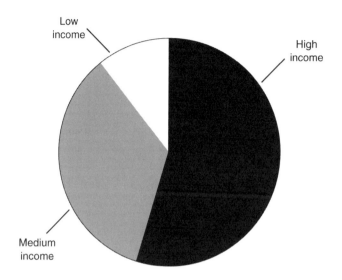

Source: Author's calculations based on individual FSRs.

Table 2. Financial Stability Reports Included In the Survey

Country	Publishing Institution	Frequency	Starting Year
Argentina	Banco Central de la Rep. Argentina	Semi-annual	2004
Australia	Reserve Bank of Australia	Semi-annual	1999
Austria	Österreichische Nationalbank	Semi-annual	2001
Belgium	National Bank of Belgium	Annual	2002
Brazil	Banco Central do Brasil	Semi-annual	2002
Canada	Bank of Canada	Semi-annual	2002
Chile	Banco Central de Chile	Semi-annual	2004
China	People's Bank of China	Annual	2005
Colombia	Banco de la República Colombia	Semi-annual	2002
Croatia	Croatian National Bank	Semi-annual	2005
Czech Rep.	Czech National Bank	Annual	2004
Denmark	Denmarks Nationalbank	Annual	2002
Euro Area	European Central Bank	Annual	2004
Estonia	Eesti Pank	Semi-annual	2003
Finland	Suomen Pankki	Annual	2003
France	Banque de France	Semi-annual	2002
Germany	Deusche Bundesbank	Annual	2004
Ghana	Bank of Ghana	5x per year [1]	2005
Greece	Bank of Greece	Annual [2]	2004
Hungary	National Bank of Hungary	Semi-annual	2000
Hong Kong SAR	Hong Kong Monetary Authority	Semi-annual	2003
Iceland	Central Bank of Iceland	Semi-annual	2000
Indonesia	Bank Indonesia	Semi-annual	2003
Ireland	Central Bank and Financial Services Authority of Ireland	Annual	2000
Israel	Bank of Israel	Annual	2003
Japan	Bank of Japan	Annual	2005
Kenya	Central Bank of Kenya	Annual	2004
Korea	Bank of Korea	Semi-annual	2003
Latvia	Bank of Latvia	Semi-annual	2003
Macao	Monetary Authority of Macao	Semi-annual	2005
Netherlands	De Nederlandsche Bank	Semi-annual	2004
New Zealand	Reserve Bank of New Zealand	Semi-annual	2004

Country	Publishing Institution	Frequency	Starting Year
Norway	Norges Bank	Semi-annual	1997
Philippines	Bangko Sentral ng Pilipinas	Semi-annual	1999
Poland	National Bank of Poland	Semi-annual	2001
Portugal	Banco de Portugal	Semi-annual	2004
Russia	Bank of Russia	Annual	2001
Singapore	Monetary Authority of Singapore	Semi-annual	2003
Slovak Republic	National Bank of Slovakia	Annual	2003
Slovenia	Bank of Slovenia	Annual	2004
South Africa	Reserve Bank of South Africa	Semi-annual	2004
Spain	Banco de España	Semi-annual	2002
Sri Lanka	Central Bank of Sri Lanka	Annual	2004
Sweden	Sveriges Riksbank	Semi-annual	1997
Switzerland	Schweizerische Nationalbank	Annual	2003
Turkey	Türkiye Cumhuriyet Merkez Bankasý	Semi-annual	2005
United Kingdom	Bank of England	Semi-annual	1996

Note: Additionally, in Norway and the United Kingdom there are also FSR-like reports published by the unified supervisory agencies. In Russia, the central bank publishes two different reports qualifying as stability reports.
[1] Available on the website since 2005 as Volume 5. Earlier volumes not available to the author.
[2] A chapter on banking sector and its supervision included in the annual report. Given the extent of the chapter and its relatively self-contained nature, it is classified as an FSR since 2004 for the purpose of this text.

Table 3. Correlations between FSR Publication and Other Characteristics

	FSR published	FS in a separate organizational unit	Official FS among objectives	Independent monetary policy	Banking supervision in the central bank	Advanced economy	FSAP took place or requested by authorities 1/
FSR published	1.00	0.91	0.13	-0.31	-0.26	0.55	0.37
FS in a separate organizational unit	0.91	1.00	0.14	-0.25	-0.29	0.54	0.33
FS among official objectives	0.13	0.14	1.00	0.02	0.01	0.17	0.08
Independent monetary policy	-0.31	-0.25	0.02	1.00	0.24	-0.61	-0.26
Bank supervision in central bank	-0.26	-0.29	0.01	0.24	1.00	-0.24	-0.16
Advanced economy	0.55	0.54	0.17	-0.61	-0.24	1.00	0.27
FSAP took place or requested [1]	0.37	0.33	0.08	-0.26	-0.16	0.27	1.00

Source: The author's calculations based on individual FSRs.
Note: Each row and column corresponds to a dummy variable indicating whether the respective feature is present (1) or not (0). The values in the table are pairwise correlation coefficients for these dummy variables. FS refers to financial stability.
[1] FSAPs up to end-2004.

Selected Features of FSRs

To assess FSRs, Čihák 2006 has identified five main elements of the report: its aims; the overall assessment presented; the issues covered; the data, assumptions, and tools being used; and other features such as the reports' structure; and three key characteristics: clarity, consistency, and coverage.[11] Table 7 (located at the end of this chapter) presents this "CCC framework" in a matrix format.

This section focuses on definitions of financial stability in FSRs, objectives of an FSR, its role in central bank accountability, and the overall assessments in FSRs. The CCC framework also contains other important elements, such as the scope and method of analysis. Those are covered in more detail in Čihák 2006.

How Do FSRs Define Financial Stability?

A basic question faced by a reader trying to understand an FSR is what the central bank means by the term *financial stability*. Some FSRs attempt to define the term while also recognizing that financial stability is a complex concept. Many FSRs make clear that they are not focused on problems in individual institutions but rather on system-wide issues. Furthermore, there is a general understanding that financial stability refers to smooth functioning of the components of the financial system (financial institutions; markets; and payments, settlement, and clearing systems). The prevailing view is that the analysis of financial stability covers phenomena that (1) impair the functions of the financial system; (2) create vulnerabilities in the financial system; and (3) lead to a negative impact on the financial system and thereby on the economy as a whole. Beyond that, the exact definitions of financial stability vary across the FSRs.

The survey of FSRs in Čihák 2006 suggests that financial stability can be defined narrowly or broadly.[12] At one end of the spectrum, some FSRs define financial stability as the antithesis of system-wide financial crises in which the financial system fails to function and the institutional underpinnings of a monetary economy—payments and settlements systems, and the acceptability of bank deposits as money—are disrupted. Such episodes can be very costly, so policymakers need to assess the (usually low) risks of their occurrence. Financial crises of this sort are of particular concern to central banks because they disrupt the transmission mechanism of monetary policy (see Table 1). Table 4 illustrates this definition: financial crises are results of significant shocks in a situation when the system has large exposures (bottom right cell in the table); all other situations are identified with financial stability.

The definition of financial stability has obvious impacts on the scope of the financial stability reports. The broader the definition of instability, the more potential threats to stability (and the longer the report).[13]

Table 4. Definitions of Financial Stability: Overview

| | | Significant Exposures? | |
		Not apparent	Apparent
Significant shocks?	No	Financial stability	Financial stability
	Not now, but plausible	Financial stability	Financial fragility
	Yes	Volatility (turbulences, bubbles)	Financial crisis

Source: The author, based on a survey of the literature.
Note: The table covers only definitions based purely on risks and exposures. It does not cover some of the broader definitions mentioned in the text, in particular those incorporating efficiency.

Many FSRs use broad definitions of financial instability (see Table 5 for examples). In particular, most also include situations when the system—even though not in a state of crisis—is fragile, i.e., has significant exposures to plausible risks. Using such a broad definition of instability calls for the use of additional instruments. In particular, stress tests are used to distinguish whether the system has significant exposures to the plausible risks. If the stress tests suggest the existence of such exposures, the system is deemed fragile; otherwise, it is considered stable (robust).

Some FSRs also include, under the heading of instability, those situations when a system is subject to significant shocks, even though it does not seem to have major exposures. These include major volatility in financial markets (asset price bubbles), with uncertain impacts on financial institutions. Including these situations under the heading of instability is potentially more controversial than including the situations of fragility because the system does not have apparent exposures. However, some FSRs do this partly in recognition of the limitations of the available tools to uncover hidden exposures, e.g., those relating to institution-to-institution contagion or correlations of exposures across a range of portfolios. These FSRs, while noting the absence of apparent exposures, maintain that it is prudent to watch closely the sources of risk.

Some FSRs define financial stability even more broadly, as the situation when the efficiency of financial intermediation between ultimate borrowers and ultimate lenders is not subject to significant adverse shocks. If this definition is adopted, the remit of policy-makers is correspondingly broader, and their analysis more encompassing. The assignment of responsibility to the central bank for safeguarding financial stability is less clear-cut if this definition is chosen. Supervisory and competition authorities, for example, would naturally have a close interest (see Table 1).

Table 5. Examples of Definitions of Financial Stability in FSRs

	Definition	Where?
Canada	Explicit definition not provided, but a box on the inside cover lists components of the financial system and notes that serious disruptions to one or more of these components "can create substantial problems for the entire financial system and, ultimately, for the economy as a whole." The same box also notes that "inefficiencies in the financial system may lead to significant economic costs over time and contribute to a system that is less able to successfully cope with periods of financial stress."	Box on the inside cover
Denmark	Explicit definition not provided, but the FSR contains an implicit definition in a description of its purpose, namely "to assess whether the financial system is so robust that any problems in the financial sector do not	Introduction

	spread and impede the functioning of the financial markets as efficient providers of capital for companies and households." It also notes that "The approach is to consider the general risks to the financial system rather than the situation of the individual financial institutions."	
Euro Area	"A condition where the financial system is capable of performing well at all of its normal tasks and where it is expected to do so for the foreseeable future."	Preface
Iceland	The FSRs made several references to Andrew Crockett's definition (*see supra* note 1) that financial stability broadly hinges upon the stability of the key institutions and markets that make up the financial system. "This requires (1) that the key institutions in the financial system are stable, in that there is a high degree of confidence that they continue to meet their contractual obligations without interruption or outside assistance; and (2) that the key markets are stable, in that participants can confidently transact in them at prices that reflect the fundamental forces and do not vary substantially over short periods when there have been no changes in the fundamentals."	Various places in the FSR
Norway	"Financial stability means that the financial system is robust to disturbances in the economy and is able to mediate financing, carry out payments and redistribute risk in a satisfactory manner. Experience shows that the foundation for financial instability is laid during periods of strong growth in debt and asset prices. Banks play a central part in extending credit and mediating payments and are therefore important to financial stability."	Box on the inside cover
Sweden	"The analysis of financial stability concerns the ability to withstand unforeseen shocks to financial companies as well as to the financial infrastructure, that is, the systems that are required for making payments and for trading and delivering financial products. The analysis of financial companies concentrates on the four major Swedish banking groups because it is these that are of crucial importance for the payment system's stability."	Foreword
Switzerland	"A stable financial system can be defined as a system where the various components fulfill	Introduction

| | their functions and are able to withstand the shocks to which they are exposed. This report focuses on two vital elements in the system: the banking sector and financial market infrastructure." | |
| United Kingdom | Explicit definition not provided, even though implicitly the overview section reviews the elements that the Bank of England assesses (e.g., the major institutions' profitability, capitalization, resilience to shocks). | ... |

Source: the author, based on the individual country FSRs.

Most FSRs include a general definition of stability. With the possible exception of the Swiss National Bank's FSR, no FSR includes an operational definition of stability, which would narrow the range of indicators to be considered when assessing stability of the financial system. This issue is particularly relevant for FSRs using the broader definition of financial instability that includes resilience to shocks, because the distinction between stable and unstable systems is likely to depend on the degree of plausibility of the potential shocks to which a system is subjected. The absence of an operational definition of financial stability contrasts sharply with the framework for price stability, where an operational definition of price stability has played a key role in recent years, with a trend towards setting more explicit inflation targets (Table 6).

Financial stability is a more complex concept than price stability, and expecting that it can be boiled down to a single indicator and a single target range would not be realistic (reflecting also the fact that research in this area is not as developed as in the area of price stability). Nonetheless, clarifying a set of basic indicators that need to be looked at and a set of threshold values would be a useful way of clarifying the framework underlying the assessment of financial stability. Of course, having a summary indicator or a basic set of indicators does not mean that there is no role for other indicators or for nonquantitative factors.

The Swiss National Bank's FSR, which highlights a "stress index" as a key summary indicator, is the first example of an FSR going in this direction. Another example is a new, revamped version of the Bank of England's FSR that the bank unveiled in July 2006. It includes a summary table highlighting the key vulnerabilities for the UK financial system (e.g., low risk premia, global imbalances, and UK household debt), and indicating for each of these vulnerabilities whether their probability and their impact significantly/slightly increased/decreased or remained broadly unchanged.

Table 6. Schematic Comparison of Price Stability and Financial Stability

	Price Stability	Financial Stability
General definition	Clear	A range of definitions
Operational definition	Clear (variable and target), especially in inflation targeting	Typically not specified
Legal base for central bank's role	Based on law	Based on interpretation of law
Scope of central bank's responsibility	Full responsibility	Partial/shared responsibility, exact boundaries in some countries unclear, in others delineated by a memorandum of understanding
Research	Well developed	Developing

Note: This is, of course, only a schematic comparison that does not apply to all countries. For example, numerous central banks do not have an explicit inflation target. Nonetheless, the adoption of such targets has clearly been a trend in recent years.

Why Publish an FSR?

There are arguments both for and against the publication of an FSR. Before undertaking publication, a central bank should consider the sensitivity of information to be included and the expense of the project, weighed against the benefits that accrue from such a publication in pursuing financial stability.

Reasons Not to Publish an FSR

Before discussing reasons for publishing FSRs, it is useful to list the main reasons *against* publishing an FSR. Based on a survey of the literature and on discussions with staff of central banks that do not publish FSRs, the main reasons not to publish an FSR can be grouped into the following three categories:

- *Financial sector issues are too sensitive to be discussed openly in the public.* It is possible to conceive of circumstances in which publication of a central bank analysis at a time of increasing risk to financial stability might precipitate the very shocks or crisis that the central bank is trying to avoid, by inducing liquidity problems in particular markets or financial institutions. That danger is reduced if the central bank has established a track record of unbiased analysis during a period of low risks to financial stability. The experience of FSR-publishing central banks so far does not provide an example of an FSR that triggered liquidity problems in the system.

- *Central banks have an incomplete degree of control over policy outcomes in the area of financial stability.* One of the basic rules of good inflation reports is "say what you do—do what you say." For FSRs, however, what the central bank can do has arguably much less of an impact on financial stability than it can have on achieving an inflation target, partly because achieving financial stability requires actions from other parties, such as other agencies and market players. However, because the desired outcome depends on a number of parties, not the least including the market players, putting out a high-quality report is important. If the report is persuasive, it may be able to trigger a desired action by the market players.

- *Preparing and publishing FSRs requires resources.* The resource intensity of the exercise may be an important argument, particularly in central banks in smaller countries with limited resources. It would be unwise to launch an FSR when its quality could not be sustained or the report could not be produced regularly. However, three mitigating factors should be taken into consideration. First, the drafting team of FSRs in most central banks is relatively small, from four to ten people. Second, in small central banks with limited resources it may be useful to choose a relatively narrower operating definition of financial stability—as recommended in the case of Norges Bank[14]—which means that the scope of the report can be relatively smaller and require less staff. Third, for most central banks the choice is not really whether to produce such a report. Given the importance of financial sector stability for their overall objectives, most central banks have to monitor financial sector stability and thus typically produce regular reports on the subject for internal purposes. The real question in most cases therefore is what the costs would be to turn such reports into full-blown publications.

Reasons to Publish an FSR

On close inspection, none of the above reasons against publishing an FSR appears strong. What, then, are then the main reasons *for* publishing an FSR? Based on the survey of FSRs, the ultimate objective of the FSR for most central banks is contribution to financial stability. Some FSRs even recognize reduction of financial instability as the ultimate objective. For example, the Bank of Canada flags in a cover box of its FSR that it is "one avenue through which it seeks to contribute to the longer-term robustness of the domestic financial system."

How can FSRs contribute to financial stability? They can do so by:

- Improving the understanding of (and contributing to dialogue on) risks to financial intermediaries in the economic environment;

- Alerting financial institutions and market participants to the possible collective impact of their individual actions;

- Building a consensus for financial stability and the improvement of the financial infrastructure.

An FSR can add value to work undertaken by private agents in the financial sector itself because a central bank can draw on its macroeconomic expertise and its role in payments and settlements.

Some FSRs list a range of general aims that relate to the above mechanism of contributing to financial stability and can be seen as subordinate to the "ultimate objective." In particular, FSRs often stress the objective of monitoring and presenting to the public the central bank's appraisal of developments relevant for the financial sector and of their impact on financial sector stability. Other often-stated objectives include encouraging an informed debate on financial stability issues, disseminating information for transparency purposes, and influencing market participants. Some central banks see their FSRs as a tool to encourage greater cooperation between supervisory and regulatory authorities. Some see their stability reports as a way of building trust in the financial services industry, based on permanent monitoring of risks and pointing out of dangers to participants (for examples, see Čihák 2006).

Publication of FSRs is only one of a number of tools that public authorities have to affect financial stability. The authorities can help achieve financial stability by (1) ensuring integrity of payment systems; (2) regulating and supervising financial intermediaries to limit risk exposures and ensure that there are appropriate buffers; (3) working on crisis management, mitigating effects of international spillovers, and minimizing risk of asset price collapses; and (4) monitoring new risks.[15] The FSR should especially play a key role in monitoring of new risks.

An additional reason for publishing an FSR is the positive impact that such a regular publication may have on the central bank itself. FSRs typically do not mention this as an explicit aim, but it is certainly important in the consideration of whether to start publishing an FSR. Bowen, O'Brien, and Steigum argue that publication subjects the central bank's analysis to scrutiny by a wide range of possible critics; it therefore provides a discipline for surveillance work as to its quality, frequency, and timing; and it demonstrates that the central bank is fulfilling its remit.[16] Hence publication can fulfill an important role in improving the accountability and transparency of the central bank.

Role in Central Bank Accountability

For central banks that have financial stability among their objectives (or are able to derive it from their objectives), it is useful to think about the FSRs as one of their accountability instruments. As Allen, Francke, and Swinburne have noted, the FSR could serve as a vehicle to allow stakeholders to form a view about how effectively the central bank is undertaking its broader financial stability responsibilities.[17] The concept of stakeholders is viewed here in a broad sense, including the industry and the general public. In some cases, there may be a specific accountability with respect to a relevant overseeing body. In Norway, for example, the FSR is submitted first for a discussion at a meeting of Norges Bank's executive board, and the main conclusions of the FSR are then summarized in a submission to the Ministry of Finance. In most countries, a launch of the FSR is accompanied by presentations to the media, market analysts, and in some cases academics. In most cases, FSRs are prominently displayed on the central bank's website, typically in a special section entitled "Financial Stability." FSRs are also made available in hard copies.

Central banks follow a gradual approach to launching FSRs. For example, Norges Bank's staff started preparing internal reports in 1995. In 1997 the bank started publishing semiannual external reports. The reports first appeared in the central bank journal as extracts from a fuller report. Since 2000 they have been published in a special publication.

FSRs are part of a broader communications strategy of the central bank. The strategy comprises a number of other reports, each with different aims and audiences. Virtually all central banks publish an annual report and a general publication focused on macroeconomic developments (e.g., an inflation report in inflation-targeting countries).

In the financial sector, there may also be several central bank publications. For example, the European Central Bank supplements its *Financial Stability Review* with *EU Banking Sector Stability* and *EU Banking Structures.* In the United Kingdom, the Bank of England publishes a separate *Payment Systems Oversight Report*, which is featured prominently alongside its *Financial Stability Review*. In Brazil, the central bank's FSR is accompanied by a set of reports on the composition and evolution of the national financial system and on the payments system. In Croatia, in addition to the FSR (*Macroprudential Analysis*), the central bank also publishes a more descriptive report focusing on changes in the structure and functioning of the banking system and its supervisory and regulatory mechanism (*Banks Bulletin*). In Poland, in addition to its *Financial Stability Review* and *Financial Stability Report*, the central bank also publishes the *Financial System Development Report*, which focus on the structure of the system. A number of FSR-publishing central banks also have separate reports on supervisory developments. Several FSR-publishing central banks also issue separate brochures on financial stability that are less technical and addressed to a more general audience than an FSR.

Overall Assessments in FSRs

Most of the overall assessments in FSRs have been positive. In a survey of the latest issues of the FSRs, virtually all (96 percent) have started off with a positive overall assessment of soundness of the domestic system (characterizing the health of the financial system as being, e.g., "in good shape," "solid," or at least "improving"). There are several possible reasons why the positive assessments are so prevalent:

- *As good as it gets.* The global financial system has been characterized by a period of relative calm. There has been no major financial crisis in recent years, and liquidity has been abundant globally. In that sense, FSRs have not yet been put to a real test.

- *Selection bias.* Countries with robust financial systems and well-designed frameworks are more likely to start publishing FSRs than those with weaker financial systems and frameworks. Therefore the prevalence of positive overall assessments in FSRs may simply reflect the fact that the systems reviewed in FSRs are in general in a better shape than those for which FSRs are not available.

- *Presentation bias.* Some central banks may prefer to present the financial system in a positive light, partly because problems may be seen as a result of bad policies, and partly because of the fear that a negative assessment might trigger a decline in confidence in the system. The drawback of this approach is that (1) if problems are unreported for a while, they may accumulate and become more difficult to address than if they were addressed earlier; and (2) a central bank's credibility may be impaired if the reports are perceived as biased. Central banks therefore typically hedge their assessments by noting possible warning signals and external and other risks faced by the system. Some FSRs include these warning signals only as "small print" in later parts of the report, while others have clear "red flags" in the overall assessment. As an example, Bowen, O'Brien, and Steigum, in their generally positive survey of the Norwegian FSR, note that the discussion of weaknesses in the financial system is sometime limited, and illustrate it by a moderate tone used when commenting on unfavorable developments in the insurance sector, which culminated in a government intervention in the fall of 2001.[18] Only in 2002 did the FSR recognize that the sector has gone through a turbulent period.

How Do Existing FSRs Compare to the Proposed Criteria?

How do the existing FSRs compare to the ideal characterized in Table 7? Ideally, a full assessment should be done by independent experts, such as has been done in Sweden and Norway.[19] In the absence of such a panel of experts, an assessment was carried out by the author of this chapter, using the proposed CCC framework.[20]

As summarized in Table 7, the framework comprises 26 principles, organized into 5 key elements (aims, overall assessment, issues, tools, structure and other features) and 3 characteristics (clarity, consistency, and coverage). Each FSR was assessed against each of the criteria, on a 4-point scale: 4 (fully compliant), 3 (largely compliant), 2 (partly compliant), and 1 (not compliant).[21] Simple (unweighted) averages were used to arrive at the aggregate gradings.[22]

The result of the analysis (Figure 3) is that most FSRs have an overall grading in the 2–3 range, and only three are in the 3–4 range, suggesting that there are areas for improvement in most existing FSRs. Areas for particular improvement include the specification and clarity of aims of the reports, and the clarity of the overall assessment. Also, for those reports that have been published for a longer period of time, consistency across the reports remains an issue. More specifically, the following are the main gaps in the existing FSRs:[23]

- **More standardized "core."** Many central banks should consider making the core section of their FSR more standardized across the years. In each main subsection, changes relative to the assessment in the previous FSR could be highlighted.

- **Aims.** Some FSRs do not contain even a very broad definition of aims. Of those that do, many could make the aims more specific, in particular to include the aim to help provide information to be used as one of the inputs into market participants' risk assessment procedures, and also the aim to serve as an accountability instrument.

- **Operational definition of financial stability.** Central banks often include a definition of financial stability, but they do so only in very general terms.

- **Underlying data.** FSRs mostly use charts to illustrate the points made in the text. While these are often eye-catching, it makes FSRs much more useful to users if tables with the key underlying data are also made available. These can be included as a separate attachment available on the website, as done, for example, in Sweden and New Zealand.

What factors can explain differences in the quality of FSRs, measured by their compliance with the CCC framework? To answer this question, a panel data regression was estimated for the available FSRs. The dependent variable was the overall grading of an FSR and the dependent variables were: (1) the length of time a central bank publishes an FSR; (2) level of economic development, approximated by GDP per capita; (3) the importance of the financial system in the economy, approximated by financial sector assets to GDP; and (4) a dummy variable taking on a value of one if the publishing central bank carries out banking supervision, and a value of zero otherwise.

Figure 3. How Do Existing FSRs Compare to the CCC Criteria? [1]

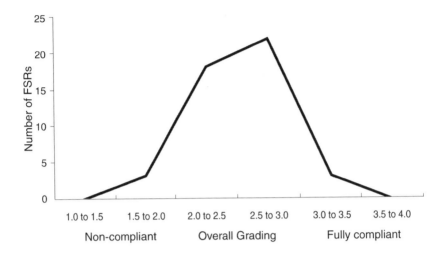

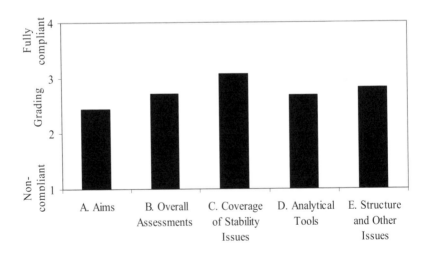

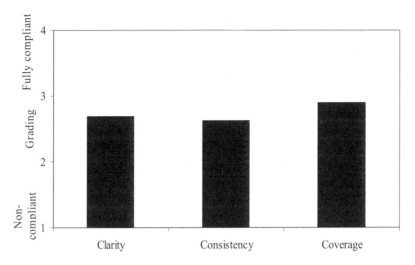

[1] FSRs published in 2005. Each of the principles in Table 7 was given the same weight for simplicity.

The calculations suggest that gradings of FSRs issued by the same central bank improve with time. As the coverage of the FSR increases, more sophisticated tools are used, and the central bank gains more experience with analyzing financial stability and presenting the results in a public document. Gradings are also positively correlated with economic development, approximated by GDP per capita, which may be a proxy for factors such as relative amount of resources available for the analysis of financial stability or the availability of market-based information. The sign for the size of the financial system is positive, but the estimate is not statistically significant. Interestingly, gradings are on average higher for central banks not directly involved in day-to-day supervision, partly reflecting the fact that the overall assessments in these reports are more candid. [24]

Conclusions

This chapter surveyed the stability reports published by central banks. It noted that there is a growing trend to publish such reports, and that the sophistication of the reports—especially the issues covered and tools used—has been on the rise.

Based on the survey of the available FSRs and a comparison with the proposed benchmarks, it can be concluded that FSRs provide useful insights into how central banks analyze financial stability. But there are areas for improvement. These include clarifying the aims of the reports, providing an operational definition of financial sector soundness, clarifying the core analysis that is presented in FSRs consistently across time, and making available the underlying data.

The survey also suggests that the clarity, consistency, and coverage of an FSR improves with time. Quality is also positively correlated with the level of economic development. The size of the financial system has a positive, but insignificant impact. Quality is higher for central banks not directly involved in day-to-day supervision.

Table 7. Proposed "CCC" Framework for Assessing Financial Stability Reports

	Clarity	Consistency	Coverage /Contents
A. Aims	A1. The definition of financial stability should be clearly indicated. A2. The aims of the report should be clearly indicated.	A3. The definition of financial stability should be a standard part of the report, presented consistently across reports. A4. The statement of aims should be a standard part of the report, presented consistently across reports.	A5. The definition of financial stability should cover both the absence of crisis and resilience to crises. Financial stability should be defined both in general terms and in operational terms. A6. The aims of the report should be comprehensive.
B. Overall assessment	B1. The overall assessment should be presented clearly and in candid terms.	B2. The overall assessment should be linked to the remainder of	B4. The overall assessment should cover the key topics.

	Clarity	Consistency	Coverage /Contents
		the FSR. B3. There should be a clear link between the overall assessments over time, making it clear where the main changes took place.	
C. Issues	C1. The report should clearly identify the main macro-relevant stability issues.	C2. The coverage of issues should be consistent across the reports.	C3. The coverage of the financial system should be sufficiently comprehensive.
D. Data, Assumptions, and Tools	D1. It should be clear what data are used to arrive at the results presented in the report. D2. It should be clear what assumptions are being used to arrive at the results presented in the report. D3. It should be clear what methodological tools are being used to arrive at the results presented in the report.	D4. The results should be presented in a consistent manner across the reports.	D5. The report should use available data, including those on individual institutions. D6. The report should use the available tools.
E. Structure and other features	E1. The structure of the report should be easy to follow. E2. Other features of the report—such as its length, frequency, timing, public	E3. The structure of the report should be consistent across time to make it easier to follow for repeat users.	E5. The structure of the report should allow covering the key topics. E6. The other features of the report should be

	Clarity	Consistency	Coverage /Contents
	availability, and links to other central bank reports—should be designed to support its clarity.	E4. The other features of the report should be designed to support its consistency.	designed to support its coverage.

Note: All principles are assessed on a 4-point scale: 4 (fully compliant), 3 (largely compliant), 2 (partly compliant), and 1 (not compliant).

Notes

[1] *See, for example*, Andrew Crockett, "Why is Financial Stability a Goal of Public Policy?" in *Maintaining Financial Stability in a Global Economy, a Symposium* (Jackson Hole, Wyoming: Federal Reserve Bank of Kansas City, 1997) and C.A.E Goodhart, "A framework for assessing financial stability?" *Journal of Banking & Finance*, Vol. 30, No. 12 (2006), at 3415–22. As regards the costs, see Glenn Hoggarth, Glenn, Ricardo Reis, and Victoria Saporta, "Costs of Banking System Instability: Some Empirical Evidence," Bank of England Working Paper No. 144 (London: Bank of England, 2001) (suggesting that average output losses during banking crises amount to 15–20 percent of annual GDP). As regards the frequency, see Michael Bordo, Barry Eichengreen, Daniela Klingebiel, and Maria Soledad Martinez-Peria, "Is the crisis problem growing more severe?" *Economic Policy*, Vol. 32 (2001) at 51–82 (They point out there was only one banking crisis in 1945–70, but nineteen in 1971–2000. The frequency of financial crises appears to have declined in the 2000s, however.)

[2] Martin Čihák, "How Do Central Banks Write on Financial Stability?" IMF Working Paper No. 06/163 (Washington, D.C.: International Monetary Fund, 2006) [herineafter Cihak 2006].

[3] Table 2 contains a list of the FSRs surveyed in this chapter. The survey also involved publications by more than 100 other central banks to determine whether these documents or their parts satisfy the criteria for an FSR. The survey reviewed 157 central bank websites listed at http://www.bis.org/cbanks.htm (last visited December 31, 2005).

[4] Some central banks issue two publications on the risks and exposures in the financial sector: for example, the European Central Bank publishes its *Financial Stability Review* and a more narrowly focused report on banking sector stability in the European Union; the National Bank of Poland publishes the end-year *Financial Stability Rep*ort and the more narrowly focused mid-year *Financial Stability Review*. The analysis in this text focuses on the broader designed publication as the FSR.

[5] See, for example, Counterparty Risk Management Policy Group, "Towards Greater Financial Stability: A Private Sector Perspective," July 27, 2005, available at www.crmpolicygroup.org. The authors of the report include private-sector practitioners from leading Wall Street houses. The report contains numerous recommended actions in three categories: (1) "actions that

individual institutions can and should take on their own initiative"; (2) "actions which can be taken only by institutions collectively in collaboration with industry trade groups"; and (3) actions which require complementary and/or co-operative actions by the official sector." (p.11)

[6] In 2005 the Bundesbank moved to stand-alone FSRs.

[7] See the list of the identified FSRs in Table 2. In some countries, e.g., Norway and the United Kingdom, a report similar to an FSR is published also by a supervisory agency. In the Euro area, FSRs are published both by the European Central Bank and many of the member central banks.

[8] Given the lack of consistent information on internal FSRs, this survey focuses on the publicly available ones.

[9] For an overview of institutional frameworks for financial stability analysis in a number of countries, see Juliette Healey, "Financial Instability and the Central Bank—International Evidence," in R. A. Brealey et al., eds., *Financial Instability and Central Banks—A Global Perspective*, Centre for Central Bank Studies (London: Bank of England, 2001); Sander Oosterloo and Jacob de Haan, "A Survey of Institutional Frameworks for Financial Stability," *Occasional Studies*, Vol. 1, No. 4 (Amsterdam: De Nederlandsche Bank, 2003).

[10] *See* Healey, *supra* note 9.

[11] As explained in more detail in Čihák 2006, the approach is based on the work of Fracasso, Genberg, and Wyplosz, who surveyed inflation reports by 19 inflation-targeting central banks. Their study assessed the quality of the inflation reports by using the following criteria: clarity, consistency, and coverage of key issues (policy objectives, decision making, analytical framework, input data, presentation of forecasts, and evaluation of past forecasts and policy). The study found a positive link between report quality and policy predictability. *See* Andrea Fracasso, Hans Genberg, and Charles Wyplosz, "How do Central Banks Write? An Evaluation of Inflation Targeting Central Banks," CEPR/Geneva Reports on the World Economy Special Report 2 (London: Centre for Economic Policy Research, 2003).

[12] For a theoretical discussion of the concept of financial stability, see Garry Schinasi, *Safeguarding of Financial Stability: Theory and Practice* (Washington, D. C.: International Monetary Fund, 2006).

[13] The fact that a broader definition of instability is correlated with longer stability reports may seem paradoxical at first, but becomes obvious on a closer observation. It is mostly because the FSRs, despite their name, are really reports about potential risks to stability rather than about stability itself.

[14] *See* Alex Bowen, Mark O'Brien, and Erling Steigum, "Norges Bank's Financial Stability Report: A Review" (Oslo: Norges Bank, 2003).

[15] *See* Franklin Allen, Lennart Francke, and Mark Swinburne, "Assessment of the Riksbank's Work on Financial Stability Issues" (Stockholm: Sveriges Riksbank, 2004).

[16] *See supra* note 14

[17] *See supra* note 15.

[18] *See* supra note 14.

[19] *See* Allen, Francke, and Swinburne, *supra* note 15; and Bowen, O'Brien, and Steigum, *supra* note 14.

[20] Carrying out full-fledged assessments under the CCC framework requires good knowledge of the financial systems being covered. Given this author's lack of country-specific expertise (in most cases), the assessment presented here focused on clarity and consistency of the FSRs; it did not examine in detail the principles relating to coverage that would require underlying analysis of the financial system (in particular, principles B4 and C3, requiring an FSR to cover the key topics in a sufficiently comprehensive way) and of the available data (principle D5).

The lack of detailed country-specific knowledge was to some extent compensated by the sheer volume of FSRs being reviewed. As part of this project, about 160 documents from 47 countries have been reviewed, comprising more than 10,000 pages.

[21] The principles relating to consistency across reports were assessed only for those central banks where three or more issues of the FSR are available.

[22] Not all the principles are likely to carry the same weight in practice. However, it is difficult to attribute *a priori* weights in a transparent manner.

As more data become available, it might be possible to "back-test" the assumption of equal weights and see if better results (e.g., in terms of a correlation between the aggregate grading and a measure of financial sector stability) can be achieved for different combinations of weights.

[23] This list of areas for possible improvement focuses on the issues discussed above. The survey also results in suggestions for improvement in analytical tools, discussed in Čihák 2006.

[24] The underlying results are available from the author upon request. Ideally, one would also like to know whether the quality of an FSR is related to the inputs into the financial sector work (in terms of resources). However, good data on the inputs are unavailable. Partial data on some of the FSR-publishing central banks suggest that the combination of GDP per capita and the relative size of the financial sector (which are both included in the regression) might be used to approximate the inputs going into the financial stability report.

IV. RATIONALE FOR REGULATION OF DERIVATIVES AND HEDGE FUNDS

8

Reassessing the Rationale and Practice of Bank Regulation and Supervision after Basel II

JAMES R. BARTH, GERARD CAPRIO, JR., AND ROSS LEVINE

In recent decades, countries around the world have liberalized the interest rate and portfolio restrictions that had been adopted during the Great Depression and immediately following World War II, and moved instead to rely more on a system of prudential regulation and supervision. Gradually, however, bank supervision has grown more intrusive and discretionary. In the United States, hardly a bastion of a socialist approach to government intervention, about two dozen supervisors report to work daily in their offices—at Citibank. And surveys of bankers recently reveal that the cost of regulatory compliance for the first time is their most important concern.

Capital requirements and powerful supervisors have replaced reserve requirements and interest rate controls as the tools of choice for promoting safe and sound banking. Basel II, the 2006 revision of the Basel Core Principles on Banking Supervision (BCP), significantly reinforced this trend. The unfortunate effect of Basel II will be to make capital requirements more complex and bank supervision even more intrusive. Indeed, supervisors will be validating and constraining banks' modeling of risks and, to the extent that one takes Basel II's pillar 2 seriously, imposing capital requirements for individual banks above and beyond that suggested by mere formulae.

The danger that arises from Basel II is that supervisors (whether in central banks or not) might not be able to do this job well, and will in the process become more exposed to political forces and possible corruption, in particular in countries where the degree of their discretionary powers is high and transparency is low. A political backlash might then ensue, especially in countries that significantly boost the resources for bank supervision to implement Basel II, resulting in sharp limits on supervisory independence. Central banks housing the supervisory function might then find that their independence to conduct monetary policy is impaired as well.

There is still time, however, to reassess the rationale and practice of bank regulation and supervision. To do so, we can now rely on a worldwide database on banking regulation, compiled and analyzed by the authors of this chapter, to evaluate what actually works. Using this database, which is described in some detail in the next section, it is possible to examine whether the threat from Basel II is one that merits serious consideration.

Drawing on the database and its subsequent analysis, this chapter summarizes the evidence in regard to what works best in bank regulation. The major findings are that (1) there is no robust evidence that stricter capital requirements help in securing better outcomes in the banking sector, and (2) stronger supervisory powers lead to worse outcomes except in the very best institutional settings.

The two pillars of Basel II that have received the most attention—more complex capital requirements and increased supervision—at best do not hurt a banking system, and at worst might do some harm or distract officials' attention from more important areas of focus. But on a more positive note, there is considerable evidence from the World Bank database that market discipline, the third and much-neglected pillar of Basel II, can be effective in improving the banking system, and that incentives matter in ensuring the safety and soundness of banking.

Accordingly, this chapter proposes a model in which supervision supports market monitoring, rather than supplanting it. Moreover, there are important interactions between the political and institutional variables that have an impact on supervision, with more open and transparent systems providing superior performance. There is, therefore, a need for disclosure of supervision and supervisory actions as much as possible, with less supervisory discretion. At present, the BCP focus exclusively on the information that must be disclosed to the supervisor. And in the more sophisticated variants of Basel II, bank supervisors are to become experts in risk modeling, which demands far higher mathematical skills than most supervisors hitherto have demonstrated.

Rather than focusing almost exclusively on training bank supervisors to have state-of-the-art risk management skills (for Basel pillar 1) and using discretionary powers to shape bank behavior (pillar 2), substantially greater emphasis should be placed on disclosing information to the public, providing private investors with the incentives to use this information to monitor banks, and developing the legal mechanisms that permit private investors to exert sound governance over banks after monitoring them. The role of supervisors should then be to verify the accuracy of this information, punish those providing faulty or misleading disclosures, and assist in the intervention and potential closure of banks according to the information revealed by the market. In other words, the key components of bank regulation, according to the empirical findings of the database, are disclosure, incentives for market discipline, supervisory verification and support of the market, and diversification requirements.[1]

The greatest danger for supervision (and for central banks that have a role in it) is that it will follow an unworkable model, despite evidence to the contrary, because this apparently is the model that supervisory groups prefer, notwithstanding the lack of supporting empirical evidence. Most supervisory agencies will never have sufficient human capital or budgets to implement Basel II successfully, especially as the increased demand for scarce risk-management skills increases the premium on these skills, and the push for more resources for supervision (which we expect in some cases is a consideration behind the popularity of Basel II) could have the reverse effect of increasing political interest in revisiting and weakening supervisory agencies' charters. And most countries do not have the institutional framework in which granting greater discretion to supervisors will produce benign results. Although attempting to improve certain factors—the strength of democratic institutions, the independence and skills of the media, and the degree of transparency—is warranted, there are few experts in institutional reform, and it is likely that the process will take some time. In the meantime, central banks and other supervisory agencies that abuse the trust that society instills in them risk a loss of power and independence. Thus central banks with supervisory powers (as well as other supervisory agencies) should move to adopt a model of banking supervision that is workable, and hence will not only provide benefits to the economy at large but to the agencies themselves.

Bank Supervision: What the Data Say

Those interested in central bank governance need to take into account all the functions that central banks perform, not just their monetary policy functions. Yet the literature on central bank independence reads as if central banks *only* conduct monetary.[2] As seen in Table 1, however, the majority of central banks also serve as either the sole supervisor or as one of several supervisory agencies. Bank supervision therefore needs to be taken into account, at least for about 90 countries, when recommendations are made on how central banks should be governed.

This section looks first at how countries should supervise their banking systems. It then makes recommendations as to how the supervisory agency in their central bank should be governed. Employing the sensible approach of James Madison, the fourth president of the United States, the strategy is that "you must first enable the government to control the governed; and in the next place oblige it to control itself."[3] Hence it is first necessary to look at what is the best way to supervise banks, and then discuss the controls on the supervisors.

Table 1. Countries with the Central Bank as a Supervisory Authority

	Central Bank only (69 countries)	Central Bank Among Multiple Supervisors (21 countries)	Central Bank Not a Supervisory Authority (61 countries)
Africa (33 countries),	Botswana, Guinea, South Africa, Burundi, Lesotho, Sudan,Egypt, Libya, Swaziland, Gambia, Namibia,Tunisia, Ghana, Rwanda, Zimbabwe	Morocco, Nigeria	Algeria, Congo, Madagascar, Benin, Côte d'Ivoire, Mali, Burkina Faso, Equatorial Guinea, Niger, Cameroon, Gabon, Senegal, Central African Republic, Guinea Bissau, Togo, Chad, Kenya
Americas (21 countries)	Argentina, Guyana, Trinidad and Tobago, Brazil, Suriname, Uruguay	United States	Bolivia, Ecuador, Nicaragua, Canada, El Salvador, Paraguay, Chile, Guatemala, Peru, Colombia, Honduras, Venezuela, Costa Rica, Mexico
Asia/Pacific (31 countries)	Bhutan, Kyrgyzstan, Samoa, Cambodia, Malaysia, Saudi Arabia, Fiji, New Zealand, Singapore, Hong Kong, China, Pakistan, Sri Lanka, India, Papua New Guinea, Tajikistan, Israel, Philippines, Tonga, Jordan, Qatar, Turkmenistan, Kuwait, Russia, United Arab Emirates	China, Thailand, Taiwan, China	Australia, Korea, Lebanon, Japan
Europe (39 countries)	Armenia, Ireland, Romania, Azerbaijan, Italy, Serbia and Montenegro, Belarus, Lithuania, Slovenia, Bulgaria, Moldova, Spain, Croatia, Netherlands, Ukraine, Greece, Portugal	Albania, Macedonia, Czech Republic, Slovakia, Germany	Austria, France, Poland, Belgium, Hungary, Sweden, Bosnia and Herzegovina, Iceland, Switzerland, Denmark, Latvia, Turkey, Estonia, Luxembourg, United Kingdom, Finland, Norway,
Offshore Centers (26 countries)	Aruba, Macau, China, Oman, Bahrain, Mauritius, Seychelles, Belize	Anguilla, Montserrat, Antigua and Barbuda, Saint Kitts and Nevis, Commonwealth of Dominica, Saint Lucia, Cyprus, Saint Vincent and The Grenadines, Grenada, Vanuatu	British Virgin Islands, Isle of Man, Malta, Gibraltar, Jersey, Panama, Guernsey, Liechtenstein, Puerto Rico

Source: Barth, Caprio, and Levine, 2006

Until recently, authorities interested in improving their supervisory or regulatory framework could only rely on the opinions and theoretical positions of international experts—what used to be called "armchair empiricism." To be sure, expert opinion can be valuable, but that expertise is derived almost entirely from the experiences of advanced countries, and the supervisory approach that those experts recommend—let us call it the Basel approach—represents a system that has been agreed upon with little or no empirical evidence. The Basel approach places a significant amount of emphasis on official supervision and on capital regulation, neither of which played much of a role when these advanced countries were in their industrialization stage. Countries attempting to adhere to the advanced parts of Basel II will need to step up substantially the resources devoted to bank supervision and embark on a difficult path of obtaining and keeping scarce risk-management skills in the supervisory agency, again not a choice that has been made in the past by a country in its high-growth phase.

Developing countries, either explicitly or implicitly, are being encouraged to follow in the recent footsteps of their rich country counterparts. This is a fine path to follow, even if difficult to do, *if it will lead to stronger financial systems*. However, it is important to ask whether this is the best path for a developing country. Even better, it would be useful not just to ask if this is a good thing, and not just rely on expert opinion, but instead to use actual data to try and describe what has been working around the world in the area of banking supervision. Measurement of the results of supervision is key. As Lord Kelvin put it:

> When you can measure what you are speaking about, and express it in numbers, you know something about it; but when you cannot measure it, when you cannot express it in numbers, your knowledge is of a meager and unsatisfactory kind: it may be the beginning of knowledge, but you have scarcely, in your thoughts, advanced to the state of science. ... If you cannot measure it, you cannot improve it.[4]

More than ten years ago the authors began assembling the first cross-country database on commercial bank regulation and supervision. Based on guidance from bank supervisors, financial economists, and our own experiences, we began putting together an extensive survey of bank regulation and supervision. The original survey, Survey I, had 117 country respondents between 1998 and 2000. The first update in

2003, Survey II, characterized the regulatory situation at the end of 2002, and had 152 respondents. Survey III was made available in July 2007, with responses from 142 countries. Survey III is special because barring a postponement in Europe on par with that in the United States; it represents the last look at the world before many countries formally begin implementing Basel II, the revised Capital Accord.

The Survey of Bank Regulation and Supervision Around the World assembles and makes available a database to permit international comparisons of various features of the bank regulatory environment. Current and previous surveys and responses are on the World Bank website and the earlier surveys, responses, and indices are available on a CD containing the research of Barth, Caprio, and Levine (hereinafter BCL).[5] The initial survey in 1998–99 was composed of about 180 questions, and was substantially expanded to approximately 275 questions in 2002. Changes to the current survey were more limited, with many aimed at achieving greater clarity and precision, and others made in anticipation of Basel II. Although the most recent version has over 300 questions, much of the expansion was in the form of making explicit separate categories for responses or otherwise clarifying issues. Some of the entirely new questions in the latest survey explicitly or implicitly refer to Basel II, such as those enquiring as to the plans for the implementation of Basel II, and if so then the variant of the first pillar to be adopted. Similarly, some of the questions relating to capital, provisioning, and supervision have been modified to keep abreast of current thinking and emerging practice in these areas.

The latest survey continues to group the survey questions and responses into the same twelve sections as previously, namely,

- Entry into banking

- Ownership

- Capital

- Activities

- External auditing requirements

- Internal management/organizational requirements

- Liquidity and diversification requirements

- Depositor (savings) protection schemes

- Provisioning requirements

- Accounting/information disclosure requirements

- Discipline/problem institutions/exit, and

- Supervision.

Also, the majority of questions are structured to be in a yes/no format, or otherwise require a precise, often quantitative, response. Experience suggests that simple and precise questions increase the response rate and reduce the potential for misinterpretation.

The databases now enable us to assess what works and what does not in the area of bank supervision, as a result of the most recent update of the database and its analysis in BCL (2006). The argument and conclusions of this chapter are based on BCL (2006).

This database, now available for 152 countries, includes information on the powers permitted to banks; bank entry requirements; capital regulations; bank supervisory powers; deposit insurance; liquidity requirements; private monitoring, accounting practices, and disclosure requirements; external governance; and the structure of supervision. The database was created from extensive interviews with bank supervisors in order to understand the quality of a country's regulatory environment. In addition, questions related to the incentives of the various actors in the banking sector were included in the survey.

It is important to be clear that this database does not, and cannot, measure the effectiveness of supervision "on the ground." First, the database is based on a survey—it is not an attempt to rate the supervisory systems of different countries. Rather than an evaluation, the survey is composed of a long list of (about 300) highly detailed questions, many of which can be answered simply in the affirmative or the negative, regarding characteristics of the supervisory environment, and it was completed by national authorities in consultation with the authors of BCL.

Second, there is no good way to evaluate how supervision functions in reality. Evaluations of regulatory systems, such as the Basel Core Principles Assessment, usually done in the context of a World Bank-IMF Financial Sector Assessment (FSAP), are not always published, and may be subject to bias due to the political process through which they are cleared. For example, as of 2005, based on both the published and unpublished assessments, one of the highest scoring regions on the Basel Core Principles Assessment was Sub-Saharan Africa. This ranking is highly implausible, as that region is mostly composed of exceedingly poor countries whose financial reforms are relatively recent, and their supervisory agencies are generally starved of resources. It is likely therefore that this ranking is not without some political bias, and in fact Bank-Fund staff have suggested that certain industrial-country authorities have been sympathetic to the appeals of certain developing countries, such as those from their former colonies. Moreover, staffing these assessments is difficult, and environments that have more tropical diseases and other hazards generally do not get the best supervisors to check BCP compliance, making it easier to override their judgments at IMF headquarters.

There are many ways to use the BCL database. Supervisory authorities can use it to benchmark their systems, and researchers can use it to see what works regarding bank regulation. BCL adopted a specific methodology: rather than examine each of the many individual regulations, it compiled broad indices of bank supervision. For example, the index of bank supervisory powers includes a long list of the powers possessed by supervisors.[6] BCL compiled a variety of other indices related to allowable bank activities, bank entry requirements, capital regulation, prompt corrective action powers, the degree of private monitoring, and moral hazard, among others. Although these indices combine several individual survey questions, the advantages of this aggregation are important. First, it is econometrically impossible to include all the many individual variables at once in a regression. Second, at least in initial investigations with the database, it is more interesting to look for some "big picture" results before even attempting to delve into the details. Third, the current focus of many authorities is whether and how to adopt Basel II, and with these broader indices, BCL was able to test the performance of the proposed three pillars of Basel II.[7] Ultimately, this approach also allowed BCL to test broad views of supervision—the framework that is elaborated in the next section—and to reconsider how financial supervision might be viewed.

Using the database, BCL examined the impact of the regulatory regime on the development of the banking sector, its efficiency, its stability, the integrity of the lending process (basically, the degree of corruption in the banking sector), and the governance of the banking sector. Stated another way, rather than select one measure of what is meant by a "good" supervisory framework, BCL looked at a variety of measures.

Turning to the first measure of the effectiveness of the regulatory environment, BCL first regressed the development of the banking sector on a matrix of supervisory variables, as well as some exogenous control factors, and found a positive relationship between the regulations that boost private monitoring and banking development. This finding holds when controlling for the possibility that the level of banking development affects the enactment of bank regulations (reverse causality) and controlling for other regulations and national institutions. Regulations that forced reliable, comparable information disclosure and that gave markets the incentive to monitor banks were found to promote bank development.

BCL also redid this analysis after removing some outliers and still found highly significant results. Even more interesting, perhaps, is that when examining the relationship between bank development and supervision, BCL found precisely the opposite result: more supervisory powers were associated with less bank development, although in a multivariate framework, which is when accounting for other supervisory variables, the negative relationship fades. Unfortunately for proponents of strengthening supervision the "Basel way," there is no evidence of a positive link. Interestingly, Rafael La Porta and his colleagues reach a similar conclusion with respect to securities market regulation, namely that private monitoring supports securities market development, and official supervision does not help.[8]

However, there is some good news for this group: when BCL took account of a variety of variables that describe the level of development of democratic institutions—constraints on the executive, other checks and balances in government, and so on— it find some evidence, although not strong, that supervision can help with banking sector development. The bad news is that the level of development of institutions is only strong enough in a very few (about 10) of the most advanced countries to avoid doing much harm. The problem for many other countries is that democracy is poorly developed, or transparency is so limited, that supervisory powers can be used to reinforce the position of the ruling authorities or of wealthy groups, rather than to promote the safety and soundness of the financial system. For example, during the Suharto era in Indonesia, it would have been unlikely that even state-of-the-art supervisory powers would have allowed Bank Indonesia to enforce disciplinary actions against banks with connections to the Suharto family. The resignation last year of former Bank of Italy governor Antonio Fazio, in the wake of allegations of improper usage of supervisory powers to block foreign entry into the banking system and to assist a favored domestic banker, is a vivid demonstration that not all wealthy countries appear to meet this standard of institutional development. Had one particular bank CEO not been subject to wiretapping for other crimes, it is doubtful that there would have been any repercussions for the former governor.

As noted above, BCL investigated other measures for assessing the supervisory environment. Rather than review all of these results in detail, the findings are summarized as follows:

- First, as regards bank capital regulations, which in effect represent the first pillar of Basel, what stands out is the absence of any positive relationship between more stringent capital requirements and any of the variables here about which we care.[9]

- Second, supervisory power, a proxy for pillar 2, also displays an absence of any positive effect, and in some cases has a negative impact.

- Third, in sharp contrast, private monitoring, the third and much neglected pillar of Basel, appears due for a promotion to pillar 1 because it has a desirable effect on all of the variables except for bank stability.[10]

On the other hand, for those concerned about stability, what helps is reducing activity restrictions, reducing the moral hazard associated with deposit insurance, and increasing diversification requirements.

Still, the message from empirical research by BCL as to how to promote stability is to encourage banks to diversify their risks and to discourage or curtail deposit insurance, which tends to reduce the incentive of market participants to monitor banks. Also, activity restrictions on banks, which when present can lead to greater concentration in fewer lines of business, reduce the stability of the banking system. This is an important message: The advanced features of risk management in Basel II were not necessary to have spared developing countries from the losses of more than a trillion dollar in the last two decades of banking crises. Rather, the culprits were easy to see: excessive concentrations of risk and highly skewed incentive systems, which in some cases accommodated outright looting of the banking system. All of these dire signs were visible without sophisticated risk-management tools, yet many did not want to see them, which raise a problem that any supervisory system needs to address—namely, human weakness. Greater transparency, so that as many eyes will be able to see a problem as possible, might at least contribute to earlier recognition of problems and perhaps to less costly resolutions of those problems.

The strength of the BCL study is that it uses different cross-country, bank-level, and firm-level datasets and employs different econometric techniques, each of which may have different drawbacks but when taken together provide the same basic message: bank regulations and supervisory practices that force banks to disclose accurate information to the public tend to (1) boost the development of the banking system as measured by private credit relative to GDP; (2) increase the efficiency of intermediation as measured by lower interest margins and bank overhead costs; and (3) reduce corruption in bank lending as measured by survey information from firms around the world.[11] These results are not just statistically significant but matter economically as well. For example, Beck, Demirguc-Kunt, and Levine (2006) estimate that the probability that a firm reports bank corruption as a major obstacle to firm growth would decrease by over half if a country moved from the 25th percentile to the 75th percentile when measuring the degree to which regulations force information disclosure and foster private-sector monitoring. Furthermore, rules on information disclosure have an especially strong effect on reducing corruption in lending in countries with well-functioning legal institutions. Thus, private investors need both information and legal tools to exert sound governance over banks, as well as incentives. If Mexico changed its very generous deposit insurance to the sample average, the improvement of incentives would have led to a lower probability of suffering a systemic crisis by as much as 12 percentage points.[12]

As summarized in BCL, the bulk of "hands on" or interventionist government policies lowers bank development, encourages less-efficient banks, exacerbates corruption in bank lending, and intensifies banking system fragility. Specifically, countries that grant their official supervisors greater disciplinary powers have lower levels of bank development and greater corruption in lending. Governments that heavily regulate bank activities and restrict entry into banking have banks with higher interest rate margins and larger overhead costs.[13] Furthermore, countries with greater government ownership of the banking industry have less banking system development. And as noted, restricting banks from diversifying into non-lending activities and prohibiting banks from lending abroad increases banking system fragility.

One caveat to this research is that it is still in its infancy. Further probing of the database might reveal, for example, whether the absence of any impact of higher required capital ratios was due to a convergence in capital ratios and definitions of capital. Alternatively, it might just be demonstrating what the literature has acknowledged for some time, namely that increases in capital ratios above levels deemed optimal by banks might induce a deliberate increase in risk taking to show the same risk-adjusted return on capital, or other means of avoidance. Further refinements in the database are welcomed, and the World Bank commissioned the authors to provide an updating of the survey, which was completed in July 2007.

Interpretation and Implication for Central Banks

In recent years, following the high inflation of the 1970s and 1980s, it has become generally accepted that central banks should be independent agencies in order to allow them to perform better their key function of maintaining monetary and financial stability.[14] However, there has been less attention paid to the governance and independence of the supervisory function, whether it is housed in a central bank (as is still the case in a number of countries) or in a separate agency. Yet this latter issue is both important and timely, as supervision is in the process of changing significantly, and there is a serious threat, as well as an opportunity, on the horizon regarding the design of bank supervision.

Essentially, there are two opposing views of supervision and regulation. The first, often referred to as the public-interest view, dates back to Arthur C. Pigou[15] and is based on the reality of market failures, as well as on the assumption that governments have the incentive and the ability to correct these failures.[16] In sharp contrast, the private-interest school, usually associated with Stigler,[17] views regulation as a product determined by supply and demand. Although market failures are also assumed to exist, according to Stigler government officials will attempt to maximize their own welfare. Since the industry being regulated has a pronounced interest in the outcome, it is to be expected that industry members will attempt to influence officials. And as public officials often are motivated by a desire to retain their positions, and occasionally by the desire to enrich themselves personally, industry may well be successful in obtaining the kind of regulation that it wants.

Figure 1 provides a broader framework with which to analyze supervision. According to the public-interest view, supervision is relatively straightforward, a technical matter of getting the rules and procedures correct. Thus it is consistent in this view for developing and emerging markets to borrow best practice from advanced countries because only the rectangle labeled "regulators and supervisors" is of concern. In the private-interest view, regulation is much more complex, and what is outside this rectangle is of great importance, as suggested in the figure. At each level in the diagram, there is a principal-agent problem: just as banks have imperfect methods at their disposal to control clients, banks supervisors and regulators, the next level up in the diagram, face similar issues when trying to control banks. Regulators face information asymmetries, and their reward differs from that of the bank owners and managers. Politicians similarly face control issues in trying to influence government regulators.[18]

Figure 1. A Framework for Bank Regulation

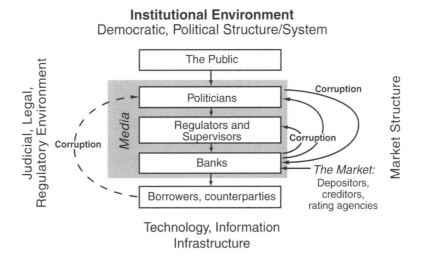

Perhaps the most difficult control problem is faced by the public, which would like to have both politicians and supervisors behave so as to maximize social welfare. But the public's control mechanism, periodic elections, is a highly imperfect tool. Much discussion of supervision takes for granted that its aim is to improve public welfare. Yet Figure 1 illustrates that other forces may be important. Beyond the series of agency problems (the straight lines with vertical arrows pointing down), the framework for bank regulation and supervision is further complicated by possible corruption, as powerful individuals try to influence the flow of society's savings (the upward-pointing arrows). Bankers may try to influence regulators and supervisors with offers of jobs or other emoluments. Perhaps even more commonly, banks may try to buy influence with politicians who in turn can affect the actions of regulators and supervisors.

John Wallis, in a study of corruption in U.S. history, refers to this channel as venal corruption, illustrated by the upward-curved arrows (in the figure) from banks to politicians and also to regulators and supervisors.[19] Perhaps more insidious is what he describes as systematic Corruption (with a capital C, and depicted by the downward-curved arrows), which is when politicians try to use their influence to maintain or augment their political position, such as by leaning on or conspiring with bankers to extend credit only to those supporting the ruling party and restricting entry to those who will play by these rules, as captured in the curved line pointing from politicians to banks. This type of corruption could evidence itself in a variety of forms, including government willingness to restrict entry into the banking system in return for favors from the existing bankers. An example is Porfirio Diaz, who came to power in Mexico in 1876 as the seventy-sixth ruler in just a 50-year period and was intent on staying in power. As described by Stephen Haber and Barth, Caprio, and Levine,[20] Diaz immediately shut off bank entry, limiting the number of banks to two at the national level and one at the state level. He then put family relations, important cabinet ministers, and state governors on the boards of the banks and turned the business of regulation over to them. These banks lent only to bank directors. Needless to say, the support for Diaz among his coterie was impressive, and when he requested, for instance, that a railroad be built so that his troops could move around the country more efficiently (and to help economic development in specific areas), these bank directors responded with alacrity.

Concern about systematic corruption pre-dates Polybius and Macchiavelli, the eighteenth century Whigs in Britain, and it was certainly a great preoccupation of the U.S. "Founding Fathers," including Alexander Hamilton and especially James Madison. Although many lines may complicate Figure 1, the crucial point is that it is potentially misleading to examine banking policies without considering the private interests of those setting and implementing policies in each country. Notwithstanding how well a given set of technical recommendations work in one country, it would be dangerous to presume that taking those recommendations—as respresented by the rectangle in the Figure labelled "Regulators and Supervisors"—and inserting them in another institutional environment will work equally well.

It is also critical to consider the institutional setting, as these institutions influence the degree to which the above forces become important or are held in check. Figure 1 frames the sequence of principal-agent relationships and political connections within an even broader institutional setting. For example, the presence and quality of checks and balances in government influence the degree to which politicians behave in a public- or private-interest manner. The power and independence of the judiciary as well as statutes shape the level of corruption, the extent to which rules and regulations are actually followed, and the ability of private market participants to exert corporate control over banks. An independent and active media can play a key role in monitoring corruption and investigating and publicizing wrongdoing in each of the relationships in the sequence of agency problems depicted in Figure 1—or as U.S. Supreme Court Justice Louis Brandeis put it, "Sunshine is the best disinfectant." Furthermore, the level of information technology affects the accuracy, speed, and flow of information about banks and borrowers, which can influence both official and private oversight of banks. This framework suggests that an array of factors influences how banking policies affect social welfare.

The private-interest view, including the importance of the broader institutional context, is consistent with the empirical results reported in the prior section. For example, although the public interest-view would predict that limits on bank activities or entry would have a positive impact, BCL found that when supervisors impose those limits to improve the safety and soundness of the banking sector, they had a negative impact on bank development and stability (activity restrictions) and efficiency (entry limits), as the private-interest view would argue. Similarly, the public-interest school would promote stronger supervisory powers so that supervisors could ensure a safer system. But as discussed above, strengthening supervision leads to less bank development, no improvement in stability, and significantly more corruption in the lending process (after holding constant the degree of economy-wide corruption).

Several implications follow. First, in considering whether supervision should be conducted by a central bank (or a separate supervisory agency) or how the supervisory function should be governed, one issue that is rarely addressed is how different this function is, compared with monetary policy, in terms of its impact on economies and societies. Monetary policy as conducted in most countries focuses on such economic aggregates as inflation, employment, and sometimes (though this is controversial) asset prices. Although there may be large groups that want low interest rates and others that benefit from high interest rates, and although at any one time there are individual winners and losers from specific monetary policy actions, the impact of these decisions are highly dispersed across society. More than at any time in history, there appears to be remarkable consensus around the world that societies benefit from relatively low inflation rates. In short, it is easy to believe that officials are acting in the public interest when they take monetary policy decisions and, accordingly, easy to believe that central banks should be independent. To be sure, in recent years more emphasis has been given to making monetary policy more transparent, but still the degree of transparency is relatively low.

In contrast to monetary policy, the effects of bank supervision are much more specific. Although supervisors can adopt actions or practices that have a systemic impact, the day-to-day business of a supervisor is bank-specific. Whereas pillar 1 of Basel II prescribes a complex, formulaic approach to determining minimum capital ratios, pillar 2 offers, or at least is described by Basel officials as offering, much discretion to supervisors.[21] Indeed, the fact that Basel II is so highly complicated essentially reduces the transparency of any supervisory activity. Perhaps the clearest contrast between monetary policy and bank supervision is that none of the authors of this paper can recall ever hearing about a monetary policy official who was bribed for taking a certain monetary policy action, whereas the occurrence of corruption in supervision is less infrequent, in particular in countries with a weak institutional setting. To be sure, regulators might respond to other rewards as well. For example,

Charles Calomiris reviews the regulatory record of the Greenspan Fed, and proposes an algorithm for Fed decision making in which

> [t]he Fed supports beneficial deregulation so long as doing so does not (1) stir up significant political opposition to the Fed within Congress or the Administration, which might threaten its monetary policy independence, (2) harm the large commercial banks (...who are key allies of the Fed in its political battles in Washington), or (3) undermine the Fed's competitive position vis-à-vis other regulators. Furthermore, these three constraints (opposition by politicians, opposition by big banks, and erosion of Fed regulatory power) may lead the Fed not only to fail to support beneficial deregulation, but to actively support harmful regulation, or in the case of antitrust regulation, to fail to enforce beneficial regulation (i.e., against undesirable anticompetitive mergers).[22]

The first implication of this discussion is that in order to increase the likelihood that bank supervision will lead to an improvement in a society's welfare, it is important that supervision be made as transparent as possible. Central banks that maintain a supervisory function, whatever the views on the optimal degree of transparency for monetary policy, should focus on this issue. The greater the discretion for supervisors, the greater the required degree of transparency and the more developed the institutional and incentive environment should be.

A second implication is that it is critical that the supervisory function be reconsidered. As seen above, empirical analysis finds no positive impact from stringent capital requirements or increased supervisory powers, but a significant payoff from improved market monitoring and better market-oriented incentives. These findings suggest a very different role for bank supervision—one that supports market monitoring by forcing banks to disclose material and lawful information, verifying the accuracy and timeliness of the information disclosed, and penalizing bankers for deliberately disclosing faulty or misleading information. This framework for supervision is much more amenable to greater transparency because it is easier for outsiders to understand. In other words, central banks that wish to preserve their independence in the sphere of monetary policy and still maintain their supervisory function should want to ensure, first, that the approach to supervision is effective in its various possible goals and, second, that the approach is as transparent as possible. The less transparent the approach to supervision, the more it will require oversight, including by other parts of government, with the risk being that monetary policy will also become involved. Also, intervention in the supervisory process by politicians is more attractive when there is less "sunshine." Central bankers who wish to reduce interventions in the monetary policy process should find it appealing to adopt this model. Another approach would be for central banks that still have responsibility for supervision to shed this function, though we presume that central bankers who attach great importance to the synergies between supervision and monetary policy would favor retaining this function but adopting an approach that would work, namely relying more on market discipline.

Unfortunately, there is a less optimistic finding that bears on this debate. What determines the supervisory choices that countries make? Do countries not pick the best supervisory framework due to ignorance, or due to other factors? BCL investigated the determinants of the choices that countries make on bank supervision and found that domestic political factors are overwhelmingly important. Countries with more open, competitive, and democratic political systems tended to choose an approach to bank supervision that puts more emphasis on private monitoring. These systems also tended to be more open to bank entry, to impose fewer restrictions on what banks can do, and to have fewer and smaller state-owned banks. Countries with closed political systems tended to choose a supervisory environment that would keep the banking system uncompetitive because it reinforces the government's own power.[23] In short, neither the opinions of experts nor empirical evidence might influence the decisions that countries make about bank supervision.

One implication of this last finding is that both the authors and readers of this chapter have less influence than they would like on what countries choose. A second implication is that much more research needs to focus on how governments make their supervisory choices and on what influences those choices. Certainly some might argue that with the increased availability of information about what other countries do, the greater ease (lower cost) of delivering experts or research results around the world, and the prominent role of international agencies and treaties (WTO) have caused international forces to become more important in affecting what countries do. However, research by the World Bank suggests that thus far many countries, though they have adopted "headline" regulations, such as the 8 percent minimum capital ratio, have done far less in implementing the underlying regulations that would make this effective—exactly what an approach that recognized the important role of politics would predict.[24]

Conclusions

The trend towards a heavier hand of government in the financial system began during the Great Depression and accelerated in the immediate postwar period, but it has been transformed since the late 1970s. Countries rely much less on direct controls on banks and more on official supervision. Basel II will greatly increase the role of government in the banking sector, which in effect will give technical "advice" to banks on the intricacies of capital (and risk) management and extensive discretion to supervisors. This chapter reviewed findings that this approach does not work but that one relying more on market discipline and incentives, with more of a supporting role for supervision, is preferable. Moreover, the chapter has argued that the governance of central banks should be determined by their functions, and that the governance requirements of supervision are significantly different from that for central banking, at least to the extent to which the Basel view of supervision is followed.

Basel II is an exceptionally complex proposal because it tries to replace market forces, which as Soviet planners discovered requires an ever-increasing level of detail and oversight. Even in the run-up to Basel II, a backlash against heavier regulation was already building. Surveys of bankers report the cost of regulation as a growing concern, and the United Kingdom has created a commission to review the regulatory reach of government in banking. Thus it is timely for central bankers to rethink their role in the sector, before it is too late. Implementing the Basel approach will be quite expensive—how else (if at all) to get highly quantitative skills into supervision—and is likely to increase opposition to supervision and to agencies that supply it. Central bankers should instruct the Basel Committee to go back to the drawing board. The foundation of a regulatory system that supports the development, efficiency, stability, integrity, and governance of the banking system is comprised of information and its disclosure, incentives for market discipline, supervisory verification and support of market monitoring, and diversification requirements. All central banks, regardless of their role with respect to supervision, should care about the regulation of the banking sector. But for central banks with supervisory responsibility, an approach to regulation that focuses on market monitoring and incentives with a supportive role for supervision will be more conducive to safeguarding the relatively high degree of independence that those central banks enjoy today, as well as to achieving better outcomes in banking.

Notes

[1] As noted below, the authors' research found that diversification requirements in banking are critical for most economies, since most financial systems are small and have a high degree of covariant risk. *See* James R. Barth, Gerard Caprio, Jr., and Ross Levine, *Rethinking Bank Regulation: Till Angels Govern* (New York and Cambridge: Cambridge University Press, 2006).

[2] *See, e.g.,* Alberto Alesina and Lawrence H. Summers, "Central Bank Independence and Macroeconomic Performance: Some Comparative Evidence," *Journal of Money, Credit and Banking*, Vol. 25, No. 2 (May 1993), at 151-162.

[3] The quote in its entirety, from *Federalist Papers*, Number 51: "If men were angels, no government would be necessary. If angels were to govern men, neither external nor internal controls would be necessary. In framing a government which is to be administered by men over men, the great difficulty lies in this: you must first enable the government to control the governed; and in the next place oblige it to control itself."

[4] From his *Popular Lectures and Addresses (1891-94)*, as quoted in *Bartlett's Familiar Quotations*.

[5] James R. Barth, Gerard Caprio, Jr., and Ross Levine, "The Regulation and Supervision of Banks around the World: A New Database," in Robert E. Litan and Richard Herring, eds., *Brooking-Wharton Papers on Financial Services* (Washington, DC: Brookings Institution, 2001), at 183-250; "Bank Supervision and Regulation: What Works Best?" *Journal of Financial Intermediation,* Vol. 13 (2004), at 205-248; *Rethinking Bank Regulation: Till Angels Govern* (New York and Cambridge: Cambridge University Press, 2006)[hereinafter BCL 2006]. The data are available on the web at http://econ.worldbank.org/WBSITE/EXTERNAL/EXTDEC/EXTRESEARC H/0,,contentMDK:20345037~pagePK:64214825~piPK:64214943~theSiteP K:469382,00.html.

[6] The questions in the survey include: Does the supervisory agency have the right to meet with external auditors to discuss their reports without the approval of the bank? Are auditors required by law to communicate directly to the supervisory agency any presumed involvement of bank directors or

senior managers in illicit activities, fraud, or insider abuse? Are off-balance sheet items disclosed to the supervisors? Can supervisors take legal action against external auditors for negligence; force a bank to change its internal organizational structure; order a bank's directors or management to constitute provisions to cover actual or potential losses; suspend the directors' decision to distribute dividends; suspend the directors' decision to distribute bonuses; and suspend the directors' decision to distribute management fees? It also asks who can legally declare—such that the declaration supersedes some of the rights of shareholders—that a bank is insolvent; and who has authority to intervene—that is, suspend some or all ownership rights—in a problem bank. Regarding bank restructuring and reorganization, can the supervisory agency or any other government agency supersede shareholder rights, remove or replace management, and remove and replace directors? See Barth Caprio, and Levine (2006), *supra* note 1, for more detail.

[7] Note that they do not test Basel II in practice, because it has not yet been implemented, but rather they test the effectiveness of capital regulation, supervisory powers, and market monitoring, which correspond with the three pillars of the proposed system.

[8] Rafael La Porta, Florencio Lopez-de-Silanes, and Andrei Shleifer, "What Works in Securities Laws?" *Journal of Finance*, Vol. 61 (2006), at 1–32.

[9] Note that the term "lending integrity" rather than corruption is used, so that a positive sign will be "good" and a negative sign "bad." This variable is based on a separate survey of borrowers who were asked about the extent to which they had to pay a bribe in order to get a bank loan.

[10] Some would say that they only care about the latter, but that view ignores the tendency for a financial system that does not promote development to become destabilized by a variety of special schemes that will be created in order to promote the excessive extension of credit—as occurred, for example, in the 1960s and 1970s in many low- and middle-income countries.

[11] For corroboration, see also Barth, Caprio, and Levine (2004), *supra* note 5; Asli Demirgüç-Kunt, Luc Laeven, and Ross Levine, "Regulations, Market Structure, Institutions, and the Cost of Financial Intermediation," *Journal of Money, Credit, and Banking*, Vol. 36 (2004), at 593-622; Thorsten Beck, Asli Demirgüç-Kunt, and Ross Levine, "Law, Endowments, and Finance," *Journal of Financial Economics*, Vol. 70 (2003), at 137-181; Beck, Demirguc-Kunt, and Levine (2005) for corroboration.

[12] James Barth, Gerard Caprio, and Ross Levine, "Bank Regulation and Supervision: What Works Best?," NBER Working Paper No. 9323, November 2002, and *Journal of Financial Intermediation* 13, (2004), at 205-48.

[13] *See*, for example, Demirgüç-Kunt, Laeven, and Levine, "Regulations, Market Structure, Institutions, and the Cost of Financial Intermediation," *supra* note 11. They compute that if Mexico had the same level of restrictions on bank activities as Korea, its interest rate margins would be a full percentage point lower.

[14] Alesina and Summers, "Central Bank Independence and Macroeconomic Performance," *supra* note 2; A. Posen, "Why Central Bank Independence Does Not Cause Low Inflation: There is No Institutional Fix for Politics," in R. O'Brien, ed., *Finance and the International Economy* (Oxford: Oxford University Press, 1993), at 40-65; K. Rogoff, "The Optimal Commitment to an Intermediate Monetary Target," *Quarterly Journal of Economics,* Vol. 100 (1985), at 1169-1189; C.E. Walsh, *Monetary Theory and Policy*, 2nd ed. (Cambridge, MA: MIT Press, 2003). .

[15] *See* Arthur C. Pigou, *The Economics of Welfare*, 4th Edition (London: Macmillan, 1938).

[16] *See* Barth, Caprio, and Levine (2006), *supra* note 5, for a more elaborate explanation.

[17] George Stigler, "The Theory of Economic Regulation," *Bell Journal of Economics and Management Science,* Vol. 2 (1971), at 3-21; and *The Citizen and the State: Essays on Regulation* (Chicago: University of Chicago Press, 1975).

[18] To be sure, one can argue that we should be thankful when they cannot directly influence regulators too easily.

[19] John Wallis, "The Concept of Systematic Corruption in American History," in Edward L. Glaeser and Claudia Goldin, eds., *Corruption and Reform: Lessons from America's History*, (Chicago: University of Chicago Press, 2006).

[20] Stephen Haber, "Political Institutions and Economic Development: Evidence from the Banking Systems of the United States and Mexico," mimeo, Stanford University, 2004; BCL 2006, *supra* note 5.

[21] Astoundingly, some members of the Basel Committee even described the purpose of pillar 2 as allowing supervisors to set the "optimal" capital ratios for individual banks.

[22] Charles W. Calomiris, "The Regulatory Record of the Greenspan Fed," mimeo (Washington, D.C.: American Enterprise Institute, 2006).

[23] See Barth, Caprio, and Levine (2006), chapter 5, for examples, with the clearest being from nineteenth century Mexico. The contrast between that example and the U.S. system in the same era is made by Haber et al. (2003).

[24] World Bank, *Finance for Growth: Policy Choices in a Volatile World*, World Bank Policy Research Report, (Washington D.C.: Oxford University Press, 2001).

9 | Derivatives Law in the United States: Who Regulates? What Is Regulated?

PHILIP MCBRIDE JOHNSON

Many attorneys practicing in the areas of securities, banking, and financial services encounter from time to time an issue that invokes federal derivatives laws and their principal administrator, the Commodity Futures Trading Commission (CFTC). Other attorneys work for or with companies that use the derivatives markets to manage their price risks. For these attorneys, a handbook of basic information is useful. This chapter has been prepared to meet that need.

The term *derivatives regulation* has effectively displaced the older reference to *commodities regulation*, mainly because of the rich variety of futures contracts, options, and other financial instruments that can be traded today. In addition to tangible assets like grain, gold, and oil, trading occurs in economic measurements of stock market performance, weather patterns, inflation rates, air quality, housing prices, natural catastrophes, and discrete events. While few of these phenomena would be considered "commodities" in any other context, they are treated as such for regulatory purposes.[1] As a result, the first rule for counsel who encounters this regime is: Make no assumptions that other legal disciplines will provide guidance.

This chapter describes the general structures of the trading vehicles that must comply with federal derivatives regulation, the various players who receive special regulatory attention and vetting, and the types of conduct that can raise criminal as well as civil exposures. It also describes the regulator and the parties that are subject to regulation. The chapter is meant to be an introduction; greater detail can be found in more specialized publications.[2]

What Is Regulated?

The principal legal authorities for derivatives regulation are the Commodity Exchange Act[3] (the CEAct) and the regulations of the Commodity Futures Trading Commission[4] (the CFTC). There is no meaningful regulation of the derivatives markets at the state or local levels, and the CFTC, with certain exceptions, acts as the sole and exclusive regulator of that activity at the federal level.

(In the case of (1) options directly on securities, (2) futures contracts on single securities or smaller stock indices, (3) options on foreign currencies if listed on a national securities exchange, and (4) the marketing of participations in collective investment vehicles using commodity futures or options, the federal securities laws can also apply but they are beyond the scope of this chapter.)

For a transaction to be regulated under the CEAct by the CFTC, it must involve both a statutory *commodity* and either a *futures contract* or an *option*. The latter two terms—referring to the structure of the trading instrument itself—are not defined in the CEAct or in the CFTC's regulations and, as a result, what is or is not a regulated trading instrument has been the subject of considerable litigation, with the courts acting as final arbiter.

Commodity Defined

The term *commodity* includes a long list of specific farm products (the markets began almost exclusively as agricultural venues), but section 1a(4) of the CEAct also sweeps in "all other goods and articles ... and all services, rights, and interests in which contracts for future delivery are presently or in the future dealt in."[5] As a result, *almost anything can be a commodity,* including mathematical calculations or measurements of phenomena, services and other intangibles or contingencies that would not fall within that term in any other real-life context.

Futures Contracts

The CEAct and CFTC regulations do not cover all forms of commodity transactions. Generally speaking, they do not apply to transactions involving the immediate transfer of title to an asset (often called "cash" or "spot" transactions) nor to transactions where transfer is simply deferred to a later date (known as forward contracts). Deferred transfers or forward contracts are most common among buyers and sellers that deal regularly in that commodity, such as grain merchants or government bond dealers.

However, the CEAct authorizes the CFTC to take enforcement action against any manipulation of the price of a commodity whatever the nature of the transaction by reason of sections 6(c)–(d) and 9(a) of the CEAct.[6] Such misconduct may also constitute a criminal felony under federal law.

While a futures contract has not been defined by the CEAct or the CFTC, it is generally understood to include any instrument by which (1) the price for a transaction is established immediately, (2) completion is set for a later date or time, and (3) some mechanism exists and is commonly used to substitute a cash payment in lieu of the physical conveyance of the commodity between the parties. To make it easy to convert, or "offset," the delivery mode into a cash settlement, most futures contracts (although not all) have standardized specifications and typically are available through a central market of some sort. However, a trading instrument allowing conversion into a cash-settled form may be a future contract even when offered by a single merchant if there is a mechanism, such as a standing offer by the merchant to buy back the contract either at any time or on some timed basis.

Unlike a genuine sale and transfer of an asset, a futures contract is simply an agreement to perform at a later date. Hence, neither party owns anything at the outset and, as a result, does not owe anything either. Gain or loss will occur solely on the basis of price movements in the futures market during the holding period. To illustrate, if the buyer (called a "long" in the trade) and the seller (a "short") of the futures contract agree to a purchase price of US$ 10, neither will gain nor lose money if the market value remains at that level. However, the buyer/long will gain if the value of the commodity increases above US$ 10 (because the commodity's true value has risen above what the buyer is obliged to pay) while the seller/short will gain if the value of the commodity falls below the agreed price (because the seller can acquire the commodity for less than the buyer has agreed to pay).

The economic behavior of a futures contract tends to be of the equal-and-opposite type. That is, one party's gain tends to be equal or comparable to the other party's loss. Because both parties take on similar market risk (albeit in opposite directions), there is seldom any fee or consideration paid between them upon entering the arrangement.[7] Moreover, because possession of a futures contract does not convey any ownership interest in the commodity (that to occur later absent cash settlement), there is no immediate payment between the parties based upon the commodity's starting value. As in the illustration above, if the commodity was worth US$ 10 at initiation of the futures transaction, neither party is entitled immediately to receive or obliged immediately to pay that US$ 10 and, therefore, no part of the purchase price is exchanged at inception.

However, both parties are at market risk and are responsible for changes in the value of the commodity during the life of the futures contract. To address this risk, most futures markets require the deposit by both parties of a specific sum of money to act as collateral for any daily losses they suffer. Called *margin*, these deposits are compared each day with those gains and losses; where one party's holdings have gained in value, the deposit may be reduced proportionately and where a party's holdings have sustained losses, the deposit may be increased proportionately. In every case, the objective is to assure that the accounts always have more money on deposit than is owed at that time.[8]

Options

While futures contracts generally create equal but opposite obligations between the parties, exposing each to an equivalent level of market risk (albeit in different directions), an option imposes far greater burdens on the seller (a "writer" in the trade) than on the buyer (the "holder"). The option seller/writer must stand ready and willing to complete the transaction during the entire life of the option,[9] whereas the buyer/holder can simply abandon the transaction if it would not be profitable to complete it (to "exercise" the option).

Unremarkably, the writer demands compensation for the added risk, in an amount that is negotiated with the buyer and acts as a sort of stand-by commitment fee (called a "premium").

Options can be acquired that profit from rising value (a "call" option) or from declining value (a "put" option). A call option behaves like a long futures contract in that it rewards the holder in rising markets (though it does not carry a corresponding downside risk), while a put option rewards the holder in falling markets (but, again, does not bear a corresponding upside risk).

Whether an option becomes profitable depends on not only changes in its value but also the cost of the premium. To illustrate, if a writer makes a commitment to complete the transaction at US$ 10 on or before a certain date if the holder so requests, the holder may exercise the option if it achieves a profit greater than US$ 10 plus the cost of the premium already paid to the writer (e.g., in the case of a call option, a price increase to US$13, minus a US$2 premium = US$1 profit). The writer remains exposed to this market risk no matter how high the price goes, while the holder may simply walk away if exercise would not be profitable.

Like futures contracts, options are versatile in that they can offer profit when prices are falling as well as rising. In the illustration above, a call option was used. In a put option, the holder has the right to sell the commodity to the writer for a certain sum even if the value of the commodity has fallen below that level. The writer, as before, must stand ready to pay the agreed amount (and to incur a loss) upon the holder's demand no matter how low the price declines. That commitment also carries a premium that the holder negotiates with the writer, and the economics are the same (but in reverse) as described above.

While holders of options normally have unlimited potential profit with relatively limited loss (the premium), options can be designed to replicate the two-way behavior of a futures contract. A party that has acquired a right to buy something at US$10 (the holder of a call option) but has written an option to sell that same thing at US$10 (the writer of a put option) will experience the same effects as if it possessed a long futures contract in that gains will occur if prices rise and equivalent losses will occur if prices fall. To replicate a short futures contract, the party would acquire a put option and write a call option.

The CEAct and CFTC regulations do not apply directly to options on any security or on a foreign currency but, in the latter case, only if it is listed for trading on a market that has been registered with the Securities and Exchange Commission as a national securities exchange.

Other Derivatives

There are two other principal forms of derivatives that, as a rule, are not offered by a CFTC-regulated exchange: *swaps* and *hybrid instruments*.

Swaps have essentially the same economic attributes as futures contracts, generating gain for one party and loss for the other party in generally corresponding amounts depending on price movements. Like futures, they are typically settled through cash payments between the parties. Swaps originated in the banking community where lenders with large portfolios of fixed-rate loans but wishing to have more adjustable-rate loan exposure on their books would hypothetically "swap" some of their fixed-rate loans with another financial institution in exchange for some of the latter's variable-rate loans. The loans themselves were not transferred, but each operated as if that had occurred and, at intervals, would calculate whether its adapted portfolio had made or lost money as compared with the other lender's experience, and the net difference would be paid by the loser.

Swaps have now spread into nearly all industries; crude oil swaps, for example, proliferate during periods of energy price volatility. To illustrate, in a crude-oil swap one party would agree to pay at stated intervals a fixed amount per barrel (e.g., US$ 50) while the counterparty agrees to pay the actual market value of a barrel of oil on the reconciliation date. The first party receives a net amount if the price has risen above the fixed level, while the counterparty gets a net payment if the fixed price exceeds current market levels.

Swaps tend to arise from private transactions rather than exchange trading. While at one time the CFTC considered whether to regulate them as futures contracts, the law now allows a wide spectrum of entities to employ swaps without fear of CFTC repercussions.

Hybrid instruments are equity or debt securities whose value is affected by some external factor. To illustrate, there exist a wide array of exchange-traded funds where the pay-out to investors may be affected by changes in the value of a portfolio of securities, the price of a commodity, or the severity of a natural disaster. Because these instruments may be said to contain an imbedded futures contract or option, the CFTC took an interest in them in its early years (at the time, over-the-counter futures trading was illegal) and agreed not to challenge them only if the impact of indexation did not predominate over other influences on the price. More recent congressional action, however, has allowed hybrid securities without CFTC regulation even if they are 100 percent commodity-impacted. And unlike the swaps exclusion from CFTC jurisdiction, which pertains only within a select group of participants, hybrid instruments may be offered to the general public.

Who Regulates?

The Commodity Futures Trading Commission

In 1922 the U.S. Congress enacted legislation to regulate the nation's grain futures markets and assigned primary responsibility to the U.S. Department of Agriculture (USDA). In the ensuing years, other farm products were listed for trading on the exchanges, and the USDA supervisory role was expanded to reach that activity as well. By the 1970s, however, futures exchanges had moved beyond the agricultural sector to offer futures contracts on various foreign currencies, precious metals, and energy sources. Developmental work was also underway to trade futures contracts on debt instruments that were designed to track changes in interest rates.[10]

Recognizing that the USDA's expertise did not extend to these new products, Congress enacted legislation in 1974 creating the CFTC as an independent agency of the United States with five commissioners (one to serve also as chairman) appointed by the President and confirmed by the Senate.[11] As noted previously, its jurisdiction extends far beyond the farm sector to include nearly anything—tangible or intangible—that can be offered in the form of a futures contract or of a commodity option. With the exception of certain securities-related derivatives,[12] the CFTC's authority preempts all other federal, state, and local regulators, allowing for a unified and cost-efficient regime.

Although the regulation of the markets for futures and commodity options has been placed in the hands of an agency having no affiliation with the USDA, the CFTC retains a particular interest in farm products because the Commission is overseen in Congress principally by the House and Senate committees responsible for agricultural policy and which display a special concern for the integrity and efficiency of the farm futures markets. At the same time, the CFTC has close relations with other branches of the Government—the Securities and Exchange Commission, the Department of the Treasury, the Federal Reserve Board, for example— to consult on futures matters affecting their interests.

The CFTC's headquarters are in Washington, D.C., and it has major offices in New York City and Chicago. A smaller office exists in Kansas City, Missouri. Policy is set by the members of the CFTC, and all rules, regulations, and orders (other than in initial adjudicatory proceedings) issue from the same group. Its principal operating units are the Division of Market Oversight (DMO), the Division of Clearing and Intermediary Oversight (DCIO), and the Division of Enforcement (DOE). DMO oversees the exchanges' compliance with duties imposed by the CEAct and CFTC regulations, while the DCIO supervises the operations of clearinghouses and conformity by various registered intermediaries with their legal duties. The DOE conducts investigations and brings proceedings with respect to violations of the CEAct or CFTC regulations. At this writing the CFTC's annual budget is roughly US$ 112 million.

In addition, the CFTC administers an unusual reparations program allowing futures and options customers to make claims to the CFTC for damages against registrants. Hearings are conducted before officers or judges on the CFTC's staff and, if violations are found, an award for actual damages may be made in favor of the claimant.

The Regulated Markets

For many years, lawful futures trading was confined by the CEAct to federally regulated central exchanges known as *contract markets*, which were authorized to offer any form of futures contract (until recently, however, only with agency vetting and approval), to both the general public as well as to professional investors and commercial users. Copious regulations evolved to mandate the behavior of these contract markets and, while many of the prescriptive rules have been replaced by broader core principles,[13] the obligations remain for these exchanges to operate in a fair and orderly manner and to police their participants against trading abuses, market manipulations, and other forms of misconduct.

Today it is possible to trade futures contracts outside the facility of any organized exchange if it occurs between certain limited classes of defined participants dealing directly with each other. In addition, it is now possible to operate an exchange where trades can be matched randomly without contract market status if trading is limited to certain futures contracts and participation is confined as well to only specific groups of users. One such alternative is a *derivatives transaction execution facility* (DTEF), which must restrict its futures offerings to commodities having very little risk of being manipulated and which must confine participation to defined institutions and wealthy individuals or other traders utilizing very highly capitalized brokers. Another alternative style of exchange, where participation is even more restricted but the product qualifications are roughly the same as for DTEFs, is an *exempt board of trade*. Finally, an exchange can exist to trade commodities that are more vulnerable to price manipulation if it operates through an electronic trading facility and is open to participation only by persons that are commercially involved with the underlying commodity; it is known as an *exempt commercial market*.

Clearinghouses

Since the 1930s, every regulated futures market has employed the services of a clearinghouse to process daily transactions and, more important, to financially guarantee them once the matching process has been completed and verified. For many years these clearinghouses were either operating units within, or controlled affiliates of, the exchanges they served. The CFTC, which had no formal role in relation to the clearinghouses, nevertheless oversaw the clearinghouses as a part of its supervision of the affiliated exchanges themselves.

More recently, however, it has become permissible to create and to operate clearinghouses independent of control by any particular exchange. To accommodate the unaffiliated clearinghouses, Congress created a new registration system to qualify as a *derivatives clearing organization* (DCO).

To understand the primary function of a clearinghouse, which is substantially different from the services provided by "clearing agencies" in the securities markets, it is important to visualize the structure of credit protection in the futures markets. As noted earlier, buyers and sellers of futures contracts must deposit with their brokers margin funds to support their market positions, and this serves as the first line of credit support for the process. Their brokers, which may be full members of the clearinghouse or may be standing between the customer and such clearing members, have an obligation to provide funds if the customer defaults on its margin obligation. The same guarantee proceeds to the clearing member if the intermediating broker fails to pay and, in the unlikely failure of the clearing member, the coffers of the clearinghouse itself constitute the final recourse. To fund its role as last-resort obligor, the clearinghouse will often maintain reserves consisting of substantial cash, with assessment rights against all clearing members and possibly a layer of insurance coverage. As a result, transactions are supported successively by greater and greater capital resources, and every default to date has been satisfied in full through this mechanism.

Clearinghouses do not generally regulate the markets in the way that is expected of a CFTC-approved exchange. They tend to be operated as a financial services organization and leave to the futures markets the task of devising and enforcing trading and ethical standards. Most clearinghouse rules deal with the credit-guarantee function, including recourse in the event of defaults which is often swift and decisive.

Other Private Regulators

For many years, all self-regulation within the futures community was centralized within the exchanges, which generally allocated responsibility among themselves based on which firms belonged to what exchanges, and the oversight included both members' on-exchange activity and their other business dealings such as the operation of brokerage or advisory firms. Today, however, substantially all of the policing of the activity of industry professionals away from the exchanges is conducted by the National Futures Association (NFA), for which membership is mandatory. The NFA was organized under a special provision of the CEAct and, in addition to surveilling its members off-exchange conduct, the NFA administers the CFTC's registration (licensing) programs for various categories of its members.[14]

The Registrants

The principal focus of the CFTC's registration program is on the point of contact between customers and the various intermediaries offering them brokerage services, advice, or an opportunity to participate in certain collective investment vehicles using commodities.

Futures Commission Merchants

Registration is required of any natural or legal person that solicits or accepts orders from customers for futures activity and that, in addition, receives cash, securities, property, or other value to margin or guarantee the contemplated transactions. Such a futures commission merchants (FCM) performs what is broadly viewed as full brokerage services and must maintain substantial net capital, follow rigid recordkeeping duties, adhere to reporting requirements in relation to its customer accounts (including specific risk warnings), and be subject to audit by both the NFA and the CFTC. In addition, each FCM must maintain its customers' funds in accounts separate (segregated) from its own and must generally use such funds solely for the customers' benefit.

Commodity Trading Advisor

Registration is required for any natural or legal person that provides trading advice regarding futures on a CFTC-regulated exchange or involving commodity options to clients for profit or gain unless the advice is solely incidental to some other services being provided such as banking, brokerage, publishing, or news reporting. Registration is not required if the advice is given without regard for the client's particular circumstances, such as a conveying a general market view to multiple clients without linking it to those clients' specific strategies or positions. If such a commodity trading advisor (CTA) is given power of attorney to make unilateral trading decisions for a client, however, the regulatory demands become considerable. For example, the CTA is generally required to provide the client with extensive information regarding its background, prior trading performance, and other matters.

Commodity Pool Operator

Registration is required for any natural or legal person engaged in the business of operating a collective investment vehicle and which receives funds or other value from prospective participants for the purpose of trading futures contracts on a CFTC-regulated exchange. Note that it is the commodity pool operator (CPO), not the pool itself (each pool is generally required to be organized separate from the commodity pool operator), that must register and, having once done so, can operate as many commodity pools as it desires. There are a number of exemptions and exceptions that counsel can identify and utilize. Generally, the CPO must provide prospective participants with a disclosure document similar to a prospectus, make periodic reports on the commodity pool's performance, and maintain substantial records regarding its activities. Units of participation in a commodity pool may also be treated as securities, and therefore subject to registration and reporting requirements under the federal securities laws.

Floor Participants

Registration is also required of natural persons acting as *floor brokers* who execute customer orders on the trading floor of a CFTC-regulated exchange or as *floor traders* who engage on the trading floor solely in transactions for their own accounts. Floor brokers and floor traders have traditionally been either owners or lessees of exchange memberships granting them access to trading arena. As physical floor trading recedes as a business model and exchanges convert from membership organizations to open stock corporations, these categories may be effectively eliminated. Where floor brokers form partnerships or other collaborations, usually in order to share or allocate brokerage fees or operating costs among themselves, registration is required of the *broker association* as well, although the relevant exchange, not the CFTC, performs the registration function.

Other

Registration as an *agricultural trade option merchant* (ATOM) is required for natural or legal persons marketing options on farm products to commercial users. And (although none are believed to exist today) a merchant offering bulk precious metals on a leveraged basis must register as a *leverage transaction merchant* LTM).

Introducing Brokers

Registration as an *introducing broker* (IB) is required of any natural or legal person not an employee of an FCM that directs (introduces) customers to an FCM in exchange for compensation or some other form of gain, but does not receive customer funds. This person must either meet minimum capital requirements (modest compared to FCM capital rules) or must be guaranteed financially by an FCM. Since these IBs do not actually service customer accounts, their recordkeeping and reporting duties are less stringent than for FCMs.

Registration as an IB is also required for any person not employed by a commodity trading advisor or a commodity pool operator to solicit advisory clients or pool participants.

Associated Persons

Registration as an *associated person* (AP) is required for any natural person employed by an FCM or an IB for the purpose of soliciting or accepting customer orders. There are no minimum capital requirements, and most recordkeeping and reporting duties are imposed on the employing FCM or IB. However, these APs can be prosecuted for fraud and other misbehavior in their dealings with customers.

Registration as an AP is also required for any person employed by a CTA or CPO for the purpose of soliciting advisory clients or pool participants, as well as solicitors for an ATOM or an LTM.

In addition to fitness standards, APs are generally required to successfully complete a proficiency examination demonstrating their knowledge of the markets.

Serious Offenses and their Consequences

Every violation of the CEAct or of CFTC regulations can be prosecuted as a felony with fines of US$ 1 million or more and up to five years of imprisonment. These penalties are raised from time to time and need to be reviewed periodically.

Most offenses do not rise to the level warranting criminal proceedings but the civil consequences can be severe as well. The CFTC, using an administrative proceeding or by application to a federal court, may exact a ban on use of the markets by a violator and assess a civil penalty of US$ 130,000 per violation (raised from time to time) or in the alternative an amount equal to treble the violator's gain. Conduct may be enjoined, and restitution to injured victims may be ordered.

Although not disciplinary in nature, the CFTC's reparations tribunal offers victims of CEAct violations an opportunity to recover actual damages from liable registrants.

Finally, the NFA and each of the regulated exchanges have codes of conduct applicable to their members and members' employees which, if violated, can result in expulsion (including forfeiture of a valuable membership), suspension for a period of time, large fines, and corrective steps.

The three principal missions of the CFTC are:

- Prevention and detection of fraud against market users;

- Prevention and detection of market manipulations; and

- Maintenance of competitive and transparent markets

Intermediaries continue to play a vital role in the interface between market users and the markets themselves, and the CFTC seeks to assure their honest treatment of users through disclosure of risks, accurate performance data, and safeguarding of users' funds. And, because the futures and commodity option markets are often relied on for the pricing and hedging of commercial transactions, the CFTC endeavors to assure that their prices are determined by the economic forces of supply and demand and not by the aberrant efforts of one or a few large traders. To perform these services, the markets must have high visibility, or transparency, and the CFTC seeks to assure that prices are readily available to the trading and hedging communities.

Speculating or Hedging: The Policy Implications

To the extent that the futures and commodity option markets are employed to speculate on (to predict) the future price of goods, services, or other forms of commodity, they resemble the dynamic of other investment markets where the principal aim is to anticipate the direction of prices and to profit from favorable changes. It is generally the national policy that within any investment group assuming the same market risks, no special advantages or handicaps should be allowed to exist. In the securities industry, for instance, investors are not permitted to use certain nonpublic (inside) information that is material to market decisions until it has been made available to the rest of the investor community. But the futures and commodity option markets also serve as a form of privately funded insurance system where parties having an exposure in their ordinary business dealings to a particular risk may hedge against that danger by acquiring futures or options positions that will gain in value from the same events that will inflict commercial losses on their regular business. This form of protection would not be possible if every hedger were required, in advance of acquiring the hedge, to announce to the world why it has become necessary to do so. The market would react immediately by driving prices away from the hedger's needs.

Similarly, in the securities industry there are traditional restrictions on the right to short a stock, that is, to sell a stock prior to acquiring it. One concern has been that this practice would tend to put downward pressure on security prices while nearly all investors aspire to enjoy rising prices; another concern is the risk of default if the security cannot be or is not acquired by the agreed delivery date. But the futures and commodity option markets exist to serve, in equal measure, those who worry about falling prices and those favoring rising prices and, to provide a hedge for the former, short selling must be freely available.

The differences in margin between securities and futures/options activity were discussed earlier. To summarize, securities margin generally applies *after* the sale is complete and delineates how much of the purchase price may be borrowed by the buyer under federal regulations designed to control the amount of credit extended in these circumstances. But margin in the futures/options context is a deposit made *before* the transaction is carried out and constitutes a form of performance bond to be applied against any intervening changes in market price; in other words, this margin is *excess funds* in the trader's account.

Role of Other Government Authorities

As a general matter, the CFTC enjoys exclusive jurisdiction to set and to enforce regulatory standards for the exchanges offering futures contracts or commodity options as well as for individuals and entities providing services related to those markets as brokers. advisors, portfolio managers, and the like. The only major exception exists in the case of futures contracts based upon single corporate securities or upon smaller indices of corporate securities, where the

SEC acts as co-regulator with the CFTC, and all rules or policies require their joint concurrence.

A less formal relationship exists between the CFTC and USDA with respect to futures and options on farm products, and between the CFTC and the Department of the Treasury when government security futures or options are involved. In addition, the rules of a futures market establishing the level of margins for stock-index futures contracts may be rejected or changed by the Federal Reserve Board.

For all intents and purposes, there is no material involvement by the states in the regulation of futures or options activity occurring on the CFTC-regulated exchanges. In the case of transactions conducted directly between parties that are eligible to trade futures contracts or options outside the regulated markets, however, states may set standards but may not invoke local gaming or bucket-shop laws to invalidate the transactions, although at this writing no state has become an active regulator of this activity.

Role of Other Laws

As a general matter, the Commodity Exchange Act and CFTC rules preempt other legislation at the federal and state levels that might relate to the same or similar activity. With respect to federal statutes, however, actions may be brought under the federal antitrust laws when the conduct involves anticompetitive behavior, such as the manipulation of commodity prices on an exchange or in the commercial realm. Similarly, violations of the Racketeer Influenced and Corrupt

Practices Act (RICO) can be asserted in appropriate cases. And actions may also be brought under state antifraud laws of general applicability (i.e., not specifically related to the futures business). Finally, the CFTC is accorded an active role in the winding up of futures entities under the federal Bankruptcy Act.

Notes

[1] The author contributed the statutory language that accomplishes this result by proposing successfully the inclusion within the definition of *commodity* in the 1974 amendments to the Commodity Exchange Act (7 U.S.C. § 1 *et seq.*) of the phrases "and all other goods and articles ... and all services rights, and interests" that are or become subject to futures trading.

[2] *See*, for example, *CCH Commodity Futures Law Reporter* and Philip McBride Johnson and Thomas Lee Hazen, *Derivatives Regulation,* 4th ed. (Aspen Law & Business, 2004).

[3] 7 U.S.C. § 1 et seq.

[4] 17 C.F.R. § 1 et seq.

[5] 7 U.S.C. § 1a. *See also* note 1, *supra.*

[6] 7 U.S.C. §§ 9 and 13b, and 13 respectively.

[7] While there is no fee charged between the parties at inception, use of a broker to arrange the transaction may result in payment of a commission to that broker.

[8] The same term—*margin*—is used in the securities business as well but bears a far different meaning. Typically, securities margin is imposed following an outright purchase of stocks or bonds where the buyer wishes to borrow part of the cost, usually from a broker. Federal Reserve Board regulations and Securities and Exchange Commission rules dictate how much of the purchase price may be borrowed for this purpose—currently about 50 percent for shares and 20 percent for security options—and the partial payment actually made is referred to as margin. But unlike the futures trader who acquires nothing upon entry into the transaction except a promise of later performance, the securities buyer takes title to the actual securities and may pledge them to the broker or other lender as collateral for the loan. Moreover, when securities are bought on margin, only the buyer (the borrower) must post margin; the seller does not. With futures, both sides must meet margin requirements. Finally, a securities account on margin contains a *deficit* (the unpaid balance on the loan) while a futures account should always have an *excess* of funds above the amount of current

obligations. To reduce confusion, some futures exchanges refer to margins as "performance bonds."

[9] Some options may be exercised by the holder at any time during their life ("American-style" options) while others can be exercised only on a set date ("European-style" options). Because American-style options offer the holder more flexibility and a greater chance for gain, they are usually considered to be more valuable than European-style options.

[10] The author was principal legal advisor in the creation of the world's first interest-rate futures contracts, a genre which now accounts for roughly 53 percent of international futures volume.

[11] The author served as the CFTC's chairman and commissioner from 1981 to 1983.

[12] The Securities and Exchange Commission regulates options directly on securities and options on foreign currencies if the currency options are listed on a national securities exchange, and co-regulates with the CFTC futures contracts on single stocks and narrow-based stock indexes.

[13] *See., e.g.*, CEAct § 5(d), 7 U.S.C. § 7(d).

[14] The author was founding counsel for the NFA.

Hedge Funds and the SEC: Observations on the Why and How of Securities Regulation

TROY A. PAREDES

The hedge fund industry is well over a trillion dollar business. Estimates put the number of hedge funds at around 9,000 today, up from an estimated 3,600 funds managing roughly US$450 billion as recently as 1999.[1] As the industry grows, so does its impact. Hedge funds add liquidity to financial markets and, as others have put it, hedge funds act as "shock absorbers" that can stabilize financial markets during crises.[2] Further, hedge funds promote the integrity of securities markets by engaging in the types of trading that make securities markets more efficient, and they provide opportunities for businesses and investors to shift and manage risk. More efficient and liquid financial markets promote capital formation and business enterprise.

A concern, on the other hand, is that hedge fund activities may also upset financial markets. In particular, the industry's growth has fueled worries about so-called *systemic risk*,[3] dating back, most notably, to the collapse of Long-Term Capital Management (LTCM) in 1998 and the private bailout of LTCM that the Federal Reserve Bank of New York orchestrated to fend off a chain reaction that threatened global markets if LTCM defaulted.[4] More recently, the multi-billion dollar loss at Amaranth Advisors that was tied to a natural gas trade by a single individual at the hedge fund renewed concern that a fund can collapse easily and quickly with widespread consequences, although none resulted from Amaranth's collapse.[5]

Separately, there have been a noticeable number of enforcement actions for fraud and insider trading brought by the U.S. Securities and Exchange Commission (SEC or Commission) against hedge funds. Hedge funds were also implicated in the market-timing and late-trading scandals that plagued the mutual fund industry in the early 2000s. And while hedge funds have been increasingly active as shareholders—arguably increasing firm value by holding managers and boards more accountable[6]—there is growing concern that hedge funds are manipulating business transactions through what Professors Bernard Black and Henry Hu have termed "empty voting," a variation of vote buying.[7]

Compensation of hedge fund managers also has been noticed. Successful hedge fund managers can make tens if not hundreds of millions of dollars per year, even in down markets. One study found that the average compensation of the top 25 managers of hedge funds was approximately US$250 million in 2004.[8]

Despite all of this, concerns about hedge funds have to be kept in proper perspective. Not only do the funds perform a number of key functions that stabilize financial markets, promote capital formation, lead to more efficient securities markets, and facilitate risk management, but the abuses and collapses that have punctuated the industry, while notable, are not indicative of widespread hedge fund behavior. To the contrary, most hedge funds are not engaged in fraudulent or other illicit behavior, and the vast number of hedge fund managers are disciplined traders who make calculated, although risky and speculative, trades.[9]

Against this backdrop, this chapter addresses three topics that bear on one key aspect of the hedge fund industry: the SEC's recent efforts to regulate hedge funds.[10] The first section of this chapter summarizes the regulation of hedge funds under the U.S. federal securities laws that is intended to protect hedge fund investors. The discussion highlights four basic choices facing the SEC: (1) do nothing; (2) substantively regulate hedge funds directly; (3) regulate hedge fund managers; and (4) regulate hedge fund investors.[11] The second section assesses the boundary between market discipline and government intervention in hedge fund regulation. To what extent should hedge fund investors be left to fend for themselves? The final section highlights two factors—politics and psychology—that impact regulatory decision making and help explain why the SEC pivoted in 2004 to attempt to regulate hedge funds when it had abstained from doing so in the past.

Hedge Funds and U.S. Federal Securities Regulation

Hedge funds are characterized not only by the nature of their investments[12] but also by the degree to which they are not regulated by the SEC. Hedge funds typically are structured so that they avoid the principal regulatory requirements of the U.S. federal securities laws. The resulting light regulation of such funds is not the product of shenanigans or the exploitation of loopholes. Rather, the Securities Act of 1933 (which regulates public offerings), the Securities Exchange Act of 1934 (which imposes ongoing disclosure and other requirements on public companies), the Investment Company Act of 1940 (which regulates mutual funds), and the Investment Advisers Act of 1940 (which regulates investment advisers) contain longstanding, purposeful exclusions within which hedge funds typically fall.[13]

In 2004, in a divisive and controversial 3-2 vote for an administrative agency that prefers to act unanimously (Commissioners Atkins and Glassman dissenting), the SEC changed course and decided to regulate hedge funds.[14] The SEC's subsequent hedge fund rule did not substantively regulate hedge fund activities directly, but required hedge fund managers to register with the SEC as investment advisers under the federal Investment Advisers Act.

Section 203(b)(3) of the Investment Advisers Act provides that an investment adviser, such as a hedge fund manager, does not have to register under the Act if, among other things, the adviser has fewer than 15 "clients." For purposes of Section 203(b)(3), a hedge fund manager has been able to count a fund as a single client. For example, a hedge fund with 100 investors has counted as a single client of the hedge fund manager for the 15-client threshold of Section 203(b)(3). Consequently, a hedge fund manager could manage up to 14 hedge funds, with an unlimited number of investors in the funds, without having to register as an investment adviser under the Investment Advisers Act.

The SEC's 2004 rule set out to change this. The SEC adopted a new rule—Rule 203(b)(3)-2 under the Investment Advisers Act—to require a hedge fund manager to "look through" the manager's fund to count each hedge fund investor as a client.[15] As a result of the new rule, hedge funds would eclipse the 15-client threshold, and hedge fund managers thus would have to start registering with the SEC as investment advisers. As registered investment advisers, hedge fund managers would have to (1) make certain disclosures with the SEC; (2) deliver basic information to investors; (3) adopt procedures concerning proxy voting by the fund; (4) adopt a code of ethics; (5) implement certain internal controls and compliance procedures; (6) meet certain requirements governing the custody of client funds and securities; and (7) designate a chief compliance officer. Most important, hedge funds would have to maintain specified books and records and make them available to the SEC for examination and inspection.[16]

This revised regulatory regime, which went into effect in February 2006, lasted only about six months. In *Goldstein v. SEC*, the federal Court of Appeals for the D.C. Circuit vacated the SEC's new hedge fund rule, calling it "arbitrary" and effectively reinstating the earlier Investment Advisers Act regime under which hedge fund managers can avoid registering.[17]

The SEC did not challenge the *Goldstein* decision,[18] but it did consider and ultimately propose a different rule in late 2006.[19] Some background is needed before explaining the SEC's more recent proposal.

The Securities Act of 1933 provides that securities offerings generally must be registered with the SEC.[20] There is, however, an important safe harbor from the Securities Act's registration requirements for offerings that are limited to "accredited investors" in private placements.[21] Accredited investors include institutional investors and individual investors who meet certain financial qualifications. Specifically, an individual qualifies as an accredited investor by having a net worth (or joint net worth with a spouse) that exceeds US$1,000,000 or an income exceeding US$200,000 in each of the past two years (or joint income with a spouse exceeding US$300,000 in each of the past two years) if such individual reasonably believes such income thresholds will be met in the present year.[22] The logic is that accredited investors are able to fend for themselves—that is, they can assess the risk of a particular investment or bear the risk of financial loss—because they are sufficiently sophisticated or wealthy. Consequently, there is no compelling need for the federal securities laws to protect them—hence the safe harbor exclusion from the Securities Act's registration requirements for offerings limited to accredited investors.[23]

As a matter of practice, hedge funds limit the offering of their securities to accredited investors.[24] Yet regulators and others have worried that individuals who satisfy the current financial thresholds for accredited investor status are not in fact able to protect themselves. Indeed, the financial thresholds have been fixed for over two decades.[25]

In its post-*Goldstein* rulemaking, the SEC proposed a new definition of accredited investor.[26] The Commission proposed a new class of accredited investor—the "accredited natural person"—that would apply to securities offerings of hedge funds.[27] An individual would qualify as an accredited natural person by meeting the financial thresholds described above and owning US$2.5 million or more in investments (individually or with a spouse).[28] This US$2.5 million threshold would be adjusted for inflation in later years.

Amending the definition of accredited investor might be seen as a relatively technical development; it is certainly a less intrusive change than the SEC's 2004 rule. The Commission's accredited investor proposal should have a relatively modest impact on the industry as a whole, even though the rule change would deny some investors the chance to invest in hedge funds and thus cut off some capital inflows, particularly for smaller or newer funds.

The SEC's new proposal, however, is important for reasons aside from its impact on hedge funds. The Commission's approach informs our understanding of securities regulation by illustrating the range of levers the SEC can pull under a policy of protecting investors. One option would be for the SEC to do nothing else and leave the regulatory regime in place as it existed before 2004. A second option would be for the SEC to regulate hedge funds directly. For example, one could imagine (although the SEC has not proposed this) regulating the types of investments hedge funds can make, how much leverage they can take on, and how managers are compensated. A burdensome regime along these lines presently governs mutual funds under the Investment Company Act of 1940. A third option would be for the SEC to regulate hedge fund managers, as it sought to do earlier by requiring their registration under the Investment Advisers Act.

The proposed definition of an accredited natural person illustrates a fourth option. Namely, the SEC can regulate investors.[29] By redefining who qualifies as accredited, the SEC effectively regulates who can invest in hedge funds.[30] This proposal does not confer upon the SEC greater regulatory authority, as the short-lived 2004 requirement for investment adviser registration did, but it does target the particular concern that unsophisticated investors, who are not especially wealthy, might invest in hedge funds.

Such investor-side regulation is not new. The SEC has for some time drawn distinctions between various categories of investors, including not only "accredited investors," but also "qualified clients," "qualified purchasers," "sophisticated" investors, and "qualified institutional buyers." The proposed "accredited natural person" adds another category.[31]

The SEC's proposal to limit hedge fund investing to individuals wealthier than traditional accredited investors was widely viewed as reasonable in academic and legal circles since the accredited investor financial thresholds were set 25 years ago.[32] If anything, perhaps the financial thresholds under the definition of accredited investor should have been revisited generally, instead of singling out hedge funds.

Individual investors have viewed things differently. Of the roughly 600 comment letters the SEC received, a notable number rejected the SEC proposal to establish the new accredited natural person category, prompting the SEC to proceed more slowly than initially envisioned. The SEC explained the accredited natural person category in terms of enhanced investor protection:

> [M]any individual investors today may be eligible to make investments in privately offered investment pools as accredited investors that previously may not have qualified as such for those investments. Moreover, private pools have become increasingly complex and involve risks not

generally associated with many other issuers of securities. Not only do private pools often use complicated investment strategies, but there is minimal information available about them in the public domain. Accordingly, investors may not have access to the kind of information provided through our system of securities registration and therefore may find it difficult to appreciate the unique risks of these pools, including those with respect to undisclosed conflicts of interest, complex fee structures and the higher risk that may accompany such pool's anticipated returns.[33]

In their criticism, individual investors have emphasized the other side of the investor protection coin. Many see the SEC's proposal as unwanted paternalism that denies less-wealthy individuals (i.e., *retail investors*) an opportunity to invest in an important asset class, namely, hedge funds, as well as private equity funds.[34]

Two basic, and related, arguments underpin investors' resistance to the SEC's proposal. First, diversification is widely touted as the best investment strategy for individual investors. However, the proposed standard for an accredited natural person crimps an individual's ability to diversify into certain private offerings. Relatedly, hedge funds, as well as private equity funds, can yield outsized, above-market returns, even on a risk-adjusted basis (i.e., *alpha*). Accordingly, individual investors might want exposure to such investment vehicles to earn higher returns. In this view, investor participation in hedge (and private equity) funds can itself be seen as a form of investor protection.

Second, regulatory efforts that preclude retail investors from investing in hedge funds and other private investment vehicles bolster concerns that the financial game is rigged. Individual investors understandably wonder why an entire category of investments is set aside for wealthy individuals and institutional investors only. To many retail investors, claims of investor protection ring hollow. Rather, they view a proposal such as the accredited natural person definition as further tilting the playing field in favor of the rich and powerful by preserving for them the best investment opportunities. The backdrop here is that retail investors want the same opportunities as wealthy individuals and large institutions, because the fact that wealthy individuals and institutions invest in these private vehicles is evidence of their attractiveness, including for the less-wealthy.[35] As the private placement market continues to grow generally, retail investors will increasingly find that they are excluded from a substantial segment of securities markets, and not just from hedge funds.[36] Individual investors may lose confidence in the integrity of securities markets when they recognize that two markets exist—one market that is open to all investors, including retail investors (i.e., publicly traded securities and mutual funds); and one that is open only to wealthy individuals and institutional investors (i.e., private placements, including investments in hedge funds, private equity funds, and venture capital funds, as well as privately held operating companies). In such a situation, investors' trust in the integrity of the legal regime that entrenches the divide is at risk also.[37]

In sum, individuals caught the SEC's attention when they expressed a preference for greater participation in private pools of capital, including hedge funds, even if it means less investor protection from the Commission.[38] Put differently, it is one thing for the SEC to demand more disclosure and to enforce antifraud requirements aggressively to reduce informational asymmetries so that investors can make better informed decisions in deciding how to allocate their capital. It is quite another for the SEC to protect investors by denying them investment opportunities that the SEC deems to be too risky.[39]

It is beyond this chapter's scope to consider how investor-side regulation might feature still more prominently in securities regulation.[40] Suffice it to say that more refined investor-side regulation—such as the SEC offered when crafting an accredited investor definition for hedge funds that would not upset the private placement market more broadly—should not be overlooked as an option, notwithstanding that it ultimately may be difficult to achieve politically.

Government Intervention versus Market Discipline

A primary goal of the SEC is to protect investors. Without question, hedge fund investors have limited information, particularly when it comes to understanding a hedge fund's investments. But it does not follow that more regulation of hedge funds or their managers is warranted to protect hedge fund investors.[41]

Hedge fund investors are accredited investors and, if the SEC's 2006 proposal is ultimately adopted, individuals will have to meet an additional investment requirement to qualify as accredited natural persons. The federal securities laws presume that accredited investors, including accredited natural persons, are able to protect themselves, militating against more government intervention on their behalf. That such well-heeled, sophisticated investors choose to invest in a hedge fund that provides its investors with little information should not trigger more SEC oversight. Neither the complexity of hedge fund strategies nor the fact that hedge fund investors may lose money because of fraud or risky trading is grounds for more hedge fund regulation. To the contrary, the risk of loss incentivizes investors to do the kind of due diligence that positions them to protect their own interests, and hedge funds and their managers are already subject to antifraud requirements. Just as hedge fund investors can evaluate the information they do possess about a fund's investment strategy, back office operations, controls, track record, valuation techniques, and disclosure practices, they can assess and "price" the risk of having imperfect information. Indeed, if they are uncomfortable with the investment, investors can simply walk.

Of course, institutional investors and wealthy individuals do not always perfectly price the risk of a particular investment. Due diligence is costly, and sometimes people are simply wrong in their assessments. In addition, as behavioral finance has taught us, when making investment decisions, people are boundedly rational and suffer from various cognitive biases.[42] Consequently, even sophisticated investors with good information make mistakes. Furthermore, in recent years investing in hedge funds has become fashionable. As investors develop a taste for hedge funds, they may rush to invest without doing adequate diligence and analysis.

Notwithstanding these breakdowns in market discipline, the SEC has not engaged in a more textured study of what it means for investors to be able to fend for themselves, in large part because a more textured analysis is too indeterminate and comes at the expense of capital formation. The SEC does not delve into the details of investor behavior. Instead, the regulator has relied on certain financial-based proxies—reflected in the definition of accredited investor—as acceptable measures of investor self-protection. Such a bright-line approach to accredited investor status in turn spurs the private placement market by reducing the risk for issuers when tapping this market.[43] As the SEC's proposed definition of an accredited natural person illustrates, there is room to debate where the appropriate line is separating when the SEC should intervene and when it should not. But it is worth underscoring that a boundary limiting SEC oversight in deference to market discipline is engrained in federal securities regulation and is part of the longstanding accepted structure of the regulatory regime.[44]

This does not mean, however, that the SEC has no role to play when market discipline predominates. The securities regulator can always look to expand its reach by moving the regulatory line delineating the boundary between SEC oversight and market discipline. The SEC has proposed doing just this by raising the financial hurdle an individual must clear to qualify as accredited to invest in hedge funds. Under the SEC's proposal, fewer individuals would be accredited and thus fewer individuals would be viewed as able to fend for themselves when investing in a hedge fund. Notably, although the SEC's accredited natural person proposal narrows the potential pool of hedge fund investors, the SEC does not propose to regulate a fund or its manager so long as the fund's investors solely comprise institutional investors and accredited natural persons. This is a qualitatively different approach from the SEC's vacated 2004 rule, which provided for SEC regulation of hedge fund managers, even when all investors were accredited.

Instead of (or in addition to) relocating the boundary between government intervention and market discipline, the SEC can actually facilitate market discipline so that it is more informed and effective. The SEC wields considerable influence as the dominant securities regulator in the United States, and it is highly respected. The Commission could take advantage of its status and reputation in adopting a best-practices mode of regulation.[45] That is, the SEC could express its view of best practices without imposing legal requirements. The SEC could articulate best practices formally through SEC releases or informally through the speeches and writings of individual commissioners and division directors. For example, the SEC could stress best practices for the hedge fund industry. Imagine the potential impact on the industry if the SEC chairman, particularly if joined by other commissioners and the directors of the Division of Investment Management and the Division of Corporation Finance, pushed a set of hedge fund best practices in a series of speeches, interviews, TV appearances, and op-eds in publications such as the *Wall Street Journal* and the *Financial Times*.[46]

By endorsing particular best practices, including those coming from the private sector,[47] the SEC would provide concrete guidance to investors to use in assessing investment options. Such guidance would be a yardstick against which investors could evaluate a specific investment opportunity. Investors could then allocate their capital as they saw fit with the benefit of the SEC's input. Further, a hedge fund manager could take the initiative in adopting the SEC-endorsed practices to distinguish the manager and the manager's fund as cooperative and willing to go above and beyond what the law requires.[48] Particularly if larger, more-established hedge funds follow the best practices, other funds may feel pressured to as well.

This is not to say that all best practices urged by the SEC would (or should) be followed. The ultimate outcome would be left for the market participants to determine in the shadow of what the SEC has urged is the right thing to do. More to the point, for best practices to be voluntary in fact and not only in name, the SEC would have to sit tight and refrain from regulating if the best practices it endorsed were not widely accepted.[49]

A best-practices approach to hedge fund regulation has gained some traction. In February 2007, the President's Working Group on Financial Markets (PWG)—chaired by the secretary of the Treasury and consisting of the chairmen of the Federal Reserve Board, the SEC, and the Commodity Futures Trading Commission—issued a set of principles and guidelines concerning hedge funds and other private pools of capital.[50] The PWG advanced a market-oriented approach to hedge fund oversight that relies on market discipline both to protect hedge fund investors and to ensure that private pools of capital undertake effective risk management for the benefit of hedge fund creditors and counterparties and to limit systemic risk. In September 2007, the PWG announced the creation of two committees—the Asset Managers' Committee made up of hedge fund managers and the Investors' Committee made up of hedge fund investors—to come up with best practices for hedge fund managers and hedge fund investors.[51] The committees' proposals will be put out for public comment before being finalized. This is a unique public-private partnership, with the PWG turning to private-sector committees to fashion best practices that the PWG, after notice and comment, presumably expects to sanction.[52]

When the SEC does regulate more substantively, it still can allow room for flexibility and private ordering by finessing the government intervention/market discipline boundary. Regulators often view themselves as having two choices: impose one-size-fits-all mandates or sit tight and do nothing.[53] However, a third choice lies between those two poles. That is, regulators, such as the SEC, can use default rules.

The virtue of default rules is that they allow parties to contract around the default requirement to order their affairs to fit their particular needs and preferences.[54] Further, the ability to opt out of the regulatory regime provides an important safety valve when regulators otherwise would overregulate. A default rule that required a hedge fund manager to register under the Investment Advisers Act or disclose why it has chosen not to register would have been a particularly apt alternative to the SEC's earlier rule mandating investment adviser registration for hedge fund managers. Just as hedge fund investors can evaluate other aspects of a fund's operations, the investors could assess the value of investment adviser registration against the backdrop default that managers must register with the SEC.[55]

Although used sparingly in the United States, some precedent exists for such a default-rule approach to securities regulation. Two specific examples can be found in the Sarbanes-Oxley Act of 2002 (Sarbanes-Oxley). Sarbanes-Oxley requires public companies to adopt a code of ethics for senior financial officers or explain why no code was adopted.[56] The Act also requires public companies to have a financial expert on the audit committee or explain why it does not.[57] Another example is the SEC's 2005 rule permitting, but not requiring, that mutual funds impose a 2 percent mandatory redemption fee on short-term trading.[58] More recently, the SEC sought comment on a proposal that would allow shareholders to opt out of the SEC's regime under Rule 14a-8 of the Securities Exchange Act and decide for themselves what procedures the company would adopt for including nonbinding shareholder proposals in the company's proxy materials.[59] On other occasions, the SEC has explicitly favored mandates over a more liberal regulatory approach. For example, in a 3-2 vote, the SEC in 2004 adopted rules requiring mutual fund boards to have an independent chairman and a supermajority of independent directors, rejecting a proposal that instead would have required a mutual fund to disclose whether its board met these heightened independence standards but without requiring them to do so.[60]

In the future, when it does regulate, the SEC should give more serious consideration to using defaults over mandates, and in some instances the SEC should do nothing more than take a stance by exhorting particular best practices.

The Politics and Psychology of Securities Regulation

The third topic concerns the SEC as an institution and a decision-making body, focusing on the impact that politics and psychology can have on regulatory judgment.[61] Although the discussion focuses on the Commission, the observations apply to any legislative or regulatory body and to risk regulation generally.

Why did the SEC reverse its long-held practice in 2004 and decide to regulate hedge funds? Nobody knows for sure what impacts a particular regulator's decision making. Group decision making complicates the analysis. That said, the SEC's decision to regulate hedge funds is consistent with two views. First, that the securities regulator did not want to get caught flat-footed and criticized again, as it had been by the scandals at Enron, WorldCom, and elsewhere, by seeming to take a lax regulatory stance with respect to hedge funds in the post-Enron era. Second, on the heels of the earlier scandals, the risk of fraud and other hedge fund abuses loomed disproportionately large at the SEC, prompting it to act when in the past the regulator had abstained from doing so. Both of these claims play out against the backdrop that regulators generally see themselves as there to do something—which is to say, to regulate.

Because much has been written on the political economy of regulation, the comments that follow are targeted. When considering the political economy of securities regulation, it is important to recognize that the investor class in the United States is expanding. Today, about 50 percent of households are invested in stock, as compared to roughly 19 percent in 1983, 32 percent in 1989, and 40 percent in 1995.[62] Not only do more households own stock today than ever before, but, as one would expect, individual wealth increasingly is tied up in stock, as well as other securities.[63] Further, the relatively newly expanded but very active business and financial media— CNBC, for example, is a phenomenon of the 1990s stock market boom, and News Corp. recently launched the Fox Business Network—brings more attention and scrutiny to securities markets and their regulation than before. Regulatory decision making is bound to be impacted as securities markets increasingly enjoy widespread participation and as securities and corporate-related questions become leading topics of serious public and political debate. The predictable result is a more pronounced "democratization" of securities regulation as regulators are more responsive to public pressure and the political agenda.[64] What is the consequence? The populist politics of securities regulation generally characterizes more regulation, more aggressive government enforcement of securities laws, and lower barriers to private litigation as "pro-investor."[65] This, however, is a stingy reading of "pro-investor" that does not fully account for the cost of government regulation and litigation when it hampers U.S. financial markets and capital formation.[66]

The SEC's desire to protect its regulatory domain contributes to this dynamic.[67] On several occasions, for example, Congress has held hearings on hedge funds, and some legislation has even been introduced, although it has not advanced very far.[68] The SEC may have correctly believed that it had to do something to fend off a Congress that may be anxious to fill any perceived regulatory void with new legislation. The SEC has an institutional interest in assuring its position as the predominant securities regulator in the United States and staking out its turf against potential incursions by Congress or the states.[69] Further, the SEC may set itself up for blame if it fails to regulate and a scandal emerges or the market melts down. The SEC can thus protect its own reputation by regulating more aggressively, even at the risk of going too far.

The comparative advantage of an administrative agency over other lawmakers—namely, the agency's subject matter expertise and its independence and impartiality[70]—is compromised when its members are responsive to political pressure or public demands in how they regulate or join lawmakers in competing to regulate. Under these circumstances, the risk is that regulators will tend to overregulate.

To avoid painting with too broad of a brush, it is worth recognizing that there may be times when the SEC needs to supply regulation when there is demand for it.[71] First, a strong regulatory response may be needed at times, such as during a period of crisis as followed Enron's collapse, to buttress investor confidence.[72] Second, the sort of "democratic" securities regulation contemplated here might help offset more conventional public-choice concerns, counterbalancing regulatory capture or other special-interest influences on securities regulation that can result in too little government oversight of securities markets.[73] Third, the SEC may need to regulate enough to avoid stirring public outrage for taking a lax stance and to preserve its own legitimacy as a regulatory body. If the SEC does not respond to the boom in the hedge fund industry, especially given some of the headline-grabbing conduct involving the funds, investors may lose faith in the SEC for allowing the industry to go unchecked. More generally, Main Street may simply demand that power be held accountable, and hedge funds are increasingly powerful.[74] The consequences here extend beyond the SEC, because if investors lose faith in the SEC, they may lose faith in the integrity of U.S. securities markets.

The SEC's decision to regulate hedge funds fits the general contours of the above take on the political economy of securities regulation. There is, however, an interesting twist. As described in the first section of this chapter, the politics of hedge fund regulation have shifted, at least insofar as less-wealthy individuals have rejected the SEC's proposal to limit further who can invest in hedge funds. While individual investors may welcome SEC efforts to regulate hedge funds or their advisers, they have not welcomed SEC efforts to regulate the investors themselves. This has caused pause at the SEC, which, as noted above, solicited additional comment on its proposed definition of accredited natural person.[75]

Psychology also impacts regulatory decision making.[76] For example, there is a psychological (or behavioral) explanation for the *precautionary principle* of risk regulation.[77] Simply put, the precautionary principle holds that it is better to be safe than sorry—a proactive regulatory policy of anticipation and preemption. The benefit of a precautionary approach to regulation is that it can lead regulators to take prophylactic steps instead of sitting back and only reacting to problems once they arise. However, taking precautions can also lead to excessive regulation as regulators try to avoid some perceived harm, often on the basis of limited information.

Further, the precautionary principle is misleading as a regulatory lodestar. As Professor Cass Sunstein has emphasized, precautionary steps with respect to one risk inevitably lead to other risks.[78] The difficult question, then, is what risks should regulators regulate to avoid and what risks should regulators tolerate? What risks weigh most heavily in the regulatory balance? To a large degree, the answer depends on the value placed on various outcomes. For example, when the two goals are at odds, how much investor protection is one willing to trade in exchange for promoting capital formation? The answer not only depends on value judgments, but also on various psychological influences that affect human judgment and decision making by making certain risks more fearful, even when in fact they are not as threatening as they seem.

Investor losses, hedge fund collapses, and jarring frauds are salient events that are readily recalled when crafting regulation, particularly in light of the journalists and politicians who play up the losses and abuses. Accordingly, these events likely will feature more prominently in regulators' decision making than the actual magnitude of the events warrant. This disproportionate impact of especially salient events on decision making is associated with what is called the *availability heuristic*, whereby salient risks are more available to one's mind and thus receive more attention than they deserve, as well as the *representativeness heuristic* and *probability neglect*, according to which people tend to overstate the probability that some bad recent occurrence will happen again.[79] Furthermore, regulators may be inclined to regulate in response to a perceived risk because regulators may view themselves as being there to regulate, after all.

The other side of the regulatory scale includes the costs of more aggressive securities regulation. These costs are generally described in such sterile and impersonal terms as the risk that more regulation will undercut the flexibility, efficiency, and liquidity of financial markets. These risks are not nearly as stirring as the supposed costs of not regulating. Additionally, regulators may be overconfident in their skill at regulating with the right touch, believing that they can get the benefits of investor protection without the attendant costs. Perhaps regulators' assessments would be different if the costs of regulation were presented to them more concretely in terms of fewer jobs, lower returns for investors, or fewer investment opportunities.

The bottom line is that regulators, as well as the public and the media, often have an exaggerated concern over fraud and investor losses and, at least by comparison, a dulled sensitivity to the costs of greater investor protection. This is not to say that regulators do not account for the costs of regulation, but only that the costs often do not receive their appropriate due. This is especially true in the wake of a wave of scandal, such as Enron ushered in, or when there is some considerable unknown, as with hedge funds. As a result, regulators' assessments of the costs and benefits of regulating can become skewed toward avoiding a particularly salient harm. In practice, this means more investor protection—indeed, perhaps too much investor protection at the expense of other goals, such as capital formation.[80] This might explain why the SEC chose to regulate hedge funds in 2004 when it did not do so earlier.

To craft an effective securities law regime, regulators must appraise objectively and rationally the costs and benefits of regulating; their judgment cannot be obscured by cognitive biases. An unbiased, more probabilistic analysis of the consequences of risk regulation should lead to a more effective regime that better advances regulatory goals. Even an SEC that emphasizes investor protection may by its own lights overregulate if it irrationally fears another series of scandals.

Recognizing that regulators are human and imperfectly rational introduces a new set of regulatory challenges. How do regulators guard against the kind of unconscious biases that can frustrate good decision making? There are no easy answers to this challenge. However, some possibilities worth considering include more rigorous cost-benefit analysis, "harder-look" judicial review of administrative agency decision making, new organizational structures that might be mined from the experiences of companies, and the use of internal "prediction" markets.[81] Indeed, a best-practices approach to regulation and the use of opt-out defaults can provide an effective safety value against the risk of overregulation rooted in regulator psychology or, for that matter, politics.

Conclusion

This inquiry into the SEC's recent attempts to regulate the hedge fund industry suggests a few basic insights into the "why and how" of securities regulation. First, investor-side regulation is an option as an investor protection strategy. Second, instead of adopting mandates, regulators could adopt defaults or simply urge best practices without adopting any new legal requirements. Third, regulators need to be aware of, and guard against, the impact of politics and psychology in securities regulation. Although the focus in this chapter has been on the SEC, these core points inform the crafting of financial regulation more broadly in both the United States and abroad.

Notes

Note: I would like to thank the participants at the International Monetary Fund's 2006 Seminar on Current Developments in Monetary and Financial Law, for which this chapter was prepared, for their helpful comments and insights. Further, I gratefully appreciate helpful thoughts offered by Bill Bratton, Kathleen Brickey, Michelle Brough, Steve Choi, Scott Kieff, Don Langevoort, Frank Partnoy, Steve Schwarcz, David Skeel, Randall Thomas, and Peter Wallison. This chapter also benefited from comments I received at workshops at the George Washington University Law School and the University of California Hastings College of the Law. For a more extensive analysis of some of the ideas and themes in this chapter, see Troy A. Paredes, "On the Decision to Regulate Hedge Funds: The SEC's Regulatory Philosophy, Style, and Mission," 2006 *University of Illinois Law Review* 975. All mistakes are mine.

[1] *See* Counterparty Risk Management Policy Group II, *Toward Greater Financial Stability:A Private Sector Perspective* (2005), at B-10, available at www.crmpolicygroup.org/docs/CRMPG-II.pdf [hereinafter *Toward Greater Financial Stability*].

[2] *See, e.g.*, John G. Gaine, President, Managed Funds Association, "Comments of Managed Funds Association for the U.S. Securities and Exchange Commission Roundtable on Hedge Funds," May 2003, available at www.mfainfo.org/images/pdf/MFA-Comments-SEC-5.6.03.pdf.

[3] Regarding systemic risk, see generally *Toward Greater Financial Stability*, *supra* note 1; Nicholas T. Chan et al., "Systemic Risk and Hedge Funds," MIT Sloan Research Paper No. 4535-05 (2005), available at http://ssrn.com/abstract=671443; Steven L. Schwarcz, "Systemic Risk," Duke Law School Legal Studies Paper No. 163 (2007), available at http://papers.ssrn.com/sol3/papers.cfm?abstract_id=1008326. For an important speech on the topic by the president and chief executive officer of the Federal Reserve Bank of New York, see Timothy F. Geithner, "Hedge Funds and Derivatives and Their Implications for the Financial System," September 15, 2006, available at www.newyorkfed.org/newsevents/speeches/2006/gei060914.htm; *see also* Greg Ip, "Geithner's Balancing Act: The Fed's Go-To Man for Financial Crises Takes on Hedge Funds," *Wall Street Journal* (February 20, 2007), at C1. For a summary of the concern over systemic risk, see Randall Smith and Susan Pulliam, "As Funds Leverage Up, Fears of Reckoning Rise," *Wall Street Journal* (April 30, 2007), at A1.

Professor Steven Schwarcz has defined systemic risk as follows:

> [T]he risk that (i) an economic shock such as market or institutional failure triggers (through a panic or otherwise) either (x) the failure of a chain of markets or institutions or (y) a chain of significant losses to financial institutions, (ii) resulting in substantial financial-market price volatility (which price volatility may well reflect increases in the cost of capital or decreases in its availability).

Schwarcz, "Systemic Risk," *supra*, at 14 (citation omitted).

For a concise set of recommendations for financial firms to follow for managing their exposure to hedge funds and thus mitigating systemic risk, see Edwin Laurenson et al., "Best Practices for Financial Firms Managing Risks of Business with Hedge Funds," 38 *Securities Regulation & Law Report* (BNA) 1477 (2006).

[4] *See generally* Roger Lowenstein, *When Genius Failed: The Rise and Fall of Long-Term Capital Management* (New York: Random House, 2000); Franklin R. Edward, "Hedge Funds and the Collapse of Long-Term Capital Management," 13 *Journal of Economic Perspectives* 189 (1999). For a thorough report prepared by the President's Working Group on Financial Markets in the wake of LTCM's collapse, see *Hedge Funds, Leverage, and the Lessons of Long-Term Capital Management:Report of the President's Working Group on Financial Markets* (1999), available at www.ustreas.gov/press/releases/reports/hedgfund.pdf.

[5] *See, e.g.*, Ann Davis, "How Giant Bets on Natural Gas Sank Brash Hedge-Fund Trader: Up in Summer, Brian Hunter Lost US$5 Billion in a Week as Market Turned on Him," *Wall Street Journal* (September 19, 2006), at A1; Ann Davis et al., "What Went Wrong at Amaranth: Mistakes at the Hedge Fund Include Key Trader's Confusing Paper Gains with Cash Profits," *Wall Street Journal* (September 20, 2006), at C1; Phil Izzo, "Getting a Grip on Hedge Fund Risk: Economists See Risk to Financial Markets and Say More Regulation Is Warranted," *Wall Street Journal* (October 13, 2006), at C3; Gretchen Morgenson and Jenny Anderson, "A Hedge Fund's Loss Rattles Nerves," *New York Times* (September 19, 2006), at C1. Amaranth's loss ended up posing no systemic problem. *See, e.g.*, Gregory Zuckerman, "How the Amaranth Wreck Was Contained: J.P. Morgan and Citadel Swooped In, Assumed Risk, Proving Markets' Resilience," *Wall Street Journal* (October 5, 2006), at C3.

[6] *See, e.g.,* William W. Bratton, "Hedge Funds and Governance Targets," Georgetown Law and Economics Research Paper No. 928689 (2006) available at http://ssrn.com/abstract=928689; Alon Brav et al., "Hedge Fund Activism, Corporate Governance, and Firm Performance," ECGICFinance Working Paper No. 139/2006 (2006), available at http://ssrn.com/abstract= 948907; Marcel Kahan and Edward B. Rock, "Hedge Funds in Corporate Governance and Corporate Control," University of Pennsylvania Institute for Law and Economics Research Paper No. 06-16 (2006), available at http://ssrn.com/abstract=919881; Randall S. Thomas and Frank Partnoy, "Gap Filling, Hedge Funds, and Financial Innovation" (2006), Vanderbilt Law and Economics Research Paper No. 06-21, San Diego Legal Studies Paper No. 07-72, available at http://ssrn.com/abstract=931254.

[7] *See* Henry T.C. Hu and Bernard Black, "Empty Voting and Hidden (Morphable) Ownership: Taxonomy, Implications, and Reforms," 61 *Business Lawyer* 1011 (2006); Henry T.C. Hu and Bernard Black, "The New Vote Buying: Empty Voting and Hidden (Morphable) Ownership," 79 *Southern California Law Review* 811 (2006); *see also* Kara Scannell, "How Borrowed Shares Swing Company Votes: SEC and Others Fear Hedge-Fund Strategy May Subvert Elections," *Wall Street Journal* (January 26, 2007), at A1. For an analogous analysis, see Shaun Martin and Frank Partnoy, "Encumbered Shares," 2005 *University of Illinois Law Review* 775.

[8] *See* Riva D. Atlas, "Hedge Funds Are Stumbling but Manager Salaries Aren't," *New York Times* (May 25, 2005), at C5.

[9] For a fascinating treatment of the history of speculation in the U.S. economy more generally, see Lawrence E. Mitchell, *The Speculation Economy: How Finance Triumphed over Industry* (San Francisco: Berrett-Koehler, 2007).

[10] This chapter does not address systemic risk or hedge funds' role in corporate governance.

[11] The SEC also can monitor hedge fund activity indirectly through its regulation of broker-dealers.

[12] Examples of typical hedge fund investment strategies include convertible arbitrage; emerging markets; long/short equity; event-driven; fixed income arbitrage; statistical arbitrage; and global macro. Hedge funds characteristically use leverage, short selling, and derivatives in attempting to

exploit market inefficiencies in search of so-called *alpha* (i.e., risk-adjusted above-market returns). Hedge funds typically seek *absolute returns* (i.e., positive returns in both up and down markets) instead of simply trying to outperform some market index.

[13] For an overview of these statutes, see Louis Loss, Joel Seligman, and Troy Paredes, *Securities Regulation*, 4th ed. (New York: Aspen, 2006), at 326-425. For accounts of hedge fund regulation outside the United States, see International Organization of Securities Commissions, *The Regulatory Environment for Hedge Funds: A Survey and Comparison* (2006), available at http://www.iosco.org/library/pubdocs/pdf/IOSCOPD226.pdf Kara Scannell et al., "No Consensus on Regulating Hedge Funds: Officials Around Globe Aim to Protect Markets but Differ on Methods," *Wall Street Journal* (January 5, 2007), at C1.

[14] Registration Under the Advisers Act of Certain Hedge Fund Advisers, Inv. Adv. Act Rel. 2333 (2004). More information concerning the SEC's interest in hedge funds is available on the SEC's Web site at http://sec.gov/spotlight/hedgefunds.htm. For a more recent assessment of the hedge fund industry by the SEC Chairman, see Christopher Cox, Chairman, U.S. Securities and Exchange Commission, Testimony Concerning the Regulation of Hedge Funds Before the U.S. Senate Committee on Banking, Housing, and Urban Affairs, July 25, 2006, available at http://sec.gov/news/testimony/2006/ts072506cc.htm. Another recent overview of hedge fund issues was provided by the SEC staff. *See* Susan Ferris Wyderko, Director, Office of Investor Education and Assistance, U.S. Securities and Exchange Commission, Testimony Concerning Hedge Funds Before the Subcommittee on Securities and Investment of the U.S. Senate Committee on Banking, Housing, and Urban Affairs, May 16, 2006, available at http://sec.gov/news/testimony/ts051606sfw.htm.

[15] The rule included an important exception. A hedge fund manager did not have to register under the Investment Advisers Act if the hedge fund contained a "lock-up" of at least two years during which the fund's investors could not withdraw their capital. The stated purpose of this provision was to distinguish between hedge funds, on the one hand, and private equity and venture capital funds, on the other. Private equity and venture capital funds typically have longer lock-up periods than hedge funds, and the SEC did not intend to subject the managers of private equity and venture capital funds to registration. This provision gave established hedge funds a competitive advantage over upstarts. Less well-known managers of newer or smaller

funds would have a more difficult time convincing investors to lock up their capital for two years, as the threat of capital withdrawals is an important means by which investors hold managers accountable. *Cf.* Daisy Maxey, "At Hedge Funds, Study Exit Guidelines: Amaranth Case Shows Disclosure and Redemption Policies for Investors Can Differ Greatly," *Wall Street Journal* (September 23, 2006), at B4. Thus, while managers of more-established funds could realistically attempt to opt out of the SEC's registration requirement, managers of less-established funds would have to bear the burden of registration.

[16] Hedge funds still could avoid the demands of the Securities Act of 1933, the Securities Exchange Act of 1934, and the Investment Company Act of 1940. Even before the 2004 rule, hedge fund managers had to comply with antifraud and fiduciary obligations under federal and state law.

[17] *Goldstein v. SEC*, 451 F.3d 873 (D.C. Cir. 2006). Basically, the court found that the SEC acted arbitrarily and outside its authority in redefining "client" to mean a fund's investors instead of the fund itself. *See* Loss, Seligman, and Paredes, *supra* note 13, at 406-07.

[18] *See* SEC Press Release 2006-135 (August 7, 2006).

[19] Prohibition of Fraud by Advisers to Certain Pooled Investment Vehicles; Accredited Investors in Certain Private Investment Vehicles, Sec. Act Rel. 8766 (2006) [hereinafter Accredited Natural Person Proposal]. The SEC has adopted the new antifraud provision it proposed under the Investment Advisers Act, but as of this writing has not yet adopted the aspects of the proposal that relate to accredited investors. *See* Prohibition of Fraud by Advisers to Certain Pooled Investment Vehicles, Inv. Adv. Act Rel. 2628 (2007).

After the 2004 hedge fund rule was vacated, many hedge fund managers withdrew from registration with the SEC. *See, e.g.*, Siobhan Hughes, "More Hedge Funds Leave the Ranks of SEC's Registry," *Wall Street Journal* (December 15, 2006), at C4.

[20] *See* Loss, Seligman, and Paredes, *supra* note 13, at 580-801.

[21] *See* Loss, Seligman, and Paredes, *supra* note 13, at chapter 3.C.7 (4th ed., forthcoming 2008).

[22] In August 2007, the SEC proposed revising the Regulation D definition of accredited investor by, among other things, (1) adding an "investments-owned" standard allowing individuals with investments exceeding a certain level to qualify as accredited, even if they do not meet the present income or wealth thresholds, and (2) requiring future inflation adjustments to the accredited investor financial thresholds for individuals, including individuals investing in hedge funds. *See* Revisions of Limited Offering Exemptions in Regulation D, Sec. Act Rel. 8828 (2007) [hereinafter Regulation D Proposal]. As of this writing, the SEC has not yet taken final action in the rulemaking.

[23] For more on the role of such financial thresholds in limiting the reach of the federal securities laws and SEC oversight of securities offerings, see *infra* the second section of this chapter, "Government Regulation versus Market Discipline."

[24] Hedge funds also often have minimum investment requirements that preclude many accredited individual investors from investing. The claim that hedge fund investors need more regulation to protect them is weak given their accredited status. Indeed, more government regulation may lead to moral hazard, in effect undercutting market discipline. This argument was leveled against the SEC's 2004 rule requiring hedge fund manager registration under the federal Investment Advisers Act. *See* Troy A. Paredes, "On the Decision to Regulate Hedge Funds: The SEC's Regulatory Philosophy, Style, and Mission," 2006 *University of Illinois Law Review* 975, 990-98 (criticizing the SEC's 2004 rule as unnecessary because hedge fund investors can protect themselves adequately). *But see id.* at 999-1001 (recognizing the argument that hedge fund regulation might be warranted to ensure against a loss of investor confidence—a sort of systemic concern that might justify more government oversight, even if hedge fund investors do not need greater protection).

If a hedge fund did offer its securities to the public, the fund would be subject to more demanding regulation under the federal securities laws. For examples of public offerings by hedge (and private equity) funds or their investment managers, see Alistair MacDonald, "Hedge Funds to Tap the Public: Two More Firms Plan Listing on Exchange," *Wall Street Journal* (January 10, 2007), at C2; Gregory Zuckerman et al., "Hedge-Fund Crowd Sees More Green as Fortress Hits Jackpot with IPO," *Wall Street Journal* (February 10, 2007), at A1; Eleanor Laise, "Hedge Funds Beckon Small Investors," *Wall Street Journal* (February 14, 2007), at D1. For a private offering with a structure somewhere between a conventional private offering and a public offering, see Henny Sender, "Live at Apollo Management: Plan to Cash In, Limit Scrutiny," *Wall Street Journal* (July 17, 2007), at C1.

[25] The SEC estimates that the accredited investor financial thresholds, if adjusted for inflation, would have increased to approximately US$1.9 million (net worth), US$388,000 (individual income) and US$582,000 (joint income) as of 2006; that when Regulation D was adopted in 1982, approximately 1.87 percent of U.S. households met the accredited investor definition; and that the percentage of households meeting the definition had increased to nearly 8.5 percent by 2003. The SEC estimates that roughly 1.3 percent of households would meet the accredited natural person standard. *See* Accredited Natural Person Proposal, *supra* note 19, at 23-24.

[26] *See id.* at 14-32. The SEC's 2004 hedge fund rule would have impacted the accredited investor concept indirectly. As a registered investment adviser, a hedge fund manager would have been subject to certain rules under the federal Investment Advisers Act that generally prohibit an investment adviser from charging a performance fee (for example, the 20 percent or so "carry" or profits interest that hedge fund managers typically charge) from any investor who is not a "qualified client" (i.e., an investor whose net worth does not exceed US$1.5 million or who does not have assets worth at least US$750,000 under management with the fund's adviser). Under relevant rules, a registered adviser has to look through the fund to determine whether its investors are qualified clients who can be charged a performance fee. Thus many accredited investors who would not qualify as qualified clients, even though they are accredited, would have been kept from investing in hedge funds as hedge fund managers took steps to ensure they did not forego their performance fee.

An interesting issue beyond this chapter's scope concerns whether the carry should be treated as capital gains or ordinary income for tax purposes. *See generally* Victor Fleischer, "Two and Twenty: Taxing Partnership Profits in Private Equity Funds," *New York University Law Review* (forthcoming 2008).

[27] The proposed accredited natural person standard would also apply to securities offerings of private equity funds, but not venture capital funds.

[28] This investment threshold would exclude the value of an individual's personal residence or place of business or other real estate that is not held for investment purposes.

[29] For an interesting proposal for regulating investors instead of issuers, see Stephen Choi, "Regulating Investors Not Issuers: A Market-Based Proposal," 88 *California Law Review* 279 (2000).

[30] In the SEC's view, the accredited natural person standard better limits hedge fund investing to individuals who are sophisticated; able to bear the economic risk of the investment; and able to negotiate adequately for information from the fund or at least price the risk of having imperfect information. *See also infra* the second section of this chapter, "Government Regulation versus Market Discipline."

[31] The SEC has proposed yet another category of accredited investor under Regulation D for all private offerings, not just those involving hedge funds. The SEC's proposal would allow limited advertising of private offerings to investors who qualify as "large accredited investors." *See* Regulation D Proposal, *supra* note 22. This rule release also solicited additional comment on the SEC's proposed definition of accredited natural person for hedge funds.

[32] Instead of proposing an additional investment requirement, the SEC could have proposed increasing the income or wealth thresholds for hedge fund investing while leaving these thresholds fixed for other private offerings under Regulation D.

[33] *See* Regulation D Proposal, *supra* note 22, at 17. The SEC's accredited natural person proposal reflects an important subtlety. The Securities Act of 1933 provides investors with information so they can assess their investment choices. The SEC does not pass on the merits of particular issuers or their offerings. Armed with information, investors may make smart decisions or they may make dumb decisions, but they make their own decisions. By way of contrast, in proposing the accredited natural person definition, the SEC explicitly references the substantive merits of investing in hedge funds, at least insofar as the SEC refers to their "complicated investment strategies" and "unique risks."

The private offering exemption typically emphasizes the characteristics of the individual investors—that is, their sophistication and wealth—without regard to the nature or merits of the investment. For example, there was no heightened investor qualification standard for investing in Internet startups that privately placed their securities in the 1990s during the technology boom. Indeed, there likely would have been a backlash if the SEC had tried to impose a differentiated standard for the private offering exemption based on a belief that investing in "dot-coms" was too risky. However, this is precisely what the SEC has proposed when it comes to hedge funds. *See, e.g.*, Regulation D Proposal, *supra* note 22, at 48 ("We believe that the different amounts applicable under the definitions [of accredited investor and accredited natural person] are targeted to address concerns about the nature of different types of offerings."). When crafting the accredited natural person definition, the SEC passed judgment on the merits of investing in hedge funds, deciding that hedge fund investing is riskier than other investments and thus requires more demanding financial hurdles before individuals can invest without the protections of the Securities Act. Yet the SEC is not qualified to judge the nature or riskiness of different investments, be they investments in hedge funds, private equity funds, venture capital funds, public operating companies, or private operating companies. (This is not to say that the SEC never does so. Consider, for example, the heightened regulation of so-called *penny stocks*. *See, e.g.*, Louis Loss and Joel Seligman, *The Fundamentals of Securities Regulation*, 5th ed. (New York: Aspen, 2005), at 1093–96. More to the point, even if the SEC were qualified to make such judgments, it is not clear that hedge fund investing is in fact always more complex or risky than these alternatives, including holding publicly traded stock. This calls into question the legitimacy of a special accredited investor standard for private pools of capital.

[34] In soliciting additional comment on its proposal, the SEC explained: "We received numerous comments disagreeing with the proposed definition of accredited natural person. Most of those submitting comments argued that the proposal limits investor access to private pooled investment vehicles and questioned the dollar amount of the investments standard." Regulation D Proposal, *supra* note 22, at 49. *See also* Kara Scannell, "On the Outside of Hedge Funds Looking In," *Wall Street Journal* (September 1, 2007), at B1 (reporting on comments on the SEC's accredited natural person proposal).

[35] Since the federal securities laws were adopted in the 1930s, there has been concern that individuals do not actually read the information they are provided and, if they do, do not understand it. William O. Douglas, who later became chairman of the SEC before becoming a U.S. Supreme Court Justice, was among the first to raise this worry:

> But those needing investment guidance will receive small comfort from the balance sheets, contracts, or compilation of other data revealed in the registration statement. They either lack the training

or intelligence to assimilate them and find them useful, or are so concerned with a speculative profit as to consider them irrelevant.

William O. Douglas, "Protecting the Investor," 23 *Yale Review* 521 (1934), at 523-24. For more contemporary analyses of the understandability of disclosures, see, for example, Troy A. Paredes, "Blinded by the Light: Information Overload and Its Consequences for Securities Regulation," 81 *Washington University Law Quarterly* 417 (2003) (focusing on the amount of information); Steven L. Schwarcz, "Rethinking the Disclosure Paradigm in a World of Complexity," 2004 *University of Illinois Law Review* 1 (focusing on the complexity of information). In short, individual investors routinely do not make informed decisions even when there is wide-scale disclosure, as mandated by the federal securities laws for registered offerings. As a practical matter, however, any concern is largely mitigated because securities markets are sufficiently efficient, along the lines of the well-known efficient capital markets hypothesis. In this view, securities professionals in effect protect unsophisticated retail investors because the buying and selling of informed professional traders ultimately incorporates available public information into securities prices. As then-Professor Frank Easterbrook and Professor Daniel Fischel put it: "The uninformed traders can take a free ride on the information impounded by the market: they get the same price received by the professional traders without having to do any of the work of learning the information." Frank H. Easterbrook and Daniel R. Fischel, "Mandatory Disclosure and the Protection of Investors," 70 *Virginia Law Review* 669 (1984). Index investing validates this point.

This raises an interesting rationale for relaxing restrictions governing who invests in hedge funds. It is presumed that investors qualifying as accredited, even under the conventional definition, can protect their own interests. *See infra* the second section of this chapter, "Government Regulation versus Market Discipline." Perhaps retail investors, then, should be allowed to "piggyback" on the work and diligence of accredited investors when it comes to hedge funds just as they effectively piggyback on the analysis and trading of securities professionals when it comes to publicly traded securities. With respect to a particular fund, retail investors could "free ride" on the market discipline that accredited investors presently bring to bear when they invest. If market discipline adequately protects accredited investors, why does it not adequately protect retail investors investing along side of them? This argument may have growing force as hedge fund investors are increasingly comprised of institutional investors. *Cf.* Houman B. Shadab, "The Challenge of Hedge Fund Regulation," *Regulation* (Spring 2007), at 41 (summarizing improving transparency of hedge funds). That said, it is worth noting that minimum investment requirements keep smaller investors out of many (perhaps the most attractive) funds, limiting the opportunity to piggyback.

[36] For data on private offerings, see Securities Industry Association, *2006 Securities Industry Fact Book,* at 10-13 [hereinafter *2006 Securities Industry Fact Book*].

[37] *See also* Brian G. Cartwright, General Counsel, U.S. Securities and Exchange Commission, "The Future of Securities Regulation," Remarks Before the University of Pennsylvania Institute for Law and Economics, October 24, 2007, available at http://sec.gov/news/speech/2007/spch 102407bgc.htm (discussing what Cartwright referred to as "deretailization").

This is not to say that retail investors necessarily believe that public offerings take place on a level playing field. For example, it became clear during the wave of corporate scandal in the early 2000s that wealthy individuals and institutional investors have preferred access to allocations of initial public offerings; and even after the SEC adopted Regulation FD in 2001 to address so-called *selective disclosure*, professional traders and analysts still have access to better information than retail investors.

[38] If desired, one way to expand individual investor access to hedge funds is obvious: do not raise the accredited investor financial thresholds under Regulation D and perhaps even lower them. Indeed, the financial thresholds for individuals to qualify as accredited could be lowered not just for hedge funds but for all private placements exempt from SEC registration requirements.

Alternatively, the SEC could consider a blended approach. For example, the SEC could consider limiting the amount a person can invest in a hedge fund depending on the person's wealth, income, or sophistication. A different approach would be to set different financial thresholds for accredited investor status depending on whether the manager of the fund has registered with the SEC under the Investment Advisers Act. The logic here is that less-wealthy individuals who are deemed unable to fend for themselves under the 1933 Securities Act should have greater access to hedge funds when the government steps up to protect them, as through investment adviser registration. In effect, hedge fund manager registration under the Investment Advisers Act would compensate for the fact that the hedge fund is not registering its own securities offering under the Securities Act. A manager of a fund that prefers to tap into smaller individual investors could simply register as an investment adviser. A third option is to loosen the restrictions on mutual funds so they can more freely adopt investment strategies that resemble those of hedge funds. This would give individual investors more exposure to hedge fund-like strategies through mutual funds, which are governed by the Investment Company Act. Presently, the ability of mutual funds to sell short, acquire securities on margin, and enter derivatives contracts, as hedge funds do, is limited. The director of the SEC's Division of Investment Management recently spoke to this in a speech to industry insiders:

> [W]ith the proper safeguards, I believe the potential benefits from hedge fund-type strategies should not be limited to only wealthy investors. To the extent that there are limitations under the Investment Company Act, the Division staff will work with you through the exemptive application and no-action processes to develop products that not only provide investors greater access to beneficial investment strategies, but also provide them the protections that are necessary. For example, with regard to long/short funds, the staff came out with a no-action position stating that a registered [mutual] fund may take short positions, provided that it has placed liquid securities that could be used to close out its short position in a segregated account with its custodian.

Andrew J. Donohue, Director, Division of Investment Management, U.S. Securities and Exchange Commission, Remarks Before the 4th Annual Hedge Funds and Alternative Investments Conference, May 23, 2007, available at http://sec.gov/news/speech/2007/spch052307ajd.htm. For examples of mutual funds that have adopted hedge fund-like investment strategies, see Eleanor Laise, "Mutual Funds Adopt Hedge-Fund Tactics," *Wall Street Journal* (February 21, 2006), at D1; Eleanor Laise, "Mutual Funds Add Exotic Fare to the Mix," *Wall Street Journal* (April 4, 2007), at D1. For an analysis of other investments open to retail investors that may be viewed as alternatives to hedge funds, see Steven M. Davidoff, *Black Market Capital*, Wayne State University Law School Research Paper No. 07-26 (2007), available at http://papers.ssrn.com/sol3/papers.cfm?abstract_id=1012042; Eleanor Laise, "The Hedge-Fund 'Clones': Wall Street Concocts Products with Fewer Barriers, but Will Returns Match?" *Wall Street Journal* (July 21, 2007), at B1. For a proposed retail fund of hedge funds structure, see Houman B. Shadab, "Fending for Themselves: Regulatory Reform to Create a U.S. Hedge Fund Market for Retail Investors" (2007), available at http://papers.ssrn.com/sol3/papers.cfm?abstract_id=1019629

[39] If the SEC were to lower the standards for investing in private offerings so they were more accessible to retail investors, political pressure would surely mount for more regulation when (not if) individuals lose billions of dollars in the collapse of a hedge fund or the bankruptcy of a large private operating company. This is troubling because more regulation would likely interfere with capital formation, a side of the SEC's mission that often gets overlooked as investor protection gets stressed.

[40] In discussing whether to allow certain foreign broker-dealers to do business in the United States while satisfying only streamlined U.S. broker-dealer registration requirements, one senior SEC official suggested that such foreign broker-dealers could be limited to doing business with market professionals or large sophisticated investors. *See* Erik R. Sirri, Director, Division of Market Regulation, U.S. Securities and Exchange Commission, Remarks Before the FIA and OIC New York Equity Options Conference, September 20, 2007, available at http://sec.gov/news/speech/2007/spch092007ers.htm.

[41] Whether hedge fund regulation is warranted to serve some other goal is beyond this chapter's scope.

[42] For more on behavioral finance, see generally Robert J. Shiller, *Irrational Exuberance* (Princeton: Princeton University Press, 2000); Andrei Shleifer, *Inefficient Markets: An Introduction to Behavioral Finance* (Oxford: Oxford University Press, 2000); Lynn A. Stout, "The Mechanisms of Market Inefficiency: An Introduction to the New Finance," 28 *Journal of Corporation Law* 635 (2003).

[43] An integral benefit of such clear-cut proxies is that they create a more certain and predictable regulatory environment in which issuers and investors can operate. The shortcoming is that proxies are always imperfect measures.

[44] *See, e.g., SEC v. Ralston Purina Co.*, 346 U.S. 119 (1953) (finding that a private offering exempt from the registration requirements of the Securities Act exists when the investors are able to "fend for themselves"). It also is worth stressing that this demarcation is thought to further the goal of capital formation by reducing the regulatory burden in those instances where market discipline adequately holds issuers and their managers accountable.

An important distinction is needed. The above discussion is from the particular perspective of whether hedge fund investors can adequately protect their own interests. That is, it focuses on the relationship between hedge funds and their investors. Hedge funds have been criticized in recent years for activities that, although benefiting the hedge fund's investors, may harm investors in other enterprises and other market participants. Even if greater SEC oversight to protect hedge fund investors is not warranted, hedge funds should not get a free pass from law compliance. Hedge funds are, and should be, subject to federal and state law regulating activities such as market timing, late trading, vote buying, insider trading, and market manipulation. This chapter takes no position on whether laws, regulations, and judicial doctrines governing such behavior should be revised in light of the hedge fund industry's recent growth.

One area receiving heightened attention concerns PIPEs (private investments in public equities). In a typical PIPE transaction, a public company (i.e., the issuer) sells equity securities in a private placement that is not subject to the registration requirements of the federal Securities Act. The issuer later files a resale registration statement under the Securities Act, allowing the initial investors, who acquired their securities in the private placement, to resell the securities to the public. The SEC has brought a number of enforcement actions alleging that hedge funds, as initial investors, have engaged in insider trading in the issuer's publicly traded securities and have violated the Securities Act registration requirements by selling short the privately placed securities expecting to "cover" the short sale with the newly registered securities once the subsequent registration statement goes effective. *See, e.g.*, Kara Scannell, "SEC Pushes for Hedge-Fund Disclosure: Advisers' Kinship to Firms' Workers, Investors Is Studied," *Wall Street Journal* (September 19, 2007), at C2.

[45] *Cf.* International Organization of Securities Commissions, *Principles for the Valuation of Hedge Fund Portfolios* (2007) (offering best practices for hedge fund valuation).

By way of analogy, the Delaware courts follow a best-practices approach for state corporate law, especially when it comes to the fiduciary duties that delineate the obligations of directors and officers. Delaware judges, through their opinions, speeches, and articles, articulate their vision of good corporate governance but do not hold corporate actors legally liable when they fail to adhere to these practices. *See, e.g.*, Edward B. Rock, "Saints and Sinners: How Does Delaware Corporate Law Work?" 44 *UCLA Law Review* 1009 (1997); *see generally* Troy A. Paredes, "A Systems Approach to Corporate Governance Reform: Why Importing U.S. Corporate Law Isn't the Answer," 45 *William and Mary Law Review* 1055, 1087-96 (2004). The following from then-Delaware Supreme Court Chief Justice E. Norman Veasey illustrates the Delaware judiciary's approach:

All good corporate governance practices include compliance with statutory law and case law establishing fiduciary duties. But the law of corporate fiduciary duties and remedies for violation of those duties are distinct from the aspirational goals of ideal corporate governance practices. Aspirational ideals of good corporate governance practices for boards of directors that go beyond the minimal legal requirements of the corporation law are highly desirable, often tend to benefit stockholders, sometimes reduce litigation and can usually help directors avoid liability. But they are not required by the corporation law and do not define standards of liability.

Brehm v. Eisner, 746 A.2d 244, 256 (Del. 2000) (citation omitted).

[46] The SEC's 2003 proposal to grant shareholders greater access to the corporate ballot for nominating directors has served as an SEC-endorsed best practice, although it was proposed as a mandate. *See* Security Holder Director Nominations, Sec. Ex. Act Rel. 48,626 (2003). The SEC's proposal faced stiff opposition, particularly from the business community, and was not adopted. However, the SEC's proposal brought greater attention to the issue of director nominations, and there has been a notable market reaction as more and more companies have adopted some version of so-called *majority voting*. *See generally* William K. Sjostrom, Jr., and Young Sang Kim, *Majority Voting for the Election of Directors* (2007), available at http://papers.ssrn.com/sol3/papers.cfm?abstract_id=962784.

[47] The private sector has already fashioned best practices for the hedge fund industry. *See, e.g.*, Managed Funds Association, *2005 Sound Practices for Hedge Fund Managers*, available at www.managedfunds.org/downloads/MFA%202005%20Sound%20Practices.pdf; *Toward Greater Financial Stability*, *supra* note 1.

     The Hedge Fund Working Group, which is based in London, has offered best practices for the European hedge fund industry. *See* Alistair MacDonald and Deborah Solomon, "Hedge Funds from Europe Take a Crack at Self-Policing," *Wall Street Journal* (October 11, 2007), at C1.

[48] *Cf.* Eric A. Posner, "Law and Social Norms: The Case of Tax Compliance," 86 *Virginia Law Review* 1781 (2000) (developing a signaling theory of law compliance).

[49] A best-practices approach to regulation does present some challenges. A fundamental challenge is deciding what the best practices are. The five SEC commissioners may not reach agreement on hedge funds or any other topic. A best-practices strategy would depend on effective coordination at the SEC.

In addition, there is a real risk that a hedge fund's failure to follow SEC-endorsed best practices would provide a roadmap for private litigation, and courts might slowly start to incorporate best practices into legal requirements. For example, one could imagine courts coming to view a hedge fund's failure to follow disclosure or valuation best practices as evidence of fraud.

[50] A copy of the Agreement Among PWG and U.S. Agency Principals on Principles and Guidelines Regarding Private Pools of Capital is available on the Treasury Department's Web site at www.treas.gov/press/releases/hp272.htm.

[51] *See, e.g.*, Carrie Johnson, "U.S. Aims to Limit Funds' Risk," *Washington Post* (September 26, 2007), at D03; Deborah Solomon, "The Obedience Rules for Hedge Funds," *Wall Street Journal* (September 26, 2007), at C3.

[52] This interesting public/private approach is not new for hedge funds. In 1998 the private sector bailed out LTCM under pressure from the Federal Reserve. It will be worth watching to see just how involved the PWG is in shaping the committees' recommendations.

[53] Even when "do nothing" is the best course, it might not be a realistic option for political or other reasons.

[54] It is worth noting that defaults often are "sticky," in which case defaults act more like mandates. *See, e.g.*, Omri Ben-Shahar and John Pottow, "On the Stickiness of Default Rules," 33 *Florida State University Law Review* 651 (2006); Russell Korobkin, "Inertia and Preference in Contract Negotiation: The Psychological Power of Default Rules and Form Terms," 51 *Vanderbilt Law Review* 1583 (1998); Russell Korobkin, "The Status Quo Bias and Contract Default Rules," 83 *Cornell Law Review* 608 (1998); Kathryn E. Spier, "Incomplete Contracts and Signalling," 23 *RAND Journal of Economics* 432 (1992). One account of stickiness can be traced back to Ronald Coase, who most famously illustrated that the initial legal allocation of entitlements—such as the "right" to have your hedge fund manager register as an investment adviser under the Investment Advisers Act—may be

sticky because of transaction costs. *See* Ronald H. Coase, "The Problem of Social Cost," 3 *Journal of Law and Economics* 1 (1960).

[55] Even when investment adviser registration is an "opt-in" instead of an "opt-out" default, many managers choose to opt in by voluntarily registering under the Investment Advisers Act.

The SEC's investment adviser registration rule did include a sort of opt-out default. If a hedge fund required its investors to commit their capital to the fund for at least two years—the two-year lock-up provision—the fund's manager did not have to register under the Investment Advisers Act. Indeed, many funds began to institute two-year lock-ups. *See, e.g.*, Gregory Zuckerman and Ian McDonald, "Hedge Funds Avoid SEC Registration Rule," *Wall Street Journal* (November 10, 2005), at C1; Eleanor Laise, "Dissecting Hedge-Fund Secrets," *Wall Street Journal* (February 4, 2006), at B5. The rule, though, did not allow a hedge fund manager whose fund did not have a two-year lock-up to choose not to register. A true default would have allowed any manager to opt out, subject to the discipline of the market if it did so.

[56] Sarbanes-Oxley Act § 406. Such a comply-or-explain approach, which essentially is a default, is popular in the United Kingdom.

[57] *Id.* § 407.

[58] Investment Company Act Rule 22c-2(a)(1).

[59] Shareholder Proposals, Sec. Ex. Act Rel. 56,160, at 50-58 (2007).

[60] Investment Company Governance, Inv. Co. Act Rel. 26,520 (2004). A particularly provocative suggestion for a default has come from the private sector Committee on Capital Markets Regulation, which had the support of U.S. Treasury Secretary Henry Paulson. In its November 2006 report the Committee recommended allowing shareholders to opt out of private securities class actions in favor of alternative dispute resolution, such as arbitration with or without class actions. *See Interim Report of the Committee on Capital Markets Regulation*, at 109-14 (November 2006), available at www.capmktsreg.org/pdfs/11.30Committee_Interim_ReportREV2.pdf [hereinafter Committee on Capital Markets Reg'n Report].

[61] For other interesting work studying the SEC as an institution and decision-making body, see, for example, Anne M. Khademian, *The SEC and Capital*

Market Regulation: The Politics of Expertise (Pittsburgh: University of Pittsburgh Press, 1992); Susan M. Phillips and J. Richard Zecher, *The SEC and the Public Interest* (Cambridge, MA: MIT Press, 1981); Stephen J. Choi and A.C. Pritchard, "Behavioral Economics and the SEC," 56 *Stanford Law Review* 1 (2003); Donald C. Langevoort, *The SEC as a Lawmaker: Choices About Investor Protection in the Face of Uncertainty* (2006), Georgetown Law and Economics Research Paper No. 947510, available at http://ssrn.com/abstract=947510; Jonathan R. Macey, "Administrative Agency Obsolescence and Interest Group Formation: A Case Study of the SEC at Sixty," 15 *Cardozo Law Review* 909 (1994); A.C. Pritchard, "The SEC at 70: Time for Retirement?" 80 *Notre Dame Law Review* 1073 (2005). For a complete history of the SEC, see Joel Seligman, *The Transformation of Wall Street: A History of the Securities and Exchange Commission and Modern Corporate Finance*, 3rd ed. (New York: Aspen, 2003).

[62] *2006 Securities Industry Fact Book*, *supra* note 36, at 64.

[63] *Id.* at 65-67. For more historical data, see Loss, Seligman, and Paredes, *supra* note 13, at 18-29. One might argue that as more people have more of their wealth tied to securities, a swifter and more aggressive regulatory response to perceived concerns with securities markets is warranted. This argument dovetails with the *precautionary principle* of regulation described below.

[64] The assumption is that the public will have different risk perceptions than the experts at regulatory agencies. Individual investors, for example, likely are particularly attuned to investor losses as compared to the cost of greater investor protection. *See generally* Paul Slovic, *The Perception of Risk* (London: Earthscan Publications, 2000); Cass R. Sunstein, "The Laws of Fear," 115 *Harvard Law Review* 1119 (2002).

[65] Two recent illustrations have received a great deal of media attention. First, the SEC was criticized for not being "pro-investor" when it read the Private Securities Litigation Reform Act of 1995 as creating a more demanding pleading requirement than some had urged in securities fraud class actions. *See* Brief for the United States as Amicus Curiae Supporting Petitioners, *Tellabs, Inc. v. Makor Issues and Rights, Ltd.*, No. 06-484 (Feb. 9, 2007). In defense of the SEC, the agency was interpreting a statute that, by its terms, requires plaintiffs to plead a "strong inference" of scienter in securities fraud cases in order to root out vexatious litigation. Second, a number of quarters publicly pressured the SEC to file an amicus brief

favoring so-called *scheme liability* in *Stoneridge Investment Partners, LLC v. Scientific-Atlanta, Inc*. Scheme liability would open to liability an issuer's outside adviser or counterparty involved in a transaction when the issuer misreports the transaction, even though the adviser or counterparty does not itself make any material misstatement or omission. Scheme liability would substantially expand the reach of Rule 10b-5 under the Securities Exchange Act of 1934, the primary federal antifraud provision, and arguably unwind the Supreme Court's earlier decision in *Central Bank of Denver, N.A. v. First Interstate Bank of Denver, N.A.* that there is no private right of action for aiding and abetting securities fraud. Again, the claim was that the SEC should be "pro-investor" and side with the investor-plaintiffs. The SEC ultimately voted 3-2 to file a brief supporting the investor-plaintiffs, but the Solicitor General did not file the requested brief and ultimately filed a brief in favor of the defendants. Notably, the chairmen of the House Judiciary Committee and the Financial Services Committee filed their own brief in favor of scheme liability.

[66] The November 2006 report of the Committee on Capital Markets Regulation addresses the concern that U.S. capital markets are losing their competitive edge, in part because of a more burdensome legal environment in the aftermath of the Sarbanes-Oxley Act of 2002 and more aggressive government enforcement. *See* Committee on Capital Markets Reg'n Report, *supra* note 60. Shortly after the Committee on Capital Markets Regulation issued its report, New York City Mayor Michael Bloomberg and U.S. Senator Charles Schumer (New York) issued a similar report, prepared by McKinsey and Company, on the need to sustain the financial leadership of New York and the United States. *See, e.g.*, Aaron Lucchetti, "Moving the Market: Identity Crisis for New York?" *Wall Street Journal* (January 22, 2007), at C3. The report responds to concerns that U.S. financial firms are being adversely impacted as U.S. capital markets become relatively less attractive as compared to foreign markets because of, among other factors, a more demanding U.S. regulatory and enforcement environment in the aftermath of Enron's collapse and the enactment of Sarbanes-Oxley. To the extent that U.S. capital markets lose some of their competitive edge, it uniquely impacts New York as the center of the U.S. financial system. The U.S. Chamber of Commerce was next to weigh in, issuing a report in early 2007 on U.S. competitiveness in global financial markets. *See, e.g.*, Kara Scannell, "Panel Urges Steps to Boost Allure of U.S. Markets," *Wall Street Journal* (March 12, 2007), at A1.

[67] *See, e.g.*, Macey, *supra* note 61.

[68] The *New York Times* recently reported on criticism of hedge funds coming from certain Republican presidential candidates. *See* "In Debate, Hedge Funds Take Some Hits," *New York Times, DealBook* (Andrew Ross Sorkin, ed.) (October 10, 2007), available at http://dealbook.blogs.nytimes.com/2007/10/10/in-republican-debate-hedge-funds-take-some-hits/

[69] Indeed, investment adviser registration for hedge fund managers may have been a less intrusive government response than alternatives that could have come from Congress had the SEC not taken any steps to regulate the industry.

[70] For a classic treatment of the role of independent administrative agencies with subject matter expertise, see James M. Landis, *The Administrative Process* (New Haven: Yale University Press, 1938); see also Seligman, *supra* note 61, at 60-62 (discussing Landis's views in the context of securities regulation and the SEC).

[71] Further, securities regulators may learn from the public's views and thus should not disregard populist pressure out of hand. *See, e.g.*, Slovic, *supra* note 64. Neither, for that matter, should securities regulators disregard the views of corporate America and Wall Street.

[72] That said, regulating in the name of investor confidence, instead of zeroing in on the more concrete substantive merits of a proposal, can lead to loose regulatory analysis that can have longstanding adverse consequences for securities markets. *See* Choi and Pritchard, *supra* note 61, at 33 ("The SEC often uncritically states that it seeks to protect investors—and in particular, that absent the SEC's efforts, investor confidence in the market will deteriorate. Rarely, however, does the SEC verify that its assumptions are correct. The SEC instead simply asserts that investor confidence demands its latest regulatory intervention."). During her tenure at the SEC, Commissioner Cynthia Glassman stressed the need for more rigorous economic analysis at the agency. *See, e.g.*, Cynthia A. Glassman, Commissioner, U.S. Securities and Exchange Commission, "Observations of an Economist Commissioner on Leaving the SEC," Remarks Before the National Economists Club, July 6, 2006, available at http://sec.gov/news/speech/2006/spch070606cag.htm

[73] For public-choice analyses of securities regulation, see, for example, Phillips and Zecher, *supra* note 61; Donald C. Langevoort, "The SEC as a Bureaucracy: Public Choice, Institutional Rhetoric, and the Process of Policy

Formation," 47 *Washington and Lee Law Review* 527 (1990); Macey, *supra* note 61. *Cf.* Brody Mullins and Kara Scannell, "Hedge Funds Coming of Age Politically," *Wall Street Journal* (April 19, 2007), at A6 (discussing increasing political activity of the hedge fund industry).

By way of illustrating the role of special interests in securities regulation, the accounting industry successfully lobbied in the late 1990s and 2000 to blunt SEC efforts to fashion more demanding independence requirements for outside auditors; and in the early to mid-1990s, business interests successfully lobbied to prevent the Financial Accounting Standards Board from requiring the expensing of stock options, a particular concern of high-tech companies. *See* Seligman, *supra* note 61, at 714-41.

It is worth noting the possibility that at least some hedge funds may have welcomed the SEC's foray into hedge fund regulation. First, established funds may have welcomed hedge fund manager registration because it seemed to erect an entry barrier that disadvantaged smaller, less-established competitors. *See supra* note 15.

Second, SEC regulation today may have fended off an even more aggressive future crackdown by the SEC, let alone Congress, if hedge fund manager registration averted some lurking hedge fund meltdown. As it stands, given the present reliance on market discipline, one can reasonably anticipate a heavy-handed regulatory or legislative response if there is a major hedge fund collapse with widespread consequences. Consider, for example, the attention focused on the regulation of credit rating agencies in the aftermath of the credit crunch in the subprime market in 2007. *See, e.g.,* John C. Coffee, Jr., "The Mortgage Meltdown and Gatekeeper Failure," *New York Law Journal* (September 20, 2007), at 5; *see also* Erik R. Sirri, Testimony Concerning Recent Events in the Credit and Mortgage Markets and Possible Implications for U.S. Consumers and the Global Economy, Before the Financial Services Committee, U.S. House of Representatives, September 5, 2007, available at http://sec.gov/news/testimony/2007/ts090507 ers.htm

Third, greater SEC oversight may have lent legitimacy to the industry and assuaged the "fear factor"—that is, the free-floating anxiety of some investors and lawmakers that hedge funds simply are too secretive and shadowy, particularly given their impact on financial markets, to be lightly regulated.

[74] *Cf.* John C. Coates IV, "Private vs. Political Choice of Securities Regulation: A Political Cost/Benefit Analysis," 41 *Virginia Journal of International Law* 531, 572-73 (2001) (explaining the "suspicion of secret

power"). I appreciate Professor Donald Langevoort's highlighting this point to me.

[75] *See* Regulation D Proposal, *supra* note 22.

[76] *See generally* Choi and Pritchard, *supra* note 61.

[77] Regarding the precautionary principle of risk regulation, see generally Cass R. Sunstein, *Laws of Fear: Beyond the Precautionary Principle* (Cambridge: Cambridge University Press, 2005) [hereinafter Sunstein, *Laws of Fear*]; Frank B. Cross, "Paradoxical Perils of the Precautionary Principle," 53 *Washington and Lee Law Review* 851 (1996); David A. Dana, "A Behavioral Economic Defense of the Precautionary Principle," 97 *Northwestern University Law Review* 1315 (2003); Cass R. Sunstein, "Beyond the Precautionary Principle," 151 *University of Pennsylvania Law Review* 1003 (2003) [hereinafter Sunstein, "Beyond the Precautionary Principle"]; Cass R. Sunstein, "Precautions Against What? The Availability Heuristic and Cross-Cultural Risk Perception," 57 *Alabama Law Review* 75 (2005).

[78] *See, e.g.*, Sunstein, "Beyond the Precautionary Principle," *supra* note 77, at 1020-29.

[79] *See generally* Daniel Kahneman and Shane Frederick, "Representativeness Revisited: Attribute Substitution in Intuitive Judgment," in Thomas Gilovich et al. eds., *Heuristics and Biases: The Psychology of Intuitive Judgment* (Cambridge: Cambridge University Press, 2002), at 49, 60-73; Amos Tversky and Daniel Kahneman, "Availability: A Heuristic for Judging Frequency and Probability," in Daniel Kahneman et al. eds., *Judgment Under Uncertainty: Heuristics and Biases* (Cambridge: Cambridge University Press, 1982), at 163, 175-78. For more particularized treatment of these biases in the context of the precautionary principle, see, for example, Dana, *supra* note 77, at 1321-36; Sunstein, "Beyond the Precautionary Principle," *supra* note 77, at 1035-54. For a critical analysis that questions these biases, see Charles Yablon, "The Meaning of Probability Judgments: An Essay on the Use and Misuse of Behavioral Economics," 2004 *University of Illinois Law Review* 899.

[80] During other periods, such as a sustained bull market, other biases, including overconfidence, may be triggered, resulting in too little regulation and government oversight and enforcement that is too lax. Indeed, politics

also cut against more regulation during rising markets. There is no investor demand for more regulation when the economy is booming and investment portfolios are growing. Lawmakers, understandably, do not want to be seen as interfering with "good times" when there is no palpable risk to regulate.

[81] For analyses of these and other proposals, see, for example, Sunstein, *Laws of Fear, supra* note 77; Michael Abramowicz, "Information Markets, Administrative Decisionmaking, and Predictive Cost-Benefit Analysis," 71 *University of Chicago Law Review* 933 (2004); William N. Eskridge and John Ferejohn, "Structuring Lawmaking to Reduce Cognitive Bias: A Critical Review," 87 *Cornell Law Review* 616 (2002); Robert W. Hahn and Cass R. Sunstein, "A New Executive Order for Improving Federal Regulation? Deeper and Wider Cost-Benefit Analysis," 150 *University of Pennsylvania Law Review* 1489 (2002); Jeffrey J. Rachlinski and Cynthia R. Farina, "Cognitive Psychology and Optimal Government Design," 87 *Cornell Law Review* 549 (2002); Mark Seidenfeld, "Cognitive Loafing, Social Conformity, and Judicial Review of Agency Rulemaking," 87 *Cornell Law Review* 486 (2002); Cass R. Sunstein, "Cognition and Cost-Benefit Analysis," 29 *Journal of Legal Studies* 1059 (2000).

Concerning judicial review of SEC decision making, the U.S. Court of Appeals for the D.C. Circuit ruled that the SEC, in adopting new mutual fund board independence requirements, violated the Administrative Procedure Act when it failed adequately to consider the costs of enhanced board independence and the alternative proposed by two dissenting commissioners. *Chamber of Commerce of the United States of Am. v. SEC*, 412 F.3d 133 (D.C. Cir. 2005); *see also Chamber of Commerce of the United States of Am. v. SEC*, 443 F.3d 890 (D.C. Cir. 2006). For two cases finding that the SEC had overstepped its authority in adopting new rules concerning, respectively, hedge funds and broker-dealers, see *Goldstein v. SEC*, 451 F.3d 873 (D.C. Cir. 2006), and *Fin. Planning Ass'n v. SEC*, 482 F.3d 481 (D.C. Cir. 2007).

V. FINANCIAL DISCLOSURE, LIABILITY OF SUPERVISORS, AND LEGAL RISK IN FINANCIAL MARKETS

CHAPTER

11

"To Protect or Not to Protect, That Is the Question": Statutory Protections for Financial Supervisors—How to Promote Financial Stability by Enacting the Right Laws

ROSS DELSTON AND ANDREW CAMPBELL

This chapter considers the possible legal protections that should be extended to financial supervisors.[1] It begins with a discussion of why such protections are necessary, then describes how the Basel Core Principles and the IMF Transparency Code address the issue. It then examines two approaches that have been enacted into law, in New Zealand and Spain, respectively. Aspects of the role played by human rights legislation are also be examined, and suggested statutory objectives for use internationally are provided.

Introduction

It is now generally accepted as a best practice that statutory protections are necessary to ensure that financial supervisors are able to undertake their jobs effectively and properly. Why are such protections necessary?

When financial institutions, particularly banks and other depository institutions, get into trouble on their way to outright failure, supervisors typically are engaged in a number of ways, including the application of a range of sanctions such as the appointment of a conservator, the imposition of fines and other penalties, and, ultimately, revocation of license. During the period prior to the institution's failure, supervisors must act quickly and effectively to prevent, remediate, or mitigate the problems of the institution. When their actions are examined after the event, supervisors will often be criticized for actions taken and also may be criticized for failure to take particular courses of action. Because of the nature of their powers and responsibilities, which are discussed

315

further below, such criticism will inevitably lead to legal challenges to the actions taken by financial supervisors.

Financial supervisors are most at risk of legal challenge when they attempt to enforce laws, impose sanctions or other penalties, or to take control of a troubled institution. Supervisors will often have no option but to take such action to protect the depositors of the institution, other creditors, and the overall health of the financial system. In situations where depositors lose some or all of their savings or other creditors lose their claim in the assets of an ongoing institution, it is quite possible that financial supervisors will be subject to civil or, in some countries, criminal action.

The threat of litigation will inevitably have an effect on how financial supervisors perform. The threat is likely to be greater when there is a systemic banking crisis with a large number of insolvent banks. In such a situation the supervisor will undoubtedly have to revoke a number of banking licenses and liquidate banks. But even in the case of the failure of a single bank, the threat still exists.

This has led financial supervisors in a number of countries to consider steps to protect financial supervisors in their work.

Supervisory Powers and the Basel Core Principles

In 1997 the Basel Committee on Banking Supervision (the Committee)[2] promulgated the Basel Core Principles for Effective Banking Supervision (the Basel Core Principles, or BCP) which were revised in October 2006. "The Core Principles are a framework of minimum standards for sound supervisory practices and are considered universally applicable."[3]

In theory, international standards such as the BCP (and other standards such as the 40+9 Recommendations of the Financial Action Task Force on Money Laundering) constitute "soft law." However, in practice—through the Financial Sector Assessment Program (FSAP)[4] of the IMF and World Bank and the offshore financial center (OFC) assessment program of the IMF, and through technical assistance provided by the IMF and World Bank among others—the BCP have moved closer to the realm of "hard law," with the kind of force more typically found in international conventions. Indeed, in many countries the standards have been implemented into the domestic legal framework, thereby becoming hard rather than soft law for the particular jurisdiction.

The need for supervisors to have strong powers to operate effectively is recognized by Core Principle 23—Corrective and remedial powers of supervisors:

> Supervisors must have at their disposal an adequate range of supervisory tools to bring about timely corrective actions. This includes the ability, where appropriate, to revoke the banking licence or to recommend its revocation.

In addition to the Core Principles, the Basel Committee has produced criteria for use in the assessment of a country's compliance with the Core Principles. These assessment criteria are set forth in some detail in the Basel Core Principles Methodology (BCP Methodology).

The range of sanctions referred to in the BCP Methodology that should be available to banking supervisors and, by extension, to other financial supervisors, are found in Essential Criterion 4 of BCP 23:

- Restricting the current activities of the bank
- Withholding approval of new activities or acquisitions
- Restricting or suspending payments to shareholders or share repurchases
- Restricting asset transfers
- Barring individuals from banking
- Replacing or restricting the powers of managers, Board directors or controlling owners
- Facilitating a takeover by or merger with a healthier institution
- Providing for the interim management of the bank
- Revoking or recommending the revocation of the banking licence.

These sanctions are in addition to Essential Criterion 3 of BCP 23, which provides that the supervisor should have

> an appropriate range of supervisory tools for use when, in the supervisor's judgment, a bank is not complying with laws, regulations or supervisory decisions, or is engaged in unsafe or unsound practices, or when the interests of depositors are otherwise threatened. These tools include the ability to require a bank to take prompt remedial action and to impose penalties.

Further, according to Essential Criterion 6 of BCP 23 a supervisor is to be empowered to apply penalties and sanctions "not only to the bank but, when and if necessary, also to management and/or the Board, or individuals therein."

The list of sanctions above demonstrates the strength of the powers provided and the effects, financial and otherwise, that their use may have on a wide number of individuals, including bank managers, shareholders, depositors, employees of the failed banks, and others. It is therefore possible, indeed it is likely, that there will be a large number of aggrieved parties when any such supervisory action is taken. The range of individuals who claim to have been adversely affected will depend on the exact circumstances of each case, but it is inevitable when a bank fails that some will lose out. Aggrieved parties will often look for someone to blame for their losses and sometimes for a defendant with sufficient assets to sue. Financial supervisors will often be the target.

Statutory Protection

To be effective, the exact scope of the protection being provided must be clearly set out in statutory form, with no scope for ambiguity.

Why must such protection be statutory? Because the rights of aggrieved parties (parties who consider themselves to have been harmed by governmental action) are being limited by any such protections, both the aggrieved parties and the supervisors need to be aware of their exact legal positions and to ascertain whether the supervisor has, in fact, acted within the scope of the legal protection as enacted in the law. Only a statutory provision will be capable of achieving this clarity. In some cases, this type of protection may even be embodied in a constitutional provision as, for example, in the Basic Law of Germany.

The issue of legal protection for the financial supervisor was considered to be sufficiently significant that it is referred to in Core Principle 1, which provides:

> A suitable legal framework for banking supervision is also necessary, including provisions relating to authorisation of banking establishments and their ongoing supervision; powers to address compliance with laws as well as safety and soundness concerns; and *legal protection for supervisors.* (emphasis added)

According to the BCP Methodology, the following essential criteria are necessary to ensure that both the supervisory authority and its staff are adequately protected: First, the law must provide protection to the supervisory authority and its staff against lawsuits brought against them for any actions taken and/or omissions made in the discharge of their duties. This is subject to a "good faith" requirement (this aspect is discussed further below). Second, it is also necessary to ensure that the supervisory authority and its staff receive adequate protection against the costs involved in defending any claims brought against them. The protection will apply when they are "discharging their duties" and will therefore presumably not apply where a supervisor is either acting *ultra vires,* i.e., falling outside the scope of their authority.

The reference in BCP 1 to "legal protection for supervisors," raises three questions. First, is it a good idea to protect both the authority and its staff, or is it sufficient to protect the staff alone? Second, is it necessary or desirable to protect the sovereign, the state, or the government as a whole? Third, why is an indemnity necessary or desirable; is it because the costs alone, even if the result is a procedural or substantive victory, can have a chilling effect on the conduct of financial supervisors?

Transparency Code

Before answering these questions, reference should be made to a second international standard, dealing with transparency, that refers to statutory protections. The connection between transparency and statutory protections for financial supervisors may not be immediately obvious. In recent years, however, a growing acceptance of the benefits of transparency has been emerging globally, and the availability of information that can be understood by members of the public can assist in creating an environment in which there is less suspicion of administrative action and where information supplied to the public will be more likely to be believed. It is good practice to ensure that all aspects of the activities of regulatory agencies are covered by the transparency requirement.

The IMF, in cooperation with the Bank for International Settlements,[5] developed the Code of Good Practices on Transparency in Monetary and Financial Policies (the Transparency Code).[6] The Transparency Code was adopted by the IMF in September 1999 and is one of the standards that may be included when undertaking an FSAP.

The design of the Transparency Code rests on two principles. The first of these is that it is possible for monetary and financial policies to have a greater efficacy where the public knows what the instruments and goals of the policies are. This is coupled with a demonstration by the authorities of a credible commitment to achieving these goals. The second relates to good governance and provides that central banks and other financial agencies should be accountable for their actions. This is especially true where they are granted a considerable amount of autonomy.

The Transparency Code provides that information about legal protections for officials and staff of the central bank in the conduct of their official duties be publicly disclosed,[7] and this requirement is extended to officials and staff of financial agencies as well.[8] In other words, it should be clear in advance to all affected parties what the legal position is in relation to both who is protected, to what extent they are protected, and what any limits on the protection may be. Of course, any such information must be set out in clear and accessible language so that members of the public can easily understand it, and this is something that is also provided for in the Transparency Code.

It is also good practice to ensure that the transparency extends to setting out the reasons why the protections are being provided.

According to the supporting document to the Transparency Code,[9] the rationale for public disclosure of information about the legal protections being provided to the officials and/or staff of financial agencies rests upon the need of "to ensure that such officials and staff can perform the official duties without fear of being personally subjected to legal action."[10] The Supporting Document to the Transparency Code goes further than simply concentrating on the need for public disclosure and contains a survey of the statutory protection accorded to officials and staff of financial agencies in a number of jurisdictions.[11] What this reveals is that there are significant differences in approach to the degree of protection provided, but unfortunately it does not provide information on the actual degree of transparency in each of these jurisdictions.

Human Rights Issues

As seen above, the Basel Core Principles include "legal protection for supervisors," and the Methodology makes it clear that this protection extends both to the supervisory authority and to its staff. Essential Criterion 1 to Principle 1(5) states: "The law provides protection to the supervisory authority and its staff against lawsuits for actions taken and/or omissions made while discharging its duties in good faith" while Essential Criteria 2 to Principle 1(5) provides: "the supervisory authority and its staff are adequately protected against the costs of defending their actions and/or omissions made discharging their duties in good faith."

This requires, therefore, that the supervisory agency itself be protected from civil suit. Some countries, such as India, have extended the supervisory protection even further so that no suits are permitted—not just against the agency and the supervisors in their individual capacities, but also against the state. Is this in accord with the rule of law and established principles of human rights? An answer may be found in one such international standard, the Convention for the Protection of Human Rights and Fundamental Freedoms as amended by Protocol No. 11 (Rome, 4.XI.1950), popularly known as the European Convention on Human Rights (ECHR).[12]

The ECHR established the European Court of Human Rights (the Court) and contains a series of obligations and prohibitions to protect human rights and promote fundamental freedoms. The ECHR has become the best-known attempt to promote human rights; many legal jurisdictions, not just in Europe, have used it has the basis for their national human rights legislation.

Article 6.1 of the ECHR states: "In the determination of his civil rights and obligations ... everyone is entitled to a fair and public hearing within a reasonable period of time by an independent and impartial tribunal established by law." The ECHR has interpreted this to mean that individuals have a right of access to a court of law to redress grievances.

For example, in *Bellet v. France*, the Court stated: [13]

> The fact of having access to domestic remedies, only to be told that one's actions are barred by operation of law does not always satisfy the requirements of Article 6 para. 1 (art. 6-1). The degree of access afforded by the national legislation must also be sufficient to secure the individuals' "right to a court," having regard to the principle of the rule of law in a democratic society. For the right of access to be effective, an individual must have a clear, practical opportunity to challenge an act that is an interference with his rights (see the de Geouffre de la Pradelle judgment previously cited, p. 43, para. 34).[14]

The next question to be asked is whether providing statutory protection for supervisors is consistent with upholding the human rights of those who are likely to be affected by the supervisors' decisions. Is it legal under the ECHR to provide such statutory protection?

As seen above, the ECHR provides an entitlement to everyone to have a fair and public hearing by an independent and impartial tribunal established by law. Is this right absolute or is it permissible under the ECHR to have exceptions or limitations? The jurisprudence of the Court has held that the right to have access to a court of law is not an absolute right and, of particular importance for the purpose of this chapter, that the interests of the state can, in appropriate circumstances, be taken into consideration.

Where the Court is considering whether the right of access of a claimant can be restricted, there are three tests that the court takes into account. The first is to determine whether the claim actually relates to a human rights issue. Political rights, for example, are not within the scope of Article 6.1, but claims for a breach of statutory duty are. Second, it is important to realize that Article 6.1 does not address substantive law issues which may prevent a litigant from having access to an appropriate court. However, the Court has indicated that it would not be consistent with the rule of law to simply "remove from the jurisdiction of the courts a whole range of civil claims or confer immunities from civil liability on large groups or categories of persons."[15] Third, it is possible for a state to limit the right of access to a court by the use of appropriate statutory provisions provided the need to have a balance between the protection of the rights of an individual and the interests of the community as a whole is taken into account. In one case,[16] the Court determined that a statutory immunity granted to the United Kingdom Department of Health and Social Security (as it was known at that time) was not an impairment of the right of access to an independent and impartial tribunal.

The state therefore, under the ECHR, is not prevented from providing statutory immunity for supervisors. It can do this without violating the human rights of an individual provided that certain conditions are met.

However, providing that the statutory protections are built into the legal provisions, there is an argument that the rights of individuals to bring actions should not be restricted. Because claimants would have to prove that the defendant has acted either in bad faith or not in the ordinary course of their duties to have a successful claim, they should surely have the right to a tribunal to air their case. The costs involved in bringing such a case and the relatively low chance of success would deter frivolous claims.

Therefore, in providing for such protections, states must ensure that in protecting supervisors in their individual capacity, and in some cases the supervisory agency in its institutional capacity, that they do not block all means for individuals to seek redress for damages.

Statutory Protection in Two Jurisdictions

The following section is an examination of two jurisdictions—New Zealand and Spain—that have provided statutory protections for financial sector supervisors. New Zealand is a common law jurisdiction; Spain is civil law.

These two jurisdictions provide a clear illustration of different approaches. In particular, they demonstrate that there is not, as yet, an internationally agreed approach to this issue and that there appears to be a fundamental issue that needs to be addressed—that is, whether the supervisory authority as a body should, or should not, have the same degree of statutory protections as are provided to the members of the authority's staff. In New Zealand the supervisory authority and its staff are protected, which is in keeping with the Basel Core Principles. In Spain the law provides a right of action against a supervisory authority to those who suffered alleged damage.

A Common Law Approach: New Zealand

New Zealand provides an example of a common law jurisdiction that provides extensive statutory protection. Under the Reserve Bank of New Zealand Act 1989, protection is provided to the Reserve Bank and its officers, employees, and agents. Section 179 (2) provides that "no person to whom this section applies is personally liable for an act done or omitted to be done in the exercise or performance in good faith of that person's functions, duties, or powers under this Act."

The protection therefore is not absolute but subject to a number of conditions. First, it includes the concept of acting within the scope of authority. Second, it contains a good faith requirement for the protections to apply. Third, it explicitly states that the employee shall not be personally liable for damages. Additionally, in section 179A, it indemnifies officers, employees, and agents of the Reserve Bank.

The indemnity for the Reserve Bank and its officers and employees provides in section 179 A (1) as follows:

> (1) The Crown indemnifies the persons listed in subsection (2) for any liability that arises from the exercise or purported exercise of, or omission to exercise, any power conferred by this Act unless it is shown that the exercise or purported exercise of, or omission to exercise, the power was in bad faith.

The indemnity therefore covers all persons who may be working for, or on behalf of, the Reserve Bank, including agents and members of advisory committees. It will also extend to any exercise or purported exercise or omission to exercise *any* power under the Act. It is important to note, however, that it excludes any exercise of a power that is carried out in bad faith.

The indemnity is given by the Crown, i.e., the sovereign, not the Reserve Bank, and therefore presumably would provide greater certainty to those covered by the indemnity.

A Civil Law Approach: Spain

Under Spanish law, government agencies can be liable for damages caused by their employees in certain situations. These are set out in statutory form in the Legal Procedure of Public Administrations and the Administrative Common Procedure Act of 26th November 1992.

Section 139, entitled Principles of Responsibility provides:

> 1. Citizens will be entitled to receive an indemnification from the relevant Public Administrations [government agencies] in connection with any damage that they may suffer in any of their assets and rights, except in cases of force majeure, provided that damage arises as a result of the normal or abnormal operation of public services.

2. In any event, any alleged damage shall have to be actual, financially assessable and individualized as to a person or group of persons.

The emphasis under the Spanish legislation is on the rights of citizens to seek redress from the government (public administration). An interesting feature is that it provides broad coverage to citizens against both normal and abnormal actions of government officials. Arguably, this acts as an incentive for citizens to proceed against the government rather than individual civil servants.

Comparing the Two Approaches

The New Zealand approach emphasizes the protection of both the agency itself and the individuals who will undertake the particular actions. The degree of protection provided is therefore very high. Under the Spanish approach, the law seeks to provide members of the public with a specific right against a public body. Under the Spanish system an aggrieved citizen who can prove actual financial damage is able to make a claim against the relevant government agency.

The New Zealand approach clearly provides a high level of protection and is in accordance with precise language of BCP 1 and the BCP Methodology. But does it go too far in the opposite direction, potentially breaching international standards on access to courts, as discussed above in connection with the ECHR?

Good Faith and Bad Faith

The concept of "good faith" has already been mentioned several times in this chapter. But what exactly does it mean? According to the *Oxford Dictionary of Law*, 5th edition, it is: "Honesty. An act carried out in good faith is one carried out honestly. Good faith is implied by law into certain contracts, such as those relating to commercial agency." Under English law a good example is provided by section 90 of the Bills of Exchange Act 1882, which provides that "[a] thing is deemed to be done in good faith, within the meaning of this Act, where it is in fact done honestly, whether it is done negligently or not." This principle is based on even earlier case law such as *Crook v. Jadis* (1834) 5 B. & Ad. 910.

It is therefore clear, at least from English case law, that negligence by itself does not amount to bad faith. What is required is to establish some degree of dishonesty. Under English law—and this is generally the case in common law jurisdictions,—there is another facet to bad faith, which is termed misfeasance.[17] This concerns the situation where a public official uses his or her power for an ulterior or improper purpose that is considered to be contrary to the overall public good. Such behavior falls within the concept of bad faith. Arguably, it is necessary to extend the concept of bad faith to include abuses of power by public officials.

Of course, those who wish to bring a claim based on bad faith will be required to prove it. It will not be for the person who has undertaken the act to prove that he or she did in fact act without bad faith.

The issue of good faith therefore centers on the concept of honesty and the need for the public official to have acted with a proper purpose. It would seem, under the English common law at least, that provided a person has acted honestly and with proper purpose he or she should be protected by the statutory protections provided.

What Should the Law Contain?

Having looked at the Basel Core Principles, the legal issues involved in protecting financial supervisors, and two approaches to legislation, an appropriate law should contain provisions:

- Limiting protection to actions taken by supervisors within the scope of their authority.
- Limiting protections to actions taken in good faith, or, alternatively, excluding actions taken in bad faith.
- Extending coverage to all individuals, including members of the board of directors, officers, and employees, as well as agents, consultants, and contractors such as public accounting firms. The reason for such wide coverage is that anyone left out will potentially become an even greater target.

- In addition to providing protections for the individuals listed above, possibly also protecting the financial supervisory agency or central bank, but it should not be a blanket grant of immunity that would cover not only those two categories but also the actions of the state itself so as to block the access of an aggrieved party to a court of law.
- Providing an indemnity by the central bank, the state or sovereign, or other relevant authority or agency that covers all of the costs of defending any suits that may be brought against an authority or any of the other parties listed in the third bullet above.

Conclusions

Although more countries have enacted statutory protections and indemnities for financial supervisors in recent years, many, particularly those with civil law regimes, do not currently have such protections, and this is something that needs to be addressed. In so doing, countries should consider the application of such protections to financial sector supervisors, as well, rather than limiting protections to banking supervisors. It is becoming increasingly common for jurisdictions to consider the use of a single unified regulator with responsibility for the entire financial sector. Adequate legal protections are necessary to enable such a unified financial supervisor to function effectively, as recognized by the Basel Committee with respect to banking supervisors.

Because financial sector supervisors often must act with considerable speed, especially during a systemic crisis when many banks may be insolvent or nearly insolvent, decisions that were necessarily taken quickly may not always stand up to scrutiny when viewed after the crisis has abated. Accordingly, there may be many aggrieved parties who would wish to take legal action after the full extent of the government's actions can be assessed. Provided the supervisor has acted in good faith, within the scope of authority, and with access to courts to redress the claims of aggrieved parties, the protections should apply.

Legislators may balk at singling out central bankers or financial supervisors for such protections. What about other civil servants, such as police and other law enforcement officials, and tax collectors? There may be valid reasons for extending protection to these groups too, but it is beyond the scope of this chapter to consider this issue.

Would enacting such protections act as a curb on corruption or would corrupt officials be insulated as a result of such protections? This is an ongoing problem to which there is no easy answer. It is hoped that the provision of such protections would have the effect of curbing corruption. But the problem of corruption is not one that should act as a brake on the introduction of appropriate statutory protections for financial supervisors.

Notes

Note: Although any mistakes appearing herein are our own, the authors would like to thank the following for their assistance with this chapter: Roy Baban, Steve Dawe, Eric Robert of the IMF Legal Department; Jose Antonio Alepuz of the Bank of Spain; Dr. Amrita Mukherjee of the University of Leeds; Dr. Dalvinder Singh of the University of Warwick; and Peter Whitten.

[1] For the purposes of this chapter, the term *financial supervisor* includes all of the directors, officers, employees, and agents of the financial supervisory agency and anyone else acting on its behalf.

[2] The Committee is based at the Bank for International Settlements. For more information, see www.bis.org.

[3] BCP, p. 2, para. 5.

[4] *See* www.imf.org/external/np/fsap/fsap.asp.

[5] A representative group of central banks, financial agencies, other relevant international and regional organizations, and selected academic experts were also involved in the consultations.

[6] *See* www.imf.org/external/np/mae/mft/code/index.htm#IV.

[7] Section 4.4.1.

[8] Section 8.4.1.

[9] *See* www.imf.org/external/np/mae/mft/sup/index.htm.

[10] Section 8.4.1.

[11] Section 8.4.1. Box 3-3.

[12] *See* http://conventions.coe.int/Treaty/en/Treaties/Html/005.htm.

[13] *Bellet v. France*, judgment of 20 November 1995, para. 36, 21/1995/527/613.

[14] *de Geouffre de la Pradelle v. France*, judgment of 16 December 1992 (Series A no. 253-B).

[15] *Fayed v. United Kingdom,* 15 EHRR CD 32 para 65.

[16] *Ashingdane v. United Kingdom*, May 28 1985, 7 EHRR 528, para. 59.

[17] Under English law the tort of misfeasance can be traced back to at least 1364.

12 | Achieving Financial Stability Through Disclosure

ROBERTA S. KARMEL

Effective securities regulation contributes to financial stability by establishing a sound environment for capital formation. It fosters the efficient allocation of resources within an economy, without the need for government direction of those resources. In the United States the federal securities laws are predicated on the theory that full disclosure by companies will enable participants in the public securities markets to price securities efficiently, and that this pricing mechanism will then foster the efficient allocation of resources among businesses competing for capital. Such efficient pricing should reduce speculation and undue price volatility. In order for full disclosure to be an effective basis for regulation, however, the disclosure must be free from fraud.

This chapter first discusses the general objectives of securities regulation. It then surveys the choices of regulatory strategy that governments can make. The final section examines the full disclosure system of the U.S. federal securities laws, including an outline of the reforms to the disclosure system since the bursting of the technology bubble in 2000-2001: the Sarbanes-Oxley Act of 2002 (Sarbanes-Oxley),[1] rulemaking by the Securities and Exchange Commission (SEC), and decisions of the courts.

Objectives of Securities Regulation

Capital Formation

The United States, the United Kingdom, and a few other countries utilize the securities markets as a primary mechanism for capital formation.[2] By contrast, some other countries—notably Germany and Japan—depend upon banks and internally generated profits for capital.[3] The different systems of corporate finance have led to different corporate structures as well as different regulatory systems. In countries where the stock market provides the basis for capital formation, investor confidence is of great importance, and a primary purpose of securities regulation is to foster such confidence. In recent years many academics have attacked the proscriptive nature of securities regulation and argued for more market-based systems of regulation, but none of these alternative theories have displaced the idea that successful securities regulation must be based on investor trust in the markets.[4] Indeed, after the stock market scandals of 2001-2002, the U.S. Congress reacted to a perceived loss of investor confidence in the public securities markets by passing the highly regulatory Sarbanes-Oxley Act.

According to the International Organization of Securities Commissions (IOSCO), the three core objectives of securities regulation are protecting investors; ensuring that markets are fair, efficient, and transparent; and reducing systemic risk.[5] The overarching purpose of securities regulation is investor protection. This is because investors entrust their capital to the management of professionals, and they are vulnerable to misconduct by intermediaries. Even supposedly sophisticated investors are not always able to comprehend the complex nature of securities transactions and can be the victims of overreaching by public companies and securities industry intermediaries. Although much of securities regulation today is by government agencies, most jurisdictions also rely on self-regulation to some extent.

Disclosure Regulation and Corporate Governance Standards

Although some systems of securities regulation depend to some degree on merit regulation—or governmental control of which corporations qualify to tap the capital markets—the United States has a disclosure-based system. Disclosure is a keystone of most other securities regulatory systems as well. In the United States the securities laws generally regulate disclosure by public companies, both when such companies engage in capital-raising transactions and on an annual and periodic basis, and the fiduciary obligations of corporate officers and directors is generally covered by state corporation law. Even in jurisdictions where there is not a similar federal legal system, there generally is a separation between securities regulation and corporate law. In the European Union, for example, securities laws directives are covered by the Financial Services Action Plan and the Lamfalussy process, whereas corporate law is covered by the Corporate Law Action Plan.[6]

Stock exchange listing requirements have acted as a bridge between these two disciplines in the United States, as well as in other countries.[7] Many of the shareholder protections now embodied in the Securities Exchange Act of 1934 (Exchange Act), such as the need to provide shareholders with annual financial reports and to hold annual meetings, originated in listing standards of the NYSE.[8] Sarbanes-Oxley specifically required stock exchanges to impose corporate governance standards on listed companies with regard to director independence and committee structure.[9] In jurisdictions where offerings are conducted over a stock exchange, the exchanges traditionally judged whether an issuer was fit to go public and, in addition, vetted prospectuses used in the offering process. Further, exchanges sometimes demanded changes in a company's board before a public offering could occur, or other merit-based or corporate governance changes in a company's structure.

In regulating broker-dealers, the SEC, like other financial regulators, has adopted capital-adequacy rules, but unlike bank regulators, for example, it does not believe its mission is to prevent financial failures, but rather only to protect customers who have property on deposit with broker-dealers. Accordingly, the SEC has utilized disclosure, as well as substantive capital-adequacy regulation, to protect broker-dealers' customers in connection with safeguarding customer funds and securities.

Choices of Regulatory Strategies

Command-and-Control Regulation by Government

An increasing amount of securities regulation operates by way of command and control regulation imposed by securities regulatory agencies. The entire panoply of regulations of the national market system—by the SEC in the United States and the Financial Service Action Plan initiatives in the EU—are examples of this type of regulation. Another example of command and control regulation is capital-adequacy requirements for financial institutions, although the trend is toward risk assessment requirements rather than arbitrary ratios of obligations to capital. Where consolidated regulation has been put in place, such as in the United Kingdom, regulation is imposed by an agency which, for all practical purposes, operates as a monopoly. In other countries, such as the United States, where functional regulation and federal-state regulation prevail, there is a certain amount of competition between regulators. Some have argued that such regulatory competition is healthy; others are more skeptical.[10]

Although there have been some deregulatory initiatives with respect to securities exchange regulation,[11] the worldwide trend seems to be to impose an increasing amount of complex rules upon market participants. Although disclosure frequently has been a substitute for regulation in the past, proscriptive rules have in many areas replaced disclosure.[12] Similarly, competition is not frequently utilized as a substitute for government regulation.

Since the bursting of the technology bubble in the late 1990s, regulations by government agencies and self-regulatory organizations (SROs) covering the securities markets and regulated entities in those markets have been proliferating. This outbreak of regulatory fervor has been justified as needed to correct the abuses of the late 1990s, but it may also be the result of competing regulators trying to outdo one another in cracking down on malefactors.[13]

Recourse to Courts or Arbitration

In the United States, after-the-fact regulatory standards frequently are imposed by way of securities litigation. Such adjudications establish norms for future conduct. This litigation can be instituted by the SEC or private parties, and the standards developed tend to be more flexible than rules. In the United States and elsewhere there is also a considerable amount of arbitration between customers and securities firms and between securities firms. Since arbitrators are not required to adhere to precedent, this type of adjudication leads to standards that are less clear than SEC or judicial opinions.

Competition

Competition is a recognized alternative to government regulation, and was utilized in the 1970s to eliminate rate setting in securities regulation and other regulatory areas.[14] The SEC is required to take competition into account in determining market-structure issues,[15] and clearing agent issues,[16] but it generally opts for regulation rather than competition.[17] In many jurisdictions, there is a single national exchange and clearing agency, and a single government regulator. Accordingly, intra-country competition may not be a consideration in promulgating regulation, but global competition may become an important influence on regulators in all countries.

Self-Regulation

Much regulation has traditionally been imposed on markets and market participants by SROs. Although in some economic areas, governments have been privatizing former state-owned enterprises, in the securities field government has been seizing power from SROs. Some regulation formerly conducted by exchanges, such as the vetting of prospectuses, is now generally conducted by government securities regulators. Listing standards are likewise becoming government-mandated standards.[18] When the Financial Services Authority (FSA) was created in London, a variety of SROs were eliminated in favor of government regulation.

Although self-regulation continues to be a popular way for governments to impose controls on the securities industry, it has also become suspect. When the Public Company Accounting Oversight Board was created by Sarbanes-Oxley to regulate auditing by accountants for public companies, it was established as neither a government agency nor an SRO, but the claim that this agency is not a state actor can be challenged.[19] If such an agency is not, as a legal or practical matter, an SRO, then its advantages over a government regulator are questionable. Further, its constitutionality is currently being challenged.[20]

The Full Disclosure System of the Federal Securities Laws of the United States

When the first of the U.S. federal securities laws, the Securities Act of 1933 (Securities Act),[21] was passed, there was a debate between advocates of controlling the sale of securities by issuers that were dishonest or in unsound condition[22] and advocates of disclosure as a means to prevent the sale of poorly capitalized companies.[23] State blue sky laws, which preceded the federal securities laws, generally prevented a corporation from making a public offering unless it was fair, just and equitable, as determined by a state official.[24] The Securities Act permitted any corporation to go public if it made full disclosure of its business and affairs to investors.[25]

Shortly after the Securities Act was passed, William O. Douglas, who was to exert considerable influence on the SEC as an early chairman, criticized the full disclosure philosophy of the statute. In his view, it was a failure because it "presupposes that the glaring light of publicity will give the investors needed protection," but investors "either lack the training or intelligence to assimilate ... and find ... useful [the balance sheets, contracts or other data in the registration statement] or are so concerned with a speculative profit as to consider them irrelevant."[26] Douglas espoused a regulatory theory that was an integral part of a whole program of industrial regulation and organization for a modern and complex economy. Control over access to the market, he argued, "would be an administrative control lodged not only in the hands of the new self-disciplined business groups but also in the hands of governmental agencies whose function would be to articulate the public interest with the profit motive."[27] Regulation of corporate governance by the SEC was injected into statutes passed after the Securities Act and intended to curb abuses by specific industries,[28] but the SEC was not given authority to regulate the structure of corporate boards generally, even when major amendments to the Exchange Act in 1964 gave the SEC power to direct a continuous disclosure system for all public companies, as opposed to its previous authority over only exchange-listed companies.[29] One possible exception, the proxy provisions of the Exchange Act,[30] generally has been regarded primarily as disclosure rather than regulatory provisions.[31] Similarly, the SEC's regulatory authority over tender offers[32] has been interpreted as giving the SEC little authority to determine the outcome of contests for corporate control.[33]

The Securities Act regulates the distribution or underwriting of securities and is based on the premise that if companies going public make full disclosure, this disclosure can be evaluated by investors who can then fend for themselves. In addition to authorizing the SEC to dictate the disclosures that need to be made in initial public offerings, and the financial statements that such companies must provide to investors, the Securities Act specifies private remedies for investors who suffer damages by reason of false or misleading information in prospectuses.[34] The Exchange Act requires all companies that have made a public offering, are listed on an exchange, or have US$10 million in assets and 500 shareholders to register its securities with the SEC.[35] Thereafter, such companies must file and send to shareholders an annual report that includes year-end audited financial statements,[36] file quarterly unaudited financial statements and make periodic disclosures of materially important events. In addition to these SEC requirements mandating full disclosure of an issuer's business, financial condition, management and other matters, the stock exchanges impose continuous disclosure requirements on listed companies. These obligations are enhanced by a ban against trading on nonpublic material corporate information and general anti-fraud provisions giving investors civil remedies against corporations that fail to fulfill their disclosure obligations.[37] In addition to the liability the Securities Act and the Exchange Act impose on public corporations, their principal officers, directors, and reputational gatekeepers such as auditors and underwriters are also at risk of liability if full disclosure is not provided to investors.[38]

The SEC has articulated its ideas and policies concerning disclosure in a variety of regulations, including registration forms and detailed instructions on how to comply with those forms.[39] It has also promulgated numerous interpretations of the disclosure provisions [40] and enforced its views regarding disclosure in civil and criminal prosecutions against violators of the laws and regulations regarding disclosure.[41] In addition, the SEC staff gives comments to issuers on their disclosure documents, and this informal administrative process often informs regulated entities and their advisors of the staff's evolving views on disclosure policies.

Since 1980 the SEC has endeavored to integrate the disclosure provisions of the Securities Act and the Exchange Act, in order to provide investors with a single disclosure template for transactional and periodic disclosures.[42] This policy culminated in 2005 in the Securities Offering Reforms.[43] The SEC's integrated disclosure policy is based on the efficient-market hypothesis—the doctrine that once an issuer has established itself in the public securities markets and is widely followed by analysts, its stock market value reflects all publicly disclosed information about the issuer. Further, if the pricing mechanism for securities is efficient, securities prices should be less volatile and speculation should be kept at bay.

Changes to Public Company Disclosure After Sarbanes-Oxley

Unfortunately, the SEC's full-disclosure regulations and other regulatory tools for dealing with speculation did not prevent the technology bubble of the late 1990s. One consequence was that in Sarbanes-Oxley the Congress directed certain reforms of the disclosure system. These changes included CEO and CFO certifications; auditor attestations as to internal controls; better disclosures as to non-GAAP financial measures; more rapid disclosures of material changes in the issuer's business and affairs; and disclosures regarding codes of ethics and board composition. In addition to passing regulations to implement these statutory amendments, the SEC embarked on an ambitious rule-making proceeding to improve disclosures regarding executive compensation.[44]

Sarbanes-Oxley requires the SEC to adopt rules requiring the principal executive and financial officers of SEC registered issuers to certify annual and quarterly reports filed with the SEC. The signing officer must certify that he or she has reviewed the report; it does not contain untrue or misleading statements; it fairly presents in all material respects the financial condition and results of operations of the issuer; and the signing officers are responsible for establishing and maintaining internal controls, have designed such controls to ensure that material information is made known to such officers and others, and have evaluated such controls.[45] Further, there are criminal penalties provided for false certifications.[46]

A related mandated disclosure is that companies include in their annual reports an explanation of their internal controls.[47] Under the SEC's final rules, an issuer's annual report must include a statement of the management's responsibility over internal controls and reporting; a statement on the framework used to evaluate those controls over the past year; management's assessments of the effectiveness of these controls over the past year, with an identification of any material weaknesses; and a statement that the issuer's auditors have attested to the management's assessment of internal controls.[48]

The filing of false or misleading financial statements with the SEC has long been subject to a variety of sanctions in SEC proceedings, criminal cases, and private litigation. Whether a CEO or CFO could be held liable for such statements generally depended on an analysis of the particular facts of a case.[49] The new certification requirement probably will make it easier to prosecute these top executive officers in such situations, but they will not prevent the filing of fraudulent financial statements.[50] The legal requirement that corporations have adequate systems of internal controls dates back to the 1977 amendments to the Exchange Act discussed above.[51] Further, the need for directors to be concerned about internal control systems in fulfilling their duty-of-care responsibilities has been enunciated in Delaware case law.[52] Sarbanes-Oxley adds another layer of legal obligation to this standard by imposing direct responsibility on executive officers for the establishment and maintenance of internal control systems. There is no question that internal control systems are extremely important and are the predicate for accurate and reliable financial reporting in today's complex business environment. But there is a question as to whether the new certification requirements are appropriately ensuring the reliability of financial statements by adding layers of costly and time consuming bureaucratic review within public companies.

The regulations for internal-controls attestation have proved extremely controversial because of their enormous expense due to the manner in which auditors have interpreted their responsibilities in order to make such an attestation. Both smaller public companies and foreign issuers have protested the attestation requirement, and the SEC has postponed the implementation of attestation for such issuers.[53] Further, the SEC has embarked upon rule making to determine whether the requirement can be altered for such issuers.[54]

Section 401(b) of Sarbanes-Oxley instructed the SEC to adopt disclosure rules for financial information that is not calculated in accordance with GAAP. The SEC then adopted rules for the use of non-GAAP financial information in the preparation of an annual report.[55] These rules essentially require companies that report any non-GAAP financial measures to reconcile these figures to GAAP financial measures.

Section 409 of Sarbanes-Oxley requires that issuers disclose "on a rapid and current basis" such information concerning material changes in their financial conditions or operations as the SEC determines is necessary or useful for the protection of investors. This instruction to the SEC to move in the direction of a continuous rather than a periodic disclosure system led to new rules regarding the timing for the filing of annual and periodic reports and an amendment to the list of items requiring the filing of a special report.

Prior to the enactment of Sarbanes-Oxley, public companies were required to file their annual reports on Form 10-K with the SEC within 90 days of the end of a fiscal year and quarterly reports on Form 10Q within 45 days of the end of each quarter. Reports of material events were required to be filed on Form 8-K within 10 days at the end of the month in which the event occurred. The requirement that reports be filed on a rapid and current basis has changed these time frames. Currently, "accelerated filers"[56] must file annual reports within 60 days after the end of a fiscal year, and (beginning December 15, 2006) must file quarterly reports within 35 days of the end of each quarter. For the time being, other filers are not required to file reports on this speedier schedule.

Important new events were added to the triggers for the filing of an 8-K by public companies.[57] These new disclosure requirements include the following occurrences:

- Entry into a material definitive agreement not made in the ordinary course of business;

- Termination of a material definitive agreement;

- Creation of a direct financial obligation or an obligation under an off-balance sheet arrangement;

- Triggering events that accelerate or increase a direct financial obligation or an obligation under an off-balance sheet arrangement;

- Costs associated with exit or disposal activities, or other action that disposes of long-lived assets or terminates employees under certain plans;

- Material impairments;

- Notice of delisting or failure to satisfy a listing rule or standard;

- A decision that previously issued financial statements are no longer reliable;

- Departure of directors and officers;

- Unregistered sales of equity securities of more than 1 percent of a company's shares;

- Material modifications to rights of security holders;

- Amendments to articles of incorporation or bylaws or changes in fiscal year.

The last three items previously were reported in an issuer's quarterly reports. Further, the 8-K now has to be filed 4 days after an event as opposed to the previous 5 business day or 15 calendar day requirements.[58]

The provision with regard to the filing of a Form 8-K within 4 business days after a company's entry into a material definitive agreements outside its ordinary course of business has been further amended by the SEC's recent rule making on executive compensation and related party disclosure.[59] Disclosure of employment compensation arrangements for purposes of Form 8-K reporting is now limited to those compensation arrangements with executive officers and directors that are unquestionably or presumptively material. But material arrangements beyond employment agreements may have to be reported.[60]

It is interesting that Sarbanes-Oxley did not require, and the SEC did not change, the dates for the filing of insider transactions or accumulations of stock by potential tender offerors. Although there have been suggestions in the past for closing the 10-day window of the Williams Act, and change of control transactions do add volatility to securities prices, the SEC seems to be disinclined to put a damper on such transactions by requiring prompter announcements of stock accumulations.[61] Similarly, Sarbanes-Oxley did not require, and the SEC did not change, the timing for the filing of reports of purchases or sales of public company securities by officers, directors, and ten percent stockholders.[62]

One of the changes in the administration of SEC disclosure policy accomplished by Sarbanes-Oxley was a requirement that every three years the agency review the Section 401(b) periodic reports of all issuers listed on a stock exchange or traded on NASDAQ (which has since become an exchange).[63] During the bubble years, the SEC was not conducting such reviews and, for example, never reviewed any of Enron's filings. Since the SEC has long promoted the idea of integrated disclosure based on the annual and periodic reporting requirements, this failure to review annual reports was a serious lapse. The SEC now gives issuers comments on annual reports and in other ways has paid more attention to disclosure issues in documents in addition to prospectuses in initial public offerings.

The most important disclosure reform of the SEC since 2002 is its new regulation of executive compensation. Although the details of this rule making are beyond the scope of this paper, it is a good example of the use of disclosure by the SEC as a substitute for substantive regulation. The purpose of the regulation is compensation disclosure, rather than control or limitations on compensation. The theory of the new regulation is that enhanced transparency will enable investors to protect themselves. Although suggested by some, the SEC did not attempt to require an advisory shareholder vote on executive compensation.[64]

Disclosure by SEC-Regulated Financial Institutions

The SEC, like other financial regulators, imposes capital-adequacy requirements on the broker-dealers subject to its jurisdiction. But the SEC's mandate has never been to assure the safety and soundness of broker-dealers or to prevent their financial collapse, but rather to safeguard customer funds in the possession of such firms. The Exchange Act requires broker-dealers to meet such operational and financial adequacy standards the SEC may establish.[65] In that connection, the SEC has promulgated the net capital rule, requiring a broker-dealer to maintain a sufficient asset base for its operations.[66] The SEC also requires the segregation of customers' funds and securities from its proprietary accounts.[67]

Yet, after widespread broker-dealer failures as the result of the paperwork crisis of the late 1960s and early 1970s, and the insolvency of many broker-dealers at that time, Congress and the SEC broke with the general policy of bank regulators to maintain confidentiality with regard to the financial condition of banks in order to prevent bank runs, and required broker-dealers to publicly disclose their financial condition to their customers. Congress felt that during the period from 1967 to 1970, "there was a notable absence of adequate disclosure of financial condition by broker-dealers to their customers."[68] At about this time, the SEC's chief accountant called for amending broker-dealer audit requirements to provide substantially greater disclosure to public customers. Although the SEC's rule making to accomplish this policy did not go as far as the staff's recommendations, it did eliminate the broker-dealer's option of filing the auditor's letter on internal controls on a confidential basis.[69]

When the Exchange Act was amended in 1975, Section 17(e) was added to provide that every registered broker-dealer annually file with the SEC a balance sheet and income statement certified by an independent public accountant and such other financial statements and information as the SEC should require, and further, should send such information to its customers. The SEC implemented this provision by adopting a new regulation requiring the filing of certain reports with the SEC by broker-dealers, and furnishing to customers within 45 days thereafter an audited balance sheet with a footnote containing the firm's required net capital under the SEC's net capital rule.[70] Although other provisions of the Exchange Act and other SEC rules help assure the ability of broker-dealers to meet their obligations to customers and other broker-dealers, these disclosure provisions gave customers the necessary confidence to entrust their funds and securities to broker-dealers and probably avoided more stringent command and control regulations concerning capital adequacy.

Although the SEC does not regulate the capital adequacy of banks, it does require banks that are publicly held to make disclosures concerning their financial condition. The SEC developed a special template for such disclosures by banks,[71] and some of the SEC's views concerning accounting matters brought the SEC into conflict with bank regulators. Such tensions have come to the fore with regard to the issue of capital adequacy requirements regarding market risk as between banks and securities firms.[72] Very generally, bank regulators have frequently been reluctant to mandate the kind of full disclosure by banks that the SEC has required, in part because the SEC is concerned more about shareholders of banks and bank regulators are concerned more about bank depositors. Yet it is unclear whether maintaining confidentiality concerning impaired assets merely postpones the inevitable collapse of a failing bank, thus increasing financial instability.

The regulation of capital adequacy of both broker-dealers and banks is fairly well-settled in most jurisdictions, but recently there has been concern about the possible destabilizing effects of investments by hedge funds and other unregulated entities. A recent rule-making proposal by the SEC to require the registration of hedge funds so that the SEC could obtain more information about them was struck down by the Court of Appeals for the D.C. Circuit.[73] The reactions of the SEC and the Congress to this decision and the future possible regulation of hedge funds are currently unclear, but in the event of problems in the capital markets due to the collapse of highly leveraged hedge funds more attention might be given to this issue. Regulators and hedge funds might well be advised to opt for disclosure of their activities rather than more prescriptive regulation.

Court Actions

The articulation of disclosure policy in U.S. securities regulation is often found in both private civil actions and civil and criminal prosecution by the Government. In 2000–2001, in the aftermath of the bursting of the technology bubble, hundreds of cases were filed in the federal courts against companies, officers, directors and reputational gatekeepers charging violations of the anti-fraud provisions of the federal securities laws. These cases influence the drafting of prospectuses in public offerings, annual report filings by public companies, proxy solicitations, and other disclosures. Since many of these cases are brought by private litigants, who are sometimes likened to private attorneys general, they serve to correct distortions in the securities markets caused by faulty disclosure.

Conclusion

The securities laws of the United States have attempted to substitute disclosure for command and control prescriptive regulation to the extent the Congress and the SEC have considered effective. With regard to the regulation of public companies, the SEC historically has not attempted to control which issuers can tap the capital markets or regulate their internal affairs. Rather, it has compelled full disclosure so that investors can choose where to invest their capital. Sarbanes-Oxley has imposed corporate governance structures on public companies and their boards where previously state law allowed greater freedom of choice in these matters, but even Sarbanes-Oxley instructed the SEC to require stock exchanges to change their listing standards to deal with these corporate governance issues, rather than act directly.

Sarbanes-Oxley also required certain changes in the SEC's disclosure regulations, including the timing of disclosures by public companies. In general, these changes move such disclosures to more current disclosure filings. In the past, many companies reached the same end-goal of rapid and current disclosure by issuing press releases, but in today's Internet world, the SEC has mandated quicker filings and has also asked public companies to post their filings on their web sites. These changes are moving the U.S. disclosure system in the direction of a continuous reporting regime as opposed to a transactional reporting regime.

In the regulation of broker-dealers, the SEC also has used disclosure to customers as a means to avoid prescriptive regulation regarding safe and sound practices or capital adequacy, although the securities laws do contain the net capital rule and other rules safeguarding customers' property. A future challenge for financial regulators in the United States and around the world will be determining what type of disclosures hedge funds and other unregulated investors should be required to make in order to avoid undue speculation and volatility in the markets.

Notes

[1] Sarbanes-Oxley Act of 2002, Pub. L. No. 107-204, 116 Stat. 745 (2002) (codified in scattered sections of 11, 15, 18, 28, and 29 U.S.C.); *see* the author's interpretation of the background for this statute in Roberta S. Karmel, "Realizing the Dream of William O. Douglas–The Securities and Exchange Commission Takes Charge of Corporate Governance," 30 *Delaware Journal of Corporate Law* 79 (2005) [hereinafter "Realizing the Dream"].

[2] *See* Lawrence A. Cunningham, "Commonalities and Prescriptions in the Vertical Dimension of Global Corporate Governance," 84 *Cornell Law Review* 1133, 1136–48 (1999) [hereinafter "Commonalities and Perceptions"]. In some transitional economies this has also been true. *See* J. Robert Brown, Jr., "Of Brokers, Banks and the Case for Regulatory Intervention in Russian Securities Markets," 32 *Stanford Journal of International law* 185 (1996).

[3] *See* Cunningham, "Commonalities and Perceptions," *supra* note 2 at 1139–43 (explaining the bank/labor model).

[4] *See* Robert Prentice, "Whither Securities Regulation? Some Behavioral Observations Regarding Proposals for Its Future," 51 *Duke Law Journal* 1397, 1500–02 (2002).

[5] International Organization of Securities Commissions, *Objectives and Principles of Securities Regulation* (September 1998).

[6] *See* Roberta S. Karmel, "Reform of Public Company Disclosure in Europe," 26 *University of Pennsylvania Journal of International Economic Law* 379 (2005).

[7] *See* Special Study Group on Federal Regulation of Securities, American Bar Association, Section of Business Law, "Special Study on Market Structure, Listing Standards and Corporate Governance," 57 *Business Lawyer* 1487 (2002).

[8] *Id.* at 1496–1500.

[9] *See* Karmel, "Realizing the Dream," *supra* note 1, at 121–23.

[10] U. S. General Accounting Office, *Securities Markets: Competition and Multiple Regulators Heighten Concerns about Self-Regulation*, GAO-02-263 (May 3, 2003) (discussing regulatory inefficiencies resulting from broker-dealer membership in multiple SROs, and conflicts that SROs face in their dual roles as market operators and regulators); Securities Industry

Association, *Reinventing Self-Regulation*, Part III.D.2 (2000) (recognizing a need to minimize duplicative and inconsistent regulations, and reduce regulatory competition among SROs), available at www.sia.com/ market_structure/html/siawhitepaperfinal.htm; Roberta Romano, "Empowering Investors: A Market Approach to Securities Regulation," 107 *Yale Law Journal* 2359 (1998) (proposing the extension of competition among states for corporate charters to two of the three principal components of federal securities regulation); Paul G. Mahoney, "The Exchange as Regulator," 83 *Virginia. Law Review* 1453 (1997) (arguing that a system of competing regulators furthers investor welfare).

[11] *See, e.g.,* Commodity Futures Modernization Act of 2000, Pub. L. No. 106-554, 114 Stat. 2763 (2000) (amendments in scattered sections of 7 U.S.C.).

[12] *See* Sarbanes-Oxley § 301, 116 Stat. 745 (codified at 15 U.S.C. § 78j–1 (Supp. II 2002)) (requiring an audit committee comprised solely of independent directors); SEC, "Certification of Disclosure in Companies' Quarterly and Annual Reports," Securities Release No. 33-8,124, 17 C.F.R. Parts 228, 229, 232, 240, 249, 270 and 274 (August 29, 2002); NYSE Corporate Governance Rule Proposals as Approved by the NYSE Board of Directors August 1, 2002, available at www.nyse.com/pdfs/ corp_gov_pro_b.pdf. *Compare* to European corporate governance codes, which lay down rules or recommendations that are not of mandatory application, but companies must either comply with them or explain publicly why they are not complying with some of their provisions. European Corporate Governance Forum, *Statement of the European Corporate Governance Forum on the Comply-or-Explain Principle* (2005) available at http://europa.eu.int/comm/internal_market/company/docs/ecgforum/ecgf-comply-explain_en.pdf .

[13] *See* Roberta S. Karmel, "Reconciling Federal and State Interests In Securities Regulation in the United States and Europe," 28 *Brooklyn Journal of International Law* 495, 519–24 (2003).

[14] In 1975, Section 6 of the Exchange Act was amended to prohibit fixed commission rates. Pub. L. No. 94-29, §4, 89 Stat. 976 (codified as amended at 15 U.S.C. § 78f(e) (1994)). Similarly, the Airline Deregulation Act of 1978 abolished the Civil Aeronautics Board, which fixed prices and limited the entry of new airlines. Pub. L. No. 95-504, 92 Stat. 1705 (codified as amended in scattered sections of 49 U.S.C.); *see also* Alfred E. Khan, "Deregulation: Looking Backward and Looking Forward," 7 *Yale Journal on Regulation* 325 (1990).

[15] Exchange Act, § 11A(a)(1)(C)(ii),15 U.S.C. § 78k–1(a)(1)(C)(ii) (2000).

[16] Exchange Act, § 17A(b), 15 U.S.C. §§ 78q–1(2002); *Bradford Nat. Clearing Corp. v. Securities and Exchange Commission*, 590 F.2d 1085 (D.C. Circuit 1978).

[17] When Regulation NMS was recently adopted, there were two vigorous dissenters who expressed their view that the SEC did not take competition as an alternative to regulation sufficiently into account. SEC, "Dissent of Commissioners Cynthia A. Glassman and Paul S. Atkins to the Adoption of Regulation NMS," Exchange Act Release No. 51,808, 70 *Federal Register* 37,496, 37,632–44 (June 29, 2005).

[18] Sarbanes-Oxley Act § 301, 116 Stat. 745 (codified at 15 U.S.C. § 78j–1 (Supp. II 2002)).

[19] *See* Donna M. Nagy, "Playing Peekaboo with Constitutional Law: The PCAOB and Its Public/Private Status," 80 *Notre Dame Law Review* 975 (2005).

[20] *See Free Enterprise Fund v. The Public Company Accounting Oversight Board*, 2007 U.S. Dist. LEXIS 24310 (D.C.D.C. March. 21, 2007).

[21] 15 U.S.C. § 77a–z (2000).

[22] An early draft of the Securities Act would have allowed a government agency to determine whether issuers were of unsound condition or insolvent. *See* Donald A. Ritchie, *James M. Landis: Dean of the Regulators* (Cambridge, MA: Harvard University Press, 1980), at 45 [hereinafter Ritchie]. Such authority would have been similar to the ability of state blue sky merit regulators to prevent a public offering of securities if an issuer's capital structure is substantively unfair or presents excessive risks to investors. See American Bar Association, Ad Hoc Subcommittee on Merit Regulation of the State Regulation of Securities Committee, "Report on State Merit Regulation of Securities Offerings," 41 *Business Lawyer* 785, 787 (1986) [hereinafter ABA Blue Sky Report].

[23] Full disclosure regulation is based on the often quoted theory that "[p]ublicity is justly commended as a remedy for social and industrial diseases. Sunlight is said to be the best of disinfectants; electric light the most efficient policeman." Louis D. Brandeis, *Other People's Money and How the BankersUse It* (New York: Frederick A. Stokes, 1914; reprint, Boston: Bedford Books of St. Martin's Press, 1995), at 92.

[24] *See* ABA Blue Sky Report, *supra* note 22.

[25] A specified list of disclosure items, including the provision of a profit and loss statement and balance sheet, was attached to the Securities Act as Schedule A to avoid congressional tinkering although this list was the "guts of the bill," according to one of its drafters. *See* Ritchie, *supra* note 22, at 47.

[26] William O. Douglas, "Protecting the Investor," 23 *Yale Law Review* 521, 523–24 (1934).

[27] *Id.* at 231.

[28] The Public Utility Holding Company Act of 1935, 15 U.S.C. §§ 79 to 79z-6 (2000), imposed various substantive controls upon capital structure. The Investment Company Act of 1940, 15 U.S.C. §§ 80a-1 to 80a-64(2000), created a corporate governance structure for mutual funds and, in particular, a requirement for control by independent directors. 15 U.S.C. § 80a-10(a) (2000). The Exchange Act required the registration of stock exchanges and broker-dealers but did not give the SEC any control over their governance. Similarly, when the Maloney Act authorized the creation and regulation of national securities associations, 15 U.S.C. § 70o-3, the SEC was not authorized to regulate the corporate governance of the National Association of Securities Dealers (NASD). A limited power to affect the board structure of these self-regulatory organizations was contained in amendments to the Exchange Act passed in 1975. Exchange Act § 6(b)(3), 15 U.S.C. § 78f(b)(3) (2000), Exchange Act § 15A(b)(4), 15, U.S.C. § 78o-3 (2000).

[29] Securities Acts Amendments of 1964, Pub. L. No. 88-467, 78 Stat. 565; *see* Exchange Act Release No. 7,425, 29 *Federal Register* 13,455 (September 30, 1964).

[30] Exchange Act, § 14(a), 15 U.S.C. § 78n(a)(2000).

[31] *See J.I. Case Co. v. Borak*, 377 U.S. 426, 431 (1964); *Roosevelt v. E.I. Du Pont de Nemours & Co.*, 958 F.2d 416, 421–22 (D.C. Circuit 1992).

[32] Exchange Act, §§ 13(d)–(e), 14(d)–(f), 15 U.S.C. §§ 78m(d)–(e)(2000), 78n(d)–(f)(2000).

[33] *See CTS Corp. v. Dynamics Corp. of America*, 481 U.S. 69, 94 (1987); *Schreiber v. Burlington Northern, Inc.*, 472 U.S. 1 (1985).

[34] 15 U.S.C. §§ 77k, l (2000).

[35] 15 U.S.C. §§ 78l(b),(g),o(d) (2000).

[36] 15 U.S.C. § 78m (2000).

[37] SEC Rule 10b-5 provides:

> It shall be unlawful for any person, directly or indirectly, by the use of any means or instrumentality of interstate commerce, or of the mails or of any facility of any national securities exchange, (a) To employ any device, scheme, or artifice to defraud, (b) To make any untrue statement of a material fact or to omit to state a material fact necessary in order to make the statements made, in the light of the circumstances under which they were made not misleading, or (c) To engage in any act, practice, or course of business which operates or would operate as a fraud or deceit upon any person in connection with the purchase or sale of any security. 17 C.F.R. § 240.10b-5 (2000).

See generally Roberta Karmel, "Outsider Trading On Confidential InformationCA Breach In Search of a Duty," 20 *Cardozo Law Review* 83 (1998) [hereinafter "Breach in Search of a Duty"].

[38] *See In re WorldCom, Inc. Sec. Litigation*, 346 F. Supp. 2d 628, 662 (S.D.N.Y. 2004) (Stating that "[o]verall, no greater reliance in our self-regulatory system is placed on any single participant in the issuance of securities than upon the underwriter. Underwriters function as 'the first line of defense' with respect to material misrepresentations and omissions in registration statements. As a consequence, courts must be particularly scrupulous in examining their conduct.") (internal citations omitted); *See also In re Enron Corp. Securities, Derivative & ERISA Litigation*, 235 F.Supp.2d 549, 589 (S.D. Tex. 2002) (Widening Section 10(b)'s net, the Enron court concluded that "the statute's imposition of liability on 'any person' that 'directly or indirectly' uses or employs 'any manipulative or deceptive device or contrivance' in connection with the purchase or sale of security should be construed 'not technically and restrictively, but flexibly to effectuate its remedial purposes.'") (citing *Affiliated Ute Citizens of Utah v.United States*, 406 U.S. 128, 151 (1972)).

[39] *E.g.,* SEC Form S-1 (instructing proper completion of this "long form" registration statement and explaining an "[e]stimated average burden hours per response [of] 1,162.00"); SEC form S-3 (instructing proper completion of this "short form" registration statement and explaining an "[e]stimated average burden hours per response [of] 459.00"); SEC Form 10-K (asking a registered company to annually give a comprehensive overview of their business); Regulation S-K, 17 C.F.R. § 229 (2006) (explaining the general disclosure requirements under the Exchange and Securities Acts); Regulation

S-X, 17 C.F.R. § 210 (2006) (outlining accounting rules for filings with the Commission).

[40] *See, e.g.,* Commission Guidance Regarding Management's Discussion and Analysis of Financial Condition and Results of Operations, Securities Act Release No. 8,350 (Dec. 19, 2003) (codified at 17 C.F.R. pts 211, 231 and 241) available at www.sec.gov/rules/interp/33-8350.htm.

[41] *See, e.g.,* SEC, "SEC Brings Settled Charges Against Tyco International Ltd. Alleging Billion Dollar Accounting Fraud," SEC Litigation Release No. 19,657 (April 17, 2006) (settling with TYCO for a civil penalty of US$ 50 million), available at www.sec.gov/litigation/litreleases/2006/lr19657.htm; Complaint, *Securities and Exchange Commission v. TYCO International LTD* (outlining TYCO's alleged disclosure violations), available at www.sec.gov/litigation/complaints/2006/comp19657.pdf; *see* SEC, "SEC Charges HealthSouth Corp., CEO Richard Scrushy With US$ 1.4 Billion Accounting Fraud," Litigation Release 18,044 (March 20, 2003) [hereinafter "HealthSouth CEO"], available at www.sec.gov/litigation/litreleases/ lr18044.htm; *see also* "Hot Topic: Probing Stock-Options Backdating," *Wall Street Journal* (May 27, 2006), at A5. For the status of investigations against the more than one hundred companies ensnared in the options backdating scandal, see "Options Scorecard," Wall Street Journal Online, available at http://online.wsj.com/public/resources/documents/info-optionsscore06-full.html.

[42] *See* Richard F. Langan, "The Integrated Disclosure System, Registration and Periodic Disclosure Under the Exchange Act of 1934," 1556 *PLI/Corp* (Practicing Law Institute Corporate Law and Practice Course Handbook Series), at 251 (2006).

[43] SEC, "Securities Offering Reform," Securities Act Release No. 8591, 70 *Federal Register* 44,722 (August 3, 2005) (codified at 17 C.F.R. parts 200, 228, 229, 230, 239, 240, 243, 249, and 274) (attempting to eliminate barriers to open communications outmoded by technological advances. Additionally, the new rules reflect the importance of electronic dissemination of information).

[44] SEC, "Executive Compensation Disclosure," Securities Act Release No. 8,765, 71 *Federal Register* 78,338 (December 29, 2006) (to be codified at 17 C.F.R. parts 228 and 229) [hereinafter Executive Compensation Release].

[45] Sarbanes-Oxley Act, § 303, 116 Stat. at 778 (codified at 15 U.S.C. § 7242 (Supp. III 2003)). These provisions have been implemented by Rules 13a-14, 13a-15, 17 C.F.R. §§ 240.13a-14, 13a-15 (2006). *See* SEC, "Certification of

Disclosure in Companies' Quarterly and Annual Reports," Securities Act Release No. 8,124, 67 *Federal Register* 57,276 (September 9, 2002).

[46] Sarbanes-Oxley Act, § 906, 18 U.S.C. § 1350 (Supp. II 2002).

[47] This disclosure is required by Sarbanes-Oxley, § 404, 15 U.S.C. § 7241 (Supp. 2002).

[48] *See* SEC, "Management's Report on Internal Control over Financial Reporting and Certification of Disclosure in Exchange Act Periodic Reports," Exchange Act Release No. 47,986, 68 *Federal Register* 36,636 (June 5, 2003).

[49] Liability could have been predicated on the theory that the officer or director was a direct participant in an accounting fraud, an aider and abettor, or a control person. *See, e.g., In re Medimmune, Inc., Sec. Litig.*, 873 F. Supp. 953 (D. Md. 1995); *General Electric Co v.Rowe*, 1992 WL 277997 (E.D. Pa. 1992); *In re Par Pharmaceutical, Inc. Sec. Litig.*, 733 F. Supp. 668 (S.D.N.Y. 1990).

[50] *See* "HealthSouth CEO," *supra* note 41.

[51] Exchange Act § 13(b), 15 U.S.C. § 78 m(b) (2000), added by the Foreign Corrupt Practices Act of 1977, Pub. L. No. 95-213, 91 Stat. 1494 (1978) (codified as amended at 15 U.S.C. §§ 78m(b), 78dd-1, 78dd-2, 78dd-3, 78ff (2000)).

[52] *See Stone v. Ritter*, 911 A.2d 362 (Del. Supr. 2006); *In re Caremark Inter. Inc. Derivative Litig.*, 698 A.2d 959 (Del. Ch. 1996).

[53] SEC, "Management's Report on Internal Control Over Financial Reporting and Certification of Disclosure in Exchange Act Periodic Reports of Non-Accelerated Filers and Foreign Private Issuers," Securities Act Release No. 8,545, 70 *Federal Register* 11,528 (March 2, 2005); Rachel McTague, "SEC May Delay Internal-Control Reporting by Non-U.S. Firms, Donaldson Says in London," 37 *Securities Regulation & Law Report* (BNA) 195 (January 31, 2005); Rachel McTague, "SEC Staff Likely to Recommend Rule to Ease Deregistration for Foreign Firms," 36 *Securities Regulation & Law Report* (BNA) 2050 (November 22, 2004).

[54] *See* SEC, "Concept Release Concerning Management's Reports on Internal Control Over Financial Reporting," Exchange Act Release No. 54,122, 71 *Federal Register* 40,866 (July 18, 2006) (seeking comment on "special issues applicable to foreign private issuers that the Commission should consider in developing guidance to management on how to evaluate the effectiveness of a company's internal control over financial reporting").

[55] *See* 17 C.F.R. §§ 244.100–102 (2006); SEC, "Conditions for Use of Non-GAAP Financial Measures," Securities Act Release No. 8,176, 68 *Federal Register* 4,820 (January 22, 2003).

[56] "Large Accelerated Filer Defined by Exchange Act Rule 12b-2(2)," 17 C.F.R. § 240.12b-2 (2006):

> The term large accelerated filer means an issuer after it first meets the following conditions as of the end of its fiscal year:
>
> 1. The issuer had an aggregate worldwide market value of the voting and non-voting common equity held by its non-affiliates of US$700 million or more, as of the last business day of the issuer's most recently completed second fiscal quarter;
>
> 2. The issuer has been subject to the requirements of section 13(a) or 15(d) of the Act for a period of at least twelve calendar months;
>
> 3. The issuer has filed at least one annual report pursuant to section 13(a) or 15(d) of the Act; and
>
> 4. The issuer is not eligible to use Forms 10 KSB and 10 QSB for its annual and quarterly reports.

[57] *See* SEC, "Additional 8-K Disclosure Requirements and Acceleration of Filing Date," Securities Act Release No. 8,400, 69 *Federal Register* 15,594 (March 25, 2004).

[58] Wally Suphap, "Getting it Right Versus Getting it Quick: The Quality-Timeliness Tradeoff in Corporate Disclosure," 2003 *Columia Business Law Review* 662, 678 (2003) (explaining that "[s]ince 1936, Form 8-K has undergone a series of substantive changes. In 1977, the SEC made significant amendments to create the general structure of the form that exists today, including filing deadlines that require reporting of some corporate events within five business or fifteen calendar days after their occurrence, depending on the nature of the event. In recent years, the SEC has amended Form 8-K at various times to add or delete items.") (internal citations omitted)

[59] *See* "Executive Compensation Release," *supra* note 44.

[60] *See* Regulation S-K Item 404, Transactions with Related Persons, Promoters and Certain Control Persons, 17 C.F.R. pt. 229.404 (2006).

[61] *See generally* "A Breach In Search of a Duty," *supra* note 37, at 124–33 (outlining the argument for closing the Williams Act's "ten day window," its evolution, and SEC reluctance to "pursue this legislative initiative more

aggressively before and after Congress abandoned takeover reform legislation.").

⁶² SEC, "Ownership Reports and Trading by Officers, Directors and Principal Security Holders," Exchange Act Release No. 46,421, 17 C.F.R. parts 240, 249, 274 (August 27, 2002) ("adopting rule and form amendments to implement the accelerated filing deadline applicable to change of beneficial ownership reports required to be filed by officers, directors and principal security holders under Section 16(a) of the Securities Exchange Act of 1934, as amended by the Sarbanes-Oxley Act of 2002.").

⁶³ Sarbanes Oxley Act § 408, 15 U.S.C. § 7266 (Supp. 2002).

⁶⁴ Roel C. Campos, Commissioner, U.S. Securities and Exchange Commission, Remarks at the SEC Open Meeting (July 26, 2006) available at www.sec.gov/news/speech/2006/spch072606rcc.htm; *see also* Protection Against Executive Compensation Abuse Act, H.R. 4291, 109th Congress (1ˢᵗ Sess. 2005) (introduced by Rep. Barney Frank seeking federally mandated shareholder votes on executive compensation). For a discussion of the federalism implications of national corporate governance proposals, *see* "Federalism vs. Federalization: Preserving the Division of Responsibility in Corporation Law," 1543 *PLI/Corp* (Practicing Law Institute Corporate Law and Practice Course Handbook Series), at 221, 267 (2006).

⁶⁵ Exchange Act § 15(b)(7), Registration and Regulation of Brokers and Dealers, 15 U.S.C. § 78o (2000).

⁶⁶ Rule 15c3-1, Net Capital Rule, 17 C.F.R. § 240.15c3-1 (2005).

⁶⁷ Rule 15c3-3, Customer ProtectionCReserves and Custody of Securities, 17 C.F.R. § 240.15c3-3 (2005).

⁶⁸ House Subcommittee on Commerce and Finance, "Securities Industry Study Report," H.R. Rep. No. 92-1519, at 51, 92d Cong., 2d Sess. (1972).

⁶⁹ *Id.* at 52. *See* SEC, "Reports to be Made by Certain Exchange Members, Brokers, and Dealers and Related Audit Requirements," Exchange Act Release No. 9,658, 37 *Federal Register* 14,607 (June 30, 1972); SEC, "Broker-Dealer Financial Disclosure Requirements to Each Customer," Exchange Act Releases No. 9,404, 35 *Federal Register* 25,236 (December 3, 1971).

⁷⁰ *See* SEC, "Focus Broker-Dealer Reports," Exchange Act Release No. 11,935, 40 *Federal Register* 59,706 (December 30, 1975).

[71] SEC, *Securities Act and Exchange Act Industry Guide 3, Statistical Disclosure by Bank Holding Companies*, available at www.sec.gov/about/forms/industryguides.pdf.

[72] Hal S. Scott, *International Finance: Transactions, Policy, and Regulations,* 13th ed. (New York: Foundation Press, 2006), at 342–43 (explaining "market risk" and capital adequacy requirements).

[73] *Goldstein v. Securities and Exchange Commission*, 451 F.3d 873 (D.C. Circuit 2006) (holding that a rule, promulgated by the SEC, requiring investors in a hedge fund be counted as clients of the fund's adviser for purposes of the fewer-than-fifteen-clients exemption from registration under IAA invalid because it conflicts with purposes underlying the statute).

VI. ANTI-MONEY LAUNDERING— TERRORIST FINANCING AND FINANCIAL STABILITY

13 The Broader Impact of Terrorism on Financial Stability

RICHARD BARRETT

The immediate impact of terrorism, seen so graphically in pictures of mourning families and twisted metal, represent only one side of their cost; the wider loss of revenue and investment can devastate a local economy and undermine the financial stability of a country, or even a region. And on top of the direct and indirect costs of terrorist attacks are the costs incurred in trying to prevent them. Whether immediate and local, such as the reinforcement of security at key installations, or longer term and broader, such as the implementation of regulations designed to attack the financing of terrorism, these costs add considerably to the overall financial impact of terrorism.

Terrorism and counterterrorism represent a constant cycle of action and reaction. The asymmetry of terrorists' actions allows them to concentrate their resources far more effectively than their counterterrorist opponents. Terrorists can ensure a strong correlation between expenditure and impact, while those trying to stop them have to guard against a range of possible attacks and protect many different targets without knowing whether they are truly at risk.

It costs terrorists little to cause major loss of life and widespread fear and disruption. According to an official British government report, the attack on the London transport system in July 2005, in which 52 random people were killed, cost the terrorists around US\$ 15,000;[1] an insignificant figure compared to the costs that resulted from it (US\$ 750 million in lost tourist revenues alone, by some estimates).[2]

The sums spent on dealing with terrorist incidents, and more especially the cost of preventing new ones, has been on a steady upward curve since the attacks in the United States on September 11,

2001. The United Kingdom estimates that its annual spending on counterterrorism will reach close to US$ 4 billion by 2008, double what it was before the 2001 attacks. Usama bin Laden, referring to these attacks just before the November 2004 U.S. presidential elections, boasted that while they had cost al-Qaeda US$ 500,000, they had cost the United States US$ 500 billion.[3] He may well be right. In so far as they can be calculated, the immediate costs of the attack in loss of life, property, and production were put at US$100 billion, and the indirect costs, in terms of other lost revenues, new protective measures, and the refocusing of government policy, will be many times higher.[4] President Bush requested a US$ 42.7 billion budget allocation for the Department of Homeland Security alone for 2007, much of it to finance counterterrorist initiatives, compared with US$19.5 billion for 2002; and this figure takes no account of the huge accumulated costs of the military campaigns in Afghanistan and Iraq.

The global nature of al-Qaeda-related terrorism, which encourages attacks against its opponents wherever they are located, gives states no option but to develop and pay for some sort of a counterterrorist policy. While these costs may not threaten the financial stability of countries such as the United States, countries with much smaller economies must also take measures to protect their people and critical infrastructure from attack. Furthermore, they may face the indirect costs of terrorism even when attacks happen far away. The indirect consequences of terrorism can affect inward investment, tourism, communications, energy prices, distribution costs, property values, and consumer confidence. For example, the attack on the huge Abqaiq oil installation in Saudi Arabia in February 2006, even though unsuccessful, caused an immediate US$ 2 spike in the price of oil;[5] the Bali attacks in October 2002 and October 2005 not only affected tourism in Indonesia—the loss of revenue after the 2002 attack equalled 2–3 percent of GDP—but also throughout South East Asia.[6] One can only imagine the widespread economic consequences of a "dirty bomb" (one containing radioactive, chemical, or biological substances) detonating in an urban environment—a known objective of al-Qaeda.

Terrorists are, of course, well aware of the broader consequences of their attacks, and plan them accordingly. The attacks on New

York's World Trade Center in 1993 and 2001 were deliberately aimed at an iconic symbol of American economic power, and in two recent statements Ayman al-Zawahiri, regarded as the second-in-command of al-Qaeda, made the economic objectives of the terrorist campaign explicit. In March 2006 he said that "the first front for Al-Qaeda was to inflict losses on the Crusader West, in particular on its economic being"; in September he added that "the focus must be on their [the West's] economic interests, in particular to stop their stealing the oil of the Muslims."

While states can judge how much they should spend on local counterterrorist protection depending on other calls on their money and their assessment of the risk of attack, they have less control when it comes to implementing international counterterrorism initiatives, such as those introduced by the United Nations, or to introducing multilaterally agreed standards, such as those recommended by the Financial Action Task Force (FATF).

The United Nations Security Council first introduced mandatory sanctions against the Taliban and al-Qaeda in Afghanistan in 1999, and since then it has broadened the regime to apply to a list of designated individuals, groups, and entities associated with the Taliban and al-Qaeda without any geographic restriction. This global sanctions regime requires all member states of the United Nations to impose an assets freeze, an arms embargo, and a travel ban on those named on the Security Council list. All states must have legislation and mechanisms in place that allow them to apply the sanctions within their jurisdiction, or risk whatever penalty the Security Council might impose for a failure to do so. The Security Council also expects all states to achieve minimum standards of implementation, given that terrorists will look for ways to evade the regime by exploiting its weakest links.

Similarly, the nine FATF Special Recommendations on Terrorist Financing propose further unavoidable expense for states. These recommendations, eight of which were drawn up in the immediate aftermath of the 2001 attacks in the United States, were supported by the Security Council in Resolution 1617 (2005), which "strongly urges all Member States to implement the comprehensive international standards" embodied in them. To do so effectively may be a task beyond the capacity of most states, and this may be why, in terms of practical application, the recommendations have been largely ignored or put in the "too difficult" tray. But the pressure on states to make some effort to adopt the recommendations has increased since they were introduced in 2001, and it is conceivable that noncompliant states might find it harder to conduct international financial transactions if they do nothing at all. But apart from the difficulties and expense of introducing and implementing the necessary legislation associated with the nine special recommendations, there are less direct costs involved.

In particular, Special Recommendation VI, concerning alternative remittance, could have a real consequence for the financial stability of certain states if implemented. The recommendation proposes that all persons or entities "that provide a service for the transmission of money or value should be licensed or registered and subject to all the FATF Recommendations that apply to banks and non-bank financial institutions." It is hard to imagine how this might be done without raising costs to a level that would either force providers underground or force the millions of migrant workers and others who currently use these systems to find cheaper alternatives. Many states rely heavily on overseas remittances for their financial viability, and without money from relatives abroad many families would become destitute. World Bank estimates (and they can only be estimates because of the lack of records) put the amount of money remitted worldwide in 2004 as US$ 207 billion, second only in total to the amount of foreign direct investment and far more than official development assistance.[7] While a good portion of this money will have passed through banks and other registered financial institutions, many migrant workers are from countries without a developed retail banking system and in any case will be attracted by the comparative speed, simplicity, and low cost of alternative and informal systems. A strict implementation of this measure might therefore have consequences quite different from the intended ones, causing difficulties and hardships that might actually promote conditions conducive to terrorism.

As well as international agreements, certain national counterterrorist regulations may cause financial difficulties for would-be trading partners. For example, the Container Security

Initiative (CSI), introduced by the U.S. Bureau of Customs and Border Protection in 2002, was designed to increase security for container cargo shipped to the United States by extending the "zone of security outward so that American borders are the last line of defense, not the first." About 90 percent of world trade is transported by container, and almost half of all imports to the United States (by value), amounting to 9.6 million containers in 2004, arrives in this way.[8] The CSI certainly does not intend to make it harder for ports in developing countries to trade with the United States if they do not have the "regular, direct, and substantial container traffic to ports in the United States" that qualifies them to join the initiative; nor does the CSI intend to add prohibitive costs to ports that may have the traffic but lack the necessary screening equipment or other required security measures. But inevitably, exporters who use one of the fifty ports that were part of the CSI program as of October 2006 will have an advantage over those that do not. One of the advertised benefits of CSI is that "the integrity of the shipment[s] is better ensured by using pre-arrival information and nonintrusive inspection equipment at foreign port locations, thus expediting their clearance upon arrival in the United States." This may therefore oblige ports in developing countries to increase their security budgets or face a possible loss of competitiveness.

If the additional costs of counterterrorism since September 2001 have been offset by a reduction in terrorist attacks (and the costs they incur), the money spent may have done more to promote financial stability than to undermine it. But there appears to be no end in sight to the threat of terrorist attacks, nor to the measures taken to prevent them, and this continuing upward spiral of action and reaction sucks all states into its vortex. Pressure will increase for more resources for law enforcement and intelligence work, greater protection for key sites and other vulnerable targets, better screening at border entry points, more public information campaigns, more effective examination of financial transactions, and the movement of value in both the private and the public sectors.

There is no demonstrable correlation between poverty and terrorism, and economic development may not be a key factor in preventing the growth of terrorism in any particular country. For example, the Kingdom of Saudi Arabia was spending US$ 5.5 billion a year on security in 2003 and no doubt spends even more today, but it still faces a hard core of terrorist supporters; and the British Home Secretary acknowledges facing a threat that is "enduring—the struggle will be long and wide and deep."[9] But the poorer and less developed a country, and the less effective its government, the more likely that terrorists will try to find recruits there. International initiatives should not force states to divert money from education and other key development budgets unless the counterterrorist benefits are obvious and proportionate to their cost.

Much has been written about the direct and indirect economic consequences of terrorist attacks, and there is some understanding of the direct and indirect costs of the measures taken to prevent them. But particularly in the febrile atmosphere following the 2001 attacks in the United States, international bodies have paid too little attention to the cumulative financial burden of terrorism and counterterrorism on the developing world. It would be a hard and long journey for many developing countries to reach the standards expected of them, even with outside assistance, and as the demands of counterterrorism increase, many of those countries may decide that they no longer see the effort as being worth the gain. There is little prospect of defeating global terrorism without the willing engagement of all members of the international community, and it is perhaps time to review what is being demanded of states in terms of cost and effect. This may best be achieved through a close partnership between those people who have an understanding of financial and economic issues and those who have an understanding of terrorism.

Notes

[1] House of Commons, *Report of the Official Account of the Bombings in London on 7th July 2005*, at 23, available at www.official-documents.gov.uk/document/hc0506/hc10/1087/1087.pdf

[2] *See* statement by the Tourism Industry Emergency Response Group, July 22, 2005

[3] Statement by Usama bin Laden, October 29, 2004, "The Towers of Lebanon," available at http://english.aljazeera.net/English/archive/archive?ArchiveId=7403.

[4] Library of Congress, Congressional Research Service, "The Economic Effects of 9/11: A Retrospective Assessment," September 27, 2002; and "The Cost of Iraq, Afghanistan and Enhanced Base Security Since 9/11," October 07, 2005.

[5] Jerusalem Center for Public Affairs, "Global Oil Supply Security and Al-Qaeda's Abortive Attack on Abqaiq, Saudi Arabia," Jerusalem Issue Brief, March 16, 2006, available at http://www.jcpa.org/brief/brief005-19.htm; see also http://www.theoildrum.com/story/2006/2/24/11925/2060.

[6] James M. Lutz and Brenda J. Lutz, "Terrorism as Economic Warfare," *Global Economy Journal,* Vol. 6, Issue 2 (quoting from Zachary Abuza, *Militant Islam in Southeast Asia: Crucible of Terror*) (Boulder, CO: Lynne Rienner, 2003), pp. 166, 233.

[7] *See* http://web.worldbank.org/WBSITE/EXTERNAL/NEWS/0,,content MDK:20648762~menuPK:34480~pagePK:64257043~piPK:437376~theSite PK:4607,00.html.

[8] U.S. Customs and Border Control, CSI Fact Sheet, October 2, 2007.

[9] Quoted by Eliza Manningham-Buller, Director General of the UK Security Service in speech at Queen Mary's College, London, November 9, 2006. Available at http://www.timesonline.co.uk/article/0,,2-2447690,00.html.

14 The Impact of Weak AML/CFT Frameworks on Financial Stability

ZENÓN ALBERTO BIAGOSCH

Strong frameworks for anti-money laundering (AML) and combating financing of terrorism (CFT) can have a powerful influence on preserving a nation's financial stability. On the other hand, countries with weak AML/CFT regimes are subject to the negative effects that large international criminal organizations can have on their economic growth and financial stability. Thus the strengthening of AML/CFT systems is a subject of vital importance to individual nations and the international community.

This chapter first describes the breadth of the problem caused by criminal and terrorist organizations. It then discusses steps that have been taken to strengthen AML/CFT, with a particular focus on the experience of Argentina. Finally, the chapter offers a proposal for regional and international standards to strengthen AML/CFT frameworks.

The Problem

All nations pursue sustained economic growth. Their success, however, is strongly linked to how effectively their governments ensure stability of the financial system. One of the challenges faced today by individual countries, as well as by the international community, is that financial stability can be undermined by the activities of criminal organizations.

In Argentina the directors of the Central Bank are responsible, under the bank's charter, for "supervising the good performance of the financial market." To achieve this objective and to ensure the sustained stability of the country's financial system, the Central

Bank's regulatory and supervisory powers in regard to liquidity and solvency have been supplemented with policies to prevent and control money laundering and terrorist financing. (These policies are described later in the chapter.)

To understand the relationship between AML/CFT and financial stability, three factors must be taken into account:

- Criminal organizations can exert great economic power in the absence of a proper AML/CFT system. In fact, they can undermine the economic and political stability of a country—and, consequently, its financial stability.

- States are devoting an increasing amount of funds to control money laundering and terrorist financing.

- There is a growing need for international standards on banking supervision related to AML/CFT in order to protect and reinforce financial stability.

Individual nations and the international community are facing criminal organizations that carry out transactions involving huge amounts of money. The breadth of the problem is illustrated by data from several sources:

- Relying on IMF data, the USA PATRIOT Act stated that money laundering ranges from 2 to 5 percent of the world's gross domestic product, approximately US$ 600 billion.[1]

- In its annual report on drugs and crime, the United Nations reported in 2006 that 5 percent of the world's population 15–64 years of age uses drugs. In addition, drug trafficking amounted to US$ 320 billion in 2003, exceeding 90 percent of the worldwide gross domestic product.[2]

- The Financial Action Task Force in June 2005 declared that trafficking in people and illegal immigration amounts to approximately US$ 10 billion.[3]

- The Basel Committee's 2002 research on fraud related to the banking sector analyzed 89 international banks and showed that their losses reached around €1.4 billion millions euros due to internal and external fraud.[4]

- Research by the Association of Certified Fraud Examiners estimated that U.S. losses for fraud could reach more than US$ 600 billion.[5]

- The World Bank estimated that bribes paid worldwide were over US$ 1 billion in a single year.[6]

These data demonstrate that national governments and the international community are facing the equivalent of supra-states, in the form of criminal organizations, that generate more wealth than many countries. Their economic power not only affects the stability of worldwide financial systems; it is also used to fund their activities. The conduct and transactions of cross-border criminal organizations harms economic growth, undermines the peace of society, and, in many cases, evades the most sophisticated security structures in the world.

The activities of criminal organizations affect different aspects of society. The most relevant aspects are related to economy and finance, policy, and society. The economic-financial aspect is basically affected in three ways: (1) a reduction in the resources of the formal economy; (2) investments contrary to economic expectations; and (3) disregard for achieving normal profit. In other words, illegal funds are, in general, invested for speculation, accumulation, or concealment. This causes a drop in the rate of international economic growth and may even damage the regular functioning of financing and capital markets.

The inflow or outflow of funds of criminal origin may adversely affect a country's market stability, with three major consequences:

- A change in variables such as interest rate, exchange rate, the price of properties, liquidity, and quotation of shares and debt instruments;

- A decreasing level of transparency, soundness, confidence, and reliance on financial markets;

- Transfer of a domestic problem to the worldwide economic and financial systems.

Criminal organizations can affect the political-institutional aspect of states because they can afford any costs to obtain their objectives, particularly because they do not intend to obtain profits. In general, they are willing to corrupt the executive, legislative, and judicial powers and law enforcement functions through bribery. Such corruption is one of the heaviest prices the international community has to pay for having to live with transnational criminal organizations.

Additionally, governments are forced to invest growing resources to implement compliance controls. In this regard, it would be advisable to estimate through research how much governments spend in that respect; in other words, how much societies must pay to fight criminal organizations.

Since the attacks of September 11, 2001, in the United States, there has been a worldwide trend toward preventing such crimes and punishing the perpetrators. In many cases, states have been forced to increase their budgets to enforce these measures. Further, it has been necessary to adopt stronger legislation and even to interfere with the private sector, in many cases disrupting the normal operation of private business. Because the population is aging in the more developed countries, a smaller working population must pay higher contributions for the security measures.

International Regimes

Over the last few years, several international bodies, both public and private, have proposed or implemented a number of recommendations to prevent and reduce risks arising from different kinds of criminal conduct, to combat increasingly complex and sophisticated crimes, and to protect the stability of states and their markets. The proposed guidelines include the following:

- Recommendations of the Financial Action Task Force and its new methodology of evaluation;

- Resolutions of the United Nations Security Council;

- Basel II statement on operating risks, and a revision of the Basel Core Principles;

- The Sarbanes-Oxley Act of 2002 in the United States, and the implementation of the resulting regulations by the Public Company Accounting Oversight Board;

- New principles of corporate governance promulgated by the Organisation for Economic Co-operation and Development;

- New accounting rules such as the International Financial Reporting Standards;

- Updated International Standards on Auditing of the International Federation of Accountants;

- Revision of the methodology of the Committee of Sponsoring Organizations of the Treadway Commission.

The Case of Argentina

Central bankers and banking supervisors should continue doing their best to implement international standards and, particularly, regional AML/CFT regulations. In the case of Argentina, the Central Bank and the Superintendence of Financial and Exchange Institutions have adopted new AML rules over the last two years and enforced a new regulation on prevention and control of terrorist financing. This new AML/CFT regulatory framework is in line with international standards.

In addition, the Central Bank of Argentina has established a specific mechanism to monitor and prevent money laundering and terrorist financing, which includes the following elements:

- Implementation of a banking supervisory regime that focuses on AML/CFT;

- Implementation of a qualified and trained group of inspectors in AML/CFT;

- Planning of supervisory activities over the financial system according to a risk-based approach;

- Arrangement of an examination schedule on the basis of a risk matrix of the financial system itself;

- Rating financial entities' in-house monitoring structures.

Regional Standards: Latin America

Most international observers view banking supervision as the axis of prevention. However, international organizations have produced few specific documents in regard to a methodology for specialized AML/CFT banking supervision. The need for international standards in banking supervision that focus on AML/CFT is to protect and strengthen the financial stability that is a primary goal of all countries. For that reason, the Central Bank of Argentina is making efforts to reach a regional agreement on standards and best practices on specialized banking supervision intended to fight money laundering and terrorist financing.

The implementation of the rules applicable to financial systems differs greatly among Latin American countries. However, they all comply with regulatory standards issued by international organizations such as the Financial Action Task Force (FATF), Financial Action Task Force on Money Laundering in South America (GAFISUD), and the Inter-American Drug Abuse Control Commission (CICAD) of the Organization of American States (OAS). For that reason, there should be supplementation and emphasis on effective regional surveillance mechanisms, such as:

- The FATF and GAFISUD New Methodologies of Mutual Evaluation;

- The CICAD/OAS Mechanisms of Multilateral Evaluation;

- Article 4 of the IMF Articles of Agreement and the Financial Sector Assessment Program (FSAP) of the IMF and World Bank;

- Due diligence principles for business and correspondent activities with Latin American banks provided by the U.S. financial system in line with the USA PATRIOT Act.

In short, the Central Bank of Argentina proposes that a mechanism for AML/CFT supervision be implemented both on a regional and international basis. This does not mean that the regulatory standards in effect, such as those provided by the Financial Action Task Force, should be replaced. On the contrary, they could be supplemented with a banking supervisory mechanism. This initiative is based on four pillars:

- Regulation. The regulatory framework should be homogeneous and supported by the existing standards such as those provided by the Financial Action Task Force.

- Specialized supervision. An AML/CFT-oriented supervisory scheme should be designed, based on a risk matrix to be implemented by qualified and trained inspectors.

- Rating. Specific rating mechanisms should be implemented, focusing on the components to be rated and rating systems applicable to financial entities. (Argentina has traditionally rated financial entities in terms of their liquidity and solvency position to protect its financial system's stability. These entities should now be rated in terms of their compliance with regulations on the prevention and control of money laundering and terrorist financing.)

- Use of information. There should be clear guidelines on the use of information and to what extent it may be shared—for instance, channels for sharing information within public and private sectors, and between them, and the ratings assigned. Special attention should be paid to the legal frameworks of different jurisdictions.

Adopting the standards with the above-mentioned characteristics would allow governments to:

- Reinforce AML/CFT regulations and make financial entities aware of this concern;

- Provide financial systems with the necessary tools to do business on a more reliable basis, particularly in countries accepting the proposed standards;

- Generate information that can be shared among the private sector and among regulatory bodies;

- Identify those countries or entities that do not endorse the standards proposed;

- Reduce the level of uncertainty in relationships, considering that the new guidelines could help to distinguish the particular characteristics of countries in each region and at the same time generate specific procedures to take into account the reality existing in each country.

The International Monetary Fund and the World Bank have been providing technical support for the supervisory methodology currently being implemented in Argentina. Indeed, this is a priority item on the agendas of both the Central Bank of Argentina and the Superintendence of Financial and Exchange Institutions, which are in charge of supervising the financial services community and warning them against criminal operations.

Notes

Note: The views expressed in this paper are those of the author and should not be attributed either to the Central Bank of Argentina or to the Superintendence of Financial and Exchange Entities.

[1] USA PATRIOT Act (Public Law 107-56), Sec. 302.

[2] United Nations Office on Drugs and Crime, *World Drug Report 2005.*

[3] FATF, *Money Laundering & Terrorist Financing Typologies 2004-2005,* at 67.

[4] Basel Committee on Banking Supervision. The 2002 Loss Data Collection Exercise for Operational Risk: Summary of the Data Collected, p.12, Table 8.

[5] Association of Certified Fraud Examiners, *2006 ACFE Report to the Nation on Occupational Fraud & Abuse*, (p. 4):

[6] United Nations Office on Drugs and Crime, "Datos sobre la Corrupción." Available at www.unodc.org.

<table>
<tr><td>CHAPTER

15</td><td>Elements of an Effective AML/CFT Framework: Legal, Regulatory, and Best Institutional Practices to Prevent Threats to Financial Stability and Integrity</td></tr>
</table>

CHAPTER 15	Elements of an Effective AML/CFT Framework: Legal, Regulatory, and Best Institutional Practices to Prevent Threats to Financial Stability and Integrity

IAN CARRINGTON AND HEBA SHAMS

In 1989 the G-7 Summit established the Financial Action Task Force (FATF). The original mission of the FATF was to study the problem of money laundering by criminal organizations and to propose measures for standardizing anti-money laundering (AML) regimes. The FATF's first recommendations were issued in 1990, then updated in 1996 and again in 2003. In 2001 the FATF took on the added task of recommending measures for combating the financing of terrorism (CFT).

Today the core question remains: How to implement an AML/CFT system that works.

This chapter addresses this question, arguing that the key challenge in implementing AML/CFT regimes is in obtaining, maintaining, and transmitting relevant information. International AML/CFT standards aim at addressing this challenge by harmonizing measures across countries, imposing obligations to obtain and maintain information, removing barriers to information sharing, and establishing channels for information flow.

International AML/CFT standards have entered a new stage of maturity. When FATF issued its revised standards in 2003 and a new round of compliance evaluations was launched worldwide by various assessor bodies,[1] it was clear that it is no longer considered progress for countries to declare political support for the international standard or merely to issue laws and regulations. What really counts is the *effective implementation* of AML/CFT measures. This new emphasis, while not absent in the 1996 version of the recommendations, has brought to the fore important questions regarding the operational effectiveness of an AML/CFT regime.

The AML/CFT standard created by the FATF is an amalgamation of measures: (1) criminalizing money laundering and terrorist financing, (2) setting up freezing, seizing, and confiscation systems, (3) imposing preventive regulatory requirements on a number of businesses and professions, (4) establishing a financial intelligence unit (FIU), (5) creating an effective supervisory framework, (6) setting up channels for domestic cooperation, and (7) setting up channels for international cooperation.

The AML/CFT system purports to achieve a multiplicity of objectives:

- removing profit from crime through confiscation;

- detecting crime by following the money trail;

- targeting third-party or professional launderers who through their services allow criminals to retain the proceeds of their crime;

- targeting the upper echelons of the criminal organization whose only connection to the crime is the money trail; and

- protecting the integrity of the financial system against abuse by criminals.[2]

Assessing the effectiveness of a system that is so composite in nature and that aims to achieve such diverse objectives has so far proven to be both conceptually and practically difficult. To date, there is no clear formula to assess whether an AML/CFT system has been effective in achieving its objectives. In the absence of a reliable measure of how much money is being laundered or how much terrorist money is circulating, the question of effectiveness becomes even more elusive when it is couched in terms of "curbing" money laundering and terrorist financing. It is therefore impracticable to try to measure the success of a specific AML/CFT measure by attempting to establish the extent to which the measure has contributed to reducing the amount of money being laundered or terrorist funds being funneled.

Starting from the premise that access to information is the main challenge that faces the governments around the world in seeking to fight money laundering and terrorist financing, or more specifically to attain the multiple objectives described above, this chapter first demonstrates how AML/CFT standards address this challenge by facilitating the flow of information by imposing measures for obtaining, maintaining, and sharing information on a myriad of public and private institutions.

The chapter then explores (1) the role of the private sector under the international standard in obtaining, verifying and maintaining information; (2) the role of the supervisory authorities in ensuring the effective performance of these functions; and (3) the mechanisms for ensuring interagency information flow. It also explores such issues as the importance of political commitment for the effective functioning of these measures and the need for risk-based proportionality between the measures adopted and the money laundering and terrorist financing threat.

The findings in this paper are based on the authors' experience in working with countries that are developing AML/CFT measures. They are also based on the findings from AML/CFT assessments conducted by the IMF and the World Bank, as well as other assessor bodies. Because both technical-assistance work and assessments are generally subject to confidentiality, the findings will be discussed and analyzed in general terms, and no reference to specific countries will be made unless the example is drawn from sources that are in the public domain.

The Challenge of Information Flow

Information is a prerequisite for the effective enforcement of laws and regulations. Law enforcement authorities need information in order to implement the law and ensure that violations do not occur or, when they occur, do not go unsanctioned. Information is needed at all stages of the enforcement process in order to detect violations and subsequently to prove the violations to the requisite standard of proof either in an administrative or a judicial process.

Procedural laws have always provided for rules to access privately held information for law enforcement purposes. Because of the severe nature of penal sanctions, laws of criminal procedure have been particularly protective of the rights of the individual in regulating the access of law enforcement authorities to information for the purposes of criminal investigations and prosecutions. These procedural safeguards require time and naturally entail time lags in the information-gathering process.

Since the 1970s, however, a number of developments took place that altered governments' approach to law enforcement needs for information: (1) technological developments and liberalization led to the globalization of economic activities, including economic crime;[3] (2) cross-border movement of funds in particular became intensely global both in volume and speed; and (3) for various reasons, economic crime has reached higher levels of magnitude involving both activities and proceeds that are crossing national borders.[4]

In response, law enforcement strategies began to analyze criminal activities in market terms and develop an understanding of criminal organizations by reference to the behavior of legitimate economic enterprises. The assumptions in this regard are that criminal organizations, like legitimate ones, need funding for their operations and that criminals are economic agents that engage in criminal activities because of economic incentives.

These assumptions and the analysis based on them have led to law enforcement strategies that focus on attacking the financial streams of criminal organizations and removing the profit from crime through confiscation/forfeiture measures as a way of removing the economic incentive. This shift in strategy meant that law enforcement authorities needed enhanced access to reliable information on financial and commercial transactions in order to be able to carry out asset-tracing investigations.[5]

In view of the globalization of fund flows and the increasing use by criminals of the regular channels of commerce to move their assets or to reinvest them, it became accepted that the needs of law enforcement authorities for transaction information, especially about financial transactions, could not be met by the traditional means of discovery and disclosure. Traditional methods, such as production orders, were slow and had a high evidentiary threshold that did not meet the needs of law enforcement for expeditious action carried out at an early stage of the detection process.

It also became apparent that some of the information that law enforcement authorities needed in order to reconstruct the financial trail was often not being gathered by the businesses and professions involved in executing the transactions. For example, financial institutions did not always retain records of verified customer identification of parties making wire transfers.[6]

The problems that faced law enforcement authorities in implementing asset-based law enforcement strategies were present at the domestic level but were exacerbated once the crime or the proceeds crossed national borders. When they did, law enforcement authorities were confronted with the problems arising from differences in legal systems and with the procedural safeguards that foreign jurisdictions applied to protect their sovereignty. Differences in legal and regulatory systems also meant that the information that businesses and professions gathered about their financial and commercial transactions varied from country to country, and law enforcement authorities could not confidently assume that the financial trail would be possible to reconstruct once it is routed through foreign jurisdictions.

To illustrate these challenges, this section will offer two cases: one real, the BCCI example, and one hypothetical.

The BCCI Case

The case of the Bank of Credit and Commerce International (BCCI)[7] offers the best example of the abuse of the banking sector to carry out cross-border criminal activities of shocking magnitude. Regulators found it to be involved in money laundering, support of terrorism, bribery, tax evasion, and other criminal acts.

BCCI is also an illustrative case of the challenges of access to information faced by law enforcement authorities when the matter involves financial information in multiple jurisdictions. While the facts of this case have been widely publicized and are therefore familiar to most readers, the account presented here will recount only the facts that illustrate the issues of information flow.

The BCCI was specifically structured to evade effective government control. It was made up of multiple layers of corporate entities connected to each other through a complex web of affiliates, subsidiaries, and holding companies. This segmented corporate structure ensured that corporate records were spread worldwide and that the regulation and audit of BCCI was fragmented across different jurisdictions without any single jurisdiction having consolidated access to all the bank's records.

When the criminality of BCCI was finally uncovered, the New York district attorney had great difficulty in obtaining any documents held outside the jurisdiction of New York. These problems were particularly challenging in relation to documents held outside the United States in the United Kingdom, Luxembourg, Grand Caymans, Panama, and Abu Dhabi. The prosecutor's main hurdle was the fact BCCI had ensured that most of the important documents were kept in jurisdictions that adhered to strict bank secrecy.

One example of this conundrum can be seen in the attempts of the New York prosecutors to obtain the records that Price Waterhouse relied upon to certify the financial statements and balance sheets that were filed by BCCI in the state of New York. Price Waterhouse at the time of the investigation declined to do so on the basis that the entity that audited BCCI was based in Bermuda and was legally separate from Price Waterhouse U.S. The New York district attorney later lamented, "So here you have financial statements, profit and loss, filed in Washington, filed in Virginia, filed in Tennessee, filed in New York, and audited by auditors who are beyond the reach of law enforcement."[8]

A Hypothetical Case

To understand the information needs of law enforcement authorities and the challenges that faces them in meeting these needs, consider the following hypothetical case.[9]

An employee of a British bank based in Singapore commits bank fraud in the 1980s and wire transfers some of the stolen money to the United States, where the funds are invested in an account of a brokerage firm in New York. He then instructs the brokerage firm to sell all the securities purchased on his behalf and wire the funds to a bank in a bank-secrecy haven. His lawyer in the bank-secrecy haven then uses part of the funds to purchase a house in Germany, where the perpetrator eventually settles. Singaporean authorities open an investigation in the case with the aim of convicting the offender and recovering the funds in order to restitute the victims.

Tracing the funds is essential for the Singaporean authorities not only to confiscate and repatriate the assets but also to locate the offender, who has gone to live in his new house in Germany. In attempting to trace the assets, the authorities are confronted with the lack of records on the originator and beneficiary of the wire transfers sent out of Singapore to the United States. This case hypothetically occurred prior to the international standards on AML/CFT that included customer due diligence (CDD) for wire transfers.

Even when the Singaporean authorities eventually manage to obtain information on the destination of funds from Singapore to the United States, and later to the bank-secrecy haven, it is still impossible to obtain any information from the bank-secrecy haven, which protects every piece of financial information relating to the perpetrator. Unknown to the Singaporean authorities, the fraudster becomes aware of the investigation into his affairs and liquidates his property in Germany, carries the cash across borders, and establishes himself under false identity in a remote but comfortable country. The process of requesting international assistance lasts five years until it is abandoned without significant results.

To sum up, law enforcement authorities in performing their functions of fighting economic crime are confronted by two fundamental informational challenges: (1) availability and reliability of the information necessary to detect and prove economic crimes, and (2) access in a timely fashion to such information wherever it is around the world.

The next section discusses how AML/CFT measures can build a reliable system for detecting financial flows for law enforcement purposes to avoid these problems.

Standard AML/CFT Measures Facilitate Information Flow

AML/CFT standards arose as a direct response to the informational challenges faced by law enforcement, such as those identified above. The FATF 40+9 Recommendations provide a comprehensive system of minimum interventions that countries can implement to address the informational deficit that law enforcement authorities face in pursuing economic crime. The recommendations create a comprehensive, multidisciplinary, asset-based enforcement model.

Under the FATF's 40+9 Recommendations, international AML/CFT standards recommend that countries adopt three types of interventions:

1. Impose obligations on key players to obtain and verify certain pieces of information in relation to specific transactions. The subjects of these regulatory obligations include financial institutions broadly defined, and other categories of businesses and professions such as real estate agents and casinos (Recommendations 5 and 12).

2. Impose obligations on the same key players to maintain records of such information for a specific period of time. The standard also requires that such records should be retrievable in a timely fashion (Recommendations 10, 12 and SRVI).

3. Create a legal environment that enables the sharing of this information between various parties to the extent that is relevant to the fight against money laundering and terrorist financing—in other words, to the extent that it is relevant to the function of competent authorities in pursuing and

preventing economic crime. This category of interventions includes removing unjustified barriers to information flows, such as detrimental financial and professional secrecy provisions, as well as creating channels for the sharing of information between the regulated institutions and the competent authorities, among the competent authorities, and between the competent authorities and their foreign counterparts (Recommendations 4, 13, 16, 31 and 36-40).

Even Recommendation 26, which relates to creating a financial intelligence unit designed to receive, analyze, and disseminate information relating to suspicious activities, fits within these three categories of interventions necessary to create financial and commercial transparency and to allow law enforcement authorities optimum access to the necessary information.[10]

Getting the Institutional Buy-In

The effectiveness of any regulatory regime depends, in part, on the extent to which it is understood and accepted by those persons on whom it has an impact. A significant challenge, therefore, is fostering the acceptance of a regulatory regime among key stakeholders. In the broad context of the regulation of financial sector activities, these key players include policy makers, consumers of financial products and services, financial institutions, regulators, and other government agencies. Acceptance among stakeholders is more likely to occur if they understand the wider environment in which regulation occurs and the varied interests that must be satisfied. Borrowing customers of a bank, for example, are more likely to understand the factors that influence the terms and conditions imposed on their loans and other financial services when they appreciate the bank's duty towards its shareholders, depositors, and the wider community. The chances of successfully implementing a regulatory strategy are therefore enhanced under circumstances in which the stakeholders understand the competing interests and the various issues on which the regulator must focus.

The challenge of understanding these factors is amplified in the case of a regulatory regime geared to address AML/CFT risks. First, the factors that influence the design of the regulatory framework go beyond the basic prudential concerns of financial sector regulation to include concerns related to illicit activity in the wider society. Second—and this is especially the case in smaller economies and societies—the design of an AML/CFT regulatory framework is influenced not only by local circumstances but also by international criminal activity and financial flows that may have very little to do with the local market. It can sometimes be quite challenging for regulators to ensure that local stakeholders understand how seemingly remote events can influence the regulatory measures adopted by the local authorities.

Parliament

Parliamentarians need to be convinced of the level of priority that should be accorded to developing an AML/CFT infrastructure. Support at this level is critical because a successful regime will depend on the passage of comprehensive and timely legislation and the provision of the resources necessary to make the regime effective. In this regard it would be useful for members of parliament to understand the obligations that arise from the relevant UN conventions, resolutions of the UN Security Council, and other regional commitments. To the extent that countries either directly or through membership in an FATF-style regional body (FSRB) subscribe to the FATF recommendations, there is an increased obligation to develop robust AML/CFT regimes. Government officials should also be aware that a number of governments have shown a willingness to impose various sanctions on other countries that are deemed to be inadequately applying the FATF recommendations. The United States has utilized Section 311 of the PATRIOT Act to designate countries or institutions as "primary money laundering concerns." Such designations, in conjunction with rules subsequently issued by the Financial Crimes Enforcement Network (FINCEN), will often have the effect of severely restricting the ability of U.S. financial institutions to deal with these countries or institutions.

Government Officials

Government officials will need to understand the various roles they are expected to play in the system and how it relates to other aspects of their work. Regulators, for example, will need to develop methodologies for the integration of AML/CFT oversight into their existing supervisory regimes and determine how much of their resources to devote to the management of this risk. All entities will need to understand the role of the FIU, which will inevitably be a new institution or function within the government's institutional arrangements. It will be important for all parties within the government bureaucracy to understand the fundamental requirements and protocols that are associated with their new responsibilities. This will be especially important in the arrangements for the handling and processing of information as it flows from reporting institutions through the FIU and on to law enforcement and prosecution authorities.

Reporting Institutions

Even in the best of times, reporting institutions are prone to perceive themselves as being subject to onerous regulatory obligations. The imposition of an AML/CFT infrastructure creates another layer of obligations to which they will be subject. They, like the policymakers, will need to be sensitized to the need to play their important role as the gatekeepers of the system and should also be aware of the sanctions that can arise if they fail to meet their legal obligations. They will need to understand that money laundering and the financing of terrorism will thrive to the extent that there are areas of weakness in the system and that such weak points may either be their own institution or institutions with which they have a business relationship. In countries with a robust sanctioning regime, financial institutions that fail to establish effective AML/CFT regimes face not only reputational risks but may also be subject to heavy fines. In extreme cases of AML/CFT failures, regulators have closed an institution. One of the most severe actions taken by regulators in response to concerns about management of AML/CFT risk was that taken by Japanese regulators against Citigroup in 2004. The Japanese regulators ordered Citigroup to close its private bank operations over their concerns about the failure of the bank's AML internal controls.[11]

Public

Perhaps the most difficult stakeholders to bring on board are the members of the public since they are a diverse and disparate constituency. But they are also the stakeholders who are likely to suffer the greatest inconveniences from AML/CFT as they conduct their everyday business. It is therefore important to have a program of public outreach that helps members of the public to understand concerns related to the potential abuse of the financial system by persons engaged in illicit activity and the measures necessary to combat such abuse. A critical issue to address in outreach programs is the importance of providing adequate levels of information to covered persons/institutions because some AML/CFT requirements may be contrary to the general expectations about the privacy of some types of personal information.

The Role of the Private Sector

Obtaining Information

An AML/CFT regime should establish strong disincentives to the use of the financial and other covered sectors to facilitate illicit activity. To this end, the framework should create an environment that promotes high levels of transparency in the conduct of business by covered entities.[12] A major cornerstone in this regard is ensuring that covered institutions have thorough and pertinent information about their customers and the nature of their customers' business.

Before discussing the measures that institutions should take to obtain the information necessary to manage AML/CFT risk, it is important to consider the measures that should be taken by government authorities. Measures taken by covered institutions will be built on the frameworks first established by the government. It is important that the framework for the formation of companies and other vehicles used in the conduct of business activity promotes high levels of transparency. There should be arrangements that allow for the identification of all persons who participate in the ownership of corporate entities, serve as directors, or are in positions to exert significant control over corporate vehicles or other entities. It is therefore important for countries to enact legislation that minimizes opportunities for persons to obscure the extent and nature of their participation in corporate or other forms of business activity. A recent FATF paper on the misuse of corporate vehicles reemphasizes the importance of a framework that requires institutions to obtain, in a timely manner, accurate and comprehensive information on the beneficial ownership of companies and to determine who are the trustees, settlors, and beneficiaries of trusts. The paper found that it is less important where such information is maintained, once it is comprehensive, up to date, and readily available to competent authorities.[13]

The other major component for obtaining such information is the action taken by the covered institutions themselves. There is often a perception that AML/CFT requirements place new and onerous responsibilities on covered institutions. While the advent of an AML/CFT regime will indeed impose a number of new requirements, there are a number of objectives that can be satisfied by measures that traditional financial institutions are likely to already have in place. In protecting their own commercial and financial interests, these institutions have a strong incentive to undertake due diligence on a customer, whether it is a bank managing its credit risk or an insurance company understanding a customer's risk profile before pricing a product offer. This type of information will not be adequate to meet the requirements of a comprehensive Know Your Customer (KYC) regime,[14] but it represents an important starting point as institutions try to obtain information on their customers in line with their AML/CFT obligations. Designated nonfinancial businesses and professions (DNFBPs)[15] are the exception in the context of the responsibilities that are associated with requirements for robust customer due diligence (CDD). In many instances the nature of their relationship with their customers in the performance of their core business activity does not present risks that necessitate the performance of due diligence. This is particularly so for dealers in precious metals and stones and real estate agents. Casino operations are perhaps the one area of DNFBP activity that has traditionally been more proactive in undertaking some forms of CDD, for they are more vulnerable than other DNFBPs to losses through the fraudulent activity of their customers.

There are a number of core questions that covered institutions are expected to ask themselves as they contemplate the establishment of a customer relationship:

- Who is this person?

- What type of activity does this person want to conduct with my firm?

- What type and pattern of activity can I expect?

- Is this person representing a third party?

- How can I verify the information presented to me?

An important standard for an AML/CFT framework is its usefulness in the context in which it takes place. In addressing the issue of verifying a customer's identity, FATF requires that countries should use "reliable, independent source documents, data or information" and cites the Basel Committee's "General Guide to Account Opening and Customer Identification" as guidance on the types of documents that would be acceptable for this purpose.[16] The paper suggests that government-issued identification documents such as passports, birth certificates, identity cards, and social security records would be appropriate for verifying identity, but it also points out that other documents "of an equivalent nature" may be used as well. While the use of such documents is clearly recommended in countries where they are commonplace, there are a number of countries where significant segments of the population do not possess such documents. In such instances the legal and regulatory framework should be designed in a manner that successfully bridges the requirements of the standard in way that is reasonable given the country's circumstances.

There is often a strong temptation to design legal and regulatory instruments and practices in a manner that conforms closely with the standards and best practices in developed societies. If this is attempted in an environment where such conformity is virtually impossible to achieve, there is a danger of establishing legal and regulatory requirements with which most institutions cannot comply, which runs the risk of the framework being ineffective. It would clearly be more desirable to design a system that meets the test of independence and reliability within the local context. One country in which few citizens have state-issued identification has developed a system in which customers are identified on the basis of assurances provided by senior, well-respected community leaders. While this is not an ideal approach, to require government-issued identity documents in this instance would not only exclude persons who lack such documents from the formal financial sector but could also provide an incentive for the development of informal financial activity, which itself could become a source of AML/CFT vulnerability.

A crucial aspect of the CDD process is the establishment of a customer profile that assists institutions in understanding the type of activity that they should reasonably expect to be conducted through the customer's accounts or facilities. It is only by establishing such a profile at the beginning and in the early stages of the relationship that an institution's suspicion can be subsequently aroused by unusual or suspicious customer behavior. Such a profile is therefore the foundation for the subsequent function of monitoring customer activity and determining whether a suspicious activity report should be filed.

Maintaining Information

The principle reason to gather information is to ensure that accurate information is held on customers and their activities. This includes not only the information originally obtained on the customer but all subsequent information obtained, particularly information that relates to transactions conducted for or on behalf of the customer. Again, this is not a requirement that arises solely in the context of AML/CFT because there are many incentives, from a commercial perspective, for companies to maintain good records of customer activity and transactions. From an AML/CFT perspective, information needs to be comprehensive enough to facilitate detailed investigations into customer activity and should be easily accessible by the covered institutions and ultimately the competent authorities. The standard establishes minimum periods for the maintenance of identification and transaction records and stresses that records should be maintained for periods beyond these minimums, if specifically requested by competent authorities.

It is important to update the original CDD information on the customer, particularly in instances where information comes to light that can potentially alter some aspect of the original customer profile. The standard requires that where an institution has reason to doubt the accuracy of information held on the customer, it should undertake a new CDD process.

A crucial aspect of maintaining information is the ongoing monitoring of customer activity. This function will initially identify unusual activity, which will be further examined to determine if it meets the test of suspicion. Institutions are challenged to determine what types of monitoring systems are most appropriate for their needs. Factors that will influence their decision are the volume, nature, and complexity of their regular business transactions. In some instances, it is possible that a system based on manual oversight may be an effective monitoring mechanism, but as institutions grow in size and transactions become more frequent and complex, it is inevitable that this function will have to be computerized. The challenge for institutions, particularly those in relatively small and unsophisticated economies, or those who deal with relatively few transactions, is to recognize when they have reached the point where it is necessary to computerize the function. At this stage it is challenging to choose the software that is the best suited to the institution's needs. A system that generates a large number of "false positives" is not effectively serving the need of the institution or the FIU. It should be the goal of covered institutions to produce a favorable ratio between the number of transactions that are originally identified as suspicious and the number of reports that are eventually filed with the FIU. The use of an automated system should not be seen as a replacement for human judgment and intervention, which are indispensable in making a final determination whether a transaction can be explained in the context of information held or known about the customer or whether it merits the filing of a suspicious transaction report (STR). The bottom line is that regulators will want to be convinced that an institution is able, with a reasonable degree of consistency, to identify suspicious activity that merits reporting to the FIU.

Transmitting Information

A significant feature of AML/CFT regimes is the number of interfaces between various groups or stakeholders, including members of the public, covered institutions, the FIU, investigatory authorities, and the officials who will eventually prosecute cases. Each group has its core functions and specific interests and each has a distinct view of its responsibilities in respect of information in its possession.

One overriding concern is the need to treat information with the appropriate level of confidentiality. In the conduct of everyday commercial and private activity there is an expectation of reasonable levels of privacy by all parties. Customers often wish to limit the amount of personal information they provide to a financial institution or make publicly available, and often have legitimate reasons for wanting to do so. Use of instruments such as trusts, for example, is sometimes driven not only by financial planning objectives but also by a desire to protect information that the settlors prefer to keep out of the public domain. In many instances these vehicles obscure the link between an asset and the person or persons with a beneficial ownership interest in the asset. Financial institutions also place priority on protecting the confidentiality of customer-specific information, and government agencies such as supervisors, FIUs, and prosecutors are no less concerned about the confidentiality of information, especially when such information could be market-sensitive or could be related to a criminal investigation or prosecution. A fundamental challenge to the transmission of information, therefore, is to establish a framework for the sharing of information that is acceptable to all parties and meets reasonable AML/CFT objectives.

Authorities should seek to establish quite clearly that all reasonable expectations to privacy will be respected. This is not only necessary for the efficient conduct of everyday business activity. It should also foster the levels of confidence that will encourage persons, both natural and corporate, to continue their use of the formal financial system. In a number of countries authorities have to balance requirements of AML/CFT legislation with confidentiality principles implicit in data-protection laws. However, notwithstanding the importance of an appropriate framework for confidentiality in the normal conduct of business, it is equally important to communicate to members of the public and the business community that there will be occasions when it will be necessary for persons and institutions to share such information. A major challenge in this regard is establishing a framework that provides for sharing of information while continuing to respect confidentiality to the extent possible.

The sharing or transmittal of information commences at the start of the business relationship. Customers should expect that their ability to initiate a business relationship with a covered institution will depend, in some measure, on the extent to which they are willing to provide information requested by the institution. If a customer is unwilling to provide information that is critical to the CDD process, the law should prohibit the institution from establishing the relationship. There are also times during the course of a business relationship when customers will be required to provide specific information to assist institutions to meet their AML/CFT obligations.

The information required for sending funds by wire transfer is a case in point. FATF Special Recommendation VII requires not only that specific customer information be obtained by the originating institution but also that such information should remain with the transfer throughout the payment chain. If the originating institution cannot obtain the information, it should decline to effect the transfer. Recipient institutions have a similar obligation to ensure that the requirements of the standard are met under these circumstances.

There should also be clear legal provisions indicating the circumstances under which covered institutions have an obligation to provide information to the FIU and other competent authorities and to provide explicit protection against civil and criminal liability for reporting institutions, their directors, and their employees, and obligating such parties to treat all reports in strict confidence.

The sharing of information when reporting institutions file suspicious transaction reports presents specific challenges that require institutions to strike an important balance. Reporting institutions are not expected to perform the role of investigatory authorities, and the test to be met before taking a decision to file a report is that there are reasonable grounds for suspicion on the part of the reporting institution. In making a determination in this regard, it is expected that an institution will review its information on the customer, consider the customer's general profile, and where possible make discreet enquires that may be necessary to clarify the information being reviewed. The process of making inquiries is a sensitive one because it is important not to "tip off" the customer about the reasons for the enquiries. In fact, it is a requirement that there be an explicit prohibition against disclosing the fact that a report is being made to the FIU.

In attempting to meet their obligations to file STRs, institutions sometimes engage in defensive reporting. This is a practice in which they report all cases where there is the slightest level of suspicion about customer conduct. In taking this action, institutions are driven by a concern that they may be sanctioned if deemed to be failing to meet their reporting obligations. Defensive reporting is in fact counter-productive because it inundates the FIU with information of varying quality and makes the FIU's job of analyzing the data more difficult that it should be. Reporting institutions are therefore challenged to find the right balance between meeting their reporting obligations and being a responsible partner by providing the FIU with quality data on which to undertake its analysis.

Corporate Governance Infrastructure

As already discussed, many of the measures that institutions are expected to employ in satisfying AML/CFT obligations are not unique to an AML/CFT regime. Such measures can operate in conjunction with an underlying infrastructure that provides general support for the operation of the covered institution. An important aspect of this infrastructure is the institution's corporate governance framework. AML/CFT requirements will only be successfully executed to the extent that there is a framework of clear and effective policies and procedures, clear lines of accountability, appropriate control mechanisms, and internal and external audit functions. Financial sector regulators have often determined that failures within licensed institutions can be linked to either a failure to establish effective risks-management systems or the failure to adequately use effective systems that are already in place. In a number of instances, regulators have given as a rationale for the imposition of AML/CFT-related sanctions the failure of institutions to maintain critical aspects of their corporate governance.

In December 2005 the Office of the Controller of the Currency (OCC) in the United States fined the Arab Bank US$24 million for failures in its internal controls related to the Banking Secrecy Act and general anti-money laundering compliance. The OCC found that the bank failed to (1) adequately implement a program to monitor funds transfers for suspicious activity, (2) obtain sufficient information about funds transfers to determine if it was necessary to file an SAR, and (3) adequately audit the program established to monitor funds-transfer procedures.[17] The OCC was therefore concerned that the corporate governance arrangements failed not only at the primary level of establishing appropriate monitoring mechanisms but also at a secondary level in relation to weaknesses in the audit function.

In October 2006 the Financial Crimes Enforcement Network (FINCEN) assessed a civil penalty against the Foster Bank in the amount of US$8.5 million. FINCEN found that the bank "failed to implement an adequate Banking Secrecy Act compliance program, including an anti-money laundering program with internal controls, independent testing and other measures to detect and report potential money laundering, terrorist financing and other suspicious activity."[18]

Role of the Supervisor

In general, supervisors should seek to create and maintain an environment in which institutions are able to conduct legitimate business activity. They should ideally see themselves as partners with the institutions they supervise and should seek, to the extent possible, to minimize unnecessary regulatory burdens not only in the interest of the efficiency of the system but also to avoid creating incentives for the emergence of informal or parallel systems. Notwithstanding this broad objective, supervisors also have an obligation to protect the integrity of the financial and wider business community. They must develop a supervisory framework that is effective for the institutions for which they have supervisory responsibility and should seek to understand the AML/CFT risk profile of these institutions in an effort to develop appropriate supervisory strategies. An important aspect of the supervisor's function is the articulation of supervisory objectives and strategies in a manner that makes clear what is expected of industry. Instruments such as regulations and guidance notes are commonly used to give more detailed expression to the basic framework as established in the primary legislation. In the context of risk-based approaches to the management of AML/CFT risks, it is very important for supervisors to give industry a clear indication of the extent to which such approaches will be accepted.

In the practice of supervision, strategy comes into play as early as the licensing stage. The basic fit-and-proper tests that are commonly applied by financial sector supervisors are a useful starting point. However, supervisors need to go beyond this type of assessment and consider whether the applicant for a license is appropriate from the perspective of its potential AML/CFT risk profile. An entity that is likely to be conducting significant portions of its business with persons from jurisdictions with weak AML/CFT laws and oversight regimes would, for example, raise certain concerns about AML/CFT vulnerabilities. As with all other areas of general supervisory concern, it is important to get it right at the licensing stage because addressing problems after an institution is up and running is far more difficult.

It is important for supervisors to have the necessary powers to undertake their responsibilities. This includes the power to request information from licensees, the power to undertake on-site inspections, and the power to apply sanctions. The international standard requires countries to have in place "effective, proportionate and dissuasive criminal, civil or administrative sanctions" that can be applied to both legal and natural persons. Actions taken by supervisors internationally have demonstrated the use of a wide range of sanctions, tailor-made to address specific supervisory concerns.

In November 2005 in the United Kingdom, the Financial Services Authority (FSA) announced that it had imposed a fine of £175,000 on Investment Services UK Limited (ISUK) "for conducting its business without due skill, care and diligence and for failing to control its business effectively in relation to anti-money laundering (AML) systems and controls." In addition to the fine imposed on the business, the FSA fined its managing director £30,000, indicating that "he failed to act with due care, skill and diligence, failed to ensure that his firm complied with AML requirements and was knowingly concerned in the actions taken by ISUK."[19]

In December 2005 four U.S. government agencies took joint action against ABN AMRO, imposing penalties totaling US$80 million. In a joint public announcement the agencies indicated that the penalties were based on "findings of unsafe and unsound practices; on findings of systemic defects in ABN AMRO's internal controls to ensure compliance with U.S. anti-money laundering laws and regulations, which resulted in failures to identify, analyze, and report suspicious activity; and on findings that ABN AMRO participated in transactions that violated U.S. sanctions laws."[20]

These actions demonstrate the importance of regulators having flexible sanction powers to address failures in accordance with the perceived severity of the failure and in a manner that can sanction both legal and natural persons.

A Question of Risk

Supervisors and reporting institutions both face resource constraints in the performance of their AML/CFT responsibilities. It is not possible to devote similar levels of resources to all functions and responsibilities, and judgments have to be made about how resources can be most effectively employed. While the debate about risk-based approaches has been the focus of considerable attention in recent years, it is certainly not new; both supervisors and supervised institutions have always had to make judgments on how best they can employ the limited resources at their disposal to effectively manage the risks they confront. For institutions the focus is on the risk inherent in their business lines. Supervisors, on the other hand, have a broader perspective and are more concerned about the risk faced by individual institutions and the financial system as a whole.

Supervised Institutions

A supervised entity must define its appetite for risk in the context of AML/CFT and develop strategies to manage the risk inherent in the business it conducts. It is therefore expected that institutions will be able to demonstrate that they understand the risk they take on and that they have devised internal mechanisms and controls to manage it. The FATF recommendations have provided some broad guidance in this regard and have identified activities considered to represent a level of risk that is higher than normal. These include businesses with politically exposed persons (PEPS), correspondent banking relationships, and businesses with persons or entities from countries that do not adequately apply the FATF Recommendations. This list is not exhaustive, and institutions are expected to understand their own risk profile and employ the appropriate measures to manage the risks. For example, a number of banking institutions worldwide have made the judgment that providing services to money services businesses is a high-risk activity in the context of AML/CFT and have either reduced services to these entities or have discontinued the business relationships. Six U.S. regulators were concerned enough about this development to issue a joint statement suggesting that a bank's concerns in this regard "may stem, in part, from a misperception of the requirements of the Banking Secrecy Act and an erroneous view that money services businesses present a uniform and unacceptably high risk of money and other illicit activity."[21] The regulators stressed that "a decision to accept or maintain an account with a money services business should be made by the banking institution's management, under standards and guidelines approved by its board of directors and should be based on the banking institutions' assessment of the risks associated with the particular account and its capacity to manage those risks." The action taken by the U.S. regulators underscores the importance of devising risk management strategies that are tailored to the risk profile inherent in an institution's business lines and customer relationships, and it also highlights the regulators' concerns that measures taken to manage AML/CFT risk should be proportionate to the perceived risk and should not be unnecessarily disruptive to the conduct of legitimate business activity.

It is permissible, using a risk-based approach, to determine that some lines of business represent a lower-than-average level of risk and accordingly can devote fewer resources to managing the AML/CFT risks. Institutions adopting such measures should be prepared to justify to their supervisor the basis of their analysis of the risks that they perceive to be inherent in their various business lines and customer relationships and the rationale for the choice of measures they have adopted to manage those risks.

The Supervisor

The obligation of the supervisor is to understand and manage the AML/CFT risk that can be posed by all institutions for which it has responsibility. The supervisor must adopt strategies and determine the extent to which a disproportionate amount of supervisory resources may be focused on some institutions. The supervisor's judgment in this regard will be influenced by a number of factors, including the nature of the business undertaken by an institution and the effectiveness of the oversight regimes to which the institution is subject. A risk analysis might determine, for example, that a branch of a large international bank that has strong internal controls and is subject to rigorous headquarters oversight and independent audit might represent a lower AML/CFT risk than a small, locally owned bank that is neither subject to head office supervision nor comes under the consolidated supervisory responsibility of a foreign supervisor. Another perspective of the relative AML/CFT risks posed by these two institutions might be that notwithstanding the more robust oversight mechanisms to which the first institution is subject, its higher volume of large international financial flows may make it more vulnerable to money laundering and financing of terrorism than a small bank catering primarily to a local market. On issues of risk management, there are no easy answers. However, supervisors are expected to assess and understand the risks to which their licensees are exposed and to make appropriate decisions on the most effective use of their supervisory resources.

Interagency Information Flows

AML/CFT measures create unlikely partners. An effective AML/CFT regime depends on the successful cooperation between multiple agencies spanning the entire regulatory and law enforcement system. The scope of AML/CFT measures keeps expanding, leading to an increase in the variety of agencies that must cooperate and exchange information for the system to work.

Initially, AML/CFT measures centered around the cooperation between financial sector supervisors, law enforcement authorities, and the FIU. The definition of financial institutions under the AML/CFT standards is quite broad.[22] It is not restricted to the traditional sectors of banking, insurance, and securities. Rather, it expands to include, for example, foreign exchange bureaus and all types of providers of fund transfers. Countries adopt different approaches to financial sector supervision. The majority, however, continue to assign the supervisory function to different agencies. The more dispersed the supervisory function, the more complex the process of interagency cooperation and exchange of information.

In 2003 the AML/CFT standard expanded to include a list of designated nonfinancial businesses and professions (DNFBPs), which includes casinos; real estate agents; dealers in precious stones; dealers in precious metals; lawyers, notaries, other independent legal professionals; and trust and company-service providers. With these additions comes an increase in the number of supervisory agencies involved in the fight against money laundering and terrorist financing. These agencies must then be incorporated in the stream of information flow.

FATF Recommendations on Domestic Cooperation and Information Sharing

The key Recommendation dealing with domestic cooperation between competent authorities is Recommendation 31. It states:

Countries should ensure that policy makers, the FIU, law enforcement and supervisors have effective mechanisms in place which enable them to co-operate, and where appropriate coordinate domestically with each other concerning the development and implementation of policies and activities to combat money laundering and terrorist financing.

Recommendation 31 is an open recommendation in that it defines the necessary measure by its objective, which is achieving effective cooperation. In other words, the recommendation does not tell countries what to do; it only guides them to implement effective mechanisms to achieve this objective.

Recommendation 31 does, however, offer some further guidance on the scope and nature of interagency cooperation. It defines the relevant authorities that should be integrated through mechanisms of cooperation. It suggests that countries bring into cooperative arrangements not only the FIU, the supervisory authorities, and law enforcement authorities, but also policy makers and other competent authorities. In the elaboration provided in the methodology for assessing compliance with the standard, it is clearly noted that law enforcement authorities should include customs authorities where appropriate. The involvement of customs authorities is particularly important because the focus on cross-border movement of cash and other negotiable instruments gained more prominence in the AML/CFT scheme with the introduction in 2004 of Special Recommendation IX, which specifically addressed this issue.[23]

Policy makers include any agency that has the power to influence or determine policies and practices. The exact scope of this category of stakeholders varies from country to country. Broadly speaking, it may include certain key ministries, such as the ministries of justice, foreign affairs, or finance.

Countries should also consider whether other competent authorities are relevant. For example, in countries where AML measures are not utilized to combat tax evasion, tax authorities may still be relevant because the information they possess may help in conducting financial investigations for the purposes of AML/CFT. A country may consider taking the necessary measures to achieve cooperation with tax authorities on AML/CFT issues, subject to that country's approach to confidentiality of tax information and the appropriate use of such information.[24]

Recommendation 31 also distinguishes between policy cooperation and operational cooperation, and requires countries to take measures to achieve cooperation at both levels. Countries should take measures that help achieve cooperation in the development of AML/CFT policies. At the same time, they should have mechanisms in place to secure operational cooperation in carrying out AML/CFT activities such as cooperation in investigating money laundering offenses.

In addition to Recommendation 31, in this regard one should also take note of Recommendation 26, which requires that the FIU have access, directly or indirectly and on a timely basis, to the financial, administrative, and law enforcement information that it needs to undertake its functions. This aspect of Recommendation 26 spells with clarity an integral component of a system of information sharing that is essential for the operational success of the FIU.

A similar requirement is to be found in Recommendations 33 and 34, which require countries to make it possible for their competent authorities "to obtain or have access in a timely fashion to adequate, accurate and current information on the beneficial ownership and control" of legal persons and legal arrangements.

Formal and Informal Mechanisms

Countries have adopted a variety of mechanisms to induce enhanced collaboration and information sharing among the agencies that have a role to play in fighting money laundering and terrorist financing, both at the level of policy making and at the operational level. In addition to the distinction between formal and informal mechanisms, there are four types of formal mechanisms that countries have adopted in order to facilitate interagency cooperation and information flows: legislative stipulation, formal multi-agency committees, interagency memoranda of understanding, and staff exchange arrangements.

Legislative Stipulation

Some countries have addressed issues of interagency cooperation and information sharing by legislation. This is consistent with the recommended approach in the UNODC/IMF Model Legislation on Money Laundering and Financing Terrorism [hereinafter, the Model Law],[25] which provides in article 3.1.4(4) that:

The financial intelligence unit may request in relation to any report it has received, any additional information it deems useful for the accomplishment of its functions from:

- Police departments
- Authorities responsible for the supervision of the entities and persons subject to this law;
- Other administrative agencies of the State

The information requested shall be provided within the time limits set by the Financial Intelligence Unit.

Another aspect of interagency cooperation, which may be established by legislation or other formal mechanisms such as ministerial orders, requires supervisory authorities to inform the FIU of any weaknesses identified in the suspicious-transactions reporting systems of any institution subject to their supervision and to require the FIU to inform the relevant supervisory agency of any such weaknesses that it detects in the reports submitted by a supervised institution.

This approach is also endorsed by the Model Law in article 3.1.5, which provides:

Whenever the financial intelligence unit determines that a financial institution or designated non-financial business and profession is not complying or has not complied with the obligations set out in this law, it may apprise the relevant supervisory authority accordingly.

Multi-Agency Committees and Steering Groups

Many countries employ multi-agency committees and steering groups, both in the area of policy cooperation as well as operational cooperation. Some of these committees are established formally by law, executive orders, or an interagency memorandum of understanding (MOU). Many countries have opted for creating an AML multi-agency, high-level committee with representatives from all relevant ministries and agencies charged with the task of coordinating AML policies. Some countries have added CFT to the scope of operations of these committees, while others have opted for a separate committee with similar composition but often a different lead agency. The responsibilities of such agencies often include the task of facilitating information exchange between the member agencies.

Memorandum of Understanding

As a way of delineating the boundaries of their respective responsibilities or establishing protocols for the sharing of information or other resources, competent authorities in some countries are opting to sign MOUs with other competent authorities. This is a helpful tool because it clarifies roles and responsibilities, especially in the area of AML/CFT, where fragmentation and overlap often creates jurisdictional ambiguity.

MOUs between authorities are often not based on any explicit legislative authorization but rather are part of the general prerogative available to the administrative agencies to do what is necessary to perform their functions efficiently. As a result, while some agencies may be in the habit of entering into MOUs whenever the context merits it, other agencies find the MOU totally alien. Similar trends could be discerned at country level, for MOUs are more familiar in some jurisdictions than in others.

Staff Secondment and Staff Sharing

In order to enhance institutional cooperation, many agencies opt for entering into agreements with other agencies by virtue of which they second staff to the other agency. This approach aims to establish a continuous point of contact as well as develop a common understanding of each other's institutional culture.

Some agencies, especially law enforcement bodies, also opt for creating task forces to handle specific issues or cases. Also, because of the complex technical nature of some money laundering investigations, law enforcement authorities are relying increasingly on borrowed expertise from the supervisory agencies.

Aside from these formal mechanisms of cooperation, one of the most effective tools of cooperation and information sharing is the informal personal ties that are developed between the staff of various agencies. Because AML/CFT systems are still novel and it is mandating new connections between agencies that had little interaction before, these informal ties are in many cases still nascent. In addition, some countries opt for developing ad hoc working groups, committees, and task forces to foster cooperation and information sharing on particular issues.

Causes of Failure

Collaboration between authorities is not an easy matter. Agencies come into the process with different institutional cultures, mandates, and priorities. But tackling economic crime is nearly impossible without cross-agency effort.[26] It is possible to identify the common causes for failure or constraints in interagency information flow.

One of the biggest impediments to collaboration is the overlap of jurisdiction among agencies. This is a problem in many countries, regardless of their level of development or the sophistication of their AML/CFT system. Overlap of jurisdiction often creates turf fights and competitiveness that is detrimental to the collaborative process. This tension and competitiveness is often expressed in the systematic withholding of information from the other agencies, which clearly undermines the flow of information necessary for an effective AML/CFT system.

Turf fights resulting from overlap of mandates occur among competing supervisory authorities as well as competing law enforcement agencies. For example, the AML/CFT laws of some countries assign to the newly established FIU the function of supervising the regulated institutions' compliance with AML/CFT measures while still maintaining their default supervisory authorities over the same subject matter. In their attempt to protect their supervisory turf, the FIU and the supervisory authorities may withhold from each other information relating to the regulated institution's compliance, to the detriment of the effectiveness of the AML/CFT regime.

It has been observed, especially in larger countries with complex economic systems, that there is a substantial fragmentation of supervisory and law enforcement functions, which creates difficulties for coordination. One reason is related to the overlap of jurisdiction. Fragmentation of functions often results in ambiguity in the scope of the jurisdiction of each agency, which has the same effect as the overlap of jurisdiction. Fragmentation also increases the number of agencies that need to be involved, which aggravates conflicts of cultures, mandates, and priorities.

The reverse of fragmentation of functions—that is, concentration of functions—can also be problematic. Some country assessments have found that cross-agency cooperation is undermined when all the powers and responsibilities relating to AML/CFT are concentrated in one agency. This may seem paradoxical, for it would seem that if all AML/CFT responsibilities are concentrated in one agency, there would be no need for interagency cooperation. This conclusion would, however, be incorrect, for AML/CFT measures are only means to other ends. They are meant to facilitate the achievement of the wider objectives, including protecting the integrity of the financial system and facilitating law enforcement efforts against all types of financial crimes. Without cooperation and information flow between the agencies responsible for AML/CFT measures specifically and the agencies responsible for these wider objectives, the effectiveness of AML/CFT measures cannot be achieved.

The detrimental effects of concentrating AML/CFT functions could be attributed to the fact that it tends to lower the priority level of AML/CFT issues in other agencies and therefore reduces the level of resources committed to AML/CFT and the level of expertise developed in this area.

Staff turnover also poses a problem in jurisdictions that are small or have an underpaid civil service. Under such circumstances, staff of supervisory and law enforcement agencies tend to leave the service at a high rate in order to pursue better employment opportunities. This affects informal interagency collaboration because it undermines the development of sustainable collaborative relationships between individuals in various agencies.

Some structural factors may also pose challenges for the efforts to collaborate and share information. The sheer size of a country when accompanied by severe resource constraints results in difficulties of cooperation and sharing of information between agencies that operate in various parts of the country.

Finally, each authority is governed by certain rules relating to the use and disclosure of information that becomes available to it. Some of these rules are justified either for operational reasons, such as the success of criminal investigations or intelligence gathering, or for reasons of civil rights and due process, such as the restrictions relating to self-incrimination that apply in certain jurisdictions. Such rules have implications, for example, for the sharing of information between tax authorities that receive voluntary disclosures for tax purposes and criminal enforcement agencies gathering evidence to prosecute a criminal offense.

When confidentiality rules are too strict, they hamper institutional cooperation and information flows. While some of the confidentiality rules are justified, others may be out of date and not in line with the current complexity and magnitude of economic crime, which poses a much higher demand for information sharing. Some confidentiality practices are merely the result of institutional culture as opposed to either legal provisions or operational considerations.

Identified Good Practices

The findings from country experiences also point toward a number of good practices in achieving institutional cooperation and effective information flow. For example, there is strong evidence from country studies that when AML/CFT efforts are led by a strong agency such as a key ministry or other key institutions (e.g, the central bank), cooperation is enhanced. This is particularly relevant in the early stages of setting up an AML/CFT system. When successful, the lead institution, especially when adequately represented, plays an important role in resolving jurisdictional conflicts and facilitating the flow of information.

Multi-agency committees, whether formally or informally constituted, have succeeded in performing the functions of facilitating cooperation and information sharing when they meet regularly and have a clear and realistic agenda. It is also good practice for member agencies to keep a representative on the committee who has sufficient authority to make commitments on behalf of the agency.

It is valuable to designate specialized AML/CFT units within each competent authority or to identify a specific liaison officer. This allows other agencies to easily identify the contact person. It also helps to develop expertise and institutional memory. An additional value is the harnessing of cooperative personal relationships across agencies.

Country experiences lend credence to the argument that the use of existing institutions instead of creating new ones to handle AML/CFT issues can benefit cooperation and information sharing. Building on already existing channels of cooperation where they exist between agencies has also proved beneficial. This does not preclude the creation of new channels, especially in situations where collaboration between particular agencies was minimal prior to the AML/CFT agenda.

Conclusion

Sixteen years after the development of the FATF 40 Recommendations, many countries are still facing the challenge of implementing effective AML/CFT regimes. The challenge is likely to be ongoing, in part because of the dynamic nature of financial sector activity and the widening of the AML/CFT net to cover nonfinancial institutions. Setting aside these two variables, success in this regard will still depend on the ability of countries to develop frameworks that create an environment in which relevant information can flow efficiently through the AML/CFT chain. Countries need to create legal frameworks that promote the easy availability of relevant and useful information, remove obstacles to the flow of such information, develop pathways through which such information can efficiently flow, and achieve a culture of cooperation across all private-sector and public-sector entities and persons that play a role in AML/CFT regimes.

Notes

[1] Compliance with AML/CFT assessments is conducted by the International Monetary Fund and the World Bank in the context of the Financial Sector Assessment Program, as well as by the FATF and the FATF-Style Regional Bodies (FSRBs) in a process of mutual evaluations among their members. All AML/CFT assessments are carried out in accordance with a commonly agreed methodology. Reference to "assessors bodies" is therefore a reference to the IMF, the World Bank, the FATF, and all FSRBs. Currently, there are eight FSRBs representing different regions of the world.

[2] For a discussion of these objectives and how they correspond to law enforcement strategies, see Mariano-Florentino Cuéllar, "The Tenuous Relationship between the Fight against Money Laundering and the Disruption of Criminal Finance," 93 *Journal of Criminal Law and Criminology* 311 (Winter/Spring 2003).

[3] In this paper, the term *economic crime* is used to refer to any crime committed for profit or economic gain.

[4] For a historical analysis of these developments and their link to the evolution of AML/CFT standards see Heba Shams, "Legal Globalization: Money Laundering Law and Other Cases," Sir Joseph Gold Memorial Series, Vol. 5, Chapters 2–3 (BIICL: London, 2004).

[5] For clear description of this approach to law enforcement, see wriiten statement of J. Rannazzisi before the Senate Committee on Finance "Breaking the Methamphetamine Supply Chain: Law Enforcement Challenges," (US Senate, September 18, 2007).

[6] For a good analytical discussion on the early debate relating to regulating wire transfers for AML purposes, see Sarah Jane Hughes, "Policing Money Laundering through Funds Transfers: A Critique of Regulation under the Bank Secrecy Act," 67 *Indiana Law Journal* 283 (Winter, 1992).

[7] For the details of the case, see Senator John Kerry and Senator Hank Brown, The BCCI Affair: A Report to the Committee on Foreign Relations, United States Senate (December 1992, 102d Congress 2d Session, Senate Print), 102–140.

[8] Ibid., Chapter 9.

[9] Parts of this hypothetical were drawn from a hypothetical case developed by Richard T. Preiss, "Privacy of Financial Information and Civil Rights Issues: The Implications for Investigating and Prosecuting International Economic Crime," 14 *Dickinson Journal of International Law* 525 (Spring, 1996), at 530 *et seq.*

[10] For a critical perspective on this issue of transaction transparency see Christopher Slobogin, "Transaction Surveillance by the Government" 75 *Mississippi Law Journal* 139 (Fall, 2005).

[11] "Japan Shuts Down Four Citigroup Offices," *Financial Times*, September 20, 2004.

[12] "Covered entities" are generally financial institutions and a category known as "designated non-financial businesses and professions" (DNFBPs), which includes but is not limited to, real estate agents, casinos, lawyers, accountants, trust and company service providers and dealers in precious metals and stones.

[13] Financial Action Task Force, *The Misuse of Corporate Vehicles, Including Trust and Company Service Providers*, October 2006.

[14] Refers to a comprehensive set of measures to be taken by financial institutions to satisfactorily identify their customers, and have a sound understanding of their background including their personal, business, and financial profiles and the type of transaction activity in which they are likely to engage.

[15] Designated Non-Financial Businesses and Professions is the term used by the FATF 40 + 9 Recommendations to refer to six categories of businesses and professions that should be covered by AML/CFT preventive requirements. These categories include: casinos, real estate agents, lawyers and other independent legal professionals, dealers in precious metals, dealers in precious stones, and trust and company service providers.

[16] Basel Committee on Banking Supervision, General Guide to Account Opening and Customer Identification February 2003—Attachment to Basel Committee Publication 85—Customer Due Diligence for Banks.

[17] Office of the Comptroller of the Currency, Enforcement Action—Consent Order for Civil Money Penalty (No. 2005 -101) http://www.occ.treas.gov/ftp/eas/ea2005-101.pdf

[18] FINCEN, "Enforcement Action in the Matter of The Foster Bank," Assessment of Civil Money Penalty (No. 2006-8) http://www.fincen.gov/news_room/ea

[19] Financial Services Authority, "FSA fines bond broker and managing director for anti-money laundering failures" (9 November 2008). http://www.fsa.gov.uk/Pages/Library/Communication/PR/2005/117.shtml

[20] FINCEN, "Enforcement Action in the Matter of The New York Branch of ABN Amro Bank N. V. New York, New York," Assessment of Civil Money Penalty (No. 2005 -5) http://www.fincen.gov/news_room/ea

[21] Federal Deposit Insurance Corporation, Financial Institutions Letters-Joint Statement on Providing Banking Services to Money Services Businesses—March 30, 2005 http://www.fdic.gov/news/news/financial/2005/fil2405a.html

[22] Financial Action Task Force, The Forty Recommendations (20 June 2003), 13.

[23] Special Recommendation IX requires countries to implement a comprehensive framework to monitor the cross-border movement of cash and other negotiable instruments specifically for the purposes of preventing and detecting money laundering and terrorist financing. The system is based on countries requiring travelers to either report spontaneously or disclose upon request from a competent officer their cargo of cash or other negotiable instruments above a certain threshold.

[24] See discussion below on the issue of confidentiality as an impediment to information flow.

[25] UNODC/IMF Model Legislation on Money Laundering and Financing Terrorism (December 1, 2005).

[26] On interagency cooperation in economic crime control, see Anne Puonti, *Learning to Work Together: Collaboration between Authorities in*

Economic-Crime Investigation, Dissertation, University of Helsinki, Department of Education, 2004).

VII. GOVERNANCE, DEPOSIT INSURANCE, AND MARKET DISCIPLINE

The Moral Hazard Implications of Deposit Insurance: Theory and Evidence

PATRICIA A. McCOY

Deposit insurance is a tightrope act. On the one hand, explicit deposit insurance can significantly reduce the incidence of bank runs or even stop runs altogether in countries with strong institutions and proper safeguards. On the other hand, when not done carefully, explicit deposit insurance can fuel bank crises by giving banks perverse incentives to take unnecessary risks.[1] The United States learned a painful lesson in this regard in the 1980s and early 1990s, when an overly generous deposit insurance system helped trigger the largest wave of bank failures there since the Great Depression in the 1930s.[2] As the U.S. experience suggests, any country that adopts explicit deposit insurance must grapple with the destabilizing effects of that insurance on the country's financial system.

This problem, known as "moral hazard," has taken on new significance with the rapid spread of explicit deposit insurance. Most countries are reluctant to permit banks to become insolvent without providing relief to depositors, and thus governments commonly extend depositors some sort of financial safety net. Until the early 1990s, however, this financial safety net did not include explicit deposit insurance in most countries. Instead, the vast majority of nations relied on other protections, including implicit deposit guarantees. A country signals implicit guarantees through its actions, not its words, by bailing out the depositors of failed banks and thereby sending a message that similar bailouts will be available in the future.

In the last few decades, this state of affairs began to change as countries flocked to explicit deposit insurance. In explicit insurance systems, countries formally commit in advance, usually through legislation, to guarantee some or all of the deposits in failed banks. Between 1974 and 2003, the number of countries adopting explicit deposit insurance grew more than six-fold, from 12 to 88.[3]

The proliferation of explicit deposit insurance and the attendant risk of bank crises make it more important than ever for countries considering adoption to decide whether explicit deposit insurance is appropriate and, if so, to institute full and proper safeguards against moral hazard by banks. Until recently, the question of proper safeguards was strictly a matter of theory and not of empirical fact. In recent years, however, two new datasets on deposit insurance schemes around the world—the first compiled by World Bank economists Asli Demirgüç-Kunt, Baybars Karacaovili, and Luc Laeven [4] and the second compiled by economists James R. Barth, Gerard Caprio, Jr., and Ross Levine[5]—have enriched our understanding of the effects and limitations of various facets of deposit insurance. This chapter discusses findings from research on these datasets and the implications for deposit insurance adoption and design.

The chapter opens by summarizing the growth of explicit deposit insurance systems around the world. It then surveys the rationales for deposit insurance and discusses why deposit insurance fosters moral hazard and increases the likelihood of bank crises. The final section examines how explicit deposit insurance can be designed to alleviate moral hazard.

The Prevalence of Deposit Insurance Worldwide

Today, deposit guarantees are the norm, not the exception, in banking systems around the world. When it comes to depositor protection, nations essentially have six choices:

- Enact a law expressly denying deposit insurance protection, as New Zealand has done.

- Expressly deny deposit insurance, but give priority to depositors over other claimants in failed bank insolvency proceedings. This is the approach in Australia.

- Be ambiguous about implicit coverage (which is the default position if there is no law on point).

- Signal implicit deposit guarantees through their actions by consistently bailing out failed banks and their depositors. As of 2003, 93 countries reported using this approach.

- Legislate explicit deposit guarantees with coverage limits. Eighty-eight countries had adopted this approach by 2003. Today, explicit deposit insurance is found predominantly in Europe, Central Asia, Latin America, and the Caribbean, but rarely in sub-Saharan Africa.

- Opt for explicit deposit guarantees with full coverage. This last approach occurs rarely and is usually reserved for severe systemic financial crises.[6] In 2003, only the Dominican Republic, Indonesia, Malaysia, Thailand, Turkey, and Turkmenistan had full explicit coverage.[7]

There are several reasons for the recent widespread adoption of explicit deposit insurance. Explicit guarantees have immense political appeal because they assuage citizens' concerns about the safety of their deposits and thus increase the flow of funds into banks. Financial experts from international financial institutions and elsewhere have also counseled developing countries to adopt explicit systems in recent years.[8] Finally, the European Union's adoption of explicit deposit insurance in its 1994 Directive on Deposit Insurance helped fuel the surge in explicit deposit insurance in Europe.[9]

Rationales for Deposit Insurance

As the preceding discussion suggests, explicit deposit guarantees are an increasingly common response to the problem of bank runs and contagion. Banks are uniquely prone to runs because they borrow "short" (by taking in demand deposits) and lend "long" (by making loans with longer maturities). This results in a "term mismatch" that makes the balance sheets of banks inherently unstable. If depositors descend *en masse* and insist on withdrawing more cash than the bank has in the vault, the bank will not be able to liquidate its assets fast enough to satisfy depositors' demands and a bank run can ensue. Furthermore, bank runs can cause a ripple effect and trigger full-blown contagion.

The unstable balance sheet of banks is not a quirk. Rather, it is inherent to a key economic function of banks, which is providing financial liquidity. As financial intermediaries, banks accept liquid deposits from the public and reinvest those funds in long-term, illiquid loans. In the process, banks provide borrowers with liquidity by allowing them to post their illiquid land or machinery as collateral and convert those assets into cash in the form of loan proceeds. Similarly, banks provide depositors with liquidity by giving them immediate access to their funds via demand deposits. Demand deposits, in turn, are integral to the payment system because they permit buyers to pay via bank drafts and sellers to clear those drafts quickly.[10]

When banks make loans, they assume the risk of holding illiquid assets. Under today's international capital standards, generally 80 percent or more of a bank's funds are tied up in illiquid loans and only a small fraction of a bank's deposits are on hand at any one time to satisfy withdrawals. Banks have confidence that they actually can honor depositors' demands based on the principle of *fractional reserves*, which holds (1) that depositors will normally withdraw only a small fraction of deposits on any given day and (2) that this fraction is statistically ascertainable. If the unexpected strikes, however, and withdrawals exceed cash on hand, the bank will not be able to honor all demands for withdrawal because its funds are tied up in loans that cannot be easily converted to cash. Unless the bank can tap backup sources of liquidity,[11] it will have to sell off its assets at fire-sale prices or close its doors.[12]

Absent deposit guarantees, once rumors, whether true or false, start that a bank is on the brink of failure, its depositors face a collective-action problem. In an ideal world, if depositors stood firm and all refrained from withdrawing their deposits, the bank could escape immediate liquidation and preserve the value of its asset portfolio. Rational depositors know, however, that the world is not ideal and that nothing stops other depositors from demanding withdrawal of their funds in full. Furthermore, rational depositors know that if they wait to withdraw their funds, the bank may run out of money before they reach the teller window. Thus, they will rush to the head of the line and immediately withdraw their funds in order to avoid losing their life savings. The resulting stampede will trigger a bank run, spelling the bank's demise.[13]

In other type of industries, investor exit, in the form of mass sell-offs of shares, exerts valuable market discipline. Bank runs likewise exert market discipline, at least when they are based on accurate information. However, the hair-trigger nature of bank runs makes them susceptible to false rumors, which can inadvertently topple solvent banks. When this happens, depositors are unnecessarily harmed and funds are shifted to less efficient uses.[14]

Whether the rumors behind bank runs are true or false, runs inflict severe social costs. Bank runs pose a classic prisoner's dilemma[15] that results in two types of harm to depositors, absent deposit guarantees. The first is a matter of distributive justice. Depositors at the end of the line lose their deposits altogether, while depositors at the front of the line receive their deposits in full. Second, depositors have a smaller pie to divide because the bank must liquidate assets at distress sale prices to try to satisfy the demand for withdrawals *en masse*.

In the worst case, a bank run can ripen into a panic. If a run at one bank causes depositors at other banks to fear for the safety of their own deposits, the run can spread into generalized contagion. As public trust in banks evaporates, depositors will pull their funds out of banks and hide them under the proverbial mattress, sending the banking system into severe disintermediation. As the money supply contracts, credit dries up, resulting in deflation, production cutbacks, and widespread unemployment.[16] Bank runs and panics can further paralyze the payment system by causing failed banks to default on payments in transit, thereby disrupting commerce.[17]

In the United States and numerous other countries, the advent of securitization improved the problem of term mismatch by enabling banks to liquidate their assets and thereby reduce the risk of bank runs. In recent years, increased reliance by banks on fee-generating income and access to emergency liquidity through the discount windows of central banks have also helped curb bank runs.[18] Nevertheless, bank runs and panics remain cause for concern. As recently as the 1980s in the United States, bank panics caused state deposit insurance systems to collapse in Maryland, Ohio, and Rhode Island.[19] Similarly, bank panic fears prompted the U.S. government to bail out

Continental Illinois National Bank and Trust Company in 1983 and Long Term Capital Management, a hedge fund, in 1998.[20]

Deposit insurance seeks to reverse the psychology of bank runs by assuring depositors that if their banks fail for any reason, their funds will be protected up to the limits on coverage.[21] This goal is deemed so important that numerous countries require depositors to have deposit insurance, whether or not they want it. Such widespread protection makes deposit insurance highly popular and resistant to reforms.

In the United States, federal deposit insurance has had remarkable success in stemming bank runs and losses to depositors. Even during the massive U.S. bank and thrift failures in the 1980s and early 1990s, runs were the exception, not the rule.[22] This record of success caused Milton Friedman and Anna Schwartz to proclaim in 1963: a Federal insurance of bank deposits was the most important structural change in the banking system to result from the 1933 panic and, indeed in our view, the structural change most conducive to monetary stability since state bank note issues were taxed out of existence immediately after the Civil War.[23] Unfortunately, it appears, Friedman and Schwartz spoke too soon.

The Moral Hazard Implications of Deposit Insurance

Initially, President Franklin Delano Roosevelt opposed the adoption of explicit deposit insurance in the United States in 1933 on grounds that the new program would put a premium on unsound banking in the future.[24] Fifty years later, his predictions came true when the largest banking crisis since the 1930s hit the United States. As Roosevelt warned, deposit insurance gives rise to moral hazard, something that is endemic to all insurance programs.

In the deposit insurance context, moral hazard manifests itself in two ways. First, explicit deposit insurance gives insured banks incentives to pursue added risks because they can capture any profits but shift any losses to the government. Second, explicit deposit insurance reduces incentives by depositors and shareholders to monitor their banks. As Professor William Lovett put it, "If governments and modern nations do not allow most banks to [fail], how can the leaders and managements of banking institutions be disciplined and avoid unduly risky, negligent, or adventurous lending policies (or simply poor asset-liability management)?"[25]

In a world with no deposit insurance, a bank that is considering making a risky loan knows that it will have to pay depositors more for taking on the added risk.[26] Either the bank will pay the risk premium or it will not make the loan. In a world with deposit insurance, however, insured depositors will not demand a risk premium because they know that the government will insure their deposits up to the legal limit, regardless of whether the bank makes the loan.[27] Thus, deposit insurance gives banks incentives to take added risks—either by increasing their leverage or investing in riskier assets S thereby increasing the government's exposure to losses.[28] These incentives are especially strong for undercapitalized banks.[29] Moral hazard will exist so long as the total expected profits from a bank's asset portfolio exceed the explicit costs of deposit insurance (premiums) plus its implicit costs (the costs of regulation).[30]

To appreciate the magnitude of moral hazard in the banking sphere, one must keep in mind that deposit insurance is not really insurance, but a guaranty against loss.[31] Normally, private insurance insures only against losses due to defined risks (such as death due to illness or an accident, but not due to suicide by the insured). Such exclusions give insureds an incentive to guard against preventable losses.

In contrast, explicit deposit insurance reimburses depositors for losses from bank failures of any type, regardless of the reason for failure. This refusal to employ policy exclusions rests on two premises: one, that depositors do not control the conduct of a bank and, two, that public confidence in the banking system demands an iron-clad guaranty. As a result, deposit insurance dampens depositors' incentives to monitor banks for undue risks.

Far from being a theoretical concern, moral hazard in explicit deposit insurance is significant and quite real. Worldwide, explicit deposit insurance has been shown to increase the likelihood of bank crises significantly. Combining deposit insurance with interest rate liberalization further compounds moral hazard because liberalization allows banks to charge higher interest rates and thus to lend to riskier borrowers in a quest for higher yields.[32]

Despite the serious moral hazard inherent in explicit deposit insurance and attempts to tinker with reforms, deposit insurance, once adopted, is difficult to curtail due to its enormous popularity with citizens. Furthermore, it bolsters political stability by removing the threat of widespread losses from bank runs that could topple a regime.[33] In this day of globalization, moreover, few economies are willing to jeopardize foreign confidence in their banking systems by paring back deposit insurance benefits.[34]

The United States provides an apt example of these political pressures. In 1980, Congress set the stage for the 1980s savings and loan crisis when it raised federal deposit insurance coverage from US$40,000 to US$100,000 per depositor per institution.[35] This increase was so large that federal deposit insurance coverage grew in real terms, even after adjusting for inflation, thus increasing the federal government's financial exposure. Congress raised the US$100,000 deposit insurance limit once again in 2006, when it indexed the limit for inflation and further raised the limit for many retirement accounts to US$250,000 per depositor per institution.[36] Similarly, the Federal Deposit Insurance Corporation (FDIC) has repeatedly caved in to pressures to expand deposit insurance coverage by agency fiat.[37]

Congress' 2006 amendments to the U.S. deposit insurance law increased moral hazard in other ways as well. Before that law was passed, the FDIC had one year to recapitalize the deposit insurance fund if the fund's reserve ratio fell below the target of 1.25 percent of estimated insured deposits. The 2006 legislation now permits the FDIC to lower the target reserve ratio to 1.15 percent. In addition, the new law gives the agency five years instead of the previous one to recapitalize the deposit insurance fund if the fund falls below the target reserve ratio. The new law even allows the agency to stretch out recapitalization beyond five years in extraordinary circumstances. In the opinion of the Shadow Financial Regulatory Committee, this forbearance was not good policy because the tendency of all regulatory agencies, generally abetted by Congress, is to avoid the tough decisions or defer them to a later time.[38]

In sum, the moral hazard dangers of explicit deposit insurance are ever-present and quite real. In addition, many financial innovations and deregulation serve to compound moral hazard. As banks expand into new activities that expose a deposit insurance fund to uncharted risks, the limited resources and expertise of bank regulators are further taxed. Thus, there is reason to be concerned that the risk-enhancing influence of deposit insurance could motivate some financial institutions in a deregulated environment to diversify their activities in a way that would increase the risks to which they and . . . deposit insurance agencies are exposed.[39]

Constraints on Moral Hazard

Despite the moral hazard in explicit deposit insurance, in many countries it is possible to institute deposit guarantees consistent with financial stability, though not in all. Moral hazard is why governments put elaborate banking regulation systems in place, replete with entry restrictions, activity restrictions, prophylactic rules, examinations, and sanctions.[40] Similarly, tough bank resolution policies, including prompt closure of critically undercapitalized banks and prohibitions against bailouts of failed bank shareholders, are crucial safeguards against moral hazard.[41]

These measures alone are not enough to curb moral hazard. In addition, three more things are needed to reduce the risk created by deposit insurance. First, all deposit insurance schemes need to incorporate risk-reducing features. Second, and related to the first, countries need to foster incentives to encourage large depositors, shareholders, and other creditors to monitor their banks. Finally, neither of these points matters if a country lacks the institutions to adopt and enforce these safeguards. Unless countries have strong institutional environments, explicit deposit insurance will do more harm than good to their overall financial stability.

Designing Explicit Deposit Insurance

In systems where explicit deposit insurance is appropriate—that is, in countries with strong institutional safeguards against moral hazard—strict banking regulation is not enough to constrain risk. Research has found that explicit deposit insurance removes more restraints on risk than government regulators are able to furnish.[42] Accordingly, explicit deposit insurance must specifically be designed with risk-reduction features in mind.

Fortunately, thanks to the new datasets mentioned earlier in this chapter,[43] we now have data on the effectiveness of various design features in deposit insurance schemes around the world. Many of these features are similar to features used by private insurers to control moral hazard, including coinsurance, coverage limits, and risk-based premiums.[44]

Coverage Limits

Coverage limits are a common technique used by private insurers to control risk. In explicit deposit insurance schemes, coverage limits usually take three forms. First, the limits address what types of *institutions* the deposit guarantees cover. Some systems only seek to cover the payment system and thus limit coverage to commercial banks; others also cover savings institutions.[45] Second, coverage limits address what types of *deposits* are covered. Some systems, for example, extend coverage to foreign currency deposits; other systems do not. Most systems exclude foreign deposits of domestic banks and domestic deposits of foreign banks.[46] In rare instances, some deposit insurance systems also cover interbank deposits.[47] Third, coverage limits cap the maximum amount of deposits that the government guarantees. It is rare for countries to impose *de jure* caps on the amount of deposit insurance per institution in its entirety.[48] Instead, *de jure* limits are usually expressed in terms of amounts of deposits guaranteed per depositor per bank.[49]

One way to gauge coverage limits *in toto* is to take the ratio of a country's deposit insurance coverage to its gross domestic product per capita. This ratio varies enormously from country to country. In 2002, for instance, much of Western Europe had a ratio of less than 2:1. On the high end, the ratio reached 9:1 for Peru, 10:1 for the Former Yugoslav Republic of Macedonia, and 27:1 for Nicaragua. The United States that year had a ratio of close to 3:1.[50] The U.S. level exceeded International Monetary Fund guidelines, which recommend limiting coverage to at most one or two times per capita GDP.[51]

In systems with explicit deposit insurance, the frequency of bank crises rises as the ratio of deposit insurance coverage to per capita GDP increases.[52] When the U.S. raised its policy limits on deposit insurance from US$40,000 to US$100,000 per depositor per bank in 1980, coverage shot up to approximately nine times per capita GDP. Shortly thereafter, the U.S. savings and loan crisis ensued. Today, economists estimate that the likelihood of that crisis would have dropped by 43 percent if the U.S. ratio had been the same as Switzerland's (one-half of per capita GDP, or 1:2).[53] More generally, countries with coverage exceeding four times per capita GDP are five times more likely to suffer bank crises than countries with coverage of under one time per capita GDP.[54]

The research on coverage limits strongly counsels governments to place credible coverage limits on deposit insurance guarantees in order to put large creditors of banks on notice that their deposits may not be safe. Doing so will give large creditors—including major depositors, holders of subordinated debentures, and correspondent banks—strong incentives to monitor the banks with which they do business. It is especially important not to insure interbank deposits, in order to induce monitoring by fellow banks.[55] Limiting deposit insurance coverage is even more important in developing countries, because banks in those countries tend to hold higher-risk assets on average than banks in developed countries.[56]

Coinsurance

Coinsurance is another technique for quelling moral hazard. As of 2003, 21 countries with explicit deposit insurance systems required coinsurance. In these countries, coinsurance requirements ranged from 10 to 25 percent, except in Bolivia and Russia, which required coinsurance of 50 percent.[57]

From a theoretical standpoint, it is not obvious how well coinsurance would work in the deposit insurance setting. In private insurance contracts, the person who pays the coinsurance is the one who creates the risk. Under these circumstances, coinsurance gives insureds incentives to reduce risk. In the deposit insurance context, however, banks create the risk, but depositors pay the coinsurance. Indeed, coinsurance might increase the likelihood of bank runs, by making some part of every deposit uninsured.[58] Finally, traditional coinsurance is regressive. Its brunt falls on small depositors, *i.e.*, those who are in need of the greatest protection. This may be why no low-income country requires coinsurance.[59]

For these reasons, some theorists have cast doubt on whether co-insurance would work in deposit insurance systems. Recent research, however, helps lay these doubts to rest. Studies show that explicit deposit insurance systems with no coinsurance experience more banking system instability than systems with coinsurance, other things being equal.[60] It appears, on average, that the incentives to large depositors from coinsurance to monitor bank risk outweigh any increased risk of bank runs that coinsurance might pose. Furthermore, the regressive nature of coinsurance can be resolved by insuring small deposits in full and only requiring coinsurance for larger deposits. Accordingly, serious consideration should be given to adopting coinsurance in explicit deposit insurance systems.

Risk-Adjusted Premiums

Risk-adjusted premiums are a newer technique to alleviate moral hazard. Pioneered in the United States in 1995, by 2003 twenty countries adjusted their deposit insurance premiums for risk.[61] These premiums work by forcing insured institutions to internalize the costs of the risks that they take.

Risk-adjusted premiums have their limitations. They are better suited to gauging past and current risks than future risks.[62] This means that insured institutions have incentives to engage in new risks as soon as their premiums are announced. In addition, there is usually a time lag before the government can incorporate the costs of new and unfamiliar risks.[63]

When evaluating risk-adjusted rates, it is also important to consider the yardsticks that are used for measuring risk. The most common yardsticks of bank risk—capital adequacy and examination ratings—are relatively crude.[64] In fact, capital measures do not directly measure risk at all. Instead, they measure the sufficiency of a bank's equity cushion against losses. Examination ratings measure risk more directly, but are plagued by subjectivity. Moreover, there is no satisfactory method to price the risk that an institution's activities pose to the banking system's stability overall.[65]

Finally, risk-adjusted premiums are prey to subjective judgment and political manipulation. Deposit insurance agencies have enormous discretion in setting a particular bank's premiums.[66] At best, this discretion can result in inconsistency; at worst, it can result in retaliation[67] or, conversely, persistent undercharges. The political fondness for artificially low premiums is not surprising, given the constant political pressure that legislatures and deposit insurers receive from banks to keep deposit insurance premiums low.[68]

Despite these problems, evidence suggests that risk-adjusted premiums work better than flat-rate premiums and help mitigate heedless risk-taking by banks.[69] This finding is powerful and intriguing, particularly because risk-adjusted premiums are generally set low[70] and are subject to political capture. For instance, in the United States between 1996 and 2005, risk-adjusted premiums were largely honored in the breach because most institutions paid zero premiums. That was because the U.S. Congress had prohibited the FDIC from charging premiums to well-managed and well-capitalized institutions —the vast majority of banks—so long as the reserve ratios of the two former deposit insurance funds remained above 1.25 percent.[71] In 2006, the U.S. Congress amended that law to permit the FDIC to charge premiums to all institutions. Under the new law, the premiums that the agency initially adopted for 95 percent of institutions were relatively small, on the order of 5-7 basis points.[72]

Although these premiums are modest, an analysis of U.S. risk-adjusted premiums by Luc Laeven suggests that U.S. premiums may not be seriously underpriced, at least for well-run banks.73 Apparently, even this slight degree of risk-adjusted pricing may help curb moral hazard (at least in a country such as the United States with strong rule of law and the systemic ability to diversify risk), especially when combined with the threat of much higher premiums for troubled institutions.

In certain other countries, however, there is strong evidence that risk-adjusted premiums need to be higher. Smaller countries in which banks have less opportunity to diversify risk generally need higher risk-adjusted premiums. The same is true for developing countries with weak regulation and rule of law. In these countries, risk-adjusted premiums may need to go as high as 5 percent or more of deposits. If such high premiums are unaffordable for banks, the country should not institute explicit deposit insurance.[74]

Market Discipline

In recent years, policymakers have paid increased attention to ways to exert market discipline on banks, other than bank runs. Market discipline can take many forms, including private monitoring by interested stakeholders, corporate governance, and ousters of bank managers through the market for corporate control.

Large depositors, shareholders, and other unsecured creditors all play an important role in monitoring banks. Explicit deposit insurance can and should be designed to encourage large depositors to oversee their banks.[75] Coverage limits and coinsurance help accomplish this by placing deposits over the coverage limits at risk of loss.

Nevertheless, theorists have disagreed about the wisdom of entrusting monitoring to uninsured depositors. On the one hand, uninsured depositors have incentives to insist on risk premiums. On the other hand, if large depositors with demand accounts become unsatisfied, they could exit *en masse* and trigger a bank run.[76] And even when depositors do have the expertise, will, and resources to monitor, they have a collective action problem because fellow depositors can free-ride on their oversight.[77]

In practice, monitoring by uninsured depositors works better than one might expect. In the United States, evidence shows that uninsured depositors *do* demand higher returns on their accounts. Similarly, there is evidence in the United States that uninsured depositors move their funds from troubled banks to safer institutions.[78] If uninsured depositors withdraw their deposits precipitously, a bank run of course can ensue. In the U.S. federal deposit insurance system in the past thirty years, this has only occurred once, at a wholesale bank where virtually all of the depositors were uninsured.[79]

Investors in subordinated debentures of banks are another source of market discipline. These debentures have two main features, at least in the United States: they are not secured by any specific assets of the bank and the holders take priority behind the depositors in the event the bank goes insolvent. Similar to uninsured depositors, investors in subordinated debentures of U.S. banks have been shown to demand higher returns, at least during periods of banking system distress.[80]

Bank shareholders are generally considered to be a source of moral hazard, not part of the solution, due to their interest in leveraged profits. But shareholders still have an important role to play in market discipline. Stock sales by shareholders send a signal to the market and place downward pressure on the bank's stock price. In addition, rules such as double-liability laws that make shareholders liable for a portion of depositor losses make shareholders supervise their banks more closely and bank managers more cautious about their use of depositors' funds.[81]

Management fears of job loss can dampen undue risks by banks as well. Such fears emanate from three sources. First, laws that permit hostile takeovers of banks can be used to remove deficient bank managers.[82] Second, laws authorizing government regulators to remove culpable bank managers from their posts and banning them from future work in the banking industry send a strong deterrent message to bank managers elsewhere.[83] Finally and above all, it is incumbent upon bank boards of directors to remove unsatisfactory managers from their posts.

As this last point suggests, strong corporate governance is integral to effective monitoring. Recent initiatives to install a majority of independent directors on the boards of banks are designed to boost outside scrutiny of bank managers.[84] Similarly, holding bank officers and directors liable for conflicts of interest, securities fraud, illegality, breach of the duty of care, and other types of misconduct has been found to reduce moral hazard.[85]

Strong Institutions, Rule of Law, and Transparency

The argument so far has assumed that the safeguards discussed above are feasible and enforceable. But if a country's institutions are weak, explicit deposit insurance will destabilize the country's financial system, rather than help it.

None of the safeguards described above—banking regulation, strict bank resolution techniques, design features of deposit insurance, or market discipline—will work unless they can actually be instituted and enforced. Effective banking regulation, tough resolution policies, and credible safety features in deposit insurance, for example, require more than the passage of banking laws. They also require consistent enforcement of those laws, integrity, independence from political interference, an ability to resist bribery, and government accountability to the public.

Similarly, market discipline will not succeed without financial transparency and strong rule of law. Unless depositors, bondholders, and shareholders can get current, credible, and meaningful financial information about their banks, they will not be able to discipline those banks in a timely fashion. Independent outside audits are an important component of financial transparency and so is public disclosure of bank financial statements. Transparency also facilitates credit ratings of banks by international rating agencies (although in many countries such credit ratings are still confined to the country's largest banks).

Strong rule of law is similarly crucial to private monitoring. Enforcing the liability of bank officers and directors requires a strong judiciary with the will, training, and resources to carry out the law. Similarly, without strong contract protections, investors will not have faith in bond covenants, and extended shareholder liability will be worthless. Where crime, graft, and fraud make contracts unenforceable as a practical matter, investors will flee the market altogether and uninsured depositors will trigger runs.

Recent studies have borne out the key importance of strong social institutions and respect for law. In "countries with a very good institutional environment" that is conducive to strong bank regulation, deposit insurance is less likely to "lead to additional instability."[86] In particular, laws requiring banks to have independent outside audits and to publicly disclose their financial statements have been shown to be successful at reducing moral hazard.[87]

Conversely, it is a mistake to institute explicit deposit insurance where financial "transparency, deterrency and [government] account-ability are very weak."[88] Under those conditions, adopting explicit deposit insurance will only retard a country's financial development and undermine its progress.[89]

Conclusion

This chapter tells a cautionary tale. Countries considering explicit deposit insurance should be careful of what they wish for. Unless a country has strong banking regulation, a strict failed bank resolution regime, carefully designed deposit insurance with safeguards against risk, healthy private monitoring, and, most of all, strong institutions and the rule of law, explicit deposit insurance will only be a recipe for future bank crises. Conversely, if all of these safeguards are in place, explicit deposit insurance can protect depositors while holding moral hazard in check.

Notes

[1] *See* Asli Demirgüç-Kunt and Edward J. Kane, "Deposit Insurance Around the Globe: Where Does It Work?" 16 *Journal of Economic Perspectives* 175, 176 (2002).

[2] *See, e.g.,* Edward J. Kane, *The S&L Insurance Mess: How Did it Happen?* (Washington, D.C.: Urban Institute Press, 1989).

[3] *See* Asli Demirgüç-Kunt, Baybars Karacaovili, and Luc Laeven, "Deposit Insurance Around the World: : A Comprehensive Database," World Bank Policy Research Working Paper 3628 (Washington, D.C.: World Bank, June 2005), at 3, 22 table 2, available at http://siteresources.worldbank.org/ INTRES/Resources/469232-1107449512766/DepositInsuranceDatabase Paper_DKL.pdf.

[4] The World Bank, Deposit Insurance Around the World Dataset, available at http://econ.worldbank.org/WBSITE/EXTERNAL/EXTDEC/EXTRE SEARCH/0,,contentMDK:20699211~pagePK:64214825~piPK:64214943~t heSitePK:469382,00.html.

[5] The World Bank, "Bank Regulation and Supervision," World Bank Finance and Private Sector Research Paper WPS2588, available at http://econ.worldbank.org/WBSITE/EXTERNAL/EXTDEC/EXTRESEARC H/0,,contentMDK:20345037~pagePK:64214825~piPK:64214943~theSiteP K:469382,00.html. *See also* James R. Barth, Gerard Caprio, Jr., and Ross Levine, "The Regulation and Supervision of Banks Around the World: A New Database," World Bank Policy Research Working Paper No. 2588 (Apr. 2001), available at http://www-wds.worldbank.org/external/default/ WDSContentServer/IW3P/IB/2001/06/01/000094946_01052204005474 /Rendered/PDF/multi0page.pdf.

[6] Giving blanket deposit insurance guarantees during a bank crisis is extremely expensive and does not resolve such crises more quickly. *See* Demirgüç-Kunt and Kane*, supra* note 1, at 191.

[7] *See* Demirgüç-Kunt, Karacaovili, and Laeven, *supra* note 3; *see also* Gillian G.H. Garcia, "Deposit Insurance: A Survey of Actual and Best Practices," IMF Working Paper 99/54 (April 1999), at 4, 19, also available at http://papers.ssrn.com/sol3/papers.cfm?abstract_id=880581. More recently, after the Northern Rock bank experienced a run on deposits in September 2007, Britain's central bank announced that it would guarantee all deposits at Northern Rock and any other British bank that collapsed. *See, e.g.,* Julia Werdiger, "Bank of England Offers New Infusion of Loan*s*," *New York Times* (September 19, 2007).

[8] *See* Garcia, *supra* note 7; Demirgüç-Kunt and Kane, *supra* note 1, at 176.

[9] *See* Demirgüç-Kunt and Kane, *supra* note 1, at 176.

[10] *See, e.g.*, Douglas W. Diamond and Philip H. Dybvig, "Bank Runs, Deposit Insurance, and Liquidity," 91 *Journal of Political Economy* 401, 402-03 (1983); Daniel R. Fischel, Andrew M. Rosenfield, and Robert S. Stillman, "The Regulation of Banks and Bank Holding Companies," 73 *Virginia Law Review* 301, 307 (1987); Jonathan R. Macey and Geoffrey P. Miller, "Deposit Insurance, the Implicit Regulatory Contract, and the Mismatch in the Term Structure of Banks' Assets and Liabilities," 12 *Yale Journal on Regulation* 1, 3-4, 7-8 (1995).

[11] Those sources include the market for interbank credit and resort to the discount window of the central bank as the lender of last resort. In the United States, access to the discount window traditionally has been limited and strictly administered for institutions that are financially unsound. *See* Board of Governors of the Federal Reserve, *The Federal Reserve System: Purposes & Functions,* 9th ed. (Washington, D.C. Federal Reserve Board, 2005), at 45–48; Walker F. Todd, "Central Banking in a Democracy: The Problem of The Lender of Last Resort," in Patricia A. McCoy, ed., *Financial Modernization After Gramm-Leach-Bliley* (Lexis, 2002) at 135. In the subprime mortgage crisis of 2007, however, the Federal Reserve Board urged healthy banks to borrow from that facility to remove the perceived stigma surrounding discount window loans. *See, e.g.*, Eric Dash, "Four Major Banks Tap Federal Reserve for Financing," *New York Times* (August 23, 2007).

[12] *See, e.g.,* Jonathan R. Macey and Geoffrey P. Miller, "Bank Failures, Risk Monitoring, and the Market for Bank Control," 88 *Columbia Law Review*, at 1153, 1156 (1988).

[13] *See, e.g.*, Fischel, Rosenfield, and Stillman, *supra* note 10, at 307-09.

[14] *See* Helen A. Garten, "Banking on the Market: Relying on Depositors to Control Bank Risks," 4 *Yale Journal on Regulation*, at 129, 154-55 (1986); Robert E. Litan, "Evaluating and Controlling the Risks of Financial Product Deregulation," 3 *Yale Journal on Regulation*, at 1, 35 (1985); R. Mark Williamson, "Regulatory Theory and Deposit Insurance Reform," 42 *Cleveland State Law Review* 105, 114 (1994).

[15] In a prisoner's dilemma, individuals rationally refuse to cooperate, even though cooperation would maximize everyone's benefit, because they cannot trust others to cooperate and they will suffer the worst result if they cooperate and others do not.

[16] *See* Fischel, Rosenfield, and Stillman, *supra* note 10, at 311–12; Thomas M. Hoenig, "Financial Modernization: Implications for the Safety Net," 49 *Mercer Law Review*, 787, 788 (1998).

[17] *See, e.g.*, Hoenig, *supra* note 16, at 788–89; Macey and Miller, "Deposit Insurance," *supra* note 10, at 15. Harm to the payment system from bank runs has declined as nonbank payment providers have gained market power.

[18] *See, e.g.*, Macey and Miller, "Bank Failures," *supra* note 12, at 1157B58.

[19] *See, e.g.*, Leonard Lapidus, "State and Federal Deposit Insurance Schemes," 53 *Brooklyn Law Review*, at 45 (1987).

[20] *See generally* Federal Deposit Insurance Corp., *Managing the Crisis: The FDIC and RTC Experience 1980-1994* (Washington, D.C.: Federal Deposir Insurance Corp.,1998), at 234-35, 252, 547-50 (describing depositor panic in 1982 at Penn Square Bank, N.A. and the 1984 run at Continental Illinois); Foulkes, "The Federal Deposit Insurance Corporation: The Rescue of Continental Illinois National Bank and Trust Company," *1985 Annual Survey of American Law*, at 137; The President's Working Group on Financial Markets, "Hedge Funds, Leverage, and the Lessons of Long-Term Capital Management" (April 1999), available at http://www.ustreas.gov/press/releases/reports/hedgfund.pdf; U.S. General Accounting Office, "Long-Term Capital Management: Regulators Need to Focus Greater Attention on Systemic Risk," GAO/GGD-00-3 (October 1999), available at http://www.gao.gov/archive/2000/gg00003.pdf.

[21] *See* Carter H. Golembe, "The Deposit Insurance Legislation of 1933: An Examination of Its Antecedents and Its Purposes," 75 *Political Science Quarterly* 181, 189, 192, 194 (1960).

[22] Despite federal deposit insurance, in 1983 the Continental Illinois National Bank and Trust Company, a wholesale bank in Chicago, Illinois, with mostly large, uninsured deposits, did experience a bank run. *See generally* FDIC, *supra* note 20, at 547-50; Foulkes, *supra* note 20. Otherwise, practically all of the other runs during the 1980s crisis took place at savings and loan institutions that were insured by state deposit insurance systems in Ohio, Maryland, and Rhode Island, and not by the federal government. In the aftermath, all of the state deposit insurance systems that had not already failed closed their doors and were replaced by federal deposit insurance. *See, e.g.*, Kenneth E. Scott, "Deposit Insurance—The Appropriate Roles for State and Federal Governments," 53 *Brooklyn Law Review* 27, 27–28 (1987). .

[23] Milton Friedman and Anna J. Schwartz, *A Monetary History of the United States, 1867–1960* (Princeton, NJ: Princeton University Press, 1963), at 434.

[24] Quoted in Harris Weinstein, "Moral Hazard, Deposit Insurance and Banking Regulation," 77 *Cornell Law Review* 1099, 1100 (1992). *See also* Helen A. Garten, "A Political Analysis of Bank Failure Resolution," 74 *Boston University Law Review* 429, 444–47 & n.79 (1994).

[25] William A. Lovett, "Moral Hazard, Bank Supervision and Risk-Based Capital Requirements," 49 *Ohio State Law Journal* 1365, 1365 (1989).

[26] Empirical findings bear this out. . For a review of the literature, see Demirgüç-Kunt and Kane, *supra* note 1, at 187–88.

[27] *See* Asli Demirgüç-Kunt and Harry Huizinga, "Market Discipline and Financial Safety Net Design," World Bank Policy Research Paper No. 2183 (1999), at 17–19, available at http://www.worldbank.org/html/dec/Publications/Workpapers/wps2000series/wps2183/wps2183.pdf.

[28] *See, e.g.*, Fischel, Rosenfield, and Stillman, *supra* note 10, at 314–15; Garten, *supra* note 14, at 133; Hoenig, *supra* note 16, at 789; Armen G. Hovakimian, Edward J. Kane, and Luc A. Laeven, "How Country and Safety-Net Characteristics Affect Bank Risk-Shifting," AFA 2003 Washington, D.C. Meetings (October 11, 2002), available at SSRN at http://ssrn.com/abstract=299523. Krishna G. Mantripragada, "Depositors as a Source of Market Discipline," 9 *Yale Journal on Regulation* 543, 548–49 (1992); Williamson, *supra* note 14, at 108–09.

[29] *See* Hovakimian, Kane, and Laeven, *supra* note 28, at 2.

[30] *See, e.g.,* Fischel, Rosenfield, and Stillman, *supra* note 10, at 314–15; Mantripragada, *supra* note 28, at 548–49; Williamson, *supra* note 14, at 108–09. Even in the absence of deposit guarantees, banks have a heightened propensity toward risk due to their high leverage and limited liability protection for their shareholders. Deposit insurance exacerbates this tendency toward risk. *See* Joseph E. Stiglitz, "Some Aspects of the Pure Theory of Corporate Finance: Bankruptcies and Takeovers," 3 *Bell Journal of Economics* 458 (1972).

[31] *See* Williamson, *supra* note 14, at 125 n.62.

[32] *See* Asli Demirgüç-Kunt and Enrica Detragiache, "Does Deposit Insurance Increase Banking System Stability?" IMF Working Paper 00/3 (Washington, D.C.: International Monetary Fund, January 2000) at 10–12 and table 2, available at www.imf.org/external/pubs/cat/longres/cfm?sk=3382.0

[33] *See* Macey and Miller, "Deposit Insurance," *supra* note 10, at 19–21.

[34] *See* Hoenig, *supra* note 16, at 790.

[35] *See* Depository Institutions Deregulation and Monetary Control Act of 1980, Pub. L. No. 96-221, 94 Stat. 132 (1980); Jonathan R. Macey and Geoffrey P. Miller, "Nondeposit Deposits and the Future of Bank Regulation," 91 *Michigan Law Review* 237, 241 (1992); Mantripragada, *supra* note 28, at 550.

[36] Pub. L. No. 109-171, Title II, § 2103, 120 Stat. 4 (2006) (codified at 12 U.S.C. § 1821(a)(1)(B)-(a)(1)(F), (a)(3)(A)).

[37] The main way the FDIC has expanded deposit insurance has been through its power to provide separate deposit insurance coverage for individuals who make deposits in different legal capacities, depending on the circumstances. For instance, an individual's personal accounts receive deposit insurance coverage up to the maximum limit separate from any bank accounts that he or she administers as trustee. In this manner, the FDIC can expand coverage through its rule-making authority without the need for new legislation. *See* Patricia A. McCoy, *Banking Law Manual: Federal Regulation of Financial Holding Companies, Banks and Thrifts,* 2nd ed. (Lexis, 2000 and cumulative supplements), § 11.06[2][c].

[38] Shadow Financial Regulatory Committee, "FDIC Replenishing of the Deposit Insurance Fund, 2," Statement No. 226, Feb. 13, 2006, available at http://www.aei.org/research/shadow/publications/pageID.888,project ID.15/default.asp.

[39] Litan, *supra* note 14, at 21; *see also* Hoenig, *supra* note 16, at 791 (allowing banks to directly conduct new activities expands the costs associated with safety nets).

[40] *See* Jonathan R. Macey and Elizabeth H. Garrett, "Market Discipline by Depositors: A Summary of the Theoretical and Empirical Arguments," 5 *Yale Journal on Regulation* 215, 220 (1988).

[41] *See, e.g.,* Ron Feldman and Gary Stern, "Methods for Addressing The Too-Big-To-Fail Problem: Where Does The Gramm-Leach-Bliley Act Of 199 Fit?" in *Financial Modernization After Gramm-Leach-Bliley, supra* note 11, at 31.

[42] *See* Hovakimian, Kane, and Laeven, *supra* note 28, at 13–15.

[43] *See* notes 4 and 5 *supra* and accompanying text.

[44] *See, e.g.,* Mantripragada, *supra* note 28, at 549.

[45] *See* Demirgüç-Kunt, Karacaovili, and Laeven, *supra* note 3, at 6.

[46] *See id.* at 6–7.

[47] *See* Demirgüç-Kunt and Kane, *supra* note 1, at 180.

[48] *See* Peter P. Swire, "Bank Insolvency Law Now That It Matters Again," 42 *Duke Law Journal* 469, 498–99 (1992).

[49] *Cf.* Demirgüç-Kunt, Karacaovili, and Laeven, *supra* note 3, at 7.

[50] *See id.* at 11 and figure 6.

[51] *See* Garcia, *supra* note 7, at 18.

[52] *See* Robert Cull, Lemma W. Senbet, and Marco Sorge, "Deposit Insurance and Financial Development," World Bank Policy Research Working Paper No. 2682 (March 2003), at 21 and table 2, available at http://papers.ssrn.com/sol3/papers.cfm?abstract_id=391940; Demirgüç-Kunt and Detragiache, *supra* note 32, at 13–15 and table 3.

[53] *See* Demirgüç-Kunt and Detragiache, *supra* note 32, at 13–15 & table 3 (the probability of the 1980s U.S. crisis would have fallen from 4.3 to 2.5 percent); Garcia, *supra* note 7, at 14 n.13.

[54] *See* Demirgüç-Kunt and Kane, *supra* note 1, at 184–85.

[55] *See id.* at 192.

[56] *See* Luc Laeven, "Pricing of Deposit Insurance," World Bank Policy Research Paper No. 2781 (July 2002), at 32, available at http://papers.ssrn.com/sol3/papers.cfm?abstract_id=636235.

[57] *See* Demirgüç-Kunt, Karacaovili, and Laeven, *supra* note 3, at 8.

[58] *See* Mantripragada, *supra* note 28, at 555.

[59] *See* Laeven, *supra* note 56, at 26–27.

[60] *See* Demirgüç-Kunt and Detragiache, *supra* note 32, at 13.

[61] *See* Demirgüç-Kunt, Karacaovili, and Laeven, *supra* note 3, at 9.

[62] *See* Garcia, *supra* note 7, at 12; Mantripragada, *supra* note 28, at 548–49.

[63] *See* Mantripragada, *supra* note 28, at 547.

[64] *See* Fischel, Rosenfield, and Stillman, *supra* note 10, at 316; Garcia, *supra* note 7, at 12; Sarah Jane Hughes, "Banking and Deposit Insurance: An Unfinished Agenda for the 1990s," 68 *Indiana Law Journal* 835, 851 (1993); Laeven, *supra* note 56, at 28–29; Scott, *supra* note 22, at 34.

[65] *See* Lapidus, *supra* note 19, at 46–47; Litan, *supra* note 14, at 40; *see also* William M. Isaac, "The Role of Deposit Insurance in the Emerging Financial Services Industry," 1 *Yale Journal on Regulation* 195, 207 (1984).

[66] *See* Isaac, *supra* note 65, at 207–08.

[67] *Cf. Doolin Security Savings Bank v. FDIC*, 53 F.3d 1395, 1397–98 (4th Cir. 1995) (FDIC terminated a healthy institution's deposit insurance in a dispute over the premium rating). In 2006, largely in response to the *Doolin* case, Congress barred the FDIC from imposing late fees when failure to pay is due to a dispute over the premium amount and the institution deposits security that is satisfactory to the FDIC in the event it loses the dispute. Pub. L. No. 109-171, Title II, ' 2104(c), 120 Stat. 4 (2006) (codified at 12 U.S.C. ' 1828(h)).

[68] *See* Hughes, *supra* note 64, at 851; Laeven, *supra* note 56, at 3.

[69] *See* Demirgüç-Kunt and Detragiache, *supra* note 32, at 15 n.16.

[70] *See* Laeven, *supra* note 56.

[71] Former 12 U.S.C. ' 1817(b)(2)(A)(iii), (v); *see generally* McCoy, *supra* note 37, § 11.06[4].

[72] *See* Pub. L. No. 109-171, Title II, § 2104(a), 120 Stat. 4 (2006) (amending 12 U.S.C. ' 1817(b)(2)(A)); FDIC, Assessments, Final rule, 71 *Federal Register* 69282 (November 30, 2006); Litan, *supra* note 14, at 40 ("Given typical spreads between marginal lending and borrowing rates of interest of 100 basis points or more, a maximum penalty of five basis points would provide little deterrence to the risk-seeking bank").

[73] *See* Laeven, *supra* note 56, at 50 and table 13.

[74] *See id.* at 41, 50–51.

[75] *See* Litan*, supra* note 14, at 21–22. In contrast to large depositors, small depositors lack the bargaining power, expertise, or resources to keep effective tabs on their banks.

[76] This becomes a particular concern when the failed bank resolution methods that a government employs—such as bailouts and purchase and assumption agreements giving uninsured depositors full protection—convey the impression that the government will protect uninsured depositors de facto if not de jure. With such resolution methods, a government sends the message that rational depositors do not need to monitor their banks for safety and soundness.

[77] *See* Joseph E. Stiglitz, "S&L Bailout*,"* in James R. Barth and R. Dan Brumbaugh, Jr., eds., *The Reform of Federal Deposit Insurance: Disciplining the Government and Protecting Taxpayers* (New York: Harper Business, 1992), at 1.

[78] *See* Demirgüç-Kunt and Kane, *supra* note 1, at 187–88 (reviewing empirical literature).

[79] *See* notes 20 and 22 *supra* and accompanying text.

[80] *See* Demirgüç-Kunt and Kane, *supra* note 1, at 187–88 (reviewing empirical literature).

[81] *See id.* at 192; Jonathan R. Macey and Geoffrey P. Miller, "Double Liability of Bank Shareholders: History and Implications," 27 *Wake Forest Law Review* 31 (1992).

[82] *See* Macey and Miller, "Bank Failures," *supra* note 12.

[83] For a description of removal and prohibition sanctions in the banking industry in the United States, see McCoy, *supra* note 37, at § 13.03[6].

[84] *See* Garcia, *supra* note 7, at 13.

[85] *See* Barth, Caprio, and Levine, *supra* note 5, at 22–23, 29, and table 7b. For a general description of such liability in the United States, see McCoy, *supra* note 37, at § 14.04.

[86] *See* Demirgüç-Kunt and Detragiache, *supra* note 32, at 26. *Accord* Cull, Senbet, and Sorge, *supra* note 52, at 21–22 and table 2 (concluding that only strong rule of law and supervisory independence from legal reprisal—not official supervisory power—mitigate volatility from generous deposit insurance schemes).

[87] *See* Barth, Caprio, and Levine, *supra* note 5, at 22–23, 29 and table 7b.

[88] *See* Demirgüç-Kunt and Kane, *supra* note 1, at 182; *see also* Hovakimian, Kane, and Laeven, *supra* note 28, at 24 ("countries where government corruption is high and economic and political freedom are low find it difficult to adopt and enforce appropriate restraints" on moral hazard).

[89] *See* Demirgüç-Kunt and Kane, *supra* note 1, at 190.

VIII. PAYMENTS, SETTLEMENT, AND SECURITIES INFRASTRUCTURE

The Central Bank's Role in the Payment System: Legal and Policy Aspects

CHRISTIAN A. JOHNSON AND ROBERT S. STEIGERWALD

Standing at the apex of the tiered account relationships through which interbank payments are typically settled, central banks have long played a critical role as payments intermediaries.[1] In particular, central banks have historically performed the function of "providing banks with deposits and a means of transferring them to make interbank payments,"[2] a function Jeffrey Lacker, president of the Federal Reserve Bank of Richmond, has called "the fundamental core of central banking."[3] Of course, payment systems, as the discussion in this chapter will indicate, have specific legal, technical, operational, and other institutional characteristics, which may differ from time to time (reflecting technological and other developments), from country to country (principally reflecting legal, regulatory, and policy considerations), and from system to system (reflecting the needs of payment system users and others).[4] As a result, the precise function that central banks perform in a particular payment system may vary considerably depending upon the institutional characteristics of the payment system.

Some payment systems, such as the Fedwire Funds Transfer Service in the United States, are real-time gross settlement (or RTGS) systems, in which each payment instruction is processed individually (in gross), on an instruction-by-instruction basis.[5] Each Fedwire payment is settled individually by means of a credit transfer at a Federal Reserve Bank.[6] The Canadian Large Value Transfer System (LVTS), by contrast, is a net settlement system, or more precisely, a continuous net settlement (CNS) system.[7] LVTS utilizes real-time net processing, in which net (as opposed to gross) payment obligations among system participants are settled by means of offset and/or end-of-day credit transfers at the Bank of Canada.[8] Both Fedwire and LVTS result in effective and final transfers of credit money between account holders.[9] There are, however, important institutional differences between the two systems, particularly concerning the roles of the Federal Reserve and Bank of Canada, respectively, in each system.[10] This chapter discusses only one of those differences— the operations through which legally effective settlement of interbank payment obligations takes place.

Because a payment system can be characterized as a specialized network,[11] it is possible to use concepts and terminology drawn from complex-network analysis to better understand the relationships among the many parts of the system. Using that terminology, this chapter proposes a simple descriptive typology of payment arrangements that may clarify the interaction between central banks and commercial banks in the settlement of interbank payment obligations.

The chapter starts with a brief overview of the payment system and the roles central banks have traditionally played as payment intermediaries. In particular, it discusses interbank settlement and the role of bank money as a settlement asset. The chapter shows that the concept of settlement finality, which has both legal and risk-management dimensions, is a basic attribute of payment transactions (unless those transactions are "provisional") not a unique attribute of payments made through a central bank.

The chapter then considers whether the central bank has a comparative advantage with respect to private-sector banks in its role as a payments intermediary. In particular, it highlights the inherent tension between: (1) maximizing the use of credit money emitted by the central bank (so-called central bank money) as a settlement asset; and (2) maximizing the ability of transactors to choose among alternative settlement assets (including central bank money and commercial bank monies), together with related value-added services (such as credit or custodial services). In other words, a policy preference for settlement in central bank money involves both costs and benefits.

This analysis is timely, given recent developments in payment systems, particularly in the Eurozone, where the European Central Bank (ECB) has launched the TARGET-2 Securities initiative, a proposal to extend special central bank settlement services to central securities depositories (CSDs), such as Euroclear and Clearstream.[12] Moreover, it has important implications for central bank competition with private-sector banks, especially because central banks have articulated the concept of "ultimate settlement, a conflation of the risk and legal attributes of settlement into what amounts to an implicit preference for settlement in central bank money."[13] The existence of inherent and unavoidable trade-offs in defining the proper role of the central bank in the payment system is masked, in part, because of persistent confusion regarding the various meanings of *settlement finality*. This chapter is therefore intended as a step toward a better understanding of settlement finality, as well as the importance of competitive considerations in the choice of whether to expand the central bank's role as a provider of interbank settlement assets.

A complete cost-benefit analysis of the roles central banks typically play in interbank payment systems would require careful consideration of numerous design and operational characteristics of each system, a task far beyond the scope of this chapter. Instead, the chapter is simply an introduction to one set of legal and policy considerations relating to the role of the central bank in the interbank payment system.

The Role of the Central Bank in the Payment System

Whatever else central banks may do—and the list of functions they perform is a long one—they almost always play a foundational role in the payment system.[14] Indeed, Stephen Millard and Victoria Saporta, in their background paper to the Bank of England's May 2005 conference, "The Future of Payments," observe that:

> Central banking and payment systems—systems consisting of a settlement asset, credit arrangements, infrastructure and rules over which monetary value can be transferred—are *inextricably linked*. In a number of countries, central banking institutions evolved naturally or were imposed by the state to *provide the ultimate settlement asset at the apex of the payment hierarchy*.[15]

This chapter is concerned with only a single aspect of the role central banks play in the payment system—that of providing what Millard and Saporta have called "the ultimate settlement asset at the apex of the payment hierarchy."[16] That role has two components: (1) the position the central bank occupies at the apex of a hierarchical structure of tiered accounts used to settle interbank payment obligations;[17] and (2) the provision of credit money, commonly called "central bank money," as a settlement asset for interbank transactions. Before discussing some of the costs and benefits associated with the use of central bank money as a settlement asset, it is necessary to understand these components.

In a 2001 article on the Federal Reserve's role in the payment system, Edward Green and Richard Todd note that;

> Historically, central banks have been chartered to perform two functions: One is to be an intermediary between the government and its lenders, enabling the government to obtain credit by ensuring that implicit default through inflation will occur only in genuine national emergencies. The other is to serve broad public interests as the *trustworthy and neutral apex of a hierarchy of banks that, in turn, provide the nonblank public with accounts used to settle financial, business, and personal payments by transfer of balances.*[18]

Green and Todd conclude that "[t]he *role as the apex of the banking hierarchy* puts the central bank in a unique and distinguished position in the payments business."[19]

Jeffrey Lacker offers a basis for understanding the importance of that role based upon the insight that "[i]ssuing, clearing and settling payment instruments are essentially communication and record-keeping activities."[20] In payment systems, as in other communications arrangements, Lacker argues:

> *Efficient communication arrangements often take the form of networks in which many paths connect through a central node.* A clearinghouse can be viewed as a natural club arrangement for such centralized settlement activity. A

central bank then represents a nationalized central settlement node for interbank payments. Contemporary legal restrictions more or less compel most banks to settle through the central bank."[21]

While there is much here that deserves close attention, the focus of this chapter is on Lacker's explanation for the development of the hierarchical structure characteristic of most account-based payment systems and the position the central bank (or a private-sector clearinghouse) typically occupies at the apex of that structure. It is noteworthy that this explanation does not depend upon the existence of a public-sector institution such as a central bank. Indeed, Lacker explicitly equates the structural role played by central banks with private-sector clearinghouse arrangements.[22]

Lacker's explanation for the position central banks occupy at the apex of the payment system appears to be consistent with the historical development of central banks, as described by Millard and Saporta:

> Historically, the evolution of central banking can be traced back to the market's natural demand for an efficient way to make payments. This natural demand can lead to the development of a *hierarchy or pyramid in payments with the liabilities of a proto central bank at its apex, as the "settlement asset" of choice.* In other words, central banks can emerge naturally from their payments role.[23]

This description connects the two components of the central bank's role as the provider of "the ultimate settlement asset at the apex of the payment hierarchy." Lacker's network analysis explains why the payment system is configured as a hierarchical structure, with a payments facilitator (either public or private) at the apex. Millard and Saporta connect that structural position to the role played by a settlement institution as the provider of a settlement asset. That role can, as they note, be performed either by a private-sector bank or a central bank.

In their role as payment intermediaries, central banks typically function as hubs, with spoke-like connections (account relationships) to all of the nodes (private-sector banks that have accounts at the central bank) in the system, forming a network (the interbank payment system) that is sometimes described as a star.[24] The Fedwire Funds Transfer Service is an example of a payment system in which the central bank functions as a network hub. Certain private-sector payment networks, such as the Clearinghouse Interbank Payment System (CHIPS) for U.S. dollar payments[25] and the Continuous Linked Settlement (CLS)[26] system for foreign currency settlements, exhibit a similar hub and spoke structure—though with important institutional differences not relevant to this discussion. On the other hand, banks have historically maintained so-called correspondent relationships to transfer money on a bilateral basis that do not exhibit a hub-and-spoke structure. Although correspondent banking arrangements are probably less important today than the network alternatives, at least for purposes of interbank funds transfers, they nevertheless represent an important alternative to hub and spoke arrangements.

Based upon this description, a simple typology of institutional arrangements for the settlement of interbank payment obligations in credit money emerges. Such settlements may be conducted through (1) central bank-centered networks, such as Fedwire, where a central bank serves as the network hub and provides the underlying settlement asset;[27] or (2) private-sector networks,[28] such as CHIPS[29] and CLS,[30] where the network hub, if there is one, is provided by a private sector institution (either a bank or a bank service provider) and the settlement asset, if there is one, is provided either by a commercial bank (as in the CLS system) or central bank (as in CHIPS); or (3) through direct bank-to-bank correspondent arrangements, in which there is no network hub and the settlement assets are provided by the commercial banks that participate in the arrangement.[31]

Based upon this simple typology, we can draw three important conclusions:

• Payment obligations can be discharged without the use of a settlement asset (as in net settlement systems, such as CHIPS and LVTS);[32]

- Both central banks and commercial banks take deposits and create credit money (central bank money and commercial bank money, respectively)[33] that can be used as an interbank settlement asset (as in RTGS systems, such as Fedwire, and private-sector systems, such as CLS, as well as in bilateral correspondent relationships); and
- The structure of the network through which interbank payments are conducted may have important implications for the choice of settlement asset.

In short, users of the payment system, have a choice to transmit payments through (1) a system in which the central bank functions as a hub (and settlement is in central bank funds) or (2) through some other mechanism. The next section of this chapter expands the explanation of the choice of settlement asset and clarifies one of the key attributes of a payment in any form of money, from cash to checks to credit money—namely, the finality of payment.

Assets for the Settlement of Interbank Payments

Payment obligations can be settled in a variety of ways. Each has its own unique characteristics, benefits, and disadvantages. The *Red Book*, published by the Committee on Payment and Settlement Systems (CPSS), summarizes these alternatives as follows:

> [A] variety of payment instruments and settlement mechanisms are available to discharge payment obligations between and among financial institutions and their customers. These payment instruments vary considerably in their characteristics, such as cost, technology, convenience, funds availability and finality, as well as in orientation towards consumer, commercial and interbank transactions."[34]

A settlement asset is generally defined as "an asset used for the discharge of settlement obligations as specified by the rules, regulations or customary practice for a payment system."[35]

The two major settlement assets are cash (i.e., specie and paper currency) or credit money. Cash is the oldest and probably best understood settlement asset. For thousands of years, specie in the form of gold, silver, and other precious metals, and paper currency, were used to meet payment obligations. Settling obligations through cash is particularly useful for small purchases and for payment obligations that are done in routine face-to-face transactions. In modern society, however, cash is logistically difficult to use for large transactions. Both the storage and delivery of large amounts of cash presents difficulty. For example, it would require the delivery of 200,000 US$100 bills to meet a US$20 million obligation in cash.

Credit money represents a claim on an intermediary and is considered to be just as important a settlement asset as cash:

> In the commercial world, large transactors consider bank credit to be the functional equivalent of money. In fact, bank credit may be even better than money when one considers the feasibility of closing a US$200 million acquisition with federal reserve notes."[36]

Credit money is typically divided into commercial bank funds or central bank funds.

Commercial bank funds result from deposits made in commercial banks. The depositor then receives in return a new settlement asset such as a demand deposit account that can be used as a settlement asset. Through the use of checks and wire transfers, individuals can settle payment obligations easily and efficiently.

Just as depositors deposit funds in commercial banks and receive in exchange a settlement asset, large financial institutions can also deposit funds in central banks and receive a settlement asset in the form of central bank funds. A financial institution can then direct a central bank to move these central bank funds from its own account into the account of another financial institution to settle its payment obligations, either to that financial institution or to a customer of that institution.

Participants often consider central bank funds as being risk-free because central banks are often thought to be "more creditworthy institutions than commercial banks in their own currency" and because they have "explicit state support."[37] Central bank funds are also considered to be more liquid because of a central bank's "ability to inject very large amounts of liquidity, where appropriate, in order to facilitate the smooth operation of large-value payment systems."[38]

Figure 1 is a diagram of an interbank payment system that results in the creation of credit money.

Figure 1
Interbank Payment System

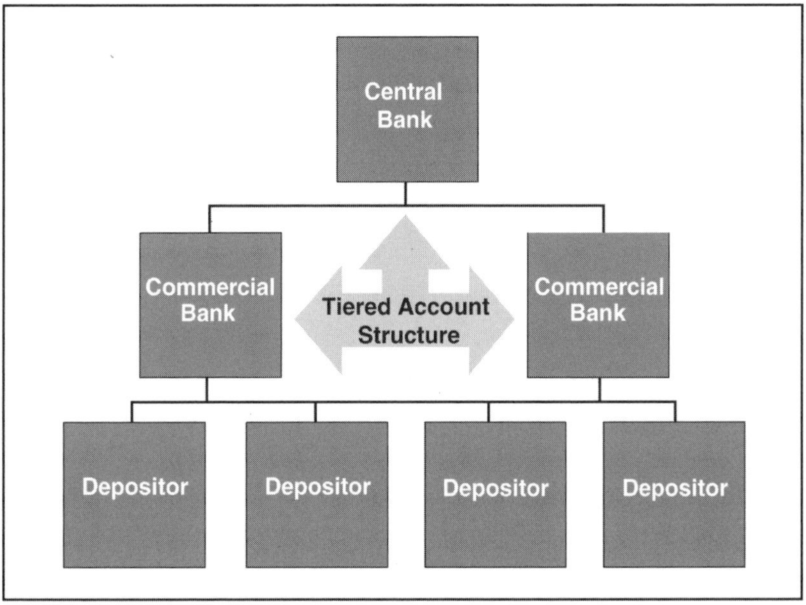

Finality

One of the principal claims for the advantage of payment and settlement in central bank funds over other settlement assets is that of finality. While the satisfaction of payment obligations through the use of central banks does enjoy a special status in some jurisdictions that is often referred to as "ultimate settlement," the advantages of finality are typically a function of the legal rules governing finality as opposed to the type of settlement asset selected.

Finality can perhaps be best understood through the use of a simple example using cash as the settlement asset. For example, when an individual purchases a newspaper using cash, finality exists, as explained by Ronald Mann: "[I]f a consumer pays with cash, the 'payment' is final at that moment, in the sense that the consumer cannot recover the cash."[39]

What is typically meant by finality is that the recipient of the settlement asset has immediate use of the funds and does not have to wait for conditional payments to become final, and it reduces buffer stock (i.e., cushion) of money for liquidity. The Committee on Payment and Settlement Systems states that "[finality] is achieved when settlement of an obligation is irrevocable and unconditional."[40]

Just because the transaction has finality, however, does not mean that an individual does not retain some possible claims. In Mann's newspaper example, he explains the newspaper's position as follows:

> Of course, the consumer might obtain a separate right to payment from the merchant by establishing some separate claim under the contract in question. That is quite a different thing from a right to retract the payment itself."[41]

The payment was final between the purchaser and the newspaper vender when the purchaser turned over the cash, meaning that the vender had immediate use of the funds and the purchaser could not stop payment or claw the payment back. However, if the newspaper was yesterday's news or otherwise deficient, the purchaser may have some claim for breach of contract against the vender, regardless of how "final" payment was.

Finality is important because it minimizes systemic risk. It avoids payments from being unwound (i.e., disallowed after reliance). It also avoids the cascading effect of unwound payments. Finally, as payment systems become more interrelated and larger, it helps minimize systemic risk and maximize legal certainty.

Finality also increases legal certainty in payment systems. It increases confidence of participants in using payment systems, and increases legal certainty regarding the treatment of payments in litigation. It can result in increased payment system volumes, providing greater liquidity. It also provides a sound foundation for systemically important payment transactions. Finally, it minimizes migration to other payment systems.

The importance of finality of payment can also be understood when it is compared with provisional settlement. The defining characteristic of a provisional or conditional payment is the ability of the transferor to stop or claw back a payment made. Finality of payment is delayed, for example, when a paper check is written on a U.S. bank. Under U.S. law, the payor may stop payment on a payer check until the presentment of the check at his bank.[42] This effectively places the recipient of the check at risk until the check has cleared the payor's bank

Provisional or conditional payment also existed in several deferred net settlement payment systems. Although these systems are now obsolete, they are illustrative of provisional settlement. For example, both CHIPS and the Canadian International Interbank Payment System (now superseded by LVTS) provided for varying periods of finality (either at the end of the day or the next business day). In contrast, in current payment systems, finality typically is achieved in real time as each payment is cleared and settled.

The legal basis for finality is not a function of whether payments are settled in cash, through commercial bank funds, or through central bank funds. Instead, it is a function of the legal rules that affect that system. The CPSS notes that "finality within an interbank payment system is generally determined by the system's rules and the legal framework within which the rules function."[43] Thus there are alternative bases for finality:

- A *contractual* basis, in which the parties to a banking relationship (namely, a bank and its customer) or the participants in a payment system may agree that payments will be considered final under the circumstances defined by the contract between or among them; and

- A *statutory or common law* basis, in which applicable law governs the finality of payments where an effective agreement does not exist among the relevant parties.

For example, finality for check and fund transfers is governed in the United States by each state's uniform commercial code, a statute that governs the majority of commercial transactions. Finality for Fedwire is determined by the new York's Uniform Commercial Code (UCC)[44] and Regulation J[45] promulgated by the Federal Reserve. Finality for CHIPS is a function of both contract law and applicable statutory law.[46] For TARGET (the real time gross settlement system for euro-denominated payments), finality is governed by the Settlement Finality Directive[47] promulgated by the European Union. National legislation also governs finality in various Eurozone countries. Finally, finality in Canada's payment system is governed by the Canadian Payments Act.[48]

If a particular form of settlement asset enjoys greater finality than a different settlement asset, such advantage is not the result of whether it is central bank funds or commercial bank funds. Instead, such a result typically stems from special statutory or regulatory rules put in place by policy makers. The Committee on Payment and Settlement notes that "[i]n general, the law does not distinguish between assets in this respect: settlement finality is no easier or harder to achieve in central bank money than in any other asset."[49]

Finality Through Interbank Payment Systems

This section discusses achieving finality through interbank systems and compares the costs and benefits of clearing and settling through central bank funds versus commercial bank funds. The costs and benefits of each should be weighed carefully before selecting one settlement asset over the other. Although central bank funds may enjoy some benefit with respect to finality over commercial bank funds, such benefits may be outweighed by other costs incurred in using central bank funds.

Payment System Characteristics and Finality

Finality is achieved in an interbank system by settling through a central bank in central bank funds, through a commercial bank in commercial bank funds, or through a combination of the two types of settlement assets. There are many different large-value payment systems currently in use throughout the world. The most common ones are Fedwire, CHIPS, LTVS (Canada), TARGET (Eurozone),[50] and CLS. The payment systems can be according to several characteristics:

- Ownership or operation: public or private;
- Operational considerations: gross, net, or hybrid;
- Settlement through central bank money or commercial bank money;
- Finality (the one constant): all systems provide for legal finality.

Table 1 summarizes these characteristics and selected large-value payment systems.

Table 1. Summary of Payment Systems

CHARACTER– ISTICS / SELECTED LARGE-VALUE SYSTEMS	Ownership/ Operation / Operational and Data Processing Environment	Form of Settlement Asset	Intraday Finality (or Provisionality) of Settlement
United States Fedwire Funds Transfer System	Federal Reserve Banks Real-Time Gross Settlement (RTGS)	Central bank money	Final settlement
Clearinghouse Interbank Payment System (CHIPS)	CHIPCo. (New York Clearinghouse Association) Continuous (Real-Time) Net	1. Netting: N/A	Final settlement

CHARACTER–ISTICS / SELECTED LARGE-VALUE SYSTEMS	Ownership/ Operation / Operational and Data Processing Environment	Form of Settlement Asset	Intraday Finality (or Provisionality) of Settlement
	Settlement (Hybrid)	2. Residual settlement in central bank money	
Canada Large-Value Transfer System (LVTS)	Canadian Payments Association Continuous (Real-Time) Net Settlement (Hybrid)	1. Netting: N/A 2. Residual settlement in central bank money	Final settlement
Eurozone TARGET	European Central Bank/ESCBs Real-Time Gross Settlement (RTGS)	Central bank money	Final settlement
Other CLS (Continuous Linked Settlement)	CLS Shareholders (Major International Banks, etc.) 1 Real-Time Gross Settlement (RTGS) 2 Designated Net Settlement (DNS)	1.Commercial bank money 2. Central bank money	Final settlement Final settlement
Derivatives Settlement Arrangements (U.S.)	N/A 1. Book Transfer 2. Interbank Wire	1.Commercial bank money 2. Central bank money 3. Other	Final settlement* Final settlement Final settlement

CHARACTER-ISTICS / SELECTED LARGE-VALUE SYSTEMS	Ownership/ Operation	Form of Settlement Asset	Intraday Finality (or Provisionality) of Settlement
	Operational and Data Processing Environment		
	Transfer (via Fedwire and/or CHIPS)	assets (e.g., IEF)	
SUMMARY	Various Forms of Ownership/ Operation; various Operational and Data Processing Environments	Central bank or commercial bank money; netting; other assets	Final settlement

*Settlement is final as of the time the relevant settlement banks undertake an irrevocable contractual commitment to make payment.

Many of these payment systems still benefit from finality, even though the settlement asset is commercial bank funds.

Finality and Commercial Bank Money

Finality occurs through the use of commercial bank money in numerous payment systems. These payments enjoy the same kind of finality as do central bank funds, except in the case of legal rules that provide ultimate settlement, as discussed below.

The most common clearing and settlement using commercial bank funds is through commercial bank book-entry transfers such as "on us" transfers or correspondent banking. CLS clears huge volumes of foreign currency trades through its account system.[51] Millions of dollars of derivatives payments are cleared each day through clearinghouses for exchange-traded derivatives such as futures and options and through over-the-counter derivatives (done typically through commercial bank book-entry transactions).[52] Internalized payment, custodial, and related transactions, such as tri-party repo transactions, also involve large sums and may benefit from the ability of commercial banks to internally coordinate all relevant aspects of the transaction.

The Advantages of Central Bank Funds: Ultimate Settlement

The case for using central banks funds is often justified based on what is referred as "ultimate settlement" enjoyed by central bank funds in certain payment systems. The CPSS states that "[t]he term 'ultimate settlement'… combines the concept of settlement being final with the concept of the settlement asset being the least risky possible."[53]

Jurisdictions have sometimes provided ultimate settlement to central bank funds through special legal rules. In some jurisdictions, payments made in central bank funds are not subject to preference payment or clawback rules, providing additional assurances that a payment cannot be unwound after the payment is completed.

It is important to understand, however, that similar finality could just as easily be given to commercial bank funds by a legislature. This has been done in the United States with respect to protecting transactions entered into through a bilateral netting contract.[54] A bankruptcy or insolvency system could also be reformed to eliminate preference payments and clawbacks for payments made in commercial bank funds. Some of this has already been done with respect to essentially eliminating the application of preference payment to swap payments under the U.S. Bankruptcy Code.[55]

Weighing the Costs of Central Bank Funds

Although ultimate settlement through central bank funds has certain advantages, there are costs associated with the external processing of payments through central accounts. These costs often are not highlighted. For example, it may be more efficient or less costly to clear certain types of transactions using commercial bank versus central bank funds. Unless one factors in these other costs, one cannot measure the true benefits of expanding the role of central banks.

Conclusion: The Role of the Central Bank

There are many considerations that should be taken into account before expanding the role of central bank funds in settlement and clearing of payment obligations. For example, using central bank funds requires a high degree of centralization. All payments would need to be cleared through a central authority, risking operational resiliency in the event there was a failure at the central bank level.

Using central bank money would also greatly expand the role of the central bank in a jurisdiction's payment system and economy. This could result in the disintermediation of private-sector banks and the weakening of the commercial banking sector of that jurisdiction.

Using central bank funds also introduces moral hazard issues. There is some concern that having access to central bank money may in turn provide "semi-automatic access to emergency liquidity from the central bank."[56]

Finally, and perhaps most importantly, ultimate settlement may not be important for many participants in the market. For all but the very largest or most systemically important transactions, participants may value the convenience, flexibility, speed, and industry knowledge that commercial banks can provide over the somewhat theoretical benefits provided by ultimate settlement using central bank funds.

There clearly is a case to be made for using central bank funds in settling systemically important payments. For other payment transactions, however, the costs of settlement at the central bank may not be offset by the benefits of ultimate settlement.

Notes

Note: The views expressed herein are solely those of the authors and not necessarily those of the Federal Reserve Bank of Chicago or the Board of Governors of the Federal Reserve System.

[1] *See, e.g.*, S. Millard and V. Saporta, "Central banks and payment systems: Past, present and future," Background Paper, Bank of England Conference, "The Future of Payments," London, May 2005, at 2; *see also,* E. Green and R. Todd, "Thoughts on the Fed's Role in the Payments System," *Federal Reserve Bank of Minneapolis Quarterly Review*, Vol. 25, No. 1 (April 2001), Appendix B at 26; J. McAndrews and W. Roberds, "Payment Intermediation and the Origins of Banking," Federal Reserve Bank of New York, Staff Report No. 85 (September 1999)(examining the important role banks have historically played as payments intermediaries).

[2] J. Lacker, "Central Bank Credit in the Theory of Money and Payments," Remarks at the Economics of Payments II Conference, Federal Reserve Bank of New York, New York, March 29, 2006, at 2–3; *see also,* S. Quinn and W. Roberds, "The Big Problem of Large Bills: The Bank of Amsterdam and the Origins of Central Banking," Federal Reserve Bank of Atlanta, Working Paper No. 2005-16 (August 2005).

[3] See J. Lacker , *supra* note 2.

[4] The Committee on Payment and Settlement Systems of the central banks of the Group of Ten countries (CPSS) defines *payment system* as: "a set of instruments, banking procedures and, typically, interbank funds transfer systems that ensure the circulation of money." CPSS, *Red Book on Payment and Settlement Systems in Selected Countries* (Basel: Bank for International Settlements, 2003); *see also* CPSS, *Core Principles for Systemically Important Payment Systems* (Basel: Bank for International Settlements, January 2001)(technical infrastructure is one of the key elements of a typical payment system).

[5] For a glossary of key terms relating to payment system design and operation, see CPSS, *A Glossary of Terms Used in Payments and Settlement Systems* (Basel: Bank for International Settlements, March 2003). For references to other materials relating to payment, clearing, and settlement systems, see C. Johnson and R. Steigerwald, "The Financial Services

Lawyer's Bookshelf: A Selected Bibliography Of Payment, Clearing And Settlement Resources," *The Journal of Payment System Law* Vol. 2, No. 6 (October 2006).

[6] The CPSS *Red Book* for the United States explains:

> The Fedwire funds transfer system, owned and operated by the Federal Reserve Banks, is a real-time gross settlement system that enables participants to send and receive final payments in central bank money between each other and on behalf of customers. Fedwire processes and settles payment orders individually throughout the operating day. Payment to the receiving participant over Fedwire is final and irrevocable when the amount of the payment order is credited to the receiving participant's account or when notice is sent to the receiving participant, whichever is earlier.

CPSS, *Red Book* (U.S.), *supra* note 4, at 443.

[7] According to the CPSS *Red Book* for Canada:

> LVTS is a real-time net settlement system that provides intraday finality for recipients. Each payment instruction is subject to real-time risk control tests. If the tests are passed, funds are made available to the recipient on an unconditional and irrevocable basis intraday. Each participant's position is calculated in real time on a payment by payment basis.

CPSS, *Red Book* (Canada), *supra* note 4, at 37 and 44.

[8] The *Red Book* states that LVTS uses "claims on the Bank of Canada to settle net payment obligations among those participants that participate directly in these systems." *Id.* at 44. This statement refers to the net imbalances among participants' multilateral positions at the end of the LVTS processing day:

> At the end of the daily cycle, the participant's ... positions are merged and the final multilateral net positions are settled across settlement accounts at the Bank of Canada.

Id. at 55. Continuous netting with intraday finality of payment, on the other hand, implies the settlement of payments without the use of any settlement asset. *See* CPSS, *Core Principles*, *supra* note 4, at 34 (payment "obligations ...are not always settled by the transfer of a settlement asset; in some cases, an offsetting process can discharge obligations."). Therefore it appears that settlement in LVTS takes place through a combination of netting without a settlement asset and settlement in central bank money for those payment instructions that are not discharged by offset. In that respect, the LVTS system is like the Clearinghouse Interbank Payment System (CHIPS) for U.S. dollar payments. CHIPS is discussed later in the chapter. *See* text accompanying note 25 *infra.*

[9] This chapter uses the term *money* to refer only to credit money, which arises from a deposit relationship between an account holder and a bank (either a central bank or a commercial bank). Coins and currency are excluded from consideration because they are not commonly used in the settlement of large-value payment obligations. *See, e.g.,* American Bar Association, Task Force on Stored-Value Cards, "A Commercial Lawyer's Take on the Electronic Purse," *Business Lawyer,* Vol. 52 (February 1997), at 653 (hereinafter the "Electronic Purse Report"). This usage is inconsistent with the definition of money contained in the Uniform Commercial Code (U.C.C.), the body of commercial law that is generally applicable to payments in the United States. *See, e.g.,* J. Sommer, "A Law of Financial Accounts, Modern Payment and Securities Transfer Law," *The Business Lawyer,* Vol. 53, No. 2 (1998), at 1181, 1193, note 61.

[10] For example, the Federal Reserve Banks own and operate Fedwire. CPSS, *Red Book* (U.S.), supra note 4, at 443. The Bank of Canada, by contrast, "does not own or operate any payment or other clearing and settlement systems." CPSS, *Red Book* (Canada), supra note 4, at 44. More importantly, as noted above, Fedwire is not a netting system. Settlement in Fedwire takes place by means of a credit transfer at a Federal Reserve Bank, not by offset or by a combination of offset and credit transfers, as in LVTS.

[11] *See, e.g.,* Lacker, *supra* note 2, at 2 (central bank payment system characterized as a communications "network in which many paths connect through a central node."); *see also,* K. Soramäki et al., "The Typology of Interbank Payment Flows," Federal Reserve Bank of New York, Staff Report No. 243 (March 2003) at 1 ("the payment system can be treated as a specific example of a complex network.").

¹² TARGET-2 is the real-time gross settlement system for euro-denominated payments. The European Central Bank (ECB) has summarized the motivation for the TARGET-2 Securities initiative as follows:

> Conscious of the need for further integration in market infrastructures, and extracting the benefits from the implementation of the TARGET2 payment system, the Eurosystem is evaluating opportunities to provide efficient settlement services for securities transactions in central bank money, leading to the processing of both securities and cash settlements on a single platform through common procedures.

European Central Bank, Press Release, "The Eurosystem is evaluating opportunities to provide settlement services for securities transactions" (July 7, 2006); *see also* European Central Bank web site at www.ecb.int/paym/t2s/html/index.en.html

¹³ *See, e.g.,* CPSS, *The Role of Central Bank Money in Payment Systems* (Basel: Bank for International Settlements, August 2003) at 14. According to the CPSS:

> The term "ultimate settlement" is sometimes used to denote final settlement in central bank money [reference deleted]. As such, the term combines two distinct concepts—finality and the nature of the settlement asset used to achieve finality in payment systems.

Id. at 14, box 2.

¹⁴ Millard and Saporta, *supra* note 1, at 2. There has, of course, been considerable variation in the functions central banks have performed over the nearly 350-year history of the central bank. This has lead some commentators to conclude that "we recognize [a central bank] when we see it." F. Capie et al., eds., *The Future of Central Banking, The Tercentenary Symposium of the Bank of England* (Cambridge: Cambridge University Press, 1994), at 5. *See also* Green and Todd, *supra* note 1 (listing common functions of a central bank).

¹⁵ Millard and Saporta, *supra* note 1, at 2 (emphasis added).

[16] *Id.; see also* J. Lacker, "Payment Economics and the Role of Central Banks," Remarks at Bank of England Conference, "The Future of Payments" (London, May 2005) at 2.

[17] Green and Todd, *supra* note 1, at 5 (central banks function "as the trustworthy and neutral apex of a hierarchy of banks that, in turn, provide the nonbank public with accounts used to settle financial, business and personal payments by transfer of balances."); *see also* H. Blommestein and B. Summers, "Banking and the Payment System," in B. Summers, ed., *The Payment System: Design, Management and Supervision* (Washington, D.C.: International Monetary Fund, 1994), at 27 (describing the payment system as an "inverted pyramid"):

> At the top of the inverted pyramid is the broad base of economic actors whose daily activity in the market economy gives rise to payment obligations. This base consists of individuals who use retail payment services provided by banks, and a variety of business enterprises.... The next level includes very specialized firms, such as brokers and dealers, ... which also rely on bank payment services.

[18] Green and Todd, *supra* note 1, at 5 (emphasis added).

[19] *Id.* (emphasis added).

[20] J. Lacker, *supra* note 2, at 2. Lacker notes that "[t]he economic function of a payment instrument is to communicate [information about past transactions] reliably." And, he points out:

> The central role of communications technologies in payment arrangements points . . . to the importance of economies of scale, common costs and joint production. These conditions can give rise to *'network effects' in which much of the benefits and costs are shared among multiple participants.*

Id. (emphasis added).

[21] *Id.* ("central banks have more or less nationalized the clearinghouses at the 'apex' of the payment system.")

[22] Lacker notes that there is a range of views regarding whether the transition to central banking from earlier networks of private-sector institutions (i.e., clearinghouses) enhanced efficiency. *Id.*

[23] Millard and Saporta, *supra* note 1, at 2. (Emphasis added)

[24] *See, e.g.,* K. Soramäki et al., "The Typology of Interbank Payment Flows," Federal Reserve Bank of New York, Staff Report No. 243 (March 2003). As Soramäki and his co-authors point out, " the payment system can be treated as a specific example of a complex network." *Id.* at 1.

[25] *See, e.g.,* CPSS, *Red Book* (U.S.), *supra* note 4, at 444; Further information about CHIPS is available online at the CHIPS web site at: http://www.chips.org/home.php.

[26] *See, e.g.,* CPSS, *Red Book* (International Payment Arrangements), supra note 4, at 462 et seq.; G. Galati, "Settlement Risk in Foreign Exchange Markets and CLS Bank," *BIS Quarterly Review* (December 2002); information available online at CLS Group web site at www.cls-group.com.

[27] For the reasons explained above (*see supra* note 8), the Canadian LVTS probably should be considered a private-sector network because settlements conducted through LVTS on the basis of offset do not involve the use of a settlement asset. To be sure, LVTS is supported by the Bank of Canada in a variety of ways, not least of which involves the use of central bank money for purposes of the end-of-day settlement of payment instructions that are not discharged by offset within LVTS. However, LVTS does not differ from CHIPS in that respect.

[28] Soramäki et al., *supra* note. 23, at 1 (referring to private sector payment systems as "ancillary networks").

[29] CHIPS is a private-sector network in which payment instructions are offset on a continuous net basis, with intraday finality of settlement:

> Since January 2001, CHIPS has been a real-time final settlement system that continuously matches, nets and settles payment orders. On a daily basis, the new system provides real-time finality for all payment orders released by CHIPS from the CHIPS queue. To achieve real-time finality, payment orders are settled on the books of CHIPS

against positive positions, simultaneously offset by incoming payment orders, or both.

CHIPS is not a bank, does not take deposits, and does not create a settlement asset in the form of credit money. Settlement in CHIPS takes place, as it does in the Canadian LVTS, through a combination of netting without a settlement asset and settlement in central bank money for those payment instructions that are not discharged by offset. *See supra,* note 7.

[30] CLS Bank International (CLS Bank) is an Edge corporation formed under U.S. law that functions as a bank, with the power to take deposits and create credit money. Settlement of foreign currency transactions through CLS takes place on the books of CLS Bank in commercial bank money—a fact that is often misunderstood because the CLS funding process involves transfers of central bank money through the national payment system for each currency cleared by CLS (although, as noted, Canadian dollar settlements through LVTS remain anomalous from this point of view, though not from a risk management perspective). The 2003 CPSS report *Role of Central Bank Money* clarifies this point:

> CLS Bank, a private utility which meets the international norms for risk management laid out by the G10 Governors, is the settlement institution for CLS—i.e. settlement is not in central bank money. However, all payments to and from CLS are made through the issuing central bank, so central bank money retains a necessary role, pivotal but not central, in the settlement of foreign exchange transactions in CLS.

CPSS, *The Role of Central Bank Money in Payment Systems, supra* note 13 at 3.

[31] The CPSS *Glossary of Terms* defines *correspondent banking* as "an arrangement under which one bank ([the] correspondent) holds deposits owned by other banks ([the] respondents) and provides payment ... services to those respondent banks." CPSS, *Glossary of Terms, supra* note 5.

[32] The legal meaning of *discharge* is defined later in this chapter for purposes of interbank payment obligations. *See* text accompanying note 33.

[33] Consistent with the terminology employed in the CPSS report *Role of Central Bank Money*, this chapter refers to *central bank* and *commercial bank monies,* respectively. CPSS, *The Role of Central Bank Money in Payment Systems, supra* note 13 at 13.

[34] CPSS, *Red Book, supra* note 4, at 439.

[35] CPSS, *A Glossary of Terms*, *supra* note 5. *Discharge* is defined as: "release from a legal obligation imposed by contract or law."

[36] ABA, Electronic Purse Report, *supra* note 9, at 668.

[37] CPSS, *The Role of Central Bank Money in Payment Systems, supra* note 13, at 13.

[38] *Id.* at 14.

[39] Ronald J. Mann, "Making Sense of Payments Policy in the Information Age," *Georgetown Law Journal*, Vol. 93 (2005), at 633, available at SSRN at http://ssrn.com/abstract=507822

[40] CPSS, *The Role of Central Bank Money in Payment Systems, supra,* note 12, at 14.

[41] Mann, *supra* note 38, at 643.

[42] New York Uniform Commercial Code § 4-403(1); *see also* 9 N.Y. Jur. 2d Banks § 382 (discussion of stop payment rights). We refer here to New York law, which governs many of the most important payments transactions in the United States. The Uniform Commercial Code (U.C.C.) is drafted by the National Conference of Commissioners on Uniform State Laws. The work of the conference is intended to promote the consistency of commercial law from state to state and, thereby, to promote legal certainty within a federal system of law. *See,* http://www.nccusl.org/Update/

[43] CPSS, *The Role of Central Bank Money in Payment Systems*, *supra* note 13, at 14.

[44] New York Uniform Commercial Code, Article 4A.

[45] 12 C.F.R. Part 210.

[46] *See* CHIPS Rules and Administrative Procedures (Sept. 2006), Rule 3.

[47] Settlement Finality Directive 98/26/EC (EU 25). For a discussion of the directive, *see* Commission of the European Communities, "Report from the Commission-Evaluation Report on the Settlement Finality Directive" 98/26/EC (EU 25), 27 March 2006, available online at:http://ec.europa.eu /internal_market/financial-markets/docs/settlement/evaluation_report_en.pdf (Feb. 28, 2007).

[48] Canadian Payments Act (R.S., 1985, c. C-21), available online at http://laws.justice.gc.ca/en/showtdm/cs/C-21.

[49] CPSS, *The Role of Central Bank Money in Payment Systems*, *supra* note 13, at 14.

[50] For a discussion of TARGET, *see* CPSS, *Red Book* (Euro Area), *supra* note 4

[51] On January 16, 2007, "CLS Bank settled 705,582 payment instructions with a gross value of US$5.22 trillion." *See* www.cls-group.com (Feb. 28, 2007).

[52] Through its clearinghouse, the Chicago Mercantile Exchange (CME) cleared over US$13.8 million exchange-traded futures and options contracts on February 27, 2007. *See* www.cme.org. The money settlements associated with those trades are conducted through a network of so-called "settlement banks" which carry accounts for the CME clearinghouse and its clearing members.

[53] CPSS, *The Role of Central Bank Money in Payment Systems,* supra note 13, at 14.

[54] 12 USC §§ 4401–4407. Under a bilateral netting contract, the parties net the termination values of the various transactions governed by the contract upon termination of these transactions.

[55] 11 USC § 546(g) (preference payments) and §548(d)(2) (fraudulent transfer).

[56] CPSS, *The Role of Central Bank Money in Payment Systems, supra* note 13, at 15.

Legal Protection of Payment and Securities Settlement Systems and of Collateral Transactions in the European Union

DIEGO DEVOS

Since the early 1990s, credit institution insolvencies (Herstatt, BCCI,[1] Banesto, Barings, Japanese banks, for example), some of which were sudden and unexpected, have led authorities responsible for the supervision of payment and securities settlement systems, as well as operators of and participants in these systems, to become more careful about the repercussions of insolvency on the functioning of these systems, and in particular on the enforceability of collateral transactions carried out through such systems.

Control of the legal risks associated with the insolvency[2] of a participant in a payment or securities settlement system is especially difficult when the insolvent party is subject to a foreign legal system. This occurrence is widespread if one takes into account the participation of branch offices of foreign banks, whether or not incorporated under the law of a member state of the European Union (the EU) or in other national systems. Furthermore, the "remote access" participation of foreign community banks,[3] an example of the free provision of services within the European Union area, increases the incidence of foreign participation in EU national systems.

In the past, it was sufficient for national payment and settlement systems to ensure that in the event of the insolvency of a domestic participant in a payment system, the *local law applicable to the system* would, for example: (1) uphold the validity and enforceability against third parties of the netting of payments (in net settlement systems); (2) uphold the contractual irrevocability of payment orders (in gross settlement systems); (3) exclude any "zero-hour" rules (backdating of the effects of insolvency decisions to the first hour of the day of the pronouncement of the insolvency decision); and (4) uphold the enforceability of collateral arrangements that had been set up.

When a foreign participant enters insolvency today, it is also necessary to ensure that the foreign law applicable to the insolvency will not invalidate the settlement of the cash or securities orders or the collateral arrangements put in place. Such issues fall within the area of *cross-border insolvency*,[4] which has become one of the most complex legal issues facing market participants.

The EU has taken steps to address these issues. The European Directive 98/26/EC of 19 May 1998 on Settlement Finality in Payment and Securities Settlement Systems[5] (Settlement Finality Directive, SFD, or the Directive) is devoted to the legal protection of payment and settlement systems as such, including the protection of collateral transactions processed in these systems. A second important instrument at the EU level is the Collateral Directive of 6 June 2002 (Collateral Directive), which aims to harmonize substantive rules on collateral arrangements irrespective of the systems or custodians through which the relevant collateral assets are held.

This chapter examines the main legal issues that may arise in cross-border insolvency, before going on to describe two other EU legal instruments likely to be of relevance. It then addresses the Settlement Finality Directive itself and reviews the provisions of the recent Collateral Directive. The final section reports on three recent legal developments in the fields of clearing and settlement systems: The Hague Convention of 13 December 2002 on the Law Applicable to Certain Rights in Respect of Securities Held with an Intermediary; the UNIDROIT Draft Convention on Intermediated Securities; and the EU Legal Certainty Group.

Insolvency of a Foreign Participant in a Payment/Settlement System

There are two main approaches used by jurisdictions to address cross-border insolvency:[6]

- the principle of the *unity of insolvency*, by virtue of which there is only one competent court to declare a debtor's insolvency, that is, the court in the place where the insolvent company has its head office, registered office, or statutory seat. This principle is generally linked to the principle of *universality* (or universal nature) of insolvency, allowing the insolvency decision to be enforceable and to produce legal effects in other states[7] where branch offices or assets of the insolvent party are located (for example, the regimes in Belgium and Luxembourg);

- the principle of the *plurality of insolvencies* (or *territoriality*), which requires a declaration of insolvency in each country where the insolvent debtor has a center of activity or even mere property. Under the territoriality approach, each insolvent branch is governed by its local insolvency law and is administered by its own receiver, and such territorial insolvency only affects assets located in the territory in question (for example, the regimes in France and Denmark).

There are also systems that combine these two approaches in some way. An insolvency pronounced in the state of the insolvent party's domicile may indeed produce effects outside the territory of that state. On the one hand, the insolvency proceeding reaches other states where the insolvent party's property is located (universality of the insolvency), but, on the other hand, it is possible to institute a separate insolvency proceeding in the jurisdiction where local branch offices or even mere assets of the foreign debtor are located (territorial insolvency). This is the so-called principle of *mitigated universality* principle in force (for example, in Germany, Austria, and the United Kingdom).

In the case of insolvency of a foreign participant in a national payment and settlement system, the solution, as far as the jurisdiction of the system is concerned, will depend on the type of insolvency regime that is applied by a court in the jurisdiction of the payment and settlement system (the local court):

- In states that apply the territoriality principle of bankruptcy, the local court will simply refuse to recognize any insolvency decision handed down in the debtor's jurisdiction and will not apply the foreign insolvency law (*lex fori concursus*). In principle, a foreign insolvency should not have any impact on the payment and settlement system.

- In states that apply the principle of mitigated universality, to the extent that there is an establishment of the foreign debtor, or even mere assets, in the territory, there will generally (but not necessarily) be the opening of territorial insolvency proceedings in the local court limited to local assets. The national insolvency law of the place of the payment and settlement system will then prevail over the insolvency law of the foreign participant.

- In states applying the unity and universality principle of bankruptcy, the local court should, in principle, recognize the foreign insolvency order by right[8] and also apply the foreign insolvency law.

The main qualifications to the automatic recognition of the foreign insolvency decision in such jurisdictions that apply the unity and universality principle will generally be as follows:

- There will be no judicial recognition if the foreign bankruptcy order is strictly limited by its terms or by nature to the territory of the foreign state.

- There will be no recognition if the application of the bankruptcy decision or foreign insolvency law is likely to be contrary to the international public policy[9] of the state of the payment and settlement system.[10] In this case, the local law will overrule the conflicting provisions of foreign law.

Here, the application of foreign insolvency law could be particularly detrimental to the proper functioning of national payment or settlement systems; it may then lead to the local court refusing to recognize the *lex fori concursus* because it would conflict with public policy.[11]

It is also worth noting that certain courts may refuse to recognize foreign insolvency decisions issued in countries that do not give reciprocal recognition to their own insolvency decisions.[12]

One good example of the practical application of the unity and universality approach is the issue of the legal enforceability of collateral that secures the credit (intra-day or overnight) granted by a system operator or a central bank (the creditor) to a foreign participant (the foreign debtor). The enforceability of the collateral against third parties is governed by the law of the location of the collateral. This law, for example, may allow for the realization of the collateral without any prior judicial authorization.

However, in the case of insolvency or of any composition proceedings[13] commenced against the foreign debtor in a court in the foreign debtor's jurisdiction, the foreign insolvency law might overrule the law applicable to the credit transaction and the related collateral because of the public policy nature of insolvency laws. This, of course, assumes that this foreign insolvency law would be recognized in the local court.

This does not mean that the validity of the main credit transaction or the collateral securing the transaction (a pledge, for example) would suddenly be governed entirely by a foreign law. One basic principle of the conflict of laws rules of most states is that a provision of collateral is governed, with regard to its proprietary aspects, in particular the enforceability against third parties and its realization, by the law of the country where the assets are located (*lex rei sitae* rule). In this case, the local law of the creditor is therefore still applicable to the assessment of the pledge's enforceability against third parties, with respect to the securities "located"[14] in the creditor's jurisdiction.

However, the foreign debtor's insolvency law—assuming it would be recognized by the local court—will have sole competence to govern two issues of crucial importance for the *effectiveness* (not the validity) of the collateral in question:

- Determination of the ranking of the creditor as collateral taker with respect to the collateral, that is, the order of preference on the proceeds of the assets encumbered by the pledge, vis-à-vis other preferential or ordinary creditors of the insolvent foreign debtor;

- The possibility of realization of the relevant collateral, that is, whether it is necessary to obtain prior authorization from the receiver or the competent courts before any realization of the assets, as well whether or not there may be a stay on any action by secured creditors, in the interest of insolvency liquidation. (The idea here is to leave a kind of 'inventory deadline' in order to freeze any legal action or forced sale by creditors before the receiver has been able to value the assets and liabilities of the insolvent foreign debtor and settle in court the disputable claims.)

These matters are essential for the creditor because in the case of the insolvency of a foreign debtor, it is important to ensure that the foreign debtor's insolvency law will give priority to the creditor over the pledged assets, without preferring other creditors such as the tax authorities, social insurance bodies, or employees. In addition, the creditor must be able to immediately realize the securities in its possession, or at least as soon as possible, in order to avoid the market risk that arises due to the possibility of a decline in the market value of the securities posted as collateral, independently of any margins which may have been constituted against such a risk. These issues are precisely addressed specifically in the Collateral Directive.

European Legal Instruments Related to the Settlement Finality Directive

In view of the diversity of existing legal systems and the complexity resulting from the combination of several laws potentially applicable to an insolvent participant in a payment or settlement system, a harmonized solution at the European level was considered highly desirable. The Settlement Finality Directive is the binding EU legal instrument that aims at addressing the specific legal issues for payment and settlement systems, including collateral constituted in those systems.

There are, however, two other EU instruments that were adopted after the Settlement Finality Directive (even though they were originally drafted before the Directive), which include provisions relevant for the protection of payment and settlement systems against the insolvency of participants:

- The European Regulation on Insolvency Proceedings dated 29 May 2000

- EU Directive (2001/24/EC) on the Reorganisation and Winding-up of Credit Institutions of 4 April 2001

It is appropriate to examine both instruments, as they were various interactions between those texts and the Settlement Finality Directive.

The European Regulation on Insolvency Proceedings Dated 29 May 2000

The work on a European Convention relating to EC insolvency proceedings ended on November 23, 1995, when a definitive text was signed (the Insolvency Convention).[15] It was the fruit of five years of intense efforts on the part of an ad hoc working group of national experts (chaired by Manfred Balz). Because it required the signature of all member states, the 1995 Insolvency Convention, following a joint initiative of Germany and Finland, was converted into the EU Council Regulation on Insolvency Proceedings (Insolvency Regulation) pursuant to Article 61 and 67 of the Rome Treaty. The Insolvency Regulation was finally adopted on May 29, 2000,[16] with the same provisions as those contained in the Insolvency Convention.[17] The Insolvency Regulation entered into force on May 31, 2002.

The Insolvency Regulation is a vast and complex instrument, including 47 articles and three annexes, and a full discussion of it is beyond the focus of this chapter. But it is worth mentioning here that the Insolvency Regulation establishes the principle of the mitigated universality of insolvency by means of a double set of rules:

- On the one hand, the first chapter of the Insolvency Regulation attributes principal competence to the jurisdiction of the member state where the debtor's domicile (or center of main interests) is situated[18] to commence insolvency proceedings (Article 3)— referred to as "main insolvency proceedings"—and provides that the insolvency law of this state will apply in the other states of the European Union (Article 4). Articles 5–15 of the Insolvency

Regulation, however, set out exceptions to the basic competence of the law of the place of the main insolvency proceedings in favor of the laws of other member states called upon to govern certain rights (real estate, employment contracts, rights in rem, etc.). It is within the latter framework that some protective provisions relevant for payment and settlement systems (and collateral) are laid down. Chapter II of the Insolvency Regulation provides for the automatic recognition of the main insolvency proceedings in the other states of the EU.

- On the other hand, Chapter III of the Insolvency Regulation authorizes other member states to open territorial proceedings—referred to as "secondary" insolvency proceedings—in their territory, if the debtor has an "establishment" there under the meaning of the Insolvency Regulation (see Articles 3.2 and 2(h)). The purpose of those proceedings is to protect such other states against the effects of the main proceedings (independently of the exceptions to the law governing the main proceedings contained in Chapter I). In addition, member states other than the state of the debtor's head office are also authorized to open territorial insolvency proceedings independently of the opening of any main proceedings (subject to the fairly liberal conditions of Article 3.4). Chapter III organizes relations between main and secondary proceedings (particularly, Articles 31–35).

It should again be noted that the Insolvency Regulation, by harmonizing the rules of conflict of laws and certain procedural rules in matters of international insolvency, is not applicable to the insolvency of credit institutions, insurance companies, investment firms, and collective investment undertakings (Art. 1.2). This exclusion is due to the existence at the time of specific draft EU instruments designed to cover the insolvency of these categories of financial institutions (particularly for banks and insurance companies), which takes into account the specific features of the financial sectors in which the categories of financial institutions operate and the principle of *home country control*, as the key rule of supervisory control for activities in such sectors.

In view of this, it is obvious that the Insolvency Regulation has only a limited effect on payment and settlement systems because most of the participants in these systems are excluded from its scope of application. The fact remains that these provisions of the Insolvency Regulation may govern systems which may admit nonfinancial institutions, as well as to relations between a financial institution that participates in a system and its clients, which are ordinary commercial undertakings. The same debate about the scope of application emerged during the Collateral Directive's discussions. Recital 27 of the Insolvency Regulation states explicitly that the Settlement Finality Directive must be considered as *lex specialis* and overrules the Insolvency Regulation as *lex generalis*.

Three provisions of the Insolvency Regulation are likely to concern payment and securities settlements systems or collateral, to the extent defined above:

- Article 5 relating to rights in rem;
- Article 6 relating to set-off;
- Article 9 relating to payment and settlement systems and financial markets.

As indicated above, these provisions act as a limitation of the exclusive application of the law of the main proceedings with certain rights governed by the law of another member state.

Rights in Rem

The first paragraph of Article 5 of the Insolvency Regulation states:

> The opening of the insolvency proceedings shall not affect the *right in rem* of creditors or third parties in respect of tangible or intangible, movable or immovable assets—both specific assets and collections of indefinite assets as a whole which change from time to time— belonging to the debtor, which are situated within the territory of another member state at the time of the opening of proceedings. [19]

The aim of Article 5.1 of the Insolvency Regulation is to ensure the maximum protection of the holders of *rights in rem* for assets located in other member states, in view of the effects of the main insolvency proceedings opened in the country of the head office (or of the center of main interests) of the debtor. The holder of the *right in rem* may thus realize the assets and claim a right of preference on the proceeds of this realization without being hindered by any restrictive rules (or conferring on him a lower rank than that of other creditors) of the law governing the main insolvency proceedings. Thus one can see the importance of this provision for situations where securities are provided as collateral (in relation or not to participation in a payment or settlement system) (compare, in this sense, Article 9.1 of the Settlement Finality Directive discussed below).

By doing this, the Insolvency Regulation also entitles the holder of the *right in rem* (or of the collateral) not to be hindered by any restrictive rules that apply in the case of insolvency under the law governing the *right in rem* itself. Applying the *lex rei sitae* rule, the law applicable to the *right in rem* normally corresponds to the law of the place of the assets subject to the *right in rem*.

In other words, the expression "does not affect" actually grants the holder of the *right in rem* the right to exercise its prerogatives (and particularly the right to realize the asset) in accordance with "ordinary" rules of the local law. The restrictive rules laid down in the local law (*lex situs*) for the insolvency of the debtor are thereby excluded.

In concrete terms, therefore, if (1) the debtor is domiciled in country A and is declared insolvent in country A, and (2) the creditor is domiciled in country B and is the recipient of a pledge of securities located in country B, the creditor may realize the collateral and be paid in accordance with the law of country B. However, the creditor in country B will not be bound by the mandatory rules ordinarily applicable in the case of insolvency of any pledgor (debtor) under law B (such as, for example, the necessity to obtain a judicial authorization prior to realization).

By adopting the "does not affect" formula, the Insolvency Regulation grants to the holder of the *right in rem* or of the security interest concerning an asset located in another country an even more favorable status than it would have under any relevant legislation in country A or country B applicable to its *right in rem* or its collateral since it "is not affected" at all by the opening of the insolvency proceedings.

This interpretation is confirmed in the draft explanatory report of the former Insolvency Convention.[20] Under paragraph 98, the draft report stated:

> The rule "does not immunise" rights in rem against the debtor's insolvency. If the law of the State where the assets are located allows these rights in rem to be affected in some way, the liquidator (or any other person) empowered to do so may request secondary insolvency proceedings be opened in that State if the debtor has an establishment there. The secondary proceedings are conducted according to local law and allow the liquidator to affect these rights under the same conditions as in purely domestic proceedings.

This passage thus clarifies the scope of the rule contained in Article 5 of the Insolvency Regulation:

- In the case of a main insolvency proceeding against the debtor, the creditor may exercise its *rights in rem* on local assets as if the insolvency proceedings did not exist.

- In order to apply any possibly restrictive provisions laid down in case of insolvency under the law of the state where the assets in question are located, a secondary insolvency proceeding must be opened. Failing this, these restrictive provisions are not applicable.

To sum up, Article 5 of the Insolvency Regulation enables the holder of collateral not only to be protected against an unfavorable "importation" of the insolvency law of the foreign debtor, but also of "not being affected" by this insolvency, so that the holder will be able to realize its collateral as if no insolvency had been opened, as long as no secondary proceedings are initiated in the country where the assets are located.

Set-off

Article 6.1 of the Insolvency Regulation states:

> The opening of [main] insolvency proceedings shall not affect the right of creditors to demand the set-off of their claims against the claims of the [insolvent] debtor, where such a set-off is permitted by the law applicable to the insolvent debtor's claim.[21]

This provision authorizes a set-off after the opening of the main insolvency of the debtor on the basis of claims arising previously,[22] even if this post-insolvency set-off would be forbidden under the insolvency law of the jurisdiction in which the main insolvency proceedings have been commenced,[23] provided that such a set-off is authorized by the law governing the insolvent debtor's claim[24] (of course, this assumes that the applicable law is different from the law of the main insolvency proceedings).

This means, in the financial area, that the contractual set-off governed by a law that authorizes post-insolvency set-off could be successfully claimed against the receiver of the (main) insolvency proceedings of a foreign debtor, despite the restrictions which might apply under the *lex fori concursus*[25] (compare Article 3 of the Settlement Finality Directive, commented on below, under paragraph 24 or Article 8 of the Collateral Directive).

Payment Systems and Financial Markets

Article 9, paragraph 1[26] of the Insolvency Regulation states as follows:

> Without prejudice to Article 5, the effects of insolvency proceedings on the rights and obligations of the parties to a payment or settlement system or to a financial market, shall be governed solely by the law of the member state applicable to that system or market.

This article substantially ensures the protection of payment and securities settlement systems and the financial markets[27] because when a foreign participant is insolvent, the effects of the insolvency proceedings on its rights and obligations in the system or market in question will be governed exclusively by the law applicable to the system, to the exclusion of foreign insolvency law.

Consequently, the validity of "netting" in the case of insolvency or of gross payments settled in real time in a real-time gross settlement systems (RTGSS) or, again, the existence or not of a "zero-hour" rule for transfers executed in the system, are to be assessed only according to the law of the system.[28] The same applies, for example, to the validity of margin calls or transfer of positions (in favor of a nonbankrupt participant, as it is organized in certain options or futures markets). This rule is also reflected in Article 8 of the Settlement Finality Directive (commented on below).

The preservation of the effect of Article 5 of the Insolvency Regulation aims at avoiding the "blind" application of Article 9, that is, the exclusive application of the law of the payment system to collateral which constitute *rights in rem* (in particular, a pledge) on assets located in a member state other than the one whose law governs the system.[29] These collateral rights will still, in principle, be governed by the *lex rei sitae* and will not be affected, in the sense of Article 5 indicated above, by the opening of the insolvency proceedings.

EU Directive (2001/24/EC) on the Reorganisation and Winding-up of Credit Institutions of 4 April 2001[30]

In 1985 the Commission presented a draft directive, formally modified in 1988,[31] with the aim of harmonizing the reorganization of credit institutions and their winding-up, according to the same principles of centralization in the home country. Furthermore, the directive will ensure mutual recognition of the measures taken by other member states, along the lines of the basic regime that exists for the creation and exercise of banking activity within the EU, by virtue of the two so-called banking coordination directives.[32] The directive relating to deposit guarantee schemes[33] had, moreover, completed the structure by organizing the mandatory affiliation of credit institutions to a deposit-guarantee scheme of the home member state, also for its branch offices established in host member states.

After a hiatus of several years, work on the reorganization/winding-up directive began again in 1993, and ended[34] with a Common Position at the EU Council level in May 2000. After the final amendments of the European Parliament, the EU Directive on the Reorganisation and Winding-up of Credit Institutions (the WUD) was finally adopted on April 4, 2001, which has now been implemented by member states since May 5, 2004 (Article 34.1).

The WUD is based on the principle of the exclusive competence of the administrative or judicial authorities of the home country of the bank in difficulty. These authorities are solely entitled to decide on the adoption of reorganization measures or the opening of a winding-up proceedings (in the broad sense) with application of the home country's law. The authorities in the host member state must recognize the effects of these measures, without being able, on their part, to take reorganization measures locally or to open territorial insolvency proceedings against the branch offices set up in their territory.

For the European banking sector (as well as for the insurance sector), therefore, the WUD applies the principles of unity and universality of bankruptcy, and thus differs quite substantially from the approach adopted by the Insolvency Regulation, which is based on mitigated universality (that is, there is a main insolvency proceeding accompanied by secondary insolvency proceedings in each state where an establishment of the debtor is located).

However, the European Council felt it necessary to depart to some extent from the application of the home country's law in favor of the law of other member states, in order to govern certain rights. This means not only providing a compromise to territorial states but, above all, also avoiding a situation in which the generalized application of the home country's law might prove to be seriously detrimental to legal certainty, particularly for financial transactions and the participation of the credit institutions in question in payment or settlement systems.

The WUD thus sets out a series of exceptions to the law of the home country, including those which deal specifically with the protection of financial transactions and payment or settlement systems. The most important provisions for the purposes of this chapter are Articles 20–33 of the WUD, which adopt a similar approach to that of the Insolvency Regulation[35] in the sense that, as waiver of the home country law, the effects of the reorganization measures or winding-up proceedings on certain rights, contracts, or systems concerning the insolvent bank will be exclusively governed by another law, that is, the one applicable to these rights, contracts, or systems.

The validity of contractual netting[36] and repurchase agreements, or repos,[37] will indeed be governed exclusively by the *lex contractus*.[38] The enforcement of proprietary rights in book-entry securities, recorded on a register, an account, or in a centralized deposit system held or located in a member state, will be exclusively governed by the law of the member state where the account, the register, or centralized deposit system in which those rights are recorded, is held or located.[39] Transactions carried out in the context of a regulated market shall be governed solely by the law of the contract governing such transactions.[40]

The WUD also applies the same regime as the Insolvency Regulation in the treatment of *rights in rem*, which "shall not (be) affect(ed) by the adoption of reorganisation measures or the opening of winding-up proceedings" when the relevant assets are "situated within the territory of another member state at the time of the adoption of such measures...." (Article 21).

Because the opening of insolvency proceedings in the home member state "does not affect" the holder of the *right in rem*, there will be an "immunization" of the holder of such a *right in rem*, taking into account the absence of any possibility of opening secondary insolvency proceedings in other member states. In such a regime, the holder of the *right in rem* should thus be exempted from any restrictive rules intending to avoid abuses to the detriment of other creditors—whether under the insolvency law of the home member state or under the law of other member states applicable to the holder's *right in rem* or security interest.[41] This is also what the

Collateral Directive is aiming to achieve (see in particular Articles 4, 8, and 9 of the WUD.

The Settlement Finality Directive[42]

The Settlement Finality Directive (Directive or SFD) is the product of a group of member states' experts who worked under the aegis of the European Commission. The group was established in 1993 to study the legal aspects of cross-border payments.[43]

The Directive proposes legislation at the EU level to eliminate, as far as possible, the legal risks to which payment systems and securities settlement systems are exposed,[44] taking into account the systemic risk[45] inherent in such systems.

The goal is, first of all, to require member states—if they have not already done so—to ensure that their domestic law ensures the satisfactory functioning of payment and settlement systems, whether operated on a net basis, in which case the validity of netting must be ensured, or on a gross basis, where the contractual irrevocability of orders needs to be guaranteed. There is also the need for the removal of any zero-hour rule in the case of the insolvency of a participant.

A second objective, equally important, is to ensure that the functioning of the relevant system, once its domestic law has been strengthened, cannot be threatened by the application of foreign insolvency legislation, in the case of participation of an institution from another member state or even from a non-EU country.

Once these protections are in place, financial institutions (mainly credit institutions and investment firms) should be able to settle their transactions in euro or other currencies without major legal risks, not only by means of national systems for domestic transactions, but also by means of cross-border payment systems such as the TARGET system[46] managed by the national central banks of the euro system and the European Central Bank or by the EURO 1 system[47] for cross-border transactions in the euro area.

The same applies to securities transactions that can be settled on a cross-border basis, either in an international central securities depositary (CSD), such as Euroclear or Clearstream, or by means of connections between national central securities depositaries, in order to allow securities held, for example, in country Y to be transferred from party A to party B, both located in country X.

Finally, monetary policy or exchange transactions of central banks—and particularly those which are members of the European System of Central Banks within the euro area—should also benefit from the legal protection brought by the Directive. The collateral provided to these central banks to guarantee, for example, extensions of credit should no longer run the risk of being rendered ineffective or unenforceable in the case of the counterparty's insolvency. This also includes intra-day credit, which is important for the satisfactory functioning of payment systems.

Scope of Application of the Settlement Finality Directive

Ratione Materiae

The provisions of the Directive apply to any payment or securities settlement system within the meaning of Article 2(a) of the Directive, that is:

- a formal arrangement (comprising common rules and standardized arrangements) between three or more participants[48] for the execution of transfer orders (on cash or securities) between the participants;

- designated as a "system"[49] by each member state, which must notify such to the Commission "after that member state is satisfied as to the adequacy of the rules of the system." Each national system must be assessed on the basis of an "accurateness" criterion, which is subject to the satisfaction of each member state. In reality, this provision is a compromise between those that favored harmonized supervision of payment and settlement systems[50] and those opposed to any harmonization on this point, who consider that the Directive should just focus on reducing the legal risks associated with these systems.

Each member state is also free to designate as a system, on a case-by-case basis, a formal arrangement (as defined above) that only includes two participants—which can cover a correspondent banking relationship—provided that this designation, in the opinion of the member state concerned, is warranted on grounds of systemic risk.[51]

In the same vein, each member state may also treat an indirect participant (or sub-participant)[52] as if it were a direct participant in a system as defined above, in order to apply the protective provisions of the Directive to bilateral relations between the direct participant and the indirect participant, provided the following conditions are fulfilled:

- The "indirect participant" must be a credit institution.

- The direct participant must be an institution that participates in a payment system. (Securities settlement systems have been excluded.)

- There must be a contractual relationship between the direct participant and the indirect participant.

  (On these three first conditions, see Article 2(g)).

- The inclusion of indirect participants in the category of "participants" in the sense of the Directive must be warranted on the grounds of systemic risk, in the opinion of the member state concerned (Article 2(f)).

- The indirect participant must be "known" to the system in which it participates via its direct participant (Article 2(f)). The system must also disclose to the member state in question (the one whose law is applicable) the participants in the said system, including any possible indirect participants, as well as any change in them (Article 10).

Ratione Personae

According to Article 2(b), direct participants in a system may be (1) credit institutions as defined in the First Banking Co-ordination Directive,[53] (2) investment firms as defined in the Directive on

Investment Services,[54] (3) public authorities and publicly guaranteed undertakings, or (4) any undertaking whose head office is outside the EU and whose functions correspond to those of the EU credit institutions or the aforesaid investment firms.

Central counterparties, settlement agents, and clearing houses are also included in the scope of application of the Directive (see Article 2(c), (d), and (e)).

All these categories of institutions are included in the general concept of "participant" in the sense of Article 2(f).

Rationae Territoriae

Contrary to the initial proposal of the Commission, the Directive is limited to EU systems, that is, those governed by the law of a member state chosen by the participants (Articles 1(a) and 2(a), second indent),[55] even though, of course, these systems may include participants with a registered office established in a non-EU country, acting through a branch office located in the EU. Recital no. 7 states, however, that member states may apply the provisions of the Directive to their domestic institutions that participate directly in non-EU payment and securities settlement systems.

The Directive has various effects on relations between EU institutions and systems and institutions or systems of non-EU countries.

First of all, the power left to member states to apply the Directive to their institutions that participate in non-EU systems does not mean that such non-EU countries would be bound by the Directive. The Directive is only binding on member states of the EU in order to ensure that their domestic law satisfies the objectives of legal soundness and certainty. However, in the case of insolvency of EU institutions participating in a system operating in a non-EU country, the non-EU system will be entitled to rely on the protective effects of the Directive. In this case, the Directive extends its effects to the domestic law of a member state, insofar as its provisions (concerning netting, irrevocability of transactions, zero-hour rules, and collateral) will also be binding on the (domestic) receiver of the insolvent institution in order to prevent the invalidation of the operations of the non-EU system. Such a regime should favor the participation of EU institutions in American, Japanese, or Swiss systems, for example.

On the other hand, in the case of insolvency of non-EU institutions participating in an EU system, the protective provisions of the Directive should prevent the receiver of the non-EU country from challenging the operating rules of the EU system or any collateral arrangements, on the grounds, for example, of their incompatibility with the mandatory rules of the insolvency law of the non-EU jurisdiction (assuming of course, that the insolvency proceedings of the non-EU country would be, as a starting point, recognized in the member state where the system is located). One should consider, in such a case, the protective provisions in question (introduced into domestic law of each member state when implementing the Directive) as part of the international public policy of the member state where the system in question is operated, preventing the application of conflicting rules of the non-EU country's law.

The Directive also authorizes member states to designate "systems" securities settlement systems, which allows "to a limited extent" the execution of orders concerning financial instruments other than "securities" as defined in Article 2(h). (See Article 2(a)); what is intended here are, for example, transfer orders on gold or other commodities, which are covered under the concept of "commodity derivatives.") A system that grants access to nonfinancial institutions can also be designated as a "system" (for example, large companies ("corporates") carrying out financial transactions), provided that, for such cases, the system in question is a securities settlement system supervised in accordance with national legislation (see Article 2(b), final paragraph). In both cases, designation as a "system" must again be warranted on the grounds of protection against systemic risk.

As one can see, Article 2 of the Directive refers to systems' criteria ("formal arrangement," justification of "systemic risk," verification "of the adequacy of the rules of the system," etc.) that appear to be fairly vague and general and therefore require a formal designation by each member state, in its implementing legislation or by means of subsequent enforcement regulations, independently of the notification of the national systems to the European Commission, required by Article 10, paragraph 1 of the Directive.

Provisions of Material Law Aimed at the Legal Protection of Payment and Settlement Systems

Article 3 of the Directive is one of the most ambiguous provisions (with Recital 13; see below)—and one of the least well drafted, from a strictly legal point of view—of the whole text of a directive not known for its clarity. The ambiguity is the result of a political compromise aimed at merging two initially separate texts, one devoted to the validity of netting, the other to the validity of transfer orders in general. The result is text that may undermine the very legal certainty which it was meant to provide.

The first objective of Article 3.1 is to ensure the validity and, particularly, the enforceability against third parties of the "netting of payments," in the event of the insolvency of a participant in a payment or settlement system operating on a net basis. Both bilateral netting and multilateral netting, by set-off, novation, or any other technique (the German "skontration," for example), are included in this provision. (See the rather economic definition of "netting"[56] in Article 2(k), referring to the conversion of reciprocal claims into a "single net" claim.[57]) Netting of forward contracts (swaps, repurchase transactions, etc.), known as "obligation netting," could also be caught, at least indirectly, if operated within the framework of a system in the sense of the Directive. One good example was the ECHO system managed in London by the ECHO Clearing House, which has now been replaced by the CLS system. The Collateral Directive is now aiming at expressly validating close-out netting provisions (as stipulated in market agreements such as the ISDA Swap Master Agreement, ISMA, Global Master Repurchase Agreement, and European Master Agreement), notwithstanding insolvency proceedings against a counterpart (Article 7).

The way in which Article 3.1 is drafted ("Transfer orders and netting shall be legally enforceable and ... shall be binding on third parties provided that transfer orders...."could be interpreted, first of all, as limiting the scope of this paragraph only to the netting of transfer orders—in other words, as applying only to payment or settlement systems that operate a liquidation on a net basis, to the exclusion of transfer orders executed in gross settlement systems (RTGS systems, for short, which operate an individual settlement of each order for its initial gross amounts, without netting).

Article 3.2, which only protects netting (without reference to transfer orders) against preferences rules (transactions during the "suspect period") would appear, at first sight, to confirm this narrow interpretation. This is corroborated by Recital 11, which stipulates that "transfer orders and *their* netting should be legally enforceable...."

Although this concept may have been in line with the Commission's initial proposal for a directive, this was definitely not the objective sought by most, if not all, member states, which wanted to protect transfer orders generally against the effects of insolvency, whether these orders would be settled on a net (which is becoming less frequent) or on a gross basis.

It is therefore appropriate to adopt a broad and reasonable interpretation of Article 3.1 that applies not only to the netting of transfer orders, but even to transfer orders, independently of any subsequent netting. But the scope of this provision is still unclear:

- If the first paragraph of Article 3.1 aims at ensuring the validity and enforceability against third parties of transfer orders entered into a system before the opening of insolvency proceedings (which is the basic hypothesis), what does this mean? Is it a protection against a revocation or against a zero-hour rule in the case of insolvency? If so, then of what use would be Articles 5 and 7, which deal specifically with these cases?

- Is it, on the other hand, a matter of ensuring that a payment order entered into a system before insolvency can always be settled validly after this time? Can one, in particular, infer from the text of the first paragraph of Article 3.1 that a payment order entered into an RTGS system before the insolvency but which is not settled immediately (after being placed in a "waiting queue" for example) can, however, be processed and settled without any hindrance after the insolvency? One should answer this question in the affirmative to the extent that the text of the first paragraph of Article 3.1 renders the validity and enforceability against third parties of transfer orders solely contingent on their prior entry into the system, which must take place before the opening of the insolvency proceedings against the participant concerned. To make any sense, this should imply the admissibility of the subsequent settlement of such previous orders.

The second paragraph of Article 3.1 deals with the case of transfer orders carried out on the day of opening of such proceedings but entered after the opening of insolvency proceedings.[58] This second paragraph was introduced in the Directive in order to remedy the legal uncertainty affecting the fate of payments orders made between the time of insolvency and the moment of its knowledge by the participants and operators of the systems concerned. It goes without saying that participants who are debtors of the insolvent participant following a bankruptcy order that was issued, for example at 11:00 AM on a working day, may be led to make further orders after this moment, being unaware of the occurrence of this insolvency. Also, it is possible to imagine that the insolvent participant orders payments after its insolvency. For example, the payments could have been entered with an order of delayed execution or the orders could have been passed by another participant in the system representing the defaulting institution, at the time when this direct participant does not yet know about the insolvency of the defaulting institution.

These orders subsequent to the declaration of insolvency are declared legally enforceable and binding on third parties "only if, after the time of settlement, the settlement agent, the central counterparty or the clearing house can prove that *they were not aware, nor should have been aware*, of the opening of such proceedings" (paragraph 2 of Article 3.1; emphasis added).

In case of dispute about transfer orders entered after the opening of insolvency proceedings against the participant, it is up to the settlement agent or the operator of the system to prove its legitimate ignorance of the insolvency at the time of settlement. The settlement agent or operator must be able to justify its legitimate ignorance by demonstrating that at the time of the orders and their execution, the competent authority in accordance with the rules stated in Article 6 of the Directive did not provide the settlement agent or operator with the news of the insolvency of the relevant participant, nor was the insolvency known to the markets (through, for example, reference to announcements in the press or on Reuters, Telerate, or Bloomberg screens).

In the same way and under the same conditions as for the transfer orders themselves, Article 3.1 allows for the protection of netting of transfer orders provided that:

- either the transfer order to be netted is entered into the system before the moment of opening of the insolvency proceedings;

- or the transfer order was introduced and settled on a net basis after the moment of opening of insolvency proceedings, to the extent that the operator of the system can prove its legitimate ignorance of the opening of such insolvency proceedings.

Article 3.2 deals with the protection of the effects of netting[59] against the possible damaging impact of rules on fraudulent transactions carried out during a certain period (six months, two years, etc.) before the opening of the insolvency proceedings (referred to variously as the "suspect period," *fraus pauliana*, regime of "preferences," "fraudulent conveyance"). It is stipulated that netting may not be unwound as a result of these rules.

Article 3.3 states that for the purposes of applying Article 3.1, the moment of entry of a transfer order into a system is defined by the operating rules of the system. This appears to be rather obvious. Unfortunately, the text adds that if the national law itself defines this moment, the rules of that system must be in accordance with such conditions. At this point, one may question the usefulness of the first sentence of Article 3.3.

Article 4 of the Directive allows member states, despite the insolvency of a participant, to authorize the debit (in cash or securities) of a settlement account of this participant[60] in order to allow for the settlement of its final position or of its transfer orders. This could be carried out either by the debit of cash amounts or securities already credited on such an account or even by means of a withdrawal on a credit line extended to the defaulting participant by the central bank or the operator of the system. In the latter case, the central bank or the operator of the system is required to obtain the prior authorization of the receiver as regards this use of credit facilities. However, the relevant credit facility so used has to be already secured by means of "available existing" collateral, taking the form of collateral security as defined under Article 2(m).

Article 5 aims to ensure the irrevocability of transfer orders. In most cases, this will be provided for in the rules of the system, which should then be protected against any rules of internal law[61] that could invalidate this irrevocability, including in the case of the insolvency of a participant. Pursuant to Article 5, from the moment of irrevocability defined in the rules of the system, a transfer order can no longer be revoked by a participant or by a third party.

Section III of the Directive contains three provisions (Articles 6–8) that deal with the opening of insolvency proceedings against a participant of a system.[62]

Article 6.1 defines the opening of insolvency proceedings as the moment when the relevant judicial or administrative authority "handed down its decision." This definition is useful for the interpretation of Article 3 (protection of netting and transfer orders entered into the system) and Article 7 (protection against any zero-hour rule).

When a decision opening insolvency proceedings is handed down by the relevant authority (for example, by a commercial court), the relevant authority must immediately transmit that decision to the appropriate authority designated by its member state to receive such notification (Article 6.2). This national authority (which may be the central bank), must in turn immediately pass this news to other member states (the authority in question must in practice notify the decision taken in its country to its foreign counterparts).[63] member states are also obliged to inform the Commission of the authorities which they have appointed for this purpose (Article 10, paragraph 1).

One must not lose sight of the fact that however useful this notification system may be, the moment of opening of insolvency proceedings remains, in principle, when the relevant authority of a country hands down its decision, not the moment when this decision is notified to the appropriate authority of that country nor the moment when the decision is passed on to the other member states, subject, of course, to the rules of national law applicable in each member state concerned.

However, a degree of protection is conferred by the rules that protect transfer orders executed (without knowledge of the insolvency) between the time of insolvency and the moment when this news is widespread on the markets (see paragraph 2 of Article 3.1, described above).

Article 7 aims at neutralizing the rules of some insolvency regimes under which an insolvency decision is deemed to have retroactive legal effects from the first hour of the day of its pronouncement (the zero-hour rule). Zero-hour rules result in the insolvent party being deemed to have lost its legal capacity from the first moment of the day on which the insolvency decision was handed down. Therefore, the transactions and payments that it carried out between the first hour of the day of insolvency and the moment when the decision declaring its insolvency was handed down, are void or voidable, and at least not enforceable against the receiver.

Zero-hour rules are of course totally inappropriate for interbank transactions at the beginning of the twenty-first century. It is imperative, especially in a gross settlement system, that a recipient can consider a payment received as final and then be able to freely dispose of or transfer it in favor of third parties. Article 7 states therefore that an insolvency proceeding cannot have retroactive effects on "the rights and obligations of a participant arising from, or in connection with, its participation in a system." This provision mainly concerns the validity of transfer orders executed and of collateral provided before the opening of the insolvency proceedings. The same type of rule is also proposed in the Collateral Directive (Article 8.1.). This rule is of general application, whatever the type of system (net or gross).[64]

This neutralizing of the zero-hour rule in the case of insolvency of a participant in a system, could, however, be subject to qualification arising from Recital 13, which states that "nothing in this Directive should prevent a participant or a third party [for example a receiver] from exercising any right or resulting from the underlying transaction which they may have in law to recovery or restitution in respect of a transfer order which has entered a system, e.g., in case of fraud or technical error, as long as this leads neither to the unwinding of netting nor to the revocation of the transfer order in the system."

As the title of the Settlement Finality Directive indicates, the idea of some member states was to ensure the finality, or rather the definitive character of the settlement (*settlement finality*) of transfer orders processed in payment or settlement systems, and not the finality or definitive status of the payments themselves (*payment finality* or *receiver/beneficiary finality*). Under this view, reflected in Recital 13, the netting of transfer orders and the orders themselves can no longer be invalidated or unwound (paragraphs 1 and 2 of Article 3.1), a transfer order can no longer be revoked after the time authorized by the system (Article 5), and insolvency proceedings against a participant can no longer retroactively affect its rights and obligations linked to its participation in a system (Article 7), as far as the system is concerned. But in this narrow interpretation the participant who gives the order, or its receiver, might always act directly against the beneficiary participant (or a subsequent beneficiary) outside the system in order to claim back or to recover the amount transferred (cash or securities) in the system. This would not only be possible in case of mistake[65] or fraud,[66] which goes without saying, but also, in all other circumstances[67] in which such a recovery claim could be available pursuant to national law.

In other words, if one took a particularly narrow view, Recital 13, together with the wording of some provisions of the Directive (Articles 3, 5, 7, 9), could be interpreted as meaning that a receiver would be authorized to act outside the system—for example by claiming back the sums paid as a consequence of a netting carried out on the day of insolvency—as long as the netting itself is not called into question "in the system."

Yet again, the payments made by the insolvent participant on the day of its insolvency but prior to the declaration of the insolvency order could be subject to recovery actions by the receiver against the beneficiaries on the grounds that the participant had retroactively lost the right to dispose of its assets. Consequently, these payments—not invalidated as such "in the system"—would be null and void or nonbinding and, therefore, subject to restitution "outside the system."

Such a narrow interpretation would be particularly shocking because it would actually go directly against the spirit and the text of the Directive, which aims precisely at avoiding, for example, the application of such a zero-hour rule or the invalidation of a netting or a transfer order (see Articles 3, 5, and 7). Furthermore, a recital cannot overrule or contradict the provisions of a directive. Member states are responsible for ensuring that the implementation into their national legislation leaves no room whatever for doubt as regards the protection granted to transfer orders executed in their systems.

Article 8 of the Directive is a conflict of laws rule stating that in the event of the insolvency of a participant in a system, the effect of the insolvency proceedings on the rights and obligations of such participant arising from, or in connection with, its participation in a system will be determined by the law of the jurisdiction which governs the system. In spite of a slightly different formulation, this rule is close to the one stipulated by Article 9.1 of the Insolvency Regulation.

This provision is important because, first, it determines by reference to the law of the system the rights and obligations of an insolvent participant for matters which are not specifically covered elsewhere in the Directive. One can refer, for example, to a transfer of contracts or of positions organized by the relevant system, in accordance with local law.

Second, and most importantly, Article 8 sets out a conflict of laws rule (for the EU judge) by stating that, in the event of insolvency proceedings being opened against a defaulting participant (incorporated in the EU or not) in an EU system, the participant's rights and obligations toward the system for matters governed by the Directive (transfers orders, netting, irrevocability, zero-hour, etc.) will be determined by the law governing that system and not by the insolvency law of the defaulting participant. In other words, additional conditions under legislation in the insolvent participant's jurisdiction regarding netting, irrevocability of payments, or the effects of the insolvency decision, will not apply if they differ from the conditions of the law of the system.

The same should apply to the exclusion of a zero-hour rule contained in the insolvency law applicable to a foreign participant to a system: it is the law governing the system, including its rules on the finality of payments in the case of the insolvency of the participant, that will exclusively govern the validity of payments made via this system, as "rights and obligations arising from the participation (of the insolvent party)" in the system in question.

Section IV of the Directive, consisting of Article 9, is devoted to the insulation of rights with respect to collateral security granted to a participant or a central bank of a member state (collateral taker), in the event of the insolvency of the collateral provider.[68]

Article 2(m) defines *collateral security* as "all realisable assets provided under a pledge ..., a repurchase or similar agreement, or otherwise,[69] for the purpose of securing rights and obligations potentially arising in connection with a system, or provided to central banks of the member states or to the (future) European Central Bank."

There is a need to differentiate between, on the one hand, the actual insulation of the collateral security against the insolvency of the debtor, which is the goal of Article 9.1 of the Directive, and, on the other hand, the determination of the law applicable to collateral on book-entry securities recorded in an account, as laid down in Article 9.2.

Insulation of Collateral Security Against Insolvency of the Collateral Provider

The aim of Article 9.1 of the Directive is twofold. Its first goal is to protect the holders of collateral security in relation to participation in a payment or securities settlement system against the negative effects of the law governing the insolvency of a foreign participant (whether or not originating from the EU).

The second objective of Article 9.1 is to ensure the legal effectiveness of collateral security to the extent that it will not be "affected by insolvency proceedings" against the debtor, whether it is a foreign or even domestic insolvency proceeding. The Directive adopts the rule introduced in the Insolvency Regulation (Article 5.1), which allows the collateral taker to realize its collateral without being "affected" by the opening of the debtor's insolvency.[70] The Directive goes even further than the Insolvency Regulation to the extent that a collateral taker will not be affected by the opening of an insolvency, even if the assets provided as collateral (a pledge for example) are located in the same member state as the one where the insolvency proceedings have been opened. By contrast, the Insolvency Regulation (or the winding-up directives) supposes that the pledged assets, in order to benefit from the "non-affected" rule, must be located in a member state other than the country where the insolvency proceedings have been opened. The creditor may, under this hypothesis, realize the collateral as if insolvency proceedings would have simply not been opened, without being bound by the restrictive domestic rules applicable to the realization of collateral in the case of insolvency. This is also the solution adopted in the Collateral Directive (see Articles 4 and 9).

In other words, supposing the insolvency of a participant is governed by the same national law as the one governing the system itself, Article 9.1 means that the collateral taker can realize its collateral (also located in the same jurisdiction) without having to obtain the prior authorization of the receiver or of the competent court, should the national law require this in the case of insolvency of the collateral provider. But it goes without saying that the collateral taker must always comply with the rules under the applicable general law to collateral with respect to the procedures of realization of its collateral—for example, the necessity to sell in an organized market, or at the best possible price. On a similar rule, see Article 4.6 of the Collateral Directive.

The same rule applies to collateral provided to central banks of member states (or to the European Central Bank) by their counterparties, without there being any requirement to have any connection whatever with "a system"[71] or that the counterparty should have the quality of "participant" in the sense of the Directive. The idea is to apply the insulating rule of Article 9.1 to all collateral security transactions of central banks acting in this capacity (see Recital 10)—including monetary policy transactions, interventions on exchange markets, or transactions linked to the management of their external reserves—whether the secured transaction is formally carried out or processed in a system. The same extension is offered for the relations between financial institutions or between financial institutions and their clients in the context of the Collateral Directive (see Article 1.2 (e) and 1.3).

Determination of the Law Applicable to Collateral Security on Book-Entry Securities

The aim of Article 9.2 of the Directive is to determine the law applicable to collateral provided in the form of book-entry records that represent securities accounts or rights in securities (this is the case of physical securities circulating by way of book-entry transfers or dematerialized securities solely represented by book-entry records on accounts). This issue of applicable law is particularly crucial and complex, especially when securities are held on account with a financial institution in one country and then held through a chain of intermediaries with a custodian in another country, which itself then holds such securities with the CSD system where the underlying securities have been directly issued and are primarily held.[72]

Should (1) the law of the country where the underlying securities are issued, or at least where the underlying certificates are ultimately held, be applied, or (2) should one apply the law of the country where the interest in the book-entry securities held on an account is recorded with an intermediary? Article 9.2 of the Directive opts for this second solution, which has been recommended for several years by several international financial market associations.[73] This is also the approach proposed by the Collateral Directive (Article 9) by reference to the place of the relevant intermediary (the one maintaining the account where the collateralized assets are recorded). This rule (PRIMA) is also proposed (with, however, a refined connecting factor referring no longer to the place of the account but, as a rule, to the law governing the account agreement) at the international level by the Hague Conference on Private International Law in its Convention on the Law Applicable to Certain Rights in Respect of Securities Held with an Intermediary.[74]

Article 9.2 of the Settlement Finality Directive thus aims at ensuring that if a participant (or a central bank of a member state) holds securities as collateral security in a register or an account[75] held with an intermediary situated in a member state, its rights as collateral taker will be governed by the law of the member state where the register or account (recording the provision of collateral)[76] is held.[77, 78]

As "local law" (the law of the jurisdiction where the relevant assets subject to collateral are located), the law of the intermediary maintaining the collateral account will govern the nature of the rights of the collateral taker on the securities, the enforceability vis-à-vis third parties (perfection governed by *lex rei sitae*) and the realization rules (see also Article 9.2 of the Collateral Directive).

Article 9.2 of SFD appears to be designed for collateral security in the form of book-entry securities, taking the form of a pledge for example. In the case of secured transactions in the form of a repo, this rule should mean, that the validity and enforceability against third parties of the transfer of ownership (with respect to the book-entry securities) will be governed by the law of the member state where the interests representing the securities transferred are recorded, without prejudice to the application of the law governing the transaction itself (applicable as *lex contractus*) with respect to the counterparts' various contractual obligations.

The implementation of the Directive into domestic law was due by December 11, 1999, and today all EU and EEA countries have implemented the Directive in their national laws, even though most EU countries seem to have followed a narrow interpretation of the Directive (in particular with respect to Article 9, by restricting its application at national level to collateral constituted in favor of a central bank or of the system's operator, but not to collateral between participants). A revision of this Directive is presently considered by the EU Commission.

Directive 2002/47/EC on Financial Collateral Arrangements of 6 June 2002

The importance of collateral transactions for the smooth and efficient functioning of domestic and international financial markets is obvious today. According to the preparatory report prepared by the EU Commission on 15 June 2000[79]:

- As of the beginning of 1999, the total value of government securities on loan or repo in the majority of EU countries was estimated at US$900 billion. The size of the market in the United States was approximately twice as large.

- An ISDA[80] collateral survey concerning the size and complexity of the market for collateralized over-the-counter (OTC) derivatives estimated that the value of the collateral held in the OTC derivatives market at the end of 1999 amounted to approximately US$250 billion.

- At the beginning of 2000, the European Central Bank held collateral of around €550 billion, of which nearly €160 billion was held on a cross-border basis.

Collateral in the form of pledge or transfer-of-title arrangements is used by financial institutions, corporations (major commercial companies active on the financial markets), central banks, and other financial public entities for trading, investment, and financing purposes as a way to manage their credit risk on counterparts and the market risks on the various assets subject to such collateral transactions, especially if the use of collateral[81] can lead to regulatory ("Basle ratios") and tax/accounting favorable treatment (neutralization of any capital gain or accrued income deriving from a transfer of assets in favor of the collateral taker that has to transfer back the assets once reimbursed at the end of the transaction).

It is therefore paramount to use collateral techniques that benefit from sound legal protection, in order to allow the collateral taker to recover in case of default (in particular in insolvency situations) the amount of its exposures on the defaulted counterpart. Such legal soundness is generally required by banking regulators for capital adequacy purposes,[82] but it is also strictly necessary from a risk-management and audit viewpoint, and carefully monitored by rating agencies as part of their credit assessment of the relevant institution acting as collateral taker. Collateral instruments must therefore be valid and binding between parties, enforceable (or good) against third parties, and the assets so provided must be easily and rapidly realized (by way of sale or appropriation or by way of set-off in the case of claims), notwithstanding any insolvency proceedings affecting the collateral provider.

This legal robustness should not only be ensured at the domestic level (assuming that both collateral taker and collateral provider would be situated in the same country, dealing domestically without any cross-border aspects) but also at the cross-border level for transactions between institutions from different countries making a collateral transaction under an agreement governed by the law of another jurisdiction related to assets located[83] or held with an intermediary CSD, international CSD, global custodian, local agent/custodian) operating in a fourth country. In such a case, the collateral taker will have to take into account the regime of at least three different laws to assess the legal soundness of the transaction:

- The law governing the collateral agreement (*lex contractus*), generally the law explicitly selected by the parties according to the Rome Convention in the EU and to basic principles of conflict of laws of most countries, as regards the validity and the binding character of the agreement between parties, which will govern the contractual aspects of their collateral arrangements;

- The law governing the proprietary aspects of such collateral transaction (being, in case of a security interest in the form of a pledge, the formalities to create a *right in rem* of the type agreed to by the parties, giving a preferential right over unsecured creditors on the proceeds of the pledged assets, and in the case of a transfer of title, the method to transfer the ownership of the assets as agreed to by the parties), including the formalities required, if any, to perfect[84] the collateral in order to make it enforceable against third parties. Such law will be determined, generally pursuant to the *lex rei sitae* (or *lex situs* in the Anglo-Saxon terminology), by reference to the local law where the assets pledged or transferred are located. This law will also govern the realization of the assets that are the subject matter of the collateral.

- The law governing the possible insolvency—whether under the form of a reorganization (aiming at restoring the financial soundness of the debtor) or of a bankruptcy proceeding (aiming at liquidating the assets of the debtor)—of the collateral provider, which will generally be determined by reference to the law of the country where the head/main office of the insolvent debtor is situated. But local insolvency proceedings may also be opened in other countries where the insolvent collateral provider may have branches or assets.[85] Such insolvency law(s) may affect the collateral, either by invalidating the collateral arrangement as constituting a preference (or a fraudulent conveyance) if made during a certain period before the bankruptcy order, or by freezing any foreclosure or realization of the assets during a certain period after insolvency, which will be subject to prior authorization of the receiver (stay), or by subordinating the preferential claim of the collateral taker to other special classes of preferred creditors (employees or tax authorities, for example), downgrading as a result the expected ranking of the collateral taker.[86]

With regard to these cross-border aspects of collateral transactions, the chapter has reviewed above[87] the European legal context already in place for achieving legal certainty for collateral (especially in case of insolvency of the collateral provider), which consists in particular of the Directive 98/26/EC of 19 May 1998 on Settlement Finality in Payment and Securities Settlement Systems [88] (in particular Article 9) as well as of Directive 2001/24/EC of 4 April 2001 on the Reorganisation and Winding-up of Credit Institutions [89] (in particular Articles 21, 23–27 "WUD"), the Directive 2001/17/EC of 19 March 2001 on the Re-organisation and Winding-up of Insurance Undertakings,[90] and the Council Regulation (EC) No.1346/2000 of 29 May 2000 on insolvency proceedings [91] (in particular Articles 5, 6 and 9). (About this legal framework, see also the fourth recital of the Collateral Directive.)

With respect to the substantive rules governing collateral transactions once being determined by application of the conflict of laws rules, without application of foreign insolvency laws of the collateral provider, it is worth mentioning that in the early 1990s most OECD countries started a general review of their domestic financial laws, generally under the pressure of G-10 or EU bodies[92] or of their national market players, in order to improve their collateral regime on the different aspects mentioned above. This trend was enhanced with the establishment of the European Central Bank in 1998, which wanted to ensure that an adequate legal framework was in place in the EU for the development of ESCB monetary policy transactions as of January 1999.

But despite such improvements at the domestic level, the collateral regime of several EU countries remains either unfavorable to the extent that (1) domestic laws would leave open some risks of recharacterization of a repurchase transaction or transfer of title into an irregular unenforceable pledge or (2) would still establish undue constraints on the establishment, use, or perfection of a pledge, or on its realization. Netting of claims by way of novation or set-off may also in some countries be void after insolvency. In addition, negative impacts of suspect period rules (in insolvency situations) may still endanger the validity of collateral transactions made in a pre-insolvency period.

This situation led the EU Commission in 1999 to create a working party, the Forum Group on Collateral, which contributed substantially to the definition of the industry's need for legal certainty for collateral transactions. Under the leadership of Mr. Guy Morton and Richard Potok, the Forum proposed a draft directive.[93] After a consultation process, on March 27, 2001, the EU Commission presented a proposal for an EU directive on financial collateral arrangements.[94]

This proposal was intensively discussed under Swedish, and more especially Belgian, EU Council presidencies, which succeeded in reaching a common position at the Brussels ECOFIN of December, 13, 2001 (only nine months after the initial proposal, which is indeed remarkably fast in EU legislative matters). After a quick and constructive co-decision process with the EU Parliament during the first half of 2002, the directive was adopted in final form on June 6, 2002.[95]

This section discusses the provisions of EU Directive 2002/47/EC on Financial Collateral Arrangements (hereafter the Collateral Directive)[96] and describes its rationale (which is also well described in the detailed recitals of the Directive, which read like a kind of "user guide"[97] to some provisions of the Collateral Directive.[98]) The discussion provides a first commentary of the Collateral Directive rather than a detailed exposition in a comparative law manner.[99] The following discussion reviews the scope of the Collateral Directive, the removal of collateral formalities, the pledge's provisions, provisions for the transfer of title, the provisions common to both collateral instruments, and the applicable law. It concludes by looking at the foreseeable achievements of the Collateral Directive.

The Scope of the Collateral Directive

The scope of the Collateral Directive was among the most sensitive topics during the consultation process and discussions at the EU legislative level. Indeed, while almost all members states' representatives were of the opinion that such a directive was necessary to remove remaining legal risks from substantive laws within the EU for the benefit of financial markets and transactions, there were also diverging views with respect to the assets to be covered and more importantly about the type of counterpart qualifying as a protected collateral taker and collateral provider.

Relevant Types of Collateral Instruments

Pursuant to Article 1.1, the Collateral Directive applies to "financial collateral arrangements" (hereafter collateral) that take the form of either a "security financial collateral arrangement" or a "title transfer financial collateral arrangement" as defined in Article 2.1. This definition covers basically any type of contractual[100] security interest (especially a pledge) where the collateral provider remains the owner of the pledged assets, and transfer of title for security purposes (including in particular repurchase transactions), where assets are transferred (against others) in full ownership but with the duty to retrocede equivalent assets at the maturity of the transaction.[101] Additional constitution of collateral by way of margin calls ("top-up" collateral aiming at marking-to-market the value of the assets to cover both parties against any market risk deriving from changes in the market value of the assets) is also protected (see, in particular, Article 8.3).

Relevant Assets

The Collateral Directive applies to collateral relating to cash or financial instruments (Article 1.4 (a)). By cash, the Collateral Directive is referring to cash credited to an account (Article 2.1 (d)), which means that in most countries the subject of a pledge of cash will be the claim in reimbursement against the institution holding the cash account, since the cash itself will become the property of the intermediary as a result of the fungibility of cash deposits, unless otherwise organized by the law governing the cash account. Banknotes as such are explicitly excluded, according to Recital 18.

By financial instruments (hereafter securities), the Collateral Directive means:

> Shares in companies and other securities equivalent to shares in companies and bonds and other forms of debt instruments if these are negotiable on the capital market, and any other securities which are normally dealt in and which give the right to acquire any such shares, bonds or other securities by subscription, purchase or exchange or which give rise to a cash settlement (excluding instruments of payment), including units in collective investment undertakings, money market instruments and claims relating to or rights in or in respect of any of the foregoing. (Article 2.1 (e))

This definition is intended to cover all debt and equity instruments (including warrants, options, and futures) as well as the securities entitlement organized in some jurisdictions (Belgium, Luxembourg, and the United States) giving to the holder of a securities account not direct and traceable property rights on the underlying securities held abroad via sub-custodians, but co-ownership rights on a pool of fungible securities. (The co-ownership right does not apply directly on each of the underlying securities held on a fungible pooled basis but on the book-entry interests in securities as recorded in the books of the intermediary.) In such systems, what is transferred or pledged is not the underlying securities but the co-ownership rights of the collateral provider on the pool of book-entry fungible securities vis-à-vis the intermediary holding the securities account. This is the sense of the term right in or in respect of any of the foregoing.[102]

Claims against the intermediary holding the securities account in question in relation to (actual or future) delivery of securities to be recorded on the account are also covered by the definition and may be subject to collateral arrangements under the Collateral Directive.

Type of Protected Counterparts

Several countries (possibly under the pressure of their ministry of justice) did not want to extend the benefit of the protective regime to nonfinancial institutions (*a fortiori* not to natural persons), while others were more favorable to the inclusion of commercial companies active on financial markets, at least those having a certain size in terms of capital/own assets and which could not be regarded as a weak party when dealing with financial counterparts.

This last conception was proposed by the Commission in its initial proposal that included a "person ... whose capital base exceeds EUR 100 million or whose gross assets exceed EUR 1000 million at the time where financial collateral is actually delivered...." (Article 2.4 (c)). But the common determination of the financial base—and the thresholds—in relation to a specific collateral transaction was too complicated in view of the above divergence of approaches.

In order to reach an agreement on the Collateral Directive, a compromise was finally found in the scope of Article 1.2. (a) to (e), including:

- All financial institutions (credit institutions, insurance undertakings, collective investments firms, investment firms, other financial institutions) under the meaning of applicable directives;

- Public bodies (including treasury agencies, financial institutions of public nature), central banks, the European Central Bank (plus the Bank for International Settlements, International Monetary Fund, European Investment Bank, etc);

- Central counterpart in clearing systems (Clearnet, LCH, etc) and settlement agent or clearing house under the meaning of the Settlement Finality Directive (operators and transfer/paying agents in securities settlement systems designated by each member state) and assimilated representatives (see Article 1.2 (d));

- "A person other than a natural person,[103] including unincorporated firms and partnerships, provided that the other party is an institution as defined" above.

Commercial undertakings are therefore included as possible counterparts in financial collateral arrangements without requiring any minimal financial conditions. However, Article 1.3 reserves the faculty for a member state to exclude from the scope of the Collateral Directive financial collateral arrangements where one of the parties is such a nonfinancial person, at the request of those countries that were opposed to such inclusion. (On the consequences of such opting-out, see below in Conclusions).

Subject to the above possible exclusion, the Collateral Directive will apply if both collateral provider and collateral taker(s) belong to the above categories (Article 1.2) if both are financial institutions or at least one financial institution dealing with one nonfinancial legal person (e.g., a company).

Removal of Collateral Formalities

One goal of the Collateral Directive is to simplify the various formalities prescribed by some national laws, especially in pledging arrangements, for the creation or the validity of a pledge between parties (such as, e.g., written agreement, delivery of the assets, certification by way of notarial/public registration), its perfection or enforceability against third parties (delivery of the pledged assets, notification, publicity by way of registration of the pledge agreement in a public register (filing as foreseen, for example, by Section 395 of the UK Companies Act 1985) that can be required in the country where the assets are located and/or in the country of the incorporation of the collateral provider, etc) or even its admissibility as evidence (notarial document, stamp, deed).

To that end, Article 3 states that "member states shall not require that the creation, validity, perfection, enforceability or admissibility in evidence of a financial collateral arrangement or the provision of financial collateral under a financial collateral arrangement be dependent on the performance of any formal act." Recital 10 gives a nonexhaustive list of such formal acts.[104]

This removal of external formalities relating to pledging and transfer of title arrangements does not mean, however, that financial collateral can be established by mere oral agreement between collateral provider and collateral taker without any externalization of their will to create such collateral. There are indeed two types of mitigating factors that are foreseen by the Collateral Directive:

• There is still a practical need to deliver the assets subject to a pledge or a transfer of title to the collateral taker, either in its account or in an account held on behalf of both parties by a third party (which can be the operator of a settlement system or any other custodian) or even to keep the assets in the account of the collateral provider but pledged in favor of a collateral taker with adequate measures to block the taking of such assets by the intermediary holding the account. Otherwise, the collateral taker would be in a situation where in case of default of the collateral provider, the collateral might have lost its object—and therefore its goal—because of the previous transfer of the assets to another party (assuming the good faith of the latter, which should be usually the case, especially in the absence of any publicity measures) if no blocking measure was put in place.

This is why the Collateral Directive is only applicable to collateral "once it has been provided" (Article 3.2; see also Article 1.5), which means once "delivered, transferred, held, registered or otherwise designated so as to be *in the possession or under the control* [emphasis added] of the collateral taker or of a person acting on the collateral taker's behalf' (Article 2.2; see also Recital 9). A typical example is the usual practice of identifying assets as being pledged through the use of designated pledged securities and cash accounts—in the name of the collateral taker or even in the name of the collateral provider as long as the assets posted in such pledged account can be blocked up to the amount of the guaranteed claim or exposure of the collateral taker—held with an intermediary. A certain form of dispossession is therefore required under the Collateral Directive (see Recital 10), which should give some comfort to those jurisdictions that were either reluctant to completely remove collateral formalities or wish to preserve this traditional feature of pledging arrangement linked to their *right in rem*'s nature implying as a rule dispossession (as in French or Belgian law).

- The second mitigating factor is the requirement of written evidence for both the collateral agreement (the Collateral Directive refers to an "arrangement," without defining what it means, which seems broader that just the pledge or transfer of title agreement, but in practice one may wonder what it is intended to cover) and the provision of such collateral (Articles 1.5 and 3.2)[105.]

The Collateral Directive specifies that such evidence of the provision of collateral "must allow for the identification of the financial collateral to which it applies. For this purpose, it is sufficient to prove that the book entry securities [evidenced by entries in a register or account maintained by or on behalf of an intermediary: Article 2.1 (f)] provided as collateral have been credited to, or form a credit in, the relevant account [as defined under 2.1 (h); see below] and that the cash collateral has been credited to, or forms a credit in, a designated account" (Article 1.5, second paragraph).

The Collateral Directive adopts a modern approach by allowing consideration of book-entries evidenced "by electronic means and any durable medium" (Article 2.3) and more generally any evidence "legally equivalent" to written evidence (Article 3.2) that seems to refer to other admissible evidence (see in that sense Recital 11: "in any other legally enforceable manner" foreseen by the *lex contractus*) under some national legislations as in commercial matters, where a court may in its discretion determine if an obligation is established, including by way of testimony and assumptions.

Security Financial Collateral Arrangement (Pledging)

Two provisions of the Collateral Directive address pledging arrangements: Article 5, establishing a right of use of the pledged assets by the collateral taker, and Article 4 on the enforcement of such pledging arrangements.

Right of Use (Article 5)

Such right of use (or reuse) on the side of the collateral taker (sometimes also known as rehypothecation, especially in U.S. practice) seems rather revolutionary for jurisdictions influenced by the French Code Napoleon to the extent that under these laws a pledgee cannot as a rule dispose in any manner of the pledged assets (especially by using them in the course of another transaction with a third party), since this is not regarded as an admissible right for a collateral taker,[106] who should instead take care of the assets still belonging to the debtor who has the right to recover them back upon payment of the secured claim of the pledgee. In case of infringement of such prohibition, the pledgee may even lose the rights held as secured creditor on the reused assets ("déchéance pour abus de jouissance"; see Article 2082 of French civil code).

However, in the international financial markets, such right of use is common among many players (especially with U.S. counterparts), who consider this latitude as a prerequisite to mobilize efficiently their collateral portfolio instead of freezing it in the framework of "classical" pledges, in cases where, for any reason,[107] transfer of title (implying by nature a transfer of full ownership with the associated right of reuse for the transferee) may not be available. The downside is, of course, that by allowing the use of the pledged assets by the collateral taker for the purposes of other transactions with third parties (outright sales, repo, margins, pledges, loans), the initial collateral provider is exposed to a credit risk on its creditor since it would have no guarantee that once fully reimbursed, the collateral taker will be able to transfer back equivalent assets to those initially pledged and reused in the meantime.

In order to give European financial institutions the same flexibility enjoyed already by some market players, it was agreed to introduce such right of use for the collateral taker in pledging arrangements under the following conditions:

- The terms of the collateral arrangement must provide for such right (Article 5.1).

- The collateral taker must incur an obligation (which can then be set-off; see the following bullet point) to transfer equivalent collateral[108] (to the one used) at the latest on the due date for the performance of the secured obligations (Article 5.2).

- On that date, either the initial pledged assets will be replaced by equivalent assets, or the value of such assets in replacement due by the collateral taker will be set-off against the amount of the secured claim owed to it by the collateral provider, in order to give to the latter a certain protection against pledgee's default.

- The equivalent collateral shall not give rise to a new pledge (that may be challenged as preference or by virtue of any suspect period rules), but instead will continue to be governed by the initial security financial collateral arrangement provided at the same time as the initial collateral (Article 5.3).

- Such right of use can no longer be sanctioned by a "déchéance" or any termination of the pledge or of the rights of the pledgee (Article 5.4).

- In case of default, close-out netting should be allowed in order to give effect, if necessary, to the set-off laid down in Article 5.2, second paragraph.

Enforcement of pledge arrangements (Article 4, paragraphs 1–4)

Contrary to the heading of the provision, the first four paragraphs of Article 4[109] aim at addressing enforcement only of security financial collateral arrangement (pledging) by requiring members states to ensure that in case of default of the collateral provider (defined by the concept of "enforcement event"[110]), the collateral taker shall be able to realize the assets pledged in accordance with the terms of the collateral agreement through one of the following methods:

- For securities, by way of sale or appropriation[111] of the assets;

- For cash (and securities if any), by way of setting off the amount of cash (or the value of the securities) against the amount of the secured obligations due to the collateral taker (Article 4.2).

As one can see, appropriation of the assets is foreseen in addition to the classical way of enforcing rights of a pledgee through the sale of the assets. This is also quite revolutionary for some jurisdictions (again generally those inspired by French civil law[112]), where appropriation of the pledged assets by the pledgee is traditionally not allowed (it is even a public policy prohibition: see Article 2078 of the French Civil Code and Articles 4 and 10 of Belgian law relating to commercial pledge) since it is viewed as eluding the formal requirement to seek the prior authorization of the competent court before realizing the assets—which is the normal rule—or, as an exception, by appropriating them[113] again upon prior judicial authorization. But such formal requirement to obtain prior judicial authorization before any enforcement has been gradually removed in the collateral laws of most countries over the past ten years, so that appropriation as such should no longer be regarded as conflicting with the key features of pledging arrangements, especially in the financial area.

It is again open to member states that did not allow appropriation on the date of the Collateral Directive (June 27, 2002) to refuse to implement in their legislation such an appropriation mechanism for pledge arrangements and accordingly—which is more debatable in our view—not to recognize it when laid down in pledging arrangements governed by another law that would organize such a technique (Article 4.3). This is another opting-out provision introduced for the sake of compromise.

All enforcement techniques (sale, appropriation, and set-off) of pledging arrangements must take place in accordance with the terms of the pledge agreement, without being subject to any other external requirement that would be laid down in national law—such as to give prior notice, to seek prior judicial authorization, to organize a public auction, or to observe a certain time period (Article 4.4)—before realizing the pledged assets in order to be paid on the proceeds (or as a result of the appropriation or set-off). As mentioned above, this simplification of the enforcement proceedings was already introduced in many European and U.S. laws in the past few years, and the objective is now to impose such simplified realization proceedings within the EU, beyond the scope of the Settlement Finality Directive focusing on designated systems and their participants. With the Collateral Directive, the aim is now to encompass all collateral transactions between financial institutions (and even with commercial companies, subject to EU member states' opting-out) whether or not made through a system.

Protection of Transfer of Title Arrangements (Article 6)

Article 6.1 states very simply that "member states shall ensure that a title transfer financial collateral arrangement can take effect in accordance with its terms," which means that the validity of a transfer of title for security purposes can no longer be put in question through its recharacterization by a court into a pledge (see Recital 13).

In the 1980s the validity of a repurchase transaction (repo)—a spot sale of securities against cash coupled with the reversed forward sale transaction where the initial buyer, in turn, resells equivalent securities to the initial seller—was challenged in the United States[114] because of the economic purposes of such a transaction, which can be regarded as credit in cash secured by way of securities transferred as collateral (one could also see it as a loan of securities secured by cash), while from a legal point of view it is a sale implying a full transfer of ownership of the securities to the buyer, even if it is a transfer of ownership for security purposes. This economic approach is generally the one adopted from a tax and accounting viewpoint that tends to analyze the transaction as a secured credit, the securities remaining accounted as belonging to the seller, who is also the beneficial owner of the income attributed during the life of the repo, unless otherwise agreed. Such an analysis was then used to challenge the legal qualification of (double) sale to recharacterize the repo into a pledge (in view of its economic purpose) generally void or nonenforceable because of nonfulfilment of the formalities required for the creation or the perfection of such pledge.[115]

The same debate took place almost everywhere in Europe and generated a wave of legislative reforms in order to remove such legal risk of recharacterization and to organize specifically the rights of the nondefaulting party in case of failure of the other party (the right to sell the assets or to purchase equivalent securities, depending on the position of the non-defaulting party; the right to keep the assets as a result of the transfer of ownership; and close-out netting of the reciprocal obligations by set-off).[116] Besides a true repo, there are other types of transfer of ownership for security purposes (transfer of title) that face the same kind of legal risks and for which it was necessary to achieve legal certainty.

Article 6.2 deals with the hypothesis of a default of a counterpart (enforcement event) triggering the application of a close-out netting, which is a setting-off of all[117] the reciprocal obligations to deliver cash and securities, including assets provided as margins, to mitigate the exposure of the nondefaulting party vis-à-vis the party in default, organized to take place automatically in case of bankruptcy or upon notice. The specific purpose of Article 6.2 is not clear because Article 7 deals more extensively with close-out netting provisions in all collateral arrangements.[118]

Common Provisions Applicable to Both Pledge and Transfer of Title: Close-out Netting and Insolvency (Article 4, paragraphs 5 and 6; Articles 7 and 8)

Article 7 aims to ensure that close-out netting provisions, stipulated in pledge and transfer of title arrangements, may apply and will remain valid and enforceable notwithstanding the opening of insolvency proceedings, either reorganization or bankruptcy, against one of the parties (Art. 7.1 (a)) or the occurrence of any competition between creditors imposing, in certain jurisdictions, an equality of treatment (*pari passu* ranking) (Art. 7.1 (b)). Such close-out netting provisions must apply in accordance with their terms without being subject to external requirements such as a prior notice or the need to obtain prior approval from a courts, unless otherwise agreed.

In the same vein, Article 4.5 stipulates the same regime for financial collateral arrangements as a whole, which must take effect in accordance with their terms notwithstanding the opening of insolvency proceedings, either reorganization or bankruptcy, against one of the parties.

Article 4.6 also states that enforcement of rights (including close-out netting) of the collateral taker as organized under Articles 4, 5, 6, and 7 "shall be without prejudice to any requirements under national law to the effect that the realization or valuation of financial collateral and the calculation of the relevant financial obligations must be conducted in a commercially reasonable manner" in order to allow for an ex post control by the court on the manner by which the collateral taker enforced its rights (see Recital 17) and to hold him liable for any abuse in the exercise of such rights. An example of such an abuse would be the sale of the relevant assets at a substantial discount from their market value when it would have been possible, without major damage for the creditor, to proceed to such realization in a different manner.[119]

Article 8 deals with the neutralization of certain insolvency rules (mainly in a bankruptcy situation because the rules in question are generally not foreseen in reorganization proceedings) to provide collateral arrangements with more legal certainty and predictability. First of all, Article 8.1(a) aims to protect both the collateral agreement and subsequent provision of assets (constituting the pledge or achieving the transfer of ownership in transfer of title) against the rules of some insolvency regimes under which an insolvency decision is deemed to have retroactive legal effects from the first hour of the day of its pronouncement—the zero-hour rule.

As indicated earlier, zero-hour rules result in the insolvent party being deemed to have lost its legal capacity from the first moment of the day on which the insolvency decision was handed down. Therefore the transactions and payments carried out between the first hour of the day of insolvency and the moment when the decision declaring its insolvency was handed down are void or voidable, and at least not enforceable against the receiver. In the United Kingdom, for instance, certain transactions (property dispositions) may be voided if they have been made between the introduction of a winding-up petition and the day when the final winding-up resolution is taken by the general assembly of creditors or shareholders as ratified by the court.[120] In the financial area, most countries where such zero-hour rules still apply have enacted special legislation to exclude its application with respect to financial transactions (see also Article 7 of the Settlement Finality Directive), but some uncertainties remain in certain jurisdictions.

It is now laid down in Article 8.1(a) that such zero-hour rules can no longer invalidate the collateral agreement or provision entered into or made on the day of the insolvency but prior to the moment when the insolvency decision being handed down. The same protection is extended by Article 8.2[121] to a collateral agreement or provision entered into or made on the day of the insolvency of one party but *after* the moment of the insolvency decision, provided that the collateral taker can prove that it was not aware, nor should have been aware, of the commencement of such proceedings or measures. A protective rule for parties acting in good faith was adopted in Article 3.1 second alinea[122] of the Settlement Finality Directive for payment orders and their settlement in payment and settlement systems.

The second important rule, which has some precedent in the Settlement Finality Directive (Article 3.2)[123] aims to exclude the application of preference rules (or, in French law, the "suspect period" rules) in order to avoid collateral agreements or subsequent provisions of collateral being declared invalid or unenforceable just because they would have been entered into or made in a certain period of time (six months, two years, and so on) preceding the insolvency order (Article 8.1.(b)). This type of protection is a major derogation to the normal insolvency regime of all member states where, in order to protect the general creditors against any last-minute attempt to defraud them, certain acts of the debtor are deemed to be fraudulent or detrimental to the general creditors and therefore are void or voidable. Those types of preference rules (applicable by reference to certain acts if carried out during a certain period) will no longer apply to collateral arrangements or provisions. (See Article 8.1: "collateral may not be declared invalid ... on the sole basis that...."). But this does not remove fraudulent-conveyances rules or other types of suspect period rules based on fraud ("Fraus pauliana") that will continue to apply (see Article 8.4) if evidence of fraud is demonstrated. The broad wording of such a provision may well appear to contradict the rules laid down in the previous paragraphs of Article 8, but in order to give some sense to this Article, paragraph 4 should be read as reserving only suspect period rules that do not apply automatically and for which evidence of fraudulent intention is required (see Recital 16).

The same protective regime against zero-hour and preference rules is made applicable to the provision of additional collateral (margins) in order to adapt constantly the contractual value of the collateralized assets to their current market value (marking-to-the-market) that takes place by providing—or delivering back to the collateral provider, if the market value would be higher than the agreed value—additional cash or securities (top-up collateral) (Article 8.3 (a)). The same also applies (Article 8.3.(b)) to substitutions of the initial assets by new ones (which may completely differ from the previous assets transferred as collateral) of substantially the same value (see, for instance, the regime of margins and substitutions in Articles 4 and 8 of the 2000 Global Master Repurchase Agreement).

Article 8.3(ii) specifically protects margin transfers and substitutions against the risk of being qualified as a new pledge created during the suspect period to cover pre-existing claims, which is generally void under certain insolvency legislations. (Transfer of title generally does not give rise to the same issue unless it is first recharacterised into a pledge.) This protection is still subject to a fraud exception according to the interpretation this chapter gives to paragraph 4 of Article 8.

Conflict of Laws (Article 9)

The aim of Article 9 is to determine the law applicable to collateral provided in the form of book-entry securities recorded in securities accounts for the purposes of the *lex rei sitae* (or *lex situs*[124]) rule. The issue of applicable law is particularly crucial, especially when securities are held on account with a financial institution in one country and then held through a chain of intermediaries with a custodian in another country which itself then holds such securities with the central securities depositary system where the underlying securities have been directly issued and are primarily held.[125] In that context, one must take into account the type of entitlement that is granted on the basis of the intermediary's books to reflect such indirect holding of securities though sub-custodians and CSDs. Usually, in cross-border holdings, the securities accounts of the investor with its intermediary recording a deposit of foreign securities will represent not the underlying securities themselves[126] but a securities entitlement consisting of interests in the underlying securities[127] (or rights in such securities) that may be protected by law to give the investor a co-ownership right in a book-entry pool of fungible securities of the same kind as those recorded in the investor's account.

Should the law of the country where the underlying securities are issued, or at least where the underlying certificates are ultimately held, be applicable? Or should one apply instead the law of the country where the interest in the book-entry securities held on an account is recorded with an intermediary? As mentioned earlier, Article 9.2 of the Settlement Finality Directive opted for the second solution. This is also the approach chosen in Article 24 of the Directive of 4 April 2001 on the Reorganisation and the Winding-up of Credit Institutions.[128] This is also the rule set by the Collateral Directive (Article 9) for book-entry securities collateral (see definition under Article 2.1 (g)) by reference to the law of the country[129] in which the relevant account is maintained).

The relevant account is defined under Article 2.1 (h) as "the register or account—which may be maintained by the collateral taker—in which the entries are made by which that book entry securities collateral is provided to the collateral taker," meaning the account where the assets (securities or rights in the securities) are recorded as being pledged or transferred, which is not so far from what Article 9.2 of the Settlement Finality Directive already stated or implied.

Since Article 9 of the Collateral Directive aimed to mirror the latest draft Convention of the Hague Conference (at the time of the EU council's works), and since it appeared that the Collateral Directive was likely to be adopted before the finalization of the work on the Hague Convention, the EU Council then decided[130] "...to establish the place of the relevant intermediary (PRIMA) principle in the Directive, without going into further details at this stage" with the intention "that, when the Conference has been finalised, Article 9 may have to be reviewed in the light of the outcome of the Convention."

Conclusions on the Collateral Directive

The Collateral Directive has been an important step forward in the realization of a single, harmonized European financial market since following its implementation it has led a number of member states to improve the legal framework of collateral transactions within the EU as a continuation of the notable progress already made in this field with the Settlement Finality Directive, the Directive on the Reorganisation and Winding-up of Credit Institutions, the Directive on Insurance Undertakings, and the Insolvency Regulation.[131] In particular, the Collateral Directive improved the substantive regime[132] of pledge and repurchase transactions and removed most of the legal risks and undue constraints on the establishment or the perfection of a pledge, or on its realization, that still existed in some EU jurisdictions.

In addition, the Collateral Directive has introduced some flexibility, especially for the benefit of pledging arrangements, by allowing the collateral taker to use the pledged assets (while protecting at the same time the collateral provider against credit risk on the pledgee) and to appropriate them in case of default, features that had been regarded as specific to transfer-of-title arrangements. By doing so, the Collateral Directive has erased the differences between pledge and transfer of title and the reasons for opting for one technique over the other. One could wonder whether in the long run these two instruments in the financial area will not merge with each other.

That being said, the Collateral Directive may suffer from the political compromise that enabled its rapid adoption by including various options for opting-out that allow some member states not to implement or even not to recognize in their national regime the inclusion of nonfinancial companies or the appropriation regime in pledging arrangements. Such dual regimes will certainly penalize the market players in the jurisdictions that would not implement such rules and also maintain a certain degree of complexity and legal uncertainty in the EU collateral framework, which is neither desirable nor expected as a result of this Directive.

The EU Commission will probably have to help member states coordinate closely in the implementation process to make sure things will evolve in the right direction.[133] Consistency in the implementation of the other EU instruments (SFD, WUD, and the Insolvency Regulation) will also have to be taken into account, as well as with other international conventions finalized or under negotiation (the Hague Securities Convention and the draft UNIDROIT Convention on Intermediated Securities).

New Developments Relating to Conflict of Laws and Harmonizations of Securities Legislation Relevant to Payment and Securities Settlement Systems

Since 2002, initiatives have been taken at the international level to enhance legal certainty for transactions on book-entry securities, in terms of applicable law (the finalization of the Hague Securities Convention at end-2002) or with respect to their substantive regime (UNIDROIT and the EU Legal Certainty Project).

The Hague Securities Convention on the Law Applicable to Certain Rights in Respect of Securities Held with an Intermediary

The Hague Convention on the Law Applicable to Certain Rights in Respect of Securities Held with an Intermediary (the Securities Convention), adopted in first instance by the 19th diplomatic session of the Hague Conference on Private International Law[134] on December, 13 2002, aims to provide greater legal certainty and predictability in cross-border transactions on book-entry securities held through intermediaries.

Unlike the EU instruments discussed above (which refer to the jurisdiction in which the relevant account is held or maintained), the Securities Convention adopts a subjective approach to determine the applicable law by reference namely to the law selected to govern the account agreement (or, if different from the custody law, by reference to the law agreed to govern proprietary aspects relating to book-entry securities) provided that the intermediary in question has an office (e.g., a branch) in the country engaged in securities accounts' business as defined (see Article 4.1 of the Securities Convention).

Until now there has been a considerable degree of legal uncertainty at the international level as to the national law governing securities credited to an account with an intermediary in a cross-border dimension due to the variety of possible governing laws (law of the issuer, law of the place where the underlying paper certificates in bearer form may be physically deposited or held, law of the register, law of the issuer CSD, law of another intermediary at upper or lower level, etc). This legal uncertainty generates, in turn, legal risks for the securities industry and the investors to the extent that the law governing the book-entry securities will determine the protection offered to the holder in case of insolvency of the intermediary as well as the formalities to comply with to create, perfect, and enforce collateral arrangements on such securities. The application of another law than the one expected by the parties to the custody relationship might indeed jeopardize the ownership rights of the investor or invalidate its collateral transactions if the requirements of such other laws were not fulfilled.

There have been ways to mitigate such legal risks—for example, collection of legal opinions confirming the application of the intermediary's law under the laws of the country where the underlying securities are deposited and/or under the laws of the collateral provider—but they remain, in a number of countries, still uncertain in case of litigation. At the EU level, some directives have been enacted since 1998[135] with provisions helping to eliminate this uncertainty, but these new rules, even though they substantially increase the level of legal certainty, remain limited to the EU without addressing the rest of the world (United States, Japan, Canada, Switzerland, China), nor all the aspects of securities holdings, nor even all market players. This is what the Hague Securities Convention aims to achieve.

This Convention was "technically"[136] signed at end-2002 by delegates of 53 states that are members of the Hague Conference, including the United States, the EU member states, Japan, Australia, Argentina, Brazil, China, and the Russian Federation. It was signed jointly by the United States and Switzerland on July 5, 2006,[137] and has officially become the [Hague] Convention of 5 July 2006 on the Law Applicable to Certain Rights in Respect of Securities Held with an Intermediary. It now has to be formally executed by one other government to enter into force. In the EU, the Hague Securities Convention's adoption should imply amendments to some EU directives already adopted.[138] However, a formal signing ceremony by the EU was suspended in 2005 because of the opposition by some circles in the EU.

Certain EU member states (essentially France, Spain, Italy, Sweden, and Poland) and the European Central bank have opposed the Securities Convention, arguing that it could lead to more legal uncertainties due to the greater flexibility offered by the Convention in the determination of the law governing the book-entry securities, by reference to the law agreed to govern the account agreement, instead of focusing on the place "where the account is (in fact) maintained."

In June 2005 the EU Council requested that the Commission conduct an impact study on the Hague Convention in relation to its scope, its impacts on third parties, securities settlement systems and public policy legislation. There was quite an intense debate about the pros and the cons of the Securities Convention in 2005,[139] which might have contributed to the resulting impact study, "Legal assessment of certain aspects of the Hague Securities Convention,"[140] which was presented by the EU Commission on July 3, 2006. In a nutshell, the Commission staff recommended that EU member states sign the Securities Convention with an adjustment to the Settlement Finality Directive, to ensure that the freedom given by the Hague Convention to select the law governing the proprietary aspects of book-entry securities will be restricted, for securities systems, to the choice of a single law applicable to the entirety of the securities-accounts part of the relevant system (which seems obvious in our view).[141] EU member states will now have to consider the findings of this study and take a position on the signature and the proposed adjustment of the related EU framework.

The EU Legal Certainty Group

In April 2004 the EU Commission promulgated a communication on clearing and settlement,[142] as a follow-up to the Giovannini reports,[143] listing a number of barriers (including legal and regulatory barriers) in this domain. The Commission suggested a framework directive on clearing and settlement to ensure freedom of services and full right of access to clearing and settlement services providers.[144] After a deep analysis of the market and active discussion with market players, the Commission finally concluded there was no need for such a Directive but called for a Code of Conduct which was adopted by securities market infrastructures (stock exchanges, clearing houses and central securities depositaries) on November 2006.[145]

In parallel, the Commission has set up three advisory working groups:

- The Advisory and Monitoring Group (CESAME) to review the barriers listed in the Giovannini reports and discuss with the Commission topics of harmonization and definitions of certain concepts, such as CSD, settlement, clearing, core or added-value services;[146]

- The Legal Certainty Group (LCG), composed of experts in each EU country but appointed on a personal basis, to identify needs for legal harmonization of substantive securities legislation;[147] and

- The Fiscal Compliance Experts Working Group (FISCO) to focus on the identification of tax barriers such as certain national laws requiring foreign intermediaries carrying out business on a remote basis to still use a domestic intermediary as withholding tax agent.[148]

In 2006 these working groups produced reports identifying barriers and possible ways to harmonize securities and tax regimes in the EU. It is now up to the Commission to decide whether it will translate all or part of those recommendations into a Community instrument (recommendation, directive, or regulation). In particular, the Legal Certainty Group released a report dated 28 July–11 August 2006,[149] which recommended to:

- Adopt new EU legislation harmonizing the legal effects of book entries made on securities accounts, on topics similar to UNIDROIT works;

- Defer the harmonization of the rules applying to the moment of transfer of ownership until there is further progress on other EU initiatives relating to corporate actions;

- Remove legal and regulatory barriers relating to the issuer's ability to choose the location of its securities, meaning that in some jurisdictions there are mandatory contraints imposed on the issuer to deposit or register its securities in that country with the national CSD, with limits on the ability for foreign intermediaries to serve similar functions.

Complementary to these recommendations, there is a proposal by the EU Commission, dated January 5, 2006, on the exercise of voting rights,[150] which presents certain links with the works of the LCG with respect to relations between the intermediaries and their clients and the issuer, particularly in intermediated holding patterns. Article 13 of this proposal states that an omnibus account should be possible in all member states without the need to segregate securities in the name of a particular beneficial owner to exercise voting rights and have access to the general meeting.

Such reforms would constitute a major improvement in the EU because a number of countries (Greece, Spain, and Portugal, for example) do not currently recognize the concept of nominee holdings through an omnibus account (which could prohibit the voting through nominee), or they prevent or penalize the holding of securities in fungible form, continuing to treat the intermediary as sole shareholder for the total position recorded on the omnibus account. Others countries, such as Sweden and Denmark, require segregation for voting purposes.

Harmonization of Market Practices and of Related Legislation and Regulation

Along with these EU initiatives, market players and infrastructure members are also conducting reviews of securities practices (ESCDA, Euroclear, for example) and have offered some harmonization proposals.[151] On the legal side, discussion is focused on barriers relating to nominee holdings, requirements for local presence, direct access to CSDs, treatment of market claims, and harmonization of record date (date of entitlement to dividends and right to vote when securities are transferred).

The need for legal harmonization can also be found in the differences in the transfer of ownership on securities. Legal transfer of ownership may be treated as taking place on the trade date (which was the case until March 2005 in France for stock exchange transactions), while other types of transactions may entail transfer of ownership only on settlement date in the relevant CSD. The latter is the common rule in most EU countries.[152] This variety of regimes has a substantial cost for market claims and tax processing, as every difference results in a different procedure. This could also generate legal risks to the extent that insolvency of a counterparty occurring between transfer of ownership on trade date according to home stock exchange rules and settlement date in a foreign settlement system where the settlement of the same transaction actually takes place, may lead to questions about ownership rights.

The UNIDROIT Draft Convention on Intermediated Securities

In 2002–2003, UNIDROIT undertook a project to create an international convention to harmonize the substantive regime applicable to intermediated book-entry securities. On the basis of a draft convention prepared by an ad-hoc working group, in April 2005 UNIDROIT convened an international conference in Rome to discuss a first draft.[153] After interim meetings on specific topics convened in Bern, Sao Paulo, and Paris, the plenary UNIDROIT conference met in March 2006, November and May 2007 and produced a revised draft convention.[154] A diplomatic conference should finalise the Convention in the course of September 2008 in Geneva.

Similar to the Commission's communication of April 2004 and its Legal Certainty Project, UNIDROIT is seeking to further enhance legal certainty in intermediated holdings of securities by addressing the following issues:

- Legal protection of account holders enforceable in case of insolvency of the relevant intermediary;

- Determination of the rights of the account holder with respect to the securities credited to its account, in particular vis-à-vis the issuer in terms of economic (cash payments, redemption) and noneconomic rights (voting rights), including the recognition of nominee-pooled holding of securities;

- Protection against misappropriation;

- Protection against upper-tier attachment proceedings at the level of the intermediaries of the relevant intermediary;

- Protection of good-faith purchasers/transferees;

- The introduction of a specific regime for Collateral transactions (see Chapter VII of the draft Convention). This part has been designed as a model law to be used especially by emerging markets.

At the EU level, the adoption of the UNIDROIT convention would require a correction of possible inconsistencies in the various EU legal instruments adopted on book-entry securities matters. The EU Commission will, however, be negotiating on behalf of the Community on points of "acquit communautaire"—matters already covered by EU legislation, in particular the Directives on Settlement Finality and Collateral arrangements.

It is fair to note that on a worldwide basis, only a few jurisdictions today offer an adequate legal framework for holding and transferring book-entry securities in a cross-border environment. For example, most jurisdictions may provide investors with a sound ownership regime on domestic securities held directly with the domestic CSD or with domestic intermediaries. But only a few legal regimes have enacted specific rules for holding and pledging, under domestic law, securities primarily issued and deposited abroad through an account of the relevant intermediary with the foreign issuer's CSD or with a local custodian.[155]

The current UNIDROIT draft convention also defines the duties of the intermediary towards the account holder (entries to the account, reversals, finality, securities shortfalls, loss sharing) in a way that sometimes overlaps with current regulatory regimes in place at the international or national level.

Regulatory Developments Relevant for Clearing and Settlement Activities

In November 2001 the Committee on Payment and Settlement Systems (CPSS) of the central banks of the Group of Ten countries and the Technical Committee of the International Organisation of Securities Commissions (IOSCO) published a set of standards, the "Recommendations for Securities Settlement Systems."[156] The objective of the 19 CPSS-IOSCO recommendations is to contribute to financial stability by strengthening the securities settlement systems (SSS) that are an increasingly important component of the global financial infrastructure. The CPSS-IOSCO also developed an assessment methodology[157] for the recommendations, which aimed to provide a clear and comprehensive methodology for the assessments made on the basis of the recommendations.

In November 2004 the CPSS and IOSCO published their "Recommendations (15) for Central Counterparties" (CCP/clearing institutions), following the same design of those applicable to securities systems with the adaptations required for the activity of a CCP that uses netting by novation to interface traders and manages its credit risk through margin requirements and marking-to-market procedures.

Depending on the locale, there are two or three types of regulatory standards applicable to a clearing or settlement system:

- The oversight standards aiming at regulating securities systems to avoid systemic risk. This is the subject of the above-mentioned CPSS-IOSCO recommendations adopted at the G-10 level in 2001 and 2004 and of the new 19 ESCB-CESR Standards adopted at EU level in October 2004 (based on CPSS-IOSCO recommendations with EU adaptations), which are currently on hold because of divergences of views between regulators concerning the so-called functional approach.

- In the Eurozone, the nine ECB/EMI users standards adopted in 1998 for the use of securities systems in ESCB monetary policy operations. They should be reviewed soon.

- National regulatory standards, where applicable.

Such standards aim at establishing best practices for clearing and settlement operators with respect to legal soundness, clearing or settlement efficiency and transparency, risk management (including credit risks where relevant), cash operations, finality, operational reliability, corporate governance, participation/access, and links with other systems.

The oversight standards are not law and are generally not directly binding on securities systems. They are adopted by the community of regulators (central banks as overseers,[158] and securities/CSDs supervisors) at G-10 or at EU level as the basic common rules to carry out their supervisory functions, without prejudice to any additional national regulatory standards that may exist.

The sanctions attached to the noncompliance with such standards (or with the resulting recommendations made by competent regulators to achieve compliance) are generally of an indirect nature:

- Regulators may make noncompliance public,[159] which will obviously affect the image of the system vis-à-vis the clients, foreign regulators, and others.

- Foreign regulators may also invoke the system's noncompliance with international standards to infer negative consequences for the approval of certain projects for which compliance with international standards is required.

- Under domestic legislation, specific sanctions (such as fines) may be foreseen if a system does not comply with the applicable standards.

There is a risk that such co-existence or superposition of different sets of regulatory rules with sanctions could be perceived by the market infrastructures and their clients as a source of confusion and uncertainty in the regulatory treatment of their activities. Such a perception will not improve if the current text of the UNIDROIT Convention (which also contains provisions of a regulatory nature) is adopted as it stands. If proposed, an EU directive on clearing and settlement should probably also contain provisions that will translate all or part of the ESCB-CESR standards adopted in 2004 and which are currently on hold.

Notes

Note: This paper is based on several studies published by the author, in particular, "Collateral transactions in Payment and Securities Settlement Systems: the EU framework" in *Revue de Droit bancaire et financier* 2002, p. 10-27; "The Directive 2002/47/EC on Financial Collateral Arrangements of 6 June 2002" in *"Mélanges en hommage à Jean-Victor Louis"* (Tribute to Professor Louis), Vol. II (Bruxelles: Editions de l'Université de Bruxelles, 2003) with relevant updates where appropriate. The opinions expressed are strictly the author's own.

[1] *See Banque & Droit,* April 1996, a special issue devoted to the insolvency of BCCI.

[2] For convenience, the term "insolvency" will be used. However, other proceedings based on a debtor's insolvency, or, more generally, on an agreement or moratorium between creditors, such as, in particular, judicial or amicable composition, voluntary winding-up, attachment proceedings, etc., must also be considered.

[3] *See* Directive 93/22/EEC of 10 May 1993 on securities investment services, *Official Journal of the European Union* [hereinafter *Official Journal*], L141, 11 June 1993, at 27.

[4] Or, if one prefers, the private international law (conflict of laws) rules of each State; on cross-border insolvency, *see* in particular M. Giovanoli and G. Heinrich, ed., *International Bank Insolvencies : A Central Bank Perspective* (Kluwer Law International, 1999).

[5] *Official Journal* L166 of 11 June 1998, p. 45 and following.

[6] Regarding these principles, *see* under Belgian law esp. Rigaux, *Droit international privé, II* (Bruxelles : Larcier, 1993) n° 1102 to 1104; N. Watté, "La faillite internationale...," note under Cass. 12 January 1990, RCJB 1993, at 454 and following, particularly page 457 n° 8; M. Delierneux, "Les succursales face à la faillite" in *Les succursales bancaires* (AEDBF Belgium 1996), at 214 discussing the respective merits of the various existing solutions.

[7] Subject, of course, to the recognition by these states of the insolvency decision and its effects on their territory, pursuant to the rules of private international law of the relevant court.

[8] Without, for example, formalities of *exequatur (judicial recognition of foreign judgements)*.

[9] International public policy has a variable content, determined most often by jurisprudence, by reference to the "essential interests of the State or of the collectivity" or to the "legal bases on which the economic or moral order of the State relies," to take the Belgian example (Cass. 25 March 1968, Pas. I, 885).

[10] To the extent this recognition would likely affect the payment or settlement systems, with adverse consequences for other participants, so as to result in the possibility of systemic risk. The argument of international public policy, however, has never, to the best of the writer's knowledge, been invoked or upheld in case law in such a context. This legal argument may be regarded as underpinning, in the writer's opinion, Article 8 of the Settlement Finality Directive.

[11] One may also think about the nonenforceability of payment orders concerning the defaulting participant on the day of its insolvency, either for payments made before the insolvency (zero-hour rule) or for those made between the time of the insolvency and the settlement of transactions of the insolvent participant.

[12] In this sense in Belgium, *see* Comm. Brussels 20 June 1975, J.T. 1975, at 641, which refers to the status of international public policy of the principles of unity and universality of insolvency; however this has been criticised by Rigaux, *Droit international privé* (Bruxelles, 1968), II, no. 1103– end.

[13] "Concordat," moratorium, "redressement judiciaire," receivership, suspension of payments, etc.

[14] As there are more and more securities that are essentially dematerialized, that is, represented exclusively from the outset by book-entries, one may consider (although hardly considered by legal doctrine so far) that the place of location of these securities is the place where the accounts, recording the relevant rights, in such securities, are held and operated; *see* in this sense Article 9.2. of the Settlement Finality Directive; see also the Convention of 5

July 2006 adopted by the Hague Conference on Private International Law on the Law Applicable to Certain Rights in respect of Securities held with an Intermediary (*see* R. Potok, "The Hague Conference on Private International Law ...," *Journal of International Banking and Financial Law (*April 2001), at 166; R. Potok and C. Bernasconi, "PRIMA Convention brings certainty to cross-border deals," *International Financial Law Review* (January 2003), at 11.

[15] The Insolvency Convention was signed by all member states except the United Kingdom, Ireland, and the Netherlands. Ireland and the Netherlands signed after the explanatory report of the Insolvency Convention was finalized. The United Kingdom, however, did not sign the Convention due to a conflict with other member states over the so-called "mad cow" crisis. Under the Convention, the deadline for signature expired on May 23, 1996.

[16] *Official Journal,* L 160 of 30.06.2000, at 1–13.

[17] Recitals have been added in order to give some limited explanations, replacing, in a limited way, the draft explanatory report of the Insolvency Convention.

[18] This is the application, first of all, of the principle of unity of insolvency.

[19] The other paragraphs of Article 5 define *rights in rem* with reference to the attributes generally attached to these rights: right of realization (pledge, mortgage), right to recover a claim assigned for security purposes, right of recovery, right to receive income ("fructus"), etc.

[20] Version of 8 July 1996, doc 6500/1/96, commentary on Article 5 under paragraphs 94 *et seq.*, pages 70 *et seq.*

[21] Article 6.2 preserves the right of the receiver or liquidator to commence actions for avoidance of transactions because of actual fraud to rights of the creditors or because of rules based on a "suspect period" ("preferences" or "fraudulent conveyances").

[22] According to the explanatory report, no. 110, at 77.

[23] As is the case under the law of certain member states (France, Belgium, Luxembourg), apart from notable exceptions (particularly concerning connected claims or for claims between financial institutions, for example).

[24] On the reasons of selection of the law applicable to the insolvent's claim, see Report, no. 108, at 76.

[25] The report explicitly confirms this interpretation. *See* no. 110, at 76.

[26] As for the two other dispositions, paragraph 2 reserves the actions for fraudulent or prejudicial acts to the creditors but, contrary to Articles 5 and 6, Article 9.2 states that these actions will be governed not by the law of the (main) insolvency proceedings, but by the law applicable to the system or market concerned.

[27] The notion of "financial market" is defined by the Report (no. 120, at 82) and is similar to the one used in the Directive on Investment Services.

[28] In principle, this law will be the law of the member state where the operator of the system is situated, which will, moreover, be generally stipulated contractually as *lex contractus.*

[29] *See* also the Explanatory Report, no. 124, at 82.

[30] *Official Journal,* L 125 of 5.5.2001, at 15

[31] *Official Journal,* C 36 of 8.2.1988, at 1.

[32] Directive 77/780/EEC of 12 December 1977 (*Official Journal,* L 322 of 17.12.1977, at 30) as modified by the Second Directive 89/646/EEC of 15 December 1989 (*Official Journal,* L 386 of 30.12.1989, at 1).

[33] Directive 94/19/EC of 30 May 1994 (*Official Journal,* L 135 of 31.5.1994, at 5.

[34] It was rumored that the work on the draft Directive had then been placed on hold due to a dispute between the United Kingdom and Spain concerning the application of this Directive to Gibraltar.

[35] *See* Articles 5–15 of the Insolvency Regulation concerning exceptions to the application of the law of the main insolvency proceedings.

[36] Article 25.

[37] Article 26.

[38] Subject, for repurchase transactions, to the enforceability against third parties of the transfer of ownership as determined by the law of the country where the relevant securities are transferred (this is the meaning of "without prejudice to Article 24"—referring to the *lex rei sitae* rule with respect to book-entry securities—introduced in Article 26).

[39] Article 24 (*lex rei sitae*). Compare with Article 9.2 of the Settlement Finality Directive or the rule proposed in the Hague Convention (see hereafter).

[40] Article 27, again subject to *lex rei sitae* as laid down in Article 24.

[41] Compare with Article 9.1 of the Finality Directive, which has also adopted such a rule of exoneration.

[42] *Official Journal*, L 166 of 11 June 1998, at 145; the initial proposition concerning "the finality of settlement and guarantees" was presented by the European Commission on May 30, 1996 (*Official Journal* C 259 of 18 July 1996, at 13) and later amended, following the first opinion of the European Parliament (JO C 259 of 26 August 1997, at 6); on the Directive, *see* D. Devos, *Euredia: European Banking & Financial Law Journal* 2 (1999), at 149–85; J. Richards and M. Evans, "The Settlement Finality Directive—The End or the Beginning of the Story," Travers Smith Braitwaite, 16th Annual Seminar on International Financial Law, International Bar Association, (May 21, 1999); M. Vereecken, "Reducing systemic risk in payment and securities settlement systems," 6 *Journal of Financial Regulation and Compliance* (May 1998), at 107 *et seq.*; P. Bloch, "The Directive 98/26/CEE concerning the finality of settlement in the payment and securities settlement systems," *Banking and Financial Law* (Mélanges AEDBF-France), II (1999), which undertakes a comparative analysis of the Settlement Finality Directive and French law on the subject.

[43] For background on the work of this group of experts, see my study on "The European Directive 97/5 of 27 January 1997 Concerning Cross-border Credit Transfers," *Revue Banque* (1998), at 43 *et seq.*, particularly note 7 at 47.

[44] *See* Recitals 1, 2 and 4 of the Settlement Finality Directive.

[45] That is, the risk that the insolvency of a participant in a payment or settlement system, or a financial market, might in turn cause the insolvency of other participants.

[46] Target is a connection of national payment systems operating a real-time settlement of gross amounts, without netting. On the Target system, *see* J. Lachand, "The Target System," *Bulletin de la Banque de France* (June 1995), at 97 *et seq.*

[47] A net payment system in euros managed by an inter-banking association named "Eurobanking."

[48] Not including a settlement agent, clearing house, or any other intermediary party of this type.

[49] The Settlement Finality Directive adds: "without prejudice to other more stringent conditions of general application laid down by national law"; on the meaning of these terms, see hereafter in the main text.

[50] *See* also Article 10.3 indicating that member states may impose supervision or authorization requirements on systems. See in this respect the regulatory standards applicable to securities settlement systems laid down in the "Recommendations for Securities Settlement Systems" of November 2001 adopted by the Committee on Payment and Settlement Systems (CPSS) together with the Technical Committee of the International Organisation of Securities Commissions (IOSCO).

[51] Article 2(a), final paragraph.

[52] That is, a credit institution or another financial institution that processes its cash or securities orders by the intermediary of a direct participant, being the member of the system in which these orders are settled.

[53] Directive 77/780/EEC of 12 December 1977, *Official Journal*, L 322 of 17 December 1977, at 30. Article 1.1.

[54] Directive 93/22/EEC of 10 May 1993, *Official Journal*, L 141 of 11 June 1993, at 27, point 2 of Article 1.

[55] It is fairly bizarrely stated, in the second indent under Article 2(a), that "participants may only choose the law of a member state in which at least one of them has its head office."

[56] Translated as "compensation" in the French version of the Directive.

[57] On the legal aspects of "netting," *see* P. R. Wood, *Principles of Netting : A Comparative Law Study* (Amsterdam : Nederlands Instituut voor het Bank– en Effectenbedrijf, 1994); *see also* my study on the matter with regard to Belgian law in *Revue Banque* (1994), at 162 *et seq.*

[58] On this point, *see* comments below on Article 6 of the Directive.

[59] To the exclusion of the transfer orders, not covered under the terms of this paragraph.

[60] For example, a current account opened at the central bank or with the system's operator.

[61] For example, based on the revocability of the agency/mandate.

[62] In reality, all the provisions of the Directive particularly deal with the incidence of insolvency proceedings opened against a participant, as shown also by Articles 3, 4, and 9, even if the bankruptcy or insolvency in general is not the only relevant possibility.

[63] There is a discrepancy here between the English text of the Directive (the original text) simply referring to "other member states" and the French text pointing more specifically to the "other member states concerned." The idea here was in fact to require the national authority of countries where the insolvency is opened to notify all the other member states of this news, without the national authority being required to assess which member states are "concerned" and therefore should receive notification.

[64] One points out, however, that it does not cover the fate of payments made after the moment of opening of insolvency proceedings, but in the ignorance of the latter, except to apply Article 3.1, paragraph two, to them.

[65] The well-known issue of undue payments or payments erroneously transferred to a wrong beneficiary.

[66] The well-known issue of fraudulent payments made particularly in infringement of the rules concerning a "suspect period" or immediately prior to the day of insolvency.

[67] *See* the words "for example" contained in Recital 13.

[68] On the legal protection offered to collateral by the Euroclear system already before the implementation of the Directive, *see* L. De Ghenghi and B. Servaes "Collateral held in the Euroclear System: a Legal Overview," *Journal of International Banking and Financial Law* (March 1999), at 83; *see* also Diego Devos, "Protection juridique des systèmes de paiement et de règlement-titres en Belgique," *Revue Banque* (2000), at 313–326.

[69] This expression more generally aims at covering any other type of security interest legally recognized in a member state, such as, for example, statutory liens on specific assets or transfers of ownership for security purposes (transfer of title) (*see* in this sense, Recital 9).

[70] As mentioned earlier in the text, this is also the solution finally adopted in the directives on reorganisation and winding-up of credit institutions and insurance undertakings.

[71] Contrary to collateral security in favor of a participant that must be provided "in connection with a system" by another participant, becoming insolvent (first section of Article 9.1). One will note that Article 2(m) of the Directive, concerning the definition of collateral security, also refers to the security of "rights and obligations potentially arising in connection with a system" without any further explanation. What is surely being intended here is, first, to catch collateral security provided in favor of the system operator, but also all collateral security provided "in connection with a system" (see Article 9.1 and 9.2) "in favor of a participant," whoever that participant may be. Article 9 applies therefore to collateral security provided in a system, to participants in that system. We consider in this respect that the EU Commission's Explanatory Memorandum of the initial draft Collateral Directive, to the extent it seems to imply that the Settlement Finality Directive, as well as the other EU legal acts described above, would not apply to collateral between participants (section 1.2, second and fifth paragraphs) but only to central banks and operators of systems, is incorrect.

[72] This is the daily management of securities held with international central securities depositaries systems such as Euroclear or Clearstream. One may

also think of the case of links between national central securities depositaries; on Article 9.2, *see* Richard Potok, "Legal certainty for securities held as collateral," *International Financial Law Review* (December 1999), at 12; *see also* "The Oxford Colloquium on Collateral and Conflict of laws," held at St John's College, Oxford University, *Journal of International Banking and Financial Law* (September 1998).

[73] *See in particular* Randall D. Guynn, "Modernising Securities Ownership, Transfer and Pledging Laws," published in 1996 by the Capital Markets Forum (Section on Business Law of the International Bar Association); for further details on this problem, *see also* the Explanatory Memorandum of Belgian law of 28 April 1999 implementing the Directive, Doc. Chambre, session 1998-1999, no. 1999/1, at 23 and 24.

[74] *See* the preparatory report of the Hague Convention prepared by Christophe Bernasconi, First Secretary at the Hague Conference's Permanent Bureau, available on the website of the Hague Conference at www.hcch.net; *see* R. Potok, "The Hague Conference..." *Journal of International Banking and Financial Law* (2001), at 166, particularly see footnote 15.

[75] *See* in this respect, Article 8.2 of the Belgian Act dated 28 April 1999 implementing the Finality Directive in Belgium (Moniteur Belge, 1 June 1999, 19563); *see* my study on this Belgian law in *Revue Banque* (2000), at 313.

[76] *Id.*

[77] See, however, Recital 21 of the Directive, which seems to reserve, in fairly sibylline terms, the application of the law of the member state where the securities are issued or in which they are originally located as regards the basic regime applicable to these securities.

[78] Which is the jurisdiction where the intermediary holding the relevant account is located.

[79] EU Commission: "Working document on Collateral from the Commission to relevant bodies for consultation," C4/PN D (2000).

[80] International Swaps and Derivatives Association, Inc.

[81] This chapter use hereafter the term *collateral* to cover the type of transaction (pledge, repo, transfer of title, margins, etc) rather than the assets subject to the security arrangement, unless otherwise required by the commented provision.

[82] *See* EU Directive 96/10/EC of 21 March 1996 amending Directive 89/647/EEC as regards recognition of contractual netting by the competent authorities, *Official Journal*, L 85, of 3.4.1996, at 17, in particular the revised Annex II, Article 3 (b), (ii) and (iii).

[83] The underlying securities related to the book-entry collateral transaction may also be held/located in other countries (where they have been initially issued and deposited) via sub-custodians (home CSD, local depositaries), which is common practice in cross-border securities business.

[84] Perfection is broadly equivalent to the French concept "opposabilité aux tiers."

[85] *See* Richard Obank, "Outlining Insolvency Practice in Europe," *Journal of International Banking and Financial Law* (1999), at 437 ; P. Wood, *Principles of Interantional Insolvency* (London: Sweet & Maxwell, 1995), sections 5–17, p.94; *see also* section 13-1.

[86] On this distinction, *see* Joanna Benjamin, *The Law of Global Custody* (London : Butterworths, 1996), chapters 6 and 7, at *49 et seq.*; *see also* Richard Potok, *Cross-Border Collateral: Legal Risks and the Conflict of Laws* (London: Butterworths, 2002). All the various national reports in Potok's book are based on the same collateral fact pattern (covering both a pledge and transfer of title arrangement).

[87] *See* also D. Devos, "La directive européenne 98/26/CE concernant le caractère définitif du règlement dans les systèmes de paiement et de règlement des opérations sur titres," *Euredia* (1999), at 149 et seq; D. Devos, "Collateral Transactions in Payment and Securities Settlement Systems: The EU Framework," *Revue de Droit bancaire et financier* (2002), at 10–27; Devos, "The European Directive of 19 May 1998 on Settlement Finality in Payment and Securities Settlement Systems" in Ferrarini and Hopt, ed., *Capital Markets in the Age of the Euro* (New York: Kluwer Law International, 2002), 361–388.

[88] *Official Journal* L 166, 11.6.1998, at 45.

[89] *Official Journal*, L 125, of 5.5.2001, at 15; on the WUD, *see* in particular Jean-Pierre Deguée, "La directive 2001/24/CE sur l'assainissement et la liquidation des établissements de crédit: une solution aux défaillances bancaires internationales?" *Euredia* (2002), at 241.

[90] *Official Journal*, L 110, of 20.4.2001, at 28.

[91] *Official Journal*, L 160, of 30.6.2000, at 1. This regulation entered into force on May 31, 2002.

[92] The so-called Lamfalussy Report, "Report of the Committee on Interbank Netting Schemes of the Central Banks of the Group of Ten Countries" (BIS, November 1990); Committee on Payment and Settlement Systems "Cross-border Securities Settlements" (BIS, 1995); "Standards on the use of securities settlement systems for the purposes of ESCB monetary policy transactions" (EMI, 1998), etc. On this influence of international standards set by regulatory bodies, see Mario Giovanoli, "A new architecture for the global financial market: legal aspects of international financial standard setting," in M. Giovanoli, ed., *International Monetary Law, Issues for the new millennium* (Oxford: Oxford University Press) at 3 *et seq.*

[93] *See* the various position papers produced by members of the Forum Group attached to the Working Document on Collateral (containing a first draft directive prepared by the Commission on the basis of the draft made by the Forum group) *circulated to members states and to market participants* in the course of a consultation organized on June 15, 2000. See also attached to this consultation the converging report prepared by a special working group (with market lawyers) established by the ECB.

[94] *Official Journal*, C 180 E, 26.6.2001, at 312 with an explanatory memorandum. This memorandum contained, however, several statements concerning the interpretation of the 1998 Settlement Finality Directive (second and third paragraphs of section 1.2) to which we can not subscribe since it contradicted this last Directive itself by giving a narrow scope of application that was not favored by the services of the Commission themselves (on this discussion, see "Collateral Transactions," *Revue de droit bancaire et financier* (2002), at 26 , footnote 73).

[95] *Official Journal* L 168, 27.6.2002, at 43.

[96] *See also* Spyros Economou, "La proposition de directive européenne sur les contrats de garantie financière," *Bulletin Joly Bourse* (2002), chron., 1; Clifford Chance, Securities Newsletter May/June 2002; Dermot Turing, "The EU Collateral Directive," *Journal of International Banking and Financial Law* (2002), at 187 G. Morton, "Modernization of EU financial law : the directive on financial collateral arrangements," 1 *Euredia* (2003), at 11; H. Seeldrayers "De Europese Richtlijn inzake zekerheidsovereenkomsten— Krachtlijnen en artikelsgewijze commentaar" *T.Fin.R.*, 2003-1, at 337 and 2003-2, at 420; F. T'Kint and W. Derjcke, "La directive 2002/47/CE concernant les contrats de garantie financière au regard des principes généraux du droit des sûretés," 1 *Euredia* (2003), at 41; H. De Vauplane and J.-J. Daigre, "Chronique financière et boursière" *Banque & Droit*, (mai-juin 2003), at 30, spéc. p. 38; W. Bossu, "De Richtlijn betreffende financiëlezekerheidsovereenkomsten: inhoudelijke analyse" in M. Tison (ed.), *Sûretés bancaires et financiers—Bancaire en financiële zekerheden*, Série: Cahiers AEDBF/EVBFR-Belgium no. 15, (Bruxelles: Bruylant, 2004), at 227.

[97] *See, for example,* Recital 14.

[98] *See* Article 2.1(n) on the definition of "close-out netting provision" that is inspired by Section 10 of the 1995 GMRA (Global Master Repurchase Agreement) on repo transactions elaborated by ISMA (compare with the same provision in the 2000 version of the same GMRA); on the PSA/ISMA GMRA, *see* G. Morton, "Cross-Border Securities (Repo, Lending and Collateralisation)," Tyson-Quah, ed., *FT Law & Tax*, at 31.

[99] *See*, however, the remarkable study of JP Deguée, already quoted above (footnote 98), which contains elements of comparative law on collateral-related matters.

[100] Excluding therefore a security interest that is only created by operation of law, such as statutory liens that are also used in some jurisdictions as collateral technique by financial institutions and operators of payment and settlement systems.

[101] On this type of collateral, see   D. Devos "Protection juridique des systèmes de paiement et de règlement-titres en Belgique," in *Revue Banque* (2000), at 318 and 319, n° 12; *see* also my study on « Les effets externes des conventions en matière financière » in *Les contrats et les tiers* (Ed. ABJE,

Jeune Barreau de Bruxelles, Vlaams Pleitgenootschap bij de Balie te Brussel, 1995), at 213 n° 18.

[102] One will find the same expression, aiming at encompassing explicitly the same type of securities entitlements, in Article 9.2 of the Settlement Finality Directive ("rights in securities"), in Article 24 of the WUD ("other rights in such instruments") and in the Hague Convention on the Law Applicable to Certain Rights in Respect of Securities Held with an Intermediary (Article 1.1 " any interest therein," and "rights…. resulting from a credit of securities to a securities account"; *see also* the notion of "interest in securities" in Article 2.1(d), (e), (f.). On this last expression, *see* Johanna Benjamin, *Interests in securities* (Oxford University Press, 2000) n° 1.05, 2.21 *et seq.*; J. Benjamin, "Conflicts of Law and Interests in Securities," in "Cross-Border Securities (Repo, Lending and Collateralisation)" by K. Tyson-Quah, *F.T Law & Tax* (1997), n° 2.3 *et seq.*, and at 16; in the context of Belgian Royal Decree n° 62 of 1967 relating to book-entry circulation of securities, governing the rights of participants in the Euroclear system, *see* L. De Ghenghi and B. Servaes "Collateral held in the Euroclear System: a legal overview," *Journal of International Banking and Financial Law* (March 1999), at 85–87; Bart Servaes, "Het immobiliseren van effecten: Het Belgisch juridisch kader," in *"Nieuw vennootschap-en financieel recht 1999"* (Jan Ronse Instituut-KU Leuven), at 513. See also our commentary of Article 9, above.

[103] One will note that some EU countries have implemented the Collateral Directive beyond its terms (based on the analysis that the Directive was setting up *minimal* harmonization rules) by applying the new collateral regime even to natural (physical) persons. *See,* for example, the Belgian Act dated 15 December 2004 relating to financial collateral; on this new law, *see, e.g.,* J.P. Deguée and D. Devos "La loi relative aux sûretés financières du 15 décembre 2004—Lignes directrices," *Revue de Droit bancaire et financier* (2005), at 155–163 and the following studies in the same publication.

[104] This Recital 10 specifies that acts that are required for the transfer or the creation of a security interest on physical securities not held in book-entry form, like endorsement for security purposes of instruments to order (bills of exchange, etc) or registration of a pledge directly on registered securities in the issuer' books, should not be regarded as such formal acts.

[105] One will find several times in these two provisions the requirement that arrangements and provision of the collateral must be evidenced in writing,

duplication that appears more as a "credo" inserted to ease adoption process but this does not really seem justified from a legislative point of view.

[106] We should, however, point out that it is agreed, even in French law jurisdictions, that with the consent of the pledgor, a pledgee may of course validly use the pledged assets (De Page, *Traité de droit civil*, VI, n° 1088-B in fine); to compare with the situation under English Law, see J. Benjamin, *Interests in Securities: a proprietary law analysis of the international securities markets* (Oxford: Oxford University Press, 2000), n° 5.46 *et seq.*, also promoting the reform of English law's equitable rules traditionally restricting rehypothecation of collateral.

[107] Reasons may be linked, e.g., to considerations of tax, accounting, capital adequacy, risks management, and legal risk; *see* Dermot Turing, 5 *Journal of International Banking and Financial Law* (2002), at 188.

[108] The term "collateral" here is used to refer to the assets and not to the legal form of the arrangement.

[109] The two last paragraphs are common to both pledge and transfer of title arrangements and will be addressed in the following section of this paper.

[110] "Enforcement event" means an event of default or any similar event as agreed between the parties on the occurrence of which, under the terms of a financial collateral arrangement or by operation of law (as it is organized, for example, in German law for transfer of title), the collateral taker is entitled to realize or appropriate financial collateral or a close-out netting provision comes into effect (Article 2.1 (1)).

[111] Appropriation is only possible if contractually foreseen, including with respect to the valuation of the assets (Article 4.2).

[112] *See* Fabrice Leduc, "Le gage translatif de propriété: mythe ou réalité," *RTD* civ. 1995, at 307, where the author concludes that pledge under French law cannot lead to a transfer of ownership on the pledged assets in favor of the pledgee.

[113] On this issue, see our above-mentioned study on the Belgian regime protecting payment and settlement systems, *Revue Banque* (2000), at 318 and 319, with the references quoted in the footnotes.

[114] *See* M. Stigum, *The Repo and Reverse Market* (Dow Jones-Irwin, 1989), especially chapter 19 (by L. Stremba), at 333; on French law, see. Luvel-Jurgensen et Guéranger, "Le réméré, la pension et le prêt de titres," *Banque*, 1992, at 144 and 246; P. de Lapasse, "Le nouveau régime juridique des opérations de pension," *Bulletin,* Banque de France, no. 7 (July 1994), at 67; A. Perrot, "Pension de titres et transfert de propriété," *Revue de droit bancaire* (1994), at 252.

[115] On this issue, see J. Benjamin, "Recharacterisation risk and conflict of laws," *Journal of International Banking and Financial Law* (1997), at 513 and its updated version in the Oxford Colloquium on Collateral and Conflict of Laws (same review, special supplement, 1998, at 29); Fentiman, "Cross-border securities collateral; Redefining recharacterisation risk," Oxford Colloquium, 1998, at 38.

[116] On this issue, see our above-mentioned study, supra note 62, *Revue de la Banque* (2000), at 318–319.

[117] By encompassing all the reciprocal exposures and claims, such close-out netting provisions aim at reducing the total credit risk on the failed counterpart to the minimal net amount, avoiding cherry-picking from the liquidator of the insolvent counterpart, that is, the selection of the favorable contracts from a general creditor's viewpoint (those in which the noninsolvent party is debtor—which are maintained and for which performance is sought—to repudiate the others, unfavorable to the insolvent party and its creditors, for which the counterpart in such last contracts would only then have an unsecured claim to lodge in the insolvency proceedings. By setting-off in case of insolvency all the contracts (that are interrelated in practice, like swaps and/or repos and/or loans) without distinction, one avoids such unbalanced treatment. On netting, *see* P.R Wood, *English and International Set-off* (London: Sweet & Maxwell, 1989); same author, "Principles of Netting: A Comparative Law Study," NIBE-Bank Juridische reeks, no. 20 (1994); *see also* my study "Le netting en droit belge," *Revue Banque* 1994, at 162.

[118] In addition, in a repo at least, not only the collateral taker but also the collateral provider may fail to transfer the due assets. Both failures should trigger a close-out mechanism, but this is probably the intended meaning in Article 6.2 by referring only to the collateral taker since both parties have in fact the capacity of collateral taker, each for the assets transferred to him.

[119] For an example, see Belgian Act of 2 January 1991 on public debt instruments, specifically Article 8 organizing simplified realization proceedings for pledge of dematerialized securities with the comments made in the Explanatory Memorandum of this provision as amended in 1996, Doc. Chambre, Session (1995–1996), 501/1, at 7–8.

[120] See Mark Evans, "Recent and prospective developments in settlement, part 2," *Journal of International Banking and Financial Law* (1999), at 425, about the zero-hour rules in the UK before the implementation of the Settlement Finality Directive and its impact on collateral provided in systems like Crest; on the impact of the new Insolvency Act 2000 concerning small companies on this UK insolvency regime, see M. French and H. Staniland, "The Insolvency Act 2000," *Journal of International Banking and Financial Law* (2001), at 174.

[121] The French translation of Article 8.2 (in fact, of the whole Directive (*see also, e.g.*, Recitals 8 and 9, Articles 2.2 and 9.2)) could be improved ("... à la date....mais après l'ouverture...").

[122] See also in that sense Article 157.2 of Belgian Banking Law of 22 March 1993 on zero-hour rules and close-out netting.

[123] "No law, regulation or practice on the setting aside of contracts and transactions concluded before the moment of the opening of insolvency proceedings, … shall lead to the unwinding of a netting."

[124] See also Christoph Keller, "Die EG-Richtlinie 98/26 vom 19.5.1998 über die Wirksamkeit von Abrechnungen in Zahlungs-sowie Wertpapierliefer-und-abrechnungssytemen und ihre Umsetzung in Deutschland," 26 *Zeitschrift für Wirtschafts-und Bankrecht* (2000), at 1269 *et seq.*, proposing the concept of *lex conto sitae* (even though we do not share the restrictive view suggested by the author for the application of Article 9.2 of the Settlement Finality Directive; *see* p. 1274).

[125] This is the daily management of securities held with international central securities depositaries systems such as Euroclear or Clearstream. Global custodians and certain other custodians are also acting through the same holding pattern. One may also think of the case of links between national central securities depositaries; see R. Guynn and N. Marchand, "Transfer of pledge of securities held through depositories," in *The Law of Cross-border Securities Transactions*, (Sweet & Maxwell, 1999), at 47; Richard Potok,

"Legal certainty for securities held as collateral," *International Financial Law Review* (December 1999), at 12; *see also* "Oxford Colloquium on Collateral and Conflict of laws held at St John's College, Oxford University," *Journal of International Banking and Financial Law* (September 1998).

[126] Such underlying securities may consist either in physical certificates kept in the vaults of a CSD or of a local custodian and circulating by way of book-entry transfers in the local CSD; or in registered securities, the title of which is noted in the issuer's books, circulating in the books of the local CSD through the intermediation of nominees (of the local CSD or of the intermediaries, in order to make the registered securities fungible for book-entry transfer purposes) that appear as the legal owners of such registered securities in the issuers' books, holding the securities in trust on behalf of beneficial owners which are the relevant intermediary's clients; or in dematerialized securities, solely represented by book-entry records on accounts held with the local CSD.

[127] *See* Roy Goode, "Security Entitlements as Collateral and the Conflict of Laws," Oxford Colloquium 1998, *Journal of International Banking and Financial Law*, at 22 and especially 25 and 26; *see also* J. Benjamin, *Interests in Securities*, no. 1.05 and 2.21 and following (see also no. 14.02–14.27).

[128] "The enforcement of proprietary rights in instruments, or other rights in such instruments the existence or transfer of which presupposes their recording in a register, an account, or a centralized deposit system held or located in a member state, shall be governed by the law of the member state where the register, account or centralized deposit system in which those rights are recorded, is held or located."

[129] Excluding, however, any rules of *renvoi* that may be applicable under the national law so determined (Article 9.1, last sentence), in order to avoid referring to another law that would apply a different solution, which would undermine the legal certainty and predictability wished on this issue.

[130] Statement of the Council's reasons, Doc 5530/3/02 of 5 March 2002, at 12 and 13.

[131] See our study, "Collateral Transactions in Payment and Securities Settlement Systems: The EU Framework," *Droit bancaire et financier* (2002), at 10–27; J. P. Deguée, "La directive 2001/24/CE sur

l'assainissement et la liquidation des établissements de credit," *Euredia* (2002), at 241.

[132] While the previous EU legal instruments mentioned were more focused on conflict of laws aspects, except the Settlement Finality Directive, which also contains substantive protection rules (for payment orders and settlement and for collateral) in the scope of designated systems.

[133] *See* Article 10 of the Directive relating to the establishment by the Commission of a report on its application by 27 December 2006 at the latest. A report is currently in preparation after a consultation process that ended on March 31, 2006 (*see* http://www.ec.europa.eu/internal_market/financial-markets/ collateral/index_en.htm).

[134] The Hague Conference is an intergovernmental body established in 1955 to work on harmonization of private international law (conflict of laws). It is based in the Hague (Netherlands) and has produced more than 35 international conventions on the law applicable to sales, trusts, judicial litigations, torts, agencies, and family matters. *See* the text of the Convention and the Explanatory Report prepared by Professors Goode, Kreuzer, and Kanda with the assistance of Ch. Bernasconi, on the Hague conference website: http://www.hcch.net/e/conventions/menu36e.html

[135] Settlement Finality Directive of 1998; Insolvency Regulation of 2000; Directives on the Reorganisation and the Winding-up of credit institutions and insurance undertakings of 2001; Collateral Directive of 2002.

[136] The signing of the Hague Convention on December 13, 2002, was only meant to signify the end of negotiations and to propose a final text to the formal signature of contracting states.

[137] *See* http://www.hcch.net/index_en.php?act=events.details&year=2006& varevent=117.

[138] *See* footnote 138 *supra*.

[139] *See* in favor of the Convention, K. Kreuzer, "Das Haager Übereinkommen über die auf bestimmte Rechte in Bezug auf Intermediär-verwahrte Wertpapiere anzuwendende Rechtsordnung," in *Le droit international privé : esprit et méthodes*, Mélanges Paul Lagarde, (Paris: Dalloz, 2005), at 523 ; J. Rogers "Conflict of Laws for Transactions in Securities Held through

Intermediaries," Boston College Law School Research Paper No 108 (2005); Bernasconi and Sigman, "Myths about the Hague Convention debunked,"*International Financial Law Review* (November 2005), at 31; D. Devos, "The Hague Convention on the Law applicable to Book-entry Securities—Relevance for the European System of Central Banks," *Liber Amicorum Paolo Zamboni Garavelli* (Frankfurt: European Central Bank, 2005), at 157; Deguée and Devos, "La loi applicable aux titres intermédiés: l'apport de la Convention de La Haye de décembre 2002," *Revue de droit commercial belge* (2006), at 5–32; Financial Markets Law Committee, "Issue 58–Hague Convention…," which is a legal assessment produced in November 2005, available on FMLC website at www.fmlc.org; *see against*, the Hague, Opinion of the European Central Bank dated 17 March 2005, OEJC., no. C 81 of 2 April 2005, at 10; H. De Vauplane and P. Bloch "Loi applicable et critères de localisation des titres multi-intermédiés dans la Convention de La Haye," in Mélanges AEDBF France IV, Revue Banque Édition (2004), at 469, also published in *J.D.I.*, 1/2005, at 3; W.A.K. Rank, "Vaststelling Hague Securities Convention: meer rechtszekerheid in het internationale effectenverkeer?" NiPR 2005, at 249.

[140] *See* http://ec.europa.eu/internal_market/financial-markets/docs/legal_assessment_en.pdf .

[141] *See* D. Devos, "The Hague Convention on the Law applicable to Book-entry Securities—Relevance for the European System of Central Banks," *Liber Amicorum Paolo Zamboni Garavelli* (Frankfurt: European Central Bank, 2005), at 157; Deguée and Devos, "La loi applicable aux titres intermédiés: l'apport de la Convention de La Haye de décembre 2002," *Revue de droit commercial belge* (2006), at 5–32.

[142] "Clearing and Settlement in the European Union—The Way Forward," Communication of 28 April 2004 from the Commission to the Council and the European Parliament, COM (2004) 0312.

[143] Alberto Giovannini complained about the insufficient progress made so far in the follow-up of the recommendations of his group; see *Financial Times* (May 16, 2005), at 17.

[144] Several EU jurisdictions retain "national-oriented protection" rules relating to the physical location of securities activities such as:
- requirements to open or maintain a local office in order to be entitled to act as withholding agent, act as general clearing

member, or to act as a recognized CSD or otherwise provide settlement and custody services to local residents;

- requirements to locate register (for registered securities) or accounts physically in the country of the issuer;
- requirements (in law or practice) that restrict local membership in CSD to local intermediaries only.

These requirementscan be imposed through laws or regulations, but also through disproportionate requirements to be fulfilled obliging de facto a nonresident firm to act in the local market through a local intermediary.

[145] *See* http://europa.eu/rapid/pressReleasesAction.do?reference= IP/06/1517&forma=HTML&aged=0&language=EN&guiLanguage=en

[146] Documents and minutes of meetings are available at http://www.europa. eu.int/comm/internal_market/financial-markets/clearing/cesame_en

[147] Documents and minutes of meetings are available on the LCG website at http://www.europa.eu.int/comm/internal_market/financial-markets/clearing/ certainty_en.htm.

[148] *See* http://www.europa.eu.int/comm/internal_market/financial-markets/ clearing/compliance_en.htm

[149] *See* http://ec.europa.eu/internal_market/financial-markets/docs/certainty/ advice_final_en.pdf

[150] "Proposal on the exercise of voting rights by shareholders of companies having their registered office in a member state and whose shares are admitted to trading on a regulated market," adopted by the Commission on 5 January 2006, COM (2005) 685.

[151] *See, e.g.,* the Euroclear consultation paper, "Harmonisation Fundamentals" (June 30, 2004), in particular section 8 and appendix 1 on legal and regulatory barriers, especially in the UK, France, Netherlands, and Belgium.

[152] In France the transfer of ownership (TO) for stock exchange trades (the situation depends on the type of trades) is organized by law (French Monetary and Financial Code, Article 431-2) by reference to the credit of the buyer's account but "at the date and in the conditions defined by (French) market rules." The Euronext Paris market rules then organized the TO at

trade date. Because of the harmonization discussions, this rule has changed in France with the adoption of Decree no. 2005-303 dated 31 March 2005, which refers to the settlement date (with the crediting of the buyer's account) as the moment of transfer of ownership. This new rule is, however, still dependent on the revision of the rules of the French market supervisor ("Autorité des marches Financiers"); on this complex regime, see H. de Vauplane, "Transfert de propriété des titres cotés: la réforme achevée … ou presque!" *Revue Banque* (May 2005), at 87.

In Belgium and the Netherlands, no specific law has been laid down to organize specifically the transfer of ownership for stock exchange or OTC trades. In these two countries it is the application of the ordinary rules of commercial legislation that leads to the transfer of ownership at settlement date.

Irish and UK laws provide for transfer of securities based on transfer of legal title on registration. The regulations covering each regime (England and Wales, Scotland, Northern Ireland—all UK—and Ireland) provide for electronic book-entry transfer of title effected pursuant to settlement of a properly authenticated dematerialized instruction attributable to one or more members (in accordance with the rules of the securities settlement system). Registration (with associated transfer of ownership) takes place at the point of settlement for the UK jurisdictions. For Ireland, a statutory equitable interest arises in favor of the transferee at the point of settlement and is extinguished (usually minutes, but no more than two hours, later) by transfer of legal title in his favor on an issuer register.

[153] The draft Convention is available on the UNIDROIT website at http://www.UNIDROIT.org

[154] This latest draft Convention is available at http://www.UNIDROIT.org/english/publications/proceedings/2006/study/78/s-78-42-e.pdf

[155] This generally supposes that the interest in such foreign securities is treated as a specific entitlement governed by the national law of the relevant intermediary (under the Hague Convention rules) distinct from any directly traceable entitlement to the underlying foreign securities, which remain governed by local ownership law.

[156] "Recommendations for Securities Settlement Systems," CPSS-IOSCO, November 2001, available on the web site of the Bank for International Settlements at www.bis.org in the CPSS publication section.

[157] "Assessment Methodology for the Recommendations for SSSs," CPSS-IOSCO, November 2002, available on the web site of the Bank for International Settlements at www.bis.org in the CPSS publication section.

[158] See the CPSS (BIS) report, "Central bank oversight of payment and settlement systems" (May 2005).

[159] The main conclusions of the assessment of clearing and settlement systems against CPSS-IOSCO recommendations are normally published even though there are not many assessments currently available. The National Bank of Belgium published its main findings in relation to the Euroclear System in its Financial Stability Review in 2005, at 105–113.

On the U.S. Commercial Law Response to the Development of Intermediated Securities Holding Systems

SANDRA M. ROCKS

This chapter offers a perspective on the commercial law response in the United States over the last half-century to the transformation in how securities are held. Except for some aspects of the American federal system, the commercial law rules governing transactions involving investment securities—whether outright conveyances or security interests—are part of a statutory scheme called the Uniform Commercial Code (UCC). Technically, the UCC is a model law that is offered to the states for adoption, and only when adopted by a state does it have the force of law. Two articles of the UCC are relevant for securities: Article 8, entitled "Investment Securities," and Article 9, entitled "Secured Transactions."[1] All 50 states and the District of Columbia have adopted versions of these two articles that are uniform in all respects relevant to this chapter. It is important to note, however, that these articles operate within a context of general contract law as well as a context in which many—but not all—of the relevant players are subject to regulatory oversight.

At one time, these two articles dealt with investment securities only in physical form. With a very narrow exception for clearing corporation activities (which for the most part was located in New York), there was no real commercial statutory law recognition of the multi-layered holding patterns that have become so prevalent today. Indeed, when the U.S. Treasury decided to take action in the face of the "paper crunch" in the 1960s—in which securities transactions in large numbers failed to settle due to the inability to deliver the paper certificates in a timely fashion as trading volume grew—it took two contradictory steps. First, it created completely dematerialized securities—simply entries on the records of Federal Reserve Banks (which served a quasi-transfer agent role). These securities could then be moved solely by electronic entry. (Many other countries have also done this, of course.) And second, for commercial law purposes—since this is not really a subject of federal law—the enacting regulations "deemed" these securities to be maintained in "bearer definitive form at the Federal Reserve Bank." Technology was obviously out in front, but the securities needed to find a home in a commercial code that knew only paper. (At that time, paperless securities would have been considered "general intangibles" in UCC parlance, a category unsuitable for a variety of reasons, not the least of which was that UCC searches and filings would have been necessary for utilizing such securities as collateral, an approach impossible to adapt to most transactions in fungible securities.)

In the regular corporate market in the United States, dematerialization did not occur, but another phenomenon had a similar effect: immobilization and intermediation. More and more securities were held by—and in some cases issued directly into—clearing corporations, to be held for participants who in turn held for their customers. The split between what one might consider legal title (i.e., the person who is the registered owner as far as the issuer is concerned) and beneficial ownership (i.e., the person to whom the economic benefits of ownership were to flow) was recognized in practice but not in explicit statutory language. Revisions to the UCC in the late 1970s attempted to recognize these phenomena by creating a definitive list of how interests in securities could be conveyed (whether outright or by way of security interest) and introduced a pro rata sharing rule for situations in which holdings were insufficient to cover the positions of investors. The definition of "security" limited the scope of the statute's applicability, notwithstanding the market's identical treatment of many different types of investments. Moreover, the rules suggested that the most determinative factor was whether the security itself was certificated or uncertificated, and each person having an interest in the security was treated as though that person had an interest in the underlying security itself, which interest could potentially be traced into the hands of any purchaser (with a limited exception for transfers within the clearing corporation context).

These shortcomings had become widely recognized by the late 1970s, and the uncomfortable fit between the federal regulations for securities maintained solely in the form of entries in the records of Federal Reserve Banks and state commercial law was a significant source of legal uncertainty. But it took a fairly significant market disruption in the late 1980s to jump-start the process of revising the law. Efforts on the state law and federal regulatory fronts played leap-frog, as drafts of proposed revisions to federal regulations were put out for comment and, with the threat of greater federal preemption hanging in the air, the appropriate groups began the process of revising Article 8 (with conforming amendments to Article 9.)

Simultaneously, various revisions to U.S. bankruptcy law—which generally annoys creditors and counterparties by interrupting enforcement of rights and sometimes avoiding transfers of interests in property—were adopted during the 1980s and 1990s to free certain market participants from these adverse consequences. Briefly, repurchase agreements, futures contracts, securities contracts, and swap agreements are now afforded special protection that allows certain counterparties to exercise their contractual remedies and access and retain the value of their collateral notwithstanding a bankruptcy proceeding in respect of the other party (and this "safe harbor" phenomenon appears not only in the U.S. Bankruptcy Code, which is available to most general corporate entities, but in the federal receivership regime governing most depositary institutions). These parallel movements had a common goal: to increase legal certainty in contexts for which systemic risk was a concern.

Principles of Commercial Law Rules Relating to Interests in Securities Held with Intermediaries

The principles outlined in this section provide a framework that accommodates market developments in securities holding and trading patterns and thus are a foundation for the legal certainty required by credit departments and regulators alike.

Principle 1. *Recognize and, to the extent possible, anticipate innovations in holding patterns and the assets that may become subject to such innovations.*

The law needs to grow with the market. In many jurisdictions today, however, the market is way out front. Unless there is a policy reason to the countrary, any project to revise the commercial law should aim to address the manner in which assets are in fact being held and transferred. The harder task is to craft rules that will have a long shelf life and thus are flexible enough to accommodate future holding patterns without resort to artifice or attenuated legal analogies. UCC Article 8 attempts to be accommodating in two ways: first, by recognizing a concept of indirect holding that is unlimited in terms of participants and the number of potential intermediaries in any given chain, and second, by being even more limitless (and this concept exists—see Cantor's Theorem) in regard to what might in the future be held in the indirect holding system as we know it. This latter accommodation was accomplished in the United States through the use of the wide-open gatekeeping definition of financial asset that includes *any property an intermediary agrees to treat as a financial asset.* (A life insurance policy is an example of a nontraditional asset being treated as a financial asset. This approach has begun to appear in the "life settlement" business, as investors seek to acquire and transfer interests in life insurance policies without the need to involve the insurer when changing "ownership.") As for the legal recognition of holding through intermediaries, under the UCC, the terminology that applies when a person has a direct relationship with the issuer is *direct holding*; when securities or other financial assets are held through one or more intermediaries, it is *indirect holding*. (See Figure 1.)

Figure 1. Overview of Securities Holding Patterns

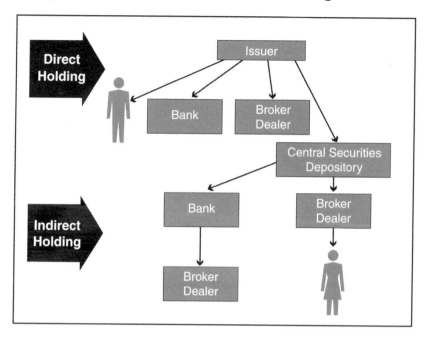

Two questions—who, as a corporate or regulatory matter, is permitted to act as an intermediary and what such intermediaries are permitted to hold and deal with on behalf of themselves and others—were left to other areas of law. (And the commercial law governing a financial asset in its natural state—that is, outside the securities account itself—was also untouched.)

Principle 2. *Recognize and/or create an appropriate concept of property interest.*

Generally speaking, in the United States the corporate and commercial law rules regarding the nature of an investor's relationship with an issuer of securities (part of the direct holding system) did not need adjustment—nominee holdings, split legal and beneficial interests, passing through of benefits, and so on were already recognized and thus easy to integrate into the indirect holding system. But the extent of intermediation that had developed and the inherent fungibility of many of the financial assets involved led to a departure from viewing an investor's interest in securities held indirectly as a property right traceable in all respects to an underlying security or other financial asset.

For indirect holding, the questions became (1) What is the nature of the beneficial "owner's" property interest? and (2) What are the basic rights a beneficial owner has against its intermediary (and others) with respect to that underlying security or other financial asset?

In reponse, a *security entitlement* (defined in Section 8-102(a)(17)) was born: "'Security Entitlement' means the rights and property interest of an entitlement holder with respect to a financial asset specified in Part 5," which rights and interests include:

- Pro rata property interest in the relevant financial assets;

- Obligation of the securities intermediary to maintain sufficient financial assets to cover positions it creates by crediting securities accounts;

- Duty of the securities intermediary to obtain and remit payments or distributions made by issuers;

- Duty of the securities intermediary to exercise rights (e.g., voting) as directed by entitlement holder;

- Duty of the securities intermediary to comply with transfer instructions of entitlement holder;

- Duty of the securities intermediary to change entitlement holder's position to another available form of holding for which such entitlement holder is eligible (e.g., one can obtain a paper certificate only when and if the terms of issuance so permit).

Much flows from this recognition. Under the UCC, the investor's rights are neither simply a derivative property interest in assets that happen to be held for customers, nor are they immune from dilution. As was just noted, an intermediary's duties include the obligation to maintain sufficient financial assets to cover the positions of its entitlement holders. Section 8-503(a) of the UCC provides:

> To the extent necessary for a securities intermediary to satisfy all security entitlements with respect to a particular financial asset, all interests in that financial asset held by the securities intermediary are held by the securities intermediary for the entitlement holders, are not property of the securities intermediary, and are not subject to claims of creditors of the securities intermediary, except as otherwise provided in Section 8-511.

Section 8-511 provides that in the event of a shortfall in financial assets, claims of entitlement holders have priority over claims of creditors other than secured creditors having control over the financial asset. (See Figure 2.)

Figure 2. Customers vs. Creditors

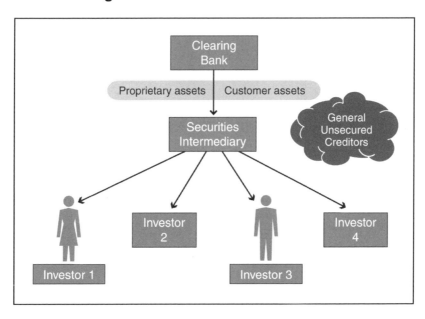

Here the claims of the investors to particular financial assets would be satisfied out of customer *and* proprietary assets before unsecured creditors would have access to any of the financial assets held by the securities intermediary.

On the other hand, Section 8-503 goes on to provide:

> An entitlement holder's property interest with respect to a particular financial asset under subsection (a) is a pro rata property interest in all interests in that financial asset held by the securities intermediary, without regard to the time the intermediary acquired the interest in that financial asset. (Section 8-503(b))

This means that investors' positions can be adversely affected by the existence of other investors

Figure 3. Customers vs. Customers

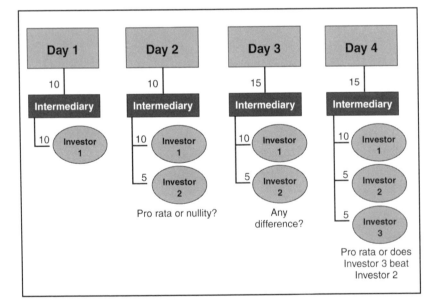

Under the UCC, on Day 2 the "overcrediting" would generally be effective, and Investor 2 would be considered as obtaining a security entitlement, Investor 1's position being diluted. On Day 3 the intermediary would be in compliance with its obligations to both investors, and Day 4 would again involve dilution, not a "trumping" by last-in-time Investor 3.

Regarding this fact pattern, is the securities intermediary allowed to overcredit? It depends. If the action is fraudulent, no; but in the United States, if the position is created by a broker-dealer pending settlement, for example, and there is an open fail to receive, the answer is yes (for a limited period of time). (And of course we are not at this point addressing "mistaken" credits or debits.)

Recognizing a new concept of property interest in a security entitlement enables the prevention of "upper tier attachment" and itself enhances certain aspects of finality—both of which are essential to the smooth functioning of the markets. The intermediary that is maintaining the securities account for the investor is the only place the investor's attachable property resides. UCC Article 8 makes clear that the customer's interest cannot, except in very limited circumstances, be asserted against any other intermediary (or purchaser), and modified a rule to clarify that a creditor can attach the customer's interest only at that level by process against the intermediary (or, if a secured party had become the entitlement holder with respect to pledged assets, by process against the secured party). This is sometimes referred to as a "no look through" approach.

This also means that in the event of an intermediary's insolvency customers will share pro rata (category by category of the financial assets), and it seems that some method of loss sharing must be made explicit in conjunction with any recognition of the effects of holding securities through an intermediary. (For U.S. stockbrokers covered by the Securities Investor Protection Act, the sharing is done without regard to the type of financial asset—all customer property is pooled and shortfalls are allocated across financial asset categories.)

Principle 3. *Provide enhanced finality.*

The United States is far from unique in recognizing the concept of a good faith or other type of protected purchaser, especially in the world of tangible movables. In such a case a rightful owner can be prevented from recovering wrongfully transferred property. But in the indirect system how can such a rule be implemented? The asset is certainly far less traceable, but that doesn't answer the question. Consider the following hypothetical:

There are two investors, one whose securities were improperly moved out by an intermediary and one who acquired a security entitlement in respect of those securities without notice that their transfer was improper. Putting the burden on the first feels unfair, and therefore there are some who might suggest that this plaintiff should enjoy the right to recapture. The question, however, is not really whether such plaintiffs should have redress. Of course they should. The question for the commercial law project is really whether the "innocent" transferee should be at risk. Of course, for the transferee to be at risk in any meaningful way presumes traceability, which is quite unlikely in the vast majority of cases. One might therefore feel comfortable supporting recapture rights under the theory that there will be few successful attempts anyway. On the other hand, in most cases the recipient has no idea where the purchased securities are coming from, and just the possibility of such a tracing or recapture right has been thought (and felt, through market experience) to constitute something of a cloud on title. The potential ripple effect in the market of tracing wrongfully transferred securities through multiple purchasers could have negative consequences exponentially exceeding the benefit to the wronged original owner. For these reasons, the policy choice made in the UCC was to permit *any* purchaser, including a secured party, who gives value (which in the United States means any sort of consideration) and obtains "control" (discussed in greater detail under Principle 4) without notice of a particular adverse claim to be protected against the assertion of that adverse claim. It is for this reason that the better, and perhaps more honest, outcome is for commercial law to provide clear and widely available adverse-claim cut-off rules that promote systemic confidence and thus work to the benefit of investors large and small.

Another aspect of finality that is of vital concern to market participants is finality notwithstanding the insolvency of a transferor. "Zero hour" and other recapture rules have a chilling effect on the market, and for that reason in the context of such an interlinked trading system they should be eliminated or limited as much as possible. These negative insolvency effects have been questioned as a policy matter in many corners, including at a major symposium sponsored some years back by the European Central Bank. The long and tortured history of the appropriate contours for "safe harbors" under the key U.S. insolvency regimes—recently expanded yet again—illustrates this as well.

Principle 4. *Provide a flexible approach to effectiveness, perfection, and priority, including the reduction or elimination of formalities.*

Flexibility has been a recognized goal in two major respects: first, in terms of what the purchaser (especially a secured party) needs to do or have done in its favor; and second, what the pledgor can continue to do.

Since the issues requiring attention arose from the indirect system, the effectiveness of physical delivery of a security in certificated form remained undisturbed. But once the indirect system became recognized for what it is—a vast electronic grid in which securities and other financial assets are moved in response to transfer or other instructions—it seemed most efficacious to accommodate these realities of the marketplace by recognizing new ways to effect transfers of interests—that is, not being limited to the ways one would typically transfer a physical certificate (e.g., physical delivery) or an intangible (e.g., notice to the obligor). In fairness, this did not begin with the development of the "security entitlement" concept. Book entries had been recognized for quite some time, but not with the full panoply of attendant rights the market required.

In the United States the concept of "control" was introduced as a statutory construct: a transfer is perfected (i.e., enforceable against third parties) if the transferee has the right, enforceable against the intermediary, to direct the disposition of the subject assets. Such control can materialize in one of three types of situations. First, a transferee who has the financial assets credited to its own securities account is considered to be in control of the financial assets. This is the situation that involves a book entry in the classic sense of a debit and corresponding credit. (See Figures 4a and 4b.)

Figure 4a.

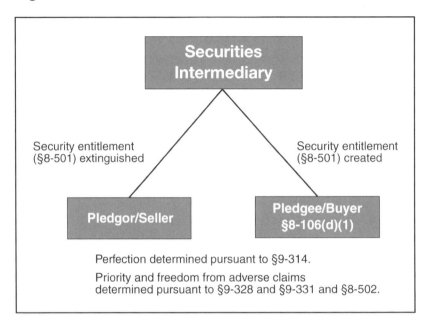

Figure 4b.

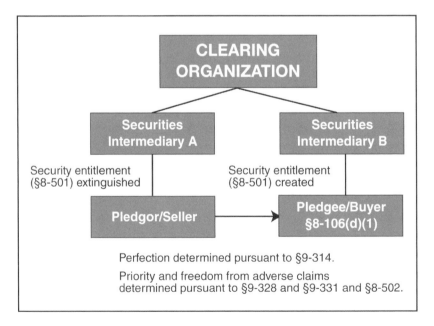

Second, the intermediary with which a securities account is maintained is considered, as a matter of law, to be in control of the financial assets carried in that securities account. (No book entry is needed in such a fact pattern. Market participants are expected to assume that an "upper tier" intermediary, often involved in the clearing and settlement of securities on behalf of its customers, would have a lien without making a notation on its books). (See Figure 5.) The UCC includes a statutory lien in favor of such intermediaries as well, which arises in the circumstance in which the intermediary extends credit to the customer in connection with the acquisition of a financial asset and is limited in scope to a security interest in the particular asset securing the particular extension of credit. (Section 9-206)

Figure 5. Control via Being the Securities Intermediary

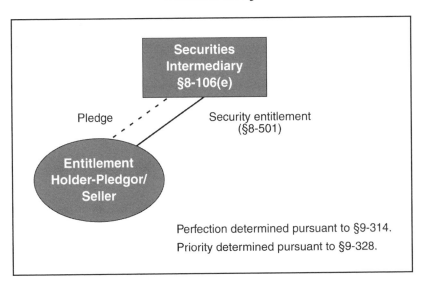

Third, a transferee who obtains the agreement of the intermediary to act on the transferee's instructions without further consent of the transferor has obtained control. (The UCC states explicitly that an intermediary is under no duty to enter into such an agreement and is prohibited from doing so without its customer's consent). Again, this third situation requires no book entry and has proved enormously useful, including for individual investors. (See Figure 6.)

Figure 6. Control via a Securities Account Control Agreement

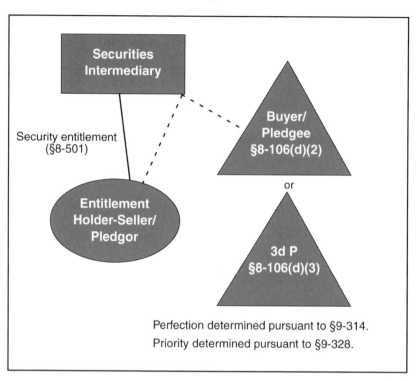

Securities Intermediary

Security entitlement
(§8-501)

Buyer/
Pledgee
§8-106(d)(2)

or

Entitlement
Holder-Seller/
Pledgor

3d P
§8-106(d)(3)

Perfection determined pursuant to §9-314.
Priority determined pursuant to §9-328.

No registration of any sort is required. (In the United States perfection by filing a UCC financing statement is an option, but this affords less priority). And a book entry is not the only way to effect a transfer of an interest. There are other settings in which the requirement of a book entry would seem inappropriate—net settlement systems do not make debits and credits for each movement of financial assets. That would defeat the whole purpose; gifts and inheritances, a bankruptcy trustee's assertion of jurisdiction over estate assets—all these are likely to need effectiveness notwithstanding the lack of a book entry.

The second aspect of flexibility mentioned above is the degree to which the pledgor can continue to have access to the property, i.e., permitting a pledgor to continue to deal with the property transferred (this is often an issue in the security interest context, for example, although other transaction forms could be involved).

The UCC concept of control does not require exclusivity: a pledgor can continue to maintain its portfolios with existing intermediaries who may not wish to extend credit, and can continue to trade its portfolios of securities, including through direct instructions to the relevant intermediary, notwithstanding a secured party's parallel right to originate such instructions. The limits, if any, and the interplay of these rights are left to the parties' agreement. The secured party may or may not be comfortable allowing debtor access, and the debtor may seek to limit the circumstances in which the secured party can take action, but effectiveness of a secured party's interest as against third parties remains intact.

Principle 5. *Recognize a secured party's right to reuse collateral.*

The line between ownership and security interest is often blurred under the law of a single jurisdiction, and in a cross-border situation it only gets more complicated. Trillions of dollars in value are involved in the reuse of financial assets transferred under securities contracts, repurchase transactions, and swap agreements, thus forming long chains of reuse. The United States has chosen to permit this explicitly whenever a secured party is in control. Reusing collateral is *what the market does.* If the U.S. experience is any guide, new commercial law approaches need to recognize this and permit it in a way that does not elevate form over substance. (This does not mean that an intermediary is permitted to use fully paid customer securities, of course. In the United States this would generally require the customer's permission; even in that case it could be subject to various legal restrictions.)

It is important to reiterate that the UCC itself sits within a nest of other law and regulations that determine, among many other things, the right of an intermediary to use nonproprietary assets, and the absence of such controls (or the infrastructure to support them) could militate in favor of commercial law adjustments.

Principle 6. *Provide flexible realization rules, including self-help.*

In the United States a secured party has the right as a matter of law to dispose of property in which it has a security interest after default, but the secured party's actions must be commercially reasonable. For commonly traded financial assets, prompt collateral liquidation without the need for any sort of judicial intervention is one of the hallmarks of the type of commercial law rule this market requires. Limiting interference of the commercial law with using self-help to realize on marketable and fungible collateral reduces the likelihood of gridlock and the systemic risk that could ensue.

Principle 7. *Where warranted, provide special protections for intermediaries.*

Three circumstances might apply here. The first is allowing special deference to the rules of regulated/supervised clearing organizations and central counterparties. (This principle is also recognized in the EU Settlement Finality Directive.) These entities or systems are key players in the smooth flow of securities trading and settlement and generally do not (in fact, are often not permitted to) maintain true proprietary positions. In the United States the concept of "clearing corporation" is limited to:

- a person that is registered as a "clearing agency" under the federal securities laws;

- a federal reserve bank; or

- any other person that provides clearance or settlement services with respect to financial assets that would require it to register as a clearing agency under the federal securities laws but for an exclusion or exemption from the registration requirement, if its activities as a clearing corporation, including promulgation of the rules, are subject to regulation by a federal or state governmental authority.

Although this category has been expanded somewhat over the years, it is still a fairly small club. Because of the important role played by these institutions and the nature and extent of their supervision (at least in the United States), the UCC includes special rules just for clearing corporations. One is found in UCC Section 8-111, which provides: "A rule adopted by a clearing corporation governing rights and obligations among the clearing corporation and its participants in the clearing corporation is effective even if the rule conflicts with this [Act] and affects another party who does not consent to the rule." This section provides essential comfort to clearing organizations that the various loss sharing, finality, and failed-settlement rules they adopt will be given effect irrespective of what Article 8 would otherwise mandate.

The second circumstance allows a departure from the usual relationship between a securities intermediary's customers and its creditors. As mentioned earlier, creditors without control are generally subordinated to customers, and secured creditors having control are superior. In the clearing corporation context, however, the rule is different. The clearing corporation is a direct holder of securities, which means that control would require re-registration or possession of certificates or control agreements with issuers. Requiring a clearing corporation's secured creditors—in practice limited to liquidity lines to provide end-of-day failed-settlement financing—to obtain control in any of those ways could be disruptive to ordinary securities processing if put in place at the outset, and impossible to accomplish in a timely manner if only put in place when an end-of-day loan was required. Given this special situation, the UCC provides, under Section 8-511(c), that all creditors of clearing corporations have priority over customers.

The third circumstance is an adjustment to the rules governing when interests in securities held indirectly are acquired free of adverse claims. Section 8-115 of the UCC ("Securities Intermediary and Others Not Liable to Adverse Claimant") provides:

> A securities intermediary that has transferred a financial asset pursuant to an effective entitlement order, or a broker or other agent or bailee that has dealt with a financial asset at the direction of its customer or principal, is not liable to a person having an adverse claim to the financial asset, unless the securities intermediary, or broker or other agent or bailee:

(1) took the action after it had been served with an injunction, restraining order, or other legal process enjoining it from doing so, issued by a court of competent jurisdiction, and had a reasonable opportunity to act on the injunction, restraining order, or other legal process; or

(2) acted in collusion with the wrongdoer in violating the rights of the adverse claimant; or

(3) in the case of a security certificate that has been stolen, acted with notice of the adverse claim.

This standard, applicable to any securities intermediary, recognizes the "conduit" nature of the intermediary's role and does not attribute the knowledge or wrongful behavior of customers or counterparties to the intermediary.

Principle 8. *Provide clear and market-sensitive choice-of-law rules.*

(The ensuing discussion concerns rights in or to securities or other financial assets held through intermediaries but does not address the relationship of parties to a transaction or the relationship between an account holder and an intermediary as a matter of contract law.)

Before the last round of UCC revisions, it would have been fair to say that while the UCC provided clear choice-of-law rules, the rules were limited in reach (by essentially applying only to secured transactions) and not market-sensitive. They were clear because the rule turned on whether the security was in certificated form, in which case the physical location of the certificate was key, or uncertificated, in which case the jurisdiction in which the issuer was organized was determinative. (This was particularly counterintuitive when applied to the U.S. Treasury and U.S. agency securities that the federal regulations had "deemed" to be maintained in bearer definition form "at a Federal Reserve Bank.") They were not market sensitive because they did not treat the securities account itself, to which a variety of securities could be credited, as relevant. This shortcoming became an even greater liability in the cross-border situation.

Figure 7. Going Global

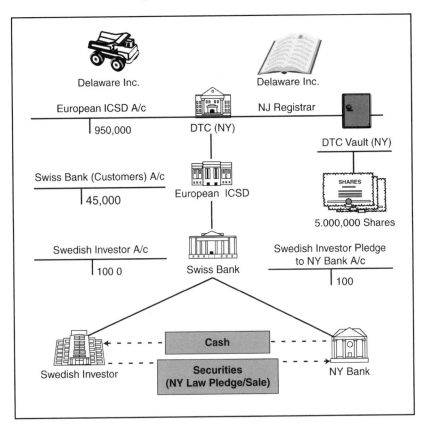

The fact pattern shown in Figure 7, or in any fact pattern involving indirect holding, participants need to know what law governs their rights against others, known and unknown. This includes the counterparty to a given sale or pledge transaction (and its insolvency representative), the intermediary or intermediaries with which the parties dealt, other entities involved in the transfer and holding of the relevant assets, and competing claimants of all sorts. And the answer needed to make sense—not point to a jurisdiction with no discernibly relevant relationship to the rights and interests being determined (e.g., the Delaware jurisdiction of organization or the New York vault, shown in Figure 7).

The response in the United States was to take an unprecedented path: the concept of *securities intermediary's jurisdiction* was developed. In general terms, the law governing the rights one acquired via a credit to one's securities account, whether an adverse claim could be asserted against a purchaser, perfection in most circumstances, and priority of a security interest, is the law of the securities intermediary's jurisdiction. This concept is not entirely intuitive, and has definitely taken some getting used to (especially for practitioners from outside the United States).

UCC Section 8-110(e) Applicable Law

The following UCC rules determine a securities intermediary's jurisdiction:

- An express selection of a securities intermediary's jurisdiction in the relevant agreement between the securities intermediary and its entitlement holder;

- An express selection of a governing law in the relevant agreement between the securities intermediary and its entitlement holder;

- An express provision in the relevant agreement between the securities intermediary and its entitlement holder that the securities account is maintained at an office in a particular jurisdiction;

- The jurisdiction in which the office identified in an account statement as the office serving the entitlement holder's account is located;

- The jurisdiction in which the chief executive office of the securities intermediary is located;

Keeping this shift in mind—from the location of the security certificate or the jurisdiction of the issuer to the securities intermediary's jurisdiction—one can see that the relevant law in Figure 7 will be determined in some way by reference to the Swiss Bank. Whether Swiss law will in fact apply or what Swiss law has to say (substantively) are beyond the scope of this chapter. But focusing on the choice of law, we've now eliminated several other jurisdictions (e.g., location of certificate, jurisdiction of issuer's organization, location of securities register, pledgor's or seller's location, and jurisdictions relevant to other intermediaries). A possibility for what a diversified portfolio might look are illustrated in Figure 8.

Figure 8. Going Global—A Closer Look

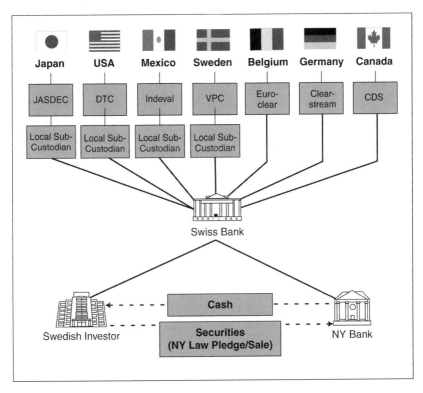

The UCC will point to the securities intermediary's jurisdiction, without regard to issuer, physical location of any certificates or any intermediary (such as a sub-custodian) other than the Swiss Bank. Moreover, the applicable law will be the local law—i.e., not including any conflicts of law rules—of the securities intermediary's jurisdiction. In the foregoing example, therefore, although New York law will apply to the pledge or sale relationship between the Swedish investor and the New York bank, the substantive law of Switzerland will apply to, among other matters, the effectiveness and priority of the pledge against most third parties. Whether this would be the result if the issue is considered under non-U.S. law is currently a source of uncertainty in most jurisdictions and for this reason this author, for one, hopes for the adoption of the Hague Convention on the Law Applicable to Certain Rights in respect of Securities Held with an Intermediary (the topic of the next chapter by Christophe Bernasconi).

Note

[1] All statutory section references herein are to these Articles.

20 | The Hague Securities Convention

CHRISTOPHE BERNASCONI

The need for uniform conflict of laws rules that effectively address the reality of how securities are held and transferred[1] today (i.e., by electronic book-entry debits and credits to securities accounts of primarily dematerialized or immobilized securities) has become critical. The last several decades have seen a dramatic increase in the value, number and speed of cross-border securities transactions, facilitated by advances in technology. The value of trades and collateral transactions in government and corporate securities in countries of the Organisation for Economic Co-operation and Development (OECD), for example, has grown to approximately US\$ 2 trillion per day.[2] Legal uncertainty as to the law governing the perfection, priority, and other effects of transfers imposes significant friction costs on even routine transactions and operates as an important constraint on desirable reductions in credit and liquidity exposures. Increased exposure to unsecured credit risk amplifies systemic risk and the potential proliferation of bankruptcies. Not surprisingly, for more than a decade the international legal and financial community has been emphasizing the need for uniform conflict of laws rules applicable to transactions involving securities held with intermediaries.[3]

To address the current uncertainties, the 19th Diplomatic Session of the Hague Conference on Private International Law (HCCH) unanimously adopted the Convention on the Law Applicable to Certain Rights in Respect of Securities Held with an Intermediary (the Hague Securities Convention or the Convention).[4] Key industry groups such as the Group of 30 (G30), composed of representatives of public and private financial institutions, promptly urged its immediate and universal ratification.[5] Such reactions reflect the importance of the Convention, constitute a strong sign of its macro-economic relevance, and prefigure the key role it will play in the safe, sound, and effective functioning of national financial systems, as well as individual private transactions. The Convention's importance was also promptly recognized in scholarly writings.[6]

Soon after its adoption, several governments, as well as the relevant bodies of the European Community, started the necessary consultations regarding a possible signing and ratification of the Convention. To date, the Convention has been signed by the United States and Switzerland;[7] both of these states are actively working towards the ratification of the Convention.[8] In other states, as well as at the level of the European Community,[9] the assessment of the Convention is ongoing.[10] In this respect, it should be noted that the process leading to the adoption of the Convention was quite unusual, and in many respects remarkable: it was negotiated, in a totally inclusive and transparent fast-track procedure that lasted only thirty months (May 2000 to December 2002), by delegations from around the world (thirty-one member states of the Hague Conference, two non-member states, eight intergovernmental organizations, nine nongovernmental organizations)—delegations that reflected all major legal systems and that included not only private international law experts, but also experts in securities industry practice and commercial law—with the active participation of important industry representative groups. Thus the Convention reflects a pragmatic approach, based on real-world needs, aimed at achieving *ex ante* certainty and predictability as to the law governing issues that are of crucial practical importance for the holding and transfer of securities held with an intermediary, in particular their effects against the intermediary and third parties.[11]

The *ex ante* legal certainty that the Convention is designed to achieve is very important under the revised capital adequacy framework commonly known as Basel II.[12] This revised framework, which was endorsed in June 2004 by central bank governors and the heads of bank supervisory authorities in the Group of Ten (G10) countries, provides a range of options for determining the capital requirements for credit risk and operational risk to allow banks and supervisors to select approaches that are most appropriate for their operations and their financial market infrastructures. Banks use a number of techniques to mitigate the credit risks to which they are exposed—for instance, by taking collateral in the securities to ensure first priority rights on default. When these techniques meet the requirements for legal certainty established by the Basel II accord, the revised approach to credit risk mitigation allows for the recognition of a wider range of strategies to alleviate credit risk for regulatory capital purposes than is permitted under the 1988 accord.[13]

This chapter briefly describes the changes that have occurred over the last several decades in the way shares, bonds, and other investment securities are held, traded, and settled. It then demonstrates the resulting need for re-examining the traditional conflict of laws rules applicable to transactions involving securities held with intermediaries. The main part of the chapter explains the content, operation, and principal advantages of the primary conflict of laws rule embodied in the Convention, and is followed by a discussion of the Convention's most significant other provisions. The chapter concludes with a brief overview of the Convention's remaining provisions.

Holding and Transfer of Securities: Changes in Market Practice; the Legal Environment; Conflict of Laws Issues

From Direct to Indirect Holding

Over the last half century there has been a marked change in the way that shares, bonds and other investment securities are held and transferred. The two principal changes are (1) the immobilization or dematerialization of securities, and (2) the shift *from* the holding of securities through the registration of ownership on books maintained by or for the issuer or the physical possession of security certificates, without the involvement of any intermediary (i.e., a *direct* holding system whereby there is a direct relationship between the issuer and the holder), *to* holding systems in which interests in securities are held (and transferred) through securities accounts maintained for customers by intermediaries, one or more of which stand between the customer and the issuer (i.e., the owner is said to hold its securities *indirectly* because its holding is reflected in an account maintained for it by its intermediary, even though in some legal systems the owner is said nevertheless to have a direct legal relationship with the issuer, and the intermediary is viewed as a mere pass-through record-keeper without any legal interest in the securities held).

In indirect holding systems there will be one or more *intermediaries*—a term that can include not only a central securities depositary (CSD) and an international central securities depositary (ICSD), where large quantities of securities of different issuers are immobilized or otherwise concentrated, but also clearing corporations, central banks, securities firms, and banks—positioned between the investor and the issuer. Typically, a CSD or ICSD will maintain securities accounts for financial institutions, broker-dealers, and other intermediaries (these account holders are often called "participants" of the CSD or ICSD). These participants, in turn, maintain securities accounts for their customers, such as institutional investors or other intermediaries. These intermediaries, in turn, maintain securities accounts for other intermediaries, and so forth, with the lowest-tier intermediary maintaining a securities account for the ultimate investor. Thus there may be a variable number of tiers between the investors at the bottom of the structure and the issuers at the top. In many systems, there is no record (i.e., no identification or segregation) of an individual account holder's interest in the underlying securities at the level of the issuer's register or that of any intermediary other than the intermediary with whom the investor has a direct relationship.[14]

Substantive Law Approaches to Securities Held with an Intermediary

Substantive law approaches to the holding of interests in securities with an intermediary vary among legal systems. Under some legal systems, the investor's intermediary[15] is contractually and/or legally obligated to hold interests in securities, corresponding to the investor's interest and to those of the intermediary's other customers, credited to a securities account maintained for it by its intermediary and so on up the chain to the highest-tier intermediary, whose holdings are reflected directly on the issuers' books; in these legal systems there is a separate interest at the level of each intermediary, and the highest-tier intermediary (or its nominee) is the registered holder of the securities on the issuer's books.

Under other legal systems, however, an intermediary acts as a mere record keeper of an investor's interest; while the investor's interest results from a credit to a securities account and is transferable through book-entry, the credit of the securities to a securities account maintained by the investor's intermediary establishes a direct relationship between the investor and the issuer. Consequently, in these legal systems, no intermediary is registered on the issuer's books as the holder of the securities. Even under the latter legal systems, the investor's interest in the securities is within the Convention since it is held through a securities account maintained for the investor by an intermediary.

The Conflict of Laws Analysis

The Traditional **Lex Rei Sitae**

The traditional rule for determining the enforceability of a transfer of property effected in the direct holding system is the *lex rei sitae* (or the *lex situs*), more specifically referred to in the context of securities as the *lex cartae sitae*. Under this rule, the effectiveness of a transfer of securities is determined by the law of the place where the securities are located at the time of the transfer. In the case of bearer securities (i.e., securities that are represented solely by physical certificates and are not registered in any name), this is taken to be the law of the place of the certificates representing the securities at the time of transfer. In the case of registered securities, the *lex rei sitae* is taken to be either the law of the place of the issuer's incorporation or organization or the law of the place where the register is maintained (whether by the issuer itself or by a registrar on behalf of the issuer) at the time of transfer.

These traditional approaches have generally produced a satisfactory result in relation to directly held securities. The approaches are, however, unsatisfactory in relation to interests in securities held with an intermediary because they require, for the purposes of determining the applicable law, "looking through" tiers of intermediaries to the level of the issuer, register, or actual certificates (the *look-through approach*). Suffice it to say, in the context of securities held with one or more intermediaries, the look-through approach may not be possible at all, and even when possible, may give rise to severe difficulties.

In today's markets, it is very common, both for intermediaries providing collateral to their financiers and the CSDs of which they are participants, and for investors providing collateral to their financiers, to hypothecate a diversified portfolio of securities issued by companies organized under the laws of diverse jurisdictions (and/or maintaining registries in diverse jurisdictions) and/or by diverse governments and governmental agencies—a practice facilitated by modern movables security laws. Rules based on a look-through approach would compel the collateral taker to determine and satisfy the perfection requirements of the domestic movables security law of each of the States where the issuers of the particular debt or equity securities are organized (or where the registries are maintained): a multitude of states for each such transaction. Moreover, where the portfolio is not static but changes composition over time, even daily or hourly (again, a practice greatly facilitated by modern movables security laws), it is impossible under such traditional conflict of laws rules for the collateral taker to efficiently manage a security interest in the portfolio. In addition, in many jurisdictions it is unclear exactly which of the rules based on a look-through approach should be applied. Would it be the law of the place of the issuer's organization, the law of the place of the securities register, the law of the place of the underlying security certificates, the law of the place of the highest-tier intermediary, or the law of the place of any other intermediary? Finally, even if the collateral taker does know which test to apply, it is often not possible to obtain the information necessary to apply the appropriate test. For example, an investor holding certificated securities through several tiers of intermediaries may not be able to discover where the certificates are actually stored.

The Place of the Relevant Intermediary Approach

Against this background of fundamental difficulties raised by the look-through approach, it was initially suggested that the Convention's conflict of laws rule should, in a continued search for a place, or *rei sitae* (real or fictional), focus on the location of the account to which the interest in the securities is credited, that is, the account maintained by the relevant intermediary, or the location of the office maintaining that account. This concept was described as the Place of the Relevant Intermediary Approach (PRIMA). It proposed that in regard to securities held with an intermediary, the law applicable to the effects against the intermediary and third parties of holdings and transfers of such securities be determined based on the place of the relevant intermediary's office at which the account is maintained, without consideration of the location of any higher-tier intermediary or the issuer or the registry or the security certificate— that is, avoiding look-through.[16]

While this approach would subject all of an account holder's interests with respect to a portfolio of securities to the law of a single jurisdiction, it nevertheless suffers from a fundamental difficulty. In the course of the Convention negotiations it became clear that there is no criterion—generally acceptable on a global basis for all categories of intermediaries and all types of securities falling within the Convention's scope—to determine definitively and beyond a doubt the location of a securities account (an intangible having no real location) or the office of an intermediary that maintains a specific securities account.[17]

Among the means and criteria mentioned as possible determinants of the location of an office that maintains a securities account were the use of tax, regulatory reporting, or accounting requirements. In certain states, intermediaries may be required to assign a code to each securities account that effectively allocates it to a particular office for tax, regulatory reporting, or accounting purposes. However, such requirements are by no means universal (indeed, they may be the exception rather than the rule). It is not the case in all states that securities accounts must appear on an intermediary's balance sheet, and, in any event, not all states have comprehensive accounting rules for assets and liabilities that do appear on an intermediary's balance sheet. Also, accounting, regulatory, and tax rules are based on considerations that are wholly unrelated to the considerations pertaining to the global business of securities custody, clearing and settlement. Therefore, it was deemed arbitrary to use the allocation of a securities account to a particular office for tax, regulatory reporting, or accounting purposes to determine the applicable law for an unrelated business purpose.

Moreover, it was found that locating an office that maintained a particular account would be increasingly impossible in light of the reality that some or all of the functions involved in the maintenance and servicing of a securities account are increasingly being undertaken from more than one office or outsourced to third parties in several locations. In light of the difficulties and uncertainties relating to the effort to "localize" a securities account or the place where it is maintained, it is suggested here that the rules, currently embodied in the European Settlement Finality and Collateral Directives,[18] provide only an illusion of certainty.[19]

In sum, if the Convention's criterion for determining the applicable law had been the location of the securities account or the location of the office where the securities account is maintained, no certainty would have been achieved, and such a test would have invited litigation in which courts would be required to make fact-intensive inquiries. The risks and burdens presented to a potential collateral taker are readily apparent.

Against this background, it became apparent in the course of the negotiations that the Convention had to move beyond the initial formulation of the PRIMA concept in order to provide the necessary *ex ante* legal certainty and predictability. It did this by abandoning the effort to attribute a location to an intermediary, a securities account, or an office at which a securities account is maintained, and replacing it with an approach giving effect to an express agreement on governing law between an account holder and its intermediary (including in this approach a *qualifying office* requirement, as described below). In so doing, the Convention adhered to the agreed rejection of rules based on *lex rei sitae* or any look-through approach, and it retained the key element of the relevant intermediary by focusing on the relationship between an account holder and the relevant intermediary with respect to a particular securities account.

The Conflict of Laws Rules Adopted in the Convention (Articles 4–6)

The Primary Rule (Article 4): An Expressly Agreed Choice of Law, Subject to a "Qualifying Office" Requirement

The Agreed Choice of Law

Article 4 is the key provision of the Convention. It sets forth the primary conflict of laws rule to determine the law applicable to all the issues falling within the scope of the Convention. The rule is not based on an attempt to "locate" a securities account, the office at which a securities account is maintained, an intermediary, the issuer, or the underlying securities. Rather, the Convention's primary rule is based on the relationship between an account holder and its intermediary: it gives effect to the express agreement by the parties to an account agreement on the law governing all the issues falling within the scope of the Convention. This choice may be expressed in either of two ways. If the parties expressly agree on a law governing their account agreement (general governing law clause), that law also governs all the issues falling within the scope of the Convention. If, however, the account holder and its relevant intermediary expressly agree that the law of a particular state will govern all the issues falling within the scope of the Convention, that law governs all these issues (whether or not there is also a separate choice of law to govern the account agreement generally).

The requirement that the agreement be express makes clear that the Convention will not give such an effect to an implied choice of a law (whether implied from the terms of the account agreement considered as a whole or from the surrounding circumstances or otherwise).[20] Under Article 4(1), only an express agreement will determine the applicable law. If an implied but unexpressed choice could have effect under the Convention, it would seriously undermine the certainty and predictability provided by the Convention.[21]

The Qualifying Office Requirement

The parties' express choice of law, however, will be effective to determine the applicable law under the Convention only if, at the time of the agreement on governing law, the relevant intermediary has an office in the selected state that meets either of two criteria set out in the Convention (the "qualifying office" requirement).

Under the first criterion (Article 4(1)(a)), the office must be one which, alone or with another office of the intermediary or a third party acting for the relevant intermediary *anywhere* (i.e., in the selected state or in any other state): (1) effects or monitors entries to securities accounts; (2) administers payments or corporate actions relating to securities held with the intermediary; or (3) is otherwise engaged in a business or other regular activity of maintaining securities accounts.[22] Under the second criterion, an office is a qualifying office if it is identified, by any specific means, as maintaining securities accounts in that state.

It must be stressed that no aspect of the Article 4(1) qualifying office requirement relates to any *specific* account maintained by the relevant intermediary or any *specific* account holder. The qualifying office need not be related to the securities account in respect of which the issue arises, and an office is a qualifying office if it satisfies any of the criteria described above, even if the securities account of the particular account holder in respect of which the issue arises is maintained at an office situated in another state (assuming that one can determine where a particular account is maintained).

The qualifying office requirement was inserted out of an abundance of caution to give heightened assurance against abuse, the potential of which was feared by some delegates. In fact, the requirement should rarely cause even a moment's pause. After all, most intermediaries are professional and responsible institutions—typically regulated entities—highly unlikely to enter into governing law agreements for the purpose of abusing a potential third party or to have difficulty satisfying the qualifying office requirement both obviously and legitimately.[23]

Explanatory Rules for Transfers by an Account Holder in Favor of Its Intermediary (Article 4(3))

Article 4(3) eliminates uncertainty over the issue of which intermediary is the relevant intermediary and which account agreement is the relevant account agreement in the context of a transfer by an account holder in favor of its intermediary, including circumstances when the intermediary holds a corresponding position in the same type and quantity of securities with an upper-tier intermediary or moves securities from one account to another with the upper-tier intermediary to comply with customer segregation requirements (whether regulatory or contractual). Article 4(3)(a) and (b) confirm that the relevant intermediary is the account holder's intermediary and that the relevant account agreement is the agreement between the account holder and its intermediary for purposes of applying Articles 4(1) and 5(1). Article 4(3)(c) confirms that the securities account to which the securities are credited immediately before the transfer is the relevant securities account for the purposes of Article 5(2) and (3). The interpretive rules of Article 4(3) apply whether or not the intermediary maintains on its own records a securities account in its own name to which are credited any securities debited from the account holder's securities account.

Appraisal of the Primary Conflict of Laws Rule

Article 4(1) reflects a policy decision to formulate a conflict of laws rule that reduces risk, promotes capital formation and investment, reflects existing and foreseeable market practice, is practical and efficient, and permits market participants to determine, in advance, which law governs all the issues falling within the scope of the Convention. Article 4(1) thereby provides *ex ante* legal certainty and predictability for the largest number of transactions. Under current market, legal, and regulatory conditions, none of the alternatives considered and rejected would have provided the degree of *ex ante* legal certainty, simplicity, logic, and clarity that the rule in Article 4(1) provides.

It should be noted that the Convention's primary conflict of laws rule works equally well in all situations involving securities held with an intermediary, independently of the nature of the right resulting from the credit of securities to a securities account and whether the right is enforceable against the relevant intermediary, any higher-tier intermediary, or the issuer.

Some voices in Europe have asserted that the possibility for the operator of a securities settlement system (SSS) to agree on different applicable laws with different participants in the system might increase systemic risk.[24] This assertion must be rejected as unrealistic. First, it is highly improbable that an SSS would agree to having the accounts that it maintains for its participants be governed by different laws, given the operational complexities that might result, in particular with respect to settlement finality. Second, there seems little likelihood that a participant could offer sufficient incentive to induce, or have such bargaining power to force, an SSS to make such an agreement. Third, it is highly likely that an SSS within the European Community would be deterred from agreeing to different governing laws with different participants by the fear that it might thereby jeopardize its designation by a member state as a "system" within the meaning of the Settlement Finality Directive.[25] Fourth, it is also quite possible that an SSS currently eligible for the settlement of collateral for Eurosystem credit operations would be deterred from agreeing to different governing laws with different participants by the concern that doing so might jeopardize its continued eligibility.[26] Accordingly, a settlement system (and particularly a European SSS) is, in practice, overwhelmingly likely to agree on the same governing law for all its accounts.[27]

It has also been asserted that the Convention's primary rule would lead to an increased impact of non-EU law (usually referring particularly to the law of New York), and that this would create a competitive advantage for U.S. institutions.[28] Again, both legs of this assertion must be firmly rejected. If there is any such risk, it is unrelated to the Convention and exists already in the absence of the Convention. Nothing currently prevents an investor based in Europe from opening an account with the New York office of a European intermediary, having European securities credited to that account, asking the intermediary to agree that New York law govern issues such as the legal nature of the rights resulting from the credit of securities to the securities account, and producing the result that some or all third-party rights be governed by New York law (as can likewise currently be done with respect to directly held certificated securities simply by the investor traveling to New York with the certificates and pledging the securities by delivery of the certificates to a lender there). In any event, opposing the Convention would not seem to be the appropriate response to an investor-held view (if such is the case) that non-EU law might be more advantageous to investors and their financiers. Furthermore, coping with New York or other law in the United States would hardly seem to be an unmanageable problem in these times of the ready availability of global legal advice and the extensive presence of affiliates and branches of many European institutions in the United States.[29]

It has also been argued that the Convention would lead to reduced investor protection.[30] This assertion, too, is without foundation. The Convention has no effect, and was not designed to have any effect, on how much protection a particular state's commercial or bankruptcy laws provide to investors as a result of their status as account holders, in particular in the event of an intermediary's bankruptcy. That is a matter for each state to decide. The Convention has no impact on where an intermediary's insolvency proceeding is likely to occur or the content of that state's insolvency law and its impact on the position of an investor. Investor protection rests on the prudent selection by investors of the intermediaries with whom they choose to do business and the effective supervision of intermediaries by those charged with regulation, not on the provisions of a private international law convention.

Finally, the following—one would think rather obvious—point cannot be overemphasized: the Convention has no impact on existing or future regulatory regimes controlling private conduct, whether toward the goal of preventing money laundering, preventing tax evasion, assuring safe and sound business practices, or minimizing systemic risk. These questions are simply not within the scope of the Convention and therefore remain unaffected by it.[31] Thus, supervisory authorities are, in the exercise of their authority, free to prohibit intermediaries from choosing any governing law ("no choice at all"), or choosing a particular governing law ("applicable law cannot be the law X, Y or Z"), or choosing a governing law other than the law specified by the authority ("the applicable law must be the law of X"). Regulators and operators of securities systems are free to impose any of such actions as a condition to participation in a securities settlement system or to classification of obligations as acceptable for meeting credit standards (e.g., eligible bank loans in the Single List of Collateral in the Eurosystem Collateral Framework), or as a qualification for "designation" or in any other context (e.g., supervisory authorities may require that the member state's law chosen to govern a system (under Article 9(2) of the Settlement Finality Directive) must also be chosen as the relevant law for purposes of the Hague Securities Convention.

The Fall-back Rules (Article 5)

If the primary conflict of laws rule does not apply, whether because the parties have expressly selected a governing law but the qualifying office requirement is not satisfied, or they have failed to make any express selection in their agreement or they have never concluded an account agreement at all, the Convention provides three fall-back rules that operate as a cascade (Article 5).[32] The determinative elements used in the fall-back rules are, in sequence:

1. The law of the place of the office that a written account agreement expressly and unambiguously identifies as the office through which the relevant intermediary entered into the account agreement (Article 5(1));

2. The law of the place of incorporation or organization of the relevant intermediary (Article 5(2)); and,

3. The law of the (principal) place of business of the relevant intermediary (Article 5(3)).

Articles 4 and 5 are complemented by Article 6, which provides that in determining the applicable law under the Convention, no account is to be taken of the place where the issuer of the securities is incorporated or organized or has its statutory seat or registered office or place or principal place of business, or of the place where certificates representing or evidencing securities are located, or of the place where a register of holders is maintained by or on behalf of the issuer. Strictly speaking, Article 6 could have been dispensed with, but the provision was added to avoid any misunderstanding as to the Convention's firm rejection of any approach that would involve looking through an account holder's intermediary to determine the applicable law.

Transfers from One Securities Account to Another, Including Through a Chain of Intermediaries

Articles 4 and 5 must be applied independently with respect to each securities account (i.e., to each relationship between an account holder and its relevant intermediary). Thus, when a chain of intermediaries stands between an account holder and the issuer, there is no single law that would necessarily govern all the issues falling within the Convention's scope with respect to all securities accounts maintained by intermediaries standing between the account holder and the issuer. Similarly, when securities are transferred from one securities account to another, including transfers through a chain of intermediaries, the independent application of Articles 4 and 5 with respect to each securities account may, and often will, result in a different law governing the Article 2(1) issues with respect to each account. The Convention rejects the idea of a "super PRIMA" that would apply the same law governing the Article 2(1) issues with respect to every securities account maintained by each intermediary standing between an account holder and the issuer or with respect to every securities account involved when a transfer of securities is made from one account to another through a chain of intermediaries (assuming such a linkage could in fact be established in current trading and settlement systems).[33]

Other Important Provisions of the Convention

The Scope of the Convention and the Applicable Law (Article 2)

The Convention is a pure conflict of laws convention. That is, it does not impose any changes on existing (or limits on future) substantive law, in particular regarding the nature of an investor's interest in securities held with an intermediary or the requirements concerning how such an interest may be provided as collateral or otherwise transferred. Second, the Convention deals only with issues relating to securities[34] *held with an intermediary*. If the securities are held *directly*—that is, there is no intermediary involved and the investor's interest is recorded on the books of the issuer or is embodied in bearer certificates in the investor's possession—the Convention does not apply.[35]

In the context of these important parameters, Article 2 defines the scope of the Convention and of the applicable law. Article 2 is best understood when read with the following guidelines in mind:

- The key provision is Article 2(1).

- Article 2(2) is merely a clarification of Article 2(1).

- Articles 2(3)(a) and (b) are subject to Article 2(2) and are merely illustrative.

- Article 2(3)(c) states an absolute exclusion.

The Convention law (i.e., the law determined by the Convention's conflict of laws regime in Articles 4, 5, and 6) is the applicable law that determines all the issues enumerated in the exhaustive but very broad and intentionally very generally worded list in Article 2(1) (the Article 2(1) issues). The list in Article 2(1) is intended to be comprehensive and to include all issues that might have practical significance. An issue not specified in Article 2(1) does not fall within the Convention's scope and, therefore, is not governed by the applicable substantive law determined by the Convention. It is not possible, in respect of a particular securities account, for some Article 2(1) issues to be governed by one law and others by a different law.

Most significant among the issues listed in Article 2(1) are the legal nature and effects *against the intermediary and third parties of rights resulting from a credit of securities to a securities account* (Article 2(1)(a)), and the legal nature and effects *against the intermediary and third parties of a disposition*[36] *of securities held with an intermediary* (Article 2(1)(b)). As discussed above, the approaches to securities held with an intermediary vary among legal systems. In some systems, the account holder's rights resulting from a credit of securities to a securities account are characterized as a form of property right. In other systems, the account holder's rights are characterized as a form of purely personal (contractual) right against the intermediary to the delivery or transfer of a given type and number of securities. In still other systems, the account holder's rights are characterized or denominated as the interest of a beneficiary under a trust, a fiduciary interest, a *Gutschrift in Wertpapierrechnung*, co-property rights in a fungible, notional, or book-entry pool of securities, security entitlements or some other bundle of property, contractual, or other rights.[37] These differences, however, do not matter under the Convention, which caters to the needs of all these approaches and applies to securities held with an intermediary regardless of how the relevant substantive law classifies the nature of the right resulting from the credit of the securities to the securities account, and independently of whether this right is against the investor's intermediary, any other intermediary, or the issuer. For the sake of clarity and to avoid any doubt, Article 2(2) explicitly confirms the Convention's applicability even in situations where, under the Convention law, the rights resulting from the credit of securities to a securities account are determined to be contractual in nature.[38]

As indicated, the Convention does not determine the law that governs issues not falling within Article 2(1). This category includes, for example, issues relating to such purely contractual or other purely personal rights and duties between an account holder and its intermediary *inter se* as the content and frequency of account statements, the intermediary's standard of care in maintaining securities accounts, risk of loss, deadlines in giving instructions, and the like (Article 2(3)(a)). Similarly, this category includes such contractual or other personal rights and duties between the parties to a disposition *inter se* as the number and type of securities agreed to be sold or their purchase price (Article 2(3)(b)). These sets of issues are outside the domain of the Convention law because they are not within the issues listed in Article 2(1), not because they are excluded by Articles 2(3)(a) and (b). These latter two provisions, which are both subordinated to Article 2(2), are not intended, and should not be read, as limitations or qualifications of the reach of Article 2(1) but merely as illustrative of those contractual or other personal rights that do not fall within Article 2(1) altogether. The law applicable to those contractual rights between an account holder and its intermediary (or between the parties to a disposition) *inter se* which do not fall within Article 2(1) is determined not by the Convention but by other conflict of laws rules of the forum.

While the issues embraced in Articles 2(1)(a) and (b) are extremely broad, the list of issues within the domain of the Convention law does not stop there. The Convention also determines the law applicable to the perfection[39] requirements of a disposition (Article 2(1)(c)) and whether an interest extinguishes or has priority over another person's interest (Article 2(1)(d)). Thus the law determined by the Convention will govern, *inter alia*, the priority between a person who acquired an interest in securities in good faith, for value, and without notice of an adverse claim (a so-called "bona fide purchaser" or "protected purchaser") and an adverse claimant. Article 2(1)(d) includes not only the simple issue of priority but also the effects of a priority decision—that is, whether the competing interests co-exist, with one being preferred over the other, or one takes free of the other altogether. The Convention does not resolve these priority and effects issues; it simply provides the conflict of laws rule to determine which substantive law will govern these matters.

Further, the Convention law also governs *whether an intermediary has any duties to a person other than the account holder who asserts, in competition with the account holder or another person, an interest in securities held with that intermediary* (Article 2(1)(e)). This includes, for example, whether the intermediary is protected if it honors an instruction from one claimant even if it is later found that another claimant has priority. It also includes the important question of whether so-called upper-tier attachments are permissible (i.e., an effort to reach an account holder's interest in securities by levying an attachment against an intermediary at a level above that of the account holder's intermediary).

The Convention law also governs the requirements for the realization of an interest in securities held with an intermediary (Article 2(1)(f)). Finally, the Convention law also governs whether a disposition of securities held with an intermediary extends to entitlements to dividends, income, or other distributions, or to redemption, sale, or other proceeds (Article 2(1)(g); see the comments below at the end of section IV, B)).

It is readily apparent that more than one sub-paragraph of Article 2(1) may embrace a particular issue. There is nothing to be gained from determining which particular sub-paragraph applies; it suffices that the issue falls within the list. For example, the granting of a security interest in securities held with an intermediary is a disposition; accordingly, under Article 2(1)(b), the Convention determines the law applicable to the "effects against the intermediary and third parties" of the security interest. A dispute requiring determinations concerning the perfection and priority of the security interest would fall within Article 2(1)(b); yet it also would likely fall within the more specific Articles 2(1)(c) and (d).

The Convention does not under any circumstances determine the law applicable to the rights and duties of an issuer of securities or of an issuer's registrar or transfer agent (Article 2(3)(c)). This exclusion encompasses the duties of an issuer with respect to all corporate actions, including voting rights, dividend rights and registration rights, and the rights of an issuer to define the steps for achieving good discharge of a note, bond, or other debt security.

Finally, the Convention has no impact on regulatory schemes relating to the issue or trading of securities, regulatory requirements placed on intermediaries, or enforcement actions taken by regulators. While there is no explicit language spelling out this exclusion, the result is clear from the fact that these issues are not specified in the list of Article 2(1) issues.[40]

The Definition of *Securities* (Article 1(1)(a))

The definition of the term *securities* set forth in Article 1(1)(a) is intentionally both very broad and very general. The term extends to all assets that are financial in nature, whether they are in bearer or registered form, and whether they are represented by a certificate or dematerialized. The term encompasses all types of debt and equity securities. The term includes financial instruments and financial assets that are standardized, negotiable, dealt in an organized market, or capable of being traded (none of these characteristics, however, is required).[41] The only personal (movable) property excluded from the term is (1) cash and (2) assets that are not financial in nature (such as land or machinery). The breadth of inclusiveness reflects the policy decision that the Convention's coverage would accommodate both the existing range of practice in diverse financial markets and future developments in market practice.

The term *securities* is in no way limited to (or otherwise related to) definitions of that term found in the regulatory regime of any state. Those definitions were developed for other purposes, and they would be too narrow for purposes of the Convention; moreover, it is highly unlikely that consensus could have been achieved on the choice of a particular regulatory definition in light of the diversity of those definitions in national regulatory regimes around the world. Thus, precedents determining that an asset is not a security in a particular state, or in a different context, should not result in exclusion from the Convention's coverage. Of course, states remain free to limit the types of financial assets that may be credited to a securities account by intermediaries that are subject to their regulation.

Despite the Convention's extremely broad definition of securities, there is no risk of undesirable over-inclusion. This is because of the existence of two substantial limitations on the scope of the Convention: first, the requirement that the securities be "held with an intermediary" (see Article 1(1)(f)), thereby excluding direct holdings and, more importantly, encompassing only assets susceptible of being credited to a securities account); and second, the limitation of the domain of the Convention law only to matters falling within the Article 2(1) list. Thus, there was no need to rely on the definition of securities to limit the scope of the Convention. Therefore, no court or legal adviser need be long delayed by the effort to determine whether an asset is a security: if an asset is credited to a securities account and is financial in nature, it is a security within the meaning of the Convention.

The definition of securities expressly excludes cash. The term *cash* is not confined to physical money but also encompasses ordinary deposit accounts, even if maintained by the intermediary who also maintains a securities account for the same account holder. The definition of securities does not extend to cash paid to the intermediary toward the cost of acquiring securities on behalf of the account holder or providing margin cover. Issues relating to rights in that cash are governed not by the Convention law, but by the applicable law determined by other conflicts rules of the forum; this is so whether the cash is credited to the securities account or to a separate cash account maintained by the intermediary. The Convention law *does*, however, govern whether a disposition of securities held with an intermediary extends to entitlements to dividends, income, or other distributions, or to redemption, sale, or other proceeds, in the form of cash or credits to a cash account— issues that are expressly mentioned in Article 2(1)(g).

Internationality (Article 3)

The purpose of Article 3 is to ensure the applicability of the Convention whenever a situation involving securities held with an intermediary relates in any way to more than one state. Only by providing for maximum applicability can the Convention achieve its goal of providing certainty and predictability. Thus, the function of Article 3 is to include, rather than to exclude; and, for this reason, all doubts about coverage should be resolved in favor of inclusion.

Article 3 does not define the applicability of the Convention by reference to specific, pre-established, and precisely delineated factors or by means of a definition of *internationality*, which would have to be satisfied at a particular point in time and against which parties and courts would have to assess facts to determine whether or not the Convention applies. Rather, the provision takes a broad descriptive approach by stating that the Convention applies in all cases involving "a choice between the laws of different states," that is, it applies unless there is absolutely no aspect of a situation (e.g., "location" of a person involved in or affected by a transaction or of an activity of such a person, "location" of a security or its issuer, presence of a governing law clause or any other governing law factor or element) that might give rise to a claim for the applicability of the law of more than one state. Only a formulation that does not depend on the development of a coherent interpretation of Article 3 by courts, but instead declares a broad scope of application which cannot be avoided by (mis)interpretation of the verbiage used, enables parties to a disposition, as well as affected third persons, to enjoy the legal certainty and predictability that the Convention seeks to provide.

It is important to stress that the principle of *fraus legis* (or similar principles such as the *bona fide* principle under English law) cannot displace the applicability of the Convention where the latter is triggered by the parties' choice in favor of the law of one state even if all the factors relevant to the situation are connected with another state.[42]

Impact of Opening of an Insolvency Proceeding (Article 8)

Article 8 fixes the boundary between the Convention law (*lex causae*) and the applicable insolvency law (*lex concursus*) in the context of an insolvency proceeding. It provides that pre-insolvency rights, which are effective and perfected under the Convention law, are to be respected as such in an insolvency proceeding (Article 8(1)), but that these rights are not thereby exempted from general insolvency rules relating, for example, to the ranking of claims, enforcement of rights, and the avoidance of unfair preferences and transactions in fraud of creditors (Article 8(2)). Accordingly, despite the opening of an insolvency proceeding, the Convention law will continue to apply to all Article 2(1) issues as regards pre-insolvency events (such as an outright sale or the grant of a security interest), and an insolvency court or administrator may not refuse to recognize the right or its perfected status merely because this right had not (also) been created or perfected in accordance with the *lex concursus*. The *lex concursus*, however, determines the effects of those rights, that is, the extent to which these rights can be used in the insolvency proceeding. For example, a security interest perfected in accordance with the Convention law during a "suspect period" may be avoided as a "preference" or "fraudulent conveyance," and its pre-insolvency priority under the Convention law may be displaced by the rule of the insolvency forum governing the ranking of claims, to the same extent as a security interest perfected in accordance with the *lex concursus* under the same circumstances.

Public Policy and Internationally Mandatory Rules (Article 11)

Article 11 carefully restricts the grounds for judicial refusal to apply the Convention law. Article 11(1) sets forth a public policy (*ordre public*) exception under which the application of the Convention law may be refused only if the effects of its application would be manifestly contrary to the public policy of the forum state, that is, depart so radically from the forum's concepts of fundamental justice that its application would be intolerably offensive to the forum's basic values.

Article 11(2) provides for the exclusive application of the forum's internationally mandatory rules, that is, those *substantive* rules (i.e., not private international law rules) of the forum (not those of other states), often referred to as *laws of immediate application*, which must be applied despite the fact that the Convention determines another law to be applicable and irrespective of the effects that application of the Convention law would have. The threshold for the application of the internationally mandatory forum rule exception, like that for the public policy exception, is very high (safeguard of fundamental moral, social, economic, or political principles). Thus, it is to be expected that both exceptions will be applied extremely rarely.

Moreover, and most importantly, both these exceptions are subject to Article 11(3), which precludes them from being used to impose any perfection requirements of the forum on any consensual security interest or other disposition (including a statutory lien falling within Article 1(2)(c)) in lieu of or in addition to the perfection requirements of the Convention law,[43] or to apply any rule of the forum relating to priorities between competing interests (unless, of course, the law of the forum is the Convention law). Article 11(3) is a crucial provision, for without the strict limitation of both the public policy and the internationally mandatory forum rule exceptions, the legal certainty and predictability provided by the Convention would be undermined and the achievement of the Convention's benefits, sought by the forum along with all other contracting states, would be thwarted.[44] As the Explanatory Report rightly emphasizes, "Article 11(3) is not at all a derogation from the Contracting state's public policy; rather, it is a clear announcement of what that policy is."[45] Like all other provisions of the Convention, Article 11(3) leaves unaffected the ability to apply the forum's regulatory laws, such as anti-money laundering or anti-tax evasion laws.[46]

Transition Provisions (Articles 15 and 16)

Chapter IV of the Convention, entitled "Transition Provisions," contains two articles (Articles 15 and 16) that deal with completely separate issues, although each reflects the fact of possible change in practice or legal outcome brought about by the advent of the Convention.

Article 15 addresses the situation of a priority dispute between an interest acquired after the Convention's entry into force for a state and an interest acquired before the Convention's entry into force for that state. For example, such a priority contest might arise where, before the Convention's entry into force for the forum, an account holder grants a security interest in securities held with an intermediary to Lender A and, subsequent to the Convention's entry into force for the forum, the same account holder grants a security interest in the same securities to Lender B.[47] Article 15 provides that the Convention's conflict of laws rule (either Article 4 or 5) applies to determine which state's law will govern this priority dispute. As a result, application of the Convention law may have an effect on "pre-Convention" interests (for example, the Convention law may determine that Lender A's pre-Convention interest is subordinate to or extinguished by Lender B's post-Convention interest). The rule should cause no difficulty in practice because parties to existing (pre-Convention) account agreements have ample opportunity to adjust their arrangements to take into account the possible application of the Convention to determine the applicable law. In any event, in most situations, potential application of the Convention law to govern that priority contest will have been anticipated.[48]

Because the Convention's references to account agreements and securities accounts include agreements entered into, and accounts opened, before the entry into force of the Convention on the international plane[49] (see Article 16(1)), it was deemed advisable to provide rules for the interpretation of such account agreements. Article 16 provides guidance for parties who have entered or are now entering into such pre-Convention account agreements, and enables currently existing and still-to-be-entered-into pre-Convention account agreements to enjoy the benefits of the Convention without the parties having to engage in the costly exercise of amending these agreements or opening new accounts. Articles 16(3) and (4) provide interpretive rules that treat certain provisions of pre-Convention account agreements as having the effect of determining, for the purposes of Article 4(1) of the Convention, the law applicable to all the Article 2(1) issues. Thus, if express words in a pre-Convention account agreement would, under the rules of the state whose law governs the contract, have the effect of determining the law governing any of the Article 2(1) issues, that law will govern all those issues, but only if the qualifying office test was met at the time of the agreement on governing law.[50] Similarly, if the parties to an account agreement (other than one to which Article 16(3) applies) have agreed, pre-Convention, that the securities account is maintained in a particular state, the law of that state will be the applicable law under the Convention, but only if the qualifying office test was met at the time of the agreement on governing law;[51] in this particular situation, the agreement as to where the securities account is maintained may be express or implied from the terms of the contract considered as a whole or from the surrounding circumstances (subject to the prohibition in Article 6).

The interpretive rules of Articles 16(3) and (4) apply only if the account agreement does not contain an express reference to the Convention. If an account agreement contains an express reference to the Convention, Articles 4, 5, and 6 are to be applied directly, without any interpretive assistance from Articles 16(3) and (4). Thus, a simple way to ensure that the benefit of legal certainty and predictability provided by the Convention extends to an account agreement concluded prior to the entry into force of the Convention is to refer expressly to the Convention in the agreement. This practice is already being followed.

Article 16 also allows for some declarations by contracting states. Under Article 16(2), a state may declare that its courts will not rely on the interpretive rules of Articles 16(3) and (4) in applying Article 4(1) to account agreements entered into during the period between the date the Convention enters into force on the international plane (Article 19(1)) and the date the Convention enters into force for that state (the gap period). If a contracting state makes such a declaration, the courts of that state will apply Articles 4, 5, and 6 to gap period account agreements without any interpretive assistance from paragraphs 3 or 4. In addition, under Article 16(3), a state may make a declaration that the courts of that state will not apply the interpretive rule of Article 16(3) if the parties to the account agreement have expressly agreed that the securities account is maintained in a different state than the state whose law would otherwise be applicable by reason of the interpretive rule of Article 16(3).[52]

Brief Overview of the Remaining Provisions

Article 12 sets forth several important interpretive and substantive provisions relating to the application of the Convention with regard to multi-unit states (i.e., states within which two or more territorial units of that state, or both the state and one or more of its territorial units, have their own rules of law in respect of any of the Article 2(1) issues; see the definition in Article 1(1)(m)). In particular, Article 12(1) sets out how the Convention's primary conflicts rule operates when the parties have designated the law of a particular territorial unit of a multi-unit state. When the parties have expressly agreed on the law of a particular territorial unit of a multi-unit state (either as the law governing the account agreement or as another law governing all the Article 2(1) issues), the applicable law is the law of that specified territorial unit, if the relevant intermediary has a qualifying office anywhere in the multi-unit state. A multi-unit state may, however, by declaration under the Convention, impose a geographically more stringent condition by requiring that the applicable law will, under Article 4, be that of the one of its territorial units agreed to by the parties only if the relevant intermediary has a qualifying office within that territorial unit.[53]

The law determined by the Convention is the applicable law whether or not it is the law of a contracting state (Article 9). Furthermore, the Convention does not leave any room for *renvoi* in the traditional private international law sense: the applicable law determined by the Convention refers to substantive rules only, not to conflict of laws rules (Article 10).[54]

Article 13 calls for uniform interpretation of the Convention. The importance of this principle is reinforced by the provision in Article 14 for Special Commission meetings to review the practical operation of the Convention. The legal certainty and predictability that the Convention is designed to provide would not be achieved, however, if judges or practitioners were to reach differing views as to the interpretation or practical implementation of the Convention.

Article 7 determines the impact, if any, under the Convention of an amendment to an account agreement if the consequence of the amendment is that the Convention law changes from the law of one state as determined under either Article 4(1) or Article 5 to the law of a different state as determined under Article 4(1). The principle embodied in Article 7 is that the new law governs all the Article 2(1) issues in respect of any interest in securities previously or subsequently credited to the securities account governed by the amended account agreement (Article 7(3)), subject to exceptions with respect to specified issues which are designed to protect certain interests in securities that were acquired before the amendment by a person who did not consent to the amendment (see Articles 7(4) and (5)).

It is expected that Article 7 will come into play only rarely since the kinds of amendments to which it would apply are likely to be infrequent. Article 7 does not come into play in a situation when the parties fail to select a new applicable law under the Convention that satisfies the requirements of Article 4(1) (including the qualifying office requirement of the second sentence of Article 4(1), which must be met at the time of the amendment). When the requirements of Article 4(1) are not met, the amendment is ignored for Convention purposes and the *status quo ante* with respect to the determination of the applicable law is preserved.[55] Furthermore, Article 7 also does not come into play when a different law becomes the Convention law as a result of a transfer of securities to another securities account. Thus, Article 7 does not come into play in the case of an outright transfer of securities to a buyer or where a security interest is implemented by means of a transfer of the securities from a collateral provider's account to a collateral taker's account. In these instances the rights resulting from the credit of securities to the buyer's and collateral taker's account, as well as all the other Article 2(1) issues, are governed by the Convention law determined with respect to the buyer's and collateral taker's account, respectively.[56]

Articles 17–24 contain the final clauses, including a provision (Article 18) that enables a regional economic integration organization (REIO), constituted by sovereign states, to sign, accept, approve, or accede to the Convention, but only to the extent it has exclusive competence over matters covered by the Convention; it is the first time that such a provision has been included in a Convention adopted under the auspices of the Hague Conference.[57]

Conclusion

The Hague Securities Convention is the result of a highly focused, inclusive, and representative effort to provide legal certainty and predictability as to the law governing issues that are of great practical importance for the holding and transfer of securities held with an intermediary. The Convention provides a clear, straightforward, pragmatic, and easily applicable solution to a technically complex issue. This *ex ante* legal certainty is essential for the effective and smooth operation of the financial markets, which are increasingly interconnected. The Convention thus brings very important benefits to market participants and the financial system as a whole. It is hoped that the example set by the United States of America and Switzerland—two of the most important and sophisticated financial markets—will soon be followed by other states and by the European Community and that this important instrument will enter into force as soon as possible.

Notes

Note: The author is First Secretary at the Permanent Bureau of the Hague Conference on Private International Law (HCCH); in this capacity, his primary responsibilities include the work relating to the Hague Securities Convention. The opinions expressed are strictly personal and not to be attributed to the Hague Conference or to its Permanent Bureau.

The following contribution is a slightly revised and updated version of an article coauthored by Christophe Bernasconi and Harry Sigman that was published in the *Uniform Law Review* (2005-1/2), at. 117–140, which was a special volume entitled "Enhancing Legal Certainty over Investment Securities Held with an Intermediary" (see www.unidroit.org/english/publications/review/main.htm). This updated version was completed on February 9, 2007; all the websites referred to in this article were last visited on January 29, 2008.

[1] In this chapter, unless otherwise indicated, the term *transfer* includes an outright transfer of ownership, a transfer by way of security, and the grant of a security interest, pledge, or other form of hypothecation; see also Article 1(1)(h) of the Convention.

[2] *See* Professor Roy Goode (United Kingdom), Professor Hideki Kanda (Japan), Professor Karl Kreuzer (Germany), with the assistance of Dr Christophe Bernasconi (Permanent Bureau), *Explanatory Report on the Convention on the Law Applicable to Certain Rights in Respect of Securities held with an Intermediary* (*Explanatory Report*), para. Int-2.

The text of the Hague Securities Convention is available at www.hcch.net (follow "Welcome" to "Conventions" to "36. Convention of 5 July 2006 on the Law Applicable to Certain Rights in respect of Securities held with an Intermediary." A two-page outline of the Convention may be found on the same page of the HCCH website. A commercial edition of the *Explanatory Report* may also be ordered via the HCCH website. Both the Convention and the Report have been prepared in the two official languages of the HCCH (English and French).

[3] *See, in particular,* Euroclear, *Cross-Border Clearance, Settlement and Custody: Beyond the G30 Recommendations* (Brussels, 1993), at 62; Randall Guynn, "Modernizing Legal Rules to Reduce Settlement Risk," *Capital Markets Forum Yearbook,* vol. I (International Bar Association, 1993, at 172–179; International Bar Association, Capital Markets Forum, Section on

Business Law, *Modernizing Securities Ownership, Transfer and Pledging Laws*, Discussion Paper on the Need for International Harmonization, with Responding Comments by Professor James Steven Rogers (United States), Professor Kazuaki Sono (Japan) and Dr. Jürgen Than (Germany), 1996, available at www.dpw.com/iba.modernization.pdf); for more references, see *Explanatory Report, supra* note 2.

[4] According to the tradition followed by the HCCH at that time, the 19th Session in fact adopted a *draft* Convention; it was only on July 5, 2006, i.e., on the day of the signing by Switzerland and the United States, that the draft became a Convention. One should thus speak of the Convention of July 5, 2006. It is recalled that under Article 19 of the Convention, the entry into force of the instrument necessitates the ratification, acceptance, approval, or accession by at least three States. The tradition according to which a Hague Convention bears the date of its first signing was abandoned with the Convention on Choice of Court Agreements, which bears the date of its adoption by the diplomatic session (June 30, 2005).

[5] Group of Thirty (G30), *Global Clearing and Settlement—A Plan of Action* (January 2003) (see http://www.group30.org). Recommendation 15 of this report addresses the need to advance legal certainty "over rights to securities, cash, or collateral"; the commentary on the Recommendation stresses that "[o]ne area of recommendation for which united support can be offered is choice of laws. National authorities should be encouraged by all interested parties to sign and ratify the just-adopted Hague Convention as soon as reasonably possible. It is of course critical to its effectiveness that the Hague Convention be ratified as quickly as possible in as many nations as possible." See also G30, *Global Clearing and Settlement—Final Monitoring Report* (Washington, D.C., 2006) (see http://www.group30.org). Appendix 3 of this report (at 33 *et seq.*) provides a summary of the work conducted by the Legal Subcommittee of the G30 (of which the author of this chapter was a member), an overview of the Convention, as well as the status of the implementation of the Convention in 15 target jurisdictions selected by the G30. As regards the status of implementation in the EU member states, the report emphasizes that "the choice-of-law rules in the Hague Convention are broader in scope [than the scope of the rules in the relevant instruments of the European Community] and so remain an important goal." On the limits of the solution adopted in the relevant EC instruments, see in particular Jean-Pierre Deguée and Diego Devos, "La loi applicable aux titres intermédiés: l'apport de la Convention de La Haye de décembre 2002," *Revue de Droit Commercial Belge (Tijdschrift voor Belgisch Handelsrecht)* 2006/1, at 5 *et*

seq., in particular paras. 9–12 ; Harry C. Sigman and Christophe Bernasconi, "Myths About the Hague Convention Debunked," *International Financial Law Review* (November 2005), at 31 *et seq.*, in particular 32 and 33 ("Myth three: The Convention would displace an existing successful European PIL regime"). On the evaluation of the current EC regime, see also *infra* note 19 and accompanying text. For the position of the International Swaps and Derivatives Association (ISDA), another highly important industry group, see www.isda.org (follow "Comment Letters, Policy Papers & Statements," then "Submissions dated 2005" to submission date 02/28/2005, "ISDA comments on ECMI project on the potential impact of the Hague Securities Convention"; "Submissions dated 2004" to submission date 07/26/2004, "The Hague Convention on the Law Applicable to Certain Rights in Respect of Securities Held with an Intermediary"; at home page, follow "Press," then "Press Releases 2006" to release date July 5, 2006, "ISDA Welcomes U.S., Swiss Signature of Hague Securities Convention").

[6] An updated selection of publications relating to the Convention can be found at www.hcch.net (follow "Welcome" to "Conventions" to "36. Convention of 5 July 2006 on the Law Applicable to Certain Rights in respect of Securities held with an Intermediary" to "Bibliography"). For a robust response to questions raised and criticism made with respect to the Convention, see the comments below under "Appraisal of the Primary Conflict of Laws Rule."

[7] For updated information, see www.hcch.net (follow "Welcome" to "Conventions" to "36. Convention of 5 July 2006 on the Law Applicable to Certain Rights in respect of Securities held with an Intermediary" to "Status table").

[8] *See* the notice "Swiss Government recommends quick ratification of Hague Securities Convention" at www.hcch.net (follow "Welcome" to "News & Events" to "2006" to "Swiss Government recommends quick ratification of Hague Securities Convention").

[9] On the same day as the signing by Switzerland and the United States (July 5, 2006), the European Commission released the results of its "[l]egal assessment of certain aspects" of the Convention. The Commission concludes in particular that "adoption of the Convention would be in the best interest of the Community" and recommends that Convention "be signed after or with at least two of its main trading partners, the USA included." In a press release issued on the same day, Internal Market and Services

Commissioner Charlie McCreevy commented as follows: "In today's global financial markets we can no longer afford uncertainty about which law is applicable to indirectly held securities. The "location of the account formula" has worked fine in Europe's transition to a fully integrated single securities market, but now that European citizens are able to reap the benefits of participation in global financial markets, we need legal rules that are sustainable world-wide. Therefore, we need to change. The USA and Switzerland are about to sign the Convention and the EU should not lag behind." See the notice "Switzerland and United States sign Hague Securities Convention" at www.hcch.net (follow "Welcome" to "News & Events" to "2006" to "Switzerland and the United States sign Hague Securities Convention"). On December 15, 2003, the European Commission had already submitted to the Council a proposal for a Council Decision concerning the signing of the Hague Convention (16292/03 JUSTCIV 273); see also the comments in note 19 *infra*. On December 14, 2006, the European Parliament (EP) adopted a "resolution on the implications of signing the Hague Securities Convention" (see http://www.europarl. europa.eu/sides/getDoc.do?pubRef=-//EP//TEXT+TA+P6-TA-2006-0608+0+DOC+XML+V0//EN). This resolution includes some rather astonishing comments, such as under point 7, that "ensuring the security of intra-European transactions must take precedence over the facilitation of transactions between the European Union and the rest of the world"—when it is evident that in the field of securities held with an intermediary, no clear-cut distinction can possibly be made between purely intra-EU holding-patterns and other ("rest of the world") holding patterns); on the main shortcomings of this resolution, both in terms of its analysis of today's market reality and of the Hague Securities Convention and the negotiating process that led to it, see also *infra* notes 11, 19, 23, 24, 31, 44 and accompanying text. It should also be noted that the EP was represented during the entire negotiation of the Convention.

[10] In Mexico, for example, on September 21, 2006, the board of INDEVAL (Central Securities Depository) formally recommended signing of the Convention. A few weeks later, the Securities Commission of Brazil also recommended signing of the Convention.

[11] In light of the broad, balanced, inclusive, and most representative nature of the negotiations of the Convention, it is somewhat puzzling that the EP's resolution (see *supra* note 9) expresses "extreme concern" at some of the solutions adopted by the Convention, that it characterizes some of these solutions as "highly inadequate" and that it calls for a "comprehensive impact

study" on the implications of an accession to the Convention—more than four years after the completion of the negotiations of the Convention and following the Commission's assessment referred to *supra* in note 9.

[12] *See* Bank for International Settlements, Basel Committee on Banking Supervision, *International Convergence of Capital Measurement and Capital Standards—A Revised Framework* (June 2004), available on the website of the Bank for International Settlements at www.bis.org; see in particular www.bis.org/publ/bcbsca.htm.

[13] The minimum standards for legal documentation that must be met for banks to obtain capital relief for any use of credit risk mitigation techniques are set in para. 118 of the Basel II framework as follows: "All documentation used in collateralized transactions and for documenting on balance sheet netting, guarantees and credit derivatives must be binding on all parties and legally enforceable in all relevant jurisdictions. Banks must have conducted sufficient legal review to verify this and have a well founded legal basis to reach this conclusion, and undertake such further review as necessary to ensure continuing enforceability."

[14] This characteristic, however, has nothing to do with regulatory matters or strictly corporate matters such as the right of the ultimate investor to receive notices, attend meetings, or vote shares.

[15] The intermediary that maintains a securities account for its customer, regardless of which level that customer may occupy, is referred to in the Convention and in this article as the "relevant intermediary."

[16] PRIMA has been adopted, for example, in the conflict of laws rules contained in Article 9(2) of the *Directive 98/26/EC of the European Parliament and of the Council of 19 May 1998 on settlement finality in payment and securities settlement systems*, and in Article 9(1) of the *Directive 2002/47/EC of the European Parliament and of the Council of 6 June 2002 on financial collateral arrangements*. The latter provision reads as follows: "Any question with respect to any of the matters specified in paragraph 2 arising in relation to book entry securities collateral shall be governed by the law of the country in which the relevant account is maintained."

[17] *See* the *Explanatory Report, supra* note 2, para. Int-41 *et seq.* and 4-3 *et seq.*; Deguée and Devos, *supra* note 5, paras. 11 and 36; James Steven

Rogers, "Conflict of Laws for Transactions in Securities Held through Intermediaries," *Cornell International Law Journal* (2006) (39), at 285–328, available on the Social Science Research Network (SSRN) at http://ssrn.com/abstract=815005, see in particular pp. 25 *et seq.* Professor Rogers brings the point home with the help of a few, but very persuasive words: "But there is a problem. An account does not have a location. Period. There is no way around that fact. An account is an abstract legal relationship between two entities. Abstract relationships do not have locations."

[18] *See supra* note 16.

[19] *See* in this respect the comment by Rogers, *supra* note 17, at 27: "The annoying reality is that abstract relations simply do not have a location. Thus, at present, the law in the European Union is stuck in the situation of having adopted a conflict of laws rule that those who have examined the matter carefully have determined simply will not work." This, in essence, also seems to be the conclusion of the Commission's evaluation of Article 9 of the Collateral Directive, when it states: "Therefore, also in the event that the Council would decide not to go forward with the [Hague] Convention, Article 9 FCD (as well as Article 9 SFD and Article 24 Winding-up Directive) would still have to be amended to improve the situation within the Community by specifying the exact criteria for determining the relevant location of account. The example of the two Member States (France and Portugal), that have developed such criteria, shows that different interpretations are indeed possible," in *Report from the Commission to the Council and the European Parliament—Evaluation report on the Financial Collateral Arrangements Directive (2002/47/EC)*, COM(2006)833 final, under heading 4.5. *See* also the earlier *Communication from the Commission to the Council and the European Parliament—Clearing and Settlement in the European Union—The way forward* (April 2004) (COM/2004/0312 final), which at least implicitly endorses this view and is to be welcomed and strongly supported:

> The implementation of the Hague Convention in the EU will enable participants to determine in advance of any action, with certainty and with only reasonable effort what national substantive law governs their rights to indirectly-held securities. In the context of its responsibilities, the Commission will make the necessary arrangements for the signature and subsequent accession to the Convention by the European Union and its ratification by the Member States. The Commission will also take the necessary steps to bring the Settlement Finality and the

Financial Collateral Directive in line with the conflicts of law provisions of the Hague Convention.

Id. at 24.

Against this background, the "commitment to the PRIMA principle" expressed by the EP in its resolution (see *supra* note 9) is inconsistent and seems to reflect a misconception of today's market reality.

[20] This is in sharp contrast to the agreement involved in the limited situation referred to in Article 16(4), final sentence; *see* the further comments on Article 16 in "Transition Provisions," *infra*.

[21] The term *express* should not be construed as a form requirement, to wit, that the account agreement must be in writing. Where a writing requirement is intended, the Convention imposes it explicitly (see Article 5(1)).

[22] The last of these three alternative modes of activity is not satisfied if the actual activity of an office consists *merely* of one of the activities listed in Article 4(2). Article 4(2) sets forth a list of activities none of which, standing alone, is sufficient for an office to be considered engaged in a business or other regular activity of maintaining securities accounts within the meaning of Article 4(1)(a)(iii). The list includes being a place that is engaged solely in representational functions or administrative functions and lacks authority to make any binding decision to enter into any account agreement, unless the functions relate to the opening or maintenance of securities accounts. The list also includes merely being the place where the technology (e.g., computers) supporting the book-keeping or data processing is located; where a call center is located; where mailing relating to securities accounts is organized; or where files or archives are located. It is important to stress that none of the listed activities is a disqualification; rather, the list merely sets a bottom line—*any* of these activities *alone* would not constitute the office as being engaged in maintaining securities accounts within the meaning of Article 4(1)(a)(iii). It is also important to appreciate that Article 4(2) comes into play only in the context of Article 4(1)(a)(iii); it has no effect in the context of either Article 4(1)(a)(i) or (ii), which function independently as safe harbors in satisfying the qualifying office requirement.

[23] Again, this reality seems to go unnoticed in the EP's resolution (see *supra* note 9), when in point 8 it refers to the "highly inadequate nature of the reality test."

[24] This assertion was made in a letter, dated November 18, 2004, submitted to Mr. A. Schaub (Director General, European Commission, Directorate General Internal Market) by the European Banking Federation (a copy of this letter was sent to the author by the EBF); *see also* a subsequent letter, dated December 13, 2004, sent by the EBF to the Civil Law Committee of the Council, available on the website of the EBF at www.ebf-fbe.eu (using the "Search" option and looking for "Hague"). Similar assertions were made by the European Central Bank (*see e.g.,* letter dated January 16, 2004, to the Committee on Civil Law Matters (General Questions), and letter dated September 7, 2004, to Paul Meijknecht, then Chairman of the Committee on Civil Law Matters, Council of the European Union; both letters are on file with the author. The joint response of the Secretary General of the HCCH, Hans van Loon, and Christophe Bernasconi to the EBF letter dated November 18, 2004 (referred to at the beginning of this note), can be found at www.hcch.net (follow "Welcome" to "Conventions" to "36" to "Miscellaneous"; *see also,* on the same webpage, an article published by Christophe Bernasconi in L'AGEFI, December 9, 2004, entitled "La Convention de La Haye, une chance pour l'Europe !" *See also* the unsubstantiated comment number 6 from the EP in its resolution (see *supra* note 9).

[25] *See* Article 2(a) of the Settlement Finality Directive (mentioned in note 16 *supra*).

[26] The Governing Council of the European Central Bank periodically updates its assessment of SSS eligibility for such settlement activity. See the website of the ECB at http://www.ecb.int.

[27] *See also* the very persuasive comments by Deguée and Devos, *supra* note 5, para. 38.

[28] *See* the references in note 24 *supra*.

[29] The December 10, 2004, issue of *American Banker* noted: "The French banking giant BNP Paribas has emerged as a significant player in U.S. retail banking through two decades of acquisitions ... [describing the recently completed acquisition, through its Honolulu-based subsidiary, of a North Dakota entity] ... with more than 150 branches in 12 western and Midwestern states,... its executive vice president for international retail banking and financial services, said in a telephone interview Tuesday that

BNP will continue to seek acquisitions on this side of the Atlantic. Its goal is to have the U.S. market generate 20% of earnings ... 'We consider [the U.S. market] as our second home market now.'" More broadly, an *American Banker* chart, "Foreign Holding Companies That Majority-Own U.S. Banks," published December 14, 2004, ranked by assets of the U.S. banks as of June 30, 2004, indicates that HSBC Holding PLC (London) and ABN Amro (Amsterdam) each held over US$ 100 billion in such assets, and that four of the top five holding companies are European-based (BNP Paribas being the fifth largest). UBS AG (Zurich) was the ninth largest. Moreover, UBS's wealth management operations in the United States, which have increased considerably in recent years, include the acquisition of PaineWebber, a leading stockbroker. *See also* Sigman and Bernasconi, *supra* note 5, at 33 and 34 ("Myth five: The Convention is an attempt by US intermediaries to gain advantages over European intermediaries").

[30] *See* the references in note 24 *supra*.

[31] *See Explanatory Report, supra* note 2, para. Int-59 and 2-35; *see also* the detailed analysis in Sigman and Bernasconi, *supra* note 5, at 31 and 32 ("Myth one: The Convention would interfere with enforcement of anti-money laundering laws, tax laws or other similar regulatory measures"; "Myth two: The Convention would disempower supervisory authorities") and 35 ("Myth eight: The Convention would override public policy"); Rogers, *supra* note 17, at 42 *et seq*. Again, the fact that the Convention has no impact on regulatory and supervisory regimes is overlooked by the EP's resolution (see *supra* note 9; point 9 of the resolution).

[32] The question of whether an agreement on the governing law does not exist due to the absence of consent (e.g., by reason of a generally applicable contract law doctrine such as lack of capacity) is governed by the conflict of laws rules of the forum other than those contained in the Convention. If, under the applicable substantive rule, consent is absent, there is in fact no agreement for the purpose of Article 4(1), and the relevant fall-back rule of Article 5 applies. If there is a consented-to agreement, a material rule depriving that agreement of legal effectiveness may be applied only in accordance with Article 11 (see further comments below).

[33] For a comprehensive description of transfers through a chain of intermediaries, see the *Explanatory Report, supra* note 2, para. 4-43 *et seq*.

[34] The definition of the term *securities* is discussed in "The Definition of *Securities*," below in this chapter.

[35] The provisions in Article 1(3)–(5) are designed to clarify whether certain persons (including certain systems and their participants) should be regarded as intermediaries for the purposes of the Convention. For a full description of these provisions, see the *Explanatory Report*, *supra* note 2, paras. 1-32 to 1-40.

[36] As defined in Article 1(1)(h), the term *disposition* covers any transfer of title, whether outright or by way of security, and any other form of security interest. Disposition includes sale and repurchase (repo), purchase and resale (reverse repo), transfers under sell/buy-back or buy/sell-back arrangements, and stock loans.

[37] For a more complete discussion of the various substantive law models, see the *Explanatory Report*, *supra* note 2, paras. Int-22 and Int-23, 2-11 *et seq.* (with further references).

[38] Unfortunately, the English and French texts of Article 2(2) do not match. While the English text correctly refers to both a "disposition of" and "an interest in" securities (and thus covers both dynamic and static situations), the French text only refers to a disposition (of either securities or an interest in securities). The history and purpose of Article 2(2) clearly reveal that the English version is correct and that the French text must be read accordingly. This result is expressly confirmed by the *Explanatory Report*, *supra* note 2, para. 2-31.

[39] In many legal systems, a security interest or other disposition, though effective as between the parties by virtue of their agreement, is not effective against a third party acquiring an interest in the subject matter unless some further step has been taken. Article 1(1)(i) defines *perfection* as the completion of any steps necessary to render a disposition effective against persons who are not parties to that disposition, including an insolvency administrator and general creditors in the debtor's insolvency proceedings. For example, for a security interest to have any effects beyond the secured party and the debtor, the applicable law may require, in addition to the secured party and the debtor entering into a collateral agreement, that the secured party take control over the securities account, have the encumbered securities credited to an account in the secured party's name, make a public filing, or take some other step. For certain dispositions, the applicable law

may not require the parties to take any particular steps beyond their agreement in order to make the dispositions effective against third parties. For example, the applicable law may deem an intermediary to have control over a securities account that is encumbered in its favor (and thus, over all securities credited to that securities account), if the intermediary is the person who maintains the securities account for the debtor/account holder, with no further step beyond the agreement being required for effectiveness of the security interest against third parties.

[40] *See* the comments in "Appraisal of the Primary Conflict of Laws Rule," above in this chapter.

[41] Clearly falling within the Convention's definition of securities are shares of stock, bonds, units in collective investment schemes, exchange-traded financial futures and options, credit derivatives, short-term promissory notes (commercial paper) issued on a money market, warrants, and American Depositary Receipts. The definition also includes financial instruments that are structured to have no element of usury, a high degree of uncertainty, or gambling as a matter of Islamic law.

[42] See *Explanatory Report*, *supra* note 2, Example 3-3 and para. 3-10.

[43] See *Explanatory Report*, *supra* note 2, para. 11-12.

[44] Again, this is not recognized by the EP's resolution (see *supra* note 9) where, in point 8, it refers to the "highly inadequate nature" of the "exemptions with regard to the public policy rules [of the Convention]."

[45] *Id.*

[46] For a more complete analysis of Article 11 and particularly of Article 11(3), see *Explanatory Report*, *supra* note 2, especially para. 11-12.

[47] The interests referred to in Article 15 need not be of the same type. Thus, the priority contest might be between two persons that have security interests, between two account holders, between an account holder and a person having a security interest, or between a person having a security interest and an attaching creditor. *See Explanatory Report*, *supra* note 2, para. 15-3.

[48] The *Explanatory Report*, *supra* note 2, paras. 15-1 and 15-4, makes clear that other than in the context discussed above, the Convention is silent as to

whether the Convention law may or must be applied to govern any other issue or be given any other effect with respect to pre-Convention interests or dispositions (except to the extent otherwise provided in Article 16, discussed below).

[49] Under Article 19(1), the Convention enters into force on the international plane on the first day of the month following the expiration of three months after the deposit of the third instrument of ratification, acceptance, approval, or accession by a state.

[50] For example, existing account agreements governed by state law or federal law in the United States frequently contain provisions either specifying the relevant intermediary's jurisdiction or selecting a governing law. These provisions have the effect, under that state or federal law, of determining the law governing at least some of the issues specified in Article 2(1). Parties who include such provisions in such account agreements can be presumed to have expected the consequences provided by that governing law and, under Article 16(3), those expectations will be fulfilled as that law will govern all the Article 2(1) issues

[51] For example, existing account agreements governed by the law of a member state of the European Community frequently indicate agreement, either expressly or implicitly, on where the relevant securities account is maintained. Parties to such agreements can be presumed to have intended that the law of that place would govern all the Article 2(1) issues. Under Article 16(4), that expectation will be fulfilled (see the further comments in the main text and the following note regarding the possibility of a declaration under Article 16(3)).

[52] Such a declaration addresses the situation when the parties to the account agreement have expressly agreed that the securities account is maintained in a particular state but the operation of Article 16(3) would designate the law of a different state as the governing law. An Article 16(3) declaration precludes Article 16(3) from having that effect. Thus, a state which considers that parties who make such an express agreement would have expected the Article 2(1) issues to be governed by the law of the location specified as the place of the maintenance of the securities account, and wishes to protect that expectation, may want to make an Article 16(3) declaration.

[53] For a more detailed presentation of Article 12, see the commentaries in the *Explanatory Report*; see also the following note.

[54] Article 12(2)(b) and Article 12(3) both provide for an internal *renvoi* in the context of multi-unit states. Article 12(2)(b) provides that if the conflict of laws rules in force in a territorial unit of a multi-unit state designate the law of another territorial unit of that state to govern perfection by public filing, recording, or registration, the law of that other territorial unit governs that issue. Under Article 12(3), a multi-unit state may file a declaration to the effect that if the applicable law, determined under Article 5, is that of the multi-unit state or one of its territorial units, the internal conflict of laws rules in force in that multi-unit state must be applied, and those rules will determine whether the substantive law of that multi-unit state or of a particular territorial unit of that multi-unit state shall apply.

[55] Thus, such an amendment does not lead to the application of Article 5(2) or (3); and no amendment can lead to the application of Article 5(1) because Article 5(1) is applicable only if the requisite condition existed at the time the account agreement was originally entered into. *See Explanatory Report, supra* note 2, para. 7-1.

[56] For a more detailed presentation of Article 7, see the commentaries in the *Explanatory Report.*

[57] Article 18 of the Hague Securities Convention closely follows Article 48 of the Cape Town Convention of 2001 on International Interests in Mobile Equipment.

The Draft Unidroit Convention on Intermediated Securities: Transactional Certainty and Market Stability

HERBERT KRONKE

This chapter describes the efforts of the International Institute for the Unification of Private Law (UNIDROIT) to deal with a major change in capital markets that has occurred over the past thirty years, specifically the intermediated holding of securities. The product of the organization's work is the draft UNIDROIT Convention on Intermediated Securities (Convention). The chapter first describes this change in the pattern of securities markets, then describes the status of work on the Convention, including a conceptual analysis of today's market in intermediated securities. It then summarizes the overarching objectives of the Convention: internal soundness and cross-border compatibility. Finally, the chapter presents a summary of the provisions and structure of the Convention.

Only a few decades ago, and in virtually all legal systems around the world, investment securities, in particular shares and bonds, were certificated. In everyday bilateral transactions a sale and purchase of securities could be carried out in a manner similar to the sale and purchase of any other movable: the seller delivered the certificate representing the underlying security against payment of the purchase price. The delivery transferred, subject to qualifications flowing from the type of security and varying according to the relevant national law, title in the securities, thus constituting settlement; the payment occurred contemporaneously unless the parties to the transaction agreed, at the seller's risk, to defer payment of the price. The fact that owners of securities kept the certificates either under their direct control or under a simple custody agreement with their bank contributed equally to the straightforwardness of the situation and the absence of risks—other than the risk of bad judgment—and serious legal problems. So long as all investors had physical possession of their securities in form of certificates and notes and trade occurred within the territorial boundaries of one country, the law hardly paid any attention. The reality of today's capital markets, however, is different.

The last thirty years have witnessed dramatic changes in the holding patterns as well as the structure and organization of securities markets. The need to reduce administrative burdens, risk, and expense by curbing the volume and movement of paper (the huge increases of the amount of capital sought to be raised on the market, as well as increases in both domestic and trans-border investment and trading, had led to the proverbial "paper crunch") induced a growing number of countries to move from direct holdings of certificated investment securities to indirect holdings of uncertificated and/or immobilized securities through one or more tiers of custodians (banks or specialized financial institutions).[1]

In 2005 the estimated value of securities held in custody with intermediaries was US$ 50 trillion. The volume of trades and collateral transactions in corporate and government securities issued by OECD member governments per day amount to US$ 2 trillion—that is, it exceeds the world's total GDP (greater than US$ 40 trillion) approximately every 20 trading days.

Holding patterns being multi-tier—i.e., each of the intermediaries holding its clients' securities in accounts maintained with other intermediaries—and stretching across national boundaries, the legal risks known from purely domestic situations (such as the principal risk, which is that one party to a transaction may perform without reciprocal performance by the other; the replacement cost risk, which is the potential failure to realize an anticipated gain and a potential liability to others in case of nonperformance by one party; or the general custody risk, that the intermediary may act improperly) have become exacerbated. Moreover, the legal frameworks within which the intermediaries operate are often not compatible. Measures to address these uncertainties in the course of each transaction produce unnecessarily high transaction costs.

The objectives of the draft UNIDROIT Convention on Intermediated Securities, therefore, are:

- The protection of market participants (both investors and intermediaries);

- The protection of the financial system; and

- Gains in economic efficiency.

History and Current Status

Following UNIDROIT practice, in 2002 a group of experts (the Study Group), made up of 16 experts from 12 countries and three international organizations set out to explore possible directions and the scope of its work,[2] and in 2004 produced a first draft. On-site consultations in 20 countries and four sessions of the Committee of Governmental Experts (CGE), held in May 2005, March 2006, November 2006, and May 2007 at which 39 delegations and 17 observer organizations substantially developed the underlying analysis and the legal concepts, produced a remarkably mature preliminary draft Convention.[3] At the end of the fourth session, which was particularly devoted to issues arising from the desired inclusion of so-called transparent systems, the Committee concluded that the text of the draft was mature for transmission to a diplomatic conference. The UNIDROIT Governing Council examined the draft and authorized transmission to a diplomatic conference, for adoption of the final text as a convention, i.e., a treaty binding those states that will ratify or accede to it. At the invitation of the Government of Switzerland the Conference will be held in Geneva, September 1–13, 2008.

Conceptual Analysis of Intermediate Holding of Securities

Put simply, there are four ways to conceptualize the legal position of the various actors in indirect holding patterns and, in particular, that of the investor/account holder. Example 2 below graphically depicts these legal positions.

In all four systems, at the top level one finds the issuer and a central securities depositary (CSD) where either dematerialized (uncertificated) securities and/or immobilized securities (issued in the form of global notes) are deposited and held. As seen in Example 2, the account holder/investor is shown at the bottom. One or more intermediaries stand between an account holder and the issuer. In other words, the investor holds his securities in an account with an intermediary who in turn may hold the securities of that investor, other clients' securities, as well as its own securities in an account with one or more upper-tier intermediaries. Ultimately, all investors' and all intermediaries' securities holdings up the chain are reflected in the CSD's omnibus account (and/or individual investors' accounts).

In the first group of legal systems, even though one or more intermediaries stand between the account holder/investor and the issuer, the intermediary has no legal significance, and the investor's rights are the functional equivalent of those of a direct owner. In terms of *property law* analysis, all account holders and investors in the securities of an issuer are co-owners of a fraction of a pool of securities. The law, moreover, imputes that the intermediary has some kind of possession or control for the account holder/investor.

In a second group of systems, the property analysis is the same but the law permits or imposes—and at least in a number of jurisdictions assures—that each investor's holdings and dispositions of securities be traceable. In other words, at the level of the CSD there are individual accounts of identified account holders who are owners of the securities credited to their accounts. Intermediaries merely act as book-keepers, pass on instructions and information or transfer dividends in a capacity of agent or similar. China, which may soon be the most important market, is based on this model.

A third group of jurisdictions uses the concepts of the law of *trusts*, where ownership is split into legal ownership and beneficial ownership. In those systems the top-tier intermediary is the legal owner bound by fiduciary duties (trustee), whereas the ultimate investor (and, as the case may be, other intermediaries in the chain) is the beneficial owner.

In a fourth group, the analysis is that there is legal ownership at the top level, i.e., vested in the CSD, whereas the investor's legal position (and that of other intermediaries) is defined as *entitlement*, a bundle of contractual and other rights defined by statute.[4] This is the model for the recent evolution in two exceedingly important markets, the United States and, in the not too distant future, Canada.

At one end of this spectrum, the account holder's rights may include the right to enforce the securities against the issuer and he is generally treated as the direct owner of the securities or may be permitted or required to be recorded as the registered owner on the issuer's books. Elsewhere within that spectrum, either the intermediary breaks the ownership chain between the account holder/investor, and the issuer or the intermediary is treated as the registered, legal, or nominal owner of the securities and the account holders are limited to enforcing the securities indirectly against the issuers through their intermediaries.

Overarching Objectives: Internal Soundness and Cross-Border Compatibility

Internal Soundness

In light of the specific risks created by the lack of physical control of certificates, the question is whether investors can be confident that their interests are robust and can be dealt with under simple, clear rules and procedures for acquisition, holding, transfer (including both outright transfer and provision of securities as collateral), and realization. Furthermore, it is clearly essential that the investor's interest should not be exposed to risks such as the insolvency of any intermediary or interference by unrelated parties.

The Study Group termed these issues of *internal soundness*. Domestic legislation or judge-made law either already addresses them or should address them. The draft Convention's objective is to contribute to modernization and harmonization of the solutions.

Even without any complexity added by any internationality of the situation, rules incapable of solving the problems arising in the following two examples would clearly be unsound.

Example 1

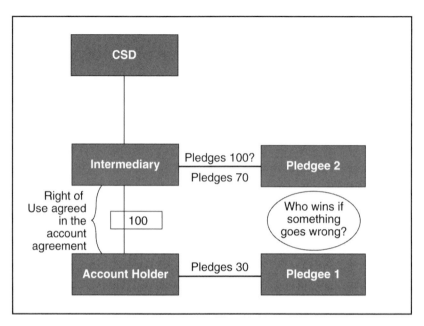

In example 1, the account holder holds 100 securities with his intermediary. Under the account agreement the intermediary is allowed to use securities credited to the account maintained with that intermediary. The account holder has pledged 30 to pledgee 1. What happens if the intermediary pledges 100, and not just 70, to pledgee 2? An internally sound system must provide plausible answers to the questions as to what the position of the pledgees is vis-à-vis each other and the intermediary, what action the intermediary is required to take to remedy the situation, and what safeguards are provided to protect the integrity of the system and prevent a virtual "inflation" of the issue.

Example 2

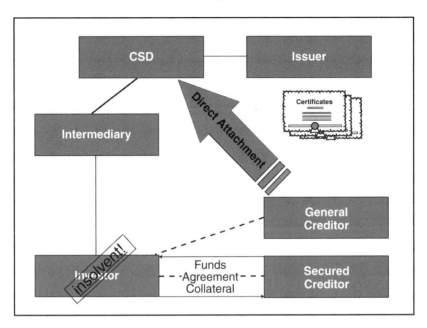

In example 2, the account holder/investor has provided securities held with his intermediary as collateral to a lender (secured creditor). Now the account holder becomes insolvent. The general creditor tries to attach the investor's securities, not at the level of his immediate intermediary (where they are still identifiable) but somewhere further up the chain, e.g., at the level of the CSD, where that intermediary has an account to which its own securities, the insolvent investor's securities, and other clients' securities are credited (but where those securities are not identifiable as "belonging" to any of them). An internally sound system prohibits upper-tier attachment. First, because securities of investors who have nothing to do with the subject matter of the attachment must not be blocked. Second, because both the account holder and a person dealing with an account holder at a lower level (e.g., a pledgee) must be able to rely on the position as it is stated for the account at that level).

Cross-Border Compatibility

Arguably, all intermediated securities holdings are or may potentially be turned into cross-border fact patterns. Therefore the draft Convention must address issues affecting the ability of different legal systems to connect successfully where securities are actually or potentially held or transferred across national frontiers. If the rules of two systems, though each achieving internal soundness, produce an unclear or unsatisfactory result in combination, this raises questions that the UNIDROIT Study Group termed, and the draft addresses, as issues of *compatibility*.

This problem goes beyond the question of which law governs a cross-border transaction, a question answered by the relevant conflict of laws rules and, it is hoped, in the future by the Hague Securities Convention (see discussion below). And we do not need to think of complex fact patterns where rules of company law, contract law, property law, insolvency law, and regulatory law have to work together. It is sufficient to recall that the very concept of *securities* varies from country to country. And it is clear that, in case of an investor in country A who provides securities issued and held by a CSD in country B and accredited to his account with his intermediary in country C to his creditor in any of A, B or C, let alone country D, legal certainty suffers significantly if what constitutes a security in country A and B were not to be characterized as a security in C (or D). This situation, however, reflects today's legal situation, even in countries with legal systems belonging to the same family.

Law and Practice: Potential Benefits of Modernization and Harmonization

Although the same commercial developments have taken place to one degree or another in most markets, domestic legal systems have maintained their insularity. The systems may be exceedingly refined and, in this respect, typical "lawyers' law" (or, even worse, "students' law"). But they produce, in the best case, problems of comprehension leading to unnecessarily high transaction costs (e.g., legal opinions) and, in worst-case scenarios, problems of actual incompatibility in a crisis and, following from that, systemic risks of market failures.

By realigning the law (where such law exists) with today's practice of holding and trading securities, many systems—even analytically sophisticated systems in developed securities markets—

stand to gain in terms of economic efficiency. Some may well improve their position as regards international competition of legal systems and the markets for which they provide the framework. Individual investors and individual intermediaries, as well as lenders who take securities as collateral, stand to gain from improved legal certainty. This, in turn, may lower the cost of credit. And most importantly from the perspective of domestic legislatures and national and international regulators, systemic risk will be reduced and overall financial markets' stability will be improved. The more these improvements occur in an internationally harmonized fashion, the better and the more incisive they will be.

What Has Been Achieved and What Remains To Be Done?

At the worldwide level, the Hague Convention on the Law Applicable to Certain Rights in Respect of Securities held with an Intermediary, adopted in 2002 but signed by Switzerland and the United States of America on 5 July 2006 and therefore bearing the title Hague Securities Convention of 2006 (Hague Convention), now provides legal certainty as regards the conflict-of-laws issues, i.e., in determining which domestic law is applicable to the holding and dispositions of securities held in the form of book entries with an intermediary. The Hague Convention is unique for a number of reasons:

- The unsatisfactory state of the lex lata and the basic features of the solution to the problems arising out of technical and operational changes in the securities industry were identified by practitioners,[5] legal scholars,[6] and legislators in Belgium and Luxembourg, homes to two major international central securities depositories (ICSDs), before work on the draft got under way. Moreover, a highly visible case in the English courts arising out of the collapse of Robert Maxwell's empire had given exposure to how unsatisfactory the state of the conflict of laws was in many jurisdictions and how much judicial instinct and caliber it took to get it right.[7]

- The delegates in The Hague were fortunate to start their discussions on the basis of a superb preparatory document, the so-called Bernasconi Report.[8]

- The financial industry was deeply involved in the consultations.

- This was the first time that the world negotiated with the European Commission, the executive arm of a regional economic integration organization to which its member states had transferred the law making power over the issues to be covered by the future instrument.

- A supra-national regulator, the European Central Bank, participated—no doubt to some extent with an agenda of its own.

- Those who will be called upon to implement, interpret, and apply the Convention will have at their disposal an official explanatory report[9] of the highest quality. The degree of predictability achieved through the new uniform conflict rules is remarkable.

However, there are deliberately accepted weaknesses in the Hague Convention deriving from the limitation of its scope. Most importantly, Article 2(1) issues, in particular the creation and perfection of security interests, are governed by the law applicable under the Convention if the relevant "event" has occurred before the opening of the insolvency proceeding (Article 8(1)). At the same time, the applicable insolvency law (*lex concursus*) designated by the autonomous conflict rules of the forum is preserved because the Convention does not contain any rule on determining the *lex concursus*. Thus in cases where the relevant intermediary is a financial institution that operates globally, it is impossible both for the account holder and any collateral taker to anticipate which law will govern the *effects* or the *use* of their—recognized, Article 8(1)— rights vis-à-vis the intermediary's insolvency administrator or the collateral provider (account holder) respectively. Will the *lex concursus* contain appropriate rules regarding any shortfalls in the intermediary's holdings? Will the *lex concursus* uphold or, on the contrary, defeat the collateral provider's default? These uncertainties highlight the need for harmonization of the basic substantive law regarding indirectly held securities.

At the regional level, the EC Finality Directive[10] and the Financial Collateral Directive[11] have addressed discrete areas and are applicable to distinct market participants and/or specific types of transaction.

The future UNIDROIT Convention is designed to provide a general legal mold in the form of substantive rules for indirect holding patterns as well as transparent systems. The greater the success of the Hague Convention, the stronger the incentive for domestic legislators to bring their domestic substantive law up to the benchmark provided by the UNIDROIT Convention because, under the Hague Convention's rule of party autonomy, investors and intermediaries will choose only national laws to govern their transactions that meet the most advanced standards for investor protection and operational soundness.

Overview of the Draft Convention

Scope and Approach: The Policy Choices

Governments and their intergovernmental organizations in charge of formulating private and commercial law instruments must make a number of policy choices each time they embark on the process of developing and negotiating a new instrument. They must respond to real needs, fix a real problem, not be overly ambitious as regards the prospective scope, and where necessary be coordinated with other instruments in adjacent areas of the law.[12]

Apart from the targeted objectives of improving internal soundness and compatibility of national legal frameworks, the Study Group made five policy decisions at the outset.

First, it was considered inappropriate to distinguish between domestic and cross-border transactions and draft an instrument only for the latter. While the definition of internationality and the limitation of the scope based on that criterion do make sense in instruments governing simple, bilateral relationships that may well be and remain domestic (such as a contract for the sale of goods—see Article 1 of the 1980 UN Convention on Contracts for the International Sale of Goods), it loses its *raison d'être* in all instances that are potentially international even if originally purely domestic. The classic example is the 2001 Cape Town Convention on

International Interests in Mobile Equipment and its equipment-specific protocols.[13] Where assets that by their very nature cross, or potentially cross, international frontiers in their daily operations or that are located outside any national territory—such as aircraft, railway rolling stock, or space assets—are used as collateral, it would not make sense to envisage a purely domestic situation and distinguish it from fact patterns that are international from the outset. In the same vein, it would have appeared artificial and unrealistic to conceptualize, in today's global environment of financial instruments and connected markets, a distinction between international and domestic holdings of securities with intermediaries.

Second, conceptual neutrality was of the essence. On the basis of the so-called functional approach, it was important not to transplant solutions—or, for that matter, even use terminology—that were clearly associated with a certain legal family and analysis (e.g., the law of trusts, or concepts of ownership rooted in a specific tradition). Article 7 of the current draft[14] is the most striking example. It accommodates effortlessly both the average civil law and common law approaches, as well as hybrids, just by describing in neutral, everyday language an investor's rights where that investor holds securities in the form of credits to a securities account with an intermediary.

Third, the drafters opted for a minimalist approach: no comprehensive uniform "custody, clearing and settlement act" is planned; consideration is given only to what is strictly needed to establish or enhance internal soundness and efficiency and cross-border compatibility. The objective is to produce as unintrusive an instrument as possible by employing fact-based rules. The instances where the draft leaves details or even basics to the non-convention law (see Article 1 (m) of the draft Convention) are numerous.

There are, however, limits to both the functional approach and the minimalist approach. As to the latter, Articles 9–16 (on the transfer of intermediated securities) are in all likelihood more detailed than their counterparts in a number of countries participating in the negotiations. As regards the functional approach, it is clear that the neutral, nonconnoted language of the instrument will have to be "retranslated" into domestically meaningful conceptual language.

Undoubtedly, a significant challenge lies here. The implementing legislation in contracting states must give full effect to the Convention's provisions, weigh carefully how far it may go beyond minimum requirements so as to not disrupt trans-border compatibility, and ensure that any conceptually diverging but functionally equal retranslation by other contracting states will be recognized as such in a domestic forum and, where applicable, applied on an equal footing. Legislatures in countries that at the time of implementation have no or very few and conceptually noncommitted rules on intermediated securities will have a much easier job than, say, France, Germany, or Japan.

Fourth, the unifying element—acceptable from early on in the consultation process to all key legal systems independently of their historic roots—is the recognition of book-entry accounts and the constitutive nature of credits to an account for any right or obligation.

Fifth, the future UNIDROIT Convention must be compatible with existing relevant international instruments both at the global and the regional level, such as the Hague Convention and, probably amended, EC Directives (see discussion below).

Guidelines for the Solution of Core Issues

The needs of market participants, both investors and intermediaries, as well as the need for governments, regulators, and central banks to assure the soundness and stability of financial markets, required that the future instrument encapsulated the following solutions of core issues.

- Book entries in the investor's account must be effective both against the intermediary—in particular, in case of the intermediary's insolvency—and third parties.

- An investor/account holder's rights attached to the securities, including in particular dividends and other distributions and voting rights, must be protected.

- The Convention must contain clear and simple rules for the acquisition and disposition of securities, including the creation of security interests, i.e., their use as collateral.

- To the extent that there are matching debits and credits to accounts maintained by the intermediary for different account holders (whether or not in respect of deliveries between those account holders), the intermediary must be able to effect a net settlement of those debits and credits. In other words, it need not make precisely matching entries in accounts which it holds with an upper-tier intermediary, but can make such entries (if any) as required to reflect the net overall change in the aggregate balances of its account holders together.

- So-called upper-tier attachment (see Example 2 above) must be prohibited. In other words, creditors of an account holder must not be allowed to attach their debtor's intermediated securities at the level of higher tier intermediaries or the issuer.

- There must be clear rules on priority in case of competing interests.

- Good-faith acquisition or, as the draft puts it, "acquisition by an innocent person," must be protected.

- The rights of an account holder and an interest that has been effective against third parties must be effective against the insolvency administrator and creditors in any insolvency proceeding in respect of the relevant intermediary.

- Measures for the protection of the integrity of the issue (against inflation by book entries) must be taken.

- Loss sharing in case of an insufficient aggregate number and amount of securities of the same description credited to securities accounts maintained by an intermediary must be regulated, including in case of insolvency of the intermediary.

Structure of the Draft Convention

In the course of the Study Group's deliberations and, thereafter, the consultations at the sessions of the Committee of Governmental Experts, the structure of the draft instruments has undergone quite substantial changes. The current version would appear to be mature and capable of being transformed into the final text of the future Convention with relatively few amendments and changes.

As is common in transnational commercial law, Chapter I (Articles 1–6) is devoted to definitions, scope of application, and principles of interpretation. The reader's attention is particularly drawn to the definitions of *securities* (Article 1 (a)), *intermediated securities* (Article 1 (b)), *intermediary* and *relevant intermediary* (Article 1 (d) and (g)), *account holder* (Article 1 (e)), *securities settlement system* and *securities clearing system* (Article 1 (n) and (o)). Article 6, the provision guiding legislators and courts, as well as investors and intermediaries, in the processes of implementing, applying, and interpreting the Convention, is current standard. Article 3 defines the sphere of application once the conflict-of-laws analysis—be it under the Hague Convention or under the forum's autonomous conflicts rules—has identified which country's law governs. Article 4 establishes that of the two branches of activities carried out by central securities depositaries (CSDs)—to wit, the notarial functions of creating, recording, or reconciling securities in their relationship with the issuers and, on the other hand, their activities as intermediaries—only the latter are within the instrument's scope. The most important addition to the draft formulated during the last session of the CGE in May 2007 is Article 5, a provision designed to accommodate the so-called transparent systems. It addresses the phenomenon that the CSD and other entities in the chain share functions, and the declaration mechanism set forth in paragraphs 2 and 3 serves the purpose of enabling parties to a transaction involving a transparent system to precisely evaluate the relevant legal implications *ex ante.*

Chapter II (Articles 7 and 8) spell out the rights of the account holders where securities are credited to their accounts.

Chapter III (Articles 9–16) lays out the ways of acquiring and deposing of securities by credit and debit to the account holder's securities account, including good-faith acquisition by an innocent person (Article 14). Other key provisions of this chapter are Article 13 (on invalidity of debits and reversal, which is important both for the protection of account holders and the stability of the system) and Article 15 (on priority among competing interests).

Chapter IV (Articles 17–25) deals with insolvency issues, prohibition of upper-tier attachment, instructions to the intermediary, the requirement that an intermediary hold sufficient securities of any description equal to the aggregate number and amount of that description credited to accounts which it maintains, limitations on obligations and liabilities of intermediaries, allocation of securities to account holder's rights, loss sharing in case of insolvency of the intermediary and, finally, the effect of debits and credits and instructions on the insolvency of operators of or participants in securities settlement systems.

Chapter V (Articles 26 and 27) deals with the relationship with the issuer of securities.

Chapter VI (Articles 28–34) contains special provisions with respect to collateral transactions, obviously an exceedingly important aspect both for the account holder/borrower and the collateral taker/lender.[15] Here the reader's attention is drawn in particular to Article 31 (on the collateral taker's right to use collateral securities as if it were the owner of them) and Article 33 (the practice of topping-up and substituting of collateral). Article 34 provides that a contracting state may opt out of this chapter by declaration. Providing for opt-out declarations, once considered to be a sin committed by unfaithful uniform-law drafters, is today looked at with greater sympathy. The negotiations of other recent transnational commercial law instruments have shown that accommodating strong feelings rooted in participating states' traditions facilitates both the intergovernmental negotiation process and domestic implementation without closing the door to making the right (i.e., the most radical and innovative) choices in the end.[16]

Chapter VII will contain general and subject-matter specific final clauses.

Conclusions

1. In its final monitoring report on global clearing and settlement, the Group of Thirty states:

> Consequently, harmonisation in both areas, conflict-of-laws and substantive law, must be pursued. As to the scope of the harmonization of substantive law, both the UNIDROIT project and the measures taken by the EU go well beyond the steps required by recommendation 15. Their successful completion and implementation will contribute significantly to the stability and efficiency of clearing and settlement. This report therefore encourages competent national authorities and market participants to support these processes. Despite the overlap in their scope, the work of UNIDROIT and the work of the recent EU Legal Certainty Group are not to be understood as substitutes for each other but as complementary. This is because, on the one hand, more countries participate in the UNIDROIT project (notably including the United States, Japan, Switzerland, Australia and Canada) and, on the other hand, because the EU Legal Certainty Group might target a higher level of harmonization and even prepare the way for a global work on additional issues, such as corporate action processing. It is, however, most important that both projects proceed in a coordinated manner. Uncoordinated results would jeopardize global harmonization in the field of substantive law regarding securities settlement for years. As far as possible, therefore, both projects must go forward at the same pace. It is therefore necessary that sufficient resources are made available to both of them. With a view of achieving full coverage of the 15 target countries, measures should also be examined that would allow the countries that are not yet involved to participate in the work on the UNIDROIT Convention.[17]

2. Governments that have not yet participated in the intergovernmental consultation process are warmly invited to consider participation in the finalization of the text, i.e., the diplomatic Conference which will be held September 1–13, 2008, in Geneva.

3. Interested governments and other interested parties such as intergovernmental organizations and international NGOs representing the financial and legal communities may contact the Secretariat (Thomas Keijser) at t.keijser@unidroit.org.

Notes

[1] *See* Roy Goode, "The Nature and Transfer of Rights in Dematerialised and Immobilised Securities," in Fidelis Oditah, ed., *The Future for the Global Securities Market* (Oxford: Clarendon Press, 1996), at 107; Madeleine Yates, Joanna Benjamin and Gerald Montagu, *The Law of Global Custody*, 2nd ed. (London: Butterworths, 2002). *See Uniform Law Review/Revue de droit uniforme* (2005), at 1–442, for national reports on Canada, China, France, Germany, Japan, the Nordic countries, Poland, Switzerland, United Kingdom, and the United States, as well as related work at the Hague Conference, UNCITRAL, the European Communities, and the first UNIDROIT draft, with articles by B. Sen, Christophe Bernasconi and Harry C. Sigman, Spiros V. Bazinas, Klaus M. Löber, Michel Deschamps, Dong Ansheng and Han Liyu, Antoine Maffei, Dorothée Einsele, Jürgen Than, Hideki Kanda, Lars Afrell and Karin Wallin-Norman, Michal Romanowski, Luc Thévenoz, and Curtis Reitz, and the FMLC Report.

[2] The UNIDROIT Study Group on Harmonised Substantive Rules Regarding Indirectly Held Securities, Position Paper, August 2003, Study LXXVIII, Doc. 8. All documents cited are also available at www.unidroit.org.

[3] UNIDROIT 2006, Study LXXVIII—Document 94, Original in English/French, July 2007.

[4] On the revision of Article 8 of the U.S. Uniform Commercial Code, see Mooney, "Beyond Negotiability: A New Model for Transfer and Pledge of Interests in Securities Controlled by Intermediaries," 12 *Cardozo Law Review* 305 (1990); Rogers, "Policy Perspectives on Revised U.C.C. Article 8," 43 *UCLA Law Review* 1431 (1996); Reitz, *supra* note 1.

[5] To name but a few, Randall Guynn, "Modernizing Legal Rules to Reduce Settlement Risk," *IBA Capital Markets Forum Yearbook* (1993), at 172; Euroclear, *Cross-Border Clearance, Settlement and Custody: Beyond the G 30 Recommendations* (Brussels, 1993), at 62; Jean-Pierre Mouy and Hubert de Vauplane, "La réforme du nantissement des titres dématérialisés," *Banque & Droit* (Juillet-Aout 1996), at 3.

[6] Ulrich Drobnig, "Vergleichende und kollisionsrechtliche Probleme der Girosammelverwahrung von Wertpapieren im Verhältnis Deutschland-Frankreich," in H. Bernstein, U. Drobnig, and H. Kötz, eds., *Festschrift für Konrad Zweigert* (Tübingen: Mohr Siebeck, 1981), at 73; Dorothée Einsele,

Wertpapierrecht als Schuldrecht (Tübingen: Mohr Siebeck, 1995); Goode, "The Nature and Transfer of Rights in Dematerialised and Immobilised Securities," *supra* note 1 at 107; Herbert Kronke, "Capital Markets and Conflict of Laws," *Recueil des Cours*, Vol. 286 (2000), at 247.

[7] *Macmillan Inc. v. Bishopsgate Investment Trust plc and Others (No. 3),* [1995] 1 WLR 978 (Ch. D.); on appeal, the Court of Appeal reverted to the classical *lex situs* rule, [1996] 1 WLR 387. For an insightful comment by Lord Millet (as he now is), see his foreword in R. Potok, ed., *Cross Border Collateral: Legal Risk and the Conflict of Laws* (London: Butterworths, 2002) at v *et seq.*

[8] Christophe Bernasconi, "The Law Applicable to Dispositions of Securities Held Through Indirect Holding Systems," Preliminary Document No. 1, November 2000, for the attention of the Working Group of January 2001.

[9] Roy Goode, Hideki Kanda, and Karl Kreuzer with the assistance of Christophe Bernasconi, *Hague Securities Convention—Explanatory Report* (The Hague: Hague Conference on Private International Law/Martinus Nijhoff Publishers, 2005).

[10] Directive 98/26/EC of the European Parliament and of the Council of 19 May 1998 on Settlement Finality in Payment and Securities Settlement Systems.

[11] Directive 2002/47/EC of the European Parliament and of the Council of 6 June 2002 on Financial Collateral Arrangements.

[12] *See* Roy Goode, Herbert Kronke, and Ewan McKendrick, *Transnational Commercial Law—Text, Cases and Materials* (Oxford: Oxford University Press, 2007), chapters 6, 18–20.

[13] Texts available at www.unidroit.org. The Convention and the Aircraft Protocol are also reproduced in Roy Goode, Herbert Kronke, Ewan McKendrick and Jeffrey Wool, *Transnational Commercial Law, International Instruments and Commentary* (Oxford: Oxford University Press, 2004), at 550–595, with commentary, at 433–453. In the meantime, the second industry-specific protocol to the Cape Town Convention was adopted, i.e., the 2007 Luxembourg Protocol on secured financing of railway rolling stock. Its text is reproduced in *Uniform Law Review/Revue de droit uniforme* (2007), at 417–678, with comments by Howard Rosen, Fabien

Owono Essono, Rafael Castillo-Triana, John Wilson, Tatjana Josipović, Bruno Poulain, Steven Harris, Gustav Kafka, Hans-Georg Bollweg and Katharina Schnell, and Benjamin von Bodungen and Konrad Schott.

[14] *See* note 3 *supra*.

[15] On this topic, see Thomas Keijser, *Financial Collateral Arrangements* (Deventer: Kluwer, 2006).

[16] With respect to secured transactions, see Roy Goode, *Convention on International Interests in Mobile Equipment and Protocol thereto on Matters Specific to Aircraft Equipment—Official Commentary* (Rome: UNIDROIT, 2002), at 28, 40.

[17] Group of Thirty, *Global Clearing and Settlement, Final Monitoring Report* (Washington, D.C.: Group of Thirty, 2006), at 41–42.

BIOGRAPHICAL SKETCHES

Biographical Sketches

Kern Alexander is Professor and Director of Research in International Financial Regulation at the Centre for Financial Analysis and Policy, the Judge Business School, University of Cambridge. He is also Senior Research Fellow in International Financial Regulation at the Institute of Advanced Legal Studies, University of London. From 2007 to 2009 he was a U.K. Economic and Social Research Council Senior Research Fellow in International Political Economy and Law, and has been a visiting professor of international economic law at the University of Zurich. He has given oral and written evidence to the House of Lords Select Committee on Economic Affairs and to the European Union Parliament's Economic and Monetary Affairs Committee on European and international economic and financial regulation issues.

Richard Barrett is Coordinator, Analytical Support and Sanctions Monitoring Team of the UN Security Council Committee for Al-Qaida and the Taliban. He is responsible for a team of experts that supports the Security Council with analysis of the threat from Al-Qaida and the Taliban and evaluates the implementation of the UN sanctions regime designed to limit their ability to mount attacks, including by making specific recommendations for improvements to the sanctions and suggesting possible new measures. He is a member of the UN Counter-Terrorism Implementation Task Force (CTITF), established to promote the implementation of the United Nations Global Counter-Terrorism Strategy, with a particular involvement in radicalization and extremism that lead to terrorism, terrorist use of the Internet, and terrorist financing. From 1975 to 2004 he served in the government of the United Kingdom, where he dealt with a variety of security issues, including the threat from international terrorism, and was posted to Amman, New York, Ankara, and Ottawa.

James R. Barth is the Lowder Eminent Scholar in Finance at Auburn University and a Senior Finance Fellow at the Milken Institute. His research focuses on financial institutions and capital markets, both domestic and global, with special emphasis on regulatory issues. Most recently, he served as leader of an international team advising the People's Bank of China on banking reform. He was an appointee of Presidents Ronald Reagan and

George H.W. Bush as chief economist of the Office of Thrift Supervision until November 1989, and has served as the chief economist of the Federal Home Loan Bank Board. He has also been professor of economics at The George Washington University, associate director of the economics program at the National Science Foundation, and Shaw Foundation Professor of Banking and Finance at Nanyang Technological University. He has been a visiting scholar at the U.S. Congressional Budget Office, Federal Reserve Bank of Atlanta, Office of the Comptroller of the Currency, and the World Bank. He has authored more than 200 articles in professional journals and has written and edited several books, including *The Great Savings and Loan Debacle* and *The Reform of Federal Deposit Insurance*. His most recent books are *Rethinking Bank Regulation: Till Angels Govern*, with Gerard Caprio, Jr., and Ross Levine (Cambridge University Press, 2006) and *Financial Restructuring and Reform in Post-WTO China*, with Zhongfei Zhou, Douglas Arner, Berry Hsu, and Wei Wang (Kluwer Law International, 2007). He is the overseas associate editor of *The Chinese Banker* and serves on the editorial boards of the *Journal of Financial Services Research*, *Review of Pacific Basin Financial Markets and Policies*, *Journal of Economics and Finance*, and *Financial Services Review*.

Christophe Bernasconi is First Secretary of the Hague Conference on Private International Law (HCCH). His primary responsibilities include the HCCH's work relating to the Hague Securities Convention (Convention on the Law Applicable to Certain Rights in respect of Securities held with an Intermediary); the Hague Apostille Convention (Convention Abolishing the Requirement of Legalisation for Foreign Public Documents); the Hague Service Convention (Convention on the Service Abroad of Judicial and Extrajudicial Documents in Civil or Commercial Matters); and the Hague Evidence Convention (Convention on the Taking of Evidence Abroad in Civil or Commercial Matters). Dr. Bernasconi holds a law degree from Fribourg University in Switzerland, an LL.M. from McGill University in Montreal, and a doctoral degree from Fribourg University. He is a member of the International Bar Association Capital Markets Forum Subcommittee on Legal Certainty for Intermediated Securities. He was also a member of the Legal Subcommittee of the G30 that monitored the implementation of the G30 Recommendations of 2003 on Global Clearing and Settlement.

He was co-rapporteur of the International Law Association's Committee on Transnational Enforcement of Environmental Law. Dr. Bernasconi has published numerous private international law articles on a variety of topics in major law journals. He is a regular speaker at international conferences and seminars, and has taught at the Hague Academy of International Law.

Zenón Alberto Biagosch graduated in management from the School of Economic Science of the University of Buenos Aires and is a certified fraud examiner of the Association of Certified Fraud Examiners (ACFE). He is currently Director of the Central Bank of the Argentine Republic and Vice-Superintendent of Financial and Exchange Entities. He has been director and vice-president of Banco de la Nación Argentina; president of Nación Seguros de Vida S.A. and Nación Seguros de Retiro S.A.; senior manager for regulation and compliance for the financial services industry at PricewaterhouseCoopers; commissioner for preventing money laundering at the Secretariat for the Struggle against Drug Trafficking; national government coordinator with the Financial Action Task Force of the Organization for Economic Co-operation and Development; and president of the Group of Experts for Controlling Money Laundering at the Organization of American States. He is member of the board of speakers of the Cambridge International Symposium on Economic Crime, which takes place every year at Jesus College of the University of Cambridge. He is also a member of the UN Counter-Terrorism Implementation Task Force and special guest of the International Monetary Fund and World Bank.

Andrew Campbell is Director of the Centre for Business Law and Practice at the University of Leeds in the United Kingdom and a solicitor of the Supreme Court in England and Wales. He specializes in international banking law, with particular emphasis on bank insolvency, depositor protection, and banking regulation. He regularly acts as consulting counsel to the International Monetary Fund. He is co-author, with Peter Cartwright, of *Banks in Crisis: the Legal Response* (Ashgate, 2002) and a co-author of *Butterworths Annotated Guide to the Financial Services and Markets Act*

(LexisNexis Butterworths, 2nd ed., 2005). He is also a co-editor, with Raymond LaBrosse, David Mayes, and Dalvinder Singh, of *Deposit Insurance* (Palgrave Macmillan, 2007). He is a member of the editorial boards of the *Journal of Banking Regulation*, the *Journal of Money Laundering Control*, the *Journal of Financial Regulation and Compliance*, and the *Journal of Financial Crime*.

Gerard Caprio, Jr., is Professor of Economics at Williams College and Chair of the Center for Development Economics there. From 1998 until January 2006 he was director for policy in the World Bank's Financial Sector Vice-Presidency. He served as head of the financial sector research team in the Bank's Development Research Group from 1995 to 2003, and previously was a lead and principal financial economist there. Past positions include vice-president and head of global economics at JP Morgan, economist at the Federal Reserve Board and the IMF, and adjunct professor at The George Washington University. He has written extensively on financial sector policy, financial reform, and banking crises in developing countries, including over 50 articles and 9 books, the most recent of which is *Rethinking Bank Regulation: Till Angels Govern* (Cambridge, 2006), with James Barth and Ross Levine. He co-authored a World Bank policy research report, *Finance for Growth: Policy Choices in a Volatile World* with Patrick Honohan, and founded and served as editor of the bimonthly electronic newsletter, *Interest Bearing Notes*. He is also a co-editor of the *Journal of Financial Stability*. Professor Caprio earned his Ph.D. in economics at the University of Michigan and his A.B. degree in economics at Williams College.

Ian Carrington has worked for nearly three decades on issues related to financial sector activity. He has been involved in loan origination in the banking sector, and has had extensive experience in the regulation of financial institutions. Mr. Carrington began his working career in the private banking sector in Barbados and later joined the Ministry of Finance and Planning as a budget analyst and the Barbados Development Bank as a project analyst. He joined the Central Bank of Barbados in 1983, and took up the position of deputy director of banking supervision in 1990; he was promoted to the position of director of banking supervision in 1997. In 2000, Mr. Carrington took up an appointment as a financial sector expert with the UN Global Program against Money Laundering in the UN's Office of Drugs and Crime in Vienna. He joined the IMF as a senior financial sector expert in 2002 and currently works in the Financial Integrity Group of the Legal Department. He undertakes AML/CFT assessments and provides technical assistance to member countries of the IMF. Mr. Carrington holds a B.S. in public administration and an MBA in banking management.

Martin Čihák is a senior economist at the International Monetary Fund. He joined the IMF in 2000, working mostly in the Monetary and Capital Markets Department, where he focused on financial sector and monetary policy issues. He has recently moved to the IMF's European Department, covering EU policy issues, while continuing his financial sector work. Mr. Čihák is a senior editor of the *Czech Journal of Economics and Finance*, one of a few peer-reviewed journals in Central and Eastern Europe, and has held various leadership positions in the Czech Economic Association. Before joining the IMF, Mr. Čihák worked in Prague, Czech Republic, as a chief macroeconomic analyst at a major commercial bank, university lecturer, advisor to a minister of justice, and external advisor to the president. He has co-authored several textbooks and published in professional journals. He holds an M.A. in economics from the Charles University, Prague, and Ph.D.s in economics from CERGE, Prague, and the University of the State of New York. He also holds an M.A. in law from the Charles University. Mr. Čihák specializes in stress testing, financial soundness indicators, and other methods of assessing financial sector soundness.

Ross Delston is an attorney and former U.S. banking regulator who specializes in anti-money laundering (AML) compliance for financial services firms. He heads GlobalAML.com, a Washington, D.C.-based consulting firm he founded. Since September 1997 he has been a legal consultant to the International Monetary Fund on AML and banking matters, and has participated in its AML assessments of seven offshore financial centers. In 2007 he was named to the AML subgroup of the Financial Services Roundtable's Blue Ribbon Commission on Enhancing Competitiveness. From 2000 to 2005 he served as consulting counsel in the IMF Legal Department, where he drafted AML and banking laws for a number of countries, and chaired a working group to draft a model AML law for Commonwealth countries. Previously, Mr. Delston was a solo legal practitioner specializing in financial regulation; Of Counsel to Jones Day; assistant general counsel for assisted acquisitions at the Federal Deposit Insurance Corporation during the U.S. banking crisis; and counsel at the U.S. Export-Import Bank, where he specialized in trade finance. His recent publications include "Regulatory Blitz for Subprime Players?" *American Banker* (November 9, 2007); "Independent Audit for Anti-money Laundering: Essential Element or Nice to Have?," (co-authored with Martin Owen), *Money Laundering Bulletin*, (June 2007); and "Memo to top executives: AML compliance affects you, too," *Money Laundering Alert* (April 2007) (co-authored with Mr. Owen). Mr. Delston is also a member of the international editorial board of the *Journal of Banking Regulation*. Mr. Delston is a graduate of The George Washington University and its law school.

Diego Devos is Deputy General Counsel of the Bank for International Settlements. In this capacity, he is supports the general counsel in the management of the legal service of the BIS and advises the various BIS Departments and services on public international and financial private law issues. Mr. Devos was previously deputy general counsel of Euroclear, where he was primarily responsible in the legal division for international/EU/Belgian regulatory issues and legal issues relating to harmonization of financial markets. Until April 2006 he was a member of the EU Legal Certainty Group, which was set up in early 2005 by the European Commission to address harmonization of substantive securities laws and legal barriers in the field of clearing and settlement. He was also a member of the drafting committee of the Hague Convention on the Law Applicable to Certain Rights in Respect of Securities Held with an Intermediary, adopted by the Hague Conference on Private International law in December 2002, and he served as a member of the drafting committee during the first session of the UNIDROIT Committee of Governmental Experts for the preparation of a draft convention on substantive rules regarding intermediated securities.

Charles Enoch received his M.A. in economics from Cambridge University and his Ph.D. from Princeton. From 1976 to 1987 he worked in a succession of jobs at the Bank of England, including in the monetary, financial, and capital markets areas, and running the office of the deputy governor during the Latin America debt crises of the 1980s. From 1987 to 1990 he was Alternate Executive Director for the United Kingdom at the IMF. On his return to the Bank of England he became senior advisor in the European and Economics departments, and led the monetary side in the initial training visits of the Bank's Center for Central Bank Studies to Central and Eastern Europe. With the establishment of the Monetary and Exchange Affairs Department in the IMF, he returned to the Fund as chief of the Review Division in early 1993, becoming head of the Banking Supervision and Regulation Division in 1998. During this period he headed missions on monetary and financial issues to a variety of countries, including leading the financial sector teams in the banking crises in Bulgaria, Indonesia, and elsewhere. In a number of these crises his work included extensive assistance in preparing banking, bank insolvency, and central bank laws. From 2000 to 2003 he worked as deputy director in the Statistics Department, also heading the Fund-Bank committee that coordinated the newly established standards and codes, and conducted outreach on the standards and codes across the membership. From 2003 to early 2007 he was deputy director in the Monetary and Financial Systems Department, responsible for the Fund's technical assistance in the monetary and financial areas. Since early 2007 he has been Deputy Director in the IMF Statistics Department.

Christian Johnson has taught courses on banking, finance, and tax at Loyola University Chicago School of Law for thirteen years. Professor Johnson has published four books and over three-dozen articles on these topics. He has lectured on finance and derivatives at the Inter-American Development Bank, the Federal Home Loan Bank System, the American Bar Association, Osgoode Law School (Toronto, Canada), the National University of Singapore, the Federal Reserve Bank of Chicago, the American Bar Association, and the Futures Industry Association. Prior to teaching, Professor Johnson was an associate at Milbank, Tweed, Hadley & McCloy in New York and Mayer, Brown in Chicago. Professor Johnson attended Columbia Law School and was the executive editor of the *Columbia Law Review* and a Harlan Fiske Stone Scholar. Prior to law school, he received his B.A. and Masters in accounting from the University of Utah and was a C.P.A. with Price Waterhouse. He is on the board of editors of the *Journal of Payment Systems Law*.

Philip McBride Johnson has devoted nearly all of his 45 years in the practice of law to the U.S. laws, regulations, and agencies governing the markets in futures contracts, options, swaps, and other derivative instruments. His past positions have included chairman of the Commodity Futures Trading Commission (CFTC) and leader of exchange-traded derivatives law practice at Skadden, Arps, Slate, Meagher & Flom LLP. He is the author of *Derivatives Regulation* (formerly *Commodities Regulation*) (3 vol., Aspen Law & Business); *Derivatives: A Manager's Guide to the World's Most Powerful Financial Instruments* (McGraw-Hill); and over 190 other published works. He was a founder and first chairman of the derivatives law committees for both the American Bar Association and the International Bar Association. From 1989 to 2004 he was a member of the regulatory advisory committee of the New York Stock Exchange, and has been a member of five CFTC federal advisory committees.

Roberta S. Karmel is the Centennial Professor of Law and Co-Director of the Dennis J. Block Center for the Study of International Business Law at Brooklyn Law School. She was a commissioner of the Securities and Exchange Commission from 1977 to 1980, a public director of the New York Stock Exchange from 1983 to 1989, and a member of the National Adjudicatory Council of the NASDR from 1998 to 2001. She was engaged in the private practice of law in New York City for over thirty years at Willkie Farr & Gallagher, Rogers & Wells, and Kelley Drye & Warren. Professor Karmel is a trustee of the Practising Law Institute and is co-chair of the International Coordinating Committee of the Section of Business Law of the American Bar Association. She is a member of the Advisory Committee on Capital Markets Law to UNIDROIT, a member of the American Law Institute, a fellow of the American Bar Foundation, and on the boards of advisors of *Securities Regulation and Law Report,* the *Review of Securities and Commodities Regulation*, and the *World Securities Law Report*. Professor Karmel is the author of over 50 articles in books and legal journals, and writes a regular column on securities regulation for the *New York Law Journal*. She is a frequent lecturer on financial regulation. She received a B.A. from Radcliffe College and an LL.B. from New York University School of Law. She was a Fulbright Scholar in 1991–92.

Herbert Kronke is Secretary General of UNIDROIT (International Institute for the Unification of Private Law), Rome, and Professor for Private Law, Commercial Law and Private International Law, University of Heidelberg, Germany (on leave). He received his academic education in Germany, Scotland, and the United States. Following graduation and practical training, he took a Dr. iur. degree. After several years as fellow of the Max-Planck-Institute for Foreign and Private International Law in Hamburg, he took a Dr. iur. habil. degree. He has been a visiting scholar at McGill University, Montréal, a visiting professor at Georgetown University Law Center, Washington, D.C., and a visiting professor at the Universidade Federal do Rio Grande do Sul, Porto Alegre (Brazil). In 1999 he taught conflict of laws (in the area of capital market law) at the Hague Academy of International Law. In 2006 the Law Faculty of the Eötvös Loránd University, Budapest, conferred the degree of doctor et professor honoris causa upon him. Professor Kronke is the author of more than 100 books and articles in the fields of the law of contracts, commercial law, company law, conflict of laws, international civil procedure and arbitration, most recently *Transnational Commercial Law—Text, Cases and Materials*, with Roy Goode and Ewan McKendrick (Oxford, 2007). He is a member of the German Institution of Arbitration and the Swiss Arbitration Association, the London Court of International Arbitration (European User Group) and the panels of the Cairo Regional Centre for International Commercial Arbitration, where he serves in ad hoc, ICC, and other institutional arbitrations.

Ross Leckow is Deputy General Counsel in the Legal Department of the International Monetary Fund. A national of Canada, Mr. Leckow has extensive experience in the legal aspects of Fund regulatory and financial operations, has contributed to the development of Fund policy in a number of areas, and has advised on a wide range of issues in the area of financial sector reform. Before joining the Fund in 1990, Mr. Leckow practiced law in the private and public sectors in Canada. He lectures frequently in the United States and abroad on issues of international financial law. His recent publications include "Law Reform and Financial Stability—the Growing Role of the International Monetary Fund," in *Reconciling Law, Justice and Politics in the International Arena* (2004); "Bringing the Disenfranchised to the Table: the Lessons of

Conditionality," in *The Measure of International Law: Effectiveness, Fairness and Validity* (2004); "Conditionality in the International Monetary Fund," in *Current Developments in Monetary and Financial Law*, vol. 3 (2005); and "The Reporting of Information under Article VIII, Section 5 of the IMF's Articles of Agreement" in *Current Developments in Monetary and Financial Law,* vol. 4 (2005).

Niall Lenihan is Assistant General Counsel at the European Central Bank (ECB). He is a graduate in law of Trinity College, Dublin, and holds a master of law from Sidney Sussex College, Cambridge. Mr. Lenihan is a licensed attorney in the New York State Supreme Court and the U.S. District Court for the Southern District of New York, a solicitor of the Supreme Court of England and Wales, and a solicitor of the High Court of Ireland. From 1991 to 1997 he was an associate with the New York law firm of Davis Polk & Wardwell, where he advised on securities offerings, corporate transactions, and litigation. In 1996 he established the Wall Street Committee on European Economic and Monetary Union (EMU), the first U.S. working group to consider the legal implications of EMU for swap, derivative, and eurobond transactions governed by New York law. In 1998 the European Commission published his study on the legal implications of EMU under U.S. and New York law. In 1998 he joined the legal division of the European Monetary Institute, and thereafter the legal services of the ECB, where he has advised on a range of financial and monetary legal matters. In 2002 he represented the ECB in the G10 Working Group on Collective Action Clauses in sovereign debt instruments. In 2004 he was appointed Assistant General Counsel of ECB Legal Services.

Ross Levine is the James and Merryl Tisch Professor of Economics at Brown University and Director of the William R. Rhodes Center in International Economics. He is a research associate at the National Bureau of Economic Research, editor of the *Journal of Financial Intermediation*, and associate editor of the *Journal of Economic Growth*. Mr. Levine received his Ph.D. in economics from UCLA in 1987. After working at the Board of Governors of the Federal Reserve System, he moved to the World Bank, where he managed research and operational programs. In 1997 Dr. Levine joined the University of Virginia, before moving to the University of

Minnesota in 1999, and then to Brown University in 2005. Professor Levine's work focuses on the linkages between financial sector policies, the operation of financial systems, and economic development. His new book, *Rethinking Bank Regulation: Till Angels Govern*, challenges current approaches to the regulation of banks.

Patricia A. McCoy is the George and Helen England Professor of Law at the University of Connecticut. She received her B.A. from Oberlin College and her J.D. from the University of California at Berkeley (Boalt Hall), where she was editor-in-chief of the *Industrial Relations Law Journal.* After graduation she clerked for Judge Robert Smith Vance on the United States Court of Appeals for the Eleventh Circuit. Later, she was a partner at Mayer, Brown, Rowe & Maw in Washington, D.C., specializing in complex securities, banking, and constitutional litigation. Professor McCoy's current research examines market failures in the financial services industry. She has written two books: *Banking Law Manual: Federal Regulation of Financial Holding Companies, Banks and Thrifts* and *Financial Modernization After Gramm-Leach-Bliley.* Professor McCoy was a visiting scholar at the MIT Economics Department from 2002 to 2003, and a member of the Federal Reserve's Consumer Advisory Council from 2002 through 2004.

Troy Paredes joined the faculty at Washington University School of Law in 2001, after practicing law as a corporate and securities lawyer in San Francisco and Los Angeles. He holds a bachelor's degree in economics from the University of California at Berkeley and received his J.D. from Yale Law School. His research interests include corporate governance, with a focus on how authority is allocated among directors, officers, and shareholders; securities regulation, including the impact of various cognitive biases and decision strategies on investing behavior; the psychology of managerial decision making; the development of corporate and securities law systems in developing economies; hedge funds; executive compensation; and intellectual property transactions. In addition to his other research and writing, he is a co-author (beginning with the 4th edition) of *Fundamentals of Securities Regulation*, with Louis Loss and Joel Seligman.

Sandra M. Rocks is counsel to Cleary Gottlieb Steen & Hamilton LLP, resident in the New York office. Her practice focuses on commercial financing, including specialties in secured transactions and bankruptcy law. Ms. Rocks is currently the American Bar Association (ABA) liaison-advisor to the Permanent Editorial Board of the Uniform Commercial Code. She has chaired the International Commercial Law and Investment Property Subcommittees of the Uniform Commercial Code (UCC) Committee of the Business Law Section of the ABA. Ms. Rocks chaired the UCC Committee's Task Force on Proposed Treasury Regulations Governing Book-Entry Securities, which studied and provided comments to the Department of the Treasury on regulations governing book-entry Treasury securities. She served as a member of the SEC's Market Transactions Advisory Committee, established to advise ways in which to reduce risk in the efficient clearance and settlement of market transactions. Ms. Rocks participated on behalf of EMTA (formerly the Emerging Markets Traders Association) in drafting sessions at The Hague Conference on Private International Law culminating in the Convention on the Law Applicable to Certain Rights in Respect of Securities Held with Intermediaries. Ms. Rocks currently participates on behalf of EMTA in the UNIDROIT project to create a convention on harmonized substantive rules regarding indirectly held securities, having previously acted as a co-coordinator for the private financial sector for UNIDROIT's study group on this project. Ms. Rocks, together with Carl Bjerre, is the author of *The ABC's of the UCC, Article 8: Investment Securities,* 2nd Edition, and has authored and co-authored various articles on UCC and securitization matters. She is a frequent speaker on Articles 8 and 9 of the UCC and related international initiatives.

Garry J. Schinasi is an advisor in the Monetary and Capital Markets Department of the International Monetary Fund. He received his Ph.D. in economics from Columbia University in 1979, and for the next decade held various staff positions at the Board of Governors of the U.S. Federal Reserve System. In 1990 he joined the IMF, where he has focused on global finance and financial stability issues. For most of this time he co-managed the IMF's surveillance of international capital markets, including co-authoring and co-editing the IMF's flagship publication *International Capital Markets: Developments, Prospects, and Key Policy Issues* (1994–2001), which was succeeded by the *Global Financial Stability Report.* Mr. Schinasi then spent two years as an advisor in the IMF's Finance Department, where he managed the development of the department's framework for assessing financial risk in the Fund, with an emphasis on sovereign credit risk. Mr. Schinasi is presently on leave from the IMF and engages in independent research on global financial stability issues, including as a consultant with not-for-profit research organizations. Mr. Schinasi has published articles in *The Review of Economic Studies, Journal of Economic Theory, Journal of International Money and Finance,* and other academic and policy journals. His book *Safeguarding Financial Stability: Theory and Practice* was published by the IMF in January 2006.

Heba Shams is a financial sector specialist at the World Bank. Prior to joining the Financial Integrity Group at the Bank in 2004, she taught international economic law and development finance law at the Centre for Commercial Law Studies, Queen Mary College, London. She has written on issues of international investment law, corruption, and money laundering. Her publications include *Legal Globalization: Money Laundering Law and Other Cases* (BIICL, 2004). She holds a *license en droit* from Cairo University, a master's degree in law from Cairo University, an LLM from King's College, London, and a Ph.D. from Queen Mary College, London.

Francisco José de Siqueira graduated in law from the Federal University of Pernambuco, in Brazil, and received a master of laws degree from the same university. Mr. Siqueira also graduated in business administration and in public administration from the Federal University of Pernambuco. He was professor of commercial law at the Catholic University of Salvador, the Catholic University of Brasília, and Brasilia's Institute of Superior Education; professor of business law of post-graduate studies at the Interamerican Center of Development, and at the Catholic University of Brasilia. Mr. Siqueira has been an attorney of the Central Bank of Brazil since 1976, where he has held the position of regional-attorney, especial consultant, and deputy general counsel. Since 2003 he has been General Counsel of the Legal Department of the Central Bank of Brazil. Since 2001 he has been a member of the Court of Fondo Financeiro para el Desarollo de la Cuenca del Plata (FONPLATA), over which he

656 • Biographical Sketches

presided from 2003 to 2004. Mr. Siqueira has published several articles, including "Responsibility of Directors of Financial Institutions," *Journal of Mercantile, Industrial, Economic and Financial Law*; "Intervention in the National Financial System: 25 Years of the Law 6.024/74," in *The Role of Central Bank in Intervention Process* (Textonovo, 1999); "Financial Institutions: Special arrangements in Brazilian Law," *Journal of Banking, Capital Markets and Arbitration Law*; and "The Industry and Microfinance of Microcredit in Brazil," prepared for the X Meeting of Lusophone's Banking Jurists (Bank of Portugal Edition, 2004).

Robert Steigerwald serves as Senior Financial Markets Advisor to the Financial Markets Group at the Federal Reserve Bank of Chicago. The Financial Markets Group includes research economists, legal and regulatory experts, experienced business practitioners, and central bank policymakers who study public policy issues relating to financial markets and large-value payment systems, with a particular emphasis on Chicago's financial market institutions. He began his legal career with Kirkland & Ellis, an international law firm based in Chicago, and later served as chief legal officer of Multinet International Bank, a clearinghouse for foreign currency transactions. In that capacity, he managed the bank's legal and regulatory affairs and contributed to the development of the clearinghouse's risk design. He also served as principal U.S. counsel in connection with the development of a multicurrency payment-versus-payment system known as "continuous linked settlement." Before taking his law degree, he worked on the precious metals and foreign currency trading desk of Shearson-American Express in New York. Mr. Steigerwald joined the Federal Reserve Bank of Chicago in February 2000 and has organized a number of public policy-oriented events, including "Five Years of the Euro: Successes and New Challenges," cosponsored by the George J. Stigler Center for the Study of the Economy and the State, University of Chicago, and most recently "Intellectual Property and Competition Issues Relating to Financial Markets," cosponsored by the Kellogg School of Management, Northwestern University. He was a lecturer in the graduate program in financial services law at Chicago-Kent College of Law from 1993 to 2000, and in 2005 was a visiting scholar at the Institute for Monetary and Economic Studies (IMES) at the Bank of Japan. His research interests include financial market clearing and settlement systems, risk and liquidity management and regulatory policy. Mr. Steigerwald received his undergraduate degree from the State University of New York at Stony Brook in and was graduated from the University of San Francisco School of Law, where he was a McAuliffe scholar and the recipient of *American Jurisprudence* awards in civil procedure and property.